Delineated & Engraved by I. Sanford, Hartford Connecticut.

OLIVER WOLCOTT,
Governor of the State of Connecticut.

Hartford, Published by Wm. S. Marsh, for a Gazetteer of Connecticut 1819.

A GAZETTEER

OF THE STATES OF

CONNECTICUT

AND

RHODE-ISLAND

WRITTEN WITH CARE AND IMPARTIALITY, FROM
ORIGINAL AND AUTHENTIC MATERIALS

CONSISTING OF

TWO PARTS

I. A GEOGRAPHICAL AND STATISTICAL DESCRIPTION OF EACH STATE; EXHIBITING A GENERAL VIEW OF THEIR MORE PROMINENT FEATURES, BOTH NATURAL AND ARTIFICIAL

II. A GENERAL GEOGRAPHICAL VIEW OF EACH COUNTY, AND A MINUTE AND AMPLE TOPOGRAPHICAL DESCRIPTION AND STATISTICAL VIEW OF EACH TOWN, WITH THEIR CIVIL DIVISIONS, SOCIETIES, CITIES, BOROUGHS AND VILLAGES, ALPHABETICALLY ARRANGED IN THEIR RESPECTIVE COUNTIES; TOGETHER WITH SUCCINCT BIOGRAPHICAL NOTICES OF EMINENT DECEASED MEN

BY

John C. Pease and John M. Niles

HERITAGE BOOKS
2012

HERITAGE BOOKS
AN IMPRINT OF HERITAGE BOOKS, INC.

Books, CDs, and more—Worldwide

For our listing of thousands of titles see our website
at
www.HeritageBooks.com

A Facsimile Reprint
Published 2012 by
HERITAGE BOOKS, INC.
Publishing Division
100 Railroad Ave. #104
Westminster, Maryland 21157

Copyright © 1991 Heritage Books, Inc.

Originally Published
Hartford:
Printed and Published by William S. Marsh
1819

— Publisher's Notice —

In reprints such as this, it is often not possible to remove blemishes from the original. We feel the contents of this book warrant its reissue despite these blemishes and hope you will agree and read it with pleasure.

The original title page indicated the inclusion of two maps, which are missing from this volume.

International Standard Book Numbers
Paperbound: 978-1-55613-544-6
Clothbound: 978-0-7884-9299-0

District of Connecticut, ss.

{L. S.} BE IT REMEMBERED, That on the twelfth day of June, in the forty-third year of the Independence of the United States of America, WILLIAM S. MARSH, of the said district, hath deposited in this office the title of a book, the right whereof he claims as proprietor, in the words following, to wit:
" A Gazetteer of the States of Connecticut and Rhode-Island; writ-
" ten with care and impartiality, from original and authentic materi-
" als. Consisting of two parts; I. A geographical and statistical des-
" cription of each state; exhibiting a general view of their more pro-
" minent features, both natural and artificial. II. A general geogra-
" phical view of each county, and a minute and ample topographical
" description and statistical view of each town, with their civil divis-
" ions, societies, cities boroughs and villages, alphabetically arranged
" in their respective counties; together with succinct biographical
" notices of eminent deceased men: with an accurate and improved
" map of each State. By John C. Pease and John M. Niles."
In conformity to the act of the Congress of the United States, entitled " An act for the encouragement of learning, by securing the co-
" pies of maps, charts and books to the authors and proprietors of such
" copies, during the times therein mentioned."
CHAS. A. INGERSOLL,
Clerk of the district of Connecticut.
A true copy of record, examined and sealed by me,
CHAS. A. INGERSOLL,
Clerk of the district of Connecticut.

PREFACE.

IN offering the following volume to the public, we have no apology to make; and little to observe, either as to our own objects or the work itself. There are, perhaps, few departments of science of more general utility, than those of geography and statistics; especially in this country, which possesses an immense territory, embracing different climates; a variety of soil, affording different productions; and where one united people, having, for the purposes of defence, foreign relations, commerce, and other national objects; a common government, are divided into distinct and separate communities; which, as it respects the common objects of legislation and the various concerns of society, are subject to local, distinct and independent authorities; which, from the influence of positive institutions, must have a tendency, not only to maintain different characteristics, habits and manners in these distinct communities, but in some measure to obstruct the dissemination of local intelligence. It is evident, that the people of the several States cannot be too intimately acquainted with each other; their local resources and advantages; the most important interests, whether of agriculture, manufactures or commerce; the most conspicuous departments of industry, and the prevailing local characteristics. A general diffusion of information upon these subjects will not only tend to unite us more effectually as one people, but may contribute to the general improvement. Several valuable works of this description have already been published in the United States; and it is gratifying to observe, that others are contemplated, and that the subject of the topography of our country is every where receiving conspicuous attention. With respect to this volume, we can only say, that it is the product of much industry; and that it embodies a vast collection of facts, will not, we think, be denied. Perhaps there has been no work of the kind undertaken upon the same principles, nor could these principles have been acted upon with success, except in a work confined to a small territory. It was our design to obtain authentic and correct topographical, and the entire statistical information from *every town*. This, as will be perceived, has given the work great uniformity; which, by depriving it of variety, may have rendered it less interesting, but we think not less useful; as that kind of information, which comes within the views of this work, can be found in the description of every town.

With the exception of the aid we have received (which we here would acknowledge,) from a statistical and topographical view of New-Haven, by the late PRESIDENT DWIGHT, published in 1811; from a view upon a similar plan, of the towns of Litchfield, Norfolk and Washington, in Litchfield county, by

PREFACE.

JAMES MORRIS Esq.; and a historical and topographical view of the towns of Haddam and East-Haddam, by the Rev. DAVID D. FIELD, published in 1814; the work has been wholly compiled from original materials. The facts have been collected either directly by ourselves, or through the aid of correspondents. Every county, and almost every important town in each State, has been visited; and a circular letter, specifying the several subjects upon which information was requested, has been addressed to one or more of the most intelligent inhabitants in every other town. The great number of gentlemen who, in this way, have furnished information for the work, are entitled to our warmest acknowledgments. We are sensible, that information obtained in this mode may, in some instances, have been erroneous; but considering the respectable sources from whence it has been derived, we have no doubt, but that in general it will be found correct. In noticing the sources of our information, we should do injustice, were we to omit to state, that for the facts relative to the first settlements of towns and much other historical information, we are extensively indebted to "Trumbull's history of Connecticut;" a work disclosing more research, and more indefatigable industry, than almost any other which has appeared in this State.

In the arrangement or plan of the work, our object has been to render it as systematic and connected as possible; the usual order of the counties and towns having been preserved.

With respect to biographical notices, as our limits did not admit of an insertion of all that might be deserving of preservation, we have selected such as we deemed most distinguished, and that could be obtained with the greatest facility; having some regard to diversity of characters, with a view to give this part of the work as much variety and interest as practicable. It will not, therefore, be understood, that all those individuals who have been noticed were deemed more distinguished, or a sketch of their lives more worthy of preservation, than many others, who have been omited. Should a second edition of the work be demanded, it might, in this as well as in other respects, receive considerable additions and improvements.

It is generally considered, that works of this description cannot be very permanent, as most of the subjects of which they treat are constantly changing. But from the condition of the improvements of almost every description in these two States, and the permanent and settled character of society, it is believed, that with the exception of some manufacturing interests, both the topographical descriptions and the statistical details will remain essentially correct for a length of time. It is from this consideration, that we have observed a minuteness and uniformity of description, which is not usual in publications of this character. Being confined to giving an account of "things as they are," we have aimed at no embellishments of style, elegance of diction or richness and brilliancy of descriptions. That a work containing such a vast collection of facts should be free from errors, will not be expected; and we trust that the intelligent and the liberal, being sensible of the difficulties attending the undertaking, will view its defects with proper indulgence. After having devoted nearly one entire year to this work, and extended it near 100 pages beyond the proposed size, it is offered to the public with the hope, that it will not be considered as altogether unworthy of the respectable patronage which it has received in almost every town in the two States.

THE AUTHORS.

CONTENTS

OF THE STATE OF CONNECTICUT.

General Geographical and Statistical View of the State of Connecticut — PAGE	1
Constitution of Connecticut	19
HARTFORD COUNTY	33
Hartford	38
Berlin	55
Bristol	58
Burlington	59
Canton	60
East-Hartford	61
East-Windsor	65
Enfield	67
Farmington	71
Glastenbury	74
Granby	76
Hartland	80
Marlborough	82
Simsbury	ib.
Southington	84
Suffield	85
Wethersfield	89
Windsor	90
NEW-HAVEN COUNTY	93
New-Haven	95
Branford	114
Cheshire	115
Derby	116
East-Haven	119
Guilford	120
Hamden	124
Meriden	125
Middlebury	127
Milford	128
North-Haven	130
Oxford	131
Southbury	132
Wallingford	133
Waterbury	135
Woodbridge	136
Wolcott	137

NEW-LONDON COUNTY	PAGE 139
New-London	141
Norwich	146
Bozrah	150
Colchester	151
Franklin	152
Griswold	153
Groton	154
Lisbon	158
Lyme	159
Montville	162
North-Stonington	163
Preston	164
Stonington	ib.
Waterford	167
FAIRFIELD COUNTY	168
Fairfield	170
Danbury	176
Brookfield	178
Greenwich	179
Huntington	180
New-Canaan	181
New-Fairfield	182
Newtown	183
Norwalk	184
Reading	186
Ridgefield	191
Sherman	192
Stamford	193
Stratford	194
Weston	199
Wilton	200
WINDHAM COUNTY	202
Windham	204
Ashford	207
Brooklyn	208
Canterbury	209
Columbia	210
Hampton	211
Killingly	212
Lebanon	214
Mansfield	216
Plainfield	217
Pomfret	218
Sterling	222
Thompson	223
Voluntown	224
Woodstock	225

CONTENTS.

	Page
LITCHFIELD COUNTY	229
Litchfield	231
Barkhamsted	237
Bethlem	239
Canaan	240
Colebrook	242
Cornwall	243
Goshen	247
Harwinton	249
Kent	250
New-Hartford	251
New-Milford	252
Norfolk	254
Plymouth	256
Roxbury	257
Salisbury	258
Sharon	260
Torrington	261
Warren	262
Washington	263
Watertown	264
Winchester	265
Woodbury	266
MIDDLESEX COUNTY	269
Middletown	271
Haddam	275
Chatham	278
Durham	280
East-Haddam	281
Killingworth	283
Saybrook	284
TOLLAND COUNTY	288
Tolland	290
Bolton	291
Coventry	ib.
Ellington	295
Hebron	ib.
Somers	296
Stafford	297
Union	300
Vernon	302
Willington	303

CONTENTS

OF THE STATE OF RHODE-ISLAND.

General Geographical and Statistical View of the State of Rhode-Island . . . . . . Page 305
PROVIDENCE COUNTY 321
Providence 324
Burrellville 335
Cumberland 336
Cranston 337
Gloucester 339
Foster 340
Johnston 342
North-Providence 343
Scituate 344
Smithfield 345
NEWPORT COUNTY 349
Newport 351
Jamestown 355
Little-Compton 356
Middletown 357
New-Shoreham . . . . ib.
Portsmouth 358
Tiverton 359
BRISTOL COUNTY 361
Bristol 363
Barrington 365
Warren . . . . ib.
KENT COUNTY 367
East-Greenwich 368
Coventry 370
Warwick 371
West-Greenwich 376
WASHINGTON COUNTY 377
South-Kingston 379
Exeter 380
Charlestown . . . . ib.
Hopkinton 383
North-Kingston . . . . ib.
Richmond 385
Westerly 386

GENERAL

GEOGRAPHICAL AND STATISTICAL VIEW OF THE STATE OF

CONNECTICUT.

CONNECTICUT is situated between 41° and 42° 2′ north lat. and between 71° 20′ and 73° 15′ west lon.

Its form is considerably irregular. It has an average length, from east to west, of about 88 miles, and a mean breadth, from north to south, of about 53 miles, comprising an area of about 4664 square miles, inclusive of navigable rivers, bays and harbours.

Connecticut is bounded on the north by the Commonwealth of Massachusetts, on the east by the State of Rhode-Island, on the south by Long-Island sound, and on the west by the State of New-York.

The State is divided into eight counties, of which the following TABLE exhibits a view; the number of towns in each; the seat of justice; the incorporated cities, boroughs, &c.

Counties.	Towns.	Seat of justice.	Incor. cities, &c.
Hartford.	18	Hartford.	Hartford City.
New-Haven.	17	New-Haven.	New-Haven City & Guilford Borough.
New-London.	14	N. London and Norwich.	N. London & Norwich Cities, & Stonington Borough.
Fairfield.	17	Fairfield and Danbury.	Bridgeport Boro'.
Windham.	15	Windham.	
Litchfield.	22	Litchfield.	Litchfield Village.
Middlesex.	7	Middletown and Haddam.	Middletown City.
Tolland.	10	Tolland.	

Surface, Soil and Geological Character.—Accuracy of geographical description, and a correct and minute delineation of the physiognomy of the earth, its surface, soil, mountains, rivers, bays, geological character, natural and agricultural productions, &c. are objects, presenting no ordinary difficulties, and which afford no prospect of attainment, without adequate and correct information, derived from authentic sources, and the result of extensive research and just observation. The description of natural objects is attended with difficulties, in proportion to the number and variety of their features, and the indistinctness of their connections and relations. Hence the difficulties of topographical description; the smallest portion of the earth frequently presents a great variety of surface, soil and character, from the influence of local causes, and an apparent and incongruous connection of natural objects, which is almost every where to be observed. At the base of a rugged granitic ridge, we often find a smooth and fertile plain; the frosty and sterile hill is often connected with the warm and fertile dale; the craggy cliff is found approaching the water's edge, upon a stream, the borders of which, elsewhere, are lined with beautiful alluvial; and perhaps this very alluvial is bounded by a lofty ridge of mountain, and upon the summit of this mountain, though vastly elevated from the stream below, there may be embosomed an extensive sheet of water. From this surprising, and often marvellous connection and diversity of the physical features of the earth, it is difficult to give an accurate description of its surface, soil and character, without a minuteness which could not be indulged, even if the materials could be obtained.

But notwithstanding the prevalence of local varieties the effect of local causes, most sections of country are characterized by certain distinct features, both as it respects their internal structure and external appearance, which *generally* prevail, and distinguish them from other districts in the immediate neighbourhood.

A concise notice of the several distinct districts of country, which this State presents, and their general and prominent characteristics, is all that can be expected in a general view of the State. The extensive argillaceous vale upon Connecticut river claims the first attention in this view. This district commences at Middletown, and extends through the State; being about 30 miles in length, from north to south, and from 10 to 16 in width, extending upon both sides of the river. The northern part of this tract bounds west upon the great greenstone range of mountain, and east upon the granitic range, in the eastern section of the State. This tract, with the exception of the alluvial upon the Connecticut, has an undulating surface, being pleasantly diversified with moderate hills and gentle declivities. The prevailing soil is a strong and fertile argillaceous loam, varying, in different sections, from a hard, stiff clay, to a light, sandy loam, according to the prevalence of aluminous or siliceous earths. This may be considered as the richest agricultural section, of the same extent, in the State, or perhaps in New-England.

West of this, is the greenstone district, consisting of the declivities of the greenstone mountain; and the vales between its several branches, of which the Farmington vale, west of this mountain, is the most considerable, commencing in the vicinity of New-Haven, and extending through the State, a distance of about 50 miles· it is from three to five miles in width. The vale of Quinipiack, in Wallingford and North-Haven, about 15 miles in length, and from two to five in breadth, belongs to this district, although the southern section of it is light and sandy. This tract is generally very fertile, and of an argillaceous character, and a rich farming district. West of the vale following the course of the greenstone mountain, in the northern part of the State, commences the declivities or subsidence of the extensive granitic mountain, extending through the State. This is an elevated, granitic, primitive region, generally rough and broken; and some sections of it frosty and sterile, particularly the evergreen district, in its northern part; but in general it is a good grazing country. West of this section, upon the borders of the Ousatonick, are calcareous vales of considerable extent, being from half a mile to five miles in breadth. This tract is very rich, and well adapted to a grain culture.

The Connecticut river vale, upon the east, is lost in the declivities of the eastern granitic range, extending through the State. From this mountain eastwardly to Rhode-Island, it is generally a mountainous or hilly country, of a primitive, geological character; but the prevailing soil is warm, strong and fertile, being excellent for grazing; and upon the Quinibaug, Shetucket, and their branches, there are numerous small but fertile vales. The granitic district, from Lyme, eastwardly, extends south to the sound; but westwardly, to the extremity of the State, or to New-York line, there is a beautiful and interesting flat, upon the border of Long-Island sound; being from one to three miles in width. The most extensive and valuable part of this flat, is west of the Ousatonick river. The soil is generally a gravelly loam, very deep, strong and fertile, and some sections of marine alluvial. West of the Ousatonick, this flat is lost in a gradual rise, extending to the north and west, which becomes elevated and hilly, but not mountainous.

Mountains.—There are five distinct and considerable mountains in the State. Three of them are of a granitic, geological character, and two of greenstone. The western or Ousatonick mountain commences in the southwestern section of the State, and extends northwardly through it; its general course following that of the Ousatonick river. This mountain has no distinct continuous ridge, but consists of a succession of eminences, and numerous spurs and branches, some of which are very elevated, particularly Mount Tom, situated between Litchfield and Washington, which has an altitude of 700 feet. The general character of this mountain is granitic; but its prevailing features are in many respects different from those of the other two granitic ranges. It is not continuous, and the summits of the eminences, although equally elevated, and more bald, are not so cold and frosty. Its declivities generally afford a warm, fertile soil; and the base of many of the eminences consists of limestone, which also abounds in many of the intervening vales. This mountain is rich in mineral treasures, particularly iron ore, which abounds in various places.

The next granitic range, in order, commences in the western section of New-Haven county, and extends northwardly through the State, into the interior of New-England. It consists of a continuous ridge, generally facing to the east. It is not very elevated, its summits being principally covered with forests. The northern section of this range is clothed with evergreens; hence it is here called the Greenwoods mountain. This evergreen region is cold, frosty and sterile. The northern section of this range is more elevated, its ascent more direct, and its declivities very rugged.

The third is a greenstone range. This mountain rises near the sound, in the vicinity of New-Haven. It has, for some distance, two branches; one of which commences at East and the other at West rock. The West rock branch extends some distance, and subsides. The west branch, and the east branch for some distance, are a succession of eminences; but the latter becomes continuous and elevated, extending in a northerly direction through the State, and far into the interior. This range has very conspicuous and peculiar features. It faces to the west, presenting, upon its west side, a bold, mural precipice, which, near the summit, consists of naked rocks, exhibited in broken fragments. Upon the east it has a gradual rise, and affords extensive and fertile declivities. The greenstone strata of this range, in their general features and mineral treasures, correspond with the trap or greenstone of the old world. They abound in minerals, particularly copper ore, which is found in various places. This mountain may with propriety be called the great greenstone range.

The fourth range of mountain commences in the eastern section of New-Haven, in the vicinity of Long Island sound, and extends northwardly, forming the western boundary of Middletown, and terminates at Rocky-hill, in Hartford. This range is of the same geological character as the last, but is not continuous; consisting of a succession of eminences or hills, which in general have but a moderate height; but there are some very bold elevations, exhibiting the more prominent features of the great greenstone range. This has usually been called the Middletown mountain, but with more propriety might be called the lesser greenstone range. These several mountains are all west of Connecticut river.

The fifth mountain is the extensive granitic range east of Connecticut river, which forms the height of land that separates the waters that fall into the Connecticut from those that run into the Thames. This mountain has, at its commencement, two branches; the principal of which rises in the eastern section of New-Haven county, and extends northeastwardly, and rising upon the east side of Connecticut river. The other branch commences near the sound, in Lymo, and extends northwardly, nearly parallel with the river; but is not continuous, consisting of broken eminences. But after the union of these branches, the mountain becomes a distinct and continuous range, becoming more elevated as it extends to the north, affording some bold elevations, of which Bald mountain, situated between Somers and Stafford, is the most distinguished. The prevailing strata of this range are primitive granite; but in many of its declivities micaceous schistus abounds.

Mineralogy.—The mineral treasures of Connecticut are valuable and extensive; but they have received but little attention, with the exception of iron ore. This is the most important mineral in the State. It abounds in Salisbury and Kent, and is of an excellent quality. It is also found in Sherman, Roxbury, Washington and Cornwall, and bog ore, of an excellent quality for castings, is found in Stafford. Copper ore abounds in various places in the greenstone range, particularly in Granby, Hamden and Cheshire. Iron pyrites has been found in Hamden and Berlin; and there are indications of galena, or lead ore, in Berlin, Cheshire, Middletown, Brookfield and Killingly. Black lead, or plumbago, has been discovered in Cornwall and Marlborough. Porcelain clay has been found in New-Milford and Cornwall, white clay in Washington, and yellow ochre also in Washington and New-Milford. Recently a valuable cobalt mine has been discovered in Chatham. From the examinations which have been made, the ore of this valuable mineral is extensive; being found principally in micaceous veins. This is a very valuable mineral, and promises to be a source of great profit.

Limestone abounds extensively in the western section of the State, particularly upon the borders of the Ousatonick river, and in the vales intervening between the mountainous eminences and ridges, which characterize this section of the State. Marble is found in New-Milford, Washington, Brookfield and Milford. That in the latter place is clouded, resembling the Italian dove marble; has a rich colour, an excellent texture, and sustains a very high polish.

Quarries of freestone exist in various places, particularly within the argillaceous district upon Connecticut river. Those most deserving of notice, in a general view, are in Chatham, Haddam and East-Hartford. There is also a quarry of excellent white fire proof stone in Stafford, suitable for furnace hearths; a singular coincidence, that stone, suitable for furnace hearths, which is rarely found, should exist in the neighbourhood of iron ore, of a suitable quality for casting.

Some small quantities of coal have been found in Berlin, and recently in Suffield. There are also some indications of coal in Middletown and Hartford.

The mineral waters of the State are numerous; but there are no watering places of much celebrity, except those of Stafford and Suffield. The first of these has deservedly acquired a conspicuous reputation, is a place of extensive resort, and is provided with very ample accommodations; the latter is also provided with convenient accommodations, and at some periods has maintained considerable reputation.

Waters.—The waters of this State are abundant and various, and afford all the advantages and conveniences which can result from an extensive sea-coast, safe and convenient harbours, numerous bays and inlets, large navigable rivers, and innumerable small streams, which intersect and fertilize the State in every direction, abounding in sites for hydraulic works.

There are three considerable rivers in this State ; the Connecticut, Ousatonick and Thames ; which, together with their numerous branches, bays, and inlets, water a considerable section of the State.

Connecticut river, from which the State takes its name, and which ranks among the most considerable rivers in the Atlantic States, intersects the State into nearly two equal sections, running through it in a southerly and southeasterly direction, a distance of 70 miles. The extreme head of its tide waters is just below the village of Warehouse-Point, about 64 miles from the mouth of the river at Saybrook bar. Sloops ascend to this place, in the season of high water. This is one of the most beautiful rivers in the world ; flowing with a placid but majestic tide, through an extensive vale, affording the most interesting scenery and landscapes, its borders being embellished by extensive and delightful tracts of alluvial, unrivalled in fertility and beauty. This river affords very important facilities for navigation and commerce, and contains numerous shad fisheries, some of which are the most valuable in the United States. The principal branches of the Connecticut, within this State, are the Tunxis or Farmington river, a very beautiful and interesting stream, which comes from the west, and the Scantic, Hockanum and Salmon rivers from the east.

The Ousatonick is the second river in this State. This river runs about 90 miles within the limits of Connecticut ; and, together with its branches, waters the western section of the State. Its navigable waters extend to Derby, about 12 miles from its mouth, and boats ascend to Southbury, in seasons of high water.

There are some valuable shad fisheries in this river ; and in many sections its borders are lined with alluvial. Its principal branches are the Naugatuck and Shepaug. The practicability and expediency of a canal upon the borders of this river, extending boat navigation into the interior, have been suggested, and we think are deserving of consideration. Navigation, upon this river, is very limited ; and a canal would supply this defect, and afford very important facilities to commerce, and essential advantages to agriculture and other important interests, particularly those of the manufacture and marketing of marble, lime, iron, timber, lumber, &c. ; articles that this region affords in abundance, and which are bulky and heavy, requiring the advantages of navigation to facilitate their transportation.

The Thames is the third river in size in Connecticut. This river, with its two great branches, the Shetucket and Quinibaug, and their numerous tributary streams, water the eastern section of the State. The Thames admits of ship navigation to Norwich, the head of tide water, about 14 miles from its mouth. The principal branches of the Shetucket are the Willimantic, the Nachaug and Hop rivers. The Shetucket, the Quinibaug, and their branches, afford some excellent shad and salmon fisheries. Salmon are taken in the Willimantic, as high as Willington; and in the Quinibaug, as far up as Thompson.

The most considerable harbours and bays in this State are those of New-London, New-Haven, Bridgeport, Stonington, Black-Rock, Norwalk, Stamford, Killingworth, Guilford, Sachem's Head, Milford, Greenwich, Saugatuck, Mystic and Niantic. These are all upon Long-Island sound; in addition to which, there are numerous safe and convenient landing places upon the navigable rivers.

Climate.—Climate depends not only upon *general*, but also upon *local* causes. Of the former, general location, or the relation which a place has to the equator, is the most important, and has the most extensive and uniform influence. There are, however, some other general causes; such as the influence of the sea, of an extensive elevated region, and of a settled and uniform current of the atmosphere, or course of winds. Causes, not of a general nature, consist principally of local situation; the physiognomy and character of the country; its being elevated or flat; inclined to, or from the equator; being wet or dry; the soil cold or warm; and the surrounding country mountainous or level, covered with forests, or in a state of cultivation. From the influence of local causes, the climate of this State, although possessing small territorial limits, is very various in different sections. The great vale of the Connecticut, and the borders of Long Island sound, enjoy a salubrious, mild and uniform climate, and will compare with the northern departments of France, and Devonshire in England. These sections are not subject to frequent storms, either in winter or summer, as is the case in many parts of the United States: and there is probably as much uniformity in the weather here, as at Philadelphia, or any other part of the Union. The rigours of winter continue from two to three months; and the rivers are usually "bound in chains of ice," for about this period; and the earth is usually covered with snow, so as to afford sleighing, from five to seven weeks.

In the climate of which we are speaking, the apple, peach and water melon come to the highest perfection. The grape vine grows spontaneously, and the mulberry tree flourishes with little attention. Destructive frosts are rarely experienced; two only are recollected within the last thirty years, that were extensively injurious to vegetation. Severe droughts are equally rare; and it is believed that there is no part of our country, where the productions of the earth are more sure, or where the fruits of agricultural industry can be relied upon with more certainty. In the northwest section of the State, where the surface is mountainous and elevated, and particularly in the evergreen district, the climate is much more cold and frosty, the winters more rigorous, the usual quantity of snow much greater, and the weather has less uniformity. And these observations are applicable, with some qualification, to the mountainous districts in the eastern part of the State. Peaches, water-melons and some other summer fruits, do not come to as great perfection here as upon Connecticut river, and the borders of Long Island sound. This, however, may not be entirely owing to the climate, as the soil is less congenial to their growth.

Natural and Agricultural Productions.—The forests of Connecticut are principally deciduous ; consisting of oak, chesnut, maple, walnut, butternut, ash, elm, beech, birch, button-wood, bass, and various other species of trees. They comprise also white and yellow pine, spruce, hemlock and other perennial trees. The oak, of which there are several different species, prevails most extensively, and is of the greatest utility. It affords a valuable and durable timber for various purposes required by the useful arts and the conveniences of life. It makes excellent ship timber ; which, for strength and durability, is surpassed only by the live oak of the southern States ; being equal to the boasted oak of England. The maple is a most valuable tree, not only for fuel and timber, but for the manufacture of sugar. This tree, which abounds extensively in some of our forests, is highly deserving of preservation, and ought to be regarded as an object of culture and particular attention, by our farmers. In those parts of the State, where this tree flourishes, every farm ought to have reserved upon it, a suitable maple orchard ; which would be equally an ornament, and a source of family convenience and economy. The most extensive and valuable forests, in this State, are in the towns of Guilford, Haddam, East-Haddam, Chatham, Southbury, Oxford, Woodbridge, Farmington, Killingly, Stafford,˙Union, Tolland, Goshen, Winchester, Colebrook and Barkhamsted.

The agricultural productions consist of grain, of which rye and Indian corn are principally cultivated, although wheat and oats receive some attention ; and in some sections, the former is a leading crop ; butter, cheese, beef and pork. The raising of cattle, sheep and swine, is an object of general attention. The products of our dairies, butter and cheese, are not surpassed by any in the United States ; and it is believed, that the business is carried on as extensively and as advantageously here, as in any section of our country.

The best grazing and dairy towns, in the State, are Pomfret, Brooklyn, Woodstock, Lebanon, Stonington, North-Stonington and Groton. east of Connecticut river ; and west of it, Goshen, Bethlem, Winchester, Norfolk, Torrington and Colebrook. Besides the articles of butter and cheese, the more direct products of the dairy business, large quantities of beef and pork are annually made in these towns, and sent abroad for a market. The towns best adapted to a grain culture, and in which the largest quantities of grain are usually raised, are East-Windsor, Enfield, Somers, Ellington, Southington, Farmington, Windsor, Simsbury and Granby, principally within the great vale of Connecticut river; and Sharon, Salisbury and Canaan, upon the borders of the Ousatonick, in the western section of the State. These are rich and fertile townships, possessing extensive resources of soil, and affording great facilities of cultivation; and it is believed, that there are few sections in the Atlantic States more favourable for a system of grain culture, particularly that of rye. It has been estimated, that 70,000 bushels of this grain have been raised in the town of East-Windsor alone, in one season. But, by mentioning these, it is not intended to have it understood, that grain is not successfully cultivated in other towns; it is raised advantageously in Cheshire, Wallingford, Southbury, Woodbury, Newtown, New-Milford, Danbury, Fairfield, Stratford, Milford, Plainfield, Windham, Mansfield, Canterbury and others. Indian corn is cultivated most extensively and successfully upon the alluvial on the Connecticut, Tunxis and Quinibaug rivers, and upon the borders of Long Island sound.

Apple orchards in this State are extensive, and a source of considerable profit. They abound most in Hartford and Middlesex counties, and in some towns upon the Ousatonick river; but are to be found in every part of the State. The most numerous and valuable orchards in Hartford county, or in the State, are in Farmington, Simsbury, Canton, Granby, Berlin, Windsor and Suffield. In these and in many other towns, a great quantity of cider is annually made, which is used extensively, as a common drink; and a small proportion of the surplus is exported; but the principal part of it is manufactured into spiritous liquor, called cider brandy. There is probably no part of the United States, in which the growth of the apple is so sure as upon Connecticut river. Here it never entirely fails. Cider is an excellent and wholesome beverage; but its quality depends in a great measure upon the attention which is bestowed upon its manufacture and preservation; and it is much to be regretted, that so important an article should in general be so much neglected.

Although confined to a general view, yet we cannot permit the culture of onions, in the town of Wethersfield, to pass unnoticed. Of this rare and valuable root nearly one and a half million bunches have been annually raised in this town; which is undoubtedly a greater quantity than is produced in any other town in the United States. Of other local agricultural interests, the cultivation of tobacco and hemp, in East-Windsor, water-melons, and other vegetables for market, in East-Hartford, and garden-seeds, raised for market by the Shakers in Enfield, are deserving of notice.

Roads.—In addition to the public roads, which are numerous, and generally well made, the State is intersected in every direction by turnpikes. The turnpike roads belong to, and were constructed by, incorporated companies. They are generally well constructed, and kept in good repair, and afford great facility to travelling, in the rough and mountainous sections of the State.

The whole number of incorporated turnpike companies in the State is about *seventy;* and the whole capital invested is between *eight and nine hundred thousand dollars.* The first turnpike company was incorporated in 1791; since which, they have been constantly increasing; so that, it is believed, there is no section of the United States so well accommodated with roads as Connecticut.

Bridges.—Both upon the public and turnpike roads, there are substantial and convenient bridges across the small streams in every part of the State; and there are several bridges across the large rivers. Of these, the Hartford bridge, across Connecticut river, at the city of Hartford, claims the first notice. This is one of the most elegant and expensive bridges in the United States. For a description of it, we must refer the reader to the article of Hartford. Next to this, are Enfield bridge also across the Connecticut, connecting the towns of Enfield and Suffield; and Washington bridge, upon the Ousatonick, connecting the towns of Milford and Stratford; for a description of which, the reader is referred to the articles of Enfield and Milford.

Progressive Population, Character and Manners of the People.—This, has always been one of the most populous States in the Union, according to its territorial limits. As early as 1756, the population of Connecticut amounted to 130,611 souls; in 1774, to 197,365; and in 1782, to 209,150. The inconsiderable increase, during this period, was owing to the ravages of war. In 1790, there were 237,946 inhabitants in the State; in 1800, 250,002; and in 1810, 261,942; being 57 persons to a square mile, which exceeds any other State in the Union, excepting Rhode-Island.

National character has generally been considered as depending both upon physical and moral causes; but we are inclined to the opinion, so ably maintained by Hume, that the influence of physical causes ought to be rejected altogether. Among the moral causes, affecting the general character of communities, those of the difficulties or facilities of obtaining subsistence, arising from the natural resources of the country, and their peculiar character, as giving a direction to industry; established institutions, of a political, religious and literary nature; and the manners, customs and prejudices of the first settlers, are the most important. The influence of the latter is much greater than would be supposed; as it is often observed, that the first settlers of a place give it its general character, although they may form but a small proportion of its inhabitants. From the causes here noticed, we can trace the more prominent characteristics of the people of this State, and of the other New-England States; which, in most respects, exhibit great uniformity; and the variety that is observable will be found to correspond with the difference of these and other obvious moral causes. The puritanical character of the first settlers of this State has had an extensive influence, which has not yet subsided; and that the early institutions must have had a permanent and lasting influence, upon the general character of the population, is evident, from the consideration that they have been maintained to the present day, without any very essential changes. The ruggedness and hardness of many sections of the State rendering great industry necessary to procure subsistence; the extensive navigable waters which the State possesses, affording important facilities to trade and intercourse abroad; the extensive, unimproved agricultural resources, to the south, the west, and formerly to the north, inviting cultivation, and promising an easy subsistence, and the rapid acquisition of wealth; these and other causes have contributed to render the people of this State remarkable for their *industry and enterprise*, which form their most important characteristics.

The enterprise of the people of Connecticut has disclosed itself through various channels; but more conspicuously by a spirit of traffic and emigration. The spirit of emigration, which has prevailed so extensively in this State, disclosed itself previously to the Revolutionary war; emigration at this period being directed to the present counties of Dutchess and Columbia, in the State of New-York, and the counties bordering upon Connecticut river in the State of New-Hampshire. After the war, the spirit of emigration revived, and was principally directed to the western section of New-Hampshire, and the territory now comprising the State of Vermont; a large proportion of the original inhabitants of these sections of our country being from Connecticut. Within the last thirty years, the current of emigration from this State has swelled to a torrent, and has been directed principally to the westward. In the States of New-York, Pennsylvania, Ohio and the immense region of the southwest, an extensive wilderness, recently the frightful abode of wild beasts and the ferocious savage, and which presented innumerable obstacles, that seemed insuperable barriers to the inroads of civilization, has been converted into fruitful fields, by the bold and active enterprise, and the hardy and persevering industry of Connecticut emigrants. In contemplating these extensive and flourishing new settlements, it may verily be said, that the "wilderness has blossomed as the rose," and become as fruitful as the gardens of Hesperides. What is a more interesting and sublime object, than to observe the progress of civilization—its rapid inroads upon the domains of the wilderness, driving back its primitive inhabitants, the wild beast and the savage—the formation of new settlements—the growth of towns—the sudden rise of villages, and the general extension of social improvements? These are the valuable fruits of enterprise and industry, in the honour of which Connecticut can claim its full share. It may be safely estimated, that at the present time the emigrants from Connecticut, and their descendants, amount to more than 700,000 souls.

A spirit of traffic has long formed a trait in the character of the people of this State. Enterprise, directed to this channel, has produced the most important results. It has led thousands of our citizens abroad. Prompted by a spirit of pecuniary adventure, they are to be found in every clime and among every people; no hazards have deterred, no obstacles discouraged, and no disasters impaired, the boldness of mercantile adventures, and the ardour with which they have been pursued. This spirit of trade, having, in some instances, elicited in individuals dispositions inconsistent with those principles of integrity which it is necessary to maintain between man and man, has, with the illiberal, the prejudiced and the ignorant, cast a stain upon the character of the State. But nothing can be more unjust, than to judge of the character of an entire community, from the conduct of a few individuals, to whom necessity, or inordinate mercenary views, may have given the character of desperate adventurers. As well might it be said, that because there were some *counterfeiters*, or other felons in community, the whole population deserved that character. Notwithstanding the influence of a spirit of traffic, which generally prevails, the people of this State are not behind their neighbours in personal integrity. And if this spirit is considered as having any unfavourable moral tendencies, the extensive intercourse which it occasions contributes essentially to introduce and diffuse social improvements and refinements among every class of people. The people of this State are, in an eminent degree, sober, peaceable and regular in their conduct, and less given to violence than most other communities. This arises from our institutions, and the regular system, and general advantages as to education, whereby all classes, and almost every individual, obtains a common education.

The people of this State have been considered as remarkably bigoted; and, from the extent and general prevalence of this opinion, have been exposed to the sneers of the illiberal and the uninformed, from the Reviewers of Edinburgh and London, to the newspaper paragraphists in the neighbouring States. Whatever may have formerly been the case, at the present time these opinions are entirely unfounded. They are to be ascribed to the puritanical character of our ancestors, and to that systematic regularity, that scrupulous decorum, which is no where so conspicuously to be observed among the mass of the people, as in this State. But, as licentiousness is no evidence of liberality of sentiment, so on the other hand, precision of conduct is not to be regarded as proceeding from prejudice, or limited and illiberal views. Ignorance is acknowledged to be the parent of prejudice; yet at the same time that the reproach of bigotry is attempted to be affixed to the people of Connecticut, they are acknowledged to be more generally intelligent and enlightened than almost any other community. But this absurdity does not exist. At the present time, freedom of inquiry, liberality of sentiment, independence of thinking and speaking, and a general spirit of toleration and charity, are perhaps no where more conspicuous than in Connecticut.

The people of this State have heretofore been regarded as remarkable for the general prevalence of a litigious spirit. This opinion also is incorrect. The citizens of this State are not now more given to litigation than their neighbours, and probably not as much so as those of the States more recently settled.

If there are any prevailing or peculiar vices belonging to the inhabitants of this State, we think that an avaricious or mercenary spirit is the most conspicuous. This probably is owing in part to the prevailing spirit and habits of trade; but principally to civil institutions, and the established principles and customs of society, which attach an undeserved importance to *property*. These causes are not peculiar to this State; yet, perhaps, from their connection with others, their influence may have been more extensive.

Commerce and Tonnage.—From the situation of Connecticut, being in the neighbourhood of New-York, the great emporium of the United States, and from other causes, its foreign trade has always been limited. What there is, is principally confined to the cities of New-Haven, Hartford, New-London and Middletown, and the boroughs of Bridgeport and Stonington, and the town of Fairfield. But the principal navigation business consists of a coasting trade, carried on with the southern States, New-York, Boston, Providence, the southern shore of Massachusetts, and the District of Maine. The principal articles of exportation are Indian corn, rye and oats, which are sent to the eastward in large quantities; and some cider, butter, cheese and various manufactures to the southern States; shad, beef, potatoes, &c. to New-York; and horses, beef, pork and lumber to the West-Indies or other foreign markets.

Of articles of manufactures, which are sent abroad for a market, spirituous liquors, distilled from domestic materials, particularly gin and cider brandy, are the most important. Gin forms a large and valuable staple for exportation, greatly exceeding any other manufactured article in the State. These articles are sent to New-York, Boston, Providence, the southern States, and in some cases to foreign countries. Large quantities of tin ware are manufactured in the State, which is principally sent abroad for a market, mostly to the southern States. Hats, shoes and other manufactures of leather are articles of exportation to the southern States. Clocks, both of wood and metal, and buttons, of metal and ivory, are articles of exportation; and also ploughs, waggons and carriages, particularly the former, of which large quantities are annually sent to the southern States. The products of the iron manufactories, castings, hollow ware, anchors, &c. are articles of exportation; also muskets, pistols and swords, saddles and harness work, cabinet furniture, combs, brooms, candles and soap, machinery, cards, wooden ware, powder, glass ware, woolen and cotton cloths, marble, freestone, wood, timber for building, ship timber and lumber, are comprised among the exports of the State. The commercial interests, unconnected with navigation, are respectable.

The whole amount of tonnage in Connecticut, in 1815, was 50,358. Since that period, there may have been such additions as to make an aggregate of 60,000 tons of shipping of every description.

Fisheries.—The fisheries of Connecticut consist principally of the smack fisheries of New-London county, and the shad fisheries of the Connecticut and Ousatonick rivers. The shad fisheries in Middlesex county are a source of profit, and form a large item in the exports of the county. Connecticut river shad are of a better quality than any other in the United States, and are worth more in market. They are sent to New-York, and most of the sea-ports in the Union. Considerable quantities of mackerel and black fish are taken in New-London county, a portion of which are sent abroad for a market. Of the shell fisheries, upon Long Island sound, the oyster fishery is the most important. These are marketed in this and the neighbouring States.

Manufactures.—Manufactures in Connecticut constitute an important interest. A manufacturing spirit was early disclosed in this State; and, with the exception of Rhode-Island, there is no State in the Union where it has been cherished with so much attention, or directed to so many objects. The establishment of manufactures depends essentially upon a dense population; which, occasioning a surplus of industry, leads to a diversion of it from agriculture, the first as well as the most important occupation of Society.

From the limited territory of the State, the denseness of its population, the enterprise and industry of its citizens, the numerous water privileges, which abound in almost every section of it, and the great facilities which it possesses for intercourse abroad, Connecticut has superior advantages for manufacturing pursuits; and it is believed that it cannot fail of becoming, at no distant period, an extensively manufacturing community. Already considerable progress has been made in various branches of manufactures; and it may be safely asserted, that, with the exception of Rhode-Island, the aggregate manufacturing industry of this State is greater, in proportion to its population, than that of any other State in the Union.

Of the various manufactures of the State, those of domestic spirits, consisting principally of gin and cider brandy, claim the first rank as articles of exportation, and for their aggregate value. The principal seat of the gin manufacture is in the county of Hartford, particularly in the towns of East-Windsor, Enfield and Windsor. There are, in this county, 21 gin distilleries, some of which are upon an extensive scale. The business is pursued extensively and advantageously, and employs a great amount of capital. The gin manufactured in the aforesaid towns is of an excellent quality, and is mostly sent abroad for a market. These towns, having engaged so extensively in this manufacture, and taken the lead of all others, it is not improbable, that some one of them may ultimately become the *Scheidam of

---

* *A town in Holland, famous for its manufacture of gin.*

America. This business furnishes a ready and advantageous market for grain and wood, and contributes in no small degree to the agricultural prosperity of the county. In addition to the spirits manufactured at these establishments, large quantities of beef and pork are fattened. It has been estimated, that nearly 1000 head of beeves have been fattened at the several distilleries in Hartford county, in one season, besides a great number of swine.

Tin-ware forms another extensive manufacturing interest. This manufacture is pursued principally in the towns of Berlin, Meriden, Southington, Simsbury and others, in Hartford and New-Haven counties. This ware is vended in almost every part of the United States, furnishing employment for a great number of persons, both at home and abroad. Clocks, buttons and shoes are manufactured for exportation in the towns of Waterbury, Plymouth and Wallingford. Hats are manufactured in Danbury, extensively; and shoes in Guilford, Durham and New-Canaan; both of which also form articles of exportation.

The tanneries in Connecticut are numerous, and at many of them the business is pursued upon an extensive scale. Large quantities of leather are annually manufactured, a considerable proportion of which is sent abroad for a market. Large quantities of saddles and harness work are annually exported from Hartford, Bridgeport, many towns in Fairfield county and other parts of the State. There are several morocco leather manufactories in Hartford, New-Haven, Norwich, &c.

Of the manufactures of wood, ploughs claim particular notice, considered as an article of exportation. The seat of this business is in the town of Enfield, where very large quantities of ploughs are annually manufactured, and sent to the southern States. Carriages and waggons are built in and exported from the towns of New-Haven, Burlington, Enfield and many others.

Litchfield county is the principal seat of the iron manufacture. The whole number of forges in the State is 48; of which 39 are in this county. The principal seats of the iron manufacture, in this county, are in the towns of Canaan, Winchester, Salisbury, Kent, New-Milford, Washington, Norfolk, Cornwall and Litchfield. In addition to the various and valuable products of the forges and furnaces, which form the most important interest in iron manufacture, sleigh-shoes, gun-barrels, axes, hoes, nail-rods and cut-nails are manufactured in various towns in this county.

There are also valuable iron manufactures in Stafford; particularly hollow-ware and castings of various kinds. There are 15 furnaces in the State, of every description; but the principal hollow-ware manufactory is in Stafford, which possesses the advantages of bog ore, of an excellent quality for casting, that abounds in various places in the town. Steel-yards and augers are manufactured in Mansfield, rifles and swords are manufactured in Middletown, and muskets, in large quantities for exportation, at the extensive gun factory in Hamden, near New-Haven. Pistols, silver-plate and jewelry are manufactured as articles of exportation, in Berlin, the two first also in Middletown; and the copper and silver smith business is carried on extensively in Hartford, and several other towns. Horn and ivory combs are manufactured in Saybrook, Mansfield and Middletown; machine and hand cards extensively in Hartford, and machinery, for carding &c. in New-Hartford, and various other towns. The manufacture of powder has received considerable attention. There are 11 powder mills in the State, a considerable number of which are in East-Hartford. The manufacture of paper has also received great attention. This manufacture is carried on principally at East-Hartford, Norwich, Windham and Coventry. There are 24 paper mills in the State; and there is a paper-hanging manufactory at Hartford, which pursues the business upon an extensive scale.

The principal seat of the glass manufactures is in East-Hartford and Coventry. There are four glass factories in the State; they manufacture bottles, and glass ware of other descriptions, which are principally sent abroad for a market.

The cotton manufacture in Connecticut is already an important interest, and promises to become an extensive business; opening a wide field for industry, affording employment to a vast amount of capital, and contributing essentially to the general prosperity of the State, by keeping its citizens and capital at home. There are, at this time, 67 cotton factories in the State, some of which are upon an extensive scale. The cotton manufacture commenced about fifteen years ago, and has experienced various vicissitudes, and had to encounter great difficulties; and although the business has at times suffered great depression, yet, in general, it has " grown with its growth and strengthened with its strength." The business was very flourishing during the war, but has been greatly depressed since the peace. It has been reviving, however, for some time past; and now exhibits renewed vigour and activity. New companies are forming, and additional capital is invested in the business; and those establishments which discontinued their operations after the late peace, and were suffered to decay, have, in general, been repaired and put in operation, many of them having been transferred to other hands. This, as well as most other great national interests, seems likely to owe its permanent establishment and ultimate prosperity to the enterprise and sacrifices of individuals. Like the vanguard of an army, those who go forward in most kinds of manufactures, are destined to be sacrificed for the general good.

In the cotton manufacture, Windham county takes the lead; there being in this county 22 cotton factories, most of which are upon a large scale. The extent of the business here, the amount of the capital invested, and the employment which it affords, gives it a rank, second only to that of agriculture, in the interests of the county; and whilst it contributes to its prosperity, it cannot fail of having a salutary effect in checking the spirit of emigration, and of maintaining its population at home.

The woolen manufacture has already become an important business in this State. There are 66 woolen factories; some of which are upon an extensive scale, and employ a large capital and considerable industry. Some of these establishments were among the first in the United States, and have acquired a reputation which has, perhaps, not been attained by any other; particularly those of Humphreysville, Middletown and Wolcottsville. The cloths manufactured at these establishments have united a fine texture with an elegant finishing; and while they have been superior, in strength and firmness, they have been considered as scarcely inferior, in style of manufacture, to first rate English cloths. The woolen manufactories of this State, in common with those of others, have experienced great depression since the peace, but are now beginning to revive; and it is believed that they will generally be able to resume their operations, and that it will soon become a prosperous and important business, and a source of profit as well as of industry. While upon the subject of woolen manufactures, the attention is invited to those which are more emphatically of a domestic character. The domestic manufactures in this State are extensive and important, and consist of woolen, linen and cotton; but the former is the most important. With the exception of the cities, almost every family manufactures the substantial woolen fabrics, for their own consumption. The domestic or household manufacture of woolen cloths is greatly facilitated and promoted, by the number of carding machines and cloth dressing establishments which abound in every direction, and which, within a few years, have become greatly improved in the business. Of the latter, there are in this State more than 200; and of the former, about 250.

Government.—It is well known, that for nearly thirty years, Connecticut and New-Haven formed two distinct colonies, having separate and independent governments. In the year 1639, the inhabitants of the towns of Hartford, Windsor and Wethersfield formed and entered into articles of association, which constituted the basis of the government of the colony of Connecticut, until 1662. This year, a number of the most distinguished citizens, having made application, obtained of Charles II. King of Great-Britain, a charter, constituting the colony of Connecticut, the limits of which were defined, a civil corporation, and investing it with the power of self-government; the authority being entrusted to a Governor, Deputy Governor, twelve Assistants and the freemen of the colony. The provisions of this charter were vague and defective, considered as the basis of a civil government, and many of them scarcely intelligible. It however granted important privileges for a colonial government; there being no other restriction upon the authority of the colony, than that its laws must not contravene those of the parent country.

The colony of New-Haven, which had heretofore been distinct and independent, was included within the colony of Connecticut, as defined by the charter; and after a resistance of several years, they acknowledged the authority of the government of Connecticut established according to the charter.

By the organization of the government under the charter, the legislative power was vested in two branches; one called the Council, consisting of the Governor, Deputy-Governor and twelve Assistants, and the other the House of Representatives, composed of the deputies of the freemen, of which the ancient towns were entitled to two each. The General Court, as these two branches were called, was authorized to make laws, to constitute judicatories, and to exercise all the essential powers of government.

After the declaration of independence, this State did not follow the example of most of the other States, and adopt a written constitution, but continued the government according to the ancient form; a statute being enacted the session following the memorable 4th July, 1776, which provided that the government should continue to be organized and administered according to the provisions of the charter. It was apparent, that this statute could have no more authority than any other act of the General Assembly; and that it might be repealed at any subsequent session; yet, by the common consent of the people, the government was acquiesced in, and continued in this form until the recent formation of a constitution.

By the ancient government, the freemen met semi-annually, in April and in September. The Governor, Deputy-Governor and twelve Assistants were elected in April, for one year; and the deputies were elected both in April and September; being chosen only for six months. Until some years since, the Council constituted the supreme judicial tribunal; being a Court of Errors. But for some years, this power has been lodged in different hands; the several judges of the Superior Court having been constituted the Supreme Court of Errors. With this exception, the government continued without any essential alteration, until the 15th of September 1818, when the present constitution of government was framed by a convention of Delegates, elected by the people for that purpose. The Delegates of this convention were elected in pursuance of a Resolve of the General Assembly, at the preceding May session; each town electing the same number that it did Representatives to the Assembly. By a resolve of the convention, it was directed that the constitution should be submitted directly to the people; and that if a majority of the qualified electors approved of it, it should become the constitution and supreme law of the State. It was accordingly submitted to the electors, assembled in their respective towns, on the 5th day of October, and was ratified by a majority of 1554. From the importance of this instrument, we have thought it better to embody it entire, than to attempt to give an abstract of its provisions.

CONSTITUTION

OF THE STATE OF CONNECTICUT.

PREAMBLE.

The people of Connecticut acknowledging with gratitude, the good providence of God, in having permitted them to enjoy a free government, do, in order more effectually to define, secure and perpetuate, the liberties, rights and privileges which they have derived from their ancestors, hereby, after a careful consideration and revision, ordain and establish the following Constitution and form of Civil Government.

Article First.

DECLARATION OF RIGHTS.

That the great and essential principles of liberty and free government may be recognized and established,

WE DECLARE,

§ 1. That all men, when they form a social compact, are equal in rights; and that no man or set of men are entitled to exclusive public emoluments or privileges from the community.

§ 2. That all political power is inherent in the people, and all free governments are founded on their authority, and instituted for their benefit; and that they have at all times an undeniable and indefeasible right to alter their form of government in such manner as they may think expedient.

§ 3. The exercise and enjoyment of religious profession and worship, without discrimination, shall forever be free to all persons in this State, provided that the right hereby declared and established shall not be so construed as to excuse acts of licentiousness, or to justify practices inconsistent with the peace and safety of the State.

§ 4. No preference shall be given by law to any christian sect or mode of worship.

§ 5. Every citizen may freely speak, write and publish his sentiments on all subjects, being responsible for the abuse of that liberty.

§ 6. No law shall ever be passed to curtail or restrain the liberty of speech or of the press.

§ 7. In all prosecutions or indictments for libels, the truth may be given in evidence, and the jury shall have the right to determine the law and the facts, under the direction of the court.

§ 8. The people shall be secure in their persons, houses, papers and possessions from unreasonable searches and seizures ; and no warrant to search any place, or to seize any person or things, shall issue without describing them as nearly as may be, nor without probable cause, supported by oath or affirmation.

§ 9. In all criminal prosecutions, the accused shall have a right to be heard by himself and by counsel ; to demand the nature and cause of the accusation ; to be confronted by the witnesses against him ; to have compulsory process to obtain witnesses in his favour ; and in all prosecutions by indictment or information, a speedy public trial by an impartial jury. He shall not be compelled to give evidence against himself, nor be deprived of life, liberty or property, but by due course of law. And no person shall be holden to answer for any crime, the punishment of which may be death, or imprisonment for life, unless on a presentment or an indictment of a grand jury ; except in the land or naval forces, or in the militia when in actual service, in time of war, or public danger.

§ 10. No person shall be arrested, detained or punished, except in cases clearly warranted by law.

§ 11. The property of no person shall be taken for public use, without just compensation therefor.

§ 12. All courts shall be open, and every person, for an injury done him in his person, property or reputation, shall have remedy by due course of law, and right and justice administered without sale, denial or delay.

§ 13. Excessive bail shall not be required, nor excessive fines imposed.

§ 14. All prisoners shall, before conviction, be bailable by sufficient sureties, except for capital offences, where the proof is evident, or the presumption great ; and the privileges of the writ of *habeas corpus* shall not be suspended, unless when in case of rebellion or invasion, the public safety may require it ; nor in any case, but by the legislature.

§ 15. No person shall be attainted of treason or felony, by the legislature.

§ 16. The citizens have a right, in a peaceable manner, to assemble for their common good, and to apply to those invested with the powers of government, for redress of grievances, or other proper purposes, by petition, address or remonstrance.

§ 17. Every citizen has a right to bear arms in defence of himself and the State.

§ 18. The military shall, in all cases, and at all times, be in strict subordination to the civil power.

§ 19. No soldier shall, in time of peace, be quartered in any house, without the consent of the owner; nor in time of war, but in a manner to be prescribed by law.

§ 20. No hereditary emoluments, privileges or honours, shall ever be granted, or conferred in this State.

§ 21. The right of trial by jury shall remain inviolate.

Article Second.

OF THE DISTRIBUTION OF POWERS.

The powers of government shall be divided into three distinct departments, and each of them confided to a separate magistracy—to wit—those which are Legislative, to one ; those which are Executive to another, and those which are Judicial to another.

Article Third.

OF THE LEGISLATIVE DEPARTMENT.

§ 1. The Legislative power of this State shall be vested in two distinct houses or branches ; the one to be styled THE SENATE, the other, THE HOUSE OF REPRESENTATIVES, and both together, THE GENERAL ASSEMBLY. The style of their laws shall be, *Be it enacted by the Senate and House of Representatives in General Assembly convened.*

§ 2. There shall be one stated session of the General Assembly, to be holden in each year, alternately at Hartford and New-Haven, on the first Wednesday of May, and at such other times as the General Assembly shall judge necessary ; the first session to be holden at Hartford : but the person administering the office of Governor may, on special emergencies, convene the General Assembly at either of the said places, at any other time. And in case of danger from the prevalence of contagious diseases in either of said places, or other circumstances, the person administering the office of Governor may, by Proclamation, convene said assembly at any other place in this State.

§ 3. The House of Representatives shall consist of electors, residing in towns from which they are elected. The number of Representatives from each town shall be the same as at present practised and allowed. In case a new town shall hereafter be incorporated, such new town shall be entitled to one Representative only ; and if such new town shall be made from one or more towns, the town or towns from which the same shall be made, shall be entitled to the same number of Representatives as at present allowed, unless the number shall be reduced by the consent of such town or towns.

§ 4. The Senate shall consist of twelve members, to be chosen annually by the electors.

§ 5. At the meetings of the electors, held in the several towns in this State in April annually, after the election of Representatives, the electors present shall be called upon to bring in their written ballots for Senators. The presiding officer shall receive the votes of the electors, and count and declare them in open meeting. The presiding officer shall also make duplicate lists of the persons voted for, and of the number of votes for each, which shall be certified by the presiding officer; one of which lists shall be delivered to the Town Clerk, and the other within ten days after said meeting, shall be delivered under seal, either to the Secretary, or to the Sheriff of the County in which said town is situated; which list shall be directed to the Secretary, with a superscription expressing the purport of the contents thereof. And each Sheriff who shall receive such votes shall within fifteen days after said meeting, deliver, or cause them to be delivered to the Secretary.

§ 6. The Treasurer, Secretary and Controller, for the time being, shall canvass the votes publicly. The twelve persons having the greatest number of votes for Senators, shall be declared to be elected. But in cases where no choice is made by the electors, in consequence of an equality of votes, the House of Representatives shall designate by ballot which of the candidates having such equal number of votes, shall be declared to be elected. The return of votes, and the result of the canvass, shall be submitted to the House of Reresentatives, and also to the Senate, on the first day of the session of the General Assembly, and each House shall be the final judge of the election returns and qualifications of its own members.

§ 7. The House of Representatives, when assembled, shall choose a Speaker, Clerk, and other officers. The Senate shall choose its Clerk, and other officers, except the President. A majority of each House shall constitute a quorum to do business; but a smaller number may adjourn from day to day, and compel the attendance of absent members, in such manner, and under such penalties as each House may prescribe.

§ 8. Each House shall determine the rules of its own proceedings, punish members for disorderly conduct, and, with the consent of two thirds, expel a member, but not a second time for the same cause; and shall have all other powers necessary for a branch of the Legislature of a free and independent State.

§ 9. Each House shall keep a journal of its own proceedings, and publish the same when required by one fifth of its members, except such parts as in the judgment of a majority require secrecy. The yeas and nays of the members of either House shall, at the desire of one fifth of those present, be entered on the journals.

§ 10. The Senators and Representatives shall, in all cases of civil process, be privileged from arrest, during the session of the General Assembly, and for four days before the commencement, and after the termination of any session thereof. And for any speech or debate in either House, they shall not be questioned in any other place.

§ 11. The debates of each House shall be public, except on such occasions, as, in the opinion of the House, may require secrecy.

Article Fourth.

OF THE EXECUTIVE DEPARTMENT.

§ 1. The supreme executive power of the State shall be vested in a Governor, who shall be chosen by the electors of the State, and shall hold his office for one year, from the first Wednesday of May next succeeding his election, and until his successor be duly qualified. No person who is not an elector of this State, and who has not arrived at the age of thirty years, shall be eligible.

§ 2. At the meetings of the electors in the respective towns in the month of April in each year, immediately after the election of Senators, the presiding officers shall call upon the electors to bring in their ballots for him whom they would elect to be Governor, with his name fairly written. When such ballots shall have been received and counted in the presence of the electors, duplicate lists of the persons voted for, and of the number of votes given for each, shall be made and certified by the presiding officer, one of which lists shall be deposited in the office of the Town Clerk within three days, and the other within ten days after said election, shall be transmitted to the Secretary, or to the Sheriff of the County, in which such election shall have been held. The Sheriff, receiving said votes, shall deliver, or cause them to be delivered to the Secretary, within fifteen days next after said election. The votes so returned shall be counted by the Treasurer, Secretary and Controller, within the month of April. A fair list of the persons and number of votes given for each, together with the returns of the presiding officers, shall be, by the Treasurer, Secretary and Controller, made and laid before the General Assembly, then next to be holden, on the first day of the session thereof; and said Assembly shall, after examination of the same, declare the person whom they shall find to be legally chosen, and give him notice accordingly. If no person shall have a majority of the whole number of said votes, or if two or more shall have an equal and the greatest number of said votes, then said Assembly, on the second day of their session, by joint ballot of both houses, shall proceed, without debate, to choose a Governor from a list of the names of the two persons having the greatest number of votes, or of the persons having an equal and highest number of votes so returned as aforesaid. The General Assembly shall by law prescribe the manner in which all questions concerning the election of a Governor or Lieutenant Governor shall be determined.

§ 3. At the annual meetings of the electors, immediately after the election of Governor, there shall also be chosen in the same manner as is herein before provided for the election of Governor, a Lieutenant Governor, who shall continue in office for the same time, and possess the same qualifications.

§ 4. The compensations of the Governor, Lieutenant Governor, Senators and Representatives, shall be established by law, and shall not be varied so as to take effect until after an election, which shall next succeed the passage of the law establishing said compensations.

§ 5. The Governor shall be Captain General of the Militia of the State, except when called into the service of the United States.

§ 6. He may require information in writing from the officers in the executive department, on any subject relating to the duties of their respective offices.

§ 7. The Governor, in case of a disagreement between the two Houses of the General Assembly, respecting the time of adjournment, may adjourn them to such time as he shall think proper, not beyond the day of the next stated session.

§ 8. He shall, from time to time, give to the General Assembly information of the state of the government, and recommend to their consideration such measures as he shall deem expedient.

§ 9. He shall take care that the laws be faithfully executed.

§ 10. The Governor shall have power to grant reprieves after conviction, in all cases except those of impeachment, until the end of the next session of the General Assembly, and no longer.

§ 11. All Commissions shall be in the name and by authority of the State of Connecticut; shall be sealed with the State Seal, signed by the Governor, and attested by the Secretary.

§ 12. Every bill which shall have passed both Houses of the General Assembly, shall be presented to the Governor. If he approves, he shall sign and transmit it to the Secretary; but if not, he shall return it to the House in which it originated, with his objections, which shall be entered on the journals of the House; who shall proceed to reconsider the bill. If after such reconsideration, that House shall again pass it, it shall be sent, with the objections, to the other House, which shall also reconsider it. If approved, it shall become a law. But in such cases the votes of both Houses shall be determined by Yeas and Nays; and the names of the members, voting for and against the bill, shall be entered on the journals of each House respectively. If the bill shall not be returned by the Governor within three days, (Sundays excepted) after it shall have been presented to him, the same shall be a law in like manner as if he had signed it; unless the General Assembly, by their adjournment, prevents its return, in which case it shall not be a law.

§ 13. The Lieutenant Governor shall, by virtue of his office, be President of the Senate, and have, when in committee of the whole, a right to debate, and when the Senate is equally divided, to give the casting vote.

§ 14. In case of the death, resignation, refusal to serve, or removal from office of the Governor, or of his impeachment, or absence from the State, the Lieutenant Governor shall exercise the powers and authority appertaining to the office of Governor, until another be chosen, at the next periodical election for Governor, and be duly qualified; or until the Governor impeached or absent, shall be acquitted or return.

§ 15. When the government shall be administered by the Lieutenant Governor, or he shall be unable to attend as President of the Senate, the Senate shall elect one of their members, as President *pro tempore*. And if during the vacancy of the office of Governor, the Lieutenant Governor shall die, resign, refuse to serve, or be removed from office, or if he shall be impeached, or absent from the State, the President of the Senate *pro tempore*, shall, in like manner, administer the government until he be superseded by a Governor or Lieutenant Governor

§ 16. If the Lieutenant Governor shall be required to administer the government, and shall, while in such administration, die or resign during the recess of the General Assembly, it shall be the duty of the Secretary, for the time being, to convene the Senate for the purpose of choosing a President *pro tempore*.

§ 17. A Treasurer shall annually be chosen by the electors at their meeting in April; and the votes shall be returned, counted, canvassed, and declared, in the same manner as is provided for the election of Governor and Lieutenant Governor; but the votes for Treasurer shall be canvassed by the Secretary and Controller only. He shall receive all monies belonging to the State, and disburse the same only as he may be directed by law. He shall pay no warrant or order for the disbursement of public money, until the same has been registered in the office of the Controller.

§ 18. A Secretary shall be chosen next after the Treasurer, and in the same manner; and the votes for Secretary shall be returned to, and counted, canvassed and declared by, the Treasurer and Controller. He shall have the safe keeping and custody of the public records and documents, and particularly of the Acts, resolutions and orders of the General Assembly, and record the same; and perform all such duties as shall be prescribed by law. He shall be the keeper of the Seal of the State, which shall not be altered.

§ 19. A Controller of the public accounts shall be annually appointed by the General Assembly. He shall adjust and settle all public accounts and demands, except grants and orders of the General Assembly. He shall prescribe the mode of keeping and rendering all public accounts. He shall *ex officio* be one of the auditors of the accounts of the Treasurer. The General Assembly may assign to him other duties in relation to his office, and to that of the Treasurer, and shall prescribe the manner in which his duties shall be performed.

§ 20. A Sheriff shall be appointed in each county by the General Assembly, who shall hold his office for three years, removeable by said Assembly, and shall become bound, with sufficient sureties, to the Treasurer of the State, for the faithful discharge of the duties of his office, in such manner as shall be prescribed by law: in case the

Sheriff of any county shall die or resign, the Governor may fill the vacancy occasioned thereby, until the same shall be filled by the General Assembly.

§ 21. A statement of all receipts, payments, funds and debts of the State shall be published from time to time, in such manner and at such periods, as shall be prescribed by law.

Article Fifth.
OF THE JUDICIAL DEPARTMENT.

§ 1. The judicial power of the State shall be vested in a Supreme Court of Errors, a Superior Court, and such Inferior Courts as the General Assembly shall, from time to time, ordain and establish: the powers and jurisdiction of which Courts shall be defined by law.

§ 2. There shall be appointed in each county a sufficient number of Justices of the Peace, with such jurisdiction in civil and criminal cases as the General Assembly may prescribe.

§ 3. The Judges of the Supreme Court of Errors, of the Superior and Inferior Courts, and all Justices of the Peace, shall be appointed by the General Assembly, in such manner as shall by law be prescribed. The Judges of the Supreme Court, and of the Superior Court, shall hold their offices during good behaviour; but may be removed by impeachment; and the Governor shall also remove them on the address of two thirds of the members of each house of the General Assembly: all other Judges and Justices of the Peace shall be appointed annually. No Judge or Justice of the Peace shall be capable of holding his office, after he shall arrive at the age of seventy years.

Article Sixth.
OF THE QUALIFICATIONS OF ELECTORS.

§ 1. All persons who have been, or shall hereafter, previous to the ratification of this Constitution, be admitted freemen, according to the existing laws of this State, shall be electors.

§ 2. Every white male citizen of the United States, who shall have gained a settlement in this State, attained the age of twenty-one years; and resided in the town in which he may offer himself to be admitted to the privilege of an elector, at least six months preceding; and have a freehold estate of the yearly value of seven dollars in this State; or having been enrolled in the militia, shall have performed military duty therein for the term of one year next preceding the time he shall offer himself for admission, or being liable thereto, shall have been, by authority of law excused therefrom; or shall have paid a State tax within the year next preceding the time he shall present himself for such admission; and shall sustain a good moral character; shall, on his taking such oath as may be prescribed by law, be an elector.

§ 3. The privileges of an elector shall be forfeited by a conviction of bribery, forgery, perjury, duelling, fraudulent bankruptcy, theft, or other offence for which an infamous punishment is inflicted.

OF CONNECTICUT. 27

§ 4. Every elector shall be eligible to any office in this State, except in cases provided for in this Constitution.

§ 5. The select men and town clerk of the several towns shall decide on the qualifications of electors, at such times, and in such manner, as may be prescribed by law.

§ 6. Laws shall be made to support the privilege of free suffrage, prescribing the manner of regulating and conducting meetings of electors, and prohibiting, under adequate penalties, all undue influence therein, from power, bribery, tumult and other improper conduct.

§ 7. In all elections of officers of the State, or members of the General Assembly, the votes of the electors shall be by ballot.

§ 8. At all elections of officers of the State, or members of the General Assembly, the electors shall be privileged from arrest, during their attendance upon, and going to, and returning from the same, on any civil process.

§ 9. The meetings of the electors for the election of the several State officers by law annually to be elected, and members of the General Assembly of this State, shall be holden on the first Monday of April in each year.

Article Seventh.
OF RELIGION.

§ 1. It being the duty of all men to worship the Supreme Being, the Great Creator and Preserver of the Universe, and their right to render that worship, in the mode most consistent with the dictates of their consciences; no person shall by law be compelled to join or support, nor be classed with, or associated to, any congregation, church or religious association. But every person now belonging to such congregation, church or religious association, shall remain a member thereof until he shall have separated himself therefrom in the manner hereinafter provided. And each and every society or denomination of Christians in this State, shall have and enjoy the same and equal powers, rights and privileges; and shall have power and authority to support and maintain the ministers or teachers of their respective denominations, and to build and repair houses for public worship, by a tax on the members of any such society only, to be laid by a major vote of the legal voters assembled at any society meeting, warned and held according to law, or in any other manner.

§ 2. If any person shall choose to separate himself from the society or denomination of Christians to which he may belong, and shall leave a written notice thereof with the clerk of such society, he shall thereupon be no longer liable for any future expenses which may be incurred by said society.

Article Eighth.
OF EDUCATION.

§ 1. The charter of Yale College, as modified by agreement with the corporation thereof, in pursuance of an act of the General Assembly, passed in May 1792, is hereby confirmed.

§ 2. The fund, called the SCHOOL FUND, shall remain a perpetual fund, the interest of which shall be inviolably appropriated to the support and encouragement of the public or common schools throughout the State, and for the equal benefit of all the people thereof. The value and amount of said fund shall, as soon as practicable, be ascertained in such manner as the General Assembly may prescribe, published, and recorded in the Controller's office; and no law shall ever be made, authorising said fund to be diverted to any other use than the encouragement and support of public or common schools, among the several school societies, as justice and equity shall require.

Article Ninth.
OF IMPEACHMENTS.

§ 1. The House of Representatives shall have the sole power of impeaching.

§ 2. All impeachments shall be tried by the Senate. When sitting for that purpose, they shall be on oath or affirmation. No person shall be convicted without the concurrence of two thirds of the members present. When the Governor is impeached, the Chief Justice shall preside.

§ 3. The Governor, and all other executive and judicial officers, shall be liable to impeachment; but judgments in such cases shall not extend farther than to removal from office, and disqualification to hold any office of honour, trust or profit, under this State. The party convicted shall, nevertheless, be liable and subject to indictment, trial and punishment, according to law.

§ 4. Treason against the State shall consist only in levying war against it, or adhering to its enemies, giving them aid and comfort. No person shall be convicted of treason, unless on the testimony of two witnesses to the same overt act, or on confession in open court. No conviction of treason, or attainder, shall work corruption of blood, or forfeiture.

Article Tenth.
GENERAL PROVISIONS.

§ 1 Members of the General Assembly, and all officers, executive and judicial, shall, before they enter on the duties of their respective offices, take the following oath or affirmation, to wit:

You do solemnly swear (or affirm, as the case may be) that you will support the Constitution of the United States, and the Constitution of the State of Connecticut, so long as you continue a citizen thereof; and that you will faithfully discharge, according to law, the duties of the office of   to the best of your abilities.
So help you God.

§ 2. Each town shall annually elect select men and such officers of local police, as the laws may prescribe.

§ 3. The rights and duties of all corporations shall remain as if this Constitution had not been adopted; with the exception of such regulations and restrictions as are contained in this Constitution. All judicial and civil officers now in office, who have been appointed by the General Assembly, and commissioned according to law, and all such officers as shall be appointed by the said Assembly, and commissioned as aforesaid, before the first Wednesday of May next, shall continue to hold their offices until the first day of June next, unless they shall before that time resign, or be removed from office according to law. The Treasurer and Secretary shall continue in office, until a Treasurer and Secretary shall be appointed under this Constitution. All military officers shall continue to hold and exercise their respective offices, until they shall resign or be removed according to law. All laws not contrary to, or inconsistent with, the provisions of this Constitution, shall remain in force, until they shall expire by their own limitation, or shall be altered or repealed by the General Assembly, in pursuance of this Constitution. The validity of all bonds, debts, contracts, as well of individuals as of bodies corporate, or the State, of all suits, actions, or rights of action, both in law and equity, shall continue as if no change had taken place. The Governor, Lieutenant Governor, and General Assembly, which is to be formed in October next, shall have, and possess, all the powers and authorities, not repugnant to, or inconsistent with this Constitution, which they now have and possess, until the first Wednesday of May next.

§ 4. No Judge of the Superior Court, or of the Supreme Court of Errors; no member of Congress; no person holding any office under the authority of the United States; no person holding the office of Treasurer, Secretary or Controller; no Sheriff or Sheriff's deputy, shall be a member of the General Assembly.

Article Eleventh.

OF AMENDMENTS OF THE CONSTITUTION.

Whenever a majority of the House of Representatives shall deem it necessary to alter or amend this Constitution, they may propose such alterations or amendments; which proposed amendments shall be continued to the next General Assembly, and be published with the laws which may have been passed at the same session; and if two thirds of each House, at the next session of said Assembly, shall approve the amendments proposed, by yeas and nays, said amendments shall, by the Secretary, be transmitted to the town clerk in each town in this State; whose duty it shall be to present the same to the inhabitants thereof, for their consideration, at a town-meeting, legally warned and held for that purpose; and if it shall appear in a manner to be provided by law, that a majority of the electors present at such meetings, shall have approved such amendments, the same shall be valid, to all intents and purposes, as a part of this Constitution.

Done in Convention, on the fifteenth day of September, in the year of our Lord one thousand eight hundred and eighteen, and of the Independence of the United States the forty-third.

By order of the Convention.

OLIVER WOLCOTT, *President.*

JAMES LANMAN, } *Clerks.*
ROBERT FAIRCHILD,

According to the constitutional provision, the House of Representatives comprises 201 members; and there are about 38,000 electors in the State.

Revenue and Expenditures.—The revenue of the State consists of the proceeds of its permanent funds, certain sources of indirect revenue, of which, duties upon writs, licences, fines and forfeitures, are the principal, and direct taxes.

The permanent funds consisting of United States stock, and of stock in the Banks of this State, amounted, in 1818, to $405,037 35; the annual dividends and interest of which may be estimated at about $25,000; and the indirect revenue, accruing principally from duties upon writs, from fines and forfeitures, duties upon licenses to retailers, the proceeds of Newgate Prison, and some other sources of indirect revenue, amount to from 15 to 20,000 dollars annually; and the nett proceeds of the direct tax, in 1818, was $33,458 58; making an aggregate revenue of from 75 to nearly 80,000 dollars, for the year 1818.

The ordinary civil list expenditures, heretofore, have amounted to from 75 to 85,000 dollars per annum, and have consisted principally of the debentures of the General Assembly, which have usually amounted (there being two sessions in a year) to about $26,000; the salaries of the judicial and executive State officers, the expenses of Newgate Prison, the State Paupers, and various other ordinary and contingent expenses.

Militia.—The militia of Connecticut, according to the returns of the Adjutant General, in 1818, amounted to 20,573; and consisted of six brigades of Infantry, one brigade of Artillery, one of Cavalry and one of Riflemen. There are 24 regiments of Infantry, 3 regiments of Horse Artillery, 2 regiments of Light Artillery, 5 regiments of Cavalry, and 2 regiments of Riflemen. In addition to these, there are four companies of Guards, two of which are Horse-Guards, and two Foot-Guards.

Literature, Seminaries of Learning, Schools and School Fund.—Connecticut has long been distinguished for its literature, and its valuable institutions of learning. It has been considered as being, in America, what Athens was in Greece, the seat of learning and the arts. Although Connecticut has undoubtedly produced her full share of men, eminent for their talents and literary acquirements, yet the reputation which the State has acquired, as it respects learning, has proceeded from a general diffusion of intelligence, among the whole body of the people, and a prevailing thirst for knowledge which pervades every class in society. In these respects this State certainly claims a pre-eminent rank, and is almost without any example in the known world. Not only does almost every person acquire the rudiments of education, but a desire for general reading prevails extensively, and newspapers and books are spread extensively among all classes. From the prevailing spirit of the people, parents in this State have been much in the habit of giving their sons a liberal or academical education; and hence the number which have engaged in the learned professions has been greater here, in proportion to the population, than in almost any other section of the world; a considerable proportion of whom have found it necessary, or deemed it expedient to go abroad to establish themselves in their professions. The advantages for obtaining an education, in the higher branches of literature in this State, are equal to those of any other section of the Union; and the advantages for common education are not surpassed by those of any other community in the civilized world. The subject of common education is not left to the *will* of individuals; but it is made a *public* concern. The principles, calculated to produce this object, form a part of the government itself. They are interwoven into its very texture and organization. The whole State is divided into civil and corporate divisions, for the purposes of primary education, called School Societies. These societies are subdivided into school districts, the limits of a single school. Both the school societies and districts are corporations, and act as such upon all subjects relating to the establishment and maintaining of schools. Of the former there are 207 in the State, and of the latter, 1431, exclusive of those in the town of Weston; information in respect to which was not obtained when this article went to press. In each district there is a school house; for the erection of which, the the district is empowered to tax all the taxable inhabitants within its limits; but the principal concerns of schooling are managed by the school societies.

For the support of the district or primary schools, very liberal provision has been made, by the well known appropriation, called the School Fund. This fund, which arose from the sale of the land reserved by Connecticut in the State of Ohio, amounts at the present time to $1,608,670. It is vested principally in individual credits, secured by bond and mortgage. In the recent constitution, this fund has been established; so that it now rests upon a constitutional provision, and is above the control of the legislature. The proceeds of this fund can be applied to no other object than the support of the primary schools. The annual dividends of this fund have been somewhat variant, but at this time amount to about $60,000; which at present is apportioned to the school societies, according to their lists.

In addition to the school fund, a certain proportion of all the taxes paid to the State is by law appropriated to the support of the common schools.

In addition to the primary schools, there are in this State numerous seminaries for instruction in the higher branches of learning. Yale

College is treated of at length, in the article upon New-Haven, to which the reader is referred. There are 6 incorporated academies. Besides these, there are 26 unincorporated academies and grammar schools, some of which are endowed with funds.

Social Libraries and Newspapers.—There are probably about 172 social libraries in the State, comprising more than 30,000 volumes. In 1818, there were 16 newspaper establishments in this State; from which, probably, more than 16,000 papers were issued weekly.

Religion.—The constitution has secured, in the most ample manner, the rights of conscience and religious liberty; all religious denominations being placed upon an equal footing, and every individual being permitted, as it respects religious faith and worship, to pursue the dictates of his own mind. There are 449 religious societies of every description in this State; of which, about 210 are Congregationalists, 74 Episcopalians, 89 Baptists, 53 Methodists, 7 Separatists, 7 Friends, 2 Universalists, 2 Sandemanians, 1 of Shakers, 1 of Rogerene Quakers, and 3 of denominations not ascertained. Many of these societies are small, and others merely nominal, particularly several of the Congregational societies being classed with that order from the principles of their organization.

History.—Some historical or chronological notices is all that can be expected under this head. The territory, comprising the State of Connecticut, was undoubtedly first visited by the Dutch; but at what period, it is difficult to determine. But it is probable, that it was soon after their settlement at New-Amsterdam, now New-York, in 1615; although they did not erect the trading house, at what is called Dutch Point, being the point of land formed by the union of Mill river with the Connecticut, at Hartford, until about the year 1633. The first information which the English colonies in Massachusetts obtained of the country upon Connecticut river, was in 1631. The first settlement was made in 1635. In 1639, the towns of Hartford, Windsor and Wethersfield entered into articles of association, and organized a government. The colony of New-Haven was first settled in 1638, and a government organized in 1639.

In 1662, the charter was obtained, and both colonies united. In 1687. the charter government was suspended by Sir Edmund Andross, and was restored after the Revolution in England, in 1688. In 1701, Yale College was established; in 1755, the first newspaper in the colony was established at New-Haven. In July 1776, the colony of Connecticut, in common with the others, became independent of Great-Britain; in 1784, the first city was incorporated; in 1792, the first bank was established; in 1806, the manufacture of cotton first began to receive attention. In 1818, a Convention of Delegates from the several towns in the State, convened at Hartford; and after a session of about three weeks, framed a constitution of civil government for the State, which was ratified by the people on the 5th of October following.

A TOPOGRAPHICAL AND STATISTICAL VIEW

OF THE SEVERAL

COUNTIES, TOWNS, CITIES, BOROUGHS, AND VILLAGES,

IN THE STATE

OF

CONNECTICUT.

HARTFORD COUNTY.

HARTFORD COUNTY is of ancient date; and its original limits comprised an extensive district of country, upon both sides of Connecticut river, the entire county of Tolland, most of the counties of Middlesex and Windham, and a part of the counties of Litchfield and New-London, having been detached from it, whereby it has been much circumscribed, although it is still one of the largest counties in the State. It is situated in the northern central section of the State, and principally in the extensive and beautiful valley of Connecticut river—bounded on the north by the county of Hampden, in Massachusetts, on the east by the county of Tolland, on the south by the counties of Middlesex, New-London, and New-Haven, and on the west by the counties of Litchfield and New-Haven. It forms nearly a square, being about 30 miles in length, from north to south, and 25 in breadth, from east to west, comprising an area of about 727 square miles, or 465,280 acres.

The following TOPOGRAPHICAL and STATISTICAL Table exhibits a compendious view of the several towns in the county; their population, according to the census of 1810; dwelling-houses; religious societies; school districts; post-offices, &c.

Towns.	Post-offices.	Population.	Dwelling houses.	Religious societies.	School districts.	Distance from Hartford.
Hartford.	1	6003	850	6	12	
Berlin.	1	2798	400	5	14	10 m. S. W.
Bristol.	1	1423	238	2	9	16 m. S. W.
Burlington.	1	1487	230	3	8	17 m. W.
Canton.	1	1374	220	3	7	13 m. N. W.
East-Hartford.	2	3240	480	4	13	2 m. E.
East-Windsor.	1	3081	500	4	19	6 m. N.

HARTFORD COUNTY.

Towns.	Post-offices.	Population.	Dwelling houses.	Religious societies.	School districts.	Distance from Hartford.
Enfield.	1	1840	274	3	11	17 m. N.
Farmington.	2	2748	400	4	15	10 m. W.
Glastenbury.	1	2766	440	4	13	8 m. S. E.
Granby.	1	2696	380	5	16	17 m. N. W.
Hartland.	1	1284	200	3	9	22 m. N. W.
Marlborough.	1	720	110	3	6	15 m. S. E.
Simsbury.	1	1966	290	2	10	12 m. N. W.
Southington.	1	1807	300	3	9	18 m. S. W.
Suffield.	1	2630	360	4	11	17 m. N.
Wethersfield.	2	3931	600	4	12	4 m. S.
Windsor.	2	2868	400	5	16	7 m. N.

The county of Hartford, whether we consider the advantages of its local situation, being intersected by a fine navigable river, and at the head of its navigation, the pleasantness, diversity, and beauty of its natural scenery and landscapes; the richness, variety, and fertility of its soil; the mildness, uniformity, and salubrity of its climate; the magnitude and multiplicity of its waters, or the general state of its improvements, in agriculture, manufactures, and the useful arts; the number and pleasantness of its villages; the means of agricultural opulence which it affords; its aggregate population, wealth, and resources; will rank before any other county in the State; and, in many of these respects, before any in New-England. With respect to its natural soil, which is the direct or indirect source of almost every interest in society, we feel authorized in hazarding an opinion, that there is not another body of land in New-England, of the same extent, lying together, equal, in quality, to that of this county. And we feel more confident in the assertion, that there is no other, that comprises an equal quantity of alluvial. The Connecticut is justly celebrated for the extent and richness of its meadows; and there is no section throughout its whole course, where they are more enlarged or valuable, than in this county. But the tracts of alluvial are not confined to the Connecticut, but abound upon most of its tributary streams, particularly the Tunxis and Scantic—the former of which is a large and interesting river. The county is intersected not only by Connecticut river, but also by the greenstone range of mountains, which terminates at the east rock, in the vicinity of New-Haven. The section on the west side of the river, extends westwardly, 14 or 15 miles, and the mountain which ranges nearly parallel with the river, is five or six miles back from it. The tract between the river and the mountain is exhaustless in the resources for agricultural improvement and wealth. The natural soil is a deep, strong, argillaceous loam, varied, in different sections, by a greater or less predominance of argil, from a hard and stiff clay,

HARTFORD COUNTY.

to a light, gravelly, and, in some places, sandy loam. It is of an undulating surface—the hills being very moderate, free from stone, and well calculated for improvement. The mountain occasions very little broken, or unimprovable lands, consisting only of a single ridge—and all the declivities of this are valuable for the growth of wood and timber, or for pasturage and orcharding, excepting the bold mural precipice which is formed upon its west side. The general character of the tract west of the mountain, is also argillaceous, although its features are considerably different, and have less uniformity. It is more hilly, and clay enters less into the composition of the soil. The western extremity of this tract is considerably mountainous, particularly the north part of it, embracing the eastern section of the granite mountains, which prevail in the county of Litchfield. Upon the Tunxis river, west of the greenstone range, in Farmington and Simsbury, there are extensive and valuable tracts of alluvial. The section of the county east of Connecticut river, is about nine or ten miles wide, and is likewise rich and fertile, and contains ample and durable resources for agricultural improvements and interests. It has its proportion of alluvial, and its geologial character is also argillaceous, but the super stratum of the soil has less appearance of the prevalence of clay, and is generally a light, gravelly, and sandy loam. The south eastern section of this tract is also somewhat mountainous.

The land in this county is well adapted to a grain culture, particularly that of rye and Indian corn, of which large quantities are annually raised. It is also well adapted to fruit, and is conspicuous for the extent, variety, and richness of its orchards. But in noticing its adaptation to these agricultural productions and interests, it is not to be inferred that it is not favourable for almost all others, of which the climate admits. It is a circumstance, which, when considering the natural resources and advantages of this county for agriculture, ought not to be passed over unnoticed, that there is probably no section in the United States, where there are less physical casualties and obstructions, which attend a cultivation of the earth, and where the fruits of the "sweat of the brow" can be relied upon with more *certainty*. Of all vegetable productions, fruit is perhaps the most precarious; yet it is scarcely within the memory of man, that apples, in this county, have entirely failed.

There is probably no section in the New-England States, less exposed to injurious results from frosts. In the year 1816, however, Indian corn was very generally injured; so much so, that there was a difficulty the next season of obtaining sound corn for seed; but this is the only instance, since our recollection, of a frost occurring so early in the fall, as essentially to injure this grain. Rye, when properly cultivated, and seasonably sown, is a sure crop, and seldom, if ever, fails. The farming interests of the county are very respectable, although it is most apparent that there is great room for improvements; a general deficiency of information upon the subject; want of enterprise; confirmed habits of error and obstinate prejudices; an unwarrantable adherence to long established usages and practices, without investigating their principles, or comparing them with other modes; and that there is a general deficiency of a *scientific system* of agriculture. But recently, a spirit of inquiry upon this important subject seems to be awakened; and aided by the exertions and encouragements of an Agricultural Society, which has been organized in the county under an act of incorporation, it is to be hoped that its salutary results will soon be extensively perceived, and the state of agricultural improvements become commensurate with the natural resources and fertility of the soil.

The waters of the county are most abundant and valuable; besides the Connecticut, the extensive and beautiful vale of which constitutes the greater part of the territory of the county, and annually overflows and fertilizes its borders; there are several of its most considerable tributary streams, which intersect this county, and discharge their waters within its limits.

The Tunxis, or Farmington river, which embodies the waters from the west and north, unites with the Connecticut, in Windsor, and is undoubtedly the largest tributary stream of the latter, throughout its whole course.— Within this county, this river is swelled by the waters of two considerable streams—the Poquaback, which unites with it in Farmington, and Salmon brook, which discharges itself in Granby. Besides the Tunxis and its branches, the principal tributary waters of the Connecticut, within this county, from the west, are embodied in Mill and Stoney rivers; the former discharges itself at Hartford, and the latter at Suffield.

Upon the east side of the Connecticut, its principal tributary streams, are the Freshwater, Scantic, Podunk and Hockanum, which, beginning at the north section of the county, discharge themselves in the same order, as they are here noticed.

Having given a compressed view of the natural features and character of this county, and its resources, agricultural productions & wealth, and alluded to the state of improvement of the same, it would be unjust, if not invidious, not to notice other interests and improvements, particularly the leading and most considerable branches of manufactures. The most important and extensive manufacturing interest in this county, is that of the distillation, or manufacturing of grain into spirits. It is, we think, keeping most distinctly within the bounds of truth, to assert that this manufacture is pursued to greater extent, and probably more advantageously, and with more practical knowledge and experience, in this county, than in any other in the United States. There are 21 grain distilleries in the county; some of which are upon a very extensive scale. Some idea of the quantity of spirit manufactured can be formed from the duties paid during the late war, which, in 1816, amounted to nearly $40,000. But at that time, the heavy duties, and other causes,

HARTFORD COUNTY. 37

growing out of the state of the times, had very much depressed the business, and many establishments had entirely discontinued their operations. Of the general policy and influence of this manufacture, in a pecuniary, moral, and social point of view, very different opinions prevail. It seems, upon a superficial examination, essentially objectionable, that so great a devastation should be made, as this manufacture occasions, of an article of prime necessity for food, thereby increasing the difficulties and expense of subsistence, if not occasioning distress and want, with the poor and unfortunate; and more peculiarly so, from the consideration that the products of this article are, with reference to the means of subsistence, not only useless, but essentially deleterious, destructive to health, to morals, and social order and happiness. But as it respects the consumption of grain, which is occasioned by its distillation into spiritous liquors, if it is regarded as an evil, it is one which, in a great measure, corrects itself, as the convenient and advantageous market, which is thereby afforded, operates as a powerful stimulous to an increased cultivation of the article. And with regard to the use of ardent spirits, it is by no means an established theorem, that its local manufacture increases its local consumption. That the manufacture of grain-spirits, in this county, has had a favourable influence upon its agricultural interests, cannot be doubted. The manufactures of Cotton and Woolen, aside from those of a domestic character, are not extensive; there are, however, 13 Cotton Factories, and 9 Woolen Factories; in addition to which there are 37 Fulling Mills and Cloth Dressing Establishments, and 38 Wool Carding Machines, for customers. There are in the county various other manufacturing establishments, of different descriptions. There are 11 Powder Mills, 8 Paper Mills, 5 Oil Mills, 83 Grain Mills, 2 Forges, and 2 Glass Works. In the southern part of the county, the manufacture of Tin-Ware is an important and extensive business. Buttons and spoons, of metal; ploughs, (sent to the southern States) horn and ivory combs, with various others, are among its manufactures, which are articles of exportation.

We cannot enlarge upon the social improvements of the county, but it is believed that there are few sections in our country, exhibiting more ample, extensive, and diversified testimonials of industry, enterprise, and perseverance; and of their necessary and salutary results, order, convenience, and competence. The great northern roads, upon each side of the river, present nearly one continued village, and corresponding improvements, of almost every description, characterized by their plainness, neatness, order, and convenience, which serve as a faithful index of the state of society; of the social and domestic habits, economy, regularity, virtues, and happiness of the people. The county contains 32 School Societies, each of which is subdivided into a convenient number of School Districts, of which there are in all 210. There are also in the county 67 Religious Societies, 30 Social Libraries, and more than 200 Mercantile Stores. Its aggregate population, according to the census of 1810, was 44,733; and the amount of taxable property, as rated in making up lists, including polls, in 1817, was $910,523.

HARTFORD.

HARTFORD, the seat of justice for the county and semi-capital of the State, is located on the west side of Connecticut river, fifty miles northwestwardly from the mouth of the river at Saybrook bar. It is in north latitude 41,44, and west longitude, 72, 50. Hartford comprises an area of about thirty square miles, making 19,200 acres; being six miles in length upon its west line, five and a half miles upon its east line, and averaging about five miles in breadth. It is bounded west on Farmington, south on Wethersfield, north on Windsor, and east on East-Hartford and East-Windsor; the north line, or boundary, extending about one hundred rods farther north, than the north line of East-Hartford. The town is divided by a small stream called *Mill river*, with high romantic banks, over which is a bridge connecting the two divisions of the town.

SURFACE, SOIL & NATURAL PRODUCTIONS. The area of this town is characteristically waving and uneven; extending only about five miles west from the river, it embraces no portion of those extensive mountainous ranges, which run through a considerable part of the interior of New-England. Although very far removed from a plain, it can scarcely be called hilly. The eminences are small, forming in general an angle of about 15 or 20 degrees.

An undulating and waving landscape is every where presented to the view, and the eye can scarcely range fifty rods upon a level surface. This character of the face of the country gives it, in the season of vegetation, a peculiar variety, diversity, and interest; and, at the same time, considering the predominating argillaceous quality of the soil, facilitates its cultivation, and greatly increases its productiveness. The extensive and valuable alluvial tract bordering upon Connecticut river, which in many places is nearly half a mile in width, is an exception to these remarks.

The soil of this town, which is characterized with much uniformity, is an argillaceous loam. It is, in general, an admixture of clay and coarse gravel, in which the former greatly predominates. In its primitive state, and before enriched and warmed by manures, either artificial or formed from the natural decay or decomposition of vegetable substances, (if it can be supposed, that there was ever such a time,) it must have been hard, stiff, and difficult of cultivation. The soil has an inexhaustible bottom, but its great defect is the predominance of clay or argillaceous earths. Hence it is easy to discover the proper mode of cultivating

HARTFORD.

and improving it, as a correct system of agriculture must always have a just reference to the natural quality of the soil. Without referring to the brilliant analytic discoveries of modern chemistry for practical purposes, the primitive or natural earths which are the component parts of all soils, are sand, argil or clay, gravel & lime. Clay is seldom united with lime or calcarious earths, but always is compounded more or less with gravel, or silicious sand. Where the clay predominates, as in this town, the obvious mode of improving the soil, is to correct the excess of argillaceous earths. And hence, on a soil of this description, *manures* of every kind have a most salutary and lasting effect. They not only render the land productive from their immediate influence, but by gradually amalgamating with the soil, counteract the excess of the clay, and form a rich mould, of a character, apparently entirely different from the natural earth. And hence too, on such a soil gravel or sand is of the greatest utility. A gentleman of this city, about ten years since, in forming a yard or square, which intervened between his house and the road, overspread the land with a course of gravel of considerable depth, taken from the bed of the river; it was then dressed with a rich course of manure, since which period, it has uniformly produced two heavy crops of grass each season, of the first quality, without having received any additional supply of manure, during this long period.

In the south part of the town, towards Wethersfield, the soil is more inclining to sand, and in some small sections this is a predominating quality. The tract of meadow upon Connecticut river, which is formed by alluvial deposits, is naturally fertile, feasible, and productive. It produces all kinds of grasses, plants, esculent roots, and grains adapted to the climate; and never fails to reward, in the most ample manner, the labours of the judicious and faithful husbandman.

There are not many forests in this town, but the natural growth of trees are oak of the various kinds, walnut or hickory, elm, ash, maple, button-wood, willow, hornbeam, sassafras, thorn, locust, butternut, birch, wild cherry, bass, alder, sumach and various shrubs, and trees of small growth.

GEOLOGY. We can give only a few notices upon this important and interesting subject.

Geological knowledge, in this country, is extremely scanty and imperfect. There is no science of so great utility, and which, at the same time, affords so amusing and interesting a study, as that which embraces an inquiry into the nature and geological structure of the globe which we inhabit, that has been so much neglected. But of late, it has made great progress in Europe; and Cuvier, Werner, Davy, Humboldt, and others, have exploredthe bowels of the earth, and disclosed its innumerable hidden secrets and treasures. And in the United States, an investigation of the internal structure of our extensive mountains, and other subjects of geological enquiry, are beginning to attract the attention of men of science, throughout the union. In Connecticut. with the exception of the scientific industry and inquiries of one gentleman,* we know of little that has been attempted, calculated to afford even a scanty knowledge of its mineralogy, and geological structure.

The internal structure of this township, has never been a subject of particular or scientific examination. The soil, with the exception of the alluvial lands on the river, is of a primitive formation, and is composed of argil, and a coarse sand, or gravel, and affords no minerals, nor any evidences of marine or alluvial deposits. From the bed of Mill river, and other streams which intersect the town, and from the general geological character of the district of country upon Connecticut river, extending from the narrows below Middletown, to Deerfield, in Massachusetts, there can be no doubt but that the whole township reposes upon a bed of *argillaceous schistus*, or *clay slate* rock. This rock is stratified, and exhibits a strata, forming an angle of about fifteen degrees with the horizon. There are several varieties of the clay slate rock; some of which are found to be of the most metalliferous kind, and to abound with minerals, and the ore of the various metals. But the clay slate formation of this town, although never particularly examined, affords no evidences of mineral or metallic treasures. It is of a primitive formation, and exhibits no appearances of marine shells, or muscular impressions.

This rock has never been penetrated to any considerable extent;

* *Professor Silliman.*

but from the principles of geology, being of the primitive order, which never rest upon secondary rocks, it would follow that it is not underlaid by any secondary formations, or rocks inclosing animal remains, shells, or marine deposits.

About two miles west from the river is an extensive quarry, or bed of wall stone; it is composed of strata of clay slate, caped with green stone, and *red sand stone*, which is nearly an indurated clay, being formed of grains of sand, connected together by a basis of clay slate. This quarry is of considerable utility, as affording the means of supplying the city, and other parts of the town in the vicinity, with stone for building, and various other purposes.

RIVERS. This township, bordering on Connecticut river, which annually overflows its banks, and fertilizes its borders, and being near the head of tide water, enjoys to a greater extent than any other town, the advantages of one of the finest rivers in the world.

Mill river is the only stream within this town, deserving of notice. It is formed from the junction of Wintonbury and Woods rivers, which unite about two miles from its mouth. The former of these streams rises in, and runs through the west Society of Windsor, of the same name; the latter has its sources in, and runs through the western part of Wethersfield. On their entering into this township, the one runs southeasterly, & the other northeasterly, nearly upon a line, whereby they intersect the township into two nearly equal parts, east and west, of these streams:

HARTFORD.

the eastern section being also intersected transversely, by Mill river, formed from the union of the two. Mill river is a rapid stream, with elevated and romantic banks, which, from its vicinity to the city, exhibits rural prospects and scenery extremely irregular, fanciful and pleasing. On or near its banks back from the city, are some elegant seats, affording the most charming and interesting prospects of the city, and the surrounding country. This stream, near its mouth, has rapid falls, that are supported by the bed of argillaceous rock, already noticed; a circumstance of the greatest importance, and of which the inhabitants have not availed themselves to the greatest extent. It affords numerous sites and privileges for mills, manufacturing establishments, machinery, and almost every kind of hydraulic works. These privileges, if not improved to the greatest extent, have not been neglected. There are one Cotton Factory, two Woolen Factories, two Grist Mills, Clothier's Works, and other Water Works, which have been erected upon this stream.

ROADS. There are few towns uniting more conveniences, or better accommodated, with respect to roads, than Hartford. Among others, the following public roads pass through, or centre in this town; most of which are turnpikes, or artificial roads.

1st. The great atlantic road to New-York, through New-Haven, distance, - - 123 miles.
2d. The same to Boston, thro' Springfield, - - 128 miles.
3d. The same do. through Stafford, - - 98 miles.
4th. The same do. through Ashford, - - 99 miles.
5th. Road to Albany, through Sheffield, - - 95 miles.
6th. Road to do. through Lenox, - - 94 miles.
7th. The road to Brattleboro,' (Vt.) through Northampton, on the west side of Connecticut river, - - - 90 miles.
8th. Road to Hanover, (N. H.) through Springfield, on the east side of the river, - 140 miles.
9th. Road to Providence, thro' Windham, - - 74 miles.
10th. Road to New-Haven, thro' Middletown, - 40 miles.
11th. do. through Berlin, - - - 34 miles.
12th. do. through Farmington, - - 38 miles.
13th. Road to Hudson, 78 miles.
14th. Road to New-London, - - - 42 miles.
15th. Road to Norwich, 40 miles.
16th. Road to Danbury, 58 miles.

The foregoing roads, whether turnpikes or not, are well made; and there are few weeks in the year in which they will not be found by travellers substantially good and pleasant in the vicinity of this town. Eighteen mails communicate with the Post-office in this town, several of which are daily; there are also thirteen different lines of stages, which communicate with Hartford. It is believed, therefore, that there is no town of its size in the United States, that unites so many facilities and conveniences for communication and intercourse abroad.

AGRICULTURE, HORTICULTURE, &c. The lands in this town indicate the cultivation of grass, as a leading agricultural interest. The grass, cultivated by the farmers of this town, is of a very fine and superior quality; and when the land is properly laid down and manured, it is produced in great abundance. The lands, which are in the highest state of grass culture, produce two crops in a season, yielding four, and in some instances five or six tons of hay to the acre, which is worth from ten to twenty dollars per ton; however, two or three tons is an average crop for grass lands, in a tolerable state of cultivation.

The agricultural interests of this town, considering the advantages of its local situation, the goodness of its market, and the natural quality of the soil, cannot be said to be very flourishing. Lands of a clay basis ought never to be cultivated to grass for more than three years in succession, unless they are dressed very copiously with manure. The plough, "heaven's second best gift to man," can no more be dispensed with upon a grass, than upon a grain farm. Without ploughing or manuring, the best lands are liable to be ruined. By turning up the sods, and exposing them to the action of the elements, rain, heat, and frosts, they become warmed, softened, & impregnated with nitrous qualities.

In this, as well as most other towns in this county, lands are suffered to remain too long in the same state, and are cropped in the same way, year after year, in succession.

To plough lands to enrich them, would be a novel idea with our farmers, although it is a necessary part of the system of agriculture of many countries.

Among the grains cultivated, Rye and Indian Corn receive the most attention. The latter is cultivated with the greatest facility, and with abundant success upon the meadows of Connecticut river, but its cultivation ought not to be encouraged. Of all culmiferous or seedling plants, it is the greatest exhauster of the soil: from the magnitude of its stalks, the extension of its roots, and the scantiness of its foliage, it takes away every thing, and leaves nothing.

Wheat, the most valuable of all grains, is much neglected, although there can be no doubt, from the description of the soil, that with proper culture and attention, the land would carry crops of it in great abundance and perfection.

Among the esculent roots cultivated, the potatoe holds a distinguished rank. It is raised with great facility, and in great abundance.

Gardening in this town, particularly in the city, has received considerable attention. A large portion of the families cultivate gardens, and do not seem disposed to depend upon the market for culinary vegetables.

There are a number of gardens here, which, whether we consider the pleasantness and beauty of situation, the style and order in which they are arranged, the neatness and attention with which they are cultivated, or the number, variety, and luxuriancy of the plants, roots, and vegetables, which they afford, are not probably surpassed by any in the State.

Summer and autumn fruits are also cultivated in gardens, and elsewhere. Among those cultivated

HARTFORD. 43

upon trees, shrubs, and plants, are apples, apricots, cherries, nectarines, peaches, pears, plums, quinces, currants, gooseberries, raspberries, and strawberries.

STATISTICS. The population of this town, at the census, in the year 1800, was 5347 persons; in 1810, 6003. At the present time, (1818) it may be estimated at 6500.

There are in Hartford,
850 Dwelling houses.
6 Houses for public worship.
12 District schools.
1 do. for Friends.
9 Printing offices.
21 Taverns, or public Inns.
18 Ale, porter, and small beer houses.
14 Houses concerned in navigation.
5 Wholesale dry goods stores.
26 Dry goods retail stores.
61 Grocery, crockery, and provision stores.
7 Druggist's stores.
5 Grain mills.
4 Clothier's works.
1 Cotton factory, of 320 spindles.
2 Woolen do. one of which is in operation, and employs 15 workmen.
2 Carding machines.
1 Machine card factory, which manufactures $10,000 worth of cards annually.
8 Distilleries.
1 Oil mill.
6 Tanneries.
5 Potteries.
1 Button factory.
1 Whip-lash factory, which manufactures $10,000 worth of the article annually.
2 Hat factories, one of which is upon an extensive scale, and employs 36 workmen.
2 Tin ware factories.
2 Looking glass factories, which together manufacture $30,000 worth of goods annually.
4 Coppersmiths, two of which carry on the business upon a large scale; one of them employing about 20 workmen.
13 Black smith's shops.
1 Bell foundery.
1 Air furnace.
1 Paper-hanging manufactory.
1 Marble paper do.
6 Book binderies.
7 Book stores.
6 Sign, coach, & house painters.
2 Portrait painters.
3 Engravers.
8 Gold and silver smith's shops.
15 Shoe factories.
1 Fine, or morocco leather do.
4 Shoe stores.
8 Cabinet furniture, and chairmakers.
19 Master house joiners and carpenters.
6 Master masons and brick layers.
4 Carriage makers.
2 Wheel wrights.
10 Coopers.
1 Pewter factory.
1 Burr mill stone manufactory.
2 Leather dressers.
2 Gold leaf manufactories.
1 Umbrella manufactory.
5 Merchant tailors.
6 Tailor's shops.
9 Millinery and mantuamaker's shops.
1 Silk dyer.
1 Sail maker.
1 Brush manufacturer.
6 Bakers.
1 Confectioner.
5 Barber's shops.
3 Auctioneers.
3 Exchange offices.

3 Lottery offices.
16 Butcher's stalls, belonging to the two public markets.

The list of the town, in 1817, was $137,845,75; there were 628 taxable polls; 26 minors; 395 horses; 370 oxen; 820 cows, &c.; 2075 acres of arable or plough lands; 7292 ¾ upland, mowing, and clear pasture; 581 bog meadow, mowed; 5127 bush pasture; 172 chaises, and 12 coaches.

The late valuation, or assessment of the lands and houses of the town, made in pursuance of the laws of the United States, in the year 1816, was $3,168,872,32. In the year 1799, 751,532,91.

The number of dwelling houses, the same year, was 593.

This statement, of the valuation of real estate, and of the number of dwelling houses, at these two different periods, is a striking evidence of the growth, and rising importance of the town. In the course of the last nineteen years, the dwelling houses have increased 227; and in the short space of seventeen years, the real estate of the town increased more than *four hundred per cent;* making an entire addition of $2,417,339,41, which is more than three times the amount of the value, at that time, of the whole real estate of the town. This has not been a period of great, or even usual prosperity. It has been marked by a succession of commercial difficulties, embarrassments, and restrictions. From 1805—6, to the close of the late war, the commercial interests of the country were more or less precarious and embarrassed, and, at times, wholly suspended.

The system of warfare carried on by the two great belligerents of Europe, either involved all other powers, or from a total disregard of all established principles, tended to abridge and sacrifice their commercial rights and interest.

This country, from the enterprise of its citizens, and the extent of its commercial interests, suffered more severely than any other. The embargo and restrictive measures ensued, which were followed by war; which, together, comprised a period of eight years, of peculiar commercial difficulties. Since the peace, the manufacturing interests that had grown up during the war, have been nearly sacrificed, and those of trade have experienced great languor. The depression of these interests necessarily affects that of agriculture; during this period, also, there has been a constant course of emigration from the State, and from this town and vicinity; yet, under these inauspicious circumstances, the property of the town has increased, by rise of real estate, and the addition of buildings, four fold; but it is not to be inferred that the size, or business of the town, has extended in this ratio. The rise of real estate proceeds from other causes; it is influenced not only by population and business, but by improvements, social refinements, and almost the whole train of artificial causes, which exist in society.

The augmentation, or rise of property, has enriched the land holders in a manner, and to an amount, of which they are scarcely sensible. They have become rich, without exertion or calculation; they have profited from the indus-

HARTFORD.

try, the enterprise, and the business of others, whether successful or profitable to themselves, or not. The improvements, the refinements, and even the luxuries and vices of society, which ruin others, have been a source of gain to them. If, under these circumstances, the town has advanced in wealth and importance, in this astonishing ratio, whatever may be thought of the influence of emigration, or other unfavourable circumstances, it may be safely calculated, that it will continue to extend its size; its interests; and its consequence.

In Hartford, there are 5 officiating Clergymen; 22 practising Attornies; 12 practising Physicians and Surgeons. There are, of militia, 1 company of Light Artillery; 2 companies of Infantry; one do. of Light Infantry; one company of Riflemen; also, one company of Horse, and one of Foot Guards. These several military companies, in style, and elegance of uniform; in correctness of discipline; and in skilfulness of military evolutions, are not surpassed by any companies of militia in the United States.

There are about 1000 Electors, or Freemen, in this town; a number which exceeds, by several hundreds, any other town in the State.

The civil divisions of Hartford are two Ecclesiastical Societies; 12 districts for Schools, and an incorporated City.

HARTFORD CITY was incorporated in 1784; it comprises an area of about seven hundred acres, being more than a mile in length upon the river, and about three fourths of a mile in breadth. Its site, if not in every respect eligible, is pleasant and interesting. The alluvial flat upon the river is narrow, being from 40 to a hundred rods, and connects with the upland with a very gradual elevation. There are several streets upon the flat, and several upon the rise of land, which, though not parallel, run in a corresponding direction with the river. These streets are intersected by a number of others, running back from the river, but do not regularly cross them at right angles. The city is irregularly laid out, and rather appears, with respect to the order of it, to have been the result of circumstances, than design or arrangement. It comprises in all twenty-four streets, of which Main-street, being the great river road, and extending through the city, from north to south, in a serpentine direction, is the principal. This street is well built, and, for more than a mile, presents an almost continued range of buildings; many of which are large and elegant brick edifices. It comprises most of the public buildings, and a considerable proportion of the population, wealth, & business of the city. The street is not paved, but has been underlaid with a stratum of stone, which renders it firm and generally dry, and it has convenient and handsome flagged side walks.

State-street, next to Main-street, claims a conspicuous notice. Running westerly from the river, it connects with Main-street by two branches, which enclose the State House square. This union forms the most central part of the city, and is its greatest theatre of activity and business. This street, towards Main-street, is compactly built, and contains many large and elegant brick buildings.

Morgan-street extends from the principal angle or curve in Main-street, eastwardly to the great bridge across the river opposite the city. This street, being in a great measure dependent upon the bridge for its population and consequence, was not of much consideration at the time that was erected; since which, in the short interval of about nine years, it has become an important section of the city. The repair, or re-building of the bridge, which has taken place the season past, giving it a more permanent and durable character, and correcting some of its inconveniences, in connection with the circumstance of the discontinuance of the ferry, must have a sensible influence upon the growth and importance of Morgan-street.

Commerce-street runs along the bank or margin of the river. It is the seat of a considerable portion of the maritime business, and many of the houses, concerned in navigation, have stores in this street.

Ferry-street extends westerly from the river, at the landing of the ferry, to Front-street. It was built at an early period, and has always been a compressed and active part of the city. An apprehension has been indulged, that the discontinuance of the ferry, thereby diverting the public travel to Morgan-street, would essentially injure this section of the city; but it is believed that there is little foundation for this idea. Ferry-street contains several mercantile houses, engaged in navigation, and a great number of respectable Grocers and Traders.

Front-street extends from the northern part of the city, to Mill river. It is considerably built, and is increasing in population; yet it sustains little, or no commercial business.

Prospect-street extends from State-street, to School-street. It is delightfully situated, and is ornamented with a number of superb dwelling-houses, and elegant and tasteful gardens.

Trumbull-street extends from the north part of Main-street, to Mill river. It contains many dwelling houses; some of which are elegant brick buildings, and is a pleasant and healthy street for a residence. An extension of this street to the New-Haven turnpike, and the erection of a bridge across the river, which would be necessary for this purpose, could not fail to add greatly to its consequence, and that of other sections of the city.

Pearl-street, extending from Main to Trumbull-street, is short, but very handsomely built, comprising a number of elegant brick edifices.

Church-street runs westwardly from Main-street; it has many neat and well built houses.

West-street is a pleasant, prospective and rural situation. It has a considerable elevation, and affords a view of the whole city, and unites the pleasantness, and, in some measure, the conveniences of the country and city.

Within the limits of the corporation, the city of Hartford contains 540 dwelling houses, which afford convenient tenements for nearly seven hundred families. The population of the city, at the census of 1810, was 3955, exclusive of the suburbs. The public buildings of the city are, a State House, four Churches, two Banking houses, a State Arsenal, (being just without the limits of the corporation,) and a county Gaol. The State House, which is situated in the central public square already noticed, is a stately stone and brick edifice of the doric order, being 114 feet by 76, including the two porticos; the walls of which are 54 feet in height. The two porticos are 38 feet by 17 each. On the basement floor is a large hall or area, extending through the building; on the left of which is a spacious and convenient court-room, on the right are two rooms occupied as public offices by the Treasurer and Controller. On the second floor are two spacious halls or apartments designed for, and occupied by, the two Houses of the Legislature; that on the right or the south wing of the building, being occupied by the Governor and Council, is called the Council Chamber; that in the north wing, being occupied by the House of Representatives, is denominated the Representatives' Chamber. The latter is provided with a small and inconvenient gallery, and the former with none at all. At the late session of the Assembly, however, a resolution was adopted, and a committee appointed to provide a gallery or bar to the Council Chamber, so as to admit spectators. Upon the second floor in the portico, at the west end of the building, is a room occupied as an office by the Secretary of State. On the third floor are several large rooms designed for committee-rooms, but which are considerably neglected. If the Legislature could be persuaded to make a small annual appropriation for the purchase of a library, to be called the State Library, one of those rooms would be a convenient apartment for this purpose; and having been occupied for a number of years by Mr. Stewart's museum, it has already become consecrated to the arts and sciences.

The new congregational meeting house, situated in Main-street, is a superb brick edifice, being 104 feet by 64; and its style and architecture, which is of the Ionic order, are among the finest specimens of the arts that are to be found in this State; in front, it has a lofty and elegant portico, supported by eight large columns, four in front and four in rear, resting upon an elevated stone base, which is approached by a flight of steps.

The two banking houses, one situated in Main, and the other in State-street, are elegant and neat buildings; and are also fine specimens of the arts. The Hartford bank, in State-street, is a brick edifice with a portico in front, supported by four stone columns resting upon an elevated basement, which is surrounded by a flight of steps. The Phœnix bank, in Main-street, directly opposite the State House, has an elegant white marble front; the other walls are of brick. It is entered by an elevated flight of steps, ornamented with an iron balustrade fence.

The State Arsenal is situated just north of the limits of the city, on the country road. It is a substantial fire-proof brick building, designed as a place of deposit for arms and military stores. It was erected during the late war, and at this time contains about seven thousand stands of arms, more than forty pieces of ordnance, and a large quantity of military stores belonging to the State.

HARTFORD BRIDGE, across Connecticut river, opposite this city, communicating with Morgan-street, is a stately and magnificent structure; of great public convenience, as well as advantage to this city. This bridge was originally erected in the year 1809, at an expence of more than $100,000, inclusive of the extensive causeways, upon the east side of the river. It was partially swept away by the freshet, in the spring of 1818, and was rebuilt the succeeding summer and autumn. The present bridge is constructed upon different principles from the former one, and is greatly improved from it. Its arches, of which there are six, of 150 feet each, are above the floor of the bridge, strengthened by strong braces, and well secured from the weather, the whole wood work being covered.

The arches rest upon six heavy stone piers, and two abutments. One of those piers was erected in building the present bridge, and the rest raised, enlarged, and strengthened. There is a safe and convenient draw, upon the west side of the river, which obviates any serious obstruction to the navigation above this city. The bridge, inclusive of the draw, is 974 feet in length, and 36 feet in width. It has convenient side walks for the accommodation of foot passengers; is provided with what are termed "dead lights," upon each side, and sky lights upon the roof, at 20 feet distance, and a suitable number of lamps.

The timber of the arches, and wood work of the bridge, is almost exclusively pine, and being strongly constructed, and well secured from the weather, it cannot fail of being permanent and durable. As the facility which it affords to travel is an advantage to the interests of this city, so the elegance and grandeur of its structure are an addition to its appearance. This bridge, whether we consider its size, its strength, or the elegance of its structure, and general magnificence of its appearance, is surpassed by few in the United States. The expense of rebuilding and repairs in 1818, was about $40,000, making the whole cost about $150,000.

There is a bridge across Mill river, which connects the two parts of the town. It has heretofore been of wood, but a new bridge is now erecting, which is to be supported by stone piers.

There are in the city of Hartford nineteen schools, three of which are public or district schools, and have been included in the number of district schools belonging to the town; fifteen of the others are private schools, and one an incorporated grammar school. One of the public schools is deserving of particular notice; it is established and conducted upon the new economical and improved method of instruction. It is the largest school in the state, and probably in New-

HARTFORD.

England; containing usually 600 scholars, all of whom are superintended by one principal instructor, and ten assistants. The scholars are divided into numerous classes, according to their acquirements, and are severally permitted to progress from class to class, according to the proficiency which they may make, which tends to encourage and stimulate them to exertion. The grammar school has a handsome fund, and has at times sustained a high reputation. Scholars are taught the English and Latin languages, and the rudiments of the sciences, whereby they are fitted for college. Several of the private schools have deservedly a very high reputation; a number are designed exclusively for young Misses, and are considerably celebrated.

At the present time there are 1132 scholars which attend the several public and private schools in the city.

Among the institutions of learning in this city, the "Asylum" for deaf and dumb persons is deserving of particular notice. It was incorporated in May 1816, and was opened for scholars in April 1817. This is the first institution of the kind in America, and its establishment has been attended with great difficulty and expense. Mr. Thomas H. Gallaudet, who is at the head of it, visited the celebrated institutions of Edinburgh and Paris, to qualify himself for its direction. On his return from the latter place, he brought with him Mr. Clerc, one of these unfortunate persons, educated at that seminary, who is now associated with Mr. Gallaudet as an instructor at this institution. There are about fifty deaf & dumb persons at the Asylum, the greater number of whom are from without the State. Tuition, board and other expenses are established at $200 per annum. However highly we may value an institution calculated to draw aside the veil which has darkened the understanding of an unfortunate portion of the human race, it is however apparent, that under present circumstances it can be of no use to those, who, to the misfortune of being deaf and dumb, add also that of being poor.

The Hartford Museum now in Main-street, nearly opposite the Episcopal Church, belonging to Mr. Steward, was first opened in the State House in 1801. It was then the only establishment of the kind in the state, excepting a few articles at Yale College.

It was so far patronised by the State, that the Legislature permitted the proprietor to occupy the two committee rooms in the State House, for the arrangement and exhibition of his Museum during the recess of the Assembly, and one room during their session. In 1808, from the industry of its ingenious proprietor and the liberality of others, the collection had so far increased, that the apartments became crowded and inconvenient, and the building which it now occupies being fitted up for the purpose, it was removed to its present situation. The room occupied by the museum is about 70 feet in length, and is neatly arranged, and handsomely filled with several thousand articles; such as paintings, waxwork, natural and artificial curiosities.

Strangers and others, who visit the Hartford Museum, will find a gratification for their curiosity and taste.

There are four News papers published in this city, one an imperial and the other three a super-royal sheet. Although concerned in one of these establishments, we do not know precisely the number of papers which are published weekly in the city, but think it must exceed six thousand.

A social library was established in Hartford in 1796. It contains at this time 2,550 volumes.

Among the useful, charitable and friendly societies, are the following:—Hartford Agricultural Society, (which however is a county institution,) Mechanic's Society, Free Mason's Society, Moral Society, Hartford Charitable Society, Female Beneficent Society, Sunday School Society, Hartford Auxiliary Bible Society, Harmony Society, Tract Society, & two Female Cent Societies.

In the city of Hartford there are two incorporated banks; Hartford bank incorporated in 1792, having at this time a capital of 1,000,000 dollars. Phœnix bank incorporated in 1814, with a capital of 1,000,000 dollars; it has a branch at Litchfield.

There is a Marine Insurance Company, incorporated in 1803, & a Fire Insurance Company, incorporated 1810. There are 5 fire Engine Companies, well regulated and provided with engines and other means of effective operation; and the Union Company incorporated in 1800, for the purpose of removing obstructions to the navigation of Connecticut river, from this city to the sound. This company has a capital of 120,000 dollars. The improvement of the navigation of the river, both below and above this place, must be an object of primary importance to the city of Hartford.

The system of towing boats up Connecticut river, proposed by John L. Sullivan, Esq. by means of a steam engine, constructed upon novel principles, has recently been submitted to the citizens of this place; and it is understood, that it is contemplated to make an experiment of its practicability and usefulness. Should this plan succeed, (and from a cursory examination of the engine, it is not perceived why it may not,) it would give facility and extension to the navigation of the river, and eventually contribute towards the growth and importance of the city.

A more correct idea, perhaps, of the navigation of Hartford cannot be obtained, than what may be formed by referring to the amount of the tonnage owned here; which, together with what is owned in Wethersfield and employed wholly in trade, that centres in Hartford, of actual and not of registered tonnage, amounts to 9,377 tons.

During the year 1816, two hundred and seventy eight ships, brigs and schooners, and more than two hundred smaller vessels ascended Connecticut river to Hartford. The same year, there were 17,600 tons of merchandise passed through the locks and canals at Hadley, 40 miles up the river from this city; and it has been estimated that 5000 tons more were carried on the river south of that place. From these facts, in connection with the circumstance that Hartford is situated at or near the head of ship navigation, upon one of the finest rivers in the world—that it has a back country, bordering upon this river, of more than 200 miles in extent, containing a dense and thriving population, the advantages of this city for business, and its commercial importance, can be determined. It is admitted that these advantages have not been improved to the extent, nor produced those results which might have been expected. There are many causes which have checked the growth and importance of this city. The city is incorporated by the name of the "Mayor, Aldermen, Common Council-men, and Freemen of the City of Hartford," who possess the municipal authority thereof. The Mayor is chosen during the pleasure of the Legislature, and the Aldermen & Common council-men for one year. The Mayor, and two senior Aldermen, constitute the City Court, and hold a session on the first Monday of every month.

HISTORY. Hartford, and the country on Connecticut river, was undoubtedly first discovered by the Dutch. In the year 1631, the English colonies of Plymouth and Massachusetts obtained the first knowledge of it from an Indian sachem; but it does not appear that they visited the country for two years. It is not known at how early a period the Dutch became acquainted with Connecticut river; but it is certain that they erected a trading house, in 1633, at the point of land formed by the confluence of Mill, with Connecticut river, which still retains the name of Dutch point. The first English settlement in this town has been ascribed to Messrs. Hooker and Haynes, in 1636; but there is the most satisfactory evidence, that it was settled the year before, by John Steel, and his associates, from Newtown, now Cambridge, in Massachusetts. In April, 1636, a General Court was held here, of which Steel was one of the principal members: whereas Mr. Hooker and Mr. Haynes did not arrive until June following.

Hartford has occupied but little space in the page of history. It was never visited by a public enemy; & although few towns were more distinguished for their patriotism during the revolutionary struggle, or entered more ardently into the "spirit of the times," it escaped the distresses of war, to which many others were exposed. It has become celebrated of late as being the place where a Convention of Delegates, from several of the New-England States, was held during the late war with Great Britain. This Convention has been a subject of much animadversion.

BIOGRAPAY. The Hon. *Jeremiah Wadsworth*, distinguished for his public employments and services during the revolutionary war; for the exalted public stations to which he was afterwards promoted; and more for his social virtues, his benevolence and philanthropy, was a native of this town. The design of this work precludes the idea of lengthy biographical details. Topography, of all the sciences, leads to the most extensive and burdensome prolixity, and it would be altogether inadmissible to encumber it with what properly belongs to another department of science. The idea of comprising biographical notices in this work was to assign to each town, according as they are entitled, the citizens of this State, who have been distinguished for their talents, learning, virtues, or public employments, whether at home or abroad, and thereby to collect and register the same. The preservation of such biographical facts, as come within these views, or the design of this work, may be of more importance than a simple record of "departed worth." It may possibly, in some instances, lead to more ample and satisfactory biographical publications, calculated to do justice to the "virtuous dead;" to exalt the reputation of the State, which depends, in a great measure, upon the number of its distinguished citizens, and to enlighten the path of posterity, by the experience and wisdom of their ancestors.

The public services of Jeremiah Wadsworth, in the momentous contest of the revolution, are well known. They are identified with, and form a part of the annals of that period. He was employed as Commissary General nearly through the war. The service was arduous and difficult, and was performed with faithfulness, perseverance and ability—with advantage to the public and to himself. After the close of the war, Col. Wadsworth retired to his residence in this city, and during the remainder of his life, was pre-eminently useful to the place, and to his fellow-citizens. Having an ample capital, and under the influence of an enlarged and liberal spirit of civil improvements, he exerted all his influence, and all his means, in promoting the interests of his native town, and the prosperity and comforts of his fellow-citizens. This city is greatly indebted to him for many of its improvements, and measurably for the rank and importance to which it has attained. But what is a more novel, and perhaps a more worthy trait in his character, is, that although blessed with opulence, and surrounded with splendour himself, he never forgot the poor and unfortunate—although exalted in society, he was never too elevated to do good. The victims of misfortune never approached his doors, without having their wants measurably supplied. Col. Wadsworth was for several years a member of Congress, and subsequently, for a long time, a member of the Council, in this State. He was born in 1743, & died 30th April, 1804, aged 61 years.

The Hon. *Chauncey Goodrich*, distinguished as a lawyer, and for the many honorable offices to which he was promoted, was a native of Durham, but was long a resident in this town. He was educated at Yale College, and became a Tutor at the same Institution, having gone through the regular course of studies with unusual reputation. He resolved to enter into the profession of law; for which purpose he went through the regular and usual course of study, required in this State. Having obtained admission to the bar, he removed to this city to establish himself in his profession. His talents were admirably calculated for forensic debate, and he soon became distinguished in his profession, and ultimately at the head of it, in this county, if not in the State. The superiority of his talents rendered him too conspicuous to be neglected in those appointments, which demand exalted abilities. Accordingly, in 1794, he was elected to represent this State, in the Congress of the United States, and continued in this situation for several years. In 1807, he was elected a senator in the Senate of the United States; whilst in this situation, in 1812, he was elected mayor of the city of Hartford, and the year after, at the annual election in April, of the supreme executive officers, he was chosen by the Freemen, Lieutenant-Governor of this State, an office which he did not live long to enjoy. He was born in 1759, and died August, 1815, aged 56.

Nathan Strong, D. D. a distinguished clergyman, was for 43 years settled in the ministry, in the first Society in this city. He was a man of strong natural talents, possessing great shrewdness and wit. He was in doctrinal points a Calvinist, and learned upon theological subjects, and well versed in general science. He was remarkable for his sound common sense; his knowledge of the human character, and of common and practical subjects, and was a sound, able and orthodox preacher. He died Dec. 25th 1816, Æ 68.

Epaphras W. Bull, Esq. distinguished for his high promise of talent, and for his patriotic zeal for the principles of republicanism, was a native of this town. He was educated to the law, and commenced his professional career with unusual brilliancy. He established himself at Danbury, where, at an early age, he was elected a member of the General Assembly, which station he occasionally filled as long as he remained in this State. In this situation he was distinguished for his zeal, and intrepidity in parliamentary debate, and displayed abilities which are scarcely to be found, but in those of riper years. Although he was a warm and active politician, and lived at a period of unusual party animosity, yet his political opponents could not but admit his brilliant talents, his dignified and commanding eloquence, which, considering his early years, were to be regarded only as the dawn of his meridian sun. He emigrated from Danbury, to a town of the same name, in the State of Ohio, situated upon Lake Erie; the settlement of which, soon after his arrival, in the fall of 1812, was broken up by the general irruption of the Indians, which, upon that frontier, followed the unfortunate and disgraceful capitulation of Gen. Hull, and the consequent occupation of Detroit, by the British. Upon the above, which occasioned the abandonment of this settlement, Mr. Bull, with others, retired to Cleaveland, where, soon after, he closed his earthly career, aged 34 years.

Dr. *Lemuel Hopkins*, a celebrated physician and poet, was born in Waterbury, from whence he removed to this city, and resided here until his death. Dr. Hopkins was an original genius, possessing a vigorous mind, a bold imagination, and characteristically eccentric, in all his intellectual features; bold in his enquiries; free from the restraints of prejudice, or authority; confident in his own opinions and views; ingenious in communicating them, and severe and sarcastic in his wit. He was the projector of the Anarchiad, a work of considerable merit, and had a principal share in writing it. Of this publication, the Analectic Magazine gives the following account. "It was a mock critical account of a pretended ancient epic poem, interspersed with a number of extracts from the supposed work. By a fable, contrived with some ingenuity, this poem is represented as having been known to the ancients, and read and imitated by some of the most popular modern poets. By this supposition, the utmost license of parody and imitation is obtained, and by the usual poetical machinery of episodes, visions and prophecies, the scene is shifted at pleasure, backwards and forwards, from one country to another, from earth to heaven, and from ancient to modern times. This plan is filled up with great spirit; the humorous is indeed better than the serious part, but both have merit, and some of the parodies are extremely happy. The political views of the authors were to support those designs which were then forming for an efficient federal constitution."

The Anarchiad was published from time to time, as matter occurred, or could be conveniently supplied. It had an extensive circulation through the union, and considerable influence upon the political opinions that were then forming, the public mind being in a state of general effervescence. Besides the part which he took in this production, Dr. Hopkins was the author of numerous fugitive poetical pieces; some of which are of a peculiarly humorous and whimsical character, particularly the "*hypocrite's hope*," and his "*epitaph*" upon the victim of a Cancer Quack. As a physician, the reputation of Dr. Hopkins stood deservedly high, and he was characterized for the freedom and liberality of his views, and his general philanthropy and benevolence. He died 14th April, 1801, aged 50 years.

Thomas Tisdall, Esq. a man of very unusual & extraordinary civil and private virtues, and an ardent, faithful and zealous patriot, was a native of Ireland, but resided in this town for forty years, preceding his death. He came into this town in or about the year 1778, during the revolutionary war, having been a paymaster in the British service; but being a republican in sentiment, and considering the war on the part of Great Britain as unjust and oppressive, he left this situation, thereby throwing himself out of employment, and the means of immediate subsistence, a sacrifice to his feelings and principles. When he came to this town, he was a young man of about 21 or 22 years of age, and had no connections or acquaintance here—without money, without friends; in not only a strange, but a foreign land; having had but small advantages as to education, and exposed to reproach from the illiberal prejudices against his countrymen, he had no resources but a firm constitution, a sound mind, and a consciousness of his own worth. But these resources never failed him; they sustained him not only at this period of darkness and discouragement, but through a long life, and raised him to the rank of one of the most distinguished citizens of this town. Mr. Tisdall never attained to any distinguished public employment, but he was one of those few who can be conspicuous in a "private station," and exalted in the humblest situation. He had a sound and discriminating mind, improved by reading, observation and experience; and although not possessed of shining talents, few have had more good sense, or a juster view of life. He was remarkable for his firmness, independence and freedom of thought: always claiming the right to judge for himself, disclaiming the authority of precedent, and above the reach of prejudice. His principles were interwoven in the texture of the constitution of his mind, and were as unyielding as adamant; and his attachments, whether relating to persons or subjects, were founded upon principle, and as inflexible and stable, as the foundation which supported them was firm and durable. He was, in the strictest sense, an "honest man." No one ever made less use of artifice and dissimulation, to disguise his faults, or gloss over his character. A consciousness of the rectitude of his life raised him far above the jesuitical arts of hypocrisy. He wished to appear precisely what he was, no more, nor no less; neither would he give to others a character which he knew they did not possess.

"*He could not flatter;*
"*An honest mind and plain,*
"*He must speak truth.*"

He was remarkable for a systematic industry and economy, and for the plainness and simplicity of his manners, and the precision, order and regularity, which characterized his whole life; these causes, producing their necessary results, put him in the possession of a good estate. The leading trait in his character was *prudence*. This was perceivable in every action. His example as a citizen cannot be too highly appreciated, at an age when "the world is deceived with show and ornament." He was constitutionally an ardent and zealous friend of civil liberty. A whig in the revolution, he was uniform and decided in his republican principles, which were of a character peculiarly rigid and austere. The lively sense which he had of the injustice & oppression, of the government of his native country, rendered him an enthusiastic admirer of the free institutions of the country of his adoption. We have had few of our native citizens more sincerely attached to the government, the liberties, and the prosperity of the United States. He died 31st August, 1818, aged 61 years.

BERLIN.

BERLIN, a post town, is situated 10 miles south-west from Hartford, and 24 miles north-east from New-Haven. It is bounded north by Farmington, east by Wethersfield and Middletown, south by Middletown and Meriden, and west by Southington.

The township contains about forty square miles, having an average length of eight miles, and an average breadth of five miles.

Its surface is uneven, being diversified with moderate hills and dales; the western border of the town is mountainous, extending upon the range of mountains which commence in the vicinity of New-Haven, and extend through the State, into the interior of New-England.

The geological structure of the town consists of argillaceous schistus or clay slate, and greenstone; being a part of the extensive geological district, upon the borders of Connecticut river, commencing at the narrows, below Middletown, (where the range of granite of the eastern section of the State seems to terminate,) & extending to Northfield, in Massachusetts. This district consists principally of the same rock, a clay slate, of a primitive formation; the range of mountain noticed above, and other eminences, are usually covered or capped with greenstone, forming mural precipices and bold ledges. The argillaceous schistus within this district consists of several varieties; at some places it is fine grained, and forms a good free stone; at others it is a coarse grained conglomerate, or pudding stone; but in this town, in Hartford, and more generally within this range, it is a simple rock, being an indurated clay. Some minerals have been found in this town; sulphuret of lead has been discovered in small quantities; on the west branch of Mill river there are the remains of some pits, or excavations, which were made during the revolutionary war, for the discovery of metals. The rock is greenstone, and contains carbonate of lime; quartz, and small quantities of silver have been found. Iron pyrites is found in several places in scattered grains; oxyd of copper, also, in small quantities. Coal has been dug in the bed of Mill river, and on both of its banks; the rock at that place is greenstone, and the coal that has been discovered has been found in small shining plates, and is very combustible and bituminous; it has been obtained only in small quantities, but our correspondent thinks that the examinations have not been made in the right place, and that, possibly, beds of this valuable mineral may abound in the neighbourhood of these discoveries.

The soil is generally a gravelly loam, but in some parts of the town the argillaceous earths predominating, it is an aluminous or clayey loam. It is fertile and productive, affording excellent pasturage, and good crops of grain. There are numerous, large and beautiful orchards in the town, many of choice and selected fruit. The making of cider is an important agricultural interest, being alike a convenience, and a source of profit to the inhabitants.

Berlin is celebrated for its manufactures and mechanic arts. The most important manufacture, is that of tin ware; it was first introduced by Mr. Edward Patterson, an Irishman, about the time of the revolutionary war, which

BERLIN.

was the first manufacture of tin in the State. For a considerable time, Mr. Patterson carried on the business alone, and peddled his own ware in a basket; but the value of the article becoming known, others engaged in the business, and the ware was soon scattered over the country. At first others, as well as Patterson, peddled it in baskets, carried by hand, or on horses; afterwards, two wheeled carts were introduced, but these, being found inadequate for long journies, were succeeded by one horse waggons, and those in some measure by very large carriages, with two and four horses. The wares manufactured of tin were vended at first in New-England and New-York, gradually extending to the southern States; and now tin pedlers may be found from Quebec to New-Orleans, and from Nova-Scotia to the Missouri. For a number of years the business was confined to Berlin; but Wallingford, Cheshire, Southington, Meriden and Bristol have, for some time past, been its rivals. For several years it has been the practice of those engaged in the business to make the ware in the summer months, in New-England, and in autumn, the ware, workmen and pedlers are removed to the south, and there continue during the winter, engaged in vending and manufacturing; but some individuals have now permanently established themselves, south of the Potomac. In general, but small capitals are invested in the business, but some individuals have engaged in it very extensively, and have realized large fortunes; many have employed twenty hands, and one person forty, in vending the ware. There are now five Tin Ware Factories, in Berlin; there are also one Cotton Factory; one Jewelery Factory; one Brass Foundery; one Silver Plate Factory; one Button Factory; and two Pistol Factories. There are eight Grain Mills; eleven Saw Mills; one Plaster Mill; three Fulling Mills; 3 Carding Machines; 12 Cider Distilleries; six Tanneries; and five Mercantile Stores.

Berlin is divided into three located or Ecclesiastical Societies; Kensington, New-Britain & Worthington; in the latter there is a pleasant and flourishing village, the principal street of which is the Hartford and New-Haven turnpike road. There is also a turnpike that passes through the town, leading from Middletown to Farmington. The population of the town, in 1810, was 2798; and there are now 500 qualified Electors, and 400 dwelling houses.

The amount of taxable polls and estate of the town is $62,161.

The valuation of the real estate, in 1816, was $1,187,873.

The valuation, in 1799, was $428,583.

There are three Congregational Churches, and one Society of Baptists, and one of Episcopalians, 14 Common Schools, two Social Libraries, five Clergymen, five Physicians, and two Attornies.

Berlin was incorporated as a town in 1785. It was previously the second Society of Farmington, by the name of Kensington. The Society was probably set off from Farmington about the year 1712; as the first minister, the Rev. Mr.

Burnham, was ordained the 10th of December of that year. A part of Wethersfield and Middletown were joined to the Society of Kensington, at its incorporation. This was the second Society, (East Windsor being the first,) that was set off from any town in the State. About this time the General Assembly passed a public law for making Societies. When Mr. Burnham was settled, there were but 14 families in the place, and the Church consisted of 10 members, seven males, and three females; previous to this period these families attended meeting at Farmington, and the women walked from 10 to 12 miles, and carried their infants in their arms. Kensington was divided about the year 1753, by the incorporation of the Society of New-Britain; and Dr. Smalley, the first Clergyman in this Society, was ordained in 1758. In 1772, the Society of Kensington was again divided by the formation of the Society of Worthington; its name being derived from one of the Committee who located the Society.

BIOGRAPHY. Major *Jonathan* Hart was a native of this town. He was a gallant & distinguished officer, & one of the victims of the unfortunate defeat of Gen. St. Clair, Nov. 4th, 1791. His life, & those of his command, were literally offered a sacrifice for the safety of the rest of the army. When all were in confusion and dismay, Major Hart was ordered to charge the enemy with the bayonet, with a view to facilitate a retreat, or rather a flight, to the shattered remains of the army. This charge was made with gallantry and spirit, under circumstances which language is too feeble to describe; the desolation of the place; the confusion of the scene; the whoops and yells of a savage foe, flushed with victory, and thirsting for blood; the general consternation which prevailed, and the groans of the dying in every direction. But the intrepid Major, and almost every man of his party, were killed in the desperate enterprise, and their bones were left to bleach upon the borders of the waters of the Wabash, the dreary abode of wild beasts and "savage men more wild than they."

BRISTOL.

BRISTOL, a post town in the south west part of the county, 16 miles from Hartford, and 28 from New-Haven, bounded on the north by Burlington, on the east by Farmington, on the south by Southington and Wolcott, and on the west by Plymouth, in Litchfield county. The township is five & a half miles in length, from north to south, and five in breadth, from east to west, comprising an area of about 27 square miles. The surface is uneven and hilly, and the soil is a gravelly loam, and considerably fertile; it produces all kinds of grain, grass and fruit, common to this region. Its forests consist of oak, chesnut, and other deciduous trees, common to the county. The geological structure of the town consists of granite and micaceous schistus. Iron and Copper ore have been discov-

BRISTOL. 59

cred, but have been neglected. The town is watered by the north and south branches of the Poquaback, a small stream which discharges its waters into the Farmington or Tunxis river.

The turnpike road, leading from Hartford to Danbury, passes thro' this town.

If discriminations are to be made, where the general characteristics of the inhabitants are marked with so much uniformity, as is the case in this State, those of Bristol deserve to be noticed for their enterprise and industry. It has been estimated that one half of the inhabitants of the town are engaged in manufacturing and mechanical employments and pursuits. The manufactures and mechanical interests of the town are various; but those of clocks and tin ware are most important. There is one clock manufactory or establishment, which is confined exclusively to the manufacture of brass clocks; this concern for the size of the town is an extensive one; there being about 2000 clocks manufactured annually. In addition to this establishment, there are a number of factories for the making of wooden clocks, which altogether manufacture, annually, large quantities of clocks of this description. These clocks, both of wood and brass, are almost all sent abroad for a market, and principally to the southern and western States. This requires the employment of a great number of persons, and opens a wide and extended field for enterprise. There are five tin ware factories which annually manufacture large quantities of various kinds of wares; these are likewise sent abroad for a market, and a multitude of persons are required to vend them. There are also two button factories in this town. From the tendency of these manufacturing and mechanical interests and pursuits, a considerable portion of the young men of the town are employed abroad. In addition to the manufactures of clocks, tin ware and buttons, there is one Woolen Factory, one Cotton Factory, eight Grain and Saw Mills, two Carding Machines, eight Distilleries for Cider, and six Tanneries; there are three Mercantile Stores.

The town contains one located Congregational Society, & Church, & one society of Baptists, which also has a house for public worship; nine School Districts, and common Schools, one small Academy for Misses, three Social Libraries, two Clergymen, and two Physicians. The population of the town, in 1810, was 1423, and there are 238 Dwelling-Houses, 235 Electors, and 115 Militia. The amount of taxable property, including polls, is $23,421. Bristol was formerly a part of Farmington, and was incorporated as an independent Society in 1747, and as a town in May, 1785.

BURLINGTON.

BURLINGTON, a post town, is situated on the western border of the county, seventeen miles west from Hartford. It is bounded on the north by New-Hartford and Canton, on the east by Farmington, south by Bristol, and on the west by Harwinton. It is about six miles in length, from north to south, and five in breadth from east to west, comprising an area of thirty square miles. The township is diversified with hills and dales, and the soil is a gravelly loam, being dry and hard. This town lies within the granite region, in the western part of the State, comprising the whole of Litchfield county, excepting a few townships upon the borders of the State of New-York, which constitute the calcarious district of Connecticut. The lands produce grain, particularly rye and oats, and are tolerably well adapted to orcharding, and some parts afford good grazing.

The Farmington, or Tunxis river, waters the northeastern section of the town, and some branches of the Poquaback run through its centre. The town is accommodated with the Farmington and Litchfield turnpike, and with one leading to Middletown, through Berlin. The inhabitants, who have a conspicuous equality in their circumstances, are principally engaged in agriculture, except the attention which is paid to domestic manufactures. There are, however, two small Woolen Factories, one Tin Ware Factory, three Distilleries, two Tanneries, two Grain Mills, three Fulling Mills, three Carding Machines, and one Oil Mill. There are two Mercantile Stores in the town, and a number of mechanic's shops engaged in waggon and chaise making; three or four of which carry on the business largely, and send their work abroad for market.

The population of Burlington, in 1810, was 1467, and there are now 220 Freemen or Electors, two companies of militia, and 230 dwelling-houses. The town contains one located Congregational Society and Church, one Society of Methodists, also one of Seventh Day Baptists. It is divided into eight School Districts; in each of which a school is maintained for several months in the year.

There are two small Social Libraries, three Physicians, and one Clergyman.

The general list of the town, including polls, is $25,645.

Burlington originally belonged to Farmington, and more recently to Bristol, and was incorporated as a town in 1806.

CANTON.

CANTON, a post town in the western part of the county, being 13 miles northwesterly from Hartford, is bounded east on Simsbury, south on Farmington and Burlington, west on New-Hartford and Barkhamstead, and north on Granby. The township is about eight miles in length, north and south, and near four miles in breadth, comprising 19,200 acres. It is considerably broken, being hilly and mountainous. One of the mountainous ranges commencing in the vicinity of New-Haven, near the sound, and extending far into the interior of New-England, runs through this town; the mountain here is considerably elevated. The rocks are principally granitic. The prevailing character of the soil is a coarse gravel, which is hard, dry and stoney. Its natural growth is principally oak, and when cultivated it is best adapted to grazing. Rye, corn, oats, and flax are principally raised. The lands are well adapted to orcharding, and considerable attention has been paid to the subject, so that cider has become one of the most important agricultural interests of the town. Farmington river runs thro' Canton, moving rapidly along at the foot of the mountain; there is one bridge thrown across it. In the southern extremity of the town there is a large pond, called Cherey's Pond; part of which is within the town of Farmington.

STATISTICS. At the last census Canton contained 1374 inhabitants. There are in the town more than 200 dwelling houses; a number of which are upon the principal street, being the Albany turnpike which runs through the town, and form a small village. There are three houses for public worship, one for Congregationalists, one for Baptists, and one for Separates or Independents. There are seven district Schools, one company of Infantry, part of a company of Artillerists, and about 180 Electors. There are three mercantile Stores, eight Distilleries, three Tanneries, three Grain Mills, four Saw Mills, two Fulling Mills, one Powder Mill, and one Tin Factory. There are several Wheel Wrights, Smiths, and other mechanics in the town, three Physicians and two Clergymen. The list of the taxable property and polls of the town, in 1817, was $27,540.

Canton was first settled in 1740, and was incorporated as a town in 1806, having, until then, been a part of Simsbury and New-Hartford, being the west section of the former, and the eastern of the latter.

EAST-HARTFORD.

EAST-HARTFORD, a post town of Hartford county, is pleasantly situated on the east side of Connecticut river, bounded north on East-Windsor, east on Bolton, south on Glastenbury, west on Connecticut river, which separates it from the city and town of Hartford, and is about ten miles in length, from east to west, and five and three-fourths of a mile in width, from north to south, containing about 36,000 acres of land.

The principal street in this town is about three-fourths of a mile from the river, and is thickly settled, from Glastenbury to East-Windsor. In the centre of this street is a beautiful and stately row of elms extending from the meeting-house, two miles north-westwardly, which, with a variety of other shade trees on its borders, renders this one of the most beautiful and pleasant situations in Connecticut.

About two miles from its eastern bounds, the Hockanum river enters the town from the northeast, and winds its course south-westerly, through nearly the centre of the town, passes a few rods from the meeting-house, and unites with the Connecticut, about a mile below the Hartford ferry. On the Hockanum, and the various smaller streams which flow into it, are numerous valuable mill seats, that give facility to manufacturing operations, which are here carried on to a very considerable extent. Over this river are six bridges, from fifty to sixty feet each in length; several other smaller streams take their rise in the eastern part of the town, & run westerly into Connecticut river.

In this town are seven Paper Mills, which are kept constantly running through the year; several of them have two engines each, and a double set of workmen are employed; also, there are eight or ten Powder Mills, in which great quantities of powder are manufactured yearly; two Cotton Factories, one Woolen Factory, two Glass Works, where vast quantities of bottles are made, and sent into various parts of the country for sale. A Hat Factory is here carried on, where the principal part of the labour is performed by machinery moved by water—for which the proprietors have a patent right. An abundance of low-prized hats are made, and sent to to the southern markets; here also are several Tanneries, Clothier's Works, Hatteries, four Carding Machines, six or eight Grist Mills—in one of which are four run of stones, several Saw Mills, and various other mechanical establishments and employments.

Adjoining Connecticut river in this town, is an extensive range of meadows, containing some of the best lands in New-England. In the spring season, these meadows are annually overflowed by the freshets of the river, which renders them very productive in grass and pasturage, for which they are principally improved. An extensive range of bridging and causeway, connected with the elegant bridge over Connecticut river, extends in a straight line across these meadows, to the main street in East-Hartford, opening a beautiful avenue into the city, and when completed and ornamented with shade trees, will form a delightful walk of a mile in extent.

Passing out of these meadows, you rise from fifteen to twenty feet into a level plain country, which extends across the whole width of the town; nearly three miles to the eastward, there is another considerable rise; from thence to Bolton, the surface is somewhat broken and hilly; between the meadows and the main-street, the soil, in general, is loam, mixed with sand, which, with the aid of manure, is abundantly productive; from thence to the next rise, eastward, the soil is somewhat light and sandy, but produces excellent rye and Indian corn. The eastern part of the town is a mixed soil of sand-loam and gravel, and has, within the last twenty-five years, been much enriched and improved by the use of plaster of Paris, which renders it very productive.

The land in this town being generally dry, and otherwise well adapted, produces the finest rye in the world. There are some valuable meadow lands, bordering upon

EAST-HARTFORD.

the Hockanum river, in the eastern part of the town.

About three miles eastward of the river is a ledge of red sand stone, or friable clay slate, which extends through the town; the stone generally lies under the surface of the ground, and quarries have been opened and worked in various places, and great quantities of fine stone for building and other uses procured. These stones, being of a soft texture, are easily shaped, and when made smooth with the chisel, make beautiful underpinning, hearth, and stepstones. A similar kind of stone is found in other parts of the town. Within these masses of rock, are frequently found white and yellow flint stones, or quartz, embedded, from the size of a pebble to that of a goose egg.

The growth of timber, in most parts of this town, when it was originally settled, is said to have been principally white and yellow pine. This has long since been nearly all destroyed; the present natural growth of forest trees consists of black, white, red and yellow oak; chesnut, walnut, white maple, buttenwood, elm, yellow and white pine, and various other kinds common to this part of the country. It has been observed that in those parts of the town, where cattle are restrained from going at large, a luxuriant growth of young timber is growing up; among which is an unusual proportion of pines.

The meadows produce abundance of hay and pasturage; on the uplands are raised large quantities of rye, Indian corn, some wheat, oats, buckwheat, flax, peas, beans, tobacco and water melons;

of this last article, immense quantities are raised on the lightest sandy land, by the aid of stable and hogspen manure; it is not uncommon to see many acres of these in the same field, and in their season, many waggon and cart loads are carried to market daily.

Two great stage roads, both of which are turnpikes, lead thro' this town from Hartford to Boston. One of these is by the way of Tolland, Stafford and Worcester; the other, called the middle road, leads through Ashford, Thompson and Dedham. Several turnpike roads, leading from the State of Rhode-Island and the eastern part of Connecticut, are concentrated in the middle road, and the travel is principally through this town. The turnpike road from Hartford to New-London passes through this town; stages daily run on each of these roads; another stage runs northerly to Walpole; another passes by the way of Lebanon to Norwich.

The number of inhabitants in this town was, by the last census, 3240; since which their numbers have probably increased. The number of dwelling-houses is about 480; the number of qualified Freemen about 500; the amount of taxable property, including polls, in 1817, was $66,235.

Previous to the late organization of the militia, there were four companies of Infantry, and one company of Artillery in this town; the Infantry are now reduced to two companies, which, with the Artillery, contain nearly 300 men, subject to do military duty.

This town being situated in the vicinity of Hartford, is not a place of much mercantile business; there are, however, nearly twenty licensed retailers, who deal principally in groceries; among these are five dry good stores. But little navigation business is carried on, though there are several masters of vessels and other seafaring men belonging to the town.

The character of the people in this town does not distinguish them from those of other river towns, being principally farmers, mechanics and tradesmen; they are a plain, economical, industrious people, generally well educated, and well bred; there are few of them possessing great wealth, but many have handsome estates, and the greater proportion possess that salutary competence, which is the happiest condition of society; avoiding, on the one hand, the distress, misery and crimes incident to a state of poverty and want; and on the other the extravagance, the fooleries, the dissipation, and the whole train of fashionable vices and disorders, which are the offspring of wealth.

The town is divided into thirteen school districts; in each of which is a school house, wherein a common school si maintained for eight or nine months in a year; some of which, in the winter season, are attended by from fifty to eighty scholars.

There are two located Congregational Societies in the town; also a small Society of Methodists, and another of Baptists; each of which has a house for public worship. In each of the located Societies, there is a Social Library, containing several hundred volumes of well selected books. The profes-sional men are two Congregational Clergymen, four Physicians, and one Attorney.

This town formerly composed a part of the ancient town of Hartford, and was incorporated with town privileges in 1784. The fertility and feasibility of its meadows, affording an easy cultivation of Indian corn, together with the multitude of fish, with which the rivers and small streams in this vicinity were abundantly stored, rendered this a favorite residence for the native Indians.

The Podunk tribe, which dwelt in this, and the adjoining town of East-Windsor, were a ferocious and warlike people; at the head of whom was Totanimo, a subtle and treacherous Chief, of no ordinary talents, who commanded 200 warriors, having no other instruments of hostility, than the bow and arrow; the latter being barbed or pointed with a sharp flint stone. This tribe, perceiving the consequences of the English settling among them, and not being willing to be dispossessed of their lands, were, for many years, very troublesome to the first settlers in these parts. Few if any traces of the customs, manners, or character of this tribe, now remain, except what may be found in records of the colony, from its first settlement, until about the year 1670, a period of about thirty-four years. The Podunk tribe of Indians has long been extinct.

BIOGRAPHY. The Hon. *William Pitkin*, formerly Governor of the colony, was a native of this town, and lived here. Several of his descendants were also men of considerable eminence in their day.

The Rev. *Eliphalet Williams* D. D. was for more than fifty years a settled minister in this town; he was highly distinguished as a man of science, a preacher and divine.

EAST-WINDSOR.

EAST-WINDSOR is a large and flourishing town, situated on the east side of Connecticut river; the post-office in the first society being 8 miles north from Hartford.

The area of the town comprises about 48 square miles, or 30,728 acres; being about nine miles in length, and having an average breadth of five and a half miles.

It is bounded on the north by Enfield, on the east by Ellington and Vernon, in Tolland county, on the south by East-Hartford, and on the west by Connecticut river, which separates it from Windsor and Hartford.

The town is generally level, although some parts of it are waving and hilly; but the eminences have but a moderate elevation. The soil is various; in the western part of the town, there are some small sections of siliceous sand, and extensive tracts of sandy loam, which is light, warm and fertile; in the eastern part, a rich, gravelly loam generally prevails; and upon the borders of Connecticut river, there is an extensive body of alluvial, remarkably fertile, and having a situation peculiarly charming and beautiful. These natural meadows comprise more than 2000 acres of the choicest land. It produces excellent grass for pasturage and mowing, and carries the largest crops of Indian Corn. The eastern and northern sections of the town are best adapted to rye, which is cultivated with facility, and in great abundance. Rye is the staple agricultural production of the town, it having been computed that 70,000 bushels have been raised in one season. There is probably no town in the State that produces an equal quantity of rye, with that which is raised in East-Windsor. There is no waste land, worthy of notice, in the town; and the principal part of the township is fertile, and well adapted to a grain culture; and the inhabitants have not been neglectful of its natural advantages, and the resources of the soil. Back from the river there are numerous forests, and extensive tracts of wood land; some of them heavily timbered, consisting principally of oak. Among other agricultural interests, the cultivation of tobacco receives considerable attention; large quantities of it being raised annually; some of which is manufactured in the town, and the rest sent abroad for a market.

The Scantic is the principal river in East-Windsor; it waters its northern section, and the Podunk, a small stream, runs through the south part of the town.

Upon Connecticut river there are several shad and herring fisheries.

The distillation of spiritous liquors, from grain, is an important business in this town. There are six Gin Distilleries in the town; four of which are upon an extensive scale, and continue the business without interruption throughout the year. Several of the largest of these establishments are situated at Warehouse Point, a flourishing village in the north part of the town. These establishments are extensively known, and the gin which they manufacture is considered of the first quality in market. There is probably no town in the United States where there is as great a quantity of spirit made from grain as in East-Windsor. The following abstract of duties p id to the collector of the district, under the laws of the United States, during the year 1816, will afford some evidence of the extent of this manufacture. The several Distilleries in this town, in that year, as appears by the statement published by the Collector of the District, paid duties to the amount of $23,913.

The civil divisions of East-Windsor are two located or Ecclesiastical Societies, and nineteen School Districts.

In the first or south Society, the principal street, which is the public river road, has a pleasant and prospective situation, and contains one Congregational Church, one Academy and Post-Office, and many handsome, and some elegant Dwelling-Houses.

In the north Ecclesiastical Society is the pleasant and flourishing village of Ware-House Point, situated upon the east bank of the Connecticut, 13 miles above Hartford, at the head of sloop navigation. The village contains one Episcopal Church, a Post-Office, four large Gin Distilleries, one of which is probably the largest in the United States, and 40 Dwelling-Houses. This village has a pleasant and healthful situation, and is not an ineligible site for a commercial town, having an extensive and fertile country around it. If aided by some improvements in the navigation of the river, it could not fail of becoming a place of mercantile business and importance, and it cannot be doubted that its natural advantages will be duly appreciated and improved.

The population of East-Windsor, in 1810, was 3081. There are now about 400 Freemen, or qualified Electors, five Companies of Militia, and about 500 Dwelling Houses.

There are nine Mercantile Stores, six Grain Mills, one Segar Manufactory, on an extensive scale, one extensive and elegant Engraving Establishment, five Saw-Mills, one Pottery of Earthern Ware, two Fulling Mills, and two Carding Machines.

There are three Churches for Congregationalists, and one for Episcopalians, two Academies, 19 District Schools, two Public Libraries, and several good private Libraries, one of near 800 volumes, three Clergymen, five practising Physicians, and two practising Attornies.

The amount of the taxable polls and estate of the town, is $76,628; the assessment of the United States in 1816, was $1,482,039 82; the assessment of 1799, was $609,420 90.

A few families settled on the east side of the river at Bissell's ferry, about the time of the first settlement in Windsor, in 1636; and a more rapid and general settlement upon the east side of the river was begun about 1677. The first Church was organized, a Meeting-House erected, and a minister settled about the year 1695. East-Windsor was incorporated as a town in 1765. The Podunk tribe of Indians inhabited the borders of the Connecticut and Scantic rivers within this town, of whom the soil was purchased by the first settlers.

BIOGRAPHY. Gov. *Roger Wolcott* was a native of this town. He received no advantages of an early education, having been bred a weaver; but from the force of native genius, and strong natural endowments, he became a man of considerable science, and of great and useful talents. He took an active part in fitting out the famous Louisburgh expedition in 1745, and was the second in command. His eldest son, *Roger Wolcott*, was a lawyer, and became a judge of the Superior Court, and died in that office in the prime of life.

He has been called the greatest man of the Wolcott family. *Eratus*, another son of Roger, altho' a plain man, and a labouring farmer, and with inconsiderable advantages as to education, acquired great influence in public affairs, and was distinguished for his talents, having become a judge of the Superior Court, although never bred to the law.

Timothy Edwards, the first minister in the town, was distinguished in his time; he was in the ministry 62 years. His only son, *Jonathan Edwards*, became celebrated as a divine; he was a man of distiguished genius, having an acute and metaphysical mind.

William Wolcott, of this town, was a man of strong natural talents. He was a judge of the County Court for 30 years, and was distinguished for uniting inflexible integrity with amiable manners.

ENFIELD.

ENFIELD, a post town, is situated in the northeast corner of the county, on the east side of Connecticut river; being 16 miles from Hartford, and 50 from New-Haven. It is bounded on the north by Long-Meadow, in Massachusetts, east by Somers, in Tolland county, south by East-Windsor, and west by Connecticut river, which separates it from Suffield.

It is nearly six miles in length from north to south, and five and a half in breadth, from east to west, comprising about 33 square miles or 21,120 acres. The township is generally of a level surface, excepting the borders of the Connecticut, which are elevated and romantic. The soil is a light, sandy loam, very feasible and generally fertile; there are some small sections of pine plains, and some tracts of clay or argillaceous loam. The natural growth of the forests is Walnut, Oak, of the various kinds, Maple, Elm, Chesnut, Butternut, various shrubs, and on the plains, yellow pine; there are a considerable number of forests in the town, and some good timber.

The agricultural productions are principally grain; rye and oats receive the most attention there is, however, some wheat growed, and Indian corn is raised to a considerable extent. From the light, dry and feasible quality of the soil, rye is cultivated with great facility, and with much success. Some sections of the town, particularly on the borders of Connecticut river, afford good lands for grazing and the culture of grass.

Besides Connecticut river, which bounds the western border of the town, *Scantic* runs through its south eastern section, affording many excellent sites for hydraulic works, and extensive alluvial tracts, which are very fertile. A firm and convenient bridge connects this town with Suffield. It was erected in 1808, and is supported by six stone piers, resting upon a rock which constitutes the bed of the river, being 1000 feet in length, and 30 in breadth. The river here has very elevated and bold banks of solid rock, which, on the west side, requires a descent to enter upon the bridge. It is an admirable site for a bridge, uniting, with a safe and secure situation, shallow water, rocky bottom, and a facility of obtaining stone for the piers, so that the whole expense did not exceed $26,000. It is the first bridge that was erected across Connecticut river in this state.

STATISTICS. Enfield, in 1810, contained 1846 inhabitants. There are now 274 Dwelling-Houses, a large proportion of which are substantial, well built houses, situated upon the principal street, running through the town parallel with the river; it has an elevated, prospective and pleasant situation. There are 225 Freemen or Electors, and two Companies of Militia. The list of the town, in 1817, was $42,576. The United States valuation, or assessment of the lands and buildings of the town, in 1816, was $603,961 87. There are six Mercantile Stores, one Druggist Store, five Taverns, five Grain Mills, two Fulling Mills, two Carding Machines, one Powder Mill, one Forge, three Tanneries, and five Distilleries; three of which are upon a large scale, and paid duties under the laws of the United States, in the year 1816, to the amount of $10,025 17.

The plough making business is prosecuted in Enfield to a great extent. In addition to supplying the demand at home, and from the neighboring towns, twenty thousand dollars worth of the article are annually sent to the southern States.

There are two Clergymen, two Physicians, and three Attornies. The town comprises but one Ecclesiastical Society, has eleven School Districts, in which schools are regularly maintained, and one small Social Library. There are three Churches, one for Congregationalists, one for Baptists, and one for a society of " Believers," commonly called *Shakers.*

The singular and extraordinary character of this people will justify a succinct history of their origin and progress; more especially as it is believed that an *impartial* account of them has never yet been published.

In the year 1706, some fanatics from France, calling themselves " prophets," visited London, and soon obtained followers there, and in other places, which they visited in England. Among others who

ENFIELD.

received the "testimony" of the French prophets, as they were called, in England, was *James Wardley*, a taylor, and *Jane*, his wife, of Bolton, in the county of Lancaster, who belonged to the society of *Quakers*. But the "new light," which they considered that they had received from their conversion to the doctrines of a new sect, soon induced them to separate themselves from that community. Having, as they represented, and probably believed, had their minds enlightened by a special revelation, they proclaimed *a knowledge and a belief of Christ's second appearance, which they affirmed was at hand.* Under the influence of the wildest fanaticism, Wardley continued to open his new testimony, and sowed the seeds of the Shaker Church. Among others who received the testimony, as it was called, was ANN LEE, of Manchester. She joined the Society of *Shakers*, for they had acquired this name at this time, in the year 1758. For the first ten or twelve years, *Ann* was not particularly distinguished from the other members of the Society; but in the year 1770, after long and continued watchings, fastings, and cries to God, she declared that she had received that manifestation from him, whereby she was enabled to discover the *real nature* of the first transgression of the first man and the first woman, which she regarded as the root and source of human depravity & wickedness. She bore testimony against all sin, and regarded herself as perfectly holy, whence she was called the holy mother, it being considered by all " believers" that *Christ* had made his *second* appearance in the person of *Ann Lee*. The religious doctrines and mode of worship of the Shakers became settled at this time, although both, and particularly the latter, have since undergone considerable modification.

Ann was now acknowledged as the spiritual mother and leader of the Society. The manner of worship in their public assemblies was singing and dancing, shaking and shouting; in addition to which they claimed to possess the power of working miracles, prophesying, speaking with new tongues, and all the various gifts of the holy ghost, known in the primitive Church. The fundamental doctrinal principles of the Shakers are a belief in the *second appearance of Christ*, in the person of the holy mother. They admit of but two persons in the godhead, God the Father, and God the Mother, which they say is according to the order of nature, being male and female. To redeem the depraved race of man, they believe that it became necessary for God to take upon him the real character of human nature as it is, male and female, and that his first appearance was in the person of man, and the second in the person of woman, whereby the work of redemption was finished and completed. The confusion and wickedness that prevailed in the Catholic Church, during the long period which preceded and followed the reformation, they ascribe to the work of redemption, not having been completed in Christ's first appearance, it being the necessary period that must intervene between the making and fulfilment of the promise of Christ, that he would establish his law of righteousness on earth. They believe in perfect holiness, and insist that salvation from *sin*, here, is necessary to salvation from *misery*, hereafter. They regard the bible as a testimony of Christ's first appearance, but deny that it contains the word of God, or of life, as they consider a belief in the second appearance of Christ, or in the spiritual character and mission of the holy mother, as indispensible to salvation. From what has been premised, it is scarcely necessary to be remarked that the Shakers can hardly be regarded as a Christian sect, as the fundamental principle of their creed has nothing to do with the Christian system. Were there no others, the Shakers would be a striking and a living monument of the weakness of human nature; of the influence of religious fanaticism, and of the facility with which the grossest delusions, and the most palpable impositions may be propagated in society.

But notwithstanding the absurd tenets of the Shakers, they are, in many respects, an exemplary and worthy people. Their religious principles necessarily affect the order of their Societies, by producing an entire separation of the men from the women; yet their communities present the most striking evidences of regularity and decorum. Their buildings are remarkably neat and convenient, and every thing appears a model of order and economy. They are characterised by a striking simplicity and plainness of manners, and are sober, industrious and economical. They are skilful mechanics, and excellent farmers and gardeners. But what is more than all this, they are a community of "honest men." Ann, and her followers, arrived in the United States in 1774, and the first Society was established at Niskeuna, in the State of New-York, eight miles northwest from Albany, two years afterwards. This is the parent of the several Shaker Societies in the United States, of which there are at least fourteen; four in Massachusetts, one in Maine, two in New-York, two in New-Hampshire, one in Connecticut, and four in the western States. The Society, in Enfield, was established in 1780, and at this time consists of fourteen Dwelling-Houses, a number of Workshops, Store-Houses, &c. making in all perhaps fifty buildings, and comprises about one hundred and eighty persons. The Society possess an excellent tract of land in the northeast section of the town, of more than one thousand acres, which is under the highest state of cultivation. Their improvements and attention to horticulture are without any example; gardening being with them not so much a family convenience, as a business of profit. They carry on various kinds of mechanical business, and their wares are justly esteemed, being always good and free from all deception. They are, for their numbers, a very wealthy and flourishing community. In the several Shaker Societies in the United States, there are now probably 5000 souls.

Enfield was settled by emigrants from Salem, in Massachusetts, in 1681, being, at that time, a part of the town of Springfield in that State.

FARMINGTON.

FARMINGTON, a wealthy post town, is situated 10 miles west from Hartford. It is bounded east by Hartford and Berlin, north by Simsbury, west by Bristol & Burlington, and south by Southington. It comprises an area of about 70 square miles, or 44,800 acres; being nearly 11 miles in length from north to south, and averaging nearly 7 miles in breadth from east to west. Farmington is characterised by features peculiarly striking and various, both as it respects its surface and soil; having a range of mountains extending through the town, extensive plains and considerable tracts of alluvial upon the borders of Farmington or Tunxis river. This river here is sixty or seventy yards in width, and the natural meadows, which it affords, are peculiarly fertile and charming.

In the south section of the town, there is a large tract of plains, being dry, light and sandy, but healthy, and well adapted to the growth of rye, of which they carry good crops when well cultivated. The soil of the uplands is a loam, composed of a red gravel, mixed with clay. The range of mountains in this town commences near the Sound in the vicinity of New-Haven, being there called east rock, and extends north into the interior of New-England; its rock is principally greenstone. It affords some valuable timber, and good pasturage upon its declivities. The forests in this town comprise the various woods common to this county.

Agriculture is the principal busines of the inhabitants, and with few exceptions, the "sweat of the brow" is amply rewarded with an abundant supply of all the comforts of life. The farmers here, like those of most of the other towns in the county, raise wheat, rye, oats, flax, Indian corn, &c; rye and corn being principally cultivated. There are many fine orchards in some sections of the town, which afford the inhabitants a large supply of cider, an excellent family beverage. Domestic manufactures receive, generally, considerable attention; and many families supply, from their own industry, most of their clothing.

One of the turnpikes from Hartford to New-Haven runs through this town; and the Talcott mountain turnpike, the great road from Hartford to Albany, the turnpike road to Danbury, also a road to Litchfield, and several other public roads centre in or pass through the town.

Farmington contains two Ecclesiastical Societies, in each of which is a Post-office, and 15 School districts.

The first Society, in its central section, is a compact settlement, comprising more than 100 houses, principally erected upon one street within the limits of something more than a mile, almost all of which are

FARMINGTON.

neat and handsome dwelling houses; and many of them elegant edifices. There are few inland towns that exhibit a corresponding appearance of populousness, wealth and splendour. Its site is at the foot of the mountain, which has a considerable elevation, and ranges along upon the east; to the west, there is a delightful landscape, having a gentle declivity, which is lost in the beautiful meadows upon the borders of the Tunxis.

There were in Farmington, in 1810, 2748 inhabitants. There are now, about 400 Freemen or qualified Electors, and about 400 Dwelling Houses, 9 Mercantile Stores, 6 Grain Mills, 6 Carding Machines, 5 Distilleries, & 6 Tanneries. There are two Congregational Churches, and one erecting for Baptists; two Ministers of the Gospel, two Physicians, and three Attorneys; there is one Academy, and fifteen district, or primary Schools, and three Social Libraries. The general list of Farmington in 1817, was $71,242. The valuation or assessment of the United States in 1816, was $1,538,873; that of 1799, was $562,417.

In the north-east part of Farmington, upon the summit of Talcott mountain, is Wadsworth's pond, a fine body of water, of about 100 rods in length, and near 50 in breadth, having considerable depth, and abounding with fish. This is a most fanciful and romantic spot, deriving beauty from the irregularity of its features, and order from an apparent incongruity of the established laws of nature. Daniel Wadsworth, Esq. of the city of Hartford, has selected this spot for a summer residence; he has made considerable improvements, having erected a neat and genteel dwelling-house for his own family, a farm-house, in which he has a Tenant, who superintends the farm, and other buildings, besides constructing wharves upon the shores of the pond, various curious avenues or walks, and erecting a tower upon the most elevated summit of the mountain. This tower affords an extensive prospect of the surrounding country, and the charming vale of the Connecticut, lies under the eye of the observer, who, enraptured with the view, cannot but feel the truth of what its own Poet hath said; that
" *No watery gleams through happier vallies shine,*
" *Nor drinks the Sea a lovelier wave than thine.*"

Parties of pleasure from Hartford, and other towns in the vicinity, frequently visit this enchanting spot.

The first settlers of Farmington were from Hartford, being emigrants from Boston, Newton and Roxbury, in Massachusetts. They began the settlement in 1640, being four years only from the first settlement in Hartford, and were probably attracted by the fine natural meadows upon the Tunxis river. The town was incorporated in 1645. The land was purchased of the Tunxis tribe of natives, a very numerous and warlike tribe, by eighty-four proprietors, and divided by them and their heirs according to their respective interests. The township, at the time of incorporation, was about fifteen miles square, and has since been divided into four towns.

BIOGRAPHY. Major *William Judd*, distinguished for his services and patriotism during the revolutionary war, and subsequently as an enlightened politician, was a native of this town. Major Judd had been regularly educated and admitted to the practice of law, which situation, together with all the advantages which young practitioners are apt to anticipate, he, at an early period of the revolutionary war, abandoned for the service of his country. He was a zealous whig, and engaged in the cause of liberty and his country with great arduor and enthusiasm. He had a Captain's commission in the Continental Army, and few officers of his rank were more active, persevering and useful. At the close of the war he received the brevet rank of Major. After the peace, in 1783, he resumed business in the line of his profession, and, for many years, was distinguished as a lawyer and an advocate. Although, for a short period, after the peace, and during the general distress, embarrassment and want of confidence which ensued, he, in common with most of the officers, became unpopular, in consequence of the act of Congress, giving them half pay for life, and the subsequent act commuting this to full pay, for five years; yet the importance of his public services, and his knowledge, integrity, abilities and patriotism, soon enabled him to attain that station in society, and in the estimation of his fellow-citizens, to which, in every point of view, he was so justly entitled. The influence of Major Judd at home, where his worth was best known, and could be best appreciated, was very conspicuous. For many years he was a representative of the town in the General Assembly, and was also, for a long time, a magistrate. After the adoption of the Constitution of the United States, and when political subjects began to agitate the public mind, Major Judd became associated with the party whose political sentiments best accorded with his own, and with what he regarded as the soundest principles of republicanism—principles combining an energetic government, with the enjoyment of the greatest portion of civil liberty. After the year 1801, the constitutional principles of the government of this State, (it being the only one, except Rhode-Island, which had not formed a constitution of Civil Government, after their separation from Great Britain,) became a subject of general discussion, and occasioned much agitation of the public mind. Upon this subject, Major Judd took a distinguished part, and maintained with firmness, but with dignity and moderation, that this State was without a constitution of Civil Government; making a distinction between a government and a constitution; thereby admitting that the existing government was *lawful* as long as the people saw fit to maintain it. In August 1804, a Convention of Delegates, from nearly one hundred towns in the State, convened at New-Haven upon this subject. Major Judd was chosen Chairman of this Convention, and as such signed an address which they submitted to the citizens of this State, recommend-

10

ing to them, to adopt legal measures to revise their government, and to organize it upon constitutional provisions. This address was drawn up with much ability, & contained an able and lucid view of this important subject.

These proceedings, in which Major Judd had taken so distinguished a part, occasioning alarm, became a subject of much animadversion with the men, who were then in authority in the State. Accordingly, the following October session of the Assembly, Major Judd, with several other members of this convention who were magistrates, was cited to appear before the Assembly, to show cause why his commission of justice of the peace should not be revoked, in consequence of his having declared, that this State was without a constitution of civil government. At the time of receiving this notice, he was much indisposed; but determining upon making his own defence, he repaired to New-Haven for this purpose. But, however, from the increase of his indisposition, he was unable himself to make his defence. The trial resulted in the revocation of his commission. After this event, whilst at New-Haven, he, with the assistance of some of his friends, prepared, in the form of a pamphlet, his defence, containing his views of the government of this State, and generally his political principles.

Before this pamphlet was out of press, he expired, and it went to the public with the obituary of the author. He died, Nov. 14th 1804, aged 63. The history of Major Judd is identified with the origin of the constitution of civil government of Connecticut, recently established. As a patriot and statesman, his memory will long be revered in his native State, whilst his important public services, during the period that "tried men's souls," cannot fail to secure to it, the veneration and respect of posterity.

GLASTENBURY.

GLASTENBURY is a post town situated upon the east side of Connecticut river, near the south east border of the county, being eight miles south east from Hartford; bounded on the north by East-Hartford, on the south by Chatham and Marlborough, on the east by Marlborough, Hebron and Bolton, and on the west by Connecticut river, which separates it from Wethersfield. The town comprises two located Societies. In 1810, it contained 2776 inhabitants, and has now 440 dwelling houses, a Post-office, four Churches or houses for public worship; two for Congregationalists, one for Episcopalians, and one for Methodists; two companies of Infantry, and a part of a company of Cavalry of Militia.

The township contains an area of about 54 square miles, having an average length of 9 miles from east to west, & being 6 miles in breadth. Its surface is uneven, and the soil various; upon the borders of Con-

GLASTENBURY.

necticut river, there are some fine meadows, back of which, upon the rise of land, the soil is a sandy loam, and some sections nearly a siliceous sand; farther east it is a gravelly loam, and some small tracts of aluminous loam. It is generally fertile and productive; its natural growth of timber is oak, chesnut and the various trees common to the district upon Connecticut river. The lands in the western section of the town, are best adapted to grain, and are cultivated with facility, and produce good crops, particularly of rye, corn and oats.

The geological structure of the township consists of sand stone or clay slate, which is less indurated, and has more of the quality of a free stone, than is its general character upon the west side of the river.

In addition to the Connecticut, which washes the western border of the town, it is watered by Roaring brook and Salmon brook, two fine mill streams; the former intersects the town nearly from north east to south west, discharging its waters into the Connecticut. Upon this stream, there is a large Cotton Factory, about one mile east of Connecticut river; and two miles farther east upon the same stream, there is a Forge and Iron works; at which iron is manufactured from the ore, anchors wrought, and various other manufactures of iron carried on. Salmon brook is a small stream, and runs through the northern part of the town in a western direction. Upon this stream, there is a Woolen Factory, Mills, Clothier's Works &c. This Factory is advantageously carried on, and the cloth made there is, in the opinion of our correspondent, equal to any that is manufactured in the United States. There are fine shad fisheries upon Connecticut river within this town. The other streams and several ponds are stored with fish.

In the eastern part of the town, there is a pond of about a mile in circumference, called "Diamond pond," from the circumstance of there being small pebbles or stones around its margin, having a peculiar brilliancy. Near the centre of the town, there is a mineral spring, which, though it has acquired no celebrity abroad, has been thought, by men of science who have examined it, to possess valuable medical qualities; and for more than one hundred years has been known in the vicinity by the name of the "Pool at Nipsuck."

Although agriculture is the leading business of the town, some attention has been paid to manufactures; and ship building, at some periods, has been carried on to considerable extent; this business, however, is on the decline. There is but one vessel building here this season.

The turnpike road leading from Hartford to New-London, passes through a part of this town.

In addition to the Cotton and Woolen Factories, and Forge and Iron Works already noticed, there are 5 Grain Mills, 3 Fulling Mills and Clothier's Works, 1 Saw Mill, 4 Tanneries, and various other mechanical establishments and employments.

The town contains 13 School Districts and Schools, 1 small Library, 2 Attornies & 3 Physicians.

The amount of taxable property, including polls, is $50,832.
The real estate of the town, together with that of Marlborough, in 1816, was valued at $1,253,024. In 1799, the real estate of Glastenbury, which at that time comprised the principal part of Marlborough, was valued at $454,080.
Glastenbury was incorporated as a town, in 1690.

GRANBY.

GRANBY is an extensive irregular township, situated in the northern section of the county, bordering upon Massachusetts, seventeen miles from Hartford; bounded on the north by Massachusetts' line, on the east by Suffield and Windsor, on the south by Simsbury and Canton, and on the west by Barkhamsted and Hartland. The average length of the township from east to west is nine and a half miles, and its average breadth from north to south, is more than six miles, comprising an area of about 59 miles, or 37,760 acres.

This township is characterised by a diversity of features, which are strikingly various; towards its eastern section, the green stone mountain ranges through it from north to south; this mountain here is perhaps more elevated than at any other place in the State, and its characteristic features more conspicuous, particularly in the vicinity of the State prison. Its western declivity, for a considerable distance from its summit, is nearly a perpendicular precipice, and its rocks are naked, and exhibited in disordered fragments. From this range of mountain, to near the eastern border of the township, the surface has a declivity to the east. This section of the town is a valuable agricultural district; the soil is a rich gravelly loam, generally warm and fertile, well adapted to orcharding, grain or grass. Immediately west of the mountain, the face of the country is hilly, and in some instances, ledgy; but the lands, though hard and stony, are fertile, and well adapted to grain and orcharding. West of this district, there is an extensive tract of plain, the soil of which is generally a light sandy loam. This tract is intersected by Salmon brook, a pleasant and lively mill stream, and extends for a considerable distance west of this stream. The lands here are well adapted to rye, and afford also good orcharding. West of this tract, and towards the extreme western border of the town, it is hilly and mountainous; the lands are rough and stoney, and the soil hard, cold and gravelly. This section of the town, bordering upon Hartland and Barkhamsted, comprises the eastern extremity of the granite range of mountain, which extends through those towns. The natural growth here is oak, maple, beach and some hemlock; upon the tract of plains east of this, it is oak and yellow pine; upon the green stone range, and the district east and west of it, the timber is oak, walnut, chesnut, &c.

GRANBY.

Various appearances of minerals have been discovered in the green stone mountain and hills of this town. Sulphuret of copper, or copper ore has been found in various places; and it is well known, that the cavern, now occupied by the State as a prison for convicts, was originally opened and worked as a mine. Copper pyrites, or ore, was found and worked; but gold, which had stimulated the cupidity of the adventurers engaged in the undertaking, disappointed their hopes; and after a very great expense and sacrifice, the business was abandoned.

The Tunxis or Farmington river washes the southeastern part of this town; and it is intersected by Salmon brook already mentioned. Both of these streams afford a number of sites for mills and other hydraulic works, many of which are advantageously occupied.

The Blanford turnpike leads through the town in a northwestern direction; and is intersected by a turnpike, leading from Connecticut river to Norfolk, where it connects with the Hartford and Albany turnpike.

The town contains two located Congregational Societies and Churches, one Society of Episcopalians, which have a house for public worship, two Societies of Baptists, and one Society of Methodists. There are 16 School districts and Schools, and a small village in the centre of each of the located Societies. The population of the town, at the last census, was 2683; and there are 380 dwelling houses, 4 companies of militia, and about 400 qualified Electors. There are two Card Factories, two Wire Factories, one Powder Mill, six Grain Mills, two Fulling Mills, three Carding Machines, three Tanneries, and four Mercantile Stores.

There are two small Social Libraries, two Clergymen, four Physicians, and four Attornies.

Granby was taken from Simsbury, and incorporated in October, 1786.

The State prison established in this town is, from its novel and peculiar character, deserving of particular notice. The character of this institution, for the imprisonment of convicts, has, by some, particularly foreigners, been regarded as a subject of reproach to the State.

Many erroneous representations have been published, which, instead of exhibiting a just picture of this institution, have presented only the frightful images of caricature.

The idea of a cavern is peculiarly gloomy and horrible; and, when we consider such a place as the abode of man, dark and dreary, excluding every ray of light, and every object of nature, the mind is apt to recoil at the picture; and, forgetting the nature of the institution, and the causes which have filled it with its miserable and gloomy tenants, to regard it as an outrage upon humanity. But upon a more cool survey, and more especially upon an investigation of the subject, however repugnant to our ideas of humanity a subterraneous imprisonment may appear, it will be found, that, practically, it is much less objectionable than we at first supposed. The object of every institution of this description is confinement; and this ought to be effected with as much regard to the health and comfort of the unfortunate subjects of crimes, and consequent punishment, as may be consistent with their security, and the economy of the public treasure. These caverns are remarkable for their healthfulness, and it is believed, that a less number of prisoners have died here, in proportion to the number which have been confined, than in any other prison in the United States. As it respects the cleanliness and comforts of the prisoners at this institution, it will not probably hold a comparison with many others; but this is more owing to the business which is pursued, (working at nails,) than to the confinement in the caverns. The security of the prisoners here is most effectual; and whether the institution is considered as an economical one or not, the use of the caverns, as a place of confinement, is not a circumstance that has any particular influence upon this subject.

On the whole, although there may be in principle, or in sentiment, objections to occupying a subterraneous prison, yet in a practical point of view, the one under consideration has many advantages; and the objections to this institution apply with more propriety and force to the description of work, at which they are employed, and to other circumstances connected with its management, than to the character of the place in which they are confined.

A succinct account of the origin of this cavern, and its establishment and occupation as a place of confinement for convicts, may be somewhat interesting.

The lands upon which Newgate prison stands, and in the vicinity, were claimed by the original proprietors of the town, in which they were formerly situated; but on account of their supposed value from the copper ore which had been found, and as gold was also supposed to abound, the title was long a subject of contention. To quiet all disputes with respect to these mines, in 1753, the General Assembly appointed a committee to investigate the subject, who confirmed the right and title of the original proprietors, and set off to them the land, or mine, which is now occupied as a public prison, and the other lands in the vicinity which were supposed to be valuable for their minerals. At this time, copper ore had been found; the ore was considered very rich, and it was also supposed, that it contained gold. From these circumstances, the fame of these mines soon reached Europe, and in 1760, a company was formed in England for the purpose of working them; and soon after, several persons, as the agents, or in the employ of this company, arrived from England for this purpose. But the company were obliged, principally, to employ men in the neighbourhood, who were entirely unacquainted with the business; from which circumstance, and various others, the work proceeded slowly, and with great difficulty. The company, however, were enabled to freight two vessels with ore, (it being their plan not to work the ore here, but to ship it to England for this purpose,) both of which were lost; one being taken by the French, and the other sunk in the channel.

These losses were so considerable, and the whole business having been little more than a succession of disasters and sacrifices, the company became discouraged, and were induced to abandon the undertaking. Since this time, the mines have not been wrought for ore. The miners, in digging and exploring, sunk numerous wells, or deep excavations. The principal one was upon Copper hill, so called, and remains at this time, being within the walls of the prison.

These caverns were first occupied as a place of confining convicts, about the commencement of the revolutionary war. There being at that time no prison in the State, other than the county gaols, and the number of convicts having considerably increased, arrangements were made for occupying these caverns as a place of confinement; but no permanent buildings were at this time erected; and it is not probable, that at first it was contemplated to convert these caverns into a State prison; their occupation for this purpose, being regarded as a temporary thing. The confining of convicts having been begun, it was continued; and this being found very inconvenient, the General Assembly, in 1790, passed an act, establishing Newgate prison as a permanent State prison, and providing for the erection of suitable buildings. At the same time, they appointed three overseers or trustees of the prison, authorized to take the charge and direction of the institution. In pursuance of this authority, the trustees erected a wooden paling, enclosing about half an acre of ground, within which was the principal cavern: they also erected a brick building directly over this cavern, into which there is an avenue from the back room in this building. Underneath the basement floor in this room, and directly over the cavern, there are two strong rooms built of stone; in these rooms, the prisoners are usually kept when they are not employed, and it is not thought necessary, that they should be confined in the cavern. Within a few years past, there has been an extensive work shop, and other buildings erected; and also a substantial stone wall, enclosing the cavern buildings and one acre of ground. This wall is twelve feet high, three feet thick at its base, and one and a half at the top.

The principal cavern is about 26 feet in depth at its entrance, which is a perpendicular descent through an aperture, stoned up square for the purpose. In this entrance, there is a large and strong ladder, resting upon the rock at the bottom, and made fast at the top, upon which the prisoners and others descend into the cavern. On reaching the bottom, you strike a smooth rock, having a gradual descent, upon the sides of which there are cavities sufficiently large to admit of small lodging rooms, which are built for the prisoners, on both sides of the main passage that leads through the area of the cavern. These rooms are built of wood and boards, and are sufficiently large to accommodate 20 men. After passing these rooms, you traverse a large cavern, enclosed on all sides by solid rock; dark, gloomy and horrible! At the extremity of this, there is a well of water 80 feet deep, which communicates with the cavern, and affords to the tenants of this subterraneous abode, a free circulation of air; although from the various windings of the avenues and other causes, it is not cold, even in the severest weather. And as strange as it may seem, it has been satisfactorily ascertained, that the mercury ranges eight degrees lower in the lodging apartments of the prisoners, in the warmest days in the summer, than it does in the coldest in the winter. This phænomenon is attributed to the circumstance, of the cavities in the rocks being stopped with snow, ice and frost in the winter, which prevents so free a circulation of air, as is enjoyed in the summer.

On the 18th of January 1811, at 8 o'clock A. M., the mercury stood in the cavern at 52 degrees; and in open air, as soon after as was practicable for a person to get up from the cavern, (which could not have exceeded five minutes,) it fell to one degree below 0. On the 17th of June, (mid-day,) the mercury stood in the cavern at 50° 10″, and in the open air at 76°. This cavern has been remarkable for its healthfulness, which has usually been ascribed to certain supposed medicinal qualities in the rocks; but it deserves consideration, whether it is not more probably owing to the uniform state of its atmosphere.

The keeper of the prison is appointed by the overseers or trustees, and is accountable to them for his conduct. He receives a regular salary of $550 per annum; he draws no rations, but has certain perquisites; he is allowed 1 sergeant, 2 corporals and 17 privates as a guard, for the security of the prisoners. The pay of the sergeant is $12 67 per month; that of the corporals $11 34; and that of the privates $10. They are all entitled to rations, and the privates receive a uniform suit of clothes, and the sergeant and corporals an allowance as an equivalent therefor.

The total expenses of the institution and disbursements for stock in 1816, amounted to $15,007 22. and the receipts the same year to } 3,428

leaving a balance against the State of $11,579 22. but at this time there were nails and stock on hand; a part or all of the latter having been purchased, and a part of the former manufactured the same year, to an estimated value of - - $5,147 44.

HARTLAND.

HARTLAND is an elevated post township in the northeast corner of the county, 22 miles from Hartford; bounded north on Massachusetts line, east by Granby, south by Barkhamsted, and west by Colebrook in Litchfield county. It contains an area of 34 square miles, being near 7 miles in length from east to west, and 5 in breadth from north to south. The township is hilly and mountainous, being embraced within the extensive granite range of mountain, which

HARTLAND.

commencing near the sound in the vicinity of New-Haven, leads thro' the State in a northeasterly direction, and extends into Massachusetts and the interior of New-England. From its elevated situation, the town is cold and frosty, or at least a considerable part of it; the soil is a gravelly loam, of a granite character, and generally rather cold and sterile; it however affords tolerable grazing, but produces but little grain; though some small sections are more warm and fertile. The timber consists of beach, maple, chesnut and evergreen, or perennial trees. The making of butter and cheese, beef and pork, and pasturing of cattle, are the principal interests of the inhabitants. The farmers in the towns east of this to Connecticut river, have been in the habit of sending their growing or young cattle, sheep &c. into this and other grazing towns, to be kept during several months in the spring & summer.

The town is watered by the east branch of the Farmington river, which passes through it, and affords some small tracts of alluvial, and many excellent mill seats. The main branch of this river passes through the southwestern section of the town. The turnpike road leading from Connecticut river to Norfolk, where it unites with the Greenwood's turnpike that extends to Albany, passes through this town.

The population of the town, in 1810, was 1284, and there are about 200 dwelling houses, 2 companies of militia, and about 150 Electors.

There are six cider Distilleries, two Grain Mills, two Fulling Mills and Clothier's Works, one Carding Machine, three Mercantile Stores, two Tanneries and four Taverns.

The town contains two Congregational Societies and Churches, and one Society of Methodists; nine School Districts and Schools, one Social Library, two Clergymen, and two Physicians. The amount of taxable property, including polls, is $27,052.

Hartland was incorporated as a town, in 1761, at which time it belonged to Litchfield county; but some years since it was annexed to the county of Hartford.

Hartland is one of the towns which were sold by the State, to the inhabitants of Hartford and Windsor. The first proprietors' meeting was holden at Hartford, July 10th, 1733. John Kendall, who removed from Lancaster in Massachusetts, in the spring of 1753, was the first settler. He located a tract of land in the great valley, on the west side of Farmington river. The following year, Thomas Giddings removed with his family from Lyme.

In 1755, Simon Baxter came into the town, and the year after, Joshua Giddings. Four additional families settled in the town in 1757. After this period, emigrants were received in considerable numbers for several years.

In 1761, the town was incorporated, and the first town-meeting was holden in July of that year. In June 1768, the Rev. Sterling Graves was ordained, being the first minister settled in the town. In 1770, Nehemiah Andrews was appointed the first Justice of the Peace; and in June the same year, the first meeting-house was erected.

MARLBOROUGH.

MARLBOROUGH is a small post town, situated in the south-eastern extremity of the county, fifteen miles from Hartford; bounded north by Glastenbury, east by Hebron in Tolland county, south by Colchester in New-London county, and west by Chatham, in Middlesex county. The area of the town comprises about twenty-two square miles, having an average length of five and a half miles, and an average breadth of four miles.

Its surface is hilly and stony; and the soil a gravelly loam, being part of the granitic section in the eastern part of the State. Small quantities of plumbago, or black lead, have been discovered. The lands are best adapted to grazing; & the making of butter and cheese, and beef and pork, are the leading agricultural interests.

There are within the town no rivers, but it is watered by a number of small streams, some of which afford very advantageous sites for mills, and other water works. Marlborough pond, in this town, is a considerable body of water; being one mile in length, and half a mile in breadth.

The Hartford and New-London turnpike road leads through the town; also, a turnpike from Middletown to Windham.

The population of the town, in 1810, was 720; and there are now one company of Infantry, and a part of a company of Riflemen of militia; 100 Electors, and 110 dwelling houses.

Manufactures have received some attention; there are one Cotton Factory and one Woolen Factory; one Carding Machine, two Fulling Mills and Clothier's Works, three Grain Mills, & one Tannery.

The town contains one located Congregational Society & Church, an Episcopal Society, and a Society of Methodists. It contains six School districts and Schools, one of which, called the central district, has been endowed with a fund of 2 or $3,000, to constitute it a grammar School.

The amount of taxable property, including polls, is $19,952.

The town contains one small Social Library, one Physician, and one Clergyman.

Marlborough was formed from Colchester, Glastenbury and Hebron, three towns belonging to three different counties; and it was incorporated in 1803.

SIMSBURY.

SIMSBURY a post town, is situated twelve miles northwest from Hartford. Simsbury was settled in 1670; the first settlers being from Windsor, of which it then formed a part. About six years after the settlement, the inhabitants, consisting of about forty families, were so alarmed at the hostility of the Indians, that they buried their effects, and returned to Windsor. The settlement being abandoned, the Indians burned the houses which had been erected, and destroyed almost every vestige of improvement, which distinguished the infant settlement from the wilderness which surrounded it; so

SIMSBURY. 83

that, when the settlers returned, they could not find the spot where they deposited their goods. This was in the spring of 1676, at which time Simsbury was a frontier settlement, although but about ten miles from Connecticut river. It was incorporated as a town at an early period, and has since been divided twice, by the incorporation of the towns of Granby and Canton; both of which belonged principally to the original town of Simsbury.

This township, at present, has an area of about 37 square miles, being seven miles in length, and about five and a half miles in breadth upon an average estimation; and is bounded north on Granby, east on Windsor, south on Farmington, and west on Canton. It is strikingly diversified, being intersected by the Farmington or Tunxis river, and embracing the range of the greenstone mountain, which here is elevated and lofty. This mountain generally has a gradual declivity upon the east, whence it is usually covered with timber. Upon its eastern side, you discover clay slate, but it is generally covered with trap or greenstone. Upon the west, it presents a bold and elevated mural precipice, wholly covered with greenstone. The rock is exhibited in broken & disordered fragments, and towards the summit is entirely naked; having no covering of earth, and not sustaining the growth of the smallest shrubs.

The Tunxis river, on approaching this mountain, ranges along upon the west of it, until it finds a chasm where it forces its passage through, forming the boundary between this town and Granby; but the mountain does not subside, but immediately rises in Granby, and soon attains its usual elevation, and presents its usual features.

Upon the Tunxis river within this town, there are tracts of meadow, or alluvial, of considerable extent, and very fertile. West from the river, the elevated lands are a light sandy plain, but considerably well adapted to the culture of rye.

East of the declivity of the mountain, the soil is generally a gravelly loam, but there are some sections of argillaceous loam; and although hilly, and somewhat stony, it is fertile, and very favourable for orcharding. This section of the town is perhaps best adapted to grass; it affords also good crops of Indian corn, and the declivities of the mountain good pasturage.

Formerly salmon and shad were taken plentifully in the Tunxis river; but for some years past, the former have disappeared altogether, and the latter are taken only in small quantities, which renders the business of fishing no object to the inhabitants.

The manufactures of the town are principally domestic, which receive great attention; the inhabitants being industrious and economical. In addition to which, there are one small Cotton Factory, three Tin ware Factories, three Wire Factories, two Grain Distilleries, three Gristmills, four Saw Mills, two Carding Machines, and two Tanneries. There are also four Mercantile Stores.

The town contains one located Congregational Society, and an Episcopal Society, each of which is accommodated with a house for public worship. It also contains 10 School districts, in each of which a school is maintained for the greater part of the year.

In 1810, the population of the town amounted to 1966; and there are now 250 Electors, two Companies of militia, and 290 dwelling houses. The taxable property, including polls, amounts to $34,009.

There are in Simsbury 1 Physician, 1 Clergyman, & 1 Lawyer.

BIOGRAPHY. Major Gen. Noah Phelps, a native inhabitant of this town, was born in 1740. He served under Gen. Amherst in the French war, and took an early and active part on the side of his country, in the war of the revolution. Early in the spring of 1775, he, with Col. Halsey, and another gentleman whose name is not recollected, proposed the capture of Ticonderoga, which they effected with a small band of volunteers raised and paid by themselves, and on their *own responsibility*, independence then not being declared. Having demolished the fort, they marched with their prisoners, about 100 in number, for Hartford, where they arrived during the session of the General Assembly in May. Gen. Phelps afterwards served as a captain in this war, and after the peace, held for many years the office of judge of Probate &c. He died March 4th, 1809.

SOUTHINGTON.

SOUTHINGTON is a post town, situated in the southwestern corner of the county, 18 miles from Hartford, and 21 from New-Haven; bounded on the north by Farmington and Bristol, on the west by Wolcott, on the south by Cheshire and Meriden, and on the east by Meriden and Berlin. The area of the township is nearly six miles from east to west, and about the same from north to south, containing about 35 square miles. The surface is uneven; the greenstone range of mountain extends along upon the east side of the town. The western section is also hilly, or mountainous, but the greater proportion of the town is but moderately hilly. The soil is various, according to the local situation of the lands, but is generally good, & well adapted to the culture of rye & Indian corn, which attain here the highest perfection; and of which there is raised annually a considerable surplus, that is manufactured into flour and corn meal, and transported to New-Haven and Middletown for a market.

There are no considerable rivers in the town, but several small streams. A branch of the Quinipiack has its source in a pond at the northwest corner of the town, and runs through it in a southeasterly direction, affording several excellent mill seats. About two miles from the centre of the town, in a southwesterly direction, it forms a junction with another branch of the Quinipiack, which has its source in Farmington, and runs in a southeasterly direction; just below this junction, there is a large flour mill and oil mill erected upon this stream.

The western turnpike road, leading from Hartford to new-Haven passes through the centre of this town; thence through Cheshire and Hamden. The Southington and Waterbury turnpike, leads from Waterbury in New-Haven county, in an eastern direction through the south part of the town to Meriden, thence to Middletown.

The inhabitants of this town are industrious and enterprising; although the greater part are engaged in agriculture, yet several kinds of manufactures and mechanical employments have received considerable attention, and been prosecuted with ardour and success. Among these, the manufactures of tin ware and buttons are the most important. The tin ware business, having been first established at Berlin, was, after the lapse of some years, transplanted to this town. There are now, three Tin Ware Factories, several Button Factories, one Woolen Factory, one Pocket-book Factory, four Flour Mills, two Oil Mills, one Fulling Mill and Clothier's Works, two Carding Machines, two considerable Tanneries, and ten Distilleries, principally of cider spirits. There are five Mercantile Stores.

The town contains one located Congregational Society & Church, one Society of Episcopalians, and one also of Baptists, all of which are accommodated with houses for public worship. It contains nine School districts and common Schools, and one Academy, not endowed, one small Social Library, two settled Clergymen, four Physicians, and two Lawyers.

The population of the town, in 1810, was 1807; and there are now 300 dwelling houses, and about 300 Freemen or qualified Electors; and two companies of Infantry, and part of a company of cavalry.

The amount of taxable property, including polls, is $43,300.

Southington originally belonged to Farmington, was incor. in 1779.

SUFFIELD.

SUFFIELD is a post town, delightfully situated upon the west side of Connecticut river, 17 miles north from Hartford, and 10 south from Springfield; bounded on the north by Massachusetts, on the east by Connecticut river, which separates it from Enfield, on the south by Windsor and Granby, and on the west by Granby and Southwick in Massachusetts. The average length of the township, from east to west, is about eight miles, and it is five in breadth, comprising about forty square miles.

The surface and soil of this town afford considerable diversity of character; its eastern section bordering upon Connecticut river, has a gradual rise for about two miles to the public road, which runs nearly in a parallel direction with the river. This is a good agricultural district, the soil being a strong, deep, argillaceous loam. There is no alluvial upon the border of the river, and the bank is generally elevated and bold, consisting of solid argillaceous schistus, or clay slate rock. From the public road westerly, the surface is generally of an undulating character, but some sections are nearly level. This district extends upon the south line of the town, to its western boundary; but upon its north section, there is a projection which extends farther west. The soil of this tract is also an argillaceous loam, and in some places it is low and frequently wet and cold, and the clay stiff and hard; when dry, it is best adapted to grass and grazing, and is well calculated for manures. That section of the township upon its northern border which extends farther west, lying north of Granby, embraces the greenstone range of mountain, which is here characterised by its usual features. The declivities of this mountain afford good grazing and orcharding, and some tracts are well adapted to grain.

The natural growth consists of oak, maple, walnut, chesnut, butternut, elm, birch &c.

Besides the Connecticut, which washes the eastern border of the town, it is intersected by Stony river, a considerable mill stream, upon which there are numerous sites for hydraulic works, many of which are advantageously occupied.

In the northwestern section of the town, there are two considerable ponds called Southwick ponds, being partly in this town and partly in Southwick in Massachusetts. These are very pleasant and beautiful bodies of water, and are well stored with fish, particularly perch and pickerel; the latter of which are taken plentifully, and with great facility in the winter season, by making holes through the ice.

Near the southern border of the township is a mineral spring, the waters of which have a strong sulphurous impregnation. It has acquired considerable celebrity in cases of of calculous and cutaneous diseases. Very ample and convenient accommodations have been provided; a large three story building, with numerous and spacious apartments, having been erected.

These waters, although undoubtedly possessed of valuable medicinal qualities, pleasantly situated, and provided with respectable accommodations, have not been a place of extensive resort; & it is believed that, for one or two seasons past, they have received less attention than at other periods, and that their celebrity is upon the decline; although circumstances might occur that would give them a reputation, which they have not yet acquired, and of which there is no apparent prospect.

Suffield comprises two located Congregational Societies, or Parishes, and two large Societies of Baptists. These several Societies are respectively provided with houses for public worship.

The principal street, in the first Society, is the great river road; it has an elevated and delightful site, and is called High-street. For one mile or more it is well settled, and contains many handsome dwelling houses, and some that are large and elegant; all of which unite the advantages of a pleasant and prospective situation. Upon this street, there are a Post-office, one Congregational and one Baptist church, and several Mercantile Stores. The west Society comprises a-number of streets, which are settled principally by independent and thrifty farmers. Here also are two Churches, one for Baptists, & one for Congregationalists.

The inhabitants of the town have been characterized by an enterprising and adventurous spirit. Various species of traffic, both at home and abroad, have been carried on. From the extent and multiplicy of these concerns, and more generally the irresponsible character of the persons engaged in them, it is not a matter of surprise, that instances of conduct should have occurred, discreditable to the authors thereof; and which, by a natural but unwarrantable association, should have had the effect of casting a shade upon the character of the community, to which such persons belonged. Yet any opinions affecting the character of the inhabitants of this town, which may have arisen from causes like these, are wholly unsupported, and illiberal in the extreme. The enterprise of a community is certainly very much to their credit, although it can scarcely be denied, that if this spirit discloses itself through such a channel as that of traffic, it is calculated to elicit dispositions and habits less consistent with the strict principles of moral integrity, than those which generally characterise labouring or *earning* communities.

But the enterprise of the inhabitants of this town, has not been confined to trade; it has disclosed itself in other channels, and has in no small degree promoted the interests of manufactures, particularly those of cotton. There are now four Cotton Factories in the town, some of which are upon a conside-rably extensive scale. There are also one Paper Mill, one Oil Mill, three Fulling mills and Clothier's Works, two Carding Machines, three Grain Mills, three Tanneries, four Mercantile Stores, and five Taverns.

The population of the town, in 1810, was 2630; and there are 360 dwelling houses, 400 Freemen or Electors, and three companies of militia.

The amount of taxable property, (estimated according to the laws regulating the making up of lists,) including polls, is $52,821; and the valuation, or assessment of lands and buildings of the town, in 1816, was $976,629.

There are in the town eleven School districts & primary Schools, and usually one Grammar School, three Social Libraries, three Physicians, four Clergymen, and two Attornies.

Suffield originally belonged to the colony of Massachusetts, and was purchased of two Sachems, at $100.

In 1660, it was granted by the General Assembly of Massachusetts to major John Pyncheon. It continued a part of the territory of that colony, and subject to its jurisdiction until 1752, being then annexed to Connecticut.

BIOGRAPHY. Gen. *Phineas Lyman*, distinguished for his services during the French war, and for many public employments, was for several years a resident in this town. General Lyman was one among the many, who have risen to distinction from the force of native talents, and surmounting all the obstacles arising from the want of education. He was bred a weaver.

but soon raised himself above this situation, and engaged in mercantile pursuits. He took a distinguished part in the dispute between this State and Massachusetts, relative to the right of jurisdiction over the town of Suffield, and the other towns upon that boundary, settled by Massachusetts. He afterwards became a councillor, then called a magistrate, which office he held for a number of years. During the French war, he had a distinguished command in the northern army for several years. In the campaign of 1755, he served as a major gen. in the provincial troops. At or soon after the close of the war, he went to England to support a claim of the officers of the provincial troops, having been authorised to act as general agent. After experiencing great difficulties and delay, (having returned once for an extension of his powers,) he succeeded in obtaining a grant of an extensive tract of land upon the Mississippi, in the vicinity of Natchez. He accordingly embarked, and sailed directly for the Mississippi, where he arrived about the year 1774. He dispatched one of his sons for his family, which during this period had remained in Suffield; but just before their arrival, the same year, Gen. Lyman died upon the tract of land of which he obtained a grant. His wife died during the passage, and his family left there soon after, on the country being reclaimed by the Spaniards.

Oliver Phelps, Esq. a man of extraordinary enterprise and extensive business, was for many years a resident of this town. He also was the "maker of his own fortunes." He was a native of Windsor, but was bred in this town, and received a mercantile education. He engaged in business in Granville, Massachusetts, and soon became a very enterprising, sagacious and successful trader. During the revolutionary war, he was employed by the State of Massachusetts in the commissary department. Whilst in this situation, his transactions were of a most extensive and responsible nature, and his own paper formed a kind of circulating medium. Afterwards he purchased a large estate, and returned to this town. In 1789 he, in connection with the Hon. Mr. Gorham, purchased of the commonwealth of Massachusetts, a tract of land in the western part of the State of New-York, at what is commonly called the Genesee country, comprising 2,200,000 acres. This is probably the greatest land purchase, or speculation, ever made by two individuals in the United States. This is a very excellent tract of land, having a mild climate, a fertile soil, and an abundance of waters, and is now comprised in the extensive counties of Ontario and Steuben. In 1795, Oliver Phelps, together with William Hart and their associates, purchased of this State the tract of land in the State of Ohio, called the western reserve; comprising 3,300,000 acres. Some years after this, he removed to Canandaigua, situated within his Genesee purchase. In 1802, he was elected a member of Congress from the western district of that State.

WETHERSFIELD.

WETHERSFIELD, an ancient and populous town, is situated on the west side of Connecticut river, four miles south of Hartford, and 34 north of New-Haven. It is bounded north by Hartford, south by Middletown and Berlin, west by Farmington and Berlin, and east by Connecticut river, which separates it from Glastenbury.

The area of the town is about six miles square, containing 23,000 acres. This is an excellent township of land, having an undulating surface, and exhibiting a beautiful diversity of hill and dale. The soil is generally a rich gravelly and sandy loam, but in the western part of the town, argillaceous loam prevails; and some small sections in the centre, may be considered as a garden mould. It is well adapted to grass and grain, & particularly to esculent roots. The tract of alluvial upon Connecticut river is extensive and beautiful, and very productive. The clay of Hartford does not extend to Wethersfield, but on the contrary, there are some small sections of silicious sand.

Among other agricultural interests in this town, the cultivation of onions has long held a conspicuous rank. This is an important agricultural pursuit, although it occupies but a small portion of land, and the service is principally performed by females. Wethersfield onions have long been justly celebrated, & are exported to the southern states and the West Indies for a market. The onions, when prepared for market, are sorted and arranged into Ropes or Bunches, consisting of a number strung together, of which it has been estimated, that there are from a million to a million and a half raised annually, and sent abroad.

This is the only town in the State which makes a business of the cultivation of this excellent root. It is peculiarly novel and interesting, on passing through the town in the month of June, to behold in every direction the extensive fields of onions. Whilst in a luxuriant state of vegetation, the growing vegetable exhales its strong savour. The atmosphere becomes impregnated, and the luscious qualities of the onion are wafted far and wide, upon every passing breeze.

The largest stream within the town is Piper's river; in addition to which, there are numerous brooks which intersect and water the different sections of the town.

On Connecticut river, there are several shad fisheries, and frequently large quantities of shad are taken. Alewives are also taken in abundance, and put up for exportation.

The business of navigation has received considerable attention in this town, and it possesses considerable tonnage. Ship building also has frequently been carried on, but the commercial and maritime interests of the town have not increased for some years past.

The civil divisions of Wethersfield are three Congregational Societies, and 12 School districts.

In the first Society, there is a pleasant village, containing a brick Congregational Church, a Post-office, several Mercantile Stores, & a number of neat and handsome dwelling houses.

At Rocky hill, in the Society of Stepney, there is a small but pleasant village. There are 12 primary Schools, one in each district, two academical Schools, and three Social Libraries.

The population of Wethersfield in 1810, was 3931, and there are now 500 Electors, 300 militia, and about 600 dwelling-houses. There are 5 Distilleries, 4 Tanneries, 3 Grain Mills, 2 Saw-Mills, 3 Fulling Mills, 2 Carding Machines, 15 Mercantile Stores, and one Ropewalk. The list of the town, in 1817, was $67,627. The assessment of the U. S. in 1816 was $1,324,178. That of 1799, - - - 636,452.

Wethersfield was one of the first settled towns in the State. In 1634, some of the people at Newtown, in the colony of Massachusetts, having visited the country upon Connecticut river, and being pleased with its beautiful meadows, were anxious to remove and commence a settlement there. The subject having been submitted to the Governor and Council, at the autumnal session of the General Court, it was debated at great length, and with great warmth; and notwithstanding the great influence of Mr. Hooker and others, who favoured the enterprise, it was decided to be inexpedient to attempt a settlement upon Connecticut river. But notwithstanding this opposition of the Court, the spring following, 1635, a number of persons engaged in the enterprise, set out for Connecticut, and arrived there in July, and erected a few huts at Pyquag, within the town of Wethersfield, and made out to subsist through the winter. The year after, the General Court having granted permission, a number of families arrived from Newtown and Dorchester, a part of which settled here, and a part at Hartford, where a settlement had also been began by John Steel and his associates, the same year with that at Pyquag.

BIOGRAPHY. The Rev. *Elisha Williams* was settled in the gospel ministry in this town.—He was made President of Yale College, in 1726. He was a man of energy and enterprise, and had a vigorous understanding.

WINDSOR.

WINDSOR, one of the first settled towns in the State, is situated on the west side of Connecticut river, north of Hartford; the Post-Office in Windsor being seven miles north from the city of Hartford, and 41 miles from New-Haven. The town was settled by emigrants from Dorchester, in the colony of Massachusetts, in the spring of 1636. Mr. Warham, their clergyman, removed in October following. There is, however, some reason to believe, that some of the Dorchester people commenced the settlement the year before. Windsor originally comprised an extensive tract of country, extending far back upon both sides of the river, which at this time forms a number of townships. The town now comprises an area of 50 square miles, or 32,000 acres; being eight and a half miles in length from north to south, and averaging about six miles in breadth, from east to west. It is bounded north by Suffield, west by Farmington, Simsbury and Granby, south by Hartford, and east by Connecticut river, which separates it from East-Windsor. The town is intersected into

WINDSOR.

nearly two equal sections, by Farmington or Tunxis river, the larger tributary stream of the Connecticut. This is a delightful river, of about 100 yards in width, the borders of which are fertile, pleasant and diversified. In the spring of the year it annually overflows its banks, and transcending its ordinary bounds, assumes the appearance of a large stream : the alluvial tracts that it affords, which are of considerable extent, are thus enriched and fertilized. But the river is by no means rapid, being navigable for flat bottomed boats for about seven miles from its mouth, and for sloops nearly the same distance, in the spring season. Above the boatable waters, there are numerous sites for mills and other hydraulic works, many of which are advantageously occupied. There are two considerable bridges erected across this stream, on the two branches of the great northern road which runs through the town. Windsor is generally of a level surface, having some extensive tracts of plains, and the other parts are of an undulating character. The soil is very various; there being a considerable quantity of alluvial, both upon the Connecticut and Tunxis rivers; large tracts of plains, which are light, dry, and inclining to a sand; but are healthy, feasible, and considerably fertile ; and in the west part of the town there is a portion of the lands that are low, flat, and inclining to be wet and marshy ; but the more prevailing character of the soil is a sandy or gravelly loam. It is free from stone, and, with few exceptions, from clay. Its natural growth is oak, walnut, maple, elm, chesnut, butternut, cherry, thorn, horn-beam, bass, birch, spruce, hemlock, yellow and white pine. The lands, in a cultivated state, produce wheat, rye, Indian corn, oats, barley, hemp, flax, beans, grass, the various esculent roots, and tobacco. Rye and Indian corn are the principal grains which are cultivated. There are a considerable portion of the improved lands, excepting the plains, that are under a grass culture, to which they are well adapted.

There are extensive orchards in the town, and cider is an important agricultural interest with the inhabitants. It is manufactured into spiritous liquor, called cider brandy, for which purpose almost every respectable farmer has a small distillery upon his own premises. This is a source of profit to the inhabitants, and the orchards, from whence it is derived, add greatly to the value of the lands, and at the same time give them the most charming and interesting appearance, exhibiting fields, having a canopy of verdure, and studded over with art.

Windsor is divided into three Ecclesiastical Societies, and sixteen School Districts. These Societies are well settled, and form considerable villages.

The first Society, in its central section, has a spacious and handsome street, containing many well built houses ; and being intersected by the river, having a beautiful grove upon its banks, which are connected by a bridge, it has a romantic and pleasing appearance. Upon the north side of the river, upon an elevated site, stands a large Congregational Church, contiguous to which are a number of Stores and handsome Dwelling Houses.

The Society of *Poquonock*, being farther back upon the Tunxis, is a delightful situation, almost unrivalled for its conveniences, and its rural scenery and objects. The road runs for several miles nearly parallel with the river, having a beautiful declivity to the meadows which line its borders to the east, and a gentle rise of land upon the west, extending back to the forests and plains. In the centre, for near a mile, there is a "purling brook," that courses along by the road, whose limpid treasures, not yielding to the severest droughts, are a grateful tribute both to man and beast. There are in this Society, both upon this stream and the river, numerous water privileges, and sites for hydraulic works. The Society of *Wintonbury* is situated in the southwest part of the town; it contains numerous roads, and many handsome and well built houses. There is a Post-office in this Society.

STATISTICS. There were in Windsor in 1810, 2868 inhabitants. There are 400 Dwelling Houses, 5 Churches, 3 belonging to the located Societies, but 1 which of is not Congregational, and 2 for Baptists; 3 companies of Infantry, and part of a company of Cavalry, of militia, and 500 freemen or Electors.

There are 4 Gin Distilleries, 5 Grain Mills, 9 Tanneries, 1 Cotton Factory, 1 Tin-ware Manufactory, 5 Mercantile Stores, 3 Clothiers' Works, and 3 Carding Machines.

There are in Windsor, 12 Taverns, or Public Inns, 16 District Schools, and one Grammar School, having a public fund, but it is not flourishing, 4 small Social Libraries, 4 Clergymen, 5 Physicians, and 3 Attornies.

The general list of the town, in 1817, was $57,068 14, there being 302 polls, 341 Horses, 394 oxen, 885 cows, heifers and steers, 3135 acres of plow land, 4153 acres of of mowing and clear pasture, 7453 acres of pasture lands, 9589 acres of uninclosed land. The valuation or assessment of the lands and houses of the town, in 1816, was $1,449,908, 47. In 1799, it was $620,261, 13.

BIOGRAPHY. The late Hon. *Oliver Ellsworth* was a native and a resident of Windsor. His eminent talents and distinguished public services are well known. He was one of the first and most eminent lawyers in Connecticut, and contributed essentially towards the establishment of our judicial system, being for several years a judge of the superior court. He was a member of Congress, both in the house of representatives and the senate, for several years; but was most distinguished for his arduous services in the judiciary of the United States, both in its organization and as one of the judges of the supreme court; which office he held for a considerable time, and succeeded Mr. Jay, as chief justice of this court. Whilst in this office, he was appointed minister to France, with William Davey and Mr. Murray, who were commissioned to negotiate a treaty of peace between the United States and the French Republic, which they succeeded in accomplishing. He died in Nov. 1807.

NEW-HAVEN
COUNTY.

NEW-HAVEN COUNTY is situated in the southern central section of the State, on Long-Island Sound. It is bounded on the north by Litchfield and Hartford counties, on the east by Middlesex county, on the south by Long-Island Sound, and on the west principally by the Ousatonick river, which separates it from the county of Fairfield, and in part by Litchfield county. The county has an irregular form, and has an average length from east to west of about 26 miles, with a medium breadth from north to south of about 21 miles, and comprises an area of more than 540 square miles, or 345,600 acres.

The following Topographical and Statistical Table exhibits a compendious view of the several towns in the county; their situation, with relation to New-Haven; population, according to the census of 1810; dwelling-houses; religious societies; school districts, and post-offices.

Towns.	Post-offices.	Population.	Dwelling houses.	Religious societies.	School districts.	Distance from N. Haven.
New-Haven.	1	6967	1050	7	25	
Branford.	2	1932	230	5	15	8 m. E.
Cheshire.	1	2288	370	3	12	13 m. N.
Derby.	2	2051	300	5	9	9 m. N. W.
East-Haven.		1209	200	2	5	4 m. E.
Guilford.	2	3845	550	7	19	15 m. E.
Hamden.		1716	260	4	9	5 m. N.
Meriden.	1	1249	200	3	7	17 m. N.
Middlebury.		847	125	2	6	22 m. N. W.
Milford.	1	2674	380	4	11	9 m. W.
North-Haven.		1239	200	3	8	8 m. N.
Oxford.	1	1453	220	3	13	14 m. N. W.
Southbury.		1413	230	3	8	20 m. N. W.
Wallingford.	1	2325	340	5	11	13 m. N. E.
Waterbury.	1	2814	400	4	19	20 m. N. W.
Woodbridge.		2080	300	4	10	7 m. N.
Wolcott.		952	150	2	7	22 m. N. W.

The local situation and advantages of the county of New-Haven are important. Lying upon Long-Island Sound, it has a very extensive maritime border, indented with numerous bays and inlets, affording important facilities to navigation and commerce. The face of the country and soil are various, corresponding with the geological character of its different sections. It is intersected by several mountainous ranges, which pass through it in a northerly direction. All the important ranges of mountains in the state, terminate in this county, and at no very considerable distance from each other. The most important of these is the great Greenstone range, consisting of two branches, one of which terminates at East Rock, and the other at West Rock, and which pass thro' nearly the centre of the county. East of these, the Middletown greenstone range extends in nearly a parallel direction; it passes thro' the eastern section of this county, for some distance, and more northwardly forms the boundary between this county and Middlesex. Eastwardly of this, & near the east border of the county, commence the granite hills, which extend northeasterly through Guilford and Haddam, and rising upon the east side of Connecticut river, form the extensive granitic range that passes through the eastern section of the State. The western section of the county comprises the termination of the granitic range, which extends through the western part of the State. The soil, in the greenstone district, is generally fertile, consisting of a gravelly and argillaceous loam. In the granitic district, both in the eastern and western section of the county, it is less fertile, and the lands are rough and stony. Upon the borders of the sound, there is some good land, and numerous and extensive tracts of marine alluvial. There are some considerable tracts of silicious sand, and light sandy loam, which, in general, are lean and sterile. The county does not possess a great proportion of first quality of land, but a considerable section of it is adapted to a grain culture, and the western part is excellent for grazing.

The agricultural interest of the county has been considerably neglected; and there is evidently great want of agricultural enterprise and intelligence, and much room for improvement. The force of established habits, the influence of prejudice, and a dread of innovation, have as sensible and injurious an operation upon the interests and prosperity of agriculture, as upon any other objects. But, although the farmers of this county, in common with those of most other parts of the State, may be wanting in enterprise, they are remarkable for their habits of industry and economy, and, in general, for the rural simplicity and plainness of their style of living.

The waters of the county, exclusive of Long Island sound, which washes its southern border for more than thirty miles, consist of the Ousatonick river, which washes its western border, and the Shepaug, Pomperaug, and Naugatuck, that discharge themselves into the former, which water its western section; the Wopowaug, the West river, the Quinipiack, Mill river, Branford, Menuncatuck, and the Hammonasett rivers, fertilize the eastern section of the county, and discharge their waters into Long-Island Sound. The latter forms its eastern boundary for some distance   There are numerous bays and inlets, and several safe and convenient harbours; the principal of which are Guilford harbour, Sachem's head, Branford, New-Haven and Milford. Upon the Ousatonick river, the principal harbour is at Derby landing. From the maritime situation of the county, its advantages for commerce are very essential; and its commercial interests are more extensive and important than those of any other section of the State. Connected with the interests of navigation, is that of ship-building, which receives considerable attention, particularly in the eastern section. The manufacturing establishments of the county are not numerous ; yet there are some very important, and upon a large scale ; and there are various mechanical employments, or certain kinds of manufactures, that are very respectable, and carried on considerably extensively. Of the former, the extensive Gun Factory in Hamden, and the large Woolen and Cotton Factories in Derby, are most deserving of notice. Of the latter, the manufacture of Tin Ware, Buttons, and Clocks, which is carried on extensively in the northern part of the county, and the manufacture of shoes, which receives considerable attention in several towns upon the Sound, are most important. There are, in the county of New-Haven, 1 Forge, 1 Furnace, 1 extensive Gun Factory, alluded to above, probably the largest private establishment in the United States, 1 Powder Mill, 3 Oil Mills, 4 Paper Mills, 2 Cotton Factories, 5 Woolen Factories, 33 Fulling Mills, and Cloth Dressing Establishments, 30 Carding Machines, and 54 Grain Mills. The county contains 30 School Societies, each of which is divided into a convenient number of School Districts, the limits of a single school, of which there are in all 193. There are also 66 Religious Societies, 28 Social Libraries, and about 210 Mercantile Stores. The aggregate population of the county, according to the census of 1810, was 37,064 ; and the amount of taxable property, including polls, as rated in making up lists in 1817, was $770,518

NEW-HAVEN.

NEW-HAVEN, the seat of justice of the county, and semi-capital of the State, is situated at the head of the bay of the same name, upon Long-Island sound, in 41° 18 north lat. and 72° 56' west lon. 34 miles southwest from Hartford, 52 miles west from New-London, and 76 northeast of New-York. It is bounded on the north by Woodbridge and Hamden, on the east by the Quinipiack river, which separates it from East-Haven, on the south by New-Haven bay and Long-Island sound, and on the west by Milford ; comprising an area, exclusive of the bay, of about eighteen square miles, having a mean length of nearly five miles, with a medium breadth of more than three and a half miles.

Surface, soil and geology. A considerable section of this township is an alluvial plain. This plain is of secondary, and apparently of recent formation; its geological structure consists of strata of siliceous sand and gravel, which may be regarded as marine deposits. The sand is considerably ferruginous, and affords no important minerals, and no stones or rock formation, except the occasional occurrence of a friable sand stone; evidently of a recent formation, and which is little more than an induration of masses of the sand and gravel composing the soil. This plain extends eastwardly to the Quinipiack, and is circumscribed northeasterly and northwardly by east rock and west rock, and several hills which are spurs of them, giving it a novel and interesting appearance. East rock is a bold bluff, or nearly a perpendicular eminence, and is the termination of the east range of the greenstone mountain; it is detached and insulated; this range for several miles being broken, or interrupted, and presenting a succession of eminences. It exhibits a naked rock in broken and disordered fragments, forming bold mural precipices. The geological character of the strata is greenstone, being a secondary formation. This eminence is partly in this town, and partly in Hamden. Contiguous to this is mill rock, of a similar description, and a spur of it. East rock is about two miles northeast from the city of New-Haven; its height is from 350 to 370 feet. West rock is about two miles west from east rock, and about the same distance northwest from the city. This is the termination of the west branch of the greenstone mountain, and presents very similar features to the other; this range, however, is more continuous, especially for several miles from its termination. West rock is also a bold perpendicular precipice, naked and bare. It is of about the same height as east rock. Contiguous to this also, there are several spurs, or smaller eminences, the largest of which is called Pine Rock, and runs off at right angles from it in an easterly direction. These several eminences, from their peculiarly bold and characteristic features, give to the scenery of New-Haven an appearance of novelty, grandeur and interest, surpassing that of almost any other town in the United States. The stones of these mountains are very valuable for building, and have latterly been used extensively for that object, in New-Haven. A considereble proportion of the long wharf is constructed of them. The western section of the town, beyond the plain, consists of a waving tract of land, being the commencement of a succession of hills, extending westwardly into Milford, and which are commonly called Milford hills. These hills are of a similar geological character; their structure consisting of greenstone strata. This section of the township is nearly five miles in length from north to south, and more than two from east to west. The soil of this section is a gravelly loam; but moderately fertile, and parts of it are lean and sterile. That of the alluvial plain is a sandy loam, light, warm, and dry. It is generally thin, and rather barren and sterile, in its natural state; but has sufficient basis to sustain manure, and is susceptible of improvement. Upon the border of the sound, it has been enriched by white fish, which are found to be a very valuable manure; and, in the interior, by barn-yard and other manures, which the town affords. Upon the borders of West river, there are extensive tracts of salt marsh, which produce very large quantities of salt hay. Attempts have been made, with some success, to improve these lands by means of draining and diking. Of what is called West Meadow, there is a tract of more than one hundred acres, that lies above, or north of the bridge across the river. An attempt was made in 1769, to prevent the salt water from overflowing this tract, by means of a dike, constructed across the meadow, having a gate at the bridge, which was shut by the tide and opened by the river, when the tide receded. When this dike was constructed, the whole of this tract was a salt marsh; and soon after the salt grass died, and was succeeded, upon about half of the tract, by white grass, as it is called; and upon the other half by spear grass and clover. A part of this tract has been plowed, and has carried good crops of corn: upon some sections of it also are several valuable orchards; & it has been remarked, that the canker-worm has never attacked these trees.

Natural and Agricultural Productions.—Upon the alluvial plain, there were never any forests, excepting those upon Mount Pleasant, an interesting eminence, comprising about 400 acres, which appears to have obtruded itself into its present situation. Upon this plain, the original growth appears to have been shrub oak. In the western section of the town, there are numerous forests. The natural growth of trees consists of oak, chesnut, hickory, elm, maple, ash, butternut, white and yellow pine, birch, thorn, red cedar, bass, wild cherry, and various shrubs or trees of small growth. But the forests within the town afford but a small proportion of the fuel which is annually consumed. Wood is bro't to New-Haven market, for more than ten miles, by land carriage. And it is estimated that about one third of the fuel consumed is brought here by water conveyance from Long-Island, the borders of the sound, and the Ousatonick river. In the year ending June 1806, it was estimated that about 2,500 cords of wood were imported into New-Haven. And, considering this but one third part of the whole quantity brought to this market, the aggregate consumption that year must have been 7,500 cords being ten cords to a house; not taking into consideration mercantile stores, mechanics' shops, &c. The pine timber used in building is imported from the Connecticut and Hudson rivers, some from the southern states, but principally from the District of Maine.

AGRICULTURE. The agriculture of this town comprises the various objects of husbandry common to this State. Wheat, rye, corn, barley, oats, flax and grass, are the principal products. The lands, although not naturally very fertile, are sucsceptible of extensive improvement. The soil is naturally very dry, and rather inclining to be hard. Wood-ashes answer an excellent purpose as a manure upon the plain, their efficacy continuing much longer than stable manure ; and they tend to correct the dryness of the soil, and also to ameliorate it, by giving it more body and consistence. White fish also are found to be an excellent manure. They are used both with and without undergoing a previous process of decomposition. When in the former mode, they are thrown into a pile, consisting of a layer of fish, and one of earth, alternately ; which, when suitably decomposed, is applied to the soil ; when in the latter mode, they are spread upon the land and plowed in, and thus dissolved and decomposed. The number of these fish with which an acre is usually dressed, is from ten to twelve thousand. They frequent the shores upon the sound in the month of June, in large shoals, and are taken with great facility. They are efficacious upon all soils, and for almost every kind of vegetation. The land in this town is in general better adapted to tillage than to grazing. It is also well adapted to the various objects of horticulture, which in general receive great attention ; there being, it is believed, as many good culinary gardens in this, as in any other town in the State. The various vegetables, roots and fruits, which, as objects of horticulture, are favoured by the climate, are cultivated in the gardens here. Of the fruit, growing upon shrubs and plants, are currants, gooseberries, raspberries & strawberries ; and of those upon trees, cultivated in gardens and elsewhere, are apples, apricots, cherries, nectarines, peaches, pears, plums and quinces.

WATERS. The waters of this town are abundant, and afford important advantages for navigation, fishing, manufacturing and other interests. New-Haven bay, at the head of which the town is situated, is an extensive body of water, being four miles in length from Long-Island sound to its head, and about 240 rods wide within the beach ; a sand bank projecting from West-Haven shore almost to the channel. At what is called the point, on the east side of the bay or harbour, is a lighthouse, erected several years since. This bay is apparently formed by the confluence of the Quinipiack, the West and Mill rivers. The channel of the harbour is the common channel of the first and last of these streams, and lies near the eastern side. The depth of the channel below the bridge, across the Quinipiack and Mill rivers, after their junction, is fifteen feet, at low water. A bar of sand, however, formed by the pier erected about one mile from the head of long-wharf, has in some measure interrupted the channel. The tide usually rises in this harbour about six feet ; and spring-tides from seven to eight feet. Upon the east side of the harbour, opposite to the beach, there is an insulated rock of considerable elevation, upon which the United States have erected a fort, for the defence of the harbour. Previously to the late war, it mounted seven guns, and contained a garrison of 22 men. It was considerably improved during the war.

From the recession of the sea, the influx of earth, from alluvial and marine deposits, and the accumulation of what is called creek weed, the harbour has undergone great change since the first settlement of the town. Upon its northwest side, the spot which was, about seventy or eighty years since, occupied as a ship yard, is now a rich meadow, covered with gardens and other improvements. About the same period, foreign vessels loaded and unloaded, on the eastern side of Fleet-street, several rods above the long wharf, where now the spot is covered with gardens.

There are three rivers in this township, which discharge their waters into New-Haven bay or harbour. Of these streams the Quinipiack is the most considerable. It has its source in Farmington, runs about 30 miles, and affords a boat navigation to North-Haven.

West river rises in Woodbridge, and runs southerly through this township; its whole course being about twelve miles. Mill river has its head waters in Cheshire, and runs about the same distance as the last. There is one pond within the town, called Beaver pond; being, when full, nearly one mile in length, and about 60 rods in breadth. There are seven bridges in this town; the harbour or Tomlinson's bridge, Dragon bridge, Long bridge, Neck bridge, Thompson's bridge, Derby turnpike bridge, and West bridge. The three first are over the Quinipiack, and the three last over West river. The harbour bridge, which is the only one deserving of particular notice, is erected below the junction of Mill river with the Quinipiack, and at the entrance of the stream into the harbour. This bridge is half a mile in length, and 27 feet in width. One half of it originally consisted of two extended piers of stone, commencing at the two shores, and each occupying one fourth of the whole distance; the remainder was a bridge erected upon wooden piers or trestles. But the timber used in the construction of the trestles, was frequently destroyed by the sea worms, and demanded continual repairs. This part of the bridge having been swept away by a freshet, in 1807, was rebuilt the same year; when the stone piers were so far extended as to occupy the whole distance, except 30 rods. The whole expense was $60,000. The stock is divided into sixty shares, more than one half of which is the property of Isaac Tomlinson Esq. who has also erected a valuable stone wharf, extending from the north side of the bridge along the western borders of the channel. From this wharf, the largest vessels employed in the navigation of the town can take in their cargoes. In 1810, the proceeds of this bridge were sold at auction for $1,500.

A great variety of fish are found in the harbour and streams of New-Haven; but few only are sufficiently numerous to make fishing an object worthy of much attention. Shad, in favourable seasons, are taken considerably plentifully in the Quinipiack, but much less so than at former periods. A little below dragon bridge, 2400 have been taken at a single draught. They are taken in considerable numbers at various places up the river, as far as Wallingford. White fish, as has before been noticed, are taken in great quantities, for the purpose of manure.

Various shell fish are taken in the harbour, and mouths of the streams, of which oysters are most abundant and valuable. The principal oyster beds are in the Quinipiack, where it has been estimated, that several hundred thousand bushels are taken annually. They are caught principally between the two lower bridges. These oysters are small, but well flavoured.

In addition to supplying the market in New-Haven and its vicinity, large quantities are opened and conveyed in kegs, into different parts of the interior of this State; into Vermont, and some sections of New-Hampshire and New-York. This fishery has raised up a considerable village upon the Quinipiack. Of the shell fish next to oysters, clams are most important, of which considerable quantities are annually taken. They are of two kinds, the long clam, and the round clam; the latter of which is taken most plentifully, and is generally most esteemed. Until about the year 1770, oysters were taken very plentifully in the harbour, but latterly the beds have been destroyed by the influx of mud. Oysters, in order to propagate, require a firm bottom, to which their spawn may adhere.

ROADS. There are nine principal roads which centre at New-Haven; one leading to New-York, one to New-Milford through Derby, one to Woodbury through Humphreysville, one to Litchfield, one to Farmington, thence to Hartford, one to Hartford through Berlin, one to Middletown, and thence to Hartford, one authorised to Norwich through Branford, Guilford and Killingworth, and one to Saybrook. The eight first are turnpikes.

There are a number of different lines of stages which communicate with New-Haven; and besides the great mail from Washington to Boston, it is accommodated with a number of others, giving it great facilities for intercourse abroad.

STATISTICS. The population of this town, at the census of 1790, was 4484; in 1800, 5157; and in 1810, 6967; being more by nearly one thousand, than any other town in the state. It has greatly increased since that period.

There are in New-Haven,
1050 Dwelling houses.
  6 Houses for public worship.
 30 Houses concerned in navigation.
  5 Printing offices.
  4 Book binderies.
 22 Dry goods stores.
 87 Grocery & provision stores.
  4 Hardware stores.
  2 Crockery stores.
  6 Druggist stores.
  4 Book stores.
  6 Shoe stores.
  2 Paper-hanging stores.
  2 Tin ware stores.

NEW-HAVEN. 101

13 Merchant tailors shops.
9 Millinery and mantuamakers' shops.
25 Master house-joiners.
11 Master masons.
3 Stone cutters.
9 Coopers.
2 Block makers.
1 Brush maker.
4 Bakers.
4 Tallow chandlers.
1 Hat factory.
17 Boot and shoe factories.
2 Tinners and copper smiths.
6 Saddle and harness makers.
1 Comb maker.
6 Cabinet furniture makers.
4 Chair makers.
6 Coach, sign & house painters.
18 Blacksmiths.
8 Chaise & wagon makers, some of which carry on the business upon an extensive scale.
2 Leather dressers.
2 Morocco do.
4 Barbers' shops.
3 Exchange offices.
4 Rope walks.
2 Sail lofts.
2 Distilleries.
8 Tanneries.
1 Nail factory.
1 Cotton Factory.
2 Paper mills.
1 Carding machine.
2 Grain mills.
1 Powder mill.
2 Fulling mills.
1 Public market, containing a number of butcher's stalls.

The amount of taxable property, including polls, as rated in making up lists in 1816, was $132,964.

There are in this town, about 700 qualified Electors; three companies of Infantry, one company of Light Artillery, and one company of horse, and one of foot guards.

There are in the town of New-Haven, 25 primary or public schools. There is an almshouse, being also a workhouse, established by the town, and under its direction and authority. All the regular poor supported by the town, are maintained here; and such of them as are able for any manual service, are employed in such occupations as circumstances will permit, & as is thought most advantageous. But a considerable proportion of the tenants of the almshouse, is made up of children, the aged, sick, disabled and deranged, who are incapable of any services, that can be productive of any profit. The almshouse is under the care of the select men, who appoint an agent to superintend, and make the necessary provisions for it. A keeper or master resides in the house, and, under the direction of the selectmen, has the immediate charge of the poor maintained here. The number of poor maintained at the almshouse, is usually from 50 to 75. In 1805, the aggregate expense of this establishment, was $2,615, of which $616 was for State paupers; and the receipts for the labour, $237. The poor supported here are comfortably provided for, and treated with great humanity.

The civil divisions of New-Haven are two located ecclesiastical Societies, and an incorporated city.

NEW-HAVEN CITY, incorporated in 1784, is situated at the head of the bay or harbour, and comprises an area of about six square miles; being about three miles in length from east to west, and two in breadth from north to south. It has a beautiful and interesting site, consisting of a level plain, the soil of which is hard and dry, and is surrounded with a novel, grand, and peculiarly interesting amphitheatre of hills, already noticed, several of which present bold and perpendicular columns of rude and naked rocks of nearly 400 feet in height. The city is regularly laid out, and consists of two parts, called the old and new townships. The old or original township was laid out in nine squares, of 52 rods upon a side. These squares are formed by streets running upon each side of them, and intersecting each other at right angles. The central square is open, having been left as a pubic square; and is one of the handsomest in the United States. It is inclosed with a handsome railing. The surrounding squares of this part of the town plot have, by a bye-law, been divided each into four, by which the number of streets has been doubled, and most of which are well built. The new township lies directly east of the old, and extends to the east river. It is a beautiful level piece of ground, and laid out in a regular and handsome manner, comprising a convenient number of streets, which cross each other at nearly right angles. Besides these two divisions, a section has lately been laid out by the Hon. James Hillhouse, upon the north part of the old town, commencing at grove-street, and extending to Mount Pleasant; and comprising a number of handsome squares, and pleasant and convenient streets. There has also a section been laid out on the west side of the harbour, commonly called the oyster point division. It contains a number of streets and building lots, but at present has but few buildings. There are in all thirty-six streets; of which the principal are Chapel, State and Church streets. These streets are compactly built, and are the seats of a considerable proportion of the commercial business of the city. They comprise the Banks, most of the public Inns, Printing-offices, Professional offices, Book and Stationary Stores, numerous Dry Goods and Grocery Stores, &c. Next to these, the most important streets are Elm, George, Broadway, College, Water and Fleet streets. These are all considerable streets; most of them well built, and some are seats of activity and business.

New-Haven, for a place of its size and importance, is characterized by an appearance of plainness, neatness and order; and presents little of that stately magnificence, or gorgeous splendour, which are to be found in most of the cities in the United States. The houses are in general two stories high, and built of wood, in a neat and handsome style, but are not expensive or elegant. Within some years past, however, several brick and stone buildings have been erected, which are elegant and stately edifices. Most of the buildings stand upon the streets forming the squares; the compact part of the city being comprised within the limits of about a mile square. The buildings are not arranged in lines; many of them being set back, leaving open fronts, which are neatly fenced, and ornamented with evergreens and flowering shrubs. Almost every dwelling-house is furnished with a piece of ground in the rear, sufficiently large for a good garden; and many for a supply of fruit trees and other purposes. These advantages and improvements afford the inhabitants many conveniences in the summer season, and at the same time contribute greatly to the pleasantness and interest of the city. Whilst noticing these objects, it is worthy of remark, that there is now standing in the garden of Abraham Bishop Esq. (which is the same that belonged to his ancestor, James Bishop, formerly deputy governor of the colony; and which, during a period of more than 130 years, has remained in the same family,) a pear-tree, that is 142 years old.

Among the objects in the city deserving of notice, is the long-wharf. This is a pier, extending from the lower part of Fleet-street to the channel. This pier is 3943 feet in length, and 45 feet in breadth, for more than half the distance, and 32 feet for the rest. The one fourth part, at the farther extremity, is constructed of stone entirely; and the other three fourths of wood, sods and earth. About half its length is lined with store-houses and their yards, to the number of 40. This is twice the length of Boston pier, and longer than any other in the United States. It has been constructed by an incorporated company, called the Union wharf Company of New-Haven; and the stock has hitherto yielded a good profit. The public buildings in New-Haven, exclusive of the collegiate buildings, consist of a State-house, which is an ancient and plain brick structure, situated upon the public square; two Congregational churches, both recently erected, and elegant brick edifices; an Episcopal church, a Methodist church, a Custom-house building, situated in Fleet-street, near the commencement of the long-wharf, recently thoroughly repaired and finished in superior style, and rendered very commodious, three Academic buildings, and six School houses.

Of the public buildings, the Episcopal church deserves a conspicuous notice. It is a large and stately stone edifice, constructed in a style of superior elegance. It is one of the finest specimens of the arts in this State; and in style of architecture, solidity of structure, richness of ornament, and the general elegance of its appearance, is surpassed by few public buildings in the United States. The stones of which it is constructed, were from the green-stone strata of East and West rock. This, together with the two Congregational Churches, is also situated upon the public square; these several public buildings being ranged upon the west side of the avenue, by which the public square is intersected.

YALE COLLEGE. Among the institutions of New-Haven, and indeed of the State, Yale College holds a pre-eminent rank, and deserves a conspicuous notice. It was founded in 1700; being the third collegiate institution established in the United States. The Association, by whom it was founded, consisted of ten of the principal clergymen in the colony; designated for this purpose by the general consent of the congregational clergy and the inhabitants. In 1701, the legislature granted them a charter, constituting them trustees of a collegiate school in his majesty's colony of Connecticut.

The institution was first located at Saybrook; and the first commencement was held there in 1702. In 1717, it was removed to New-Haven; for which purpose, a small collegiate building was erected, from the pecuniary means afforded by various individuals, but principally from the aid received from the legislature. Among the most distinguished of the early benefactors of the institution, was the Hon. Elihu Yale of London, Governor of the East-India Company. In 1718, this gentleman bestowed upon the institution several donations, amounting to £500 sterling: soon after which, as a respectful acknowledgement of such distinguished liberality, the institution was named Yale College. Subsequently it has received several very liberal individual donations. Among its more considerable benefactors, was Doct. Berkley Bishop of Cloyne, Jeremiah Dummer Esq. of Boston, James Fitch Esq. of Norwich, and his Excellency Oliver Wolcott, who, in 1807, gave the institution $2000, to be applied to the augmentation of the library. In 1811, a superb cabinet of minerals was deposited in the seminary by George Gibbs Esq. for the use of the institution. Since the establishment of the institution its charter has undergone several modifications. In 1745, it received a new charter, drawn by the Hon. Thomas Fitch, afterwards Gov. in which the style and name of the members of the corporation were changed from that of trustees, to "*The President and Fellows of Yale College.*" In 1792, the charter was further altered, by a provision, that the Governor, Lieut. Gov. and six senior Assistants, should ex officio be members of the corporation. This alteration, which has given additional weight and importance to the institution, was effected by an arrangement with the trustees; the legislature at the same time having granted to the corporation a very liberal donation. The clerical branch of the board, however, retained the power of a perpetual succession, by the right of filling its own vacancies. The charter, as modified in 1792, has been confirmed and established by the constitution of the State, ratified on the fifth of October, 1818.

In 1816, the General Assembly granted to this institution a certain proportion of the monies which might be received from the government of the United States, upon certain claims for expenses incurred during the late war. The institution has received from this grant the sum of about $7,000 This seminary is now very amply * endowed, and is in a very

---

* *The funds and other productive property of the institution afford an annual revenue of about $4000; and it possesses unproductive property, inclusive of its building, to the amount of about $175,000.*

prosperous and flourishing condition. It has, since its first establishment, been an object of the peculiar solicitude of the legislature—has repeatedly experienced its munificence, and at all times its fostering care.

Yale College has, from an early period, ranked among the first of the literary institutions in the United States; and although numerous rival seminaries have been established in the neighbouring States, yet neither its prosperity nor its reputation has declined; but on the contrary, both have increased with the age of the institution. Under the direction of its two former presidents, Doct. Stiles and Doct. Dwight, it attained a distinguished eminence, and a solid reputation, which have justly rendered it the pride of the State, and the acknowledged source of the celebrity of many of its citizens, both at home and abroad. Its distinguished reputation, and known advantages, have secured to it at all times, a large number of students from almost every section of our country; and on a review of this institution, it is gratifying to reflect, that the reputation which it has acquired is still maintained, and that no apprehensions can be indulged of its declining, so long as the institution remains under the direction of the distinguished scientific gentleman, who at present presides over it.

There are at this institution, six professorships; a professorship of divinity established in 1755; a professorship of mathematics and natural philosophy in 1770; a professorship of law, in 1801; a professorship of chemistry and natural history, in 1804; a professorship of languages and ecclesiastical history in 1805; and a professorship of rhetoric and oratory. The faculty of the college, to which the executive government is committed, consists of the president, professors and tutors.

There is a valuable and extensive library belonging to the institution, consisting of between six and seven thousand volumes; besides this, there are three libraries belonging to the students; one called the Linonian library, consisting of 854 volumes; one, the Brother's library, consisting of 860, and one, the Moral library, comprising 303 volumes. The whole number of volumes, exclusive of those possessed by the officers of the college and individual students, amounts to nearly 9000.

There is a valuable philosophical and chemical apparatus, both of which are extensive and complete; and a valuable cabinet of minerals already noticed.

The number of students in 1818, was 283.

The college edifices consist of five buildings, handsomely arranged in a line, having a spacious and beautiful court yard in front. North college is 108 feet by 40; the Lyceum is 56 by 46; the middle college 100 by 40; the chapel 50 by 40; south college 104 by 38. These buildings are all four stories in height. In the third story in the chapel, there is a philosophical chamber, containing the philosophical apparatus. The Lyceum contains seven recitation rooms, and the chemical laboratory and its appendages; and the three colleges contain ninety-six chambers.

A medical faculty has recently been connected with this institution. It consists of three professorships, besides that of chemistry; one of materia medica and botany; one of the theory and practice of physic, surgery and obstetrics; and one of anatomy and physiology. The medical institution is accommodated with a large and handsome stone building, and a botanical garden adjoining the same. There are at present about 50 medical students.

The following have been the presidents of Yale College.—The Rev. Abraham Pierson, appointed in 1701; the Rev. Timothy Cutler, appointed in 1719; the Rev. Elisha Williams, in 1726; the Rev. Thomas Clapp, in 1739; the Rev. Naphtali Daggett, in 1766; the Rev. Ezra Stiles, in 1777; the Rev. Timothy Dwight, in 1795; the Rev. Jeremiah Day, in 1817.

New-Haven is well supplied with schools; there are, in the limits of the city, 18 public schools, which were included in the number of public schools, stated as belonging to the town. There are about 750 scholars attend these schools, all of whom are under the age of fourteen years.

Besides the public schools, there is a grammar school, which has a fund that produces $233 annually. The proceeds of this fund reduces the tuition of the pupils at this school, to a small sum.

There is a decent school house belonging to the institution. There is also an academy called the new township academy, incorporated in 1809; two schools for young ladies, and one for the French language. In addition to these, there are four or five private, or subscription schools for the primary branches of education.

There are two social libraries in New-Haven, one called the *mechanics' library*, established in 1793, the other the *social library*, founded in 1807. Both of these libraries have a respectable number of volumes, and are under excellent regulations.

The Museum in New-Haven, commonly called Mix's museum, was established by Mr. John Mix, its present proprietor, in 1806—7; and first opened for public exhibition, on the 4th of July, 1807. Mr. Mix has, with unwearied perseverance and attention, and at great expense, been making continual additions to his museum since its first establishment, both by donations of individuals and purchases of his own; so that at the present time, it contains a vast collection and interesting variety of articles, consisting of most of the novel, curious and striking productions of nature and art, from the different quarters of the globe. For the period this museum has been established, it has acquired great celebrity, and is entitled to rank among the first establishments of the kind in the United States. The building containing the museum is situated upon Olive-street, at the east end of Court-street. The collection of articles occupy two rooms, one of 50 feet by 24, the other 38 by 32; both of which are completely filled, and handsomely arranged with a great number and rich variety of the productions of nature and art, worthy the inspection of the curious, as well as the common observer. On the top of the building, Mr. Mix has erected a *Camera Obscura*, on a large scale, which affords much gratification to all who view this curious and surprising invention.

Attached to the establishment of the Museum are the public gardens of Mr. Mix, known by the name of the Columbian Gardens. These are a place of much resort in the summer season, affording a pleasant and delightful walk; and visitors are accommodated with the choicest luxuries of the season, prepared by the proprietor. At the extremity of the gardens there is a bath-house, comprising fourteen separate bathing rooms, all of which are provided with the necessary conveniences and apparatus for bathing. A bathing establishment is very important in a populous town, as a means of promoting health, cleanliness and comfort, during the intense heat of summer.

The Cemetery in New-Haven is of a novel and interesting character. It is situated opposite to the north corner of the original town; and the ground is handsomely smoothed and enclosed. It is divided into parallelograms, each of 64 feet in breadth, and from 180 to 200 in length; neatly railed, and separated by alleys of sufficient width to enable carriages to pass each other. The parallelograms are divided into family burying lots of 32 feet in length and 18 in width; against each of which is an opening to admit of a funeral procession. At the division between the lots, trees are set out in the alleys, and the name of each proprietor is marked on the railing. A number of lots have been given to the several congregations, the college, and reserved for the poor. The monuments in this ground are almost universally of marble; a considerable number are obelisks; others are tables, and others slabs, placed at the head and foot of each grave. The obelisks are arranged on the middle line of lots; and thus stand in a line successively throughout each of the parallelograms. This is a very unusual burying ground, and is peculiarly solemn and impressive.

There are two banks in New-Haven: New-Haven Bank, incorporated in 1792, and at this time with a capital of $300,000; the Eagle Bank, incorporated in 1811, with a capital of $500,000. There is a Marine Insurance Company, incorporated in 1797. It has a capital of $50,000, (which may be increased at pleasure,) and is governed by nine directors. The Ocean Insurance Company, incorporated in October 1818, with a capital of $60,000, and the liberty to extend it to $100,000. The objects of it are confined to marine insurance. A Fire Insurance Company was incorporated in 1813, with a capital of $200,000.

In 1794, a chamber of commerce was formed by voluntary association. Its officers are a President, vice-president, treasurer and secretary, who are elected annually.

A Mechanics' Society was formed in 1807, called the General Society of Mechanics of New-Haven, and was incorporated in October the same year. The Society has some funds. Its objects are to regulate and promote the mecha--

nical arts and business, and to assist young mechanics by loans &c.

There are in New-Haven three news-paper establishments, at each of which a weekly news-paper is published; one an imperial and the other two a super royal sheet.

In the city of New-Haven there are more than 800 dwelling houses; in 1800, there were 4049 inhabitants; and in 1810, 5772; being an increase in ten years of 1723; which far exceeded that of any other town in the State.

The next census will probably disclose a proportional increase for the last ten years.

COMMERCE, &c. The commerce of New-Haven is very respectable. In 1816, there were 40 vessels, amounting to 5901 tons, employed in foreign trade. At the same period, there was 1431 tons employed in the coasting trade; and the total of registered vessels, exclusive of those employed in New-York, added to these sums, amounted at this period to 6697 tons.

Besides the vessels engaged in the foreign and coasting trade, there are six or seven packets that ply regularly between this place and New-York. There is also a line of steam-boats that communicate thrice a week, (excepting during the winter months,) with New-York, and likewise with New-London and Norwich.

The extent and importance of the commercial interests of this city afford a conspicuous demonstration of what has often been asserted, that commerce frequently depends more upon enterprise and industry than upon local advantages.

The maritime business of New-Haven is more extensive than that of any other town in the State, and particularly its foreign trade. This, it is believed, is more to to be ascribed to enterprise, industry and peculiar habits of the inhabitants, than to any advantages which are attached to the place. As it respects a back country, which is generally regarded as the support of commercial interests, this town is greatly inferior to Hartford, and perhaps to some others. It is situated, it is true, upon a bay of Long-Island sound; but still its harbour is far from being a very good one, or from possessing any superior advantages for navigation. Enterprise and industry have a reciprocal influence upon each other, and generally exhibit a corresponding increase and extension. And when economy and plainness, as to style of living, are associated with these characteristics, their happy results are more striking and conspicuous. There are various other circumstances, which have a salutary or injurious influence upon the prosperity of a commercial or populous town; and among these, that of the high price of rents, which depends upon a local or fictitious value that is attached to building lots, and to the style and expensiveness of buildings, deserves particularly to be noticed, as having an injurious operation. Whatever expectations may be indulged by the inexperienced, it is a fact, establishsd by the united testimony of all men of practical knowledge, that the great majority of those engaged in business of every kind, can realize but *small profits*. This is more emphatically true with respect to mechanical employments of every description. Excessive rents are a very burdensome tax upon business affording but small gains; and necessarily tend to depress and discourage those engaged in it. Mechanical pursuits are particularly favoured by moderate rents. New-Haven possesses many if not all of these advantages to a greater extent than most of our other large towns. The dwelling-houses and other buildings are in general neat but not expensive, and the rents proportionably low. The inhabitants are characterized by a commendable plainness in their style of living; and are remarkable for their systematic habits of industry and attention to business. The aggregate of mechanical industry of the town is very great, and has always been encouraged; being justly regarded as an important auxiliary to commerce, and as essentially contributing to the general prosperity. The merchants of New-Haven, for some years past, have been very enterprising, and in general the inhabitants have been governed by an enlarged and enlightened policy; and however variant their interests may have been in other respects, they have, on all occasions, exhibited a common interest in whatever has concerned their own town, and with united counsels and exertions have endeavoured to promote its growth, its prosperity and importance. And hence, for the last twenty years, it has exhibited an increase of population, buildings and business, unequalled by any other town in the State.

HISTORY. New-Haven, and the country in its vicinity, was called by the natives Quinipiack. In 1638, a tract of 18 miles in length, and 13 in breadth, comprising, besides the township of New-Haven, those of Woodbridge, Hamden, East-Haven, North-Haven, and a part of the townships of Wallingford, Cheshire and Branford, was purchased partly of Momauguin, sachem of Quinipiack, and partly of Montowese, sachem of Mattabeseck, now Middletown. The purchase was made by the Rev. John Davenport and Theophilus Eaton Esq. for themselves and others. Among the first settlers were John Davenport, Theophilus Eaton, Samuel Eaton, Thomas Gregson, Robert Newman, Matthew Gilbert, Nathaniel Turner, Thomas Fugill, Francis Newman, Stephen Goodyear and Joshua Atwater. In June, 1639, the settlers formed a compact, or regulations for their government; and in October following, organized their government accordingly, when Mr. Eaton was chosen governor. In 1640, the General Court substituted the name of New-Haven for that of Quinipiack. In 1655, a system of laws was adopted, which had been formed by Gov. Eaton, and printed in England. In 1657, Gov. Eaton died, and was succeeded by Francis Newman, who also died in 1661. In the spring of this year, Whaley and Goffe, two judges of king Charles I. came to New-Haven, and the October following removed to Hadley. New-Haven suffered considerably during the revolutionary war. It was ravaged by Gov. Tryon, July 1779, and the property burnt and destroyed was estimated, by commissioners appointed by the General Assembly for that purpose, at $84,566. The sufferers in this town, in common with those in other towns in the State, received a grant of a tract of land in the western part of the lands in the state of Ohio, reserved by this State at the cession which they made to the United States.

BIOGRAPHY. The Hon. *Jared Ingersoll* was for many years a citizen of this town. He was born in Milford, in 1722, received his education at Yale College, and took his first degree in 1742. A few years after this, having gone through with the usual course of professional studies, he commenced the practice of law in this town. His talents were of the highest order, and peculiarly adapted to forensic debate; so that he soon became distinguished in his profession, and acquired a great and solid reputation as an advocate.

Such was the reputation which he had acquired, and the estimation in which he was held by his fellow citizens, that in 1757, he was sent by the General Assembly of the colony, as their agent to the court of Great-Britain. In 1764, about the period of the passing of the Stamp Act, he went to England again. In 1770, he was appointed judge of the vice admiralty court in the middle district of the colonies; the duties of which office rendered it necessary for him to reside in Philadelphia. Accordingly he removed to that city the year after, where he resided until his office ceased, in consequence of the American revolution; whereupon he returned to this town, and continued here until his death. The most remarkable feature, in the character of Judge Ingersoll, was that of an ingenuous and dignified frankness, candour and fairness, which always characterized his deportment. This resulted from a consciousness of integrity and abilities, which led him to despise the jesuitical arts of hypocrisy and dissimulation, which are so often the only resource of small minds. As an advocate, there have been few if any individuals in this State, who have been his equals; few who have had more resources of mind, more amplitude of knowledge, more clear or comprehensive views, or more energetic powers of reasoning.

The Hon. *Roger Sherman*, distinguished for his public services, and the important offices which he held during an interesting period of our history, was for many years a citizen of this town. He was born in Newtown in Massachusetts, in the year 1721. His advantages as to education were very limited; having attended only at a common English school. In 1743, he removed to New-Milford in this State. Several years after this, he applied himself to the study of law, and was admitted to the bar in 1754. The next year he was appointed a justice of the peace, and soon after a representative in the General Assembly. In 1761, he removed to New-Haven. From this time his reputation was rapidly rising; and he

BIOGRAPHY.

soon ranked among the first men in the State. His knowledge of the human character, his sagacious and penetrating mind, his general political views, and his accurate and just observation of passing events, enabled him, on the first appearance of serious difficulties between the colonies and the parent country, to perceive the consequences that would follow ; and the probable result of a contest arising from a spirit of resistance to the exercise of unjust, oppressive and unconstitutional acts of authority, over a free people, having sufficient intelligence to know their rights, and sufficient spirit to defend them. Accordingly, at the commencement of the contest, he took an active and decided part in favour of the colonies, and subsequently in support of the revolution, and their separation from Great-Britain. In 1774, he was chosen a member of the first continental Congress ; and continued to be a member, except when excluded by the law of rotation. He was a member of the immortal Congress of 1776 ; and was one of the committee that drew up the declaration of Independence, which was penned by the venerable Thomas Jefferson, who was also one of the committee. After the peace, Roger Sherman was a member of the Convention which formed the Constitution of the United States ; and he was chosen a representative from this State, to the first Congress under this Constitution. He was removed to the Senate in 1791, and remained in this situation until his death, July 2d, 1793, in the 73d year of his age. The life of Mr. Sherman is one among the many examples of the triumph of native genius and talent, aided by persevering habits of industry, over all the obstacles arising from the want of what is generally considered as a regular and systematic education. Yet it deserves consideration, whether a vigorous mind, stimulated by an ardent thirst of knowledge, left to its own exertions, unrestrained and unembarrassed by rules of art, and unshackled by systematic regulations, is not capable of pursuing the object of acquiring knowledge more intensely and with more success ; of taking a more wide and comprehensive survey ; of exploring with more penetration the fields of science, and of forming more just and solid views. "Mr. Sherman possessed a powerful mind, and habits of industry, which no difficulties could discourage, and no toil impair. In early life, he began to apply himself with unextinguishable zeal to the acquisition of knowledge. In this pursuit, although he was always actively engaged in business, he spent more hours than most of those who are professedly students. In his progress, he became extensively acquainted with mathematical science, natural philosophy, moral and metaphysical philosophy, history, logic and theology." As a lawyer and statesman, he was very eminent ; having a clear, penetrating and vigorous mind, and as a patriot, no greater respect can be paid to his memory than the fact which has already been noticed, that he was a member of the immortal Congress of '76, which declared these colonies to be free and independent.

Samuel Bishop Esq. distinguished for the numerous and responsible public offices which he held, during a long life, and for his unimpeachable integrity, was a native of this town, and lived and died here. He was born in the year 1724, and died in August 1803, in the 80th year of his age. Almost his whole life was spent in public employments; the duties of many of which were peculiarly arduous and responsible. For fifty-four years he held the office and discharged the duties of town-clerk; and for twenty-six years was a representative of the town in the General Assembly. During the revolution, he was a zealous and decided whig, and took an active part in favour of the colonies and their separation from Great-Britain. At this period, he was a member of the committee of correspondence and of the Governor's Council of safety. For a great number of years he was a magistrate or justice of the peace; also judge of probate and chief judge of the county court. At his death, and for some years preceding, he was mayor of the city of New-Haven, and Collector of the district. The duties of all these various offices he discharged with ability, faithfulness and integrity, and to the general satisfaction of his fellow-citizens. Few men have been engaged an equal period in public employments, or in so great a diversity of them, & few have discharged their duties with equal faithfulness and integrity; few who in the circle of their action have been more extensively useful, or who have more perfectly finished the work and objects of life.

The Rev. *Timothy Dwight,* D. D. was born in Northampton, Mass. May 14th, 1752. At a very early period he disclosed unusual indications of genius, and an extraordinary propensity and aptitude for study and the acquisition of knowledge. Such was the extraordinary proficiency he had made in elementary studies, that he was admitted a member of Yale College in 1765, when he had but just entered his 13th year. At college he soon acquired the character of a good scholar, and of being remarkable for his devotion to study. He graduated in 1769, having gone through the usual course of studies with great credit. In September 1771, when he was but 19 years of age, he was chosen tutor in this seminary. He remained in this situation for six years, and discharged its duties with unusual success and reputation. During this period he composed the well known epic poem entitled the "Conquest of Canaan;" the poem having been finished when he was only 22 years of age. In 1777, it being during the revolutionary war, he was licensed as a clergyman; and the same year received the appointment of a chaplain in Gen. Parsons' brigade, and joined the army at West-Point. Soon after this, whilst in the army, he wrote his much admired patriotic and national song, Columbia. This has justly been esteemed as the best effusion of his muse. He did not continue long in the army, for, in 1778, he returned to his native town, where he remained for five years. During this period, he was employed, a portion of the time, as an instructor of youth; and occasionally officiated as a Clergyman. Whilst in this situation, he was twice chosen a representative of the town in the legislature of the State.

In 1783, having received an invitation, he became settled as a clergyman in Greenfield, a society in the town of Fairfield in Connecticut. He continued in this situation for nearly twelve years, and became highly distinguished in his profession, and as a sound, able, eloquent, orthodox and practical preacher. During his residence in this delightful and highly interesting situation, he conceived and wrote his poem, entitled "Greenfield Hill," consisting of seven parts, and a work of considerable merit. This publication, together with his Conquest of Canaan, was republished in England. Whilst in this situation also, he established and maintained an academic school, which deservedly sustained a high reputation. In the spring of 1795, Dr. Dwight was called, from this delightful abode and favourite retreat, to the presidency of Yale College, as the successor of President Stiles. In this important and responsible situation, he continued nearly 22 years; during which lengthy period he presided over the institution with great ability and astonishing success.

Notwithstanding the extensive erudition of President Stiles, and the high reputation which the institution, while he presided over it, had acquired, yet its reputation and prosperity were greatly increased during the presidency of Dr. Dwight; although a portion of this period was one of peculiar difficulties. At the accession of President Dwight, there were but about 110 students; whereas, at some periods subsequently, the number amounted to 313.

Few men have possessed the various and important qualifications necessary for a situation of this description, in so eminent a degree as President Dwight. He possessed a sound and penetrating mind, indefatigable industry, a laudable and elevated ambition for literary fame, adequate scientific acquisitions, and an extensive fund of general information. With these qualifications he united others, although more common, yet equally important; an agreeable and dignified person and deportment; a fine constitution; an unusual share of common sense; an accurate and extensive knowledge of the human character; an extensive and just observation; great practical knowledge, and an unusual portion of prudence or policy. His writings, which were published in his lifetime, consist, in addition to his poetical works, the most important of which have already been noticed, of numerous sermons or theological discourses, delivered on various important occasions. Since his death, a series of his sermons, comprising a *System of Theology*, has been published in five large octavo volumes. This edition of his sermons, which was published at Middletown in this State, in 1818, has also been published in England. He died on the 11th of January, 1817, Æ 65.

BRANFORD.

BRANFORD is a post township, situated upon Long-Island sound, 8 miles from New-Haven, and 40 miles from Hartford; bounded on the north by Wallingford, on the east by Guilford, on the south by Long-Island sound, and on the west by North and East-Haven. Its average length is 9 miles, and its average breadth 5 miles; comprising 45 square miles, or about 30,000 acres.

The township is uneven, consisting of hill and dale; upon the borders of the sound, there are some small sections that are level. The soil is more generally a red, gravelly loam; in some sections, argillaceous loam prevails. There are also some tracts of salt marsh. The natural growth consists of oak, elm, walnut, butternut, buttonwood, &c. The lands, when cultivated, produce grass, Indian corn, rye, and some wheat; but corn receives the most attention, and is principally cultivated.

There are no considerable rivers in the town. The largest stream discharges itself into the harbour, which is a small but convenient one, and admits of vessels of from 40 to 60 tons.

Upon the western boundary of the town there is a small lake, called Saltonstall lake.

There are a cluster of small islands in Long-Island sound, belonging to this town, called Thimble Islands; and another cluster called Indian Islands.

This town, being situated upon the sound, possesses great conveniences for fishing: various kinds of salt water fish, both shell and fin, are taken plentifully in almost every month in the year. Of the shell fish, the oyster and clam are the most important. The fish, with which the town is supplied, are a convenience and luxury to the inhabitants, and a source of considerable profit. In addition to the business of fishing, there are other maritime employments and interests: the coasting business has received considerable attention; there are six vessels of from 40 to 60 tons engaged in this business, which belong to this town. The maritime situation and interests of the place have a tendency to affect the character of the inhabitants, and to give a direction to their pursuits and industry.

There is a small but pleasant village in the town, consisting of about 30 dwelling-houses, a post-office, church, stores, &c. It is, from its contiguity to the sound, and the fish with which it is supplied, a place of some resort in the summer for health or pleasure.

The town is accommodated with the turnpike road from New-Haven to Middletown, which leads through its northern section.

Its population, in 1810, was 1932. There are 280 dwelling-houses, 220 qualified Electors, and two companies of militia. The amount of taxable property, including polls, is $54,739.

The manufactures and mechanical employments consist of 1 small Furnace for casting, 1 Carding Machine, 3 Fulling Mills, 4 Grain Mills, and 2 small Distilleries. There are 6 mercantile stores.

The town contains 3 located Congregational Societies and Churches, and 2 Episcopal Societies, which are also accommoda⸗

ted with houses for public worship. It has 15 School Districts and Schools, 2 small Social Libraries, 1 Episcopal and 3 Congregational Clergymen, and 5 Physicians. Branford was settled in the year 1644.

CHESHIRE.

CHESHIRE is a post township, situated in the northern section of the county, 25 miles from Hartford, and 13 from New-Haven, bounded on the north by Wolcott, and Southington, in Hartford county, on the east by Meriden and Wallingford, on the south by Woodbridge and Hamden, and on the west by Waterbury. Its average length from north to south is 7 miles, and its average breadth from east to west, nearly 6 miles; containing about 40 square miles. The northeastern section of the town is watered by the Quinipiack; its northern section by a branch of this stream, called ten mile river; and in its southern section several branches of Mill river have their sources.

The township is moderately uneven; being pleasantly diversified with hill and dale, except its western section, which is hilly and mountainous, embracing the West rock range of mountain. The prevailing soil is a gravelly loam, and is generally rich and fertile, affording grass, rye, oats, Indian corn and other productions common to this district. Of the natural growth of timber, chesnut, oak of the various kinds, and walnut, are the most prevalent. The geological structure of the township consists of argillaceous schistus and greenstone; and there are appearances of several minerals: galena, or lead ore, and copper ore have been discovered; but its mineralogy has received but little attention.

The Farmington and New-Haven turnpike passes through the centre of the town; and a turnpike which is contemplated to be laid out, to be called the Wolcott turnpike, will also pass through it.

The town contains two located Ecclesiastical Societies, and one Society of Episcopalians; each of which is accommodated with a house for public worship. It contains 12 School districts and common Schools, and an incorporated Academy.

The Episcopal Academy in this town is a very respectable institution. It was incorporated in 1801, being styled the Episcopal Academy of Connecticut. It has a fund of about $25,000, and a library, containing about 200 volumes. The institution is under the direction of a Principal and a Professor of languages. It has also a Treasurer and Secretary. The stated anniversary is the first Wednesday of October; and the average number of scholars is about 70. The academical building consists of a substantial brick edifice, 54 feet by 34. It was erected by the town, in 1796, and has a pleasant and interesting site, and is surrounded by a spacious court-yard.

The population of Cheshire, in 1810, was 2288; and there are about 350 Dwelling houses, 350 Freemen or Electors, 3 companies of Infantry, and a part of a company of Cavalry, of militia. The amount of taxable property, including polls, is $53,514. In the centre of the town there is a considerable village, having a pleasant and prospective situation. It contains forty or fifty dwelling houses, two Churches, the academical building, a Post-office, and several Mercantile Stores.

There are in the town, 4 Grain Mills, 2 Fulling Mills and Clothiers' Works, 2 Carding Machines, 1 Tinware Factory, 5 Tanneries, 5 Mercantile Stores, and 5 Taverns. There is also 1 Social Library, besides the one belonging to the Academy; an Engraving and Copper-plate Printing establishment, 4 Physicians, 2 Clergymen, 1 Episcopalian and 1 Congregationalist; and 1 Attorney. This town, originally belonging to the town of Wallingford, was incorporated in May, 1780.

DERBY.

DERBY, an ancient commercial post town, is situated upon the eastern side of the Ousatonick river, 12 miles from its mouth, at the head of navigation; 9 miles northwest from New-Haven, and 38 southwest from Hartford; bounded on the north by Oxford, on the east by Woodbridge, on the south by Milford, on the southwest by the Ousatonick river, which separates it from Huntington, in Fairfield county, and on the west by a part of Oxford. Its mean length is about 5 & a half miles, and its mean breadth 4 and a half, comprising an area of about 25 square miles. The surface is undulating, being pleasantly diversified with hills and dales. Upon the borders of the Ousatonick & Naugatuck, there are some fine tracts of alluvial. The prevailing soil is a gravelly loam; some sandy loam, and some small sections of calcareous loam. There are considerable forest lands in the township, and quantities of wood and timber are exported to the city of New-York.

The town is well watered; its southern border being washed by the Ousatonick, and the Naugatuck runs through it from north to south, and unites with the former within the town, at what is called the landing or harbour.

The Naugatuck contains some excellent privileges for mills and manufacturing establishments, which have been duly appreciated; and upon the Ousatonick, there are several shad fisheries.

There are several turnpike roads that lead through the town; the Rimmon falls turnpike, and the Ousatonick and Derby turnpikes.

The interests of the town embrace those of agriculture, manufactures and commerce. The agricultural productions consist of wheat, rye, corn, oats, grass, butter, cheese, beef, flax, flax seed, wool and some others. This was formerly a place of considerable commercial importance; the West India trade having once been flourishing, and carried on to considerable extent; but for some years past, the commerce of the town has much declined. The maritime business is done at the landing, where there is a small village, situated at the confluence of the Naugatuck with the Ousatonick. The harbour is good, and the navigation to the mouth of the river into Long Island sound, for vessels of about 80 tons; there being about 10 feet of water. The place possesses some local advantages for trade, being at the head of navigation; and the natural depot, for the surplus produce of a back country of considerable extent, upon the borders of the Ousatonick. These local advantages formerly gave the place considerable commercial consequence; but its vicinity to New-Haven is probably a circumstance that has counteracted their operation, and occasioned a decline of its trade and commercial interests. Some attempts have recently been made, to revive its commerce and business; a bank has been established, & a fishing company incorporated; but the exertions which have been made, have been attended with little or no success. The bank has now closed its operations, the business of the place being unable to sustain it; yet, notwithstanding these facts, and the inauspiciousness of present appearances, it is not improbable, that at some future period, the local advantages of the place will overcome the causes, whatever they may be, which have restricted and depressed its commercial interests, and give it that character and importance, which circumstances at an early period seemed to forebode. At the present time, the whole shipping of the place consists of four coasters, which are employed principally in a trade with the city of New-York.

Of the manufactures of this town, the large Woolen Factory, erected by the late Gen. David Humphrey, is the most important. This was one of the first establishments in the United States, and is situated upon the Naugatuck river, several miles back from the Ousatonick. The buildings connected with this establishment, and the Cotton Factory belonging to the same company, and other buildings which have been erected for the residence of the workmen, boarding houses, &c. have formed considerable of a village, which, in honour of its founder, is called Humphreysville. This establishment is upon an extensive scale; the proprietors of which, consisting of David Humphrey and his associates, were incorporated in May, 1810, by the name of "The Humphreysville Manufacturing company," with a capital of $500,000. The woolen manufactures of Humphreysville are known throughout the United States, and have acquired a reputation, at least equal to that of any other in this country. There is also a Cotton Factory at this village, belonging to this incorporated manufacturing company; a Paper Mill, and a Grain Mill. At some periods, the company have had in their employ, at the Woolen, Cotton, and other manufacturing interests at this village, nearly 200 workmen. There are three mercantile stores and a post-office at the village.

In addition to the manufactures at the village of Humphreysville, there is one Brass Foundery, two Oil Mills, six Limekilns, four Grain Mills, one of which is a Flouring Mill, one Fulling Mill and Clothiers' Works, one Carding Machine and seven Tanneries.

The population of this town, in 1810, was 2051; and there are 300 Dwelling Houses, 200 Freemen or Electors, and 3 companies of militia.

The amount of taxable property, as rated in making up lists, is $31,307.

The civil divisions of the town are two located Societies or parishes, and eight or nine School Districts. There are five religious Societies and Churches, two of Congregationalists, two of Episcopalians, and one of Methodists. In each of the School Districts, there is a School House, and a primary or common school maintained a suitable portion of the year. There are in the town, two small villages, of 30 or 40 houses each, in additon to the manufacturing village of Humphreysville.

There are 7 mercantile Stores, 2 Social Libraries, 3 Clergymen, 2 Physicians and 2 Attornies.

This place was originally called Paugassett, and belonged to the town of Milford. Some settlements were attempted in 1764, but were not permanent. In 1657—59, the lands were purchased of the natives; soon after which, the settlement made considerable progress. In 1671, the inhabitants presented a petition to the General Court, to be incorporated as a town, and renewed their application. In 1675, when at the October session, the town was incorporated by the name of Derby, at which time there were but twelve families.

BIOGRAPHY. Gen. *David Humphrey*, was a native of this town. He was a son of the Rev. Daniel Humphrey, and was born in July 1752. In 1767, he entered Yale College, and received his first degree in 1771. Whilst in college, he cultivated an attachment to the muses, and disclosed early evidences of poetical talent. During the revolutionary war, he entered the army as a captain; but at what time we are not informed.

In 1778, however, he was aid to Gen. Putnam, with the rank of major. Two years after this, he was appointed aid to the Commander in chief; having been the successful candidate of four who solicited the office. His competitors were Col. Talmadge, Gen. William Hull, and Roger Alden. He continued in this situation during the war, having the rank of a colonel, and was particularly distinguished at the memorable siege of York; and Congress, as a respectful testimony of their high estimation of his valour, fidelity, and signal services on this occasion, voted him an elegant sword. At the close of the war, he accompanied Gen. Washington to Virginia. In 1784, he embarked for France, in company with the brave but unfortunate Kosciusko; having, on the appointment of Mr. Jefferson as ambassador to France, been nominated as his secretary. In 1786, he returned to

America, and revisited the scenes of his youth in his native town. Soon after his return, he was elected by his fellow citizens to be their representative in the legislature of the State, and continued to be elected for two years, when he was appointed to the command of a regiment raised for the western service. During the period that he held this office, he remained most of the time in Hartford; and, with Hopkins, Barlow and Trumbull, assisted in the publication of the Anarchiad. On the reduction of his regiment, he repaired to Mount Vernon, and continued with Gen. Washington until 1790, when he received an appointment to the court of Portugal. In 1794, he visited America, but soon returned to Lisbon. Soon after this, he received an appointment to the court of Spain, where he continued until 1802, when he again returned to his native country. This was the end of his public life. After his return to America, he was, until his death, extensively engaged in various objects of public utility, particularly manufactures and agriculture. He is well known to have been one of the first who introduced merino sheep into this country, which has greatly improved the quality of wool, and given a strong impetus to domestic manufactures. The extensive woolen and cotton factory, which he established in this town, has already been noticed. He also did much for the promotion of agriculture; and just previously to his death was making exertions to form a society, for the purpose of procuring a farm for agricultural experiments.

Gen. Humphrey possessed considerable literary acquirements, although he published no work of magnitude; his writings consist principally of various poetical productions. Of these, the most important are an address to the armies of the United States; a poem on the happiness of America; a poem on the future glory of the United States; a poem on the industry of the United States; a poem on the love of country; and a poem on the death of General Washington. He wrote also a memoir of Gen. Putnam, various political tracts, &c. He died in New-Haven, 21st Feb. 1818, aged 66 years.

EAST-HAVEN.

EAST-HAVEN is a small township situated upon Long Island sound and New-Haven bay, four miles from the city of New-Haven, and 40 from Hartford; bounded on the north by North-Haven, on the east by Branford, on the south by Long Island sound, and on the west by New-Haven bay and the Quinipiack river. Its average length is 6 miles, and its average breadth nearly 3 miles; comprising about 17 square miles.

Upon the Quinipiack the land is level, and the soil is light and sandy. For a considerable distance into the interior, it continues level, and the soil is a sandy loam; but the eastern border is hilly and stony, and the soil a gravelly loam. The agricultural productions consist of Indian corn, some rye, barley, grass, salt hay; there being about 400 acres of salt marsh or meadow in the town. The Quinipiack river washes the western border of the town; besides which, it is watered by several small streams. Saltonstall Pond or Lake, a small body of water, is situated partly in this town and partly in Branford.

There are three considerable bridges in the town; the Dragon bridge, the Tomlinson bridge, and the Turnpike bridge. Shell fish are taken plentifully at Dragon; and there are several other small fisheries. Oysters and clams are the most important of the shell fish; and the black fish, of the " finny tribe." Large quantities of the white fish are taken for manure, for which purpose they are found to be very valuable.

The Middletown and Durham turnpike road leads through this town.

Agriculture and fishing are the principal occupations of the inhabitants; and manufactures or mechanical employments have received but little attention. There is 1 Grain Mill, 1 Fulling Mill and Clothiers' works, 1 Carding Machine, 2 Mercantile Stores, and 3 Public Inns. The population of the town, in 1810, was 1209; and there are 130 qualified Electors, one company of militia, and about 200 dwelling houses.

The town contains one located Congregational Society & Church, one Society of Episcopalians, 5 School Districts and Schools, and one small Social Library. The professional men are two Clergymen and one Physician.

The amount of taxable property, including polls, is $22,694.

East-Haven was taken from New-Haven, and incorporated in May, 1785.

GUILFORD.

GUILFORD, an ancient and populous maritime post township, is situated upon Long Island sound, 15 miles east of New-Haven, and 36 south from Hartford; bounded on the north by Durham, on the east by Hammonàssett river, which separates it from Killingworth, on the south by Long Island sound, and on the west by Branford. Its mean length from north to south is about eleven miles, and its mean breadth nearly seven; comprising about 72 square miles. The surface and face of the country are various; on the border of the sound, are some tracts of alluvial; the interior is broken and rough, being rocky and hilly; and in some sections mountainous. The rocks are primitive, consisting of granite, and other original formations. The prevailing soil is a gravelly loam, interspersed with some sections of sandy loam. It is considerably strong and fertile. In the interior of the township, and in its northern section, there are extensive tracts of forests and timber lands, consisting principally of oak, walnut, chesnut and other species of hard wood. These lands are too rough and stony for cultivation, and have therefore been suffered to remain to forests. The wood is sound and hard, and of an excellent quality, both for timber and fuel, and is now becoming valuable; being situated within a tolerably convenient distance of navigable waters. Large quantities of wood and timber are annually got to market, principally to the city of New-York. The improved lands in the town produce rye and corn; besides which, butter, cheese and cattle receive some attention. Of the hay produced, a considerable proportion is from the tracts of salt marsh, which are somewhat extensive. The farming interests of the town are not very flourishing; and there is an apparent general want of agricultural improvements and enterprise. The township is well watered; its southern border being washed by Long Island sound, and its eastern by the Hammonassett river, and the Menunkatuck, which rises in Quinapaug pond in the north part of the township, runs through it, and discharges itself into the harbour. East river, and several other small streams, accommodate different sections of the town. Some shad are taken in these rivers, and shell fish and white fish in the sound. The latter are valued only for manure, for which purpose large quantities of them are taken. They afford a rich and valuable manure, particularly for arable lands. Of shell-fish, oysters are most important; of which large quantities are annually taken, there being often from twenty to thirty oyster boats employed in the business. There are two harbours in the town, one called the town harbour, the other sachem's head harbour; the latter of which is esteemed a very safe and convenient one. The shipping of the town consists of three vessels engaged in the coasting trade, and five regular packets, which ply between this place and New-York. There is a turnpike road leading from the society of East-Guilford in this town to Durham, and thence to Hartford.

The civil divisions of the town consist of 4 located Ecclesiastical Societies, 19 School Districts, and an incorporated borough. The borough of Guilford, which was incorporated in 1815, is handsomely situated upon a tract of alluvial or maritime plain, about two miles back from the harbour, and near the Menunkatuck river. Its limits embrace the ancient town plot, which is handsomely laid out, having considerable regularity. In the centre, there is a public square, at which five considerable streets are concentrated. The several streets surrounding the square are well built, comprising many neat and handsome dwelling houses. There are, within the limits of the borough, 150 Dwelling houses, 2 Churches and a Town house situated upon the square, 5 Schools, 16 Mercantile Stores, a Post-office, several private offices, and a number of Mechanics' shops. The most considerable and important manufacturing or mechanical business in the town, is that of making shoes. There are 11 shops engaged in this business in the borough, some of which pursue it upon an extensive scale. This manufacture is carried on to a greater extent here, than in any other town in the State; and the products of the business form an important article of exportation, being principally sent to the southern states for a market. Except the shoemaking business, the manufactures of the town are inconsiderable; the greater portion of the industry of the place being engaged in the pursuits of agriculture, or the fishing and seafaring business. There are 1 Forge, 5 Grain Mills, 3 Cloth dressing establishments, 3 Carding Machines, and 4 Tanneries.

The population of the town, in 1810, was 3845; and there are about 500 Freemen or Electors, 4 Companies of Militia, and about 550 Dwelling houses. The aggregate list of the town, in 1816, was $84,945. Besides the 4 located Societies, which are Congregational, there is 1 Episcopal Society, 1 of Baptists, and 1 of Methodists; all of which are accommodated with houses for public worship. There are in the town 19 primary or common Schools, one in each district, 4 Social Libraries, 20 Mercantile Stores, 5 Clergymen, 6 Physicians, and 1 Attorney.

This town, being pleasantly situated upon the seaboard; affording in the summer months a cool and salubrious atmosphere; having an abundant supply of shell and other salt-water fish; and possessing various facilities for enjoying the air, healthfulness and pleasantness of the salt water; is, in the warm season, a place of much resort, both for health and pleasure; there being few if any towns upon the sea-coast, uniting so many agreeable and interesting objects.

Guilford was settled at an early period; the settlement having commenced in 1639, the year after that in New-Haven. The first settlers were Mr. Henry Whitefield, and several members of his church and congregation in England, to the number of about forty persons. It is represented that they selected this location, from the circumstance of the near resemblance it bore to the place from whence they had emigrated. They purchased the lands of the natives, stipulating that they should immediately abandon them. But notwithstanding this amicable arrangement with the aboriginal inhabitants, it was thought prudent, as a measure of precaution, to build one house, which should be so constructed, that, in case of necessity, it might serve as a fortress, for security & defence. This house, which was built of stone, is still standing, having been recently repaired. It is situated at the head of the great plain, upon a small eminence, and is two stories high. It is frequently visited by strangers, as an object of curiosity, and as a monument of the first settlement of the town, and of " times that are past."

BIOGRAPHY. The Hon. *Abraham Baldwin*, was a native of this town. His talents, his virtues, his patriotism, and his distinguished public services, were an honour to his native State. He graduated at Yale College, in 1772, immediately after which he was appointed a tutor at the same seminary, in which situation he continued

BIOGRAPHY.

for five years. In the year 1777, he entered the continental army, in the capacity of a chaplain, and continued therein until the close of the war. Not long after this period, he removed, at the request of Gen. Greene, to the State of Georgia. On his arrival and settlement here, he abandoned the clerical profession for that of the law. His talents and patriotism were too conspicuous to remain unnoticed even among strangers; he was soon elected a member of the legislature of that State, and in 1784, a member of the old Congress, and continued in that situation until the National Constitution superseded the system of government, (if it deserved to be called a system,) then in existence. He was also a member, and a distinguished one, of the Convention which formed the present Constitution of the United States; and upon the organization of the government, was chosen a member of Congress under the same, and so continued without interruption until he was removed therefrom for a more exalted station, being appointed a member of the Senate, in which office he continued until his death, March 4th, 1807. He died at the city of Washington, during the session of Congress, aged 53, in the midst of his usefulness, and surrounded with honours.

It is a remarkable circumstance, and an instance of assiduity and attention to public duties which scarcely have a parallel, that during his long parliamentary life, he was never known to be absent a single hour during the session of Congress, until the week preceding his death, from indisposition.

He was the founder of a college at Athens in Georgia, of which he was President for several years. He was a man of great talents, ardent patriotism, and extensive benevolence; lived in an eventful and important period of our history, and acted a responsible and important part in the establishment of our present system of government, which will go down to the latest posterity, and with it the names of its illustrious founders. Few have acted in a more extended sphere of usefulness, or filled more space in the public eye.

The Hon. *Thomas Chittenden*, for many years governor of the State of Vermont, was a native of this town. He was born 6th Jan. 1730; and at the age of twenty-one years, in 1751, he removed to Salisbury in this State, where he continued until 1773, when he, the second time, encountered the privations and hardships of a new country, by emigrating into the State of Vermont. But he was amply rewarded for his enterprise; having made a valuable location of land upon the beautiful alluvial of the Onion river, which soon became valuable, and enabled him to leave a large estate to his posterity. He was also honoured with the confidence of the public, and attained to distinguished public employments; having been elected the first governor of that State, in March, 1778. He died August 25th, 1797.

HAMDEN.

HAMDEN is a small township, centrally situated in the county, five and a half miles from New-Haven, and 32 from Hartford; bounded north by Cheshire and Wallingford, east by North-Haven, south by New-Haven, and west by the West rock range of mountain, which separates it from Woodbridge. Its average length is seven and a half miles, and its average breadth about three and a half, making about 26 square mile. A considerable section of the township is level; the western border of it is mountainous, and the eastern considerably hilly. The township is situated between the West rock range of mountain, and the east rock range. East rock is the termination of an extensive greenstone range of mountains, which extends far into the interior of New-England, leading through Cheshire, Southington, Farmington, Simsbury and Granby, into Massachusetts. It consists of a broken ridge, or a succession of hills, which become more elevated as you proceed from east rock. At Farmington, Simsbury and Granby, the ridge is more continuous and lofty, and bold in its features. West rock is the termination of the west range of the same mountain; it extends as far into the interior as the western section of Southington, where it subsides, or more properly unites with the east rock range, of which it is properly a branch. This range consists also of greenstone, and is a succession of eminences; and exhibits similar features to the other. Hamden is situated between these two ranges; the one being upon its west, and the other upon its eastern border. Mount Carmel, which is in some measure an insulated eminence, and appears to be a spur of the east rock range, lies wholly within this town. This is one of the most elevated greenstone eminences in the State. The greenstone of these mountains forms an excellent building-stone, and is extensively used for that purpose in New-Haven. In the greenstone hills of this town, various minerals have been discovered. Iron pyrites in minute pieces, and sometimes imperfectly crystalized, is found disseminated; and sulphuret of copper is sometimes found, connected with crystalized quartz. At a distant period, a large mass of native copper, weighing about 90 ℔s, was accidently discovered upon one of the greenstone hills of this town. It was preserved for a long time, and the remains of it were used not more than 15 or 20 years since, in New-Haven; it was said to be very pure, and free from alloy. It is not known precisely, upon what spot this mass of native copper was found; but copper is now known to exist in various places, in the greenstone hills of this town. Lead, in small quantities, has also been found.

The soil in this town is a gravelly loam, and generally fertile; the natural growth is walnut, oak of the various kinds, and other deciduous trees. The lands, in a cultivated state, produce rye, corn, oats &c. and carry good and heavy crops.

The town is watered by Mill river, a fine mill stream, affording numerous sites for water works.

The Farmington and New-Haven turnpike road passes through

MERIDEN.

the centre of this town, and the Hartford and New-Haven turnpike runs within its eastern limits.

The extensive Gun Factory, or establishment for the manufacture of fire arms, of Eli Whitney Esq. erected upon Mill river within this town, is particularly deserving of notice. The business at this factory, it is believed, is carried on upon novel principles. The various operations and processes, necessary in the formation of the different parts of the musket, are performed by the aid of machinery and mechanical powers. The hammering, cutting, turning, perforating, grinding and polishing, are performed, or, the performance regulated and facilitated, by machinery. This occasions such uniformity in the work, that the parts of the lock, and their different proportions and relations are so much alike, that they may be transferred from one lock and fitted to another, without any material alteration. From the mechanical principles by which every part of the manufacture is regulated at this factory, the fire arms manufactured here are characterized by a uniformity, not to be found in those made at any other place. And what is a most striking evidence of ingenuity and mechanical genius of the proprietor of this establishment, the business was undertaken without any previous knowledge of it; but genius is more than a substitute for experience.

In addition to this establishment, there are 1 Paper Mill, 1 Fulling Mill, 1 Carding Machine, 1 Distillery, 2 Grain Mills and 2 Tanneries. There are 2 Mercantile Stores, and 2 Taverns.

The town contains two located Congregational Societies and Churches, one Society of Episcopalians and one of Independents. It contains, also, nine School districts and Schools, one Social Library, two Clergymen, and two Physicians.

The population of the town, in 1810, was 1716. There are 260 Dwelling Houses, 200 Electors & 1 company of militia.

The amount of taxable property, including polls, is $36,806.

Hamden was incorporated in May 1786, previously to which, it belonged to New-Haven.

MERIDEN.

MERIDEN is a small post town, situated in the northern section of the county, 17 miles from Hartford, and about the same from New-Haven; bounded on the N. by Berlin, in Hartford county, on the east by Middletown, on the south by Wallingford, and on the west by Cheshire and Southington. Its average length from east to west is five miles, and its average breadth four and a half miles; containing twenty-two and a half square miles. The township is hilly, and some sections of it mountainous. The Middletown and Wallingford range of mountains or hills passes through the eastern border of this town. Of this range, Mount Lamentation, which is in the northeastern part of the township, is far the most elevated.

This eminence has some very striking features. In the northwest part of the town also, is an eminence which affords a considerable curiosity: there is a deep and narrow valley, having a ridge of mountain on the one side, and a bold mural ledge on the other; in which solid cakes of ice may be obtained at any season of the year. The congelations, or cakes of ice, are found under large projecting rocks. "A few years since," says our correspondent, "I found snow and ice, in this frosty vale, under the south side of a loose rock, about the 1st of September, from whence I took a small cake of ice, and carried it six or seven miles. At this time, gooseberries were but just ripe, and were growing among the rocks; and strawberries have been gathered here as late in the season as this." North of this vale is a deep, narrow and almost impervious glen; its width is only sufficient for a path and a rivulet, on each side of which are elevated ridges of mountain, forming an angle of about 45 degrees. This pass is called Cat hole, and is more than a mile in extent; in which, and in the valley noticed before, the sun shines but a few hours in the longest days. Hence the order of the seasons is entirely inverted; and spring and summer fruit is not brought to perfection until autumn. This place in every respect is characterized by features the most irregular and romantic, and has more the appearance of illusion than reality.

The soil in this town is a gravelly and sandy loam, and is considerably fertile. It produces grass, grain, &c. The Quinipiack river washes the southwestern border of the town, and several of its branches run through the interior.

The town is accommodated with the Hartford and New-Haven turnpike, which passes through its centre; also by the Middletown and Waterbury turnpike, which intersects the former.

There is a small village in the town, consisting of a Post office, a Congregational church, about 30 Dwelling houses, and a number of Mechanics' shops.

A spirit of enterprise and activity in business characterizes the inhabitants of this town. Various manufactures and mechanical employments are carried on; but those of tin ware and buttons are the most important. There are 5 distinct Factories of the former, and an equal number of the latter, for making metal buttons; and 1 Factory for ivory buttons. There are also 1 Factory for ivory combs, and 2 block tin or hard metal spoon Factories. The wares and manufactures of these establishments, like those of other towns in the vicinity, are sent abroad for a market. This furnishes employment for a number of hands; and it has been estimated that there are from 20 to 40 persons that are constantly employed in vending the wares that are manufactured in this town. Most of them are employed in the southern and western states, which afford an extensive market for the products of our industry. And this market will not be likely soon to fail; for wherever slavery prevails, mechanical ingenuity and industry will be excluded. In addition to these manufactures, there are 12 Cider Distilleries, 2 Grain Mills,

MIDDLEBURY.

1 Fulling Mill, 1 Carding Machine, and 2 Tanneries. There are 2 Mercantile Stores, and 2 Taverns. The town contains 1 Congregational Society and Church, 1 Episcopal Society, and 1 of Baptists, all of which have houses for public worship. It contains 7 School Districts and common Schools, 1 Social Library, 1 Clergyman, 1 Attorney and 1 Physician.

The population of the town, in 1810, was 1249. There are about 200 Dwelling houses, 1 Company of Militia and a fraction of another, and about 175 Electors. The amount of taxable property, including polls, is $27,425.

Meriden was incorporated in 1806; previously to which it belonged to Wallingford.

MIDDLEBURY.

MIDDLEBURY is a small township, situated in the north-western extremity of the county, being 22 miles from New-Haven, and 36 from Hartford; bounded on the north by Woodbury and Watertown, in Litchfield county, on the east by Waterbury, on the south by Oxford, and on the west by Woodbury; having an average length from north to south of 5 miles, and an average breadth of nearly 4 miles, containing about 19 square miles, or about 13,000 acres.

The township is watered by Hop river, a branch of the Naugatuck, & numerous small streams. In the southeast section of the town there is a small pond or lake, called Quasepaug, which discharges its waters into the Ousatonick.

Its surface is hilly and rocky, and its appearance rough and forbidding. The rocks are mostly granite, and the soil is a hard, coarse gravelly loam, which affords tolerable grazing; it also admits of the growth of grain, and rye is cultivated with considerable success.

The principal agricultural productions are rye, butter and cheese, and some beef and cattle. The town does little or nothing at manufactures, except those of a domestic character. It contains 2 Grain Mills, 1 Fulling Mill and Clothier's works, 1 Carding Machine, 3 Tanneries, 1 Distillery, and 1 Mercantile Store.

The general list of the town, including polls, amounts to $18,920. Its population, in 1810, was 847; and there are now 100 Freemen or Electors, 1 Company of Militia, and 125 Dwelling houses.

The town forms 1 located Congregational Society and Church, and contains besides a Society of Methodists. It is divided into 6 School Districts, each of which supports a school for several months in the year. It contains 2 small Social Libraries, 2 Taversn, 1 Physician and 1 Clergyman.

It was incorporated in 1807; previously to which, it formed a part of Waterbury, Woodbury and Southbury.

MILFORD, an ancient maritime post township, is situated on the southwestern border of the county, 9 miles west from New-Haven, and 43 from Hartford; bounded on the north by Derby and Woodbridge, on the east by New-Haven, on the south by Long Island sound, and on the west by the Ousatonick river, which separates it from Stratford. Its average length from north to south is about seven and a half miles, and its average breadth from east to west nearly five miles, comprising an area of about 34 square miles. The prevailing character of the surface is undulating, being pleasantly diversified with hill and dale. There are also some mountainous ridges, consisting principally of greenstone slate, and facing generally to the southeast, with considerable chasms or valleys between them. There is also one ridge, or rather a series of ridges, of limestone, of three or four miles in length, and about one fourth of a mile in breadth, which intervenes between the greenstone ridges. In these calcareous ridges there are exhaustless beds of valuable marble; and indeed the primitive limestone strata, of which they are in part composed, deserve that name. The following interesting account of these calcareous ridges and strata, has been given by Professor Silliman.

"About five miles west of New-Haven commences a range of serpentine, both common and noble, and mixed more or less with primitive limestone and bitterspath. As this range proceeds westward, the limestone predominates more and more over the serpentine, and soon the rock becomes primitive stratified limestone. This continues in nearly the same direction, in almost uninterrupted ridges, for three miles at least; and, as is asserted, for several miles further. Thus a circumscribed space, not exceeding one fourth of a mile in breadth, and running in length as has just been specified, intervenes between ridges of greenstone, and in some instances alternates with it; this rock forming its boundary on the north, and also on the south, and in some places coming into direct and visible contact with it. These strata of limestone are remarkably regular. Their direction and dip is the same with that of the greenstone slate. In a few instances, the limestone is interrupted by greenstone and chlorite slate. A quarry has recently been opened in these calcareous strata, for the purpose of obtaining marble; for the limestone which has been mentioned appears properly to deserve that name. The structure of the rock is schistus, and its texture minutely granular. Its prevailing colour is that of the Italian dome marble, but very much variegated by innumerable veins of calcareous spar or bitterspath of a very brilliant white, by an admixture of serpentine, forming green spots, and by black spots and clouds, which sometimes are magnetic iron ore, and sometimes appear to be serpentine of a dark hue. Marble also occurs here of a deep black, beautifully illuminated by white clouds. As far as the investigation has gone, these calcareous strata are divided into large distinct tables; so that they can be taken out, in many instances, without making any other fracture than what exists naturally. Pieces of the marble have been sawed and polished; and although only weathered pieces have hitherto been tried, the stone exhibits so fine a texture, so high a lustre, and such beautiful delineations of colour, as to justify the belief that it will prove a valuable acquisition to the country."

And it is a circumstance of no small importance, that it is situated immediately upon a stream of water, communicating directly with Milford harbour, and which is navigable to the sound. and sufficiently copious to operate the mills necessary for sawing it. The prevailing soil is a rich gravelly mould or loam of a dark colour; some sections of sandy loam, some of argillaceous, and the calcareous tracts already described. It is generally strong and fertile, and a good agricultural township. The forests, which are valuable, from their vicinity to navigable waters, consist of walnut, oak, chesnut, &c. The agricultural productions consist of corn, rye, oats, flax, as the products of tillage; and butter, chesse and beef from grazing. Of the hay which is produced, large quantities are from the tracts of salt marsh, of which there are about 300 acres in the town. From the contiguity of the town to New-Haven, considerable attention is paid to the supplying of various small meats, and esculent roots and vegetables for the market at that place.

The waters of the town are the Ousatonick, which washes its western border, and the Wapawaug, which runs through its centre from north to south, and discharges itself into Milford harbour. There are several shad fisheries in the Ousatonick, there being fifteen seines owned by individuals; and it was estimated that there were 112,000 shad taken in 1816. Shell fish and black fish are taken in the sound. The great Atlantic road from New-Haven to New-York leads through the centre of this town, upon which the Washington bridge connects the town with Stratford. This bridge is about 80 rods long, and has a draw for the accommodation of the navigation to Derby and elsewhere up the river. The town does something in navigation, and possesses four vessels engaged in foreign trade, and several in the coasting trade; there being in all 1500 tons of shipping here. There is a convenient harbour at the mouth of the Wapawaug, having sufficient water for vessels of 200 tons.

There is a considerable and pleasant village, which is of ancient date, situated upon the great turnpike road leading through the town, about nine miles west from New-Haven. It comprises, within the limits of about a mile square, nearly 100 Dwelling houses, many of which are neat and handsome buildings, a Post-office, 3 Churches, and several Mercantile Stores. The manufactures and mechanical employments of the town, independent of those of a domestic kind, are inconsiderable. There are 4 Grain Mills, one of which is a large merchant's mill, for flouring, and contains four run of stones, 3 Fulling Mills and Clothiers' works, 3 Carding Machines and 3 Tanneries.

17

The civil divisions of the town are 3 located Ecclesiastical Societies and 11 School Districts. Besides the located, there is 1 Society of Epicopalians; and a primary or common school is maintained in each of the School Districts, and 3 Grammar Schools. The population of the town, in 1810, was 2674; and there are about 400 Freemen or Electors, 3 Companies of Militia, and about 380 Dwelling houses. The aggregate list of the town, in 1816, was $54,320.

There are in Milford, 4 Churches, 8 Mercantile Stores, 2 Taverns, 3 Social Libraries, 3 Clergymen, 3 Physicians, and 2 Attornies. This is one of the ancient towns in the State, and was settled as early as 1638.

NORTH-HAVEN.

NORTH-HAVEN is a township, centrally situated in the county, being 8 miles from New-Haven, and 26 miles from Hartford; bounded on the north by Wallingford, on the east by Wallingford, Branford and East-Haven, on the south by East-Haven, and on the west by Hamden. Mean length from north to south, 6 miles, with a medium breadth of nearly 3 miles, comprising about 17 square miles. The township is generally level, but the eastern & western extremities are considerably hilly, or mountainous; the soil is mostly a light sandy loam, and produces rye, corn, &c.

There is an extensive and beautiful tract of salt and dike marsh, or meadow, in this town. These meadows produce large quantities of grass, which is usually mowed and stacked upon the land, from whence it is removed in the winter season. Upon the salt marsh, the hay is salt; but, those meadows which are protected from the salt water, by means of dikes, & are thence called dike marshes or meadows, the grass is fresh, & of a better quality.

The town is watered by the Quinipiack, which runs through it, in a southwesterly direction; thence upon the borders of New-Haven & East-Haven, and discharges its waters into New-Haven bay. This river is navigable for boats to Mansfield's bridge in this town, being 8 miles from its mouth. The tide flows to this place, and occasions a rise of 4 and a half feet of water.

There are seven or eight shad fisheries in this river, at which there are considerable quantities taken annually. There is a valuable quarry of red sandstone, which is a good freestone.

From the vicinity of this town to New-Haven, and from the light, warm, and sandy character of the soil which favours early vegetation, there are various culinary vegetables, and particularly peas, cultivated for the New-Haven market.

The town is accommodated with the Hartford and New-Haven turnpike, which leads through its western section; and also by the Middletown and Durham turnpike, which passes through its eastern section.

The population of the town, in 1810, was 1239; and there are 200

OXFORD.

Electors, 1 company of militia, and about 200 Dwelling houses. The amount of taxable property, including polls, is $26,975.

Agriculture is the principal business of the town, but some portion of the men are engaged in seafaring, or maritime pursuits. Manufactures have received but little attention. There are 1 Woolen Factory, 2 Grain Mills, 2 Fulling mills, 1 Distillery, 1 Tannery, 2 Mercantile Stores, & 5 Taverns. The town contains 1 located Congregational Society & Church, 1 Society of Baptists, and 1 of Episcopalians, all of which have houses for public worship. It contains also, 8 School districts and Schools, 2 Social Libraries, 1 Physician, 1 Congregational, and 1 Baptist Clergyman.

North-Haven was settled in 1660, by 35 men, principally from Saybrook, and was incorporated as a town, in October, 1786.

BIOGRAPHY. Dr. *Ezra Stiles*, late President of Yale College, was a native of this town. Dr. Stiles was the son of the Rev. Isaac Stiles, and was born Dec. 15th, 1727. He was educated at Yale College, took his first degree in 1746, was chosen Tutor in 1749, and continued in this situation for six years. In 1765, he was ordained minister of the second Congregational Church in Newport, R. I. In 1778, he was installed President of Yale College, where he continued until his death, May 12th, 1795, in the 68th year of his age. The literary acquirements and character of Dr. Stiles are well known, and justly appreciated; but his character as a scholar, deservingly high as it stood, is in our view, of less importance to his memory, than that conspicuous zeal and patriotic ardour in the cause of his country and of civil liberty, which distinguished him through the whole course of his life. Although at the head of the clerical order, he favoured no views of ecclesiastical aggrandizement or power. His whole life was characterized by the humanity and benevolence of his disposition and views; and his name deserves to be enrolled among the benefactors of mankind.

(See Dr. Holmes' account of the life and writings of Dr. Stiles.)

OXFORD.

OXFORD is a post township, situated in the northwestern section of the county, 14 miles northwesterly from New-Haven, and 40 southwesterly from Hartford; bounded on the north by Middlebury and Waterbury, on the east by Woodbridge and Derby, on the south by Derby, and on the southwest by the Ouatonick river, which separates it from New-town, in Fairfield county, and on the west by Southbury. Its mean length from northeast to southwest is about 8 miles, and its mean breadth nearly 5 miles; comprising about 38 square miles. The surface is uneven, being diversified with hill and dale. The prevailing soil is a gravelly loam; but in the western section of the town, it is a calcareous loam, and is generally fertile and productive. There is a large proportion of forests, the timber of which is principally oak, walnut and chesnut. Considerable quantities of wood and timber are annually got to market, principally to New-Haven; but some of which is sent to New-York. The leading agricultural productions consist of wheat, rye, and some other grains, grass, butter and cheese; small meats, fowls, esculent roots and culinary vegetables are sent to New-Haven market.

The town is well watered; the Ousatonick washes its southwestern border, and the Naugatuck runs through its northeastern section, in addition to which, there are numerous small streams. Upon the Ousatonick there are several shad fisheries. The Woodbury turnpike, leading to New-Haven, passes through this town; and also the Southbury turnpike leading to the same place, from up the Ousatonick river.

Of the mechanical employments and establishments in the town, the most important are, 1 Woolen Factory, 3 or 4 Limekilns, 1 large Hat Factoty. 2 Fulling Mills and Clothiers' works, 3 Carding Machines, for customers, 3 Grain Mills and 6 Tanneries. There are 3 Mercantile Stores and 1 Public Inn.

The population of the town, in 1810, was 1445; and there are about 200 Electors or Freemen, about 220 Dwelling houses, and 1 Company of Militia.

The amount of taxable property, including polls, as rated in the making up of lists in 1816, was $35,020.

The town contains 1 located Ecclesiastical Congregational Society and 13 School Districts; besides the located, there are 2 Episcopal Societies, and a Society of Methodists. There is a primary or common School maintained in each of the School Districts, for a suitable portion of the year. There is 1 Social Library, 1 Clergyman, 1 Physician and 1 Attorney in the town.

Oxford was incorporated, with town privileges, in October 1798, previously to which it belonged to the town of Derby.

SOUTHBURY.

SOUTHBURY is a post town, situated in the northwestern section of the county, upon the northeast side of the Ousatonick river, 40 miles southwest from Hartford; bounded on the north by Roxbury and Woodbury, in Litchfield county, on the east by Middlebury, on the southeast by Oxford, on the south and southwest by the Ousatonick river, which separates it from Newtown, in Fairfield county, and on the west by New-Milford, in Litchfield county. The average length of the township, from east to west, is 8 miles, and its average breadth 4 miles, comprising an area of 32 square miles. The surface is waving, being pleasantly diversified with moderate hills and dales. The prevailing soil is a sandy loam, generally warm and fertile. The natural growth of timber is deciduous; and it is estimated by our correspondent, that the forests embrace nearly one fourth part of the lands of the township. The agricultural productions consist of rye, corn, oats, flax, potatoes, pork, beef, cider, cider brandy and some others.

The Ousatonick washes the south and southwestern borders of the town; the Shepaug waters its western section; and the Pomperaug runs through its centre from north to south. The two latter are considerable mill streams, and discharge their waters into the Ousatonick in this town. There are several shad fisheries upon the Ousatonick. The Ousatonick middle road and the Oxford turnpike lead through the town.

The more considerable mechanical interests and employments are, 1 Tinware Factory, 4 small Distilleries, 3 Tanneries, 4 Carding Machines, 3 Clothiers' works and 4 Grain Mills. There are 6 Mercantile Stores.

The population of the town, in 1810, was 1413, and there about 200 Freemen or Electors, 2 Companies of Militia, and about 230 Dwelling houses.

The amount of taxable property, in 1817, including polls and assessments, was $39,284; of which there was $10,890 for polls, $1445 for assessments, and $26,949 of taxable estate.

The civil divisions of the town are 2 located Ecclesiastical Societies or Parishes, and 8 School Districts. Besides the located, there is a Society of Methodists, all of which are accommodated with houses for public worship; and there is a primary School maintained in each of the School Districts. There are 1 Social Library, 2 Physicians and 3 Attornies in the town.

Southbury was settled in 1672, and incorporated as a part of Woodbury, to which it then was annexed, in 1674. It was set off from Woodbury, and incorporated as a town, by the name of Southbury, in May 1787; and a few years since, it was annexed to the county of New-Haven.

WALLINGFORD.

WALLINGFORD, a pleasant post township, is situated in the northeastern section of the county, 23 miles southwest from Hartford, and 13 northeast from New-Haven; bounded on the north by Meriden, on the east by Middletown and Durham, in the county of Middlesex, on the south by Branford and North-Haven, and on the west by Cheshire. Its mean length, from east to west, is nearly 7 miles, and its mean breadth nearly 6 miles, comprising an area of about 39 square miles.

The prevailing surface of the township is undulating; being pleasantly diversified with moderate hills and dales. Upon the Quinipiack there are extensive tracts of valuable alluvial, a considerable proportion of which are annually overflown, and the eastern extremity of the township is mountainous, the Middletown range of mountain forming its boundary in that direction. This township is embraced within the greenstone and argillaceous district of the State. The mountainous tract, upon its eastern borders, consists of greenstone, having an understratum of argillaceous schistus, or clay slate, which generally prevails throughout the town. Of its mineralogy, we have obtained little information. It is said there are some indications of copper ore, and there is a valuable quarry of red sand stone, which is an excellent free stone; being an induration of sand, supported by a clay slate basis. The prevailing soil is a light gravelly loam, which in some sections approximates to a sandy loam. It is warm and fertile, and well calculated both for grain and grazing. It is also very favourable for fruit.

The agricultural productions are rye, corn, oats, grass, flax, cider, potatoes, &c. Large quantities of broom corn are annually raised and manufactured into brooms, which are sent abroad for a market. Wallingford plain, situated upon the eastern bank of the Quinipiack, is a very singular tract of land. It is nearly four miles in length, and about three fourths of a mile in breadth, and is the most extensive tract of level land in the State; and, under its present cultivation, the most sterile and barren. Its soil is a coarse sand; and it seems to be considered so barren as not to be worth cultivation, a considerable proportion of it being wholly unenclosed. Yet there is but a very small proportion of it which blows, or but what has sufficient consistence of soil, or the upper surface of the land, to sustain itsself, and to retain the vegetable substances, and other manures which collect, or are deposited upon it. Notwithstanding the sterile appearance of this land, it is believed, that by a judicious and ameliorating system of cultivation; by the use of clover, sheep, and summer fallow; or by the application of some earths or manures, calculated to correct the predominating silicious character of the soil; it might be rescued from its present condition, a waste and agricultural void, and rendered suitable and valuable for a grain culture.

The town is well watered by the Quinipiack, an interesting and valuable mill stream, which runs through the whole extent of the township. This stream is famous for its mill sites. It affords also some shad fisheries. In the southeast corner of the township is a pond, called Paug Pond. The turnpike from Hartford to New-Haven runs through the western section of this town.

There are some Manufactures in the town; 1 Woolen Factory, 2 Tin ware Factories, 2 Button Factories, 2 Metal Spoon Factories. The tin ware, buttons and other articles, are mostly sent abroad for a market, and not only promote industry at home, but enterprise abroad. Besides these manufactures, there are 3 Fulling Mills and Clothiers' works, 3 Carding Machines, 5 Grain Mills, and 4 Tanneries.

The town contains 2 located Congregational Societies or Parishes, and 11 School Districts.

WATERBURY.

In the first Society there is a considerable village, having a pleasant and prospective situation. It contains about 75 Dwelling houses, 2 Congregational and 1 Episcopal Church, a Post-office, Academy, Stores, Mechanics' Shops, &c. Besides the located Societies, there is 1 of Episcopalians, 1 of Baptists, and 1 of Methodists; all of which are accommodated with houses for public worship. There are 11 primary or common Schools, and one Academy, which usually is attended by about 45 scholars. There are 3 Mercantile Stores, 1 Social Library, 2 practising Physicians and Surgeons, 2 Clergymen, one Congregationalist and one Baptist, and 1 Attorney. The population of the town, in 1810, was 2325; and there are about 400 Electors, 2 Companies of Militia, and about 340 Dwelling houses. The amount of taxable property, as rated in making up lists, including polls, is $54,827.

Wallingford belonged to New-Haven; and, before it was incorporated as a town, was called New-Haven Village. The township was purchased by Gov. Eaton, Mr. Davenport and others of New-Haven, in 1638. But the settlement was not attempted until the year 1669, when a committee were appointed by the town of New-Haven, to manage the concerns of the settlement. The town was incorporated soon afterwards.

WATERBURY.

WATERBURY is a post township, situated in the northwest part of the county, 20 miles distant from New-Haven; bounded north by Watertown and Plymouth, east by Wolcott and Cheshire, south by Woodbridge and Oxford, and west by Oxford and Middlebury, comprising an area of about 40 square miles; having an average length of 8 miles, and an average breadth of 5 miles. Its surface is diversified with hill and dale. The soil is generally a gravelly loam, and affords tolerably good grazing, and such productions as are common to this region.

This town is watered by the Naugatuck river, which runs thro' it from north to south. This and other streams afford numerous sites and privileges for mills and other hydraulic works.

The Waterbury river turnpike passes through this town; and one leading from Middletown through Meriden extends into it.

Although in this, like the other towns in the county, agriculture is the principal business of the inhabitants; yet considerable attention has been paid to manufactures of different kinds.

The late war had a favourable influence in stimulating the naturally enterprising spirit of our citizens, to engage in various manufacturing pursuits, thereby developing new resources, and opening a more extensive and varied field of industry. Many of the germs of manufactures, to which the war afforded life and growth, have been blighted with the mildew of foreign goods, with which the peace inundated the country. Many establishments have fallen, and many individuals, who had invested their whole capitals in the business, have been sacrificed, and others severely injured. On the score of *gain,* although this was the efficient motive which influenced most of those who engaged in manufactures, the business has been generally unfortunate. But it is not uncommon, that pursuits, which are sources of loss and ruin to individuals, are often productive of the greatest and most important public and national advantages. The seeds of manufactures were sown in this country during the war; and however they may have since declined, or may languish at the present time, they cannot be exterminated. Those who engaged in the business upon a moderate scale, and conducted it upon principles of economy, have best withstood the shock. Hence the small manufacturing establishments of this town have maintained themselves. They consist of 1 Woolen Factory, 4 Button Factories, 3 of metal and 1 of ivory, and 2 Clock Factories.

There are also 5 Distilleries, 5 Grain Mills, 2 Fulling Mills, 2 Carding Machines, 1 Oil Mill, and 2 Tanneries. There are 5 Mercantile Stores and 4 Taverns.

The town contains 2 located Congregational Societies & Churches, 1 Society of Episcopalians, and 1 of Baptists. It contains 2 villages, one in the centre of the town, having 30 or 40 Dwelling houses; the other is in Salem Society, and consists of 15 or 20 Dwelling houses.

The town contains 19 School Districts and Schools. Its population, in 1810, was 2874; and there are 400 Dwelling houses, 350 qualified Electors, and 3 Companies of Militia.

The amount of taxable property, including polls, is $53,622. The professional men are 3 Clergymen, 3 Physicians and 4 Attornies at law. The town was first settled in 1686.

Dr. Lemuel Hopkins, a distinguished physician and poet, was a native of this town. (See Hartford.)

WOODBRIDGE.

WOODBRIDGE is an interior township of this county, 7 miles from New-Haven, and 40 from Hartford; bounded on the north by Waterbury and Cheshire, on the east by Hamden, on the south by New-Haven and Milford. and on the west by Derby and Oxford. Its average length from north to south is 10 miles, and its average breadth 4 miles, comprising about 40 square miles. The township is hilly and mountainous; and a portion of the lands, not being calculated for cultivation, have been suffered to remain for timber. There are considerable forests in the town, and large quantities of wood are annually carried to New-Haven for a market. The timber, being of mountain growth, is of an excellent quality, and consists of oak of the various kinds, walnut, maple, &c. The soil is a hard gravelly loam; and the lands, when cleared and cultivated, although they are rough and stony, afford good grazing; and butter and cheese, and beef and pork, are the principal agricultural productions of the town. The farmers here have paid considerable attention to sheep, for the raising of which the lands are well adapted. The town is watered by West river, running thence through New-Haven; and also by the Wapawaug, an inconsiderable stream, which runs through Milford.

There are two turnpike roads which pass through this town; one called the Rimmon's Falls turnpike, and the other the Litchfield turnpike, both of which lead to New-Haven.

There are, in this town, 4 small Distilleries for cider spirits, 3 Grain Mills, 2 Fulling Mills and Clothiers' works, 2 Carding Machines, 1 Tannery, 2 Mercantile Stores and 2 Taverns. There are 2 located Congregational Societies and Churches, and 1 of Episcopalians, 1 small Society of Methodists, 2 Social Libraries, 2 Physicians and 2 Clergymen. There are 10 School Districts & Schools.

The population of the town, in 1810, was 2084; and there are 2 Companies of Infantry, and a part of a Company of Cavalry, of Militia, about 250 Electors, and about 300 Dwelling houses. The amount of taxable property, including polls, is $49,013.

Woodbridge was incorporated in 1784, and belonged previously to New-Haven and Milford.

WOLCOTT.

WOLCOTT, a small elevated township, is situated in the northern extremity of the county, 22 miles from Hartford; bounded on the north by Plymouth, in Litchfield county, and Bristol, in Hartford county, on the east by Southington, on the south by Cheshire and Waterbury, and on the west by Waterbury and Plymouth. It comprises an area of about 18 square miles; having an average length of 6 miles, and an average breadth of about 3 miles. The township is hilly and mountainous, and is situated in the vicinity of the commencement of the granitic district, which extends through the western section of the State, and comprises a considerable part of Litchfield county.

The soil is a hard, coarse, gravelly loam, and rather sterile; the lands however afford tolerable grazing, but are rough and stony. The dairy business, or making of butter and cheese, is the leading agricultural interest.

The town is watered by Mad river, a branch of the Naugatuck, which is a small but rapid stream.

The Middletown and Waterbury turnpike road, leads through the south part of the town.

The manufactures and mechanical employments of the town, in addition to those of a domestic character, are 2 Distilleries for cider spirits, 2 Grain Mills, 1 Fulling Mill, 1 Carding Machine, and 3 Tanneries. There are 2 Mercantile Stores and 2 Taverns.

The town contains 1 located Congregational Society and 1 Episcopal Society; both of which have houses for public worship. It comprises 7 School Districts & Schools, and it has 1 Social Library, 1 Clergyman and 2 Physicians. Its population, in 1810, was 952; and there are 150 Electors, 1 Company of Militia, and 150 Dwelling houses. The amount of taxable property, including polls, is $18,504. Wolcott was incorporated in 1796.

NEW-LONDON

COUNTY.

NEW-LONDON is an ancient maritime county, situated in the southeastern section of the State, upon Long Island sound; bounded on the north by Hartford, Tolland and Windham counties, on the east by the county of Windham and the State of Rhode-Island, on the south by Long Island sound, and on the west by the county of Middlesex. Its form is very irregular, which renders it difficult to give its area with exactness. It has, however, an average length from east to west of about 26 miles, with a medium breadth from north to south of nearly 20 miles; comprising an area of about 519 square miles.

The following TOPOGRAPHICAL AND STATISTICAL TABLE exhibits a view of the several towns in the county; their situation, with relation to New-London; population, according to the census of 1810; dwelling houses; religious societies; school districts, and post-offices.

Towns.	Post-offices.	Population.	Dwelling houses.	Religious societies.	School districts.	Distance from N. Lon.
New-London.	1	3283	475	4	2	
Norwich.	2	3552	568	6	15	13 m. N.
Bozrah.		960	150	2	3	14 m. N.W.
Colchester.	2	2697	450	5	16	19 m. N.W.
Franklin.	1	1161	170	3	9	20 m. N.W.
Griswold.	1	1520	230	2	12	20 m. N.E.
Groton.	1	4451	529	7	25	1 m. E.
Lisbon.		1121	170	3	8	20 m. N.E.
Lyme.	2	4321	567	7	24	16 m. W.
Montville.	1	2187	320	4	13	8 m. N.W.
N. Stonington.	1	2524	360	4	17	14 m. N.E.
Preston.	1	1764	250	5	14	14 m. N.E.
Stonington.	2	3043	450	2	8	13 m. E.
Waterford.		2135	300	2	11	4 m. N.W.

New-London county is in some respects advantageously located, and possesses superior maritime advantages, having an extensive border upon Long Island sound, which affords numerous bays, inlets and harbours.

The face of the country, soil and geological character of this county present a conspicuous and characteristic uniformity. The surface is generally uneven, or rather hilly; but no considerable section of the county is mountainous. One of the branches of the eastern granitic range terminates in the western section of this county, near Connecticut river. Exclusive of this small section, which is principally in the town of Lyme, no portion of the county can be considered as mountainous; but it is generally hilly and elevated, and comprises a small proportion only of alluvial. The hills and elevated tracts are considerably rough and stony; and hence an inconsiderable portion of the lands are improved for arable purposes. The prevailing soil is a strong, rich, gravelly loam, corresponding with the features of the primitive granitic geology, which prevail throughout the county. The lands in general are not adapted to a grain culture; although upon the intervals and other tracts, Indian corn is raised to advantage, and to a considerable extent. Rye and wheat receive less attention; the principal agricultural interests depending upon grazing. There is very little waste land in the county; and few if any tracts having a light and sterile soil. The farming interests of the county are respectable, and its physical resources abundant and durable; although the objects of husbandry are not pursued without a greater requisition of agricultural industry than is necessary in some other sections of the State. And this industry is not wanting, as the inhabitants are remarkable for their hardy and persevering habits. But industry is not always connected with enterprise; and here, as well as in other parts of the State, and more so perhaps than in some other sections, there is an evident want of a spirit of enterprise and improvement in the important concerns of agriculture. But it is gratifying to perceive that exertions are making, by the organization of a County Agricultural Society, to excite this spirit, to direct the efforts which it may produce, and, in general, to encourage and promote the important interests of husbandry.

RIVERS. The waters of the county are abundant and valuable. Its southern border, for more than thirty miles, is washed by Long Island sound, and its western border, for a considerable distance, by Connecticut river; and the interior of the county is intersected and fertilized by the Thames; its two great branches, the Quinibaug and Shetucket; and numerous other secondary streams, some of which are tributary to the Thames, and others discharge their waters into the sound. The Yantic, distinguished for its cataract and falls, and the valuable hydraulic sites which it affords, unites with the Thames at Chelsea landing. Besides this, the Pochaug and Poquatanock discharge their waters into the Thames; and the Niantic empties into Niantic bay upon the sound. In the eastern section of the county, are the Mystic and Paucatuck rivers, the latter of which forms the eastern boundary. The principal harbours are the New-London harbour, which is one of the best in the United States, the Norwich, Stonington, Mystic and Niantic harbours. The commercial interests of the county are respectable, although not extending. The fishing business receives great attention, and is more extensively carried on here than in any other section of the State. There are usually from 50 to 60 vessels engaged in the cod, mackerel and black fisheries. Besides these, the oyster, shad, and other less important branches of the fishery business, receive considerable attention; and recently, in a few instances, the sealing business has been engaged in. The various concerns of the fishing business afford an extensive employment, and are a very productive source of industry. Connected with the maritime interests, is that of ship building, which, in some sections of the county, receives considerable attention.

A manufacturing spirit has been excited in this county, and has produced some important results. In addition to the domestic manufactures, which are very extensive and important, the woolen and cotton branches are pursued to a considerable extent, by manufacturing establishments. There are 16 Woolen Factories, and 9 Cotton Factories in the county. Of the latter, there are several which are upon an extensive scale. Besides these, there are 15 Cloth Dressing establishments, and 18 Carding Machines, for customers. Of other manufacturing and mechanical establishments, there are 2 Oil Mills, 3 Paper Mills, 2 Forges and 70 Grain Mills.

There are, in the county of New-London, 56 Religious Societies, 23 School Societies, each of which is divided into a convenient number of School Districts, of which there are in all 177; 12 Social Libraries, and about 212 Mercantile Stores.

The population of the county, in 1756, was 22,844; in 1800, 34,888; and in 1810, it contained 34,707; and the aggregate amount of taxable property, including polls, in 1817, was $643,953.

NEW-LONDON.

NEW-LONDON, the semi-seat of justice of the county, and a considerable maritime post town, is situated upon the west bank of the Thames, bordering upon the sound. 13 miles south of Norwich, 42 southeast by south of Hartford, and 53 east of New-Haven; bounded on the north by Waterford, on the east by the river Thames, which separates it from Groton, on the south by Long Island sound, and on the west by Waterford. The township is about 4 miles in length, upon an average estimation, and more than three fourths of a mile in breadth, comprising about 2,400 acres, or nearly 4 square miles.

The geological character of the township is granitic, and its surface uneven and rough, being hilly and rocky; the soil is a dry gravelly loam. Of the natural growth of timber, oak and walnut prevail most; and the agricultural productions consist of Indian corn and some other grains, butter, cheese, beef, pork, grass, potatoes and other roots, and culinary vegetables; but the lands are best adapted to grazing, and the natural quality of the soil must always, in a greater or less degree, control the agricultural pursuits and interests.

The Thames washes the town upon its eastern border, and Long Island sound upon its southern border; the waters of the former are navigable for the largest vessels, and afford one of the finest harbours in the world; it is large, safe and commodious, and has five fathoms of water. On the west side of the entrance is a light-house, on a point of land which projects considerably into the sound.

The town is accommodated with a number of turnpike roads: one leading to Hartford, one to Norwich, (the first road constructed by an incorporated company in the State,) and one to New-Haven passing through Lyme.

From the maritime location of the town, the inhabitants have been led to engage in navigation, commercial and fishing business; which pursuits occupy the attention of a considerable proportion of the earning part of the population of the place, and still greater of its industry and enterprise. The navigation business consists, principally, of a coasting trade with the southern states, and a trade with the West India islands. There are also four packets, which regularly ply between this place and the city of New-York; but the line of steam boats which has been established between these two places, and which runs daily, arriving one day and returning the next, has reduced the number of regular packets. Formerly there was considerable foreign navigation carried on at this place, but for some years past it has much declined, & become nearly extinct. At the present time, the fishing business is the most important maritime pursuit; there being 35 fishing smacks engaged therein, which belong to the inhabitants of this town. The theatre of their labours is principally from Cape Cod to Egg Harbour. Mackerel and black fish are principally taken, but some cod.

The whole registered tonnage of the district of New-London, in 1805, amounted to 13,397 tons; in 1815, to 13,182 tons.

New-London contains 14 Drygoods stores, 4 Druggists' stores, 42 Grocery and Provision stores, 2 Book stores, 1 store of Hardware, 1 of Tin ware, 2 of Saddle, Trunk and Harness work, 2 Hat stores, 1 Shoe store, 1 Silversmith's store, and about 20 houses concerned in navigation. There are 10 public Inns or Taverns.

Although this town is not distinguished for its manufactures or mechanical interests, it contains 2 Printing-offices, 3 Rope walks, 1 Distillery, 1 Pottery, 3 Tanneries, 6 House carpenters, 3 Ship carpenters, 2 Block and Spar makers, 1 Sail maker, 2 Saddlers, 6 Shoe makers, 4 Tailors, 5 Butchers, 7 Bakers, 2 Tin ware factories and manufacturers, 2 Hatters, 1 Gold and Silver smith, 3 Masons and Stone cutters, 2 Barbers, 4 Tallow chandlers, 3 Curriers and Tanners, 2 Coopers, and 2 Blacksmiths.

The population of the town, in 1810, was 3,283; and there are 350 Freemen or Electors, 3 companies of militia, and about 475 Dwelling houses.

The amount of taxable property, including polls, is $42,618.

The civil divisions of the town are one located Ecclesiastical Society, two School districts, and an incorporated city. Besides the located, there is a Society of Episcopalians, 1 of Baptists, and 1 of Methodists. These several Societies are all accommodated with houses for public worship. There is a district or primary School maintained in each of the School Districts, for several months in the year; besides which there is a free Grammar School, that usually contains from 150 to 200 scholars; a Female Academy, and a School called the Union School.

The city of New-London was incorporated in 1784, by the name of the Mayor, Aldermen, Common Council men and Freemen of the city of New-London, who possess the corporate or municipal authority of the city. The Mayor is elected by the Freemen, but holds his office during the pleasure of the General Assembly; the Aldermen and Common Council men are annually appointed by the Freemen. Since the last division of the town, it has been reduced to the same corporate limits as the city; so that in noticing the latter, we shall have no reference to its corporate extent, but only to the compact settlement, or the idea of a city in common acceptance. The city of New-London is pleasantly situated upon the west bank of the Thames, about 3 miles from its entrance into the Sound. Its site, being a declivity of land bordering upon the river, is excellent, and its harbour unrivalled. The city is irregularly laid out, and is built upon nearly thirty different streets; many of which, however, are very inconsiderable. The principal is Court-street, which, extending from Market-square, adjoining the river, in a northwesterly direction to the Court-house upon Huntington-street, divides the city into nearly two equal sections. This street is spacious and pleasant, is well built, and contains some of the public buildings and public and private offices, the naval office, the two banking houses, two printing offices, and many neat and handsome dwelling houses, and a proportion of the mercantile stores. At the east end of this street is Market-square, bordering upon the river, upon which stands the market and the public gaol. Bank-street commences at Market-square, and extends southerly, parallel with the river; and Beach-street commences at Market-square, and runs northerly, parallel with the river. Both of these streets communicate with the wharves, are the seats of most of the maritime business, and contain a great proportion of the grocery and provision stores, and a number of private offices. Main-street is situated back of Beach-street, and runs in nearly a parallel direction, extending from Court-street to the northern extremity of the city; it is well built, and contains a denser population than any other street. There is a communication between this street and Huntington-street, by Federal-street, situated in the eastern section of the city, and by Church-street, situated farther west. These streets are tolerably well built, and the latter contains the Episcopal church.

Union-street intersects Court and Church streets, and extends northerly to Federal-street. The Baptist, Methodist and Congregational meeting houses are situated upon this street, which communicates with Bank-street, by Golden-street, and the latter is intersected by Green-street. In the back part of the city, upon the height of ground, is Huntington-street, running in nearly a parallel direction with the river. This street has an elevated and prospective situation, overlooking most of the other parts of the city. It affords a pleasant and healthful residence, although it is but imperfectly built.

The city of New-London contains about 450 Dwelling houses, more than 60 Stores of every description, 4 Houses for public worship, one for Congregationalists, one for Episcopalians, one for Baptists and one for Methodists; the Naval office of the District, a Post office, two Newspaper establishments, each of which issues a weekly paper, the one a super-royal and the other a medium sheet; 2 Banks, one called New-London Bank, incorporated in 1807, with a capital of $500,000; the other called Union Bank, incorporated in 1792, with a capital of $100,000; and a Marine Insurance Company, incorporated in 1805, with a capital which cannot be less than $100,000. There are in the city 6 Physicians, 7 Attornies and 4 Clergymen.

The city is defended by Fort Trumbull and Fort Griswold; the former situated upon the New-London, and the latter upon the Groton side of the river. Fort Trumbull has undergone, at different times, important repairs, since the revolutionary war, the expense of which had amounted to $19,318 previously to the late war; during which this, and also Fort Griswold, received additional repairs.

The first English settlement in New-London was made in 1646; and the township was laid out into lots in 1648. This place was called by the natives Nameaug; and from its being the seat of the Pequot tribe of Indians, was called by the English, at an early period, Pequot. It was the seat of Sassacus, the Grand Sachem of Long Island and of part of Connecticut and Narragansett. New-London has been rendered conspicuous for its sufferings during the revolutionary war, and as the theatre of various hostile operations. On the 6th of September, 1781, a large proportion of the town was burned by Benedict Arnold. After the close of the war, in 1783, the General Assembly appointed Commissioners to ascertain and estimate the damages which had been sustained by the several towns in this State, that had been ravaged by the British troops during the war. From the investigation which was made in pursuance of this authority, it was estimated, that the

BIOGRAPHY.

damages sustained by the town of New-London, amounted to $485,980; which estimate, however, included not only buildings, but merchandize, and losses of almost every kind.

To compensate the sufferers in this, and the other towns, the General Assembly, in May 1793, granted them 500,000 acres of the tract of land reserved by Connecticut, at their cession of lands to the United States; lying south of the western part of Lake Erie, being what are now called the fire lands, in the western part of the western reserve, in the State of Ohio.

During the late war, New-London was again the theatre of hostile indications. A considerable squadron, under the command of Commodore Hardy, having chased two of our frigates into its harbour, blockaded it for a length of time. The concentration of a considerable force of the enemy, in the vicinity of this place, produced considerable alarm, and occasioned a large proportion of the militia, in the vicinity, to be called out; and subsequently, more regular and equal drafts were made, and detachments of militia, from different parts of the State, were concentrated at this place and vicinity. Besides the militia, there was a considerable body of United States' troops stationed here. The forts were well supplied, and strongly garrisoned; but, notwithstanding the "dreadful note of preparation," the enemy made no attempt upon a town, which, nearly forty years before, they had reduced to desolation, and its inhabitants to ruin, by a spirit of warfare, which belongs only to barbarians. New-London will long remain upon the page of history, alike a monument of the evils of war, and of the expense at which our glorious independence was achieved.

BIOGRAPHY. Gen. *Jedediah Huntington*, although a native of Norwich, was long a resident in this town. He died 25th September, 1818, aged 75 years; having survived every general officer of the revolution, except Gen. Starke, the hero of Bennington.

Gen. Huntington was regularly educated at Harvard College, and in early life, engaged in mercantile pursuits; but, at the commencement of the revolutionary contest, his active and enterprising mind, and ardent attachment to the cause of liberty and his country, would not suffer him to remain in the "dull pursuits of civil life," and he entered the army at an early period. In 1775, he commanded a regiment. His intelligence, activity, bravery, judgment and fidelity as an officer, secured to him advancement; the affections of the army; the respect and gratitude of his country; and the attachment and lasting confidence of Washington. He continued in the service through the war, and attained to the rank of a general officer. After the peace of 1783, securing the independence of the colonies, the object of his solicitude and of his toils, he retired to his residence in his native state, were he was employed in various civil offices, until appointed by President Washington collector of the port of New-London; the duties of which office he discharged, to the entire satisfaction of the public and the government, during a period, embracing four successive administrations.

NORWICH.

NORWICH, a wealthy commercial post town, and the semi-seat of justice of the county, is situated at the head of navigation, on the Thames or Pequot river, in north lat. 41° 34' and west lon. 72° 29'. It is 13 miles north of New-London, and 38 southeast of Hartford; bounded on the north by Franklin, on the east by the Shetucket and Thames rivers, which separate it from Lisbon and Preston, on the south by Montville, and on the west by Franklin and Bozrah. The township has an average length of 7 miles, with a medium breadth of about 3 miles, comprising an area of about 21 square miles.

The surface of the township presents an interesting diversity of hill and dale. Its geological character is primitive, and the prevailing soil is a dark coloured gravelly loam, generally strong and fertile. The natural growth consists of oak, walnut, chesnut and other deciduous trees; and the agricultural productions, of Indian corn, grass, butter, cheese, &c. Upon the borders of the Thames, Shetucket and the Yantic, there are considerable tracts of alluvial, which are very productive in Indian corn. The uplands are best adapted to grazing. The various objects of husbandry and horticulture, common to the State, are attended to in this town.

The township is well watered, its eastern border being washed, throughout its whole length from north to south, by the Thames and Shetucket; and its area intersected by the Yantic, which runs through the town in a north-easterly and southwesterly direction, and, uniting with the Shetucket, forms the harbour. This stream, about a mile from its mouth, has a very remarkable cataract. The bed of the river consists of a solid rock, having a perpendicular height of ten or twelve feet, over which the whole body of water falls in an entire sheet upon a bed of rocks below. The river here is compressed into a very narrow channel, the banks consisting of solid rock, and being bold and elevated. For a distance of fifteen or twenty rods, the channel or bed of the river has a gradual descent, is crooked and covered with pointed rocks. The rock, forming the bed of the river at the bottom of the perpendicular falls, is curiously excavated, some of the cavities being five or six feet deep, from the constant pouring of the sheet of water for a succession of ages. At the bottom of the falls, there is a broad bason, where the enraged and agitated element assumes its usual smoothness and placidity. The scenery at these falls is peculiarly novel and sublime; and the river here affords some of the finest sites for hydraulic works that are to be found in the State, or perhaps in New-England.

There is a safe and commodious harbour, formed from the union of the Yantic with the Shetucket; it consists of a spacious bason, and has sufficient depth of water to admit of vessels of considerable burthen.

There are two principal bridges in the town, one across the mouth of the Yantic, which is a permanent and commodious bridge, constructed in the form of a wharf,

NORWICH. 147

and at a great expense; and one across the Shetucket, which is a toll bridge, erected in 1817, at an expense of $10,000, and connecting the town with Preston. Besides these, there is a foot bridge across the Shetucket, about half a mile below the toll bridge, which was erected in 1818. It is 120 feet in length, and 5 feet wide, being designed only for foot passengers.

The fisheries in the Thames are important; large quantities of shad, and some salmon, being annually taken. Oysters also abound in this river. They are taken plentifully, and are of an excellent flavour.

Norwich is accommodated with several Turnpike roads; one leading to Providence, one to Hartford, through Lebanon, one to the same place through Colchester, one to New-London, one to Woodstock, one to Windham, and one authorized to New-Haven, and laid out as far as Connecticut river.

The population of Norwich, in 1810, was 3528; and there are about 400 Electors, and 4 Companies of Militia, 1 Regular Company, 1 of Artillery, 1 of Light Infantry and 1 of Cavalry.

There are in Norwich 568 Dwelling Houses, about 45 Dry Goods, Hardware, and Crockery Stores, 2 Book Stores, 2 or more Druggists' Stores, 2 Paper Mills, 1 Marble Paper Manufactory, 1 Gin Distillery, 1 Pottery, 2 Manufactories of Morocco Leather, 1 Cotton Factory, containing 1200 spindles, 1 Woolen Factory, 1 Carding Machine for customers, 5 Tanneries, 6 Grain Mills and 6 Saw Mills. There are 6 Religious Societies, 2 of Congregationalists, 2 of Methodists, 1 of Baptists and 1 of Episcopalians; 15 primary Schools; 10 practising Attornies, 6 Clergymen and 5 Physicians.

The aggregate list of the town, in 1817, was $60,371.

The civil divisions of the town are 2 Parishes or located Societies, 15 School Districts and an incorporated City.

Norwich City was incorporated in May, 1784. Its limits are extensive, and comprise a great proportion of the population of the township. It is divided into three distinct and compact sections; the first and most important is Chelsea Landing. This section is situated at the point of land formed by the junction of Shetucket and Yantic rivers, whose united waters constitute the Thames. Its site is very irregular and romantic, consisting of the declivity of a hill, which is high and rocky. The houses are built in tiers, rising one above another, having partially artificial foundations. There are here more than 150 Houses, a Post office, 4 Churches, more than 30 Stores, several excellent public Inns, various Warehouses, Mechanics' shops, &c. This is a compact settlement, and an active and busy place; being the seat of most of the commercial and maritime business of the town. The next section is called the Town; and is situated in a pleasant vale, partially surrounded with lofty hills, about two miles northwest from Chelsea. This section is more extensive, but less compact than Chelsea, consisting of a number of pleasant, rural streets. Here there is a spacious public square, a Court House, Post office, Church, and about 200 Houses and Stores. The other section, which is called Bean Hill, is situated upon the Hartford road, in the western part of the town. It consists principally of one street, is less compact and populous than either of the other, and has little commercial business; but is a pleasant and prospective situation, and affords a very agreeable residence.

In Norwich city there are about 500 Dwelling houses, 5 or 6 Houses for public worship, a Court House and County Gaol. Besides the public District Schools, already noticed, there are in the city two Schools for young ladies, and several other private Schools, for instruction in the common and higher branches of education. There is one respectable Social Library, consisting of about 500 volumes. There is one Newspaper establishment, a Bank, called the Norwich Bank, incorporated in 1796, with a capital of $200,000; a Fire Insurance Company, incorporated in 1818, with a capital of $100,000; a Mutual Assurance Company, and the Norwich Channel Company, incorporated some years since, for the purpose of improving the navigation of the river Thames, below Chelsea Landing.

Norwich, situated at the head of navigable waters, and having a considerably extensive interior country, generally well settled and flourishing, possesses very considerable advantages for commerce. Its commercial interests, however, and its general prosperity, have experienced various vicissitudes. At one period, the commercial business of Norwich was extensive and important, and rapidly increasing. The tonnage of the place, for one of its size, was very great; there having once been 6000 tons of shipping owned here. But for several years since, from the general declension of the West India trade, and from various other causes, tending to divert the industry and capital of the place into other channels, the commerce of Norwich has very much declined. There are at present but 12 vessels owned here, which are employed principally in a coasting trade to New-York and elsewhere. There is a line of steam-boats which communicates between this place and New-York. Norwich is the natural depot of the produce of a back country of considerable extent, upon the two great branches of the Thames; and, being at the head of navigable waters, and uniting other advantages, its commercial interests are respectable, although its navigation business is but inconsiderable. It is also favourably situated for the fishing business, which receives considerable attention; it possesses superior advantages for manufactures, which at no distant period, it is believed, will be improved to an extent corresponding with the private interests and public utility, that must ultimately proceed from the permanent and extensive establishment of manufactures in this country. From these and other considerations, it is believed that the population, business and importance of Norwich will progress in an equal ratio with those of most of the other considerable towns in the State.

The township of Norwich was purchased of the Mohegan sachem, Uncas, and his two sons, Owaneco and Attawanhood, by Thomas Leffingwell, John Mason, James Fitch and others, to the number of thirty-five, in 1659. About $230 were given as the purchase money. In the spring of the next year, 1660, the settlement was commenced; the first settlers consisting of the Rev. James Fitch and a considerable part of the members of his society from Saybrook. The settlement being begun, it soon received the accession of three or four families from New-London, and several from Plymouth, and other towns in Massachusetts. In 1663, the deed of the township was recorded by order of the General Assembly, its limits ascertained, and a patent granted therefor. For a number of years after the commencement of the settlement, the Mohegans were its principal security from the Pequots and other hostile tribes.

BIOGRAPHY. The Hon. Samuel Huntington, for several years Governor of this State, was a resident in this town. He was elected Governor in 1785, succeeding Matthew Griswold; and was re-elected for eleven years, and until his death. The long period in which he enjoyed the confidence of his fellow citizens, and the most distinguished honours of the State, is the best evidence of his conspicuous talents and virtues. In his public and private relations and duties, he was considered a very estimable man. He died 5th Jan. 1796, aged 65 years.

Asa Spalding Esq. of this town, was a very eminent lawyer, and a distinguished citizen. He was a native of Canterbury, and born in 1757. He was educated at Yale College; and soon after he graduated, entered upon the study of law with Judge Adams of Litchfield. Having completed his professional studies, he came to this town, previously to the close of the revolutionary war, in 1783, with a view to establish himself in business, and remained here until his death. He soon became distinguished in his profession, and ultimately at the head of it; ranking among the first lawyers in the State. His talents were solid and profound, but not brilliant; and, although he was an able, he was not esteemed an eloquent speaker. For a comprehensive and penetrating mind, for solidity of judgment, for legal science, for a faculty of investigation, which enabled him to discover the merits of the most intricate cause, however involved in obscurity and difficulty, from folly, artifice or fraud, and for persevering habits of professional industry, he has been surpassed by few. He was for many years attorney for the State, for the county in which he lived; he was also, for several years preceding his death, supported as a candidate for the office of Governor. But, however eminent as a lawyer, and however important his public consideration, Mr. Spalding was most distinguished for his private virtues, and the peculiar traits of his personal character. He was remarkable for his faithfulness and perseverance in every concern in which he engaged, and for his indefatigable industry, which no obstacles could discourage, and no difficulties impair. He was also equally distinguished for a rigid and systematic economy, which he never abandoned, and for the simplicity and plainness of his style of living. He was in an eminent degree both a *plain* and an *honest* man. And these qualities, if not necessarily associated, have, it must be admitted, a striking affinity. They are not only plants which grow in the same soil, but they flourish best in the neighbourhood of each other. His integrity, his talents, and his characteristic sincerity and regard for truth, led him to despise the arts of dissimulation and flattery, and to exhibit to the world his own character and that of others in the image of truth, and free from all disguises. Hence he had his enemies as well as friends. But if he had enemies, they were such only because " truth will often offend." From the necessary operation of those personal qualifications which we have noticed, he acquired a very large estate ; and his life adds one to the innumerable examples which demonstrate, that success in life, the acquisition of property, the attainment of character, of influence and of consideration, essentially depend upon just and regular moral and social habits, integrity, industry, economy and prudence. He died in August 1811.

BOZRAH.

BOZRAH is an inconsiderable township, situated on the northern border of the county, 33 miles from Hartford, 14 from New-London, and five from Norwich; bounded on the north by Lebanon and Franklin, on the east by Norwich, on the south by Montville, and on the west by Colchester and Lebanon. Its average length is 4 and a half miles, and its average breadth 4 miles, comprising an area of about 18 square miles. The township is uneven, consisting of hill and dale ; its geological character is granitic, and the soil a gravelly loam, which is generally rich, warm and fertile. The natural growth is oak, walnut, chesnut, &c., and the agricultural productions, grass, corn, rye, oats & flax, the latter of which is cultivated to a considerable extent, and is of an excellent quality; butter, cheese, beef and pork.

The most considerable stream, by which the town is watered, is the Yantic river, a branch of Norwich little river. There is a small pond or lake, called Gardiner's lake, partly in this town, and partly in Montville and Colchester. The Norwich and Colchester turnpike passes through the northern section of the town.

The population of the town, in 1810, was 960; and there are 150 Dwelling houses, 100 Freemen or qualified Electors, and 1 company of militia.

There are in this town, 1 Cotton Factory, 1 Forge, 3 Grain Mills, 2 Fulling Mills & Clothiers' works, 2 Carding Machines, 1 Tannery, 2 Mercantile Stores, and 3 public Inns.

The amount of taxable property, including polls, is $24,647. The town comprises one located Congregational Society & church, and one church and Society of Baptists; three School districts and Schools, and one small Social Library. The professional men are two Clergymen, & one Physician.

Bozrah was incorporated as a town, in 1786, previously to which it belonged to Norwich.

COLCHESTER.

COLCHESTER is a post township, situated in the northwestern extremity of the county, 23 miles from Hartford, and 40 from New-Haven; bounded on the north by Marlborough and Hebron, the former in Hartford, and the latter in Tolland county, on the east by Lebanon and Bozrah, the former in Windham county, on the south by Montville and Lyme, and on the west by East-Haddam and Chatham, in Middlesex county; so that the township borders upon four different counties, and eight different towns. Its average length is about 9 miles, and its average breadth nearly 6 miles, comprising an area of about 50 square miles. The face of the country is uneven, being considerably hilly, and is somewhat rough and stony; the prevailing soil is a gravelly loam, and generally hard and coarse, but tolerably strong and fertile. The geological character of the township is primitive, and its internal structure consists of granite, micaceous schistus, and other rocks of an original formation. We have ascertained nothing as to its mineralogy. Its natural growth is deciduous. The soil is best adapted to grazing; and butter, cheese, beef and cattle constitute the most important agricultural interests. Some grains are cultivated; oats, corn and rye are the principal.

The town is watered by Salmon river, and several small streams. In addition to the public or county roads, the town is accommodated with several turnpikes; New-London and Hartford turnpike, Norwich turnpike, and East-Haddam and Middletown turnpike, all lead into the centre of the town, where they intersect each other.

The only considerable manufacturing establishments are one Woolen Factory, and one Iron Works establishment, or forge. Besides these, there are three Tanneries, eight Grain Mills and eight Saw Mills. There are seven Mercantile Stores.

The population of the town, in 1810, was 2697; and there are about 350 Freemen or Electors, 2 entire companies, and a part of another company of militia, and about 450 Dwelling houses. The amount of taxable property, including polls, is $70,887.

The civil divisions of the town are 3 located Ecclesiastical Societies or parishes, and 16 School districts. Besides the located, there is a Society of Baptists, and one also of Methodists. The Methodist, Baptist and located Societies are all accommodated with houses for public worship; and one of the latter, West-Chester Society, is possessed of a fund, sufficient for the support of the ministry, and also, a free grammar School, for two thirds of the year. The several School districts are provided with School houses, and maintain primary Schools for several months in the year.

In the first located Society, there is a small, but pleasant village, having an elevated and healthful situation; it contains about 40 Dwelling houses, and a Congregational church, and an academy of considerable celebrity, called Bacon Academy, from Mr. Pierpont Bacon, its benefactor and founder. It was established in 1800, and possesses $35,000 in funds; has a large brick building, 75 feet by 34, and three stories high, which is spacious and commodious, uniting all the advantages and conveniences, required by the number of scholars that usually attend the institution, and the different branches of learning which are taught. It is a free School for the inhabitants of the Society, and is open for scholars from abroad, upon very accommodating and moderate terms. This institution is considered as one of the most flourishing academies in the State.

There are in the town, 3 Clergymen, 2 Attornies, and 5 Physicians.

Colchester was settled in 1699, being within the original limits of the county of Hartford.

FRANKLIN.

FRANKLIN is a post township, situated on the northern border of the county, 34 miles from Hartford; bounded on the northeast by Windham, and the Shetucket river, which separates it from Lisbon, on the southeast by Norwich, on the southwest by Bozrah, and on the northwest by Lebanon, in Windham county. Its average length from northeast to southwest is 5 miles, and its average breadth 4 miles, comprising about 20 square miles.

The township is diversified with hills and dales, and the geological structure and soil are of a granitic character, the latter being generally a gravelly loam; but in some small sections it is a rich, deep, chocolate coloured loam. The lands are best adapted to grazing, and the making of butter and cheese, and beef and pork, are leading agricultural interests.

The Shetucket washes the northeastern border of the town, and it is intersected by a branch of the Yantic river, an inconsiderable stream. There are several fisheries on the Shetucket.

The Hartford and Norwich turnpike passes through this town, and also one leading from Norwich to Windham.

The population of the town, in 1810, was 1161; and there are 150 Freemen or Electors, 1 Company of Militia, and a part of 2 others, and 170 Dwelling houses. There are 1 Woolen Factory, 3 Grain Mills, 1 Fulling Mill and Clothier's works, 1 Tannery, 4 Mercantile Stores, and 4 Public Inns.

The town contains 1 located

Congregational Society & Church, 1 Society of Baptists and 1 of Methodists. It has 9 School Districts and Schools, 1 Social Library, 4 Physicians and 2 Clergymen.

The amount of taxable property, including polls, is $30,287.

Franklin belonged originally to Norwich, and was incorporated in May 1786.

GRISWOLD.

GRISWOLD is a post town, situated upon the east side of the Quinibaug river, 48 miles east from Hartford; bounded south on Preston and North-Stonington, east on Voluntown, north on Plainfield and Canterbury, and west on the Quinibaug river, which separates it from Lisbon. Its average length is 8 miles, and its average breadth 4 miles, comprising about 32 square miles.

The surface is uneven, being diversified with hill and dale. The geological character of the town is granitic. There are, however, some rocks of micaceous schistus. The prevailing soil is a gravelly loam, interspersed with some sections of sandy loam; it is considerably fertile and productive. There are some low marsh lands upon the Pochaug river. The natural growth consists of chesnut, oak, walnut, maple, &c. and the agricultural productions are grass, Indian corn, some rye and oats, butter, cheese, beef and pork.

The western border of the town is washed by the Quinibaug; and the Pochaug, a sluggish stream, runs through it. There are several fisheries for shad and salmon upon the former of these streams.

The Norwich and Providence turnpike road leads through this town.

Although agriculture is the principal pursuit of the inhabitants, yet manufactures have received considerable attention. There are 3 Cotton Factories, 1 Woolen Factory, 6 Grain Mills, 2 Fulling Mills and Clothiers' works, 1 Carding Machine and 1 Tannery. There are 6 Mercantile Stores and 2 Public Inns.

The population of the town is 1520; and there are 230 Dwelling houses, 200 Freemen or Electors, and 3 Companies of Militia.

The civil divisions are 1 located Congregational Society and 12 School Districts; there is also 1 Society of Baptists; the Congregational Society is provided with a Church; and there is a School house, and a primary or common School maintained in each of the School Districts.

Jewett's City is a pleasant and flourishing village, situated upon the Quinibaug, containing about 30 Dwelling houses and a Post office. There are 2 Physicians, 1 Attorney, 1 Clergyman, and 1 Social Library in the town.

The amount of taxable property, as estimated in making up lists, including polls, is $41,909.

Griswold was originally a part of Preston, and was incorporated as a town in 1815.

GROTON.

GROTON, a large post town, is situated on the east side of the Thames, being 43 miles southeast from Hartford, and 54 miles east from New-Haven. It is bounded north by Preston, east by North-Stonington, and the Mystic, which separates it from Stonington, west by the Thames, which divides it from New-London, Waterford and Montville, and south by Fisher's Island sound.

The township has an average length of 12 miles, and an average breadth of 6 miles; and contains about 72 square miles, or 46,000 acres.

The town is watered, exclusive of the Thames, which washes its western borders, by the Mystic, the Poquonock and the Poquatonuck. The Mystic is navigable for sloops to Mystic village. The Poquonock runs through the centre of the town, and discharges its waters into Fisher's Island sound. The Poquatonock waters the north section of the town, and unites with the Thames.

The township is uneven, being hilly and stony. The soil is a rich gravelly loam, better adapted to grazing than to grain. Indian corn, however, is cultivated extensively, and with abundant success. The geological structure of the town consists of granite and other primitive formations.

The civil divisions of the town are two located Societies and 25 School Districts. There are several small villages, Groton Bank, Gales' Ferry, Mystic and Poquonock.

If any discriminations are to be made in this respect, the inhabitants of Groton, for industry and enterprise, are not surpassed by those of any other town in the State.

In addition to the pursuits of agriculture, the fishing business is carried on to a considerable extent, and domestic manufactures receive great attention.

The smack fishery is engaged in by the inhabitants, and pursued to advantage, and considerably extensively. The smacks find a market for live fish at New-York, Charleston and Savannah, as well as at the different markets in this State. The cod and smack fisheries afford employment to a portion of the inhabitants, and are sources of considerable wealth.

Whilst the men are employed in the business of fishing, the women are engaged at the loom, and other branches of domestic manufactures. It has been estimated, says our correspondent, that for seven years past, there have been, on an average, 500,000 yards of cotton cloth wove annually in Groton by private families, for manufacturing establishments in the neighbourhood and elsewhere. The average price of weaving may be considered about 8 cents per yard, and at this price, 500,000 yds. amount to the surprising sum of $40,000, as the annual product of one department of female industry; making, for the 7 years, $280,000, which is more than the value of the whole real estate of some of our towns. Domestic industry is almost necessarily accompanied with economy, simplicity, and plainness of life and manners; and it is to be hoped that these cardinal, social and domestic virtues will long withstand the deleterious and illusory ideas of "fashionable life," which are becoming diffused throughout our country far and wide.

In addition to domestic manufactures, there is 1 Woolen and 1 Cotton Manufacturing establishment in the town. There are 11 Grain Mills, 11 Saw Mills, 2 Fulling Mills, 5 Tanneries, 2 Carding Machines, 19 Dry Goods and Grocery Stores, 118 Mechanics' Shops, and 215 Corn Houses.

The population of the town, in 1810, was 4451; and there are at this time 483 qualified Electors, 268 Militia, and 529 Dwelling houses.

The amount of the taxable polls and estate of the town is $71,586.

There are 2 Congregational Churches, 2 Baptist Societies and Churches, 1 also for Methodists, 1 for Episcopalians, and 1 for Rogerene Quakers. There are 6 Clergymen, 3 Physicians, 25 Common Schools and 1 Social Library.

Groton was incorporated in 1705, having, until that period, belonged to the town of New-London. The town is conspicuous, for some events of the revolutionary war, and for the severity of its sufferings. On the 6th of September, 1781, Fort Griswold, situated on a height, on the bank of the Thames, opposite New-London city, was assaulted by the British, under the immediate command of Major Beckworth; Arnold, who directed the enterprise, being at New-London. The garrison, which consisted of 150 men, almost all of whom were inhabitants of Groton, being either militia or volunteers, under the command of the brave Col. Ledyard, made a spirited and gallant defence; the enemy being twice repulsed, and with a severe loss. On the third assault, the fort was carried; and the infamous Beckworth ordered the garrison put to the sword, after they had surrendered themselves prisoners of war. Thus 70 men, the flower of the town, were sacrificed to the vengeance of the enemy. The compact part of the town was burned at the same time, occasioning a loss to the inhabitants of $77,390.

BIOGRAPHY. *John Ledyard*, the distinguished American traveller, was a native of this town. The enterprising and adventurous spirit, by which Ledyard was characterized, disclosed itself at an early period. Before he had scarcely "ripened into perfect manhood," he was led, by his adventurous and enterprising propensities, to spend several years among the native Indians. He was one of Capt. Cook's men, and sailed round the world with that bold and adventurous navigator, and was with him at the time he was killed at the Sandwich Islands. After his return to America, he published an account of this voyage. After this, he contemplated to engage in a trading adventure to Nootka sound; and from thence, to traverse the continent of America, from the Pacific to the Atlantic, but he was disappointed in this object. But neither disappointments nor difficulties could depress his adventurous spirit, or discourage him in his favourite objects; and, accordingly, he determined to visit Europe, with a view to traverse the interior of the eastern continent, as far as Kamschatka. With this view, he crossed from England to Ostend, and proceeded from thence by Denmark to Stockholm; and from this place he walked round the head of the Gulf of Bothnia to Petersburgh. When he arrived here, his situation was peculiarly distressing; he was without shoes or stockings, and what is still worse, having no money, not even sufficient to supply these indispensable articles, and in a foreign land, and among entire strangers. From this distressing situation he was relieved by the kindness of the Portuguese ambassador, and the liberality of Sir Joseph Banks, a distinguished member of the African Association in England; the former procuring for him 20 guineas, on the credit of the latter. The Portuguese ambassador also obtained for him the privilege of accompanying a detachment that was to proceed with stores to Yakutz, in Siberia, six thousand miles to the eastward. Having penetrated this immense distance into the interior of Asia, he travelled from thence to the shore of the Kamschatkan sea, which he intended to cross, but was prevented by the ice, and was obliged to return to Yakutz. Here he experienced the mortification and personal violence of being forcibly seized by some Russian soldiers, in the name of the Empress, and conveyed upon a sledge to the frontiers of Poland, where he was turned adrift; being informed, as a consolation to his wounded feelings, that if he was found again in the Russian dominions, he would be hanged. He travelled to Koningsberg, in the most destitute and forlon condition; from whence, having again obtained pecuniary aid, upon the credit of Sir Joseph Banks, he returned to England. Here, having visited his benefactor, he was soon engaged in the service of the African Association, and had the honour of being the first person employed by them, to explore the interior of the African continent. On being asked by a member of the Association, when he would set out on his perilous geographical mission? "To-morrow morning," he replied, without the least hesitation. The Association were much pleased with the manliness of his person, his determined resolution, his inquisitive and adventurous spirit, his indefatigable perseverance, his unequalled fortitude in enduring hardships, and his sagacity and intelligence. Having set out upon this arduous and dangerous enterprise, he arrived at Cairo in Egypt in August, 1788. Whilst here, he constantly visited the slave markets, to obtain information, upon the various subjects connected with his mission, and the views of the Association, of the travelling merchants of the caravans. His ideas and observations upon the Egyptians were published after his death, in the Reports of the Association, and are remarkable for their originality, and evince a very acute discernment, a just and critical observation, and a sound and discriminating mind, improved by extensive experience, and free from local prejudices. The sufferings of Ledyard were great, beyond conception. On speaking upon this subject, previously to his setting out upon his African mission, he says, "I am accustomed to hardships; I have known both hunger and nakedness, to the utmost extremity of human suffering; I have known what it is to have food given to me as charity to a madman; and I have, at times, been obliged to shelter myself under the miseries of that character, to avoid a heavier calamity. My distresses have been greater than I have ever owned, or ever will own, to any man. Such evils are terrible to bear, but they never yet had power to deter me from my purpose. If I live, I will faithfully perform, in its utmost extent, my engagements to the Society; and if I perish in the attempt, my honour will still be safe, for death cancels all bonds." And it was decreed that the latter should be his destiny. Whilst here, he experienced repeated vexations from the disappointments and delays, as to the departure of the caravan for Sennar, that he was to accompany, which, it is thought, contributed to throw him into a violent bilious fever, with which he was seized; and to relieve himself, he most unadvisedly took a large dose of vitriolic acid, and to remove the pain which this occasioned, a powerful emetic. These violent medicines were too much for the firmest constitution, and the hardy traveller fell a victim to them. Thus died John Ledyard, one of the most distinguished travellers of the age, and a very extraordinary man. When we consider the extent of his travels, and the circumstances attending them; that most of them were undertaken under appearances peculiarly discouraging; without the assistance or patronage of the wealthy and the great; and without any adequate pecuniary means to sustain them; when we consider the unparalleled hardships which he endured, the difficulties which he encountered, and the continual perils "by land, by sea, and from false brethren," to which he was exposed; what an astonishing conception does it give us of his unbounded curiosity, of his bold and adventurous spirit, of his enlarged and comprehensive views, and his determined resolution and unyielding perseverance, which no obstacles could discourage, and no difficulties impair? He ranks first among American travellers; and the name of Ledyard will go down to posterity, with those of Park, Lucas, Houghton, and other adventurers, who have found a grave in attempting to explore the interior secrets of the African continent, that degraded part of the globe. Such was John Ledyard, an American, and a native of this State; yet so entirely has he been neglected by his country, that he is almost unknown, and no account of his life and travels has yet appeared in his native land, although the character, travels and life of Ledyard could not fail of doing honour to his country. For this short and imperfect account, we are indebted principally to the Quarterly Review.

Nathan Daboll late of this town, was a very distinguished mathematician. He was the author of a very valuable system of Arithmetic, designed for common schools, which has been very extensively used, and generally approved of, as a simplified and improved treatise, facilitating the learning of the rudiments of this important science. From his mathematical acquirements and exertions, he was eminently a useful citizen.

LISBON.

LISBON is a small irregular township, situated upon the northern border of the county; at the point of land, or fork of the Quinibaug and Shetucket rivers, 7 miles from Norwich, and 45 from Hartford; bounded on the north by Windham and Canterbury, in Windham county, on the east by Griswold, on the south by Preston, and on the west by Norwich and Franklin. The form of the township is irregular, and its dimensions cannot be ascertained with accuracy; but it comprises an area of about 17 square miles. It is uneven, and considerably hilly; upon the borders of the rivers, there are small intervals, or tracts of alluvial.

The town is well watered by the Quinibaug and Shetucket rivers, which circumscribe it upon all sides, except its northern boundary. There are sevearl considerable bridges across these rivers, and several fisheries of shad and salmon.

The natural growth of timber consists of oak, walnut, chesnut, and other trees common to this region. The agricultural productions are Indian corn, some rye, butter and cheese, &c. The prevailing character of the soil is a gravelly loam, occasionally interspersed with a sandy loam, especially in the vallies, and it is considerably fertile and productive.

There are two turnpike roads that pass through the town; one leading from Norwich to Providence, in Rhode Island, and the other from the former place, to Woodstock &c.

The more considerable manufacturing and mechanical employments, aside from those of a domestic character, consist of 1 Cotton Factory, 1 Woolen Factory, 1 Bellows Manufactory, 4 Grain Mills, 2 Fulling Mills, and 1 Carding Machine. There are 2 Mercantile Stores and 3 Taverns.

The population of the town, in 1810, was 1123; and there are 170 Dwelling houses, 150 Freemen or Electors, and 1 company of militia.

The civil divisions of the town are two located Congregational Societies, and eight School districts; there is also a Society of Baptists, two houses for public worship, & eight common Schools. There are two Physicians and two Clergymen, one Baptist, and one Congregational.

The amount of taxable property, including polls, is $29,932.

Lisbon belonged, previously to its incorporation as a town in 1786, to Norwich.

LYME.

LYME, an extensive maritime post township, is situated at the mouth of Connecticut river, on the east side; 40 miles southeast from Hartford, and about the same distance east from New-Haven; bounded north on East-Haddam and Colchester, east on Montville and Waterford, south on Long Island sound, and west on Connecticut river.

The following lines and courses, circumscribe and define the limits and extent of the township: from the end of black point to Waterford corner, in a N N E course by Niantic bay, is 2 and a half miles; thence north upon Waterford line, 6 miles; thence N N W upon the line of Montville, about 4 miles; thence nearly north, upon the same line or boundary, about 2 miles; thence west upon the line of Colchester, nearly 3 miles; thence south upon the line of East-Haddam, 3 miles; thence west upon the line of East-Haddam, nearly 7 miles; the line or boundary upon Connecticut river, is about 10 miles; and that upon the sound, is about 8 miles; comprising an area of about 100 square miles, being the largest township in the State. Its surface is strikingly diversified. About one half of the township is level, or moderately hilly, comprising the borders of the sound; its bays and inlets; the large tracts of marine alluvial, or salt marsh; the numerous and extensive intervals upon the rivers, and other sections. The other division of the township is rough; being hilly or mountainous, and stony. Of the mountainous features of the town, there are numerous granitic ledges. Near the mouth of Four Mile river, several distinct ridges commence, consisting of a succession of hills, which range northwardly, and become more elevated, as they extend into the interior. Within the township, near the Connecticut, north of Eight Mile river, commences one of the branches of the granitic mountain, which extends northwardly through the State into Massachusetts, and constitutes the height of land which divides the waters, that run westwardly into the Connecticut, from those which run eastwardly into the Thames and other streams. This mountainous ridge, also, becomes more elevated, and presents more prominent features, as it extends into the interior. The geological character of the township being granitic, the prevailing soil is a gravelly loam, but varies in different sections. The bodies of salt marsh and meadows upon the rivers, are extensive and productive; the former affording large quantities of salt hay, and the latter producing fresh hay, grain &c. The hilly and mountainous parts of the town do not admit of a general cultivation of grain, but afford good grazing; and the making of butter and cheese, are considerable agricultural interests. Of the grains cultivated, Indian corn receives the most attention. The forests comprise the deciduous trees common to this region; and among the vegetable productions there are some valuable medicinal plants, of which ginseng and Virginia snake root are most deserving of notice.

The waters of the township are very abundant. Besides the Connecticut, which washes the western border of the town, it is watered by the following streams; Whalebone, Eight Mile, Falls, Beaver, Lieutenant's, Four Miles, Bridge, Mamacock and Niantic. There is a ferry, accommodated with sail boats, upon the Connecticut, maintaining a communication between this town and Saybrook, three miles from the sound. This ferry is established and regulated by law, and is constantly attended. Besides this, there are within this town, Ely's, Brockway's and Comstock's ferries, all of which are established and maintained by law. The town is accommodated with several good harbours, of which those at the mouth of the Connecticut, Lieutenant's and Eight mile rivers are most important. The Connecticut, throughout the whole extent of the town, has sufficient depth of water, for large vessels, and in general affords safe and good landing places. A part of Niantic bay, upon Long Island sound, is situated within this town.

There are a number of ponds in the town. In the first society or parish are Rodgers' and Blackhall's ponds; in the second society, is Smith's, situated upon the line, and Bride and Pattagawonset ponds; in the third society are Hog, Norwich and Cedar Ponds.

The fishing business is carried on extensively, is an important interest, and employs, in some seasons of the year, considerable industry. The shad fisheries in the Connecticut river, which are numerous, are very valuable, and a source of great wealth to the town. Large quantities of shad are annually taken, and always have a ready market; and for some years past at a very advanced price, Connecticut river shad being esteemed better than any other in the United States. In Long Island sound, shell and black fish are taken considerably plentifully. The town has important advantages for maritime and navigation business; and there are a number of vessels owned therein, which are employed in the coasting trade.

It is accommodated with the New-London and Lyme turnpike, which passes through it from east to west; and with the Hartford and New-London turnpike, which leads through its northeast corner.

The business of agriculture, fishing and navigation, comprise the principal interests of the town; and those of manufactures can claim only a very subordinate rank. There are 2 Woolen Factories, 1 Paper Mill, 2 Hat Factories, having bowing machines, 8 Grain Mills, 11 Saw Mills, 1 Carding Machine for customers, and 3 Tanneries.

The population of the town, in 1810, was 4321, and is estimated at this time at 4500. There are about 500 Electors or Freemen; 3 Companies of Infantry, 1 of Light Infantry and 1 of Artillery, containing in all about 400 men; and 567 Dwelling houses.

The aggregate list of the town, in 1816, was $71,888, and the valuation or assessment of the lands and buildings, in 1815, under the laws of the United States, was $1,307,826.

The civil divisions of the town consist of 3 located Congregational Societies or Parishes, and 24

24 School Districts. Besides the located, there are 2 Societies of Baptists, 1 of Methodists, and 1 of Separatists; all of which, except the Methodists, are accommodated with houses for public worship.

There are, in the town, 24 primary or common Schools, 3 Social Libraries, 12 Mercantile Stores, 7 Physicians, 2 Attornies and 6 Clergymen, 3 Congregationalists, 2 Baptists and 1 Methodist.

Lyme is a very ancient town, having been settled about the year 1636; it was soon after incorporated as a part of the town of Saybrook, and as a distinct town, in 1665; and it retains at the present time its original limits, excepting about 2600 acres, which were annexed to Montville at the incorporation of that town.

BIOGRAPHY. The Hon. *Matthew Griswold*, distinguished for his many public employments, was a native of this town. Among the important and responsible offices which he was called to fill, were those of chief Judge of the Superior Court, Lieut. Governor of the State, which station he held for a number of years, and Governor, having been elected to that office in 1784. He continued in this situation but one year, being succeeded by Samuel Huntington.

The Hon. *Roger Griswold*, of this town, was the son of Matthew Griswold, and born 21st May, 1762. He was educated at Yale College, and graduated in 1780. Having been admitted to the practice of law in 1783, he soon became extensively engaged in professional business, and acquired a high reputation, as a profound lawyer and advocate. In 1789, when he was but 32 years of age, he was removed from a lucrative and extensive practice to the councils of the nation; being elected a representative from this State in the Congress of the United States. In 1801, at the close of President Adams' administration, he was nominated to be Secretary of War, but declined to accept the office. In 1807, he was appointed a Judge of the Superior Court; and, in 1809, he was elected by the General Assembly Lieut. Governor, which office he held until the spring of 1811, when the freemen elected him Governor. In this office he continued until his death, in Oct. 1812. This period, embracing the first five months after the declaration of war, was one of peculiar excitement and difficulty, and during most of which, Gov. Griswold was subject to an occasionally severe indisposition.

Roger Griswold was a member of Congress for ten years; embracing a part of the administration of Washington, the whole of that of Adams, and a part of that of Jefferson. This was a very important and interesting period, not only from the political events of this country, but from the great convulsions which agitated all Europe; and it was during this period, while in the councils of the nation, that Roger Griswold was most distinguished. During a considerable part of this time, he ranked among the first of his party, and was equally distinguished for his powerful talents in debate, and the independence and decision of his conduct. He remained but a short time in his judicial station, and still shorter in that of chief magistrate.

MONTVILLE.

MONTVILLE, a post township, is situated on the west bank of the Thames, 7 miles from its mouth, the same distance from New-London, and 35 miles from Hartford; bounded on the north by Bozrah and Norwich, on the east by the river Thames, which separates it from Preston and Groton, on the south by Waterford, on the west by Lyme, and northwest by Colchester. Its average length, from east to west, is about 8 miles, and its average breadth about 5 miles, comprising about 40 square miles.

This township is embraced within the granitic district, bordering upon the sea coast, is uneven and rough, being hilly, rocky and stony. The soil is a coarse, dry, gravelly loam, considerably strong and fertile, affording good grazing. The waters of the township are abundant and good, its eastern border being washed by the Thames and its numerous inlets; and there are several small streams discharging their waters into the Thames, that run through its interior, and accommodate its various sections. Many of the inlets upon the Thames afford good and safe anchoring places; but there is no harbour which is much used. There are two vessels only belonging to the town; and its maritime interests are proportionally inconsiderable. Some attention is paid to the fishing business; shad are taken in the Thames, in which, and in its various inlets, are also taken some shell and black fish.

There are five ponds or lakes in the town; the most considerable of which is Gardiner's lake, situated in its north western section; and a part of it is in Colchester and Bozrah.

The lands in this town being most favourable for grazing, and generally too rough and stony for a grain culture, the principal agricultural productions are cheese, butter, neat cattle and beef; some Indian corn, rye and flax are raised.

The forests consist of oak, walnut, chesnut, and some other deciduous trees. The Norwich and Hartford turnpike road leads thro' this town.

In this, like most other towns in the county, domestic manufactures are general and important. There are also some manufacturing establishments, the most considerable of which are of Woolen, there being 3 Woolen Factories. There are also 2 Oil Mills, 1 Distillery, 5 Grain Mills, 2 Clothiers' Works and Fulling Mills, 2 Carding Machines and 4 Tanneries.

In this town there was a reservation of a tract of land of 4,000 acres, for the Mohegan Indians; the remains of which still reside upon it.

The population of the town, in 1810, was 2187; and there are about 300 Electors, 3 Companies of Militia, and 320 Dwellinghouses. The amount of taxable property, including polls, as rated in making up lists in 1816, was $48,338. There are, in the town, 2 located Congregational Societies, 1 Society of Baptists, and 1 Society of Independents or Separatists. It contains also 13 School Districts and common Schools. There are 3 Houses for public worship, 5 Mercantile Stores, 3 Physicians and 3 Clergymen in the town.

Montville originally belonged to New-London, and was incorporated in 1786.

NORTH-STONINGTON.

NORTH-STONINGTON is a post township, situated in the southeastern section of the county and State, 50 miles southeast from Hartford; bounded on the north by Preston, Griswold and Voluntown, (the latter in Windham county,) east by Hopkinton, in Rhode Island, southeast by the Paucatuck river, which separates it from the State of Rhode Island, south by Stonington, and west by Groton and Preston. Its average length, from east to west is 8 miles, and its average breadth nearly 6 miles, comprising an area of about 44 square miles. This township is of a granitic character, rough, hilly and stony; the soil is a gravelly loam, considerably strong and fertile, affording good grazing. The natural growth of timber consists of oak, chesnut, walnut, &c. The agricultural productions comprise butter, cheese, beef, pork, lard, flax, wool, and some others.

The township is well watered by the Paucatuck, its branches, and other small streams, which afford numerous sites for mills and other water works.

A turnpike has been authorized, leading from New-London into the State of Rhode Island, which will pass through this town.

Agriculture is the principal business of the inhabitants, who are remarkable for their habits of industry and economy; and for the commendable simplicity and plainness of their manners and style of living. In the various calamities and embarrassments which our country has experienced, calculated to weaken the force of patriotism, and awaken a spirit of disaffection, the inhabitants of this town have been characterized by a firm and steady adherence to the interests of their country; unappalled by difficulties, and unshaken by discouragements, arising from the novel and peculiar state of the political world. Although generally agriculturalists, they have paid some attention to manufactures. There is 1 Cotton Factory, 1 Woolen Factory, 2 Fulling Mills & Clothiers' works, 2 Carding Machines, 5 Grain Mills and 3 Tanneries. There is also considerable mercantile busines done in the town, there being 16 Dry goods and Grocery Stores.

The population of the town, in 1810, was 2524; and there are about 350 Freemen or Electors, 3 entire companies of militia, and a part of another company, and about 360 Dwelling houses.

The amount of taxable property, as rated in making up lists, including polls, is $46,350.

The town contains one located Congregational Society, two Societies of Baptists, and one Society of Separates or Independents; all of which are accommodated with houses for public worship.

There are 17 primary or common Schools, one in each district, which are maintained a suitable proportion of the year; 1 Social Library, 4 Public Inns, 3 Clergymen, 1 Physician and 1 Attorney.

This town originally belonged to Stonington, & was made a distinct & independent corporation, in 1808.

PRESTON.

PRESTON, a considerable post township, 44 miles from Hartford; bounded on the north by Griswold, on the east by Griswold and North-Stonington, on the south by Groton, on the west by the Thames and Quinibaug rivers, which separate it from Norwich, Montville and Lisbon. Its average length is about 7 miles, and its breadth about 4 and a half miles, comprising an area of about 30 square miles. The township is uneven, consisting of hill and dale; it is stony and rocky, and the soil a gravelly loam, considerably fertile & productive. It is better adapted to grazing than to grain, but considerable Indian corn is raised, and some rye and oats. Butter, cheese, beef, pork and lard are among the agricultural productions, of which there are more than a supply for the inhabitants.

The western border of the town is washed by the Quinibaug and Thames. There are several small streams passing through its interior. Ames' lake or pond, an inconsiderable body of water, is situated in this town.

The population of the town, amounts to 1764 persons; and there are about 250 Dwelling houses, 250 Electors, and about 150 militia.

The amount of taxable property, including polls, is $40,428.

There are 3 Grain Mills, 5 Mercantile Stores & 3 Tanneries. The town contains 2 located Congregational Societies, 1 Society of Baptists, 1 Society of Episcopalians, and 1 of Separates or Independents; 14 School districts and Schools, and 2 small social Libraries. There are 3 Physicians, 1 Attorney and 2 Clergymen.

This town was settled in 1686.

STONINGTON.

STONINGTON, a flourishing post town, is situated in the southeast corner of the State, being 55 miles southeast from Hartford, and 62 east from New-Haven. It is bounded north by North-Stoning-

STONINGTON.

ton, east by Paucatuck river, which separates it from Rhode-Island, south by Fisher's Island sound and Paucatuck bay, and west by Mystic river, which separates it from Groton.

The area of the town is equal to about 6 square miles, or 23000 acres. The town is uneven, being hilly and rocky, but the soil, which is a gravelly loam, is rich and fertile, and admirably adapted to grazing; the dairy business, or making of cheese and butter, being the leading agricultural interest. Barley, corn and oats are cultivated.

There are no rivers within the town deserving notice; the Paucatuck, which runs upon its eastern border, and separates it from Rhode-Island, and the Mystic, that forms its western boundary, and separates it from Groton, are short but considerable streams.

There is an arm of the sea extending from Stonington harbour northeasterly, over which is Quanaduok stone bridge. A turnpike runs from New-London through Groton and Stonington, and intersects the turnpike road from Providence to Westerly, in the State of Rhode-Island.

There are 1100 tons of shipping owned in this town, which are employed either in the business of fishing, or in the coasting and West India trade, and which furnish employment to a portion of the inhabitants. The maritime situation and interests of the town have given a direction to the pursuits and habits of its citizens; and Stonington has become conspicuous, as a nursery of seamen, distinguished for their enterprise, perseverance and courage.

But although principally engaged in the pursuits of agriculture, fishing and navigation, other important interests have not been neglected. There are few towns in the State that have done more in certain branches of manufactures; there being two Woolen Factories and one Cotton Factory upon an extensive scale in the town.

The civil divisions of Stonington are 1 Ecclesiastical Society, 8 School Districts, and an incorporated borough.

Stonington Borough, incorporated by the Legislature in 1801, is situated on a narrow point of land of about half a mile in length, at the eastern extremity of Long Island sound. On its east side lies Paucatuck bay, and on its west the harbour, terminating in Lambert's Cove. It has four streets running north and south, intersected at right angles by nine cross streets, and contains about 120 Dwelling houses and Stores. It also has 2 Houses for public worship, an Academy, where the languages are taught, and 2 common schools, 2 Rope walks, commodious wharves and ware-houses for storage.

The fisheries have for a long time been prosecuted with industry and success by the inhabitants, who employ from 10 to 15 vessels in this business; which annually bring in about 7000 quintals of codfish, & 1000 bbls. of mackerel, besides most other species of fish which are taken by smaller vessels and boats. There is also a brig engaged in the sealing business, in the Pacific ocean; three packets which ply regularly between this port and New-York; a pilot boat to cruise for vessels on the coast bound in; and a number of vessels employed in the coasting trade, which carry to the southern market their fish, with the cheese, barley &c. of the adjacent country. Many fine ships and brigs are built here for the New-York market.

In the census of 1810, the town contained 3043 inhabitants; and there are now 335 qualified Electors. There are 20 Mercantile Stores, 4 Grain Mills, 3 Carding Machines, 1 Pottery & 1 Tannery. There is a Public Arsenal belonging to the United States, which is a substantial brick building; 2 Churches, one for Congregationalists and one for Baptists; 1 Academy or Grammar School; 8 district or common Schools; 3 Attornies, and 3 practising Physicians.

The general list of the town, in 1817, was $45,991.

Stonington was first settled in 1658, by emigrants from Rehoboth, in Massachusetts. The settlement was commenced upon the Paucatuck, being then called the plantation of Southerton.

This town has become celebrated for the spirited and successful resistance which it made to the attack and bombardment of Sir Thomas Hardy, during the late war. The enemy's squadron, which consisted of the Romulus 74, the Pactolus frigate of 38 guns, brig Despatch, of 18, and a bomb ship had lain off the harbour for some time; the British commodore having repeatedly threatened that he would destroy the borough, which he considered as entirely defenceless. On the 9th of August, 1814, the brig came up the harbour, within convenient cannon shot of the town, and commenced firing upon it, which occasioned the utmost alarm and confusion; it being supposed by many of the inhabitants, that the *threats* of the magnanimous commodore were now to be put in execution, and that the beautiful borough of Stonington would soon be no more.

At this critical moment, when all was confusion and dismay, a "gallant Spartan band" of volunteers were enabled to procure two 18 pounders, with which they commenced firing upon the brig, and with such effect, that, altho' they were exposed in the most imminent degree to her fire, she was compelled to cut her cables, after having sustained much damage in her hull, and suffered severely in killed and wounded.

The defence of Stonington has few examples in the annals of naval warfare, and reflects much credit on the town, and the 'heroic band' of volunteers.

BIOGRAPHY. Among the citizens of this town, who have been distinguished for their abilities, public services, virtues and patriotism, our correspondent notices the following:

Nathaniel Miner, who was a lawyer of unimpeachable integrity; much esteemed for his acquirements, his probity & exemplary life.

Dr. *Charles Phelps*, who died in 1808; he came to the town in early youth, and for many years was a Judge of the Court of the County, and of the probate Court of the District; possessing, in an eminent degree, the confidence of his fellow-citizens.

Capt. *Amos Palmer*, who was distinguished for his integrity, his republican principles, and his patriotism. He was repeatedly elected to represent the town in the legislature of the State.

WATERFORD.

WATERFORD is a maritime township, situated on Long Island sound, 4 miles from the city of New-London, and 37 from Hartford; bounded on the north by Montville, on the east by New-London and the Thames, on the south by Long Island sound, and on the west by Lyme. Its average length is 7 miles, and its average breadth 5 miles, comprising an area of 35 square miles.

The surface is uneven, being diversified with hill and dale; the soil is a gravelly loam.

The agricultural productions consist of grass, Indian corn, butter and cheese, and beef and pork. The lands are better adapted to grazing than to grain, of which there is little cultivated except Indian corn.

The eastern border of the township is partly washed by the Thames; and the Niantic and Jordan rivers, together with several small streams, run through it. The Niantic river discharges its waters into a bay of the same name, which is of three or four miles in extent, and is navigable for sloops of 20 tons.

The fishing business receives considerable attention by the inhabitants of this town; oysters, clams, black fish and mackerel are taken.

Although agriculture, fishing and other maritime pursuits are the leading occupations of the inhabitants; yet manufactures have received some attention. There are 2 Woolen Factories, 2 Fulling Mills and Clothiers' works, 3 Carding Machines, 4 Grain Mills, 1 Tannery & 4 Mercantile Stores.

The population of the town, in 1810, was 2185, and there are 3 Companies of Militia, 200 Freemen or qualified Electors, and about 300 Dwelling houses.

There are several turnpike roads that pass through this town; one leading from New-London to Hartford, one from thence to New-Haven, and one to Norwich.

The amount of taxable property, including polls, is $33,933.

This town does not contain any Congregational Society, but has two Societies of Baptists, both of which are accommodated with houses for public worship. There are 11 School Districts & Schools, 1 Social Library, 2 Clergymen and 2 Lawyers.

Waterford was incorporated in 1801. until which time it belonged to New-London.

FAIRFIELD COUNTY.

FAIRFIELD is an ancient maritime county, pleasantly situated upon Long Island sound, in the southwest section of the State; bounded on the north by Litchfield county, on the northeast and east by the Ousatonick river, which separates it from the county of New-Haven, and, for a short distance, from the county of Litchfield, on the southeast and south by Long Island sound, and on the southwest and west by the State of New-York.

The county lies in a triangular form, and has an average length from east to west of about 30 miles, and a mean breadth from north to south of about 21 miles; comprising and area of about 630 square miles.

The following TOPOGRAPHICAL AND STATISTICAL TABLE exhibits a view of the several towns in the county; their situation, with relation to Fairfield; population, according to the census of 1810; dwelling-houses; religious societies; school districts, and post-offices.

Towns.	Post-offices.	Population.	Dwelling houses.	Religious societies.	School districts.	Distance from Fairfield.
Fairfield.	2	4137	550	6	16	
Danbury.	1	3606	550	7	17	20 m. N. W.
Brookfield.	1	1037	150	2	8	24 m. N. W.
Greenwich.	1	3553	500	6	17	25 m. S. W.
Huntington.	2	2770	400	6	18	15 m. N. E.
New-Canaan.	1	1599	260	2	9	15 m. N. W.
New-Fairfield.		772	130	2	6	26 m. N. W.
Newtown.	1	2834	400	7	15	19 m. N.
Norwalk.	1	2983	400	3	13	10 m. W.
Reading.	1	1717	260	3	11	14 m. N. W.
Ridgefield.	1	2103	300	5	12	18 m. N. W.
Sherman.		949	130	2	6	30 m. N. W.
Stamford.	1	4440	600	8	11	20 m. S. W.
Stratford.	2	2895	420	6	10	8 m. E.
Trumbull.	1	1241	200	2	6	8 m. N. E.
Weston.		2618	380	5	*	8 m. N.
Wilton.	1	1728	270	2	9	13 m. N. W.

* See *Appendix.*

FAIRFIELD COUNTY.

Fairfield county is pleasantly and advantageously situated, having a maritime border upon Long Island sound, of nearly forty miles, indented with numerous bays and inlets, affording extensive advantages for commerce. This border, through most of its whole extent, affords the most charming and interesting landscapes; some sections present extensive tracts of marine alluvial; and, with the exception of the western extremity, it is in general level, and a highly pleasant and interesting country, affording many beautiful views of the sound, and being diversified with its numerous bays and inlets. Proceeding from the sound into the interior, there is a very gradual rise to the most elevated sections of the county, which overlook the intervening tract, and afford an interesting view of Long Island sound. The face of the country is, in general, agreeably diversified with hills and dales. No section of it can be considered as mountainous, although, in the northwestern part, there are ridges of considerable extent; and many of the hills are very elevated and continuous, and the vallies deep and extensive. The soil, which in general is a primitive, gravelly loam, is, with few exceptions, strong and fertile. It is, in general, well adapted to arable purposes, and a considerable proportion of the lands are assigned to a grain culture. The county of Fairfield is a rich farming district, and contains abundant natural resources of agricultural opulence. The various objects of husbandry, common to the State, are attended to here; and of the productions cultivated, more particularly or extensively than in other sections, are potatoes, and some other articles for the New-York market.

The waters of the county are abundant, and afford important advantages. In addition to the waters of Long Island sound, which washes its southeastern border, and the numerous bays, streams and inlets connected with it, the Ousatonick, (the second river in the State,) washes the eastern and northeastern border, for nearly its whole extent.

Of the small streams, which intersect and fertilize the different parts of the county, are the Still river, a tributary stream of the Ousatonick; the Pequonack, which discharges its waters into the sound at Stratford; the Saugatuck, the Ash, Noraton and Miannus rivers; Mill river, Stamford and Byram river, all of which discharge their waters into the sound; and the latter, for some distance, forms the boundary between this State and New-York.

The principal harbours in the county are Bridgeport, Black Rock, (which is one of the best in the State,) Mill river, Saugatuck, Norwalk, Stamford & Greenwich harbours.

The commercial business of the county is considerable, and consists principally of a coasting trade with New-York. There are between 20 and 30 packets, which ply regularly between the various harbours within this county and the city of New-York. In addition to this trade, there are some coasters employed in a trade with the southern states; and at Bridgeport, there is some foreign trade maintained.

This county is not distinguished for its manufactures, although, in some sections, a conspicuous manufacturing spirit exists, and has produced very important results. Of the manufactures which have received the most attention, are those of hats and flour. In some parts of the county, particularly in Danbury, the manufacture of hats is carried on very extensively, and large quantities are annually sent abroad for a market. In several towns upon the sound, particularly in Stamford, the manufacture of flour, or milling business, is carried on to great extent. There are also, several manufactures of leather, particularly of shoes, harness work and saddlery, which, in some towns, receive considerable attention as articles of exportation.

There are in this county, 1 Forge, 1 Slitting and Rolling Mill, 2 Paper Mills, 5 Cotton Factories, 9 Woolen Factories, 29 Fulling Mills and Clothiers' works, 40 Carding Machines, 80 Grain Mills, and 170 Mercantile Stores.

The county contains 74 Religious Societies, 28 School Societies, each of which is divided into a convenient number of School districts, the limits of a single School, of which there are in all 184, exclusive of Weston, & 23 Social Libraries.

The population of the county, in 1800, was 38,208; and in 1810, it was 40,950; and the aggregate list in 1817, was $903,805.

FAIRFIELD.

FAIRFIELD, an ancient maritime post town, and the semi-seat of justice of the county, is pleasantly situated upon Long Island sound, 21 miles west from New-Haven, and 58 northeast from New-York; bounded northwesterly by Norwalk and Weston, northeasterly by Stratford, southeasterly by Long Island sound, and southwesterly by the Saugatuck river, which separates it from Norwalk. The township comprises an area of about 54 square miles; having a mean length of about 9 miles, from northeast to southwest, and a mean breadth of about 6 miles.

This township, having an interesting situation upon the sound, is very pleasant, and affords some beautiful landscapes, which are scarcely surpassed. The surface is undulating, or moderately uneven, presenting an agreeable succession of moderate eminences and gentle declivities.

Upon the sound are considerable tracts of salt marsh; and, proceeding back, the surface has a gradual elevation; but no portion of the township is mountainous or broken, and it is in general free from stone.

The prevailing soil is a gravelly loam, corresponding with the primitive granitic geological character of the township. There are some sections of primitive argillaceous loam, and some tracts of alluvial. We know of no minerals in the town; but in the Society of Greenfield there are several quarries of freestone, valuable for building and other purposes. The most important is at Blue stone hill, about one mile from Greenfield Hill village.

About two miles distance from this village is a precipice of about 30 feet in height, being the termination of a granitic ridge, which runs northerly for some distance. This precipice is called Samp mortar rock, from the circumstance of there being upon its summit an excavation, in the form of a mortar, and of sufficient dimensions to contain a bushel of corn or other grain. It is evidently the work of art; and, according to the authority of tradition, was used by the native Indians, for the purpose of pounding or grinding their corn. Although with us it may seem difficult to conceive, how this mortar, consisting of so considerable an excavation, in a solid granitic stratum, could have been made without the use of iron tools; yet it can scarcely be doubted that it was the work of the natives, and for the purposes here noticed. And this opinion is strengthened from the facts, that, in the rich valley south of the rock, was a large Indian town; and at the very foot of the precipice there appears to have been a burying ground. It is probable that this mortar was the only and common mill of this town or settlement. Here the primitive inhabitants of our country, in this simple invention, and by a process equally simple yet laborious, pulverized their corn, and supplied themselves with bread stuffs. This mortar, which may be considered as a primitive grain mill, is not more important, as a monument of the aboriginal inhabitants, than as an illustration of the origin and progress of the arts. This mortar was a great improvement upon the more simple and rude method of pulverizing corn, which preceded it,—that of pounding it between two stones. To such rude and simple discoveries as this, can the most noble and useful inventions in the arts be traced.

The natural and agricultural productions of this town are such as are common to the county. The original growth of timber was, at an early period, from a common but lamentable improvidence, principally destroyed; so that the forests now existing are of a recent growth, and comprise little timber fit for building. Wood and timber are valuable in this town, and command a high price. It is observed that the texture of the present growth of timber is firmer than that which was found at the first settlement; and that the timber growing upon the sound is less porous and tougher than that which grows in the interior. Formerly, wheat was successfully cultivated here; but it cannot now be raised without a liberal use of manure. Indian corn is extensively and successfully cultivated, and may be regarded as the staple production of the town. For some years past, potatoes have been raised in great quantities, and are found a very profitable crop, from the facility which exists of sending them to New-York market. Rye, oats, grass, &c. are cultivated; and fruits of various kinds receive attention.

This is a rich, agricultural township, and in general in a flourishing state of cultivation. The soil is naturally strong and fertile;

and the town affords several unusual and important sources of manure, of which the inhabitants have recently availed themselves. Sea-weed, which washes from the bottom of Long Island sound, and lodges upon the shore, and sedge, or salt grass, which grows in the salt marshes near the sound, afford a valuable and almost inexhaustible manure. Large quantities of peat are also found in several of the swamps, which supply a valuable manure. It is collected and thrown into heaps upon the land, where it soon decomposes, giving it a suitable consistence, so that it will readily amalgamate with the soil. It is principally adapted to a dry soil, but is valuable upon almost any kind of land. This peat is also used for the purposes of fuel.

The township is well watered, being washed by Long Island sound, upon its southeastern border, and by the Saugatuck river & harbour, which form a part of its western boundary, and is navigable for vessels of considerable size for nearly three miles, by Mill and Sasco rivers, and Ash creek.

There are three harbours in the town; Black Rock, Mill river, and Saugatuck harbours. With the exception of New-London, Black Rock is one of the best harbours in the sound; being safe and commodious, and having 19 feet of water at the summer tides, below what is called the middle ground.

At the entrance of the harbour, on Fairweather's Island, belonging to the United States, and which forms the easterly chop of this harbour, a light-house has been erected; a spindle also has been placed at the "cows," a point of rocks extending a mile into the sound. Vessels can enter and depart from this harbour at any time of the tide. At the head of the bay forming this harbour, there is a small settlement, where considerable coasting business is carried on. During the late war, a small fort was erected on a hill, commanding the entrance of this harbour, by the exertions of individuals, in which the State of Connecticut a short time maintained a small body of militia, as a garrison. This fort was found very useful in protecting the coasting trade in the sound from the cruisers of the enemy. The cannon in this fort were furnished by the U. States.

Mill river harbour is very commodious for the coasting trade, but has not sufficient depth of water to admit large vessels. It is formed by the river of the same name; on which, within the distance of two miles, stand 3 large Grain Mills, 2 Fulling Mills and 2 Carding Machines. This harbour is seldom frozen with sufficient firmness to obstruct vessels from passing out into the sound.

Saugatuck harbour is formed by the river bearing the same name; it has not sufficient depth of water for large vessels, but is a convenient harbour for the smaller or ordinary coasters employed in the sound.

The commercial business of this town is very respectable; there being about 2500 tons of shipping owned here, which is employed in the coasting trade. Oysters, clams, and some other shell fish are taken in the sound, but not to any considerable extent. Former-

FAIRFIELD.

ly, they were taken in abundance; but they have greatly declined, owing, it is thought, to their being taken before they have attained their full growth; which has prevented their increase. This evil might be avoided by suitable regulations, controlling the fishery. The various kinds of fin fish found in the sound are taken here; and, in the season, shad are taken in the rivers, and various other fish. Shad are not taken extensively, nor is the fishing business of any description of importance, farther than to supply the demands of the inhabitants of the town.

The town is well accommodated with roads; the great turnpike leading to New-York passes thro' it. This road leads directly through the celebrated Pequot swamp, which is about two miles west of the Court-house.

The manufactures of this town are not extensive or important; the milling business, however, is carried on to a considerable extent. There are 9 Grain Mills, 4 of which are upon tide water, have several sets of stones each, and are employed principally in flouring wheat, which is brought from other States. Some of these mills have kilns for drying Indian corn, which is afterwards manufactured into meal for the foreign markets. The other mills are erected upon the streams of water, and are employed in customers' business. There are 2 manufacturing establishments of wool and cotton, which flourished during the war, but have since declined, 2 Fulling Mills and Clothiers' works, and 5 Tanneries. There are, in the different parts of the town, 25 retailing Mercantile Stores.

The population of Fairfield, in 1810, was 4135, and there are about 500 Electors, 3 Companies of Infantry, part of a Company of Cavalry, and the principal part of a Company of Artillery, of militia, and about 550 Dwelling houses. The aggregate list of the town, in 1817, was $86,872.

The civil divisions of Fairfield consist of 3 located Congregational Societies or Parishes, Fairfield, Greenfield and Greensfarms; and 16 School Districts. A part of the Society of Stratfield is within the limits of this town. Besides the located Societies, there is a Society of Episcopalians, a Society of Baptists and a Society of Methodists. Each of these religious Societies is provided with a house for public worship. There are 4 Clergymen, 7 Attornies, and 5 Physicians. There are 16 primary Schools, one in each District, and 3 Academies, which are well established and respectable. There are 2 Social Libraries, one in the Society of Fairfield, and one in Greenfield, which contain a respectable collection of well selected books, and are flourishing. There are four villages within the town; Fairfield, Greenfield Hill, Saugatuck and Mill river. The ancient village of Fairfield is situated upon the great stage road. It has a very pleasant site, and is considerable of a settlement, although it has never entirely recovered from the devastation which it experienced during the revolution. It is built principally upon one street; in the centre of which is an interesting green, upon which the Court House is situated. Here there is a Post office, a Congregational Church, a flourishing Academy, the County Gaol, and a number of handsome Dwelling houses.

Greenfield Hill is justly celebrated for its elevated, prospective and beautiful situation. It stands on a commanding eminence. nearly in the centre of the township; being about three miles northwardly from Long Island sound, of which it affords a view as far as the eye can reach. On this eminence, in the centre of a flourishing village, is a spacious courtyard or green, upon which stand a Congregational Church and an Academy. From the belfry of the church, in this village, may be seen ten other churches. It is presumed that no other spot in Connecticut affords a prospect so extensive and delightful; the country upon the Ousatonick may be distinctly seen at the distance of ten miles; and, in every direction, the view is extensive, diversified and interesting; the surrounding country being thickly settled, in a high state of cultivation, and in the summer months clothed with the richest verdure. In this village, vessels are daily seen passing up and down the sound, being in full view; and, at times, nearly one hundred sail of different descriptions, consisting of ships, brigs, schooners and sloops, including the steam-boat, may be seen. Here there are a number of neat and handsome Dwelling houses, and a flourishing Academy, which was established and maintained for twelve years by the late President Dwight. Whilst under his direction, it acquired a high reputation, which has since been maintained, and it is now a flourishing seminary; and a more eligible situation for youth cannot well be selected. The Custom-house for Fairfield district is kept at this place.

Mill River is a flourishing maritime village. Its trade is greater than that of any other settlement in the town, and consists of a coasting trade with New-York and the southern ports, which is carried on extensively, and generally to advantage. It also has the advantages of a considerably extensive and fertile back country. It is the most wealthy village in the town, and is not probably exceeded by any of its size in the county.

The village of Saugatuck, situated about two miles from the mouth of the river of the same name, has considerable trade, and is a flourishing and prosperous settlement; but during the winter, the harbour is obstructed by the ice. Here there is an Academy and a Post office.

HISTORY. The tract of country which now forms the town of Fairfield was discovered by the pursuit of the Pequots, in the year 1637, along the shore of Long Island sound, over the territory which now comprises the towns of Killingworth, Guilford, Branford, New-Haven, Milford and Stratford, to the great swamp, which to this day bears the name of that tribe, by Capt. Mason, who commanded the troops of Connecticut and Massachusetts. This is the swamp where the great fight took place, between the troops of Connecticut and Massachusetts, and the Pequots, in 1637; which terminated in the almost entire annihilation of that once powerful and warlike nation of savages.

Having been greatly pleased with the appearance of this country, Mr. Ludlow, who was a magistrate in the colony of Connecticut, and had accompanied Capt. Mason, in order to assist him with his counsel, in the year 1639, with eight or ten families, removed from Windsor, and commenced the settlement of the present town of Fairfield. They were shortly afterwards joined by several persons from Watertown, and others from Concord; and the inhabitants soon became numerous, and formed themselves into a distinct township, under the jurisdiction of Connecticut. They came from these several towns about the same time; and soon afterwards purchased of the Indians that large tract of country which comprises the parishes of Fairfield, Greenfield, Greensfarms, and that part of Stratfield lying within the town of Fairfield, all the town of Weston, and a considerable part of the town of Reading. After Connecticut obtained a charter, the General Assembly granted these people a patent.

Having obtained this patent, the proprietors soon after divided the territory purchased into lots, which run from near the shore of the sound, back about ten miles, reserving suitable highways, running parallel to and at right angles with these lots, the course of which was north, 28 degrees west. These highways were laid entirely straight for ten miles; but have since been altered in many places.

As but a small part of this extensive tract of land had been occupied, previously to the time when Sir Edmund Andross made his appearance in Connecticut, the inhabitants of this town adopted this plan of dividing their purchase, to prevent their wild lands back from being taken from them; supposing that, as they were actually in the occupation of the front of their lots, they might be considered as possessing the whole; so far as to render it private property, and not subject to the disposal of the British government. The lots were of different width; some being about ten rods wide, while others were fifty rods in width. Each proprietor had set to him a lot, the width of which was probably regulated by the amount of the money paid by such proprietor; as in measuring off these lots, regard was had to inches, which shows a precise arithmetical calculation. Each of these lots has to this day been called by the name of the first proprietor, although a very considerable proportion of them are owned by persons of different names. Nearly in the centre of this town was reserved a tract, one mile in extent, which was not divided, and was called the mile of common. Greenfield Hill is within the limits of this tract.

This town, at an early period, became wealthy and populous, and sent deputies to the General Assembly in Connecticut, at Hartford; while Stamford, west of it, was under the government of New-Haven.

Although the towns of Reading and Weston were formed from the town of Fairfield, yet this town, owing to the fertility of its soil, and the numerous advantages with which it is favoured for commerce, has ever stood among the first towns in Connecticut, in point of wealth and population.

This town suffered very severely during the revolutionary war. Perhaps a more aggravated instance of wanton barbarity cannot be found in the annals of civilized nations, than the burning of this place by the direction of Tryon.

" *Tryon achieved the deed malign,*
" *Tryon, the name for every sin ;*
" *Hells blackest fiends the flame survey'd,*
" *And smil'd to see destruction spread;*
" *While Satan, blushing deep, look'd on,*
" *And infamy disown'd her son!*"

The part of the town which suffered by the plundering and burning of the British was the village in the centre of the parish of Fairfield. Eighty-five dwelling houses were consumed; two churches, one elegant court house, several school houses, together with out houses, barns, &c. shared the same fate. These wretches plundered the church of a service of plate!

The distress occasioned by this event was extreme; many of the inhabitants having been compelled to flee for their lives to the parish of Greenfield, were reduced to absolute want; but were there generously and humanely entertained for a considerable time.

The event took place on the 9th of July, 1779; a day which every honourable and feeling mind, nay, every mind not benumbed with brutal apathy, will recollect with unutterable horror!

The General Assembly, soon after the burning of this village, granted to the Presbyterian Society of Fairfield, 600 pounds out of the avails of the confiscated estates of the tories, to assist that Society in re-building their meeting house.

In the year 1792, a grant of lands was made to the individuals of this, and of other towns, who sustained losses during the war by the British troops; and those who have not disposed of their lands will, by the rise of them, undoubtedly realize the full amount of their respective losses.

The Episcopal Church, (which was an elegant building,) and the parsonage house, were burnt at the same time; but the Society to which they belonged, have never received any thing from the treasury of this State, on that account.

At the session of the General Assembly, in May 1818, a lottery was granted to the Episcopal Society in this town, as a remuneration for their loss.

DANBURY.

DANBURY, the semi-seat of justice of the county, and a flourishing agricultural and manufacturing post township, is situated in the northwestern section of the county, 58 miles southwest from Hartford, 35 northwest from New-Haven, and about 65 miles north-

DANBURY.

east from New-York; bounded on the north by New-Fairfield, on the east by Brookfield and Newtown, on the south by Reading, and on the west by Ridgefield. Its mean length is 8 and a half miles, and its mean breadth more than 6 miles; comprising an area of about 53 square miles.

This is a rich agricultural township; its geological character being primitive; the rocks consisting of granite, gneiss, with some primitive limestone. The soil, or super stratum, is in general a gravelly loam, interspersed with some sections of sandy loam, and some of calcareous, and is warm, feasible and fertile.

The face of the country is undulating, and pleasantly diversified; being characterized by gentle hills and dales, with some moderate ridges, running in a northerly and southerly direction. In the calcareous strata there are some appearances of marble, some quarries of which have been opened.

Of the waters of the town, Still river is the only considerable stream; it discharges itself into the Ousatonick. Upon this stream, which passes through the centre of the town, there are several manufacturing establishments.

The natural growth of timber consists of oak, walnut, chesnut and other species of hard wood.

The agricultural interests embrace most of the staple productions, both of a system of grazing and of a grain culture. Of the latter, wheat, rye, Indian corn and oats; of the former, cattle, sheep, beef, cheese and butter are the principal.

Of the manufactures of the town, that of hats is the most important, and the business most extensively carried on. This is an important manufacturing interest, and employs a large portion of industry, and considerable capital. There are 28 Hat Factories in the town, some of which are upon an extensive scale. The products of these establishments form a respectable item of exportation; they being sent principally to the southern States for a market. Some are sent to New-York and elsewhere. Besides the manufactures of hats, there are 2 Woolen Factories upon a large scale, 3 Fulling Mills and Cloth Dressing establishments, 4 Carding Machines for customers, 3 Grain Mills, 1 Paper Mill and 4 Tanneries. There are also several lime kilns, from which considerable quantities of lime are produced.

Danbury comprises two located Congregational Societies or Parishes, and 17 School Districts. Besides the located, there are 2 Societies of Baptists, 1 of Episcopalians, 1 of Methodists, and 1 of Sandemanians. In the first located Society, there is a large, flourishing and interesting village. It is built principally upon one street, which for more than a mile exhibits an almost continued range of buildings, consisting of Dwelling houses, Mercantile Stores, Hat Factories, Mechanics' Shops, &c. Within one mile and a quarter, there are more than 100 Dwelling houses, with a great proportion of other buildings. There are also a Court house, 2 Churches and a Post office in the village. The buildings are not elegant, but exhibit an appearance of plainness, neatness and convenience. There are few interior villages in the State more compact, or that afford an equal aggregate of industry, and of mechanical and manufacturing enterprise; few more deserving of notice, for the becoming plainness and simplicity of the style of living of the inhabitants; and their persevering, industrious & economical habits. The town is well accommodated with good roads; one, which is a turnpike, leads from thence to Fairfield, one to Norwalk, communicating with the great Atlantic road to New-York, one to Ridgefield, and thence into the State of New-York, and one to Hartford, passing through Newtown.

The population of the town, in 1810, was 3606, and there are about 600 Electors or Freemen, 4 Companies of militia, and 550 Dwelling houses.

The aggregate list of the town, in 1816, was $74,556.

There are 11 Mercantile Stores, 6 Taverns, 7 Houses for public worship, 17 primary or common Schools, besides which, there are several schools for young ladies and gentlemen, of a higher order; 2 Social Libraries, 4 Clergymen, 5 Physicians and 3 Attornies in the town. The first settlement in Danbury was made in 1687, and it was incorporated in 1696. This town was among those which suffered from the barbarous and revolting mode of warfare, which, in many instances, was adopted by the British during the revolutionary contest; a considerable proportion of it having been burned by the British troops, 26th April, 1777, together with a large quantity of military stores.

BROOKFIELD.

BROOKFIELD, a post town, situated in the north part of the county, is bounded north by a part of New-Milford, in Litchfield county, northeast by the Ousatonick; river, which separates it from New-Milford, east by Newtown, south by Danbury, and west by Danbury and New-Fairfield.

The township is equivalent to about 17 square miles, containing 10,880 acres.

The northeastern border of the town is washed by the Ousatonick; and Still river, a considerable mill stream, runs through the town. There is a toll bridge across the Ousatonick, connecting the town with New-Milford. Upon this river there are two considerable shad fisheries.

The surface is diversified with hill and dale, but is considerably free from stone. The soil is generally a dry, hard, gravelly loam, particularly upon the hills; in some sections a light calcareous loam prevails. The lands in general are well adapted to a grain culture, and carry good crops of wheat and rye, particularly the latter, which is cultivated very successfully, and in great abundance.

The natural growth of the land is oak, hickory, chesnut, maple and other deciduous trees.

The geological structure of the town, in some sections, consists of limestone; and within these calcareous ranges there are several beds of marble. Several quarries have been opened, and large quantities of the stone got out and fitted for various uses. Two saw mills have been erected, to saw the stone, to fit it for use, or to facilitate its manufacture. Large quantities of marble monuments, tomb stones, hearth stones, &c. are yearly manufactured. There is also a manufactory of marble pots, mortars, vases, &c. These various manufactures of marble afford a stimulus to industry, and are sources of considerable wealth. Some indications of lead have been discovered; but the subject has received little attention.

In addition to the public roads, the town is accommodated with a turnpike to Bridgeport, called the Newtown and Bridgeport turnpike.

In 1810, the town contained 1037 inhabitants; and there are 180 Electors, 1 Company of militia, and 150 Dwelling houses.

The amount of taxable property, including polls, is $27,089.

There are 2 Grain Mills, 1 Fulling Mill and Clothier's works, 1 Carding Machine, 2 Mercantile Stores and 4 Taverns.

The town contains 1 located Congregational Society & Church; 1 Episcopal Society; 8 School Districts and common Schools; 1 Social Library, 1 Physician, 2 Clergymen and 2 Attornies.

Brookfield was formed from parts of New-Milford, Newtown and Danbury; and was incorporated in 1788.

GREENWICH.

GREENWICH, a maritime post township, is situated in the south-western corner of the county and State, 48 miles west from New-Haven, 84 from Hartford, and 38 east from New-York; bounded on the north and west by West-Chester county, in the State of New-York, on the east by Stamford, and on the south by Long Island sound. Its average length is 8 and a half miles, and its average breadth nearly 6 miles, comprising about 50 square miles.

The township is hilly and broken, being rocky and ledgy: the rocks are of a primitive granitic formation, exhibited, in some instances, in large and naked masses. The soil is a gravelly loam, and considerably fertile; it produces grass, wheat, rye, Indian corn, oats and flax. In addition to these more staple productions, there are various kinds of roots and vegetables raised for the New-York market, particularly potatoes, of which very large quantities are annually exported to that city.

The southern border of the town, washed by Long Island sound, is of considerable extent, and is intersected by several inlets and creeks, off which there are several small Islands. There are also several landing places; Coscob landings, of which there are two, upper and lower, and Bushes landing. At these landings, the maritime business of the town is concentrated,

HUNTINGTON.

and consists principally of a trade carried on with New-York by sloops, of which there are 12 or 15 belonging to the town. This trade is a great convenience to the farmers, as it affords them a great facility for conveying their produce to New-York.

Byram river is the most considerable stream; it runs within the town for some distance, and thence forms the boundary between the two States.

There are a number of fisheries upon the bays, creeks and inlets upon the sound, at which both shell and fin fish are taken; of the former, oysters and clams, and of the latter, black fish are the most plenty and valuable.

The principal mail and stage road, from New-Haven to New-York, passes through the centre of this town.

The manufactures, mechanical establishments and employments of the town consist of 2 Cotton Factories, 1 Woolen Factory, 1 Paper Mill, 6 Grain Mills, three of which are tide Mills, 2 Fulling Mills and Clothiers' works, 2 Carding Machines and 4 Tanneries. There are 9 Mercantile Stores.

The population of the town, at the census of 1810, was 3533; and there are 500 Dwelling houses, 400 Freemen or Electors, and 3 companies of militia.

The amount of taxable property, (estimated according to the laws for making up lists,) including polls, is $86,416.

The town is divided into three parishes, or located Congregational Societies; besides these, there are one Society of Episcopalians, one of Baptists, and one of Methodists. There are 17 School districts, in each of which there is a School house, and a primary or common School maintained, 1 Social Library, 3 Clergymen, 4 Physicians and 1 resident Lawyer.

This township was comprised within a tract, purchased of the natives in 1640, and settled under the government of New-Netherlands, (now New-York,) and was incorporated in 1665, by Peter Stuyvesant, then governor of New-Netherlands. But upon obtaining the charter of Charles 2d, Greenwich being included within the limits of Connecticut, as defined by the charter, it was afterwards granted by the colony, or the General Court, to eight persons or proprietors.

HUNTINGTON.

HUNTINGTON, a post town, is situated on the west side of the Ousatonick river, being 17 miles from New-Haven, and 45 from Hartford. It is bounded north on Newtown, south on Stratford and Trumbull, west on Reading and Weston, and east on the Ousatonick river, which separates the town from Oxford and Derby.

The township is about 10 miles long, from northwest to southeast, and averaging nearly 6 miles broad, from east to west, containing an area of about 56 square miles.

The surface is uneven, being

diversified with hill and dale; but the soil, which is a gravelly loam, is generally fertile and productive. It is adapted to a grain culture, and produces rye and other grains.

Agriculture is the principal business of the town, and furnishes employment to most of the inhabitants. Rye, corn, oats and flax are the principal agricultural interests.

The Ousatonick river washes the town on its eastern border. There are several shad fisheries upon this river, and two bridges across it, one called Zoar, and the other Leavenworth's bridge.

Bridgeport and Newtown turnpike road runs through the west part of the town.

The population of the town, in 1810, was 2770; and there are now 400 qualified Electors, 3 Companies of Militia, and 400 Dwelling houses.

The taxable polls and estate of the town, in 1817, was $60,000.

There are 5 Mercantile Stores, 4 Grain Mills, 2 Carding Machines, 18 District Schools, 6 Churches, two for Congregationalists, two for Episcopalians, one for Baptists, and one for Methodists; 1 Lawyer, 3 Clergymen and 2 Physicians.

The town was incorporated in 1789.

NEW-CANAAN.

NEW-CANAAN, a small post township, is situated 8 miles north of Long Island sound, and 77 miles south west from Hartford.

It is bounded north by the State of New-York, west by the town of Stamford, south by Stamford and Norwalk, and east, partly by Norwalk and partly by Wilton. Its extent is 6 miles in length and 4 in breadth, containing 24 square miles, or 15,360 acres.

The surface is mountainous, containing spines or ridges composed of rock and stone, which extend from north to south through the town.

The soil is a hard gravelly loam, being stony, but tolerably well timbered, and generally good for cultivation; producing wheat, rye, corn, oats, flax and buck-wheat, and affording, generally, good pasturage and grass.

There are several small streams in the town, the most considerable of which are the Five mile river, which rises in the State of New-York, and runs through the town; Nosoten, which rises within the town; one branch of Stamford Mill river, which runs through its north-west section; and a branch of Norwalk river, that runs through the east part of the town.

Although agriculture is the leading pursuit of the inhabitants, yet considerable attention is paid to manufactures, particularly to the manufacture of shoes, of which there are annually about 60,000 pair sent abroad for a market.

At the census of 1810, the population of the town was 1599. There are now 220 Freemen, 2 Companies of militia, 260 Dwelling houses, 2 Churches, one for Congregationalists and one for

Episcopalians, 6 Grain Mills, 5 Saw Mills, 3 Distilleries, 3 Tanneries, 2 Carding Machines and 7 Mercantile Stores. There are 9 School Districts and common Schools, 1 Academy, 1 located and 1 Episcopal Society, 2 Social Libraries, 1 Clergyman and 2 Physicians.

The general list of the town, in 1817, was $36,948.

New-Canaan was incorporated as a town in 1801.

NEW-FAIRFIELD.

NEW-FAIRFIELD is an inconsiderable town, situated in the northwestern section of the county, 64 miles distant from Hartford; and is bounded on the north by Sherman, on the east by New-Milford, in Litchfield county, and Brookfield, on the south by Danbury and Ridgefield, and on the west by the State of New-York. Its average length is 5 miles, and its average breadth 4 and a half miles, comprising 22 and a half square miles.

The township is broken, having several granite ridges extending through it; the soil is hard and gravelly. There are some indications of iron ore in some parts of these ridges; but, as yet, there is no mine or bed of ore opened or worked. The timber and forests consist of oak of the different kinds, and other trees common to this region. The lands, when cultivated, produce wheat, rye, oats, grass, &c., and are considerably fertile and productive.

The town is watered by Rocky river, a considerable mill stream, which runs in a northeasterly direction, and discharges itself into the Ousatonick. It contains 3 small ponds, the most considerable of which is called Bull's pond.

The population of the town, in 1810, was 772; and there are now, 130 qualified Electors, 1 company of militia, and 130 Dwelling houses.

The amount of taxable property, including polls, is $19,128.

There are 1 Grain Mill, 1 Fulling Mill and Clothiers' works, 2 Carding Machines, 1 Tannery, 3 Mercantile Stores and 3 public Inns.

The town contains one located Congregational Society & Church, one Society of Methodists, six School districts & common Schools, one small Social Library, one Physician and two Clergymen.

New-Fairfield was granted by the General Assembly, in October 1707, to sundry inhabitants of the town of Fairfield, whence it received its name; but the war, which at that time existed with the natives, prevented its being settled for some time afterwards.

NEWTOWN.

NEWTOWN, a flourishing post town, is pleasantly situated in the northern section of the county, on the southwestern border of the Ousatonick river, 48 miles southwest from Hartford, and about 26 miles northwest from New-Haven; bounded on the northwest by Brookfield, on the northeast and east by the Ousatonick river, which separates it from Southbury, in New-Haven county, on the southeast by Huntington and Weston, and on the southwest by Reading and Danbury.

The township lies in a triangular form, and comprises an area of about 50 square miles, having an average length from northwest to southeast of about 8 miles, and a mean breath of more than 6 miles. This township has an elevated location. Its surface is hilly, and many of the eminences are extensive and continuous; but no part of it is mountainous. The soil, which principally is a gravelly loam, with some sections of sandy loam, is, in general, fertile and productive. It is well adapted to a grain culture; and rye, which is extensively and successfully cultivated, forms the staple production. It is favourable for fruit, and abounds with many valuable orchards. The agricultural interests are respectable; and, being an interior township, and having paid but little attention to manufactures, they afford employment to the principal part of the industry of the place.

The township is well watered, its northeastern boundary throughout its whole course being washed by the Ousatonick, and its area intersected by the Powtatuck and several small streams. In the northwestern section of the township, is a pond of considerable extent. Upon the Ousatonick, connecting this town with Southbury, there is a toll bridge, called Bennett's bridge. This town is well accommodated with roads; there being, in addition to the public roads, several turnpikes leading through it, one from Hartford to Danbury, and one leading to Bridgeport.

The manufactures of the town are inconsiderable. There are, however, 1 Woolen Factory, 10 small Distilleries, 4 Tanneries, 5 Grain Mills, 5 Carding Machines and 4 Fulling Mills and Clothiers' works.

The population of the town, in 1810, was 2834; and there are about 400 Dwelling houses, 300 Electors, and 3 Companies of militia. The town contains 7 religious Societies; one located Congregational, one Episcopal, which is the largest in the State, one Baptist, one small Society of Sandemanians, one of Universalists, and two others. There are 15 School Districts & primary Schools and 2 Social Libraries.

In the central section of the the township there is a considerable village. It is pleasantly situated on a height of land, rising gradually from the south, and more abruptly on the east and west, being the subsidence or gradual termination of a considerable ridge, extending from the mountainous district to the north and west. The village consists principally of one street, which is very broad, and, for nearly a mile, is well built; it contains 50 or 60 Dwelling houses, 2 houses for public worship, 2

Schoolhouses, 3 Mercantile Stores, and numerous Mechanics' shops and other buildings.

The two turnpike roads, already noticed, lead through the village.

From the elevated site of this village, it affords an extensive and interesting prospect to the east, south and west, a distance of 8 or 9 miles, comprising a fertile country, in a high state of cultivation, and exhibiting, in every direction, the grateful results of rural industry.

There are, in Newtown, 2 Clergymen, 4 Physicians and 4 Attornies. The aggregate list of the town, in 1817, was $65,085.

In May 1708, the General Assembly made a grant of the tract of country comprising this township, which was then called Powtatuck, from the river of that name, by which it is intersected. At the same session it was incorporated, by the name of Newtown.

NORWALK.

NORWALK, a flourishing maritime post township, is situated upon Long Island sound, 66 miles southwest from Hartford, 32 west from New-Haven, and 48 northeast from the city of New-York; bounded on the north by New-Canaan and Wilton, on the east by the Saugatuck river, which separates it from Fairfield, on the south by Long Island sound, and on the west by Stamford. It comprises an area of about 34 square miles; having a mean length from east to west of about 7 miles, and a medium breadth from north to south of nearly 5 miles. The surface is uneven, being pleasantly diversified with hill and dale. Upon the border of the sound the hills are generally moderate; and in the interior more elevated.

The geological character is primitive, the prevailing strata of rocks consisting of granite. The general character of the soil is a dark coloured gravelly mould or loam, very feasible and fertile. It has a suitable adaptation both for grain and grazing, and is very favourable for fruit. This town is rich in agricultural opulence—abounds in the means of sustaining a dense population—from its contiguity to the sound, has a moderate, uniform and salubrious climate—a ready and convenient market, being possessed of navigable waters, rendering it always accessible from the sea, and affording, at all times, a facility of communication with New-York, whereby it unites ample advantages, and a powerful stimulus to agricultural industry and improvement. And these advantages, if they have not been improved to the greatest extent, have not been neglected.

The staple agricultural products consist of Indian corn, rye, oats, wheat, flour, flax, flax-seed, beef, pork and potatoes; most of which are articles of exportation.

The forests, which consist of oak of the different kinds, walnut, chesnut, &c. are very valuable, from the facility with which wood and timber are conveyed to the New-York market.

NORWALK.

The waters of the town are principally embodied in the Saugatuck, which washes its eastern border, forming the boundary between this town and Fairfield; and Norwalk river, a considerable stream which runs through the centre of the town, and discharges its waters into Long Island sound, forming the harbour, which is at the mouth of this stream, and has sufficient depth of water for vessels of 100 tons, and is safe and convenient. There is also another harbour at what is called Five mile river, which admits of vessels of about the same size. There are several small islands in Long Island sound, off this town, and numerous small inlets upon its borders.

Of the fishing business, black fish and shell fish are taken in the sound.

This town possesses considerable advantages for navigation, and the interests thereof are continually increasing. There are 16 vessels of every description belonging to the town, of which there are six regular packets that constantly ply between this place and New-York. One of them is employed exclusively in the conveyance of passengers. The remaining ten vessels consist of sloops and schooners, and are employed in the coasting trade to New-York and elsewhere.

In addition to the pursuits of agriculture, navigation and commerce, some attention has been bestowed on manufactures. There are 1 Woolen Factory, 2 Cotton Factories, one upon an extensive scale, 1 Slitting and 1 Rolling Mill, 5 Grain Mills, two of which are merchants' or flouring Mills, 3 Fulling Mills and Cloth Dressing establishments, 4 Carding Machines and 2 Tanneries.

The population of the town, in 1810, was 2983; and there are about 400 Electors or Freemen, about the same number of Dwelling houses, and 5 Companies of militia.

The town contains 1 located Congregational Society, 1 Society of Episcopalians, and 1 of Methodists, which are respectively accommodated with houses for public worship. It contains one considerable and flourishing village, situated upon the great stage road leading to New-York, at the head of the harbour. It is a place of considerable activity and business, being the seat of most of the commercial and navigation business of the town. It is the commercial depot and market for the northern section of the county; most of the staple products being brought here for sale, or to be freighted to New-York.

There are, in the village, nearly 100 houses, a number of trading houses, Dry goods and Grocery stores, 1 Bookstore, several private offices, a Post-office, a Newspaper and Printing establishment, 2 Churches, and several Mechanics' shops.

There are in Norwalk 13 primary Schools and 1 Academy, 16 Mercantile Stores, 7 Public Inns, 3 Physicians, 3 Clergymen and 2 Attornies.

The aggregate list of the town, in 1816, was $53,231.

Norwalk was settled in 1651, and incorporated in 1655, four years from the first settlement.

This town is memorable in the annals of the revolutionary war; having been burned by the British and Tories in 1779. The loss sustained by the inhabitants, from the destruction of buildings and other property, was estimated by a committee, appointed by the General Assembly for the purpose, at $116,238 : 36. A great proportion of the dwelling houses and stores were burnt.

READING.

READING, an interior, central post township, is situated 60 miles southwest from Hartford; bounded on the north by Danbury, on the east by Newtown and Weston, on the south by Weston, and on the west by Ridgefield. Its average length from east to west is nearly 6 and a half miles, and its mean breadth from north to south about 5 miles; comprising an area of about 32 square miles. The face of the country is characteristically diversified with hill and dale. The prevailing strata of rocks consist of granite and primitive limestone; and the soil, corresponding with the geological features of different sections of the township, is a gravelly and calcareous loam. From the calcareous strata limestone is obtained for making lime, of which considerable quantities are annually produced.

This town is rich in resources for agricultural improvements and wealth. It contains very little waste land, and the soil is generally good. The calcareous sections are fertile and productive, affording wheat, rye, oats and Indian corn in abundance; and the sections which are not so favourable for the growth of grain, are well adapted to grazing. Considerable quantities of beef and pork are marketed, and large quantities of flax are annually raised.

This being an interior township, and not having engaged to any extent in any manufacturing interest, agriculture is almost exclusively the business of the inhabitants.

There is a considerable proportion of forest lands in the town; the natural growth of timber consists of oak, walnut, chesnut, and other deciduous trees.

The waters of the township are principally embodied in the Saugatuck and Norwalk rivers; the former of which intersects it, running through its centre, and the latter washes its western section.

In addition to the public or county roads, the town is accommodated with several turnpikes; one from Danbury to Norwalk leads through it, and also one from Danbury to Greenfield, in the town of Fairfield.

Of the manufacturing and mechanical establishments of the town, there are 1 Woolen Factory, 5 Grain Mills, 2 Cloth Dressing establishments, 3 Carding Machines, 3 Tanneries and 1 Lime kiln.

The population of this town, in 1810, was 1717; and there are about 260 Dwelling houses, about 300 Electors, 2 Companies of Infantry and a part of a Company of Cavalry, of Militia.

Its civil divisions are 1 located Congregational Society and 11 School Districts; besides the located, there is 1 Society of Episcopalians, and 1 of Methodists, all of which are accommodated with houses for public worship.

There are, in the town, 5 Mercantile Stores, 5 Taverns or Public Inns, 1 Social Library, 2 Physicians and 3 Clergymen.

The aggregate list of the town, in 1816, was $48,707.

Reading was incorporated in May, 1767.

BIOGRAPHY. *Joel Barlow*, L. L. D. distinguished as a poet, politician, statesman and philosopher, was a native of this town. As the design of this work does not contemplate giving lengthy biographical accounts, we must, in this instance, confine ourselves to a notice of a few facts, exhibiting a compressed view of the life and writings of Mr. Barlow. He was born in or about the year 1755. His father, who was an independent farmer, but in moderate circumstances, died whilst he was a youth, leaving him a small patrimony, scarcely sufficient to defray the expenses of a liberal education, which he had contemplated. Having been placed in Dartmouth College in 1774, he was soon after removed from thence to Yale College, at New-Haven, where he graduated in 1778. The class into which he entered was remarkable for the great promise of talent which many of its members disclosed; among whom Barlow always ranked conspicuous. The late Asa Spalding and Uriah Tracey, his Excellency Oliver Wolcott, Alexander Wolcott, Abraham Bishop and Josiah Meigs were members of this class. He passed through the usual course of academic studies with great reputation, and at the public commencement in 1778, delivered or recited an original poem, which was the first time he had appeared before the public in his poetical character. This effusion of his muse was soon after printed, and has been preserved in a collection entitled "American Poems." Previously to this period, and whilst Barlow was in College, the revolutionary war commenced, and the natural ardour and enthusiasm of his mind, stimulated by the pervading spirit of liberty which characterized the times, led him to take a deep interest in a contest in which both the cause of civil liberty and the dearest interests of his country were so intimately concerned. During the early period of the war, the militia of Connecticut constituted an important part of the army. Barlow had four brothers in the service; and more than once, duing vacations, he armed himself with a musket, and joined them in the " bloody strife," as a volunteer. It is said he was in the battle at White Plains.

Upon his leaving College, he commenced the study of law; but, at the urgent solicitation and recommendation of some of his friends, he was induced to abandon this situation, and to qualify himself for, and accept the appointment of chaplain to the army. Whilst in this situation, he wrote several poetical effusions, strongly marked with patriotic and liberal sentiments, and calculated to encourage and animate the army, in the various hardships, privations and difficulties with which they had to contend. And whilst in the army, he conceived, planned, and in part composed, the celebrated poem which he afterwards published, entitled the "Vision of Columbus," and which was subsequently enlarged into his great national poem, the Columbiad. In 1781, he took the degree of A. M. at New-Haven, on which occasion he delivered a poem, entitled the "Prospect of Peace," which was principally embodied in the Vision of Columbus. About the same time, he married Miss Baldwin of New-Haven, a sister of Abraham Baldwin, for many years a distinguished member of Congress from Georgia, of whose life and character there is a brief notice following the account of the town of Guilford. After the peace in 1783, Barlow being out of employment, resolved to resume the study of law, for which purpose he removed to Hartford, with the expectation, probably, of making it his residence for life. Whilst in this situation, to aid him in his finances, he, in connection with Elisha Babcock, established a weekly newspaper, called the "American Mercury," which has ever since been published by Mr. Babcock.

In 1787, whilst engaged in this business, he published his "Vision of Columbus," a patriotic and popular poem. It was dedicated to Louis XVI., and met with very flattering success, being re-printed in London within a few months; it has since gone through a second edition in America, and one in Paris. About this period, in pursuance of the request of the General Association of the clergy of this State, he undertook the revision of Dr. Watts' version of the Psalms. His edition was published in 1786, and comprised several devotional pieces of his own composing.

About the time of these publications, he disposed of his interest in the paper to Mr. Babcock, and opened a book-store, the principal object of which was to effect the sale of his poem and edition of the Psalms. About this time, the Anarchiad was published at this place, in which Mr. Barlow is said to have taken a conspicuous part. On the 4th of July, 1787, and whilst the Convention which framed the Constitution of the United States was in session at Philadelphia, he delivered an oration to the Connecticut Cincinnati. Not being satisfied with his prospects in his profession, the next year he embarked for England, as the agent of a Land Company, called the Ohio Company, from whence he soon proceeded to France. Whilst in France, the Revolution commenced, which led Barlow to an intimate acquaintance with most of the leaders of the republican party, and particularly with those which were afterwards denominated *Girondists*. His philanthropy and enthusiasm in the cause of liberty led him to enter warmly into their plans, which received the support of his genius and political intelligence and experience. In 1791, he returned to England, and near the close of that year, published his "Advice to Privileged Orders," a work of solid merit, exposing, in a forcible manner, the abuses and evils of the feudal governments of Europe. In 1792, he published a small poem, entitled the "Conspiracy of Kings." From these publications, being of a political nature, and from his intimacy with the leaders of opposition, or friends of reform in England, he had become very obnoxious to the ministerial party. Near the close of the year 1792, he returned to France, as one of a committee of the London Constitutional Society, with an Address from the Society to the National Convention. He was received in France with great respect; and, soon after his arrival, had conferred upon him the rights of a French citizen. The year following, he was employed, in connection with a deputation of the National Convention, to assist in organizing the territory of Savoy, as a department of the Republic. Whilst at Chamberry, in this territory, he wrote a political address to the people of Piedmont. In this place he amused himself in writing a mock didactic poem, called "Hasty Pudding." From Savoy he returned to Paris, where he resided for about three years. During this period, he translated Volney's Ruins; being shocked at the atrocities of the Revolution, he withdrew from political affairs.

In 1795, he was appointed by President Washington consul at Algiers, with powers to negotiate a treaty with the Dey, and to redeem all American prisoners held in slavery by any of the Barbary powers. He immediately set out upon his mission, and, crossing through Spain, arrived at Algiers, where he soon succeeded in negotiating a treaty with the Dey, although surrounded with numerous difficulties. Early the succeeding year, he negotiated a similar treaty with Tripoli, and liberated all the American prisoners held in captivity. In 1797, he resigned his consulship and returned to Paris; and having engaged in some commercial pursuits or speculations, was very successful, and accumulated a handsome fortune. In the rupture which took place between France and the United States, Barlow exerted his influence and talents, to promote an amicable adjustment; for which end he addressed a letter to the people of the United States, upon the measures of the party then in power. This was soon followed by another, which was more abstract and examined, in that clear and forcible manner peculiar to its author, various political topics, and particularly certain established principles of maritime law and the rights of neutrals. His views were novel and bold, and founded upon the principles of abstract right, which he regarded as the only true policy. In 1805, after an absence of seventeen years from his native country, Barlow resolved upon re-visiting the scenes of his youth. He accordingly sold his real estate in France, which he had regarded as his adopted country, as long as it continued the country of liberty. After visiting different parts of the country, he purchased him a delightful situation in the vicinity of Georgetown, within the limits of the district of Columbia. Whilst in this situation, he enjoyed the society, friendship and esteem of Mr. Jefferson, then President of the United States; & of the other important functionaries and characters of distinction, who were residents, or engaged in public employments at the seat of government. In 1806, he published a prospectus of a national institution, or university; to establish which, a bill was introduced into the Senate; it met with considerable opposition; was referred to a select committee, who never reported, and thus this great national object ended. He now devoted his attention to the revision and improvement of his favourite poem; and in 1808, the Columbiad made its appearance in the most magnificent volume, which ever issued from an American press. The high price of this edition prevented its circulation; and the subsequent year, it was re-printed in two volumes. The same year, it was republished in London, in an elegant royal 8 vo. The Columbiad has been attacked in the severest manner, by critics of every rank; but Barlow, relying upon the solid merits of the poem, and the impartial award of posterity, either treated them with neglect or contempt. The Columbiad is an epic poem, abounding in philosophical discussion, and in enlarged, political and national views. It was expanded from the vision of Columbus which it comprises, and is the offspring of the labour of half a life. It is a great national work, and cannot fail of going down to posterity, to the latest generation. The name of Barlow will long be known and revered, when all those who have attempted to asperse it, will be forgotten. After the publication of his Columbiad, he was employed in collecting materials for a general history of the United States, a work which he had long meditated; but whilst thus occupied, in 1811, he was appointed minister plenipotentiary to the French government; whereupon he soon embarked again for France, clothed with authority and distinguished honours. He applied himself with great diligence to the duties of his new station, and made every exertion to effect the negotiation of a treaty of commerce, and indemnity for spoliation. In October 1812, he was invited to a conference with the Emperor at Wilna. He immediately set off upon this mission, and travelled day and night, exposed to the severe weather of a northern climate; subject to great fatigue, and accommodations at the public Inns being the most wretched, scarcely being able to obtain a wholesome meal, his constitution was unable to withstand these severe trials; he sunk into a state of debility, from which he never recovered. He died, December 22d, 1812, at Zarnawica, an obscure village of Poland, in the neighbourhood of Cracow. America has produced few men more justly deserving of immortality than Barlow; and none, it is believed, who have made their title to it more sure. He lived in an eventful period, and acted a conspicuous part in both hemispheres; and as a poet, a man of science, a politician, a philosopher and a philanthropist, his name will long be revered by the friends of civil liberty & of science, throughout the civilized world.

RIDGEFIELD.

RIDGEFIELD is an elevated post township, situated in the western section of the County and State, bordering upon the State of New-York, 10 miles southwest of Danbury, 70 miles southwest of Hartford, and 55 northeast of the city of New-York; bounded on the north by New-Fairfield, on the east by Danbury and Reading, on the south by Wilton, and on the west by the State of New-York. The township is of an oblong figure, being about 13 miles in length, and not more than 3 miles in breadth upon an average estimation, and comprises an area of about 37 square miles. The face of the county is characterized by a succession of ridges and vallies, ranging northerly and southerly, in a direction towards Long Island sound. Some of these ridges are considerably elevated, and afford an interesting view of the sound, although situated at a distance of 14 miles. The geological character of the township is primitive; the rocks consisting mostly of granite and primitive limestone. The prevailing soil is a gravelly loam, interspersed with some sections of calcareous loam,—is rich in resources for agricultural productions and improvements, well adapted both to a cultivation of grain and grazing, and also very favourable for fruit. The agricultural productions consist of wheat, rye, corn, oats, flax; and cheese, butter, beef, wool, &c.

The waters of the town consist of numerous small streams, of which the most considerable are several branches of Norwalk and Saugatuck rivers. Upon some of these streams, there are advantageous sites for mills or manufacturing establishments. The town is accommodated with the Ridgefield and Danbury turnpike. Agriculture is the principal business, and the manufactures of the town, exclusive of those of a domestic character. are inconsiderable. There are 1 Woolen Factory, 3 Fulling Mills and cloth dressing establishments, 1 large Tannery, 3 Grain Mills & 2 Carding Machines. There are several limekilns in the town.

Of the civil divisions of the town, there are 2 located Congregational Societies, and 12 School districts; besides the located, there is 1 Society of Episcopalians, 1 of Baptists and 1 of Methodists.

In the first located Society, there is a small but pleasant village, comprising, within the limits of about one mile, 50 or 60 Dwelling houses, 2 Churches, a Post-office, 3 Mercantile Stores, and several Mechanics' Shops.

The population of the town, in 1810, was 2103; and there are about 300 Electors or Freemen, about the same number of Dwelling houses, and 2 companies of Militia.

The amount of taxable property, including polls, is $55,357.

In the town, are 12 primary Schools and 1 Academy, 1 Social

Library, 5 Mercantile Stores, 4 Taverns, 4 Houses for public worship, 4 Physicians and 1 Clergyman.

The tract of land, comprising the township of Ridgefield, was called by the Indians *Caudatowa* high land, from its elevated situation, affording a prospect of Long Island for forty miles; and of the sound, and vessels navigating it. The Indian title was purchased in 1708, by several persons of Norwalk, to the number of twenty-five. The deed bears date the 30th of September 1708, and at the ensuing session of the General Court, it was incorporated into a distinct township, by the name of Ridgefield.

SHERMAN.

SHERMAN is a township, situated in the northwest corner of the county, 60 miles from Hartford; bounded on the north by Kent, in Litchfield county, on the east by New-Milford, on the south by New-Fairfield, and on the west by the State of New-York; having an average length of 9 and a half miles, and an average breadth of only 2 and a half miles, containing 23 and three-fourths square miles. Its surface is uneven, being characterized by elevated and lofty hills, and deep and extensive vales. The soil is various, according to the local situation of the lands, but is generally a gravelly loam. The hills, which are not suffered to remain for the growth of timber, afford grazing; and the vales, (most of which are warm and fertile,) are well adapted to the cultivation of wheat, rye and Indian corn, large quantities of which are annually raised.

Of the mineralogy of the town are some beds of iron ore, which, however, have received but little attention.

The town is watered by numerous small streams, which discharge their waters into the Ousatonick.

A turnpike road lately granted, extending from New-Milford to the State of New-York, runs thro' this town. Sherman contains one located Congregational Society, a Society of Episcopalians, and part of a Society of Baptists, and some Quakers. It contains 6 School districts and Schools, and 3 small villages, of 10 or 15 houses each.

The population of the town, in 1810, was 949; and there are 150 Freemen, 2 companies of militia, and 130 Dwelling houses.

The amount of taxable property, including polls, is $22,168. There are 1 Woolen Factory, 3 Distilleries, 2 Tanneries, 1 Grain Mill, 1 Fulling Mill, 1 Carding Machine, 1 Mercantile Store, 1 Public Inn, 2 Physicians and 1 Clergyman.

This town was incorporated in 1802.

BIOGRAPHY. Dr. *James Potter*, late President of the Medical Society, was a resident in this town. He was distinguished in his profession as a scholar, and a man of general science.

STAMFORD, an extensive and populous maritime post township, is situated on Long Island sound, in the southwestern part of the county and State, 10 miles southwest of Norwalk, 42 southwest of New-Haven, 76 southwest from Hartford, and 43 northeast from New-York; bounded on the north by the State of New-York, on the east by New-Canaan and Norwalk, on the south by Long Island sound, and on the west by Greenwich.

The township comprises an area of about 55 square miles; having a mean length from north to south of about 9 and a half miles, and a mean breadth from east to west of nearly 6 miles.

This is a pleasant and fertile township, rich in the resources of agricultural opulence, abounding in the means of subsistence, and of sustaining the primary interests of civilization, agriculture, commerce and the arts; it possesses a moderate and uniform climate, and the advantages of a ready and convenient market. The surface is undulating, exhibiting a pleasant and interesting diversity of moderate hills and gentle declivities and dales. The soil is a rich gravelly loam, feasible and fertile; being adapted both to tillage and grazing.

The staple agricultural products are Indian corn, rye and potatoes; the latter of which are extensively cultivated. From the facilities of communication with New-York, the value of potatoes is much increased, and a sure and ready market afforded; and hence their cultivation, which, under other circumstances must always be a minor object with the farmer, has become in this town an important interest. It is estimated that there are about 100,000 bushels sent to the New-York market annually from this town.

The town is well watered by several good mill streams, of which the principal are Mill river, which intersects the township, and discharges its waters into the sound, forming at its mouth a good harbour; the Noraton and the Miannus, the latter of which washes the northwestern section of the town, running thence into Greenwich. The harbour at the mouth of Mill river has, at ordinary tides, about eight and a half feet of water; besides this, there are two other harbours in the town, but the former is the principal one, and the seat of most of the maritime business. The shipping consists of six vessels, three of which are employed principally as packets between this place and New-York, and the others in the coasting trade. Black and shell fish are taken in Long Island sound, and in the bays and inlets thereof.

Connected with the navigation business of this town is the manufacture of flour, for exportation, which is carried on very extensively. There are two mills exclusively employed in this business; one of which is the largest in the State, containing 16 run of stones; the other contains 10 run. Besides these, there are 7 other Grain Mills in the town. Exclusive of the manufacture of flour, there are no considerable manufacturing interests in this town; not taking into view those of a domestic character. There are 2 Fulling Mills and Clothiers' works, 4 Carding Machines and 2 Tanneries. The mercantile business of the place is considerable, there being 14 Dry Goods and Grocery Stores.

The civil divisions of the town consist of 3 located Ecclesiastical Societies or Parishes, and 11 School Districts. Besides the located, there are 1 Episcopal Society; 2 Baptist Societies; 1 of Methodists, and 1 Society of Friends.

In the first located Society there is a delightful and interesting village, pleasantly situated upon Mill river, and the great mail road leading to New-York. It is a neat and handsome place, and comprises about 50 or 60 Dwelling houses, some of which are large and elegant, a Post office, several professional offices, 2 Churches, and several Mercantile Stores. The Post office at this place is a distributing office.

The population of Stamford, in 1810, was 4440; and there are about 450 Electors, 4 Companies of Militia, and about 600 Dwelling houses.

The aggregate list of the town, in 1816, was $91,668.

There are in the town 8 Public Inns or Taverns, 7 Houses for religious worship, 11 primary Schools, 2 Social Libraries, 4 Physicians, 7 Clergymen and 4 Attornies.

This is an ancient town, the settlement having commenced in 1641. It was called by the natives Rippowams.

STRATFORD.

STRATFORD, a pleasant and flourishing post township, is situated on the west side of the Ousatonick river, about 3 miles from its mouth, and 13 from New-Haven; bounded on the north by Trumbull and Huntington, on the east by the Ousatonick river, on the south by Long Island sound, and on the west by Fairfield. Its average length is about 6 miles, and its average breadth 4 miles, comprising an area of about 24 square miles.

The township is generally level, and free from stone; the more prevailing soil is a gravelly loam, interspersed with some sections of sandy loam. The flat, bordering upon the harbour and the river, appears to be an alluvial formation, presenting, on an examination into its interior structure, alternate strata of sand and gravel, with some strata of clay. This is a strong and rich soil; the more elevated lands in the interior are of a good soil, being warm, healthy and productive. They afford wheat, rye, corn, oats, grass and flax, the latter of which is cultivated to great advantage, and is of an excellent quality. There are also various other agricultural productions, of which cider, cider brandy, butter, cheese, beef, pork, lard and flax seed are the most considerable.

The southern border of the town is washed by Long Island sound, and the eastern by the Ousatonick river. There are several valuable shad fisheries in the Ousatonick; and almost all kinds

STRATFORD. 195

of shell fish are taken in the harbour, which consists of an arm of the sea, or of Long Island sound.

The population of the town, in 1810, was 2895; and there are 300 Freemen or Electors, 4 Companies of Militia, and about 420 Dwelling houses, including the borough of Bridgeport.

The amount of taxable property, including polls, is $54,197.

The manufacturing and mechanical employments of the town, exclusive of the borough of Bridgeport, are 1 Tin-ware Factory, 1 Tannery, 2 Carding Machines, 3 Grain Mills, 3 Merchants' Mills, for flouring wheat, grinding Indian corn and plaster of Paris.

The civil divisions of the town consist of 2 located Congregational Societies, 1 incorporated Borough, and 10 School Districts; there is also a Society of Episcopalians, and one of Methodists, all of which are respectively provided with Houses for public worship. There are 10 common or primary Schools, one in each District, and an Academy or Grammar School.

BRIDGEPORT, an incorporated borough, is situated in north lat. 41° 18' and west lon. 73° 12', on the west side of an arm of the sea, called Bridgeport harbour, distant southwest from New-Haven 17 miles, and from Hartford 51, and northeast from New-York 62 miles; bounded south on Long Island sound; it is about two miles in length from north to south, and half a mile in breadth from east to west. The harbour extends about three miles within land to the head of tide water, where it meets Pequanock river, a considerable mill stream, on which are several mills within a dozen miles, and two with six run of stones on tide water. The average width of the harbour, at high water, (it being a tide harbour,) is eighty rods. At low water, most of it is bare, leaving only a channel about a dozen rods wide. Common tides rise seven feet; spring tides nine. The depth of water on the bar at high water, in common tides, is thirteen feet; within the bar the water is much deeper, and has a muddy bottom, so that, at low water, loaded vessels lie at ease on the flats, while those in the channel, of almost every size, have sufficient depth of water, as ships of 200 tons can conveniently load at the wharves, and at high water proceed to sea. Vessels, when once within the bar, are at all times safe from dangers of the sea; and the entrance is also safe and easy, by means of a large beacon, just within the chops, 40 feet in height, on the west side of the channel, and the light-house on Fairweather's Island, both of which were procured by and erected by citizens of Bridgeport.

There is a bridge across the harbour, about a mile and a half from its mouth, 75 rods long, and 24 feet broad, built on trestles, and accommodated with a draw, for vessels to proceed above. This bridge, though originally built by the State, now belongs to an incorporated company, who are by law allowed to collect a toll upon it.

The surface on which the town is principally built, is a plain or level, about 12 feet above high water mark. There is, however,

STRATFORD.

a rise, called golden hill, commencing about 100 rods northwest of the centre of the present buildings, which, after a gradual ascent of about 20 rods, in which the perpendicular elevation is 50 feet, presents a surface of half a mile square, forming a delightful situation for an upper town, from which the eye may at a single glance take a survey of Long Island and the sound for a distance of 30 or 40 miles, with the numerous vessels plying upon the latter; and more nearly of a champaign country for several miles to the east and west of the town, forming altogether a landscape highly beautiful. The base of this hill appears to be silicious rock, much of which may be easily split into convenient building stones, while the soil upon it is of sufficient depth, and of the best mould, for trees and cultivation. Several springs of the best water issue from the southeastern side of the hill, from fountains evidently sufficient for the supply of an extensive town.

The earth in the lower town has no where been opened deeper than for wells. The lowest stratum discovered is a fine alluvial sand; next incumbent, is a coarse gravel, then a fine gravel, in the moister parts mixed with clay and some veins of iron ore. The surface is a soil formed principally of clay and sand, and naturally the most fertile, and affords excellent gardens.

Of the various roads running into the country, one only is a turnpike, called *Bridgeport and Newtown turnpike*, beginning at Bridgeport and ending at New-Milford.

On the east side of the harbour, about a mile above its mouth, the tide waters break out, and take the course of a small stream called Old Mill creek, about two miles upon which stands a large flouring mill of eight run of stones; the dam forming a bridge, across which is the great stage road from New-Haven to New-York. The land between the two branches, called the Point, is a beautiful level plain, at the lower end of which is a handsome village, called the Old Mill village, although not within the limits of the corporation.

There is a natural canal running from the Ousatonick river into Bridgeport harbour, which is at present useful, and with a little expense might be of vast importance, as it would give an inland boat navigation from Bridgeport to Derby. Oysters and clams, both round and long, together with a variety of scale and fin fish, are found plentifully in the harbour and adjoining waters.

The borough contains a population, by an actual census, of 867 persons, and the point, 222; making an aggregate population of 1089. Within the borough are 92 dwelling houses, on the point, 31, in the whole, 123; of which many are handsome two story buildings, generally painted white.

There are in the borough, 2 handsome houses for public worship, each having a good bell, one for Episcopalians and the other for Congregationalists.

The principal occupations of the inhabitants are manufactures, trade, commerce and navigation. There are 18 sail of vessels, making 1414 tons, employed princi-

STRATFORD. 197

pally in the coasting and West-India trade. Large quantities of wheat and rye flour, kiln dried Indian meal, rye, corn, oats, flaxseed, pork, beef, butter, lard, cider, cider brandy, and a vast variety of other articles, which constitute the exports of the place, afford them constant employment. The principal manufacturers are hatters, saddlers, saddle-tree makers, boot and shoe makers, gold and silver smiths, watch makers, watch case makers, plate workers and fan light makers, tinners, comb makers, carriage makers, cabinet makers, tallow chandlers and coopers. The products of the labours of many of these furnish large items in the exports of the place. Of the manufactures here noticed, which are exported for a market, hats, saddles, saddletrees, combs, boots, shoes and candles are the most important. This is the only place in Connecticut where the plate-working business is carried on; and the plate which is made here is as handsome, and of as good a quality as any in America. There are also two tanneries, at which large quantities of leather of all sorts are manufactured; three printing offices, one an extensive establishment, exclusively for books; from the others are issued two weekly newspapers; two book-binderies, each of which carries on the business upon an extensive scale, and large quantities of books are bound annually; one pottery, besides a variety of mechanics' shops upon an inferior scale. There are in the borough, 15 large warehouses, 28 mercantile stores, 1 bank, 1 prac-

tising physician, 1 surgeon, 1 lawyer and 1 clergyman.

The most singular and striking characteristic of the inhabitants, is their carefulness in avoiding litigation; and it is perhaps an unprecedented fact, that there has not been, in the space of 20 years, a single trial before the County or Superior Court, wherein the parties were both residents in this borough; and but few in which either of them has lived here.

The borough of Bridgeport is one of the most healthy places in the State, no epidemical or contagious disease having ever prevailed here, and cases of fever very rarely.

Though situated within three miles of Stratford and four of Fairfield, both among the earliest settlements of the State, at the close of the revolutionary war, there were not more than 10 or 12 small houses upon the site where Bridgeport has since been built; so that the place has grown up to its present size and consequence since that period. In 1793, the bridge was built across the harbour; in 1798, a fire-engine was provided by the inhabitants, and the village incorporated for its management; in 1800, the borough was incorporated; and in 1806, the bank established, having received a charter from the legislature of the State. In 1810, the census was taken separately, for the first time, by which it appeared that the borough then contained 572 inhabitants.

The growth of this place has been altogether natural, having never been forced, or received any aid or patronage, other than what has arisen from its own local advantages and resources; from which considerations, and from its present flourishing appearances, it is believed that it will not prove altogether an illusion, to calculate, that at some future period it will become a considerable town.

In addition to the borough of Bridgeport, there are several villages in this town; the one called Old Mill village, which is the most considerable, has already been noticed. There is also the village of Putney, and the village of Oronoque.

There are in Stratford, exclusive of Bridgeport, 2 Physicians, 2 Attornies, 2 Clergymen, and 1 Social Library.

Stratford is an ancient town, having been settled in 1639.

BIOGRAPHY. Gen. *David Wooster* was a native of this town, and was born in 1711. He was educated at Yale College, and took his first degree in 1738. He commanded the Connecticut sloop of war, in the expedition against Louisburg in 1745, which conveyed the Connecticut troops. This sloop, together with one from Rhode-Island, which accompanied it in this expedition, engaged the Renonnee, a French frigate of 36 guns, which, although superior in force to both of her assailants, was compelled to sheer off, to avoid being captured. In the French war, he was appointed to the command of one of the regiments, raised by this State for that service, sustained this command during most of the war, and acquired the reputation of a faithful, brave and good officer. From his military experience and character, and the reputation which he had acquired, he was appointed in 1775, at the commencement of the revolutionary war, commander of the Connecticut troops, and was subsequently made a Brigadier General in the continental army. This commission he soon resigned, and was afterwards appointed the first Major General of the militia in Connecticut.

In 1777, a party of the British having landed at Compo, and marched from thence to Danbury, for the purpose of destroying the military stores at that place, belonging to the public. General Wooster hastened to oppose them with such force as he could collect on the exigency of the occasion, which consisted of about 300 men. With this inconsiderable force he fell upon the British, as they were retreating, having accomplished the object of incursion, and burned a considerable part of the town. A smart skirmish ensued, in which Gen. Wooster, while gallantly fighting in the van of his little party, was mortally wounded. This event happened on the 27th April, 1777, and he died on the 2d of May following, at Danbury. A monument was voted to be erected to his memory by Congress, which, however, has never been done.

Gen. Wooster was a brave and good officer, an ardent patriot, possessed a respectable understanding, and, in his various public and private relations, sustained a character distinguished for integrity, benevolence and virtue.

TRUMBULL.

TRUMBULL, an interior post township, is situated 4 and a half miles from Bridgeport, 20 from New-Haven, and 55 from Hartford; bounded on the north and east by Huntington, on the south by Stratford, and on the west by Fairfield and Weston. Its average length is about 5 miles, and its average breadth 4 and a half miles, comprising about 22 square miles.

The township is uneven, being diversified with hill and dale; and the prevailing character of the soil is a gravelly loam, and it is considerably fertile and productive. Rye, corn, oats and some wheat are cultivated; and the lands are tolerably well adapted to the culture of grass, and to grazing.

The geological structure of the township is characterized by granitic features, and its natural growth is the same as is common to this region.

The town is watered by Pequanock, a small stream which discharges its waters into Bridgeport harbour. The Bridgeport and New-Milford turnpike road leads thro' this town.

The population of the town, in 1810, was 1241; and there are 175 qualified Electors, 1 company of militia, and about 200 Dwelling houses. There are 4 Grain Mills, 3 Fulling Mills and Clothiers' works, 3 Carding Machines, and 5 Mercantile Stores.

The town contains 1 located Congregational Society, and 1 Society of Episcopalians, both of which are accommodated with houses for public worship; 6 School districts and Schools, and 1 small Social Library. There are 2 Physicians, 1 Clergyman and 1 Attorney.

The amount of taxable property, including polls, is $25,100.

Trumbull originally belonged to Stratford, and was incorporated as a town in 1801.

WESTON.

WESTON is situated about 8 miles north from the sound. It is bounded south by the town of Fairfield, east by Trumbull and Huntington, north by Reading & Newtown, & west by Wilton and Norwalk. The extent of the township is nearly 9 miles from east to west, & 6 miles from north to south, containing about 50 square miles, or 32000 acres. The surface is uneven & hilly, and the soil a gravelly loam. The geological structure of the town, (which has probably never been examined,) exhibits many appearances of iron ore; its rock is a coarse granite, micaceous schistus, some silicious stones and felspar. The forests, which are considerably extensive, comprise oak of the various kinds, hickory, maple, bass, white-wood, chesnut, butternut &c., containing much valuable timber.

The lands, when cultivated, produce wheat, rye, oats, maize or Indian corn, buckwheat, flax, all kinds of culinary vegetables, esculent roots, and fruit from plants, vines, shrubs and trees, common to the climate. But rye, oats and corn are the staple agricultural productions.

There are several small streams

in the town, which afford many valuable sites for mills, and other hydraulic works; the most considerable of which, are the Saugatuck and its branches, Mill river, and Creker's brook. Many of the privileges which these streams afford are advantageously occupied. Agriculture is the principal business of the inhabitants, who are steady and industrious. The turnpike road from Fairfield to Danbury passes through this town.

The population, according to the last census, is 2618; and there are about 450 Electors, and 230 militia. The general list of the town, in 1817, was $57,551.

There are 9 Grain Mills, 12 Saw Mills, 1 Forge for the manufacture of iron, 4 Distilleries, 4 Tanneries, 3 Carding Machines, 3 Fulling Mills, 14 Mercantile Stores and 380 Dwelling houses.

There is an Academy, possessing a considerable fund, which renders it a free School; the number of district Schools we have not ascertained; 3 Social Libraries, 2 Congregational Societies and Churches, 1 Episcopal Church, 1 for Methodists, and 1 Society of Baptists; 3 Physicians and 1 Attorney. The town was first settled in 1738, and incorporated in 1787.

In 1808, a meteoric phenomenon occurred in this town. A solid mass, or meteoric stone, was precipitated to the earth, accompanied with a loud explosion. It appears to have been broken in the explosion; and was found in pieces or fragments. Soon after its descent, it was quite warm; and its fall was attended with the usual meteoric appearances, a brilliant light, and loud noises. Its general appearance was that of iron ore, its exterior being covered slightly with rust, and small portions of pure malleable iron were intermixed with the mass. This was a very large meteoric stone, it being supposed to have weighed 200lbs.; and in its fall it penetrated into the earth three feet. There have been few meteoric masses which have fallen, of equal size with this, although some have exceeded it. Two meteoric stones fell in Verona, one of which weighed 200, and the other 300 pounds.

WILTON.

WILTON is a post township, situated 6 miles north from Norwalk, and 34 miles westerly from New-Haven. It is bounded on the north by Ridgefield, on the east by Reading and Weston, on the south by Norwalk, and on the west by New-Canaan and Salem, in the State of New-York. Its extent is about 6 and a half miles in length, and 4 miles in breadth, comprising about 17000 acres. The surface is broken, there being two ridges which run northerly and southerly, intersecting the town. The soil is a gravelly loam, considerably productive, and best adapted to a grain culture. Wheat, rye, corn and oats are the principal agricultural productions. The lands are well adapted to fruit, and afford apples, pears, peaches, &c. The natural

WILTON.

growth of timber is similar to other towns in the county, the forests consisting principally of deciduous trees.

The town is watered by two small rivers, which unite near its centre, forming Norwalk river, and numerous small streams. It is well provided with public roads, but is not accommodated with any turnpike, except that the Norwalk and Danbury turnpike runs a short distance in the north section of the town.

There are but few mechanics in Wilton, and the pursuits of the inhabitants are almost exclusively confined to agriculture, being sober and industrious farmers.

The population of the town, in 1810, amounted to 1728; and there are about 250 Freemen or Electors, 140 militia, and 270 Dwelling houses. There are 7 Mercantile Stores, 2 Grain Mills, 4 Saw Mills, 4 Distilleries, 2 Tanneries, 1 Clothiers' Works and 1 Carding Machine. The list of the town in 1817, was $38,281.

There is 1 Congregational Society and Church, 1 also of Episcopalians, and 1 of Baptists. There are 9 Schools, an Academy, somewhat flourishing, 4 Clergymen and 2 Physicians.

Wilton was incorporated as a Society, previous to 1726, the year in which their first Clergyman was settled, belonging at that time to the town of Norwalk. It was incorporated as a town in 1802.

WINDHAM COUNTY.

WINDHAM, a considerable and flourishing agricultural and manufacturing county, is situated in the northeastern section of the State; bounded on the north by the county of Worcester, in Massachusetts, on the east by the State of Rhode-Island, on the south and southwest by the county of New London, and on the west by the county of Tolland. The south and west lines of the county are irregular; but its general form is that of an oblong square, having a mean length, from north to south, of about 29 miles, and a mean breadth, from east to west, of more than 21 miles, comprising an area of about 620 square miles.

The following TOPOGRAPHICAL AND STATISTICAL TABLE exhibits a view of the several towns in the county; their situation, with relation to Windham, the seat of justice; population, according to the census of 1810; dwelling-houses; religious societies; school-districts, and post-offices.

Towns.	Post offices.	Population.	Dwelling houses.	Religious societies.	School districts.	Distance from Windham.
Windham.	1	2416	450	4	16	
Ashford.	1	2553	420	6	21	15 m. N.
Brooklyn.	1	1200	160	2	8	12 m. N. E.
Canterbury.	1	1812	260	3	14	8 m. E.
Columbia.	1	834	130	1	6	7 m. W.
Hampton.		1274	182	3	10	8 m. N. E.
Killingly.	2	2544	350	4	21	17 m. N. E.
Lebanon.	1	2580	370	4	17	6 m. S. W.
Mansfield.	1	2570	360	5	19	7 m. N. W.
Plainfield.	1	1738	300	2	13	12 m. E.
Pomfret.	1	1905	300	4	11	15 m. N. E.
Sterling.	1	1101	179	2	9	16 m. E.
Thompson.	1	2467	450	4	14	24 m. N. E.
Voluntown.		1016	160	3	8	20 m. S. E.
Woodstock.	1	2658	400	5	*	20 m. N. E.

* See Appendix.

WINDHAM COUNTY.

The county of Windham is in general a rich and productive agricultural district. Its surface is characteristically a succession of moderate elevations, with gentle declivities; and its general inclination is to the south and east, and most of its waters run in those directions.

With the exception of some part of the borders of Long Island sound, and the beautiful vale of Connecticut river, this county has as mild and as uniform a climate as any section of the State. Although this tract is uniformly hilly, yet no part of it is mountainous, or very elevated. The prevailing soil is a primitive, gravelly loam, being a suitable mixture of gravel and siliceous earths. In the greatest portion of the county, the surface is stony, and considerably rough; so much so, in many sections, as to render it unsuitable for arable purposes. The lands in general are best adapted to grazing; and many sections afford some of the richest and most productive dairy farms in the State. The natural character and adaptation of the soil must always, in a greater or less degree, control its agricultural interests; and hence, in this county, the dairy business comprises the principal objects of husbandry, and affords its most important staples. Large quantities of cheese, butter and pork are annually sent abroad; being marketed in Norwich, Providence, Boston, New-York and the southern States.

Upon the borders of the Quinibaug and Shetucket, and their branches, there are considerable tracts of alluvial, which, with some other sections, are well adapted to a grain culture, and afford considerable quantities of oats, Indian corn and rye; particularly of the two first. In the eastern part of the county, there are some sections that are light and lean. The raising of neat cattle and sheep also receives considerable attention in this county; and in general the agricultural interests are as flourishing in this as in any part of the State; its inhabitants being remarkable for their hardy and persevering habits of industry, the salutary results of which, in the cultivation of the earth, the flourishing state of agriculture, the numerous manufacturing establishments, and the general condition and appearance of social improvements and of wealth, are every where to be seen.

The waters of the county are mostly embodied in the two principal rivers by which it is intersected, the Quinibaug and Shetucket. The first of these rivers waters the eastern section of the county, and affords some valuable tracts of alluvial. This river receives, in its course, the French, the Moosup, Little river, and various other small streams; which abound with numerous sites for hydraulic works. The Shetucket washes the western section of the county; its principal tributary streams are the Willimantic and Hop rivers, the former of which forms a part of its western boundary, and the Nachaug, which has numerous branches, and abounds with many valuable water privileges.

Shad and salmon are taken in the Quinibaug, the Shetucket, and their branches; and the latter, which have long since left the Connecticut, ascend the Quinibaug as high as French river, in Thompson.

Within the last ten years, a manufacturing spirit has disclosed itself in this county, which, by opening new fields for enterprise, new channels for capital, and developing new sources of industry, promises the most important and extensive results. This spirit has been principally directed to the cotton manufacture, which is pursued more extensively here than in any other county in this State. There are 22 Cotton Factories in this county, many of which are upon a respectable, and some upon an extensive scale. Most of these factories were established during the late war; and at that time they were very flourishing and prosperous; but from the vast and alarming influx of goods, which followed the peace, in common with other establishments throughout the country, they experienced great depression, and exhibited serious appearances of declension, many having stopped their operations; but for some time past the business has been reviving, and it is gratifying to reflect, that they have survived the crisis, and that it is no longer a problem, whether our cotton factories will be able to maintain themselves and pursue the business;—it is reduced to a certainty that they will. The most sceptical and the most prejudiced must yield to the force of facts, and the demonstrations of experience. Some attention has been paid to the woolen manufacture. There are 10 small establishments in the county; and the domestic or household manufactures of wool are extensive, and are facilitated by establishments for carding wool and dressing cloth for customers, of which there are of the former, 37, and of the latter, 23.

There are in the county 85 Grain Mills, 2 Oil Mills, and 2 Paper Mills. Besides these, there are several other manufactures in some sections of the county; raw and sewing silk, horn combs, and various manufactures of iron, such as steel-yards, screw augers, &c. receive considerable attention.

The county of Windham contains 52 Religious Societies, 31 School Societies, which are divided into a suitable number of School Districts, of which there are 187, exclusive of Woodstock; 23 Social Libraries, & 91 Mercantile Stores.

The population of the county, in 1810, was 21,611; and its aggregate list, in 1817, $678,629.

Windham county originally belonged to the counties of Hartford and New-London, and was incorporated as a county in May 1726.

WINDHAM.

WINDHAM, the seat of justice for the county, and a considerable post township, is situated 14 miles north of Norwich port, 30 east of Hartford, and 44 west of Providence; bounded on the north by Hampton and Mansfield, on the west by Columbia and Lebanon.

WINDHAM.

on the south by Franklin and Lisbon, in New-London county, and on the east by Canterbury. The township comprises an area of about 46 square miles; having a mean length from east to west of about 8 miles, with a medium breadth of nearly 6 miles.

This is a pleasant and fertile interior township; the surface is generally hilly, particularly the eastern section; but it is not mountainous or broken. Its geological character is primitive, the internal strata consisting principally of granite and schistus.

About three miles northwest from the Court-House, there is an inexhaustible quarry of stone, which are very excellent and valuable for building, and a great convenience to the town.

The prevailing soil is a dark coloured gravelly loam; some sections in the first society or western part of the town are a sandy loam.

The forests are not extensive, but sufficient for the purposes of fuel, and to supply the demands for timber, which the interests of the town require. They consist principally of hickory, oak of the various kinds, and chesnut.

The agricultural productions comprise all which are common to this region; beef, pork, butter, cheese, Indian corn, rye, oats and buckwheat are the principal. Of most or all of these productions, there is annually a considerable surplus, which is sent abroad for a market.

The waters of the town are abundant and pure. The principal streams are the Willimantic and Nachaug; the former entering this town from the northwest, and the latter from the north. They unite about two and a half miles northwest from the Court-House, in this town, and form the Shetucket, a considerable and pleasant river. These and other small streams afford numerous sites for hydraulic works. They are also supplied with fish, considerable quantities of shad and some salmon being annually taken in the Shetucket, Willimantic and Nachaug rivers. Across the Shetucket, within this town, there are three expensive bridges; one considerable bridge upon the Willimantic, and two upon the Nachaug, all of which are maintained at the expense of the town.

It is accommodated with several turnpike roads; two of which intersect each other at right angles in its centre, one leading from the State of Massachusetts to Norwich and New-London, the other leading from Hartford to Providence; there is also a turnpike leading from this place to Middletown.

The manufacturing and mechanical establishments of the town consist of 2 Paper Mills, 3 Fulling Mills and Clothiers' works, 3 Carding Machines, 8 Grain Mills and 10 Saw Mills.

The population of the town, in 1810, was 2416; and there are about 400 Electors, 3 Companies of militia, two of Infantry and one of Artillery, and 450 Dwelling houses.

This town contains two Parishes or located Ecclesiastical Societies, one called the First Society, the other Scotland Society; besides these there are two Societies of Baptists, all of which are accommodated with houses for religious worship.

In the first located Society there is an ancient and pleasant village. It has an interesting site, and is surrounded with a delightful rural scenery. It contains between 60 and 70 Dwelling houses, the Court House and Gaol of the county, 1 Church, a Post office, several professional offices, 1 small Newspaper and Printing establishment, a number of Mercantile Stores, Mechanics' shops, &c. The mercantile business of the town is considerable, there being 15 Dry goods and Grocery Stores, 13 in the first Society and 2 in the Society of Scotland.

The town contains 16 School Districts and common Schools, which are maintained a suitable portion of the year. There are 8 practising Attornies, 3 Physicians and 2 Clergymen.

The first settlement of this town was commenced about the year 1686. The Indian title to the tract of land comprising this township was acquired by John Mason and thirteen other persons, by devise from a Mohegan sachem, the son of Uncas. In 1676, it was surveyed and laid out in lots; but the settlement was not attempted until about ten years after. It was incorporated in May 1692, by the name of Windham.

BIOGRAPHY. Col. *Nathan Whiting*, distinguished for his military services during the French war, was a native of this town. He was educated at Yale College, and took his first degree in 1743. At an early period of the French war, in 1755, he commanded a regiment, under Sir William Johnson. He belonged to the detachment commanded by Col. Williams, which was ordered out to meet Baron Dieskau; and being the second officer in rank, after the fall of Col. Williams, the command of the detachment devolved upon him; and he conducted its retreat with great judgment, skill and intrepidity, whereby he preserved his men, under circumstances of extreme peril. In this affair he acquired distinguished honour. Col. Whiting was regarded as a brave, skilful and good officer, not only by his own countrymen, but by the British, who, during the war, had an opportunity of witnessing his conduct.

Col. *Eliphalet Dyer*, L. L. D. distinguished for his civil and military employments, was a native of this town. Col. Dyer was born 28th September, 1721, and was a descendant of Thomas Dyer, who emigrated from England. He was educated at Yale College, where he received his first degree in 1740. Soon after this, he entered upon the study of law, which he pursued as a profession. In 1743, when he was but 22 years of age, he was appointed a Justice of the peace; and in 1745 he was chosen a representative of the town in the General Court, and continued to be elected to this office, a few sessions excepted, until the year 1762. At the commencement of the French war, in 1755, he was appointed to the command of one of the regiments raised by the colony of Connecticut for that service. He continued in the service, having the command of a regiment, during most of the war, and acquired considerable reputation as a faithful and brave officer. In 1762, he was elected a member of the Council, and continued in this situation for several years. In 1763, he went to England, having been constituted the Agent of the Susquehannah Company, to prosecute their claims in Great-Britain. At this period a spirit of jealousy and hostility to the rising prosperity and the rights of the colonies, began to disclose themselves in the parent country; of which, and of the ultimate policy and designs of that country, Col. Dyer discovered clear indications, and communicated his views and apprehensions on his return. He was appointed a Delegate from this State to the Continental Congress, holden at Philadelphia, in 1766. He was also appointed a Delegate to the Congress of 1774, which preceded the commencement of the Revolutionary war; and during the interesting period of this momentous contest, he was, a considerable portion of the time, a member of that dignified and important body. He was appointed a Judge of the Superior Court of this State, and subsequently Chief Justice, which office he held until the year 1793, which closed a very protracted public life. He died in 1807, aged 86 years, having lived during a very interesting period of our history, and taken a part in many of the important events by which it is characterized.

ASHFORD.

ASHFORD, a post town, is situated 31 miles east from Hartford. It is bounded west on Willington, north on Union and Woodstock, east on Pomfret, and south on Hampton and Mansfield. The area of the town comprises about 59 square miles, being about 9 miles in length, & nearly 7 in breadth. The surface of the land is hilly and stony, the soil being hard and gravelly, yet considerably fertile, and well adapted to grazing. The dairy business and growing of cattle, are the leading agricultural interests of the inhabitants, although rye, corn, oats, flax &c. are cultivated.

The streams in Ashford, scarcely deserve the character of rivers, the most considerable are the Bigelow, Mount Hope and Still rivers. Crystal pond is situated in the northern part of this town, being about half in Ashford and half in Pomfret; it is one mile in length, and half a mile in breadth.

There are a number of roads either passing through or centring in this town; the middle turnpike from Hartford to Boston passes through it; the Providence turnpike leaves the Boston road one mile east of the central meeting house; the Tolland county turnpike intersects the Boston road two miles west of the aforesaid meeting house; and there is a turnpike road that runs through the north section of this town from Stafford to Woodstock.

There is a small but pleasant village in the centre of the town, and another in the east Society. The inhabitants, who, like those of the other towns in the county, are principally agriculturalists, are hardy, persevering, industrious and economical.

The population of the town, in 1810, was 2538; there are, at this time, more than 400 Freemen or qualified Electors, about 420 Dwelling houses, 7 Churches, 3 for Congregationalists, 3 for Baptists and 1 for Methodists; 8 Mercantile Stores, 1 Cotton Factory, 1 Woolen Factory, 6 Grain Mills, 9 Saw Mills, 4 Carding Machines and 5 Tanneries. There are 3 local Societies and 21 School districts in Ashford, and 3 small Social Libraries; 2 practising Attornies, 3 Physicians and 4 Clergymen.

The list of polls and rateable estate of the town, in 1817, was $75-000.

Ashford was first settled in 1700, and was incorporated in 1710.

BIOGRAPHY. The brave Col. *Thomas Knowlton*, who fell in the battle near Hærlem heights, in September 1776, was a native of this town. He was an intrepid soldier, an ardent whig, a true patriot and a worthy citizen. He was among the first who rallied round the standard of *Independence*, giving the country that warlike attitude, necessary to sustain it; and at an early period, sacrificed his life for the cause of liberty and his country, in which he had engaged with patriotic ardour and chivalrous heroism.

BROOKLYN.

BROOKLYN, a post town, is situated 45 miles east from Hartford, 80 miles northeast from New-Haven, and 30 miles west from Providence. It is bounded south on Canterbury, west on Hampton, north on Pomfret, and east on Quinibaug river, which divides it from Killingly and Plainfield.

The area of the town is nearly 6 miles in length from north to south, and 5 in breadth from east to west, containing about 29 square miles. It is uneven, consisting of hill and dale, and somewhat stony; but is very fertile, and admirably adapted to grazing.

The dairy business, which is the leading agricultural interest, is carried on in a successful manner, and very extensively. "I can assert, with confidence," says our correspondent, "that there is no town in the State, of the same magnitude, which makes annually an equal quantity of cheese and pork." A good dairy farm, properly stocked and attended to, affords great profits, and possesses, in many respects, important advantages over a grain farm. The lands are less exposed to become exhausted, and to require to be restored by manures, or an ameliorating system of cultivation.

The streams in the town are inconsiderable; the largest is Blackwell's brook, so called, which is not more than ten yards broad in common water,

CANTERBURY.

Quinibaug, which runs on the east line of the town, is a considerable stream, over which is a bridge leading to Killingly, and one also on the road to Plainfield. There is a small shad fishery on the Quinibaug river. The turnpike road from Norwich to Woodstock runs through the town from south to north.

In the centre of the town there is a small village consisting of about 20 Dwelling houses, a Congregational Church, and 2 Mercantile Stores and other buildings.

There were, at the census of 1810, 1200 inhabitants; there are 150 Freemen and 100 Militia, in the town, 160 Dwelling houses, 2 Dry goods and 1 Grocery Store, 3 Grain Mills, 3 Saw Mills, 2 Tanneries and 1 Carding Machine.

The town forms but one located Congregational Society; and contains, besides, a Society of Episcopalians, and some Baptists. It contains 8 School Districts, in each of which a school is maintained for several months in the year, and 1 small Social Library. There are 2 Clergymen, 1 Attorney and 1 Physician.

The general list of polls and taxable estate in 1817 was $32,783.

Brooklyn was formerly a Society, composed of the towns of Pomfret and Canterbury; and was incorporated as a town in May 1786, by an act of the General Assembly.

CANTERBURY.

CANTERBURY is a post township, 40 miles east from Hartford; bounded on the north by Brooklyn, on the east by Plainfield, on the south by Lisbon and Griswold, and on the west by Windham, having an average length of 8 miles, and an average breadth of 4 and a half miles, containing an area of about 36 square miles.

Its surface is uneven, though it can scarcely be called hilly, and some sections are level. The soil is a gravelly loam, and generally fertile and productive.

The natural growth of the forests is oak of the various kinds, chesnut and other deciduous trees. The lands, when cultivated, produce rye, corn, oats, wheat, buckwheat and flax in great abundance.

The town is watered by the Quinibaug river, which here is a large and beautiful stream. It annually overflows its banks, and fertilizes the fine tracts of alluvial upon its borders. These natural meadows are very fertile, and afford the largest crops, and at the same time are cultivated with the greatest facility.

There are two large bridges across this river, one called Bacon's bridge, and the other Butler's bridge. There are several shad fisheries upon this stream; the business is carried on in the proper season successfully, and to considerable extent. It is a convenience to the town, and a source of profit to the proprietors. Little river also, an admirable mill stream, runs through the town, and affords a number of sites and privileges for water-works, which are unrivalled by any in the county. In the south part of the town is a pond, called Bates' pond. It is famous on account of its waters being stored with pike, or pickerel, which are taken very plentifully with the hook.

The town is accommodated with the Norwich and Woodstock, and the Hartford and Plainfield turnpike roads; the former leads through the town from north to south; the latter from east to west; whereby they intersect each other in the village in the first society.

There are 2 located Congregational Societies, in each of which there is a small and pleasant village, consisting of a number of Dwelling houses, Stores, and a Church, or house of public worship. Although in this, as well as in the other towns in the county, agriculture is the leading pursuit of the inhabitants, yet some attention has been paid to manufactures. Exclusive of those of a domestic character, the manufactures and mechanical employments of the town consist of 1 Woolen Factory, 2 Cotton Factories, 1 Carding Machine, 2 Fulling Mills and Clothiers' Works, 1 Pottery, 7 Grain Mills, 9 Saw Mills and 2 Tanneries. There are 7 Mercantile Stores.

The population of the town, in 1810, was 1812; and there are 260 Dwelling houses, 280 Electors, and 130 Militia.

The amount of taxable property, including polls, is $44,259.

There are 14 School Districts and Schools, and 1 Social Library, recently purchased at an expense of 800 dollars, 2 Clergymen, and 3 Attornies.

The first settlers of this town consisted of several families from Massachusetts, and several from Hartford in this State. The settlement was commenced on the Quinibaug river, in 1690; the town was incorporated in 1706; when the inhabitants were for the first time led to the choice of a representative to the General Assembly. The year after, the Rev. Samuel Estabrooke was settled in the ministry, being the first clergyman in the town. He continued in this situation until his death, in 1727.

COLUMBIA.

COLUMBIA, a post town, is situated 22 miles east from Hartford. It is bounded on the north by Hop river, which separates it from Coventry, on the east by Windham and Lebanon, south by Lebanon, and west by Hebron. It has an average length of about 5 miles, and is 4 miles in breadth; comprising 20 square miles, or near 13,000 acres.

The township is uneven and hilly; and the soil is a coarse gravelly loam, being hard and dry, yet well adapted to grazing, and considerably productive. The raising of cattle, and the making of cheese, are the leading agricultural pursuits. Rye, corn, oats and flax are cultivated.

The hills are stony, consisting of granite, schistus and other primitive formations. The forests consist of oak, chesnut and other deciduous trees.

The northern border of this town is watered by Hop river, a lively Mill stream, which unites with the Willimantic. It would hardly be supposed, from the appearance of this stream, that it was the resort of salmon; yet such is the fact. At a small fishery at the mouth of this river, on its junction with the Willimantic, some salmon are caught annually in the spring of the year.

This town is accommodated with the Norwich and Hartford turnpike, and also with one from Middletown to Windham.

The town constitutes but one located Society.

Its population, in 1810, was 834; and it now contains 122 Dwelling houses, and 1 company of Militia. It contains 3 Distilleries, 2 Tanneries, 4 Grain Mills, 1 Fulling Mill, 1 Carding Machine, 6 Saw Mills, 2 Mercantile Stores, 6 District Schools, 1 Congregational Church, 1 Clergyman, 2 Attornies and 1 Physician.

The amount of taxable polls and estate of the town is $22,228.

Columbia was formerly a part of the town of Lebanon, and was incorporated in 1800.

HAMPTON.

HAMPTON is a post township, situated near the centre of the county, 8 miles northeast from Windham, and 37 east from Hartford; bounded on the north by Ashford and Pomfret, on the east by Pomfret, Brooklyn and Canterbury, on the south and southwest by Windham, and on the west by Mansfield. Its average length is 6 miles, and its average breadth more than 4 miles, comprising about 25 square miles.

The surface is uneven, being considerably hilly. The soil is a gravelly loam, the geological character of the township being granitic. It is considerably strong and fertile, and is well adapted to grazing.

The natural growth of timber consists of oak, walnut, chesnut and other deciduous trees.

Of the agricultural interests of the town, those depending upon the dairy business are the most important; butter, cheese, beef and pork are sent abroad for a market. The farmers in this town also have paid considerable attention to the raising of sheep, and considerable quantities of wool are annually produced, most or all of which is manufactured in a domestic way.

The domestic manufactures of the town are very important, and supply almost exclusively the substantial fabrics of clothing for the inhabitants. The domestic manufactures are not confined to woolen cloths, but large quantities of tow cloth are annually made, from flax raised in the town.

The township is well watered by the Nachaug, a considerable

branch of the Shetucket, and a stream called Little river, which runs through its centre. These streams afford some water privileges for mills or manufacturing establishments, of which there are 5 Grain Mills, 3 Fulling Mills and Clothiers' works and 2 Carding Machines. There are likewise in the town, 3 Tanneries, 3 Mercantile Stores and 1 Tavern.

The town comprises 1 located Congregational Society, 2 Societies of Baptists, and 10 School Districts. There is a small village near the centre of the town, consisting of about 20 Dwelling houses, a Congregational Church, &c.

There are 10 primary or common Schools, one in each District, and 1 Social Library.

The population of the town, in 1810, was $1274; and there are about 220 Electors, 2 Companies of Militia, and 180 Dwelling houses.

The amount of taxable property, as rated in making up lists, including polls, is $37,740.

The professional men are 2 Clergymen, one Congregationalist and one Baptist, 3 Physicians and 1 Attorney.

Hampton belonged originally to Windham and Pomfret, and was incorporated in October, 1786.

KILLINGLY.

KILLINGLY, a flourishing agricultural and manufacturing post township, is situated in the eastern section of the State, 45 miles east of Hartford, and 25 west of Providence; bounded on the north by Thompson, on the east by Rhode-Island, on the south by Sterling and Plainfield, and on the west by the Quinibaug river, which separates it from Brooklyn and Pomfret.

The township comprises an area of about 55 square miles, having a mean length from north to south of more than 9 miles, and a mean breadth from east to west of about 6 miles.

The face of the country is uneven, consisting of moderate elevations and gentle declivities; but no portion of it is mountainous. Upon the rivers there are considerable tracts of alluvial. There are three quarries of freestone, which are very valuable for building and other purposes. Some indications of lead ore have recently been discovered.

In the south part of the township there is a hill of considerable elevation, called half mile hill, one side of which has every appearance of having been occasioned by a disruption, from some concussion of nature.

A very extraordinary discovery was made in this town, a living frog having been dug out of the earth, 23 feet beneath the surface. It was enclosed or embodied in a stratum of clay; and, on being disengaged, left a distinct figure of the frog, resembling a mould. The frog, when discovered, was in a torpid state; but on coming to the air, it became animated, and acquired strength and power, and soon added one to the race of living animals.

KILLINGLY.

This town has extensive forests, which are considered of recent growth; the trees are of the deciduous species. The agricultural productions are pork, beef, butter, cheese, Indian corn and some others. Upon the streams of water and some other sections, the lands are well adapted to a grain culture, particularly that of Indian corn, of which considerable quantities are annually raised. This and other branches of agriculture are greatly promoted by the use of plaster of Paris, as a manure, which answers a very valuable purpose.

This township is watered by the Quinibaug, which washes its western border, by Five mile river, a branch of the former, and by several small streams, which afford numerous excellent sites for hydraulic works. Shad and salmon are taken in the Quinibaug, and small fish in the other streams.

There are three considerable ponds in the town, one of which is called Quinibaug pond, and one Killingly pond.

The Connecticut and Rhode-Island turnpike, leading from Hartford to Providence, passes through the centre of the town.

The cotton manufacture has been carried on in this town very extensively, there being four factories upon a large scale; all of which contain about 5000 spindles, and were erected at an expense, including buildings, machinery, &c. of nearly $300,000.

One of the factories is called the Danielson Manufacturing Company; one the Killingly Manufacturing Company; and one the Chesnut hill Manufacturing Company. These establishments employ a large capital, and have developed a new and extensive field for enterprise and industry. We have not ascertained the number of persons which they employ. At the Danielson Manufactory, waterlooms have been introduced, and in general the business is carried on upon the most improved principles, and very advantageously. Besides the Cotton Factories there are 1 Woolen Factory, 1 Gin Distillery, 1 Paper Hanging Manufactory, 4 Dying Houses, 3 Clothiers' works, 3 Carding Machines, 3 Tanneries, 8 Grain Mills and 8 Saw Mills.

The population of the town, in 1810, was 2542; and there are about 350 Dwelling houses, about 375 Electors, and 3 Companies of Militia.

There are in the town 3 located Congregational Societies, and 1 Society of Baptists, all of which have houses for public worship. There are 21 School Districts and primary Schools, 4 Social Libraries, 6 Mercantile Stores, 2 Post offices, one called Killingly Post office, the other Centre Post office, 5 Clergymen, 6 Physicians, and 1 Attorney.

The aggregate list of the town, in 1817, was $44,010.

This town was incor. in 1708.

LEBANON, a post town, is situated 30 miles southeast from Hartford. It is bounded north on Columbia, east on Windham and Franklin, south on Franklin, Bozrah and a part of Colchester, west on Colchester and Hebron. The township is of an average length of more than 7 miles from northeast to southwest, and nearly 7 miles in breadth, from northwest to southeast, containing nearly 49 square miles. The surface is uneven, being moderately hilly. The soil is generally a rich, deep, unctuous mould, nearly of a chocolate colour; it is very fertile, and peculiarly adapted to grass. Rye and other grains are cultivated; but the dairy business, and the growing of neat cattle are the most important agricultural interests. Like other towns in the county, the lands are parcelled out into farms, of from 50 to 200 acres, and some few of a larger size. The lands, being fertile and productive, are valued very high for an interior town, selling frequently at about $50 per acre by the farm. The timber is principally chesnut, walnut and oak.

There are no streams in the town deserving the character of rivers, but it is well watered by brooks and rivulets, some of which afford sites for mills and other hydraulic works.

The civil divisions of the town are 3 located Ecclesiastical Societies, and 17 School districts. Main-street, in the first Society, is spacious and pleasant, being for nearly two miles in length about 30 rods broad; it contains two Churches, an Academy, a Post-office, several Stores and a number of substantial and convenient Dwelling houses.

The population of the town, in 1810, was 2580; there are now about 400 Freemen, 2 companies of Infantry, a part of a company of Cavalry, and a part of a company of Artillery, and 370 Dwelling houses. There are 1 Woolen Factory, 4 Grain Mills, 4 Distilleries, 3 Tanneries, 2 Carding Machines, 7 Mercantile Stores and 6 Taverns in the town. There are 3 Churches for Congregationalists and 1 for Baptists, 17 School districts, 4 Clergymen, 4 Physicians and 2 Attornies.

The general list of taxable polls and estate, in 1817, was $67,949.

Lebanon was incorporated as a town in 1697.

BIOGRAPHY. The Hon. *Jonathan Trumbull*, distinguished for his many public employments, was a native and resident of this town. He was Governor of the State for fifteen years in succession, including the period of the revolutionary war, with all its political animosities, requiring, in the chief executive magistrate, great prudence, firmness and ability. The re-election of Gov. Trumbull for such a length of time, and a period too of such peculiar difficulties and embarrassments, is the best evidence of the estimation in which he was held by his fellow-citizens. He was a whig and a patriot in the " times that tried men's souls."

The Hon. *Jonathan Trumbull*, late Governor of the State, was the son of the above noticed Jonathan Trumbull, and was born and resided in this town. He was educated at Harvard College,

BIOGRAPHY.

where he graduated, having gone through with the usual course of collegiate studies with unusual reputation. In 1775, at the commencement of the revolutionary war, he was appointed by Congress pay-master in the northern department, and soon after secretary and aid to General Washington. He was for several years a member of the State legislature, and Speaker of the House. In 1790, he was chosen a representative in Congress from this State; and in 1791 he was appointed Speaker of the House of Representatives, in which situation he continued until 1794, when he was elected a Senator in the Senate of the United States. In 1796, he was chosen by the freemen Lieut. Governor of the State, and in 1798 Governor. He was annually re-elected to this office for eleven years in succession, and until his death, in 1809. He was 69 years of age. Governor Trumbull was a man of handsome talents, of very respectable acquirements, of amiable manners, and was distinguished for his social virtues. The confidence of his fellow-citizens, which he so long enjoyed in a very eminent degree, affords the most satisfactory evidence of his talents and virtues.

The Rev. *Eleazer Wheelock*, D. D. was a resident clergyman in the north Society in this town, which has since been incorporated into the town of Columbia. He was educated at Yale College, where he graduated in 1733. He became the Principal of a seminary which had been established in this town for the education of the native Indian youth. About the year 1770, he removed from this town to Hanover in New-Hampshire, and the seminary was transferred to that place, and became the foundation of Dartmouth College, of which the Rev. Mr. Wheelock was appointed the first President, and may be considered as the founder of the Institution. At this period, the country about Hanover was mostly a wilderness. The object of the primitive seminary was still in a measure retained; and Dartmouth College was originally designed principally for the education of Indian youth. President Wheelock presided over this Institution until his death, in 1779, aged 69 years. The Institution, from this small beginning, continued to flourish under his presidency, and attained to the character of a respectable College. On the death of President Wheelock, he was succeeded by his son, John Wheelock.

The Hon. *John Wheelock*, L. L. D. was born in this town. He succeeded to the presidency of Dartmouth College, on the death of his father, in 1779, and continued to preside over the Institution, with the exception of a short interval, until his death, in 1817. He was a man of erudition, and equally respected for his talents and learning, and beloved for his virtues. He presided over the Institution with great ability and success, and gave it a very respectable reputation. Some years since, this Institution was re-organized, having received a new charter, wherein its name was changed to that of Dartmouth University.

MANSFIELD.

MANSFIELD, a considerable and flourishing post township, is situated upon the western border of the county, 28 miles east from Hartford; bounded on the north by Willington and Ashford, on the east by Hampton and Windham, on the south by Windham, and on the west by the Willimantic river, which separates its from Coventry.

Its average length from east to west is 8 miles, and its average breadth nearly 6 miles, comprising an area of about 46 square miles.

The face of the country is uneven, being diversified with hills and dales, the eminences in general having considerable elevation. Upon the streams of water there are some small intervals. The geological character of the township is of a primitive formation, the rocks and stones consisting of granite, gneiss, and micaceous schistus; and the soil is a hard, dry gravelly loam. Some minerals have been discovered, mica, felspar and quartz.

The natural growth of timber is oak, walnut, chesnut elm, ash, maple, &c.

The agricultural productions are grass, rye, oats, Indian corn, butter, cheese, pork and beef. The white mulberry tree is cultivated in this town, for the making of silk; and it is estimated, that 2500lbs. of raw silk are annually manufactured. The silk manufacture is a branch of industry unknown in most of our towns, and is confided principally to females, who are the guardians and attendants of the silk worm, the most curious and useful of insects.

Besides the Willimantic, which washes the western border of the town, it is watered by Nachaug river and its tributary streams, the Mount Hope and Fenton, which unite their waters near the south part of the town. These streams afford various sites for mills and other water works. In the first Society, there is a small pond, called Fish pond, comprising an area of about 30 acres.

The middle turnpike road from Hartford to Boston leads through this town, and also a turnpike from Norwich to Stafford, and another from Windham to Hartford.

The manufactures of the town consist of screw-augers, steelyards, horn combs the manufacture of which is carried on to considerable extent, sewing silk, cotton, of which there are two establishments, and woolen, of which there are 2 Factories. There are also 7 Grain Mills, 10 Saw Mills, 5 Carding Machines, 1 Oil Mill, 3 Tanneries, and 7 Mercantile Stores.

The population of the town, in 1810, was 2570; and there are 500 Electors, 172 Militia, and 360 Dwelling houses.

The amount of taxable property, including polls, is $62,750.

The civil divisions of the town are 3 located Ecclesiastical Societies or Parishes and 19 School Districts. There is also 1 Society of Baptists and 1 of Methodists; each of these Societies is accommodated with a house for public worship; and in each of the School Districts there is a primary or common School maintained.

There are 3 Social Libraries. 4 Physicians and 2 Clergymen, 1 Congregationalist and 1 Baptist.

Mansfield was comprised within the original limits of the county of Hartford, and was first settled in 1703.

PLAINFIELD.

PLAINFIELD, a post township, is situated in the southeastern section of the county, 41 miles east from Hartford, and 20 west from Providence; bounded on the north by Killingly, on the east by Sterling, on the south by Voluntown and Griswold, and on the west by Canterbury and Brooklyn. The township comprises an area of about 40 square miles; having a mean length from north to south of about 8 miles, and a mean breadth of about 5 miles.

From the surface, soil and geological features, the township is divided into two sections. The eastern section is rough and broken, being hilly and stony. The hills are considerably elevated and continuous, forming ridges, extending in a northerly and southerly direction. The western section is an extensive plain, the surface being level, and the soil a light, sandy loam, which is cultivated with facility, and is fertile and productive. These plains are well adapted to a grain culture, affording excellent corn, oats, rye, &c.

When this town was first settled by the English, these plains were free from timber, admitted of immediate cultivation, and, from the great quantities of corn raised here, they were called the Egypt of the surrounding settlements. Plaster is found to be a valuable manure upon this soil; the use of which, and a proper regard to the amelioration of the soil by clover and other cultivated grasses, have maintained the land in a rich and fertile state.

The soil in the eastern section of the township is of a gravelly character, and affords good grazing. Its natural growth of timber comprises the various trees common to this region.

The Quinibaug river washes the western border of the town, and forms a considerable part of its western boundary, separating it from Brooklyn and Canterbury. Upon this river there are two bridges, one connecting this town with Brooklyn, and the other with Canterbury. The Moosup river runs through the eastern section of the town, and discharges its waters into the Quinibaug, affording in its course an unequalled number of excellent sites for hydraulic works.

The town is accommodated with the Connecticut and Rhode-Island turnpike, which passes through it; and by the Windham county turnpike, which terminates at the point of intersection with the former.

Of the manufactures of the town, those of cotton are the most important, there being 4 Cotton Factories, one of which is called the Union Factory; one the Moosup Factory, which has been burnt down, and is not yet rebuilt; the Central Factory; and one other. There are also 2 Woolen Factories. In addition to these, there are 4 Carding Machines and

2 Clothiers' works for customers, and 6 Grain Mills.

The population of Plainfield, in 1810, was 1738; and there are now about 230 Electors, one company of Infantry, one Rifle company, and a part of a company of Cavalry, of militia, and about 300 Dwelling houses.

There are in this town 2 Religious Societies, one located Congregational and one Baptist; 12 School Districts and primary Schools; and an Academy, called Plainfield Academy, incorporated in 1783, and which is now a very flourishing institution. There are also 2 Social Libraries, one containing 200 volumes of well selected books, and the other recently established, and confided to the care of the settled Clergyman.

There are 7 Mercantile Stores, 4 practising Physicians, and 2 Attornies.

The aggregate list of the town, in 1817, was $38,253.

This town was settled in 1689, principally by emigrants from Chelmsford in Massachusetts. The first settlers found the land in a great measure fit for cultivation, there being much less forest land then than what there is at this time. The Indians were very numerous in this neighbourhood, and continued for many years with the English, living in the most friendly manner.

BIOGRAPHY. The Rev. Joel Benedict, D. D. was for 32 years settled in the ministry in this town. He was ordained in 1782, and continued until his death in 1815. He was distinguished as a scholar and man of science, not only in his profession, but in mathematics and the learned languages. He had applied himself with great diligence and success to the study of the Hebrew language, and became an excellent Hebrew scholar, there being few men superior to him in biblical criticism. But he was not more remarkable for the extent of his learning than for the mildness of his manners and the placidity of his temper.

POMFRET.

POMFRET, a post township, is situated in the central section of the county, 40 miles northeast from Hartford, and 30 east from Providence; bounded on the north by Woodstock and Thompson, on the east by the Quinibaug river, which separates it from Killingly, south by Brooklyn and Hampton, and west by Ashford. Its mean length from east to west is about 7 miles, and its mean breadth nearly 6 miles, comprising about 42 square miles.

The surface is uneven and diversified, consisting of hills and dales; and the geological character of the township is granitic, the soil being a gravelly loam, and the rocks consist of granite, gneiss, micaceous schistus and other original formations. There are several quarries of free stone, valuable for building and other uses.

Although the lands in this town are hilly, and somewhat stony and rough, it is a rich and productive agricultural township. The soil is deep, strong and fertile, and admirably adapted to grazing. And, as the natural quality and adaptation of the soil must always, in a greater or less degree, control the agricultural pursuits, the leading interests of the farmers of this town are such as are dependent upon, or are promoted by a system of improving lands by grazing. The dairy business is generally attended to, and pursued to an extent and with a success that is scarcely surpassed. Not only cheese and butter, but pork, lard and beef are among the surplus productions of the farmers of this town. For some years past, and particularly during the late war, considerable attention has been paid to sheep, and wool has been added to the agricultural products of the town. But, although the lands are best adapted to grazing, they admit of the successful cultivation of grain, and considerable rye, corn and oats are raised.

The township is well watered. Besides the Quinibaug, which washes its eastern border, it is watered by Little river and numerous small streams. There are several shad fisheries in the Quinibaug; some salmon are also taken.

The town is accommodated with several turnpike roads; one leading from Hartford to Boston passes through it, and one from the former place to Providence; also one leading from Norwich to Worcester in Massachusetts.

Although agriculture is the principal business of the town, a manufacturing spirit has disclosed itself, and produced some results.

A Cotton Factory has been established upon a very extensive scale, and is one of the largest establishments in the State; there is also a Woolen Factory upon rather a small scale. In addition to these manufactures, there are 3 Fulling Mills & Clothiers' works, 2 Carding Machines, 3 small Distilleries, 4 Grain Mills and 6 Tanneries.

The town contains 2 located Congregational Societies or Parishes, and 11 School Districts. Besides the located, there is 1 Society of Baptists and 1 small Society of Friends. A common school is maintained in each of the School Districts, a considerable proportion of the year.

In the first located Society there is a small village of 20 or 30 Dwelling houses, a Post office, Congregational Church, and several Stores.

The population of the town, in 1810, was 1905; and there are 280 Freemen or Electors, about the same number of Dwelling houses, and 2 entire companies of Infantry, part of a Rifle company, part of a company of Cavalry, and part of a company of Artillery, of militia.

The amount of taxable property, as rated in making up the lists, including polls, in 1816, was $55,077.

The celebrated wolf den, which has been rendered famous by an exploit of Gen. Israel Putnam, who entered it with a torch light in one hand and a gun in the other, and shot a wolf at the extremity; and having had a rope fastened to his leg, was drawn out, together with the wolf; is in this town.

There are in the town 7 Mercantile Stores, 4 Public Inns, 3 Social Libraries, 4 practising Physicians, 3 Clergymen and 2 Attornies.

Pomfret was first settled in 1686, by emigrants from Roxbury in Massachusetts, and was incorporated, with town privileges, in 1713.

BIOGRAPHY. The Hon. *Thomas P. Grosvenor*, recently a member of Congress from the District of Columbia, in the State of New-York, was a native of this town. He was a man of talents, and became one of the leaders of the opposition in Congress. He died at the seat of Government, during the session of Congress, in the year 1817.

The Hon. *Sylvanus Backus*, late of this town, was a lawyer of considerable eminence, and for a succession of years was Speaker of the House of Representatives in this State. He died in 1817.

Maj. Gen. *Israel Putnam* was for several years a resident of that part of Pomfret which now belongs to the town of Brooklyn. Gen. Putnam was born in Salem, Mass. and emigrated to this town in 1739. He possessed strong natural talents, but his mind was never much improved, having enjoyed but very limited advantages as to education. Gen. Putnam at an early period engaged in the pursuits of agriculture, being an independent but laborious farmer. Yet even in this retired and obscure situation, his vigorous natural powers and characteristic bravery could not remain concealed; but his courage and spirit were displayed in a conspicuous manner, by the well known adventure of his descending into a cavern and killing a wolf at the imminent risk of his life. The distinguished bravery and determined resolution, which characterized General Putnam, having brought him into notice at the commencement of the French war, he received the commission of a captain in the Provincial troops, and became distinguished for his services in the campaign of 1755. In that of the succeeding year, he encountered many difficulties, endured the greatest hardships, was exposed to the most imminent perils, and displayed the greatest intrepidity, firmness and resolution, whereby he acquired great credit as an officer. In the month of August of this year, he was unfortunately taken prisoner by the Indians, in which situation he was destined to experience all the horrors of savage barbarity. He was fastened to a tree, in a situation which rendered him exposed to the fire of both of the contending armies; and, in the night, he was stripped of his clothing, and encircled with combustible materials, which were set on fire, and he would inevitably have fallen a sacrifice to the most excruciating and systematic savage torture, had it not been for the timely interposition of a humane French officer, who rescued him from this perilous and truly horrible situation. He was sent to Montreal, as a prisoner of war, and was not exchanged until 1759. After the close of the French war he retired to his farm, and resumed the laborious occupations of husbandry. He was plowing in his field when he heard of the battle of Lexington; and he forthwith dropped the implements of husbandry, and repaired to Cambridge. He however soon returned and raised a regiment of militia, which he marched to Cambridge; soon after which he was appointed Major-General in the militia of Connecticut. He was engaged in the battle of Bunker Hill, was the highest officer in rank, and was distinguished for his cool intrepidity. He gave orders to his men to reserve their fire until the enemy appeared within a convenient distance, and then to take deliberate aim, so that there should not a shot be lost. The result is well known. On the organization of the army by Congress, he was appointed to command the reserve under General Washington, and was the second in command. In August 1776, he was stationed at Brooklyn, on Long-Island. After the defeat of our army, on the 27th of that month, he retired to New-York; and, at that dark and desponding period, he did not despair of the glorious cause, but was very active and serviceable in the city and vicinity. The spring following, he was appointed to command at the Highlands, or upon the Hudson river. Here a singular incident occurred, which serves to show the decision and firmness of his character. An American royalist, who was a lieutenant in the British service, was discovered in the American camp, and taken into custody. Gov. Tryon reclaimed him as a British officer, and threatened retaliation, if he was not restored. To this demand, Gen.

Putnam returned the following laconic answer:

"Sir, Nathan Palmer, a lieutenant in your king's service, was taken in my camp as a spy, he was tried as a spy, he was condemned as a spy, and he shall be hanged as a spy.

I. Putnam."

"P. S. Afternoon.—He is hanged."

After the loss of Fort Montgomery, Gen. Washington confided to Gen. Putnam the selection of a suitable site for a permanent fortification; and to him belongs the honour of the judicious selection of West Point. Gen. Putnam spent the remainder of his military life in erecting and improving the fortifications at this place, and which continued until about the year 1780, when the infirmities of age obliged him to retire from the field of strife and glory, and with him the theatre of so many heroic achievements.

General Putnam was possessed of the most daring natural courage; not the offspring of insensibility, but of extraordinary natural vigor and energy, both of body and mind. He was bold and fearless in his enterprises, and firm, determined and persevering in their execution; neither appalled by dangers, discouraged by difficulties, nor was the firmness of his resolutions impaired by hardships and sufferings, however severe; he pursued his object with a steadiness and determination, which have had few examples. He was a brave officer, an ardent patriot and a good citizen; and having lived during the most important period of our annals, and taken a distinguished part in the events of two wars, his history is identified with that of his country, and his name is enrolled with those heroes and patriots, who, to the latest posterity, as long as the genius of liberty maintains her dominion, will be regarded as the fathers of it.

General Putnam died at Brooklyn, May 29th 1790, aged 72 years. He was buried with the honours of war, & an elegant eulogy was delivered on the occasion, by Dr. Waldo.

STERLING.

STERLING is a post township, situated in the southeast part of the county, 44 miles from Hartford; bounded on the north by Killingly, on the east by Rhode-Island line, on the south by Voluntown, and on the west by Plainfield. It contains an area of about 24 square miles, having an average length of 8 miles, and an average breadth of 3 miles. The face of the country, within this town, is generally uneven, or moderately hilly; but there are some sections of pine plains. The soil is a light, gravelly and sandy loam. The natural growth consists of the deciduous trees common to this region, together with a considerable proportion of yellow pine. The land is best adapted to a grain culture, and affords good crops of rye, corn &c.

The town is watered by a branch of the Moosup river, called Quanduck, an inconsiderable stream.

In addition to the county or public roads, the town is accommodated with the Norwich and Providence turnpike, which passes through it.

Near the centre of this town, there is a cavern called the devil's den, possessing very singular and curious features. It is situated within a ledge of rocks, and has a circular area of about 100 feet in diameter. The rock is cleft in two places, forming at each a chasm or fissure, of about 50 feet deep; through one of which, there runs a small stream of water; the other communicates with a room of about 12 feet square, at the interior part of which, there is a fire-place, and a chimney extending through the rock above, forming an aperture of about 3 feet square. In another part of the rock, there is a natural stair-case, winding around it from the bottom to the top. In the cold season of the year, a large mass of ice is formed in the room before described, by the dashing of water down the chimney, which continues there through nearly the whole of the warm months; the sun being almost excluded from this subterraneous recess.

There are in Sterling 3 Cotton Factories, one of which is upon a large scale, and contains 1600 spindles. The buildings for the accommodation of the workmen are of stone. This is one of the largest establishments in the State; the other two are less extensive. There are 3 Grain Mills, 1 Carding Machine, 1 Fulling Mill and Clothiers' works, 2 Tanneries, 4 Mercantile Stores and 2 Taverns.

The town contains one located

Congregational Society & Church, one Society of Baptists, one Academy, 9 School districts and common Schools, and one Social Library.

Its population, in 1810, was 1101; and there are 150 qualified Electors, 1 Company, and a part of another Company of Militia, and about 180 Dwelling houses. In the centre of the town there is a small village, consisting of about 30 Dwelling houses, a Church and several Stores.

The amount of taxable property, including polls, is $19,766.

Sterling was incorporated as a town in 1794.

THOMPSON.

THOMPSON, a post township, is situated in the northeast corner of the county and State, 47 miles northeast from Hartford, and 26 northwest from Providence; bounded on the north by Massachusetts line, on the east by Rhode-Island, on the south by Killingly, and on the west by Woodstock and Pomfret.

The township forms nearly a square, and comprises an area of about 50 square miles, or 32,000 acres.

The town is intersected into nearly two equal parts, by the Quinibaug river, which runs thro' it from north to south. In addition to this stream, it is watered by the French river, a tributary stream of the Quinibaug, and by Five mile river, which rises in Douglass, in Massachusetss, and enters the town at the northeast corner, and running through it from north to south, passes into Killingly, and discharges itself into the Quinibaug. Muddy brook, also, which rises in Woodstock, runs across the southwest corner of the town, a distance of about two miles. Upon these streams there are numerous bridges maintained by the town. Some salmon are taken in the Quinibaug and French rivers.

The surface of this township exhibits an interesting diversity of hill and dale; many of the hills are considerably elevated, but no portion of it can be called mountainous. The prevailing soil is a gravelly loam, strong and dry, well adapted to the culture of Indian corn, wheat and clover, and generally excellent for grazing. There is a great supply of valuable stone, for walls and buildings; and they are used extensively for wall fence, of which it is thought by our correspondent that there is more than in any other town in the State.

The forests in the town are not extensive, but are sufficient for the purposes of fuel, and afford sufficient timber for buildings and other uses.

The agricultural productions are beef, pork, butter, cheese and grain.

The Hartford and Boston turnpike road intersects the township from the southwest to the northeast corner, a distance of about 11 miles. The Thompson turnpike, leading to Providence, runs through it from northwest to southeast, about the same distance; and the Woodstock turnpike passes through it from west to east, a distance of about 8 miles.

A manufacturing spirit has disclosed itself in this town; it has been directed principally to cotton manufactures. There are 3 large Cotton manufacturing establishments, containing in all about 5000 spindles. These establishments usually employ a great number of persons, and add greatly to the aggregate industry of the town. There are 8 Grain Mills, 11 Saw Mills, 3 Wool carding Machines, 2 Clothiers' works and 3 Tanneries.

For an inland town, its commercial business and capital are very respectable. It is estimated that about 10,000 dollars are annually employed in a trade to Georgia. There is one vessel owned here, which sails out of Providence, and is employed in the coasting trade. There are 8 Mercantile Stores in the town.

Its civil divisions are 1 located Religious Society and 14 School Districts. Besides the located, there are 3 Religious Societies, one of Baptists, one of Methodists, and one of Quakers. There are 3 houses for religious worship, recently erected, one very elegant, built in 1817.

The population of the town, in 1810. was 2467; and there are 400 Electors, 1 company of Militia, in which there are 200 men enrolled, 1 Light Infantry company of about 65 members, and a part of a company of Cavalry. There are more than 400 Dwelling houses; 14 primary Schools, one in each District; 1 Social Library; 3 Clergymen, 3 Physicians, and 2 Lawyers.

Thompson was settled in 1715, being then a part of Killingly, from which it was separated, and incorporated as a town in 1785.

BIOGRAPHY. Gen. *David Learned*, of this town, was born in 1743, and died in 1797. He was highly distinguished for his eminent and useful life, and for his civil and military employments.

VOLUNTOWN.

VOLUNTOWN is situated in the southeast part of the county; bounded on the north by Plainfield and Sterling, on the east by Exeter, in Rhode-Island, on the south by North-Stonington, and on the west by Griswold, in New-London county. It has an average length of about 9 miles, and an average breadth of more than 4 miles, comprising nearly 39 square miles.

The surface is generally diversified with hill and dale, but there are some sections of pine plains, which are level. The prevailing character of the soil is that of a light, sandy and gravelly loam. It is best adapted to grain, and produces Indian corn, rye, oats, &c.; but corn is principally cultivated.

The town is watered by the Pochaug, a branch of the Quinibaug. It is a small and sluggish stream, but contains, however, some mill seats. There is a pond, situated partly in this town and partly in Rhode-Island, called Paucamack pond, a considerable body of wa-

WOODSTOCK.

ter, and is the source of the Pochaug river.

The manufacturing and mechanical interests and employments, aside from those of a domestic character, consist of 1 Cotton Factory, 4 Grain Mills, 2 Fulling Mills and Clothiers' works, 2 Carding Machines and 2 Tanneries. There are 2 Mercantile Stores and 2 Taverns.

The town contains 2 located Congregational Societies & Churches, 1 Society of Baptists, 1 small Social Library, and 8 School Districts and Schools.

Its population, in 1810, was 1016; and there are 150 qualified Electors, 1 Company of Militia, and 160 Dwelling houses.

The amount of taxable property, including polls, is $21,110.

In the centre of the town there is a small village of about 15 Dwelling houses. There are 3 Physicians in the town.

This town was first settled in 1696, having been granted to volunteers in the Narraganset war; hence its name. But it was not incorporated as a town until the year 1719.

WOODSTOCK.

WOODSTOCK is a post town, situated in the northern section of the county, bordering upon Massachusetts, 45 miles northeast from Hartford, 33 northwest from Providence, and 60 southwest from Boston; bounded upon the north by Massachusetts line, upon the east by Thompson, upon the south by Pomfret and Ashford, and upon the west by Ashford and Union. Its mean length is 8 miles, and its mean breadth 7 and a half miles, comprising an area of about 60 square miles.

This township, although its physical features are less smooth and interesting than those of many others, ranks deservedly among the first of the rich and flourishing interior towns in the State. The surface is characteristically hilly, but is not mountainous or broken, and comprises very little waste land; most or all of the eminences being capable of cultivation.

The prevailing soil is a deep, gravelly loam, which is strong and fertile, having a permanent basis, and is very favourable for manures, which have a very sensible and lasting effect. It is best adapted to grazing, but generally admits of tillage; and considerable quantities of grain are annually raised, consisting principally of rye and corn. For some years past, spring wheat has been cultivated to advantage, and to an extent affording a supply for the consumption of the town.

Of the agricultural productions, butter, cheese, beef and pork are the most important. Of these, there is annually a considerable surplus which is sent abroad for a market.

The township is well watered by numerous small streams, of which the most considerable is Muddy Brook, running through the town, and discharging its waters into the Quinibaug. This and other streams afford many valuable water privileges.

This town is accommodated with three turnpike roads, one leading to Norwich, one to Providence, and one to Somers, and thence to Connecticut river.

Agriculture, being the principal interest, affords employment for most of the industry of the town, excepting what is employed in domestic or household manufactures, which receive general attention, there being a loom in almost every house. Most of the primary and substantial fabrics of clothing are the products of domestic industry. Besides the manufactures of this description, there are some others of importance, particularly one Woolen and one Cotton Factory, in the Society of Muddy Brook, both of which have large and commodious buildings, and belong to incorporated companies. They are both upon a large scale, and the Woolen Factory is now doing business extensively. There is also an incorporated Woolen and Cotton manufacturing establishment, in what is called the old Society, which is in operation. In addition to these establishments, there are 7 Grain Mills, 1 Oil Mill, 2 Distilleries, 12 Saw Mills, 1 Fulling Mill and Clothier's works, 1 Carding Machine, 2 large Triphammers and Blacksmiths' shops, 1 Gold-smith and 2 Wheel-wrights.

This town is divided into three located Societies or Parishes; the one in its western section is called New-Roxbury Society; one of the others is called Muddy Brook Society, to which there is annexed a corner of the town of Thompson; and the other the old Society. Besides the located, there are 2 Baptist Societies; all of these several Religious Societies are accommodated with houses for public worship. The town is also divided into 18 School Districts.

Its population, in 1810, was 2653; and there are about 350 Electors, 4 companies of Militia, and about 350 Dwelling houses.

The amount of taxable property, as rated in making up lists, including polls, in 1816, was $62,028.

There are in this town 18 primary Schools, 3 Social Libraries, 6 Mercantile Stores, 6 Physicians, 3 Attornies and 5 Clergymen.

This town, together with Suffield, Enfield and Somers, was settled under the jurisdiction of the colony of Massachusetts, in or about the year 1686; and incorporated by the authority thereof, although by the charter of Connecticut they were included within the limits of this State. In 1713, the line between the two States was surveyed, and, upon certain conditions, it was agreed by Connecticut that the towns settled by Massachusetts should remain under its jurisdiction. This compromise produced general uneasiness and dissatisfaction with the inhabitants at the time; which, instead of subsiding, as was expected, continued to increase, so that in May 1747, they presented a memorial to the General Assembly of Connecticut, praying to be annexed to, or taken under, the jurisdiction thereof, whereby they might be restored to the charter privileges, granted to them in common with other citizens of this State.

The General Assembly, after having appointed commissioners to attempt to settle this dispute, with others that might be appointed by Massachusetts, without effect, adopted a resolution, that, as the agreement of 1713 had never received the royal confirmation, it was not binding; and that all the inhabitants who lived south of the line of Massachusetts, as defined by its charter, were entitled to the privileges, and ought to be subject to the jurisdiction of the government of this State. In 1752, an act was passed, securing to the several religious societies of the aforesaid towns all the rights and privileges of religious societies, according to the laws of this colony. These proceedings on the part of Connecticut produced from Massachusetts a remonstrance to his majesty. This was opposed by the agent of Connecticut, then in England, and the claims of the latter supported, which were finally recognized, and the boundary established accordingly in 1755. While this town was under the jurisdiction of Massachusetts, it was at first a part of the county of Suffolk, and deeds were recorded at Boston. On the organization of the county of Worcester, it was annexed to that county, and so continued as long as it remained a part of the territory of that State.

BIOGRAPHY. Gen. *William Eaton* was a native of this town, and was born February 23d, 1764. At a very early period, he disclosed strong indications of intellectual vigor, and of mental eccentricity. At the age of about 16 years, without the knowledge or consent of his parents, he went from home, and enlisted into the army. This was in 1780, near the close of the revolutionary war; and young Eaton continued in the army until the close of the war, a considerable part of the time in the humble station of a private soldier; but he attained the rank of a sergeant. After the peace, in 1784, he commenced the study of the Latin language; and the year after, was admitted a member of Dartmouth College, where he graduated in 1790; the period of his collegiate life having been protracted, from the circumstance of his having devoted a portion of his time to school keeping, which his want of pecuniary resources rendered necessary.

In October, 1791, he was chosen clerk of the House of Delegates of Vermont, residing at that time in the town of Windsor, where he had been engaged in school keeping. In March, 1792, he was appointed a Captain in the army of the United States; and whilst in this situation, he performed various services upon the western and southern frontiers. He continued in the army until 1797, when he was appointed Consul to Tunis. He continued in this difficult, (and it may be added perilous) situation, until 1803; during which period, he discharged the consular functions with great firmness and ability. In 1804, Gen. Eaton returned to America and visited Washington, where he disclosed the famous enterprise which he had planned to restore the Ex-Bashaw of Tripoli; and, having obtained the sanction of government, he embarked in July of the same year, in the Argus sloop of war, with the intention of engaging in this bold and hazardous undertaking, and arrived at Alexandria in Egypt, on the 25th of November following. From Alexandria he proceeded to Cairo, where he found the Ex-Bashaw, who approved of the enterprise; and after having made suitable arrangements and recruited about 500 men, (100 of which only were christians,) it was determined by Eaton and the Ex-Bashaw, to cross the desert and seize the province and city of Derne. After a difficult and fatiguing journey thro' a dreary desert, presenting innumerable obstacles, they arrived within the province of Derne, and soon attacked and captured the city, having the assistance of the Hornet sloop of war. The boldness and desperate bravery of Gen. Eaton and his little party alarmed the reigning Bashaw and his barbarian subjects, who almost thought that they were something more than human beings; but the progress of Gen. Eaton was arrested by a peace which the American consul concluded with the Bashaw. After this, Gen. Eaton returned to his native country, and was every where received with the most distinguished applause, the grateful tribute of patriotic and heroic achievments. After some time he fixed his residence in Brimfield, Massachusetts, where he continued until his death in 1811. Whilst here, he was elected a representative of the town, in the legislature of the State.

Gen. Eaton was a very extraordinary character; he possessed much original genius; was bold in his conceptions, ardent in his passions, determined in his resolutions and indefatigably persevering in his conduct. He possessed considerable literary acquirements, and the style of his writings was characteristic of his mind; bold, energetic and decisive. His courage was equalled only by his resolution, and the boldness of his enterprises, by his ability and perseverance to execute them. He was an important witness in the case of Burr's trial, and the celebrated toast which he gave, with reference to this transaction, is alike an evidence of his patriotism, and the originality of his conceptions: "Phrensy to the head that shall plot to dismember, and palsy to the arm that will not draw to defend the union."

LITCHFIELD COUNTY.

LITCHFIELD, an extensive agricultural and manufacturing county, is situated in the north-western section of the State; bounded on the north by Berkshire county, in Massachusetts, on the east by Hartford and New-Haven counties, on the south by the counties of New-Haven and Fairfield, and on the west by the State of New-York.

This county has an average length from north to south of about 33 miles, and a mean breadth from east to west of nearly 27 miles, comprising about 885 sq. miles, being the largest county in the State.

The following TOPOGRAPHICAL AND STATISTICAL TABLE exhibits a view of the several towns in the county; their situation, with relation to Litchfield the seat of justice; their population, according to the census of 1810; dwelling houses; religious societies; school districts, and post-offices.

Towns.	Post-offices.	Population.	Dwelling houses.	Religious societies.	School districts.	Distance from Litchfield.
Litchfield.	2	4639	512	8	26	
Barkhamsted.	1	1506	230	4	11	18 m. N. E.
Bethlem.	1	1118	170	3	9	8 m. S.
Canaan.	2	2203	276	4	12	16 m. N. W.
Colebrook.	1	1243	200	3	8	18 m. N. E.
Cornwall.	1	1602	200	3	11	12 m. N. W.
Goshen.	1	1641	230	2	8	6 m. N. W.
Harwinton.	1	1718	298	2	11	7 m. E.
Kent.	1	1794	270	2	10	15 m. W.
New-Hartford.	1	1507	220	1	8	12 m. N. E.
New-Milford.	1	3557	540	6	16	18 m. S. W.
Norfolk.	1	1441	240	1	10	16 m. N.
Plymouth.	1	1882	270	3	12	10 m. S. E.
Roxbury.		1217	200	3	9	15 m. S. W.
Salisbury.	1	2321	340	2	14	20 m. N. W.
Sharon.	2	2606	380	4	15	16 m. N. W.
Torrington.	1	1586	250	3	9	7 m. N. E.
Warren.	1	1096	170	2	8	8 m. W.
Washington.	1	1575	230	4	11	10 m. S. W.
Watertown.	1	1714	250	2	8	10 m. S. E.
Winchester.	1	1466	230	2	9	13 m. N. E.
Woodbury.	1	1963	300	4	14	15 m. S.

The principal part of the county of Litchfield is elevated and mountainous; several branches of the extensive granitic range intersect the county from north to south, and comprise an extensive evergreen district.

In the northwestern section there are some large and extensive calcareous vales, abounding in limestone; but most of the other sections of the county are of a granitic, geological character. The prevailing soil is a gravelly loam, generally deep, and in many sections strong and fertile, and admirably adapted to grazing. In the limestone district, the soil is a calcareous loam, rich and fertile, and excellent for arable purposes, particularly for the culture of wheat, which is raised here very successfully, and to great extent. This is the best section for wheat that there is in this State.

Upon the Ousatonick and its branches, in the southwestern section of the county, there are tracts of alluvial of considerable extent, and some small sections that are a light sandy loam.

The agricultural interests of the county are very respectable, and constantly improving. The staple productions consist of cheese, butter, pork and beef. Considerable attention is paid to the raising of neat cattle and sheep; and in the calcareous section there is a considerable surplus of grain raised, which is sent abroad for a market.

The waters of the county are abundant, and principally embodied in the Ousatonick and Tunxis rivers. The former of these, which is the second river in size in the State, intersects the county, and has numerous branches, of which the principal are the Naugatuck, the Pomperaug and the Shepaug, which afford many excellent sites for hydraulic works. The Tunxis washes the northeastern section of the county, and affords also numerous sites for water-works.

The manufacturing business receives considerable attention in this county, particularly that of iron, which is carried on more extensively here than in any other section of the State. There are 39 Forges, many of which pursue the business extensively, 5 Furnaces, 3 Anchor Shops and 2 Slitting Mills. The ore used at these establishments is obtained within the county, and abounds in various places. There are 2 Oil Mills, 1 Paper Mill, 62 Grain Mills, 4 Cotton Factories, 8 Woolen Factories, 50 Carding Machines and 46 Cloth Dressing establishments. In the county of Litchfield there are 68 Religious Societies, 31 School Societies, which are divided into 249 School Districts, 29 Social Libraries, and about 100 Mercantile Stores.

The population of the county, in 1800, was 41,214; and in 1810, 41,375.

The aggregate list, in 1817, was $881,601.

This county was incorporated in 1751; and a considerable section of it was more recently settled than any other part of the State.

LITCHFIELD, an extensive, wealthy and populous interior post township, and the seat of justice of the county, is situated in north lat. 41° 50′, being 30 miles west from Hartford, 36 northwest from New-Haven, and 100 from New-York; bounded on the north by Goshen and Torrington, on the east by the Naugatuck river, which separates it from Harwinton, on the south by Watertown, Bethlem and Plymouth, and on the west by Washington and Warren. The township contains about 72 square miles; having an average length from east to west of more than 9 miles, and a mean breadth of nearly 8 miles.

Litchfield is an elevated township; its surface presents an interesting diversity of hill and dale. The hills are in general considerably elevated; and their prevailing course is from north to south. In the eastern section of the town, near the Naugatuck river, there are mountainous ranges, extending in an eastwardly and westwardly direction. In the western section of the township, there are also some mountainous tracts, which comprise several considerable eminences, of which Mount Tom is the most elevated. From actual mensuration it has been found to be about 700 feet from the margin of the river to the summit of this eminence, upon the south side. Little Mount Tom and Mount Prospect are eminences of less elevation. From the elevation of this township, some of its eminences afford the most extensive and interesting prospects; to the east may be seen the hills upon the east side of Connecticut river, and to the west the Catskill mountains, appearing in huge and disorderly piles.

The geological character of the township is primitive; the prevailing strata of rocks consisting of granite and schistus, interspersed with some quartz, primitive limestone and other original formations. There is one quarry of slate-stone, of an inferior quality; and in the eastern section of the town there is a quarry of freestone, valuable for hearths and other uses. Some indications of iron ore have been discovered.

The prevailing soil is a dark coloured gravelly loam, with some sections of argillaceous loam. It is deep, strong and fertile; and, for an elevated tract, is warm, and favourable for vegetation. It is in general best adapted to grazing, the interests of which are pursued very extensively and advantageously.

The staple agricultural productions are cheese, butter, pork and some others. In some sections of the town considerable grain is cultivated, and the raising of cattle and sheep receives considerable attention. In 1811, there were 6784 sheep shorn in this town. The agricultural interests of the town are flourishing; and great exertions are making to improve them.

The town is well supplied with forests, comprising a great variety of trees; sugar maple, beach, button-wood, oak, birch, chesnut, butternut, walnut, elm, peperidge, wild cherry, bass, hornbeam, sassafras, &c.

The township is well watered. The Naugatuck washes its eastern border, the Shepaug its western, forming a part of its boundary, and the Bantam waters its interior, intersecting the township from northeast to southwest, passing through Great, Little and Cranberry ponds, and discharging its waters into the Shepaug, a branch of the Ousatonick. These streams afford numerous excellent sites for hydraulic works, particularly the latter, which, at the outlet of the Great pond, has some of the most valuable mill seats in the town, and which are scarcely rivalled. Great pond is an extensive and beautiful sheet of water, comprising an area of about 900 acres, and is the largest pond or lake in the State. Mount Tom pond, a part of which is in the town of Washington, comprises about 72 acres, Little pond, 15, and Cranberry 8. In the streams and ponds various small fish are taken. In the winter of 1809, 28 pickerel were taken in Southwick pond, and conveyed in casks of water and put into Cranberry pond, in this town. Their progeny now begin to be taken in considerable numbers; but it is apprehended that these formidable strangers will be likely to destroy the shiners, red fins and small perch, the former occupants of the pond.

This town is well accommodated as to roads, there being five turnpikes leading from it; one to New-Haven, sometimes called the Straits turnpike; one from the western part of the town to New-Milford, called the Litchfield and New-Milford turnpike; one passing through Harwinton to Hartford, called the Litchfield and Harwinton turnpike; one to Canaan, called the Litchfield and Canaan turnpike; and one leading from the northeast corner of the town to New-Hartford, called the New-Hartford turnpike. There is also a turnpike road running upon the eastern border of the township, contiguous to the Naugatuck river, which unites with the Straits turnpike at Salem, and extends northwardly through Winchester and Colebrook to Massachusetts.

The most important manufacture in the town is that of iron, of which there are 4 Forges, 1 Slitting Mill and 1 Nail Factory.

There are 1 Cotton Factory, 1 Oil Mill, 1 Paper Mill, 2 Carding Machines, 6 Fulling Mills, 5 Grain Mills, 18 Saw Mills, 5 large Tanneries besides several on a small scale, 2 Comb Factories, 2 Hatters' Shops, 2 Carriage Makers, 1 Cabinet Furniture Maker, 3 Saddlers, and a number of House Carpenters, Joiners, Smiths and other Mechanics.

The population of Litchfield, in 1810, was 4639; and there are about 600 Electors, 4 Companies, of Militia, 512 Dwelling houses, 8 Churches and 2 Post offices.

The commercial business is respectable, and employs considerable capital, there being 16 Mercantile Stores.

The civil or corporate divisions of the town are 4 located Ecclesiastical Societies, 26 School Districts, and an incorporated village.

Besides the located, there are 3 Episcopal Societies and one of Baptists; all of which are accommodated with houses for religious worship. There are 26 primary

LITCHFIELD.

Schools, one in each District, and an Academy, established in 1790, in the Society of South Farms. The Latin and Greek languages, Mathematics, English Grammar, Logic and Moral Philosophy are taught at this Seminary, which is very flourishing. There is in this Society a Social Library, established in 1785, and comprises from 300 to 400 vols. of well selected books.

There is a medicinal spring in the first Society, about half a mile from the Court House. Its waters have never been analyzed; but they appear to be chalybeate and sulphureous, and have been found efficacious in cutaneous diseases.

LITCHFIELD VILLAGE, incorporated in 1818, is delightfully situated upon an elevated plain, in the centre of the first located Society, affording the most extensive prospects, surrounded with interesting scenery and charming landscapes, and enjoying in the summer season the most salubrious and refreshing atmosphere.

The corporate limits of the village are about one mile and a half in length and a mile in breadth. The houses are chiefly built upon two streets, which intersect each other, forming a pleasant square in the centre. The principal street, running from northwest to southeast, is well built, comprising numerous neat, handsome and convenient dwelling houses, which are generally handsomely arranged, and some of which are elegant edifices. Within the corporate limits of the village there are 84 Dwelling houses, 9 Mercantile Stores, 2 Bookstores, several excellent Public Inns, a Printing office, a Bank, being a branch of the Phœnix Bank at Hartford, a Court House, the Gaol of the county, 2 Churches, a Post office, several Professional offices, Mechanics' shops, &c.

In addition to the public or common Schools, there is in the village a private School for young ladies, which at times has maintained a very distinguished reputation. There is also a Law School maintained here, which is very flourishing, and contains students from almost every section in the Union. It was established in 1784, by the Hon. Tapping Reeve, then one of the Judges of the Supreme Court. In 1798, the Hon. James Gould, at present one of the Supreme Judges, was associated as a joint instructor with Judge Reeve; and at this time he is the principal instructor. The number of students who have been educated at this school, from its establishment, in 1784, to 1812, was 474. This has justly been considered as the most respectable and systematic Law School in the United States.

The aggregate list of Litchfield, in 1817, was $86,872; and the valuation of the lands and buildings of the town, in 1815, made in pursuance of the laws of the United States, and which comprised 39,227 acres, was $1,255,380; being an average value of $32 per acre.

There are in this town 8 Physicians, 4 practising Attornies, and 5 Clergymen.

The tract of land comprising this township, the Indian name of which was Bantam, was purchased of the colony of Connecticut, (the Indian title having been previously extinguished,) by a company, in 1718. The purchase was divided into 60 shares, denominated Proprietor's rights, each of which was estimated at £5. The original purchasers and the first settlers were from the towns of Hartford, Windsor and Lebanon. The settlement commenced soon after the purchase; and in 1720 and 1721, there were several families upon the tract; and after this the settlement progressed rapidly. From the elevated situation of the lands in this tract, they afforded excellent hunting grounds; and many of the hills had been burned by the Indians for this purpose, and the forests entirely destroyed, which facilitated the improvements. There were, however, sufficient forests left for the purposes of the settlers.

BIOGRAPHY. The Hon. *Oliver Wolcott*, distinguished for his many public employments, was for many years a resident of this town. He was born in Windsor, Dec. 1726; and was the son of the Hon. Roger Wolcott, who was afterwards Governor of the colony of Connecticut. He was educated at Yale College, where he graduated in 1747. He was engaged in the expedition against Canada, in 1748, having the command of a company. He continued in the army during one campaign only; soon after which, he entered upon the study of physic, and having become qualified for practice, he established himself at Goshen. But he did not continue long in the practice of this profession; for, in 1751, he was appointed sheriff of the county of Litchfield, whereupon he removed to this town. He continued in this situation until 1772, a period of 21 years, when he was elected a member of the Council. The same year he was appointed Judge of the Court of Probate for the District of Litchfield; and in 1774, Judge of the Court of Common Pleas for this County. In 1775, he was chosen a member of the Continental Congress; and was continued in this situation, being a member of the immortal Congress of '76, which proclaimed the solemn declaration, that these colonies were, and of right ought to be, free, sovereign and independent.

Gov. Wolcott was one of those venerated patriots who signed that declaration, which is the charter of our national existence. He continued a member of the Council, with the exception of the period that he was a Delegate in Congress, until 1786, when he was chosen Lieut. Governor of this State. He was annually elected to this office, until the year 1796, a period of ten years, when he was chosen Governor; an office which he did not long enjoy, as he died 12th Dec. 1797. The duties of these numerous and important offices, which occupied the greater portion of his active life, he discharged with great integrity and firmness.

Gov. Wolcott possessed, in an eminent degree, a sound and vigorous mind, remarkable penetration, and a strong and efficient talent for investigation; forming no opinions but what resulted from satisfactory proof. From a consciousness of his own integrity, he never hesitated to disclose the real motives which governed his conduct. He had no intentions

BIOGRAPHY.

but what were avowed; no objects but what were apparent. No man ever had less indirection in his conduct. He was constitutionally an honest man; and being also remarkable for the firmness of his character, he never swerved from the most inflexible principles of rectitude and integrity, either from weakness, or sinister intention. It has frequently been observed, that men of the most eminent talents and virtues are often the most diffident; and the truth of this was strikingly exemplified in Gov. Wolcott. Both in public concerns, and in his private intercourse, he was singularly modest, and even diffident. He lived in an important period in our history, took a distinguished part in many great national events, and his name is associated, and will be transmitted to posterity, with those of the other patriots of our glorious Revolution.

The Hon. *Andrew Adams*, for many years a resident of this town, was born in Stratford, in 1736. He received his education at Yale College, where he graduated in 1769. Having completed his classical education, he commenced the study of law, and was admitted to the bar in the county of Fairfield. He commenced practice in his profession in Stamford, but continued there but a short time, having removed to this town in 1774. Here he entered upon the practice of law with success, and was soon appointed a Justice of the Peace. In 1776, he was chosen a Representative of the town in the Legislature of the State; and continued to be elected to this office until 1781, when he was chosen a member of the Council. About the same period, he was elected a Representative in the Congress of the United States. In May, 1793, the General Assembly appointed him Chief Judge of the Superior Court; and he held this important office, until his death, Nov. 26th, 1799. He was 62 years of age. As a lawyer and advocate, he was eminently distinguished, and was very successful in his practice; and as a Judge, he was very able and correct, having a sound and discriminating mind.

Ephraim Kirby Esq., distinguished as a lawyer and statesman, and for his services during the revolutionary war, was for many years a resident in this town.

Col. Kirby was in the service of his country during the revolutionary war, and was distinguished for his fidelity, bravery, enterprise and activity. Few officers, it is believed, of his rank, rendered more important services, or acquired a more distinguished reputation. The severe wounds which he received were the honourable testimonials of his bravery and services. After the close of the war, he engaged in the practice of law in this town, and became distinguished in his profession, both as a lawyer and advocate. Having a respectable knowledge of legal science, his views and opinions upon that subject were solid and correct; and he possessed a mind remarkably clear, comprehensive and discriminating. Whilst in the practice of law, in the year 1789, he published a volume of Reports, of the decisions of the Superior Court and Supreme Court of Errors in this State. This was a novel undertaking; being the first volume of Reports ever published in Connecticut; it was executed with faithfulness, judgment, accuracy and ability; and his Reports are now regarded as authority by the Courts of this State.

Col. Kirby was appointed to various offices in the militia of this State, and attained to the rank of Colonel. For a number of years, he was elected by the freemen of this town, as their representative in the popular branch of the Legislature of Connecticut. In this situation, he was always distinguished for the dignity of his deportment, for his comprehensive and enlightened views as a statesman, for the liberality of his principles, and for the ability, firmness and decision of his conduct.

On the elevation of Mr. Jefferson to the presidency, in 1801, Col. Kirby was appointed Supervisor of the Revenue of the United States, for the State of Connecticut. About this period, he was for several years a candidate for the office of Governor of this State. After the acquisition of Louisiana, Col. Kirby was appointed by the President a Judge in the then recently organized territory of Orleans. Having accepted of this appointment, he set out for New-Orleans; but he was not destined to reach that place, or enter upon the duties of his recent appointment. He proceeded as far as Fort Stoddard, in the Mississippi territory, where he was taken sick, and died 2nd October 1804. His remains were interred with the honours of war, and other demonstrations of respect.

As a lawyer, a man of learning and talents, Col. Kirby stood deservedly high; as a patriot, and friend of civil liberty, he was ardent, almost to enthusiasm; as a politician and statesman, his views were liberal, just and comprehensive, founded upon an accurate and extensive knowledge of the human character, and its susceptibility of improvement; and, as a citizen, few have had more social and private virtues. His memory will long be cherished by the citizens of his native State.

The Hon. *Uriah Tracy* was for many years a resident of this town. He was born in Norwich, in 1754. He was educated at Yale College, and was a member of the distinguished class, which graduated in 1778. Soon after he left College, he came to this town, and commenced the study of law with Judge Reeve, and was admitted to the bar in 1781. He soon became distinguished, as a lawyer and an advocate. He passed thro' various military offices, rising to the rank of a Major-General. In 1788, he was elected a Representative of the town in the General Assembly, and was successively reelected, until the year 1793, when he was chosen a Representative of this State in the Congress of the United States. He continued in this office until the year 1800, when he was appointed a Senator, which office he held at the time of his death, July 1807. He died at the seat of Government.

As a lawyer, Mr. Tracy was very respectable; and, as a politician, eminently distinguished. He was among the first of the party with which he acted, and was respected for his talents and his intelligence by his political opponents. He possessed a comprehensive mind, respectable scientific acquirements, and an extensive knowledge of the human character. He had also a great share of wit and humour, and knew its proper use;—to please, without wounding the feelings even of the most humble individual.

BARKHAMSTED.

BARKHAMSTED is a post township, situated 23 miles north-west from Hartford; bounded on the north by Hartland and Colebrook, on the east by Canton and Granby, on the south by New-Hartford, and on the west by Winchester. It comprises about 32 square miles, or 20,580 acres; being about 6 and a half miles in length from east to west, and about 5 miles in breadth from north to south.

The township is rough, stony and mountainous; being intersected by two elevated granitic ridges, which run through it in a northerly and southerly direction, extending to the north far into the interior of New-England. Upon the declivities of these ridges, and upon their summits, there is much broken land, some which is inaccessible. Their geological character is primitive, the prevailing strata of rock consisting of granite. In some places within this town, these ridges exhibit very lofty and sublime features. Their declivities afford considerable wood and timber, and when cleared, tolerable grazing.

. Iron ore has been discovered in these granitic strata, in different parts of the town in small quantities, but of a rich and good quality. In some sections of the town there are some strata of limestone; and what is commonly called cottonstone is found in abundance; and also freestone, which is valuable only for local uses. The soil, corresponding with the prevailing geological features, is generally a coarse gravelly loam, hard and dry; and with the exception of some intervals upon the streams, is rough and stony, and in general inadmissible for tillage. It affords tolerable grazing, the interests of which constitute the staple agricultural products of the town. The dairy business receives general attention, and large quantities of cheese and butter are made annually; a considerable proportion of which is sent abroad for a market.

The raising of neat cattle and sheep is attended to, and considerable beef is marketed. The intervals bordering upon the streams are generally rich and feasible, and afford tillage and mowing. The natural growth of wood and timber, which was once very heavy and abundant, has been greatly devastated. The mountains and hills were formerly covered with excellent timber, consisting of oak, chesnut, sugar maple, beach, pine and hemlock; a considerable proportion of which has been destroyed by the elements, wind and fire, and by the axe, under a system of improvidence, at a time when timber was considered of no value.

The waters of the town are abundant, and of an excellent quality; the two principal branches of the Tunxis, or Farmington river, run through it, and form a union in the north part of New-Hartford. The Still river runs northerly thro' Torrington and Winchester into Colebrook, whence it takes a southerly course and unites with the west branch of the Farmington river in this town, forming what is called the forks of the river. Besides these, there are numerous small streams which are tributary to them, that water the various sections of the town. Upon these streams, there are various sites and privileges for mills and other water works, and five considerable bridges.

The facilities of communication are greatly increased, considering the roughness of the country, by the number of turnpike roads with which the town is accommodated. The Greenwoods turnpike leading to Albany passes through its southwest section; the Farmington river turnpike, which communicates with the former and leads to Albany, runs through its western section in a northerly and southerly direction, following the course of the west branch of the Farmington river; the Hartland turnpike leading westwardly, and which communicates with the Greenwoods turnpike in Norfolk, passes through the northwest corner of the town. In May, 1818, a turnpike road was authorized, and has since been surveyed, leading from the Greenwoods turnpike to Newgate prison, which passes through the western section of this town, crossing the Farmington river turnpike, and running directly by the meeting house. It has not yet been opened.

Of the mechanical and manufacturing establishments of the town, there are 3 Grain Mills, 12 Saw Mills, 1 Fulling Mill and cloth dressing establishment, 1 Furnace for casting cart and waggon boxes, clock bells and some other small articles, and 2 Tanneries.

The population of the town, in 1810, was 1506; and there are about 260 Electors or Freemen, 2 companies of Militia, and about 230 Dwelling houses. The aggregate list of the town, in 1816, was $26,978.

The town contains 2 located Congregational Societies, 1 Society of Episcopalians and one of Methodists; besides which, there are some Baptists. There are 2 houses for public worship, 1 for Congregationalists and 1 for Episcopalians. It contains also, 11 School districts. There are 3 Mercantile Stores, 4 Public Houses or Inns, 3 Social Libraries and 1 Physician.

The first settler in Barkhamsted was Pelatiah Allyn from Windsor, who removed there about the year 1744, and remained the only inhabitant of the town for 10 or 12 years. In the summer he employed his time in clearing and cultivating his lands, and in the winter in hunting. His privations, sufferings, dangers and hardships, could only have been equalled by his perseverance. To have been for the long period of 10 or 12 years a solitary inhabitant of a dreary wilderness, rendered more hideous from the native ruggedness of its features, having no traces of civilization but what his own hands had produced, and exposed to the most imminent perils from its native inhabitants,—wild beasts which claimed to be "lords of the soil," and maintained an indisputable dominion over it, is a situation which it is difficult to conceive, and impossible to describe. Mr. Allyn justly deserves to be regarded as the patriarch of the town. From his industry and perseverance during this long period of voluntary exile, he had made such improvements, and placed himself in such a situation as to enable him to be eminently useful to other settlers; but, notwithstanding, the progress of the settlement was very slow and discouraging. In 1771, about 27 years from the commencement of the settlement by Mr. Allyn, there were but 20 families within the limits of the town. Israel Jones from Enfield, William Austin, Jonathan King and a Mr. Norton from Suffield, Amos Case from Simsbury, John Ives from Hamden, Joseph Shepard from Hartford and Joseph Wilder from East-Haddam, were among the first and principal settlers.

The town was incorporated in 1779. Joseph Wilder was the first magistrate, and for several years the only one in the town. The Rev. Ozias Ells, who was ordained in 1787, was the first minister. He died in 1813.

BETHLEM.

BETHLEM is a small elevated interior post township, 38 miles from Hartford, and 33 from New-Haven; bounded on the north by Litchfield, on the east by Watertown, on the south by Woodbury, and on the west by Washington. Its average length from east to west is 4 and a half miles, and its average breadth 4 miles, containing an area of about 18 square miles.

The township is considerably hilly; its surface being diversified with granitic eminences and vallies. The soil is generally a gravelly loam, and is best adapted to grazing. It however produces tolerable crops of grain.

The natural growth consists of oak, maple, chesnut, walnut, &c.

The township is watered by several branches of Pomperaug river, which afford some good sites for mills, some of which are occupied.

The population of the town, in 1810, was 1118; and there are 150 qualified Electors, 1 Company of Militia, and 170 Dwelling houses.

There are 3 small Distilleries, 1 Grain Mill, 1 Fulling Mill and Clothier's works, 1 Carding Machine, 1 Tannery, 4 Saw Mills, and 1 Mercantile Store.

The amount of taxable property, including polls, is $27,000; and the assessment of the lands and buildings of the town, in 1816, which included 11,161 acres, amounted to $306,555; being an average value of 27\frac{47}{100}$ per acre.

The town contains 1 located Congregational Society & Church, 1 Society of Episcopalians and 1 of Baptists.

It is divided into 9 School Districts, each of which is provided with a School house, and maintains a School for several months in the year.

The professional men are 1 Physician, 1 Clergyman and 1 Attorney; there is 1 small Social Library.

Bethlem was taken from Woodbury, and incorporated in 1787.

BIOGRAPHY. The Rev. *Azel Backus*, D. D. was for many years a resident clergyman in this town. Dr. Backus was educated at Yale College, where he graduated in 1787. Having qualified himself for the ministry, at an early period, he was ordained as the successor of Dr. Bellamy, in this town, and continued in this situation until the establishment of Hamilton College, in the county of Oneida, in the State of New-York, when he was appointed to preside over that Institution. Whilst in this town, he instituted a school, and took upon himself the charge and instruction of his pupils, whom he took into his own family, thereby adding parental care and solicitude to the advantages of literary and moral instruction. This school became very highly and deservedly celebrated, and was attended by students from different parts of the Union.

The distinguished reputation which he had acquired, as a divine, a man of science, and an instructor of youth, procured for him the appointment to the presidency of Hamilton College. He received the appointment about the year 1812, and continued in this situation until his death, December 26th, 1816. He was the first President of this College, and taking the charge of the Institution at its commencement, he had, during the short period that he presided over it, very arduous and complicated duties to perform. But his learning, judgment and faithfulness rendered him admirably qualified for his situation; and, under his guidance and direction, this infant seminary was rapidly rising into notice, and afforded a most flattering promise of future usefulness and reputation.

Dr. Backus was distinguished for remarkable vigour and aptitude of mind. He was an able divine, a good scholar, and a judicious and successful instructor. He was also eminent for his social virtues, the mildness of his disposition, and the complacency of his temper. He was both respected and beloved by his pupils.

CANAAN.

CANAAN, a considerable post township, is situated in the northwestern section of the county, 41 miles northwest from Hartford, bounded on the north by Massachusetts line, on the east by Norfolk, on the south by Cornwall, and on the west by the Ousatonick river, which divides it from Salisbury.

The township comprises an area of about 50 square miles; having an average length from north to south of about 9 miles, and a mean breadth of nearly 6 miles.

The face of the country is broken and mountainous, several considerable ranges, some of which are elevated, extending through the town in a northeasterly and southwesterly direction. These ranges are of a primitive granitic character. Between the mountains and hills there are extensive calcareous vales. These vales have internal strata of limestone; numerous quarries of which, in these calcareous strata, have been opened for the making of lime. The best limestone is usually found on the northern declivities of small eminences. In the northeasterly section of the township, iron ore has been discovered near the surface. A mine has been opened, and quantities of the ore raised and worked. The ore was found to be rich, as to the quantity of iron which it contained; but it is of an inferior quality.

The soil is various, being of a different quality in different sections, according to their geological character. Upon the mountains, hills and their declivities, it is generally a primitive gravelly loam; and in most of the vallies it is a calcareous loam. The former are principally reserved for forests, or improved by grazing; and the latter are admirably adapted to a grain culture, affording excellent crops of wheat, rye, corn and oats. There is considerable broken and waste land in the township, but many sections that are rich and fertile; so that it may be considered as a good and flourishing agricultural town.

The forests comprise various species of trees, principally deciduous; oak, chesnut, walnut, butternut, beach, sugar maple, soft maple, birch, hemlock, white and yellow pine, white and red cedar, spruce, red, white and black ash, elm, bass, boxwood, whitewood, peperidge, mountain ash, sassafras, alder, &c.

The agricultural productions are rye, Indian corn, oats, wheat, buck wheat, peas, beans, barley, cheese, butter, beef, pork, flax, flax-seed, &c. The staples are rye and corn, of which there are annually considerable quantities raised that are sent abroad for a market.

The western border of the township is washed by the Ousatonick river; and the interior is watered by numerous small streams, of which Blackberry river, that rises in Norfolk, and runs through the town, and Hollenbach, having its source within the town, and both of which discharge their waters into the Ousatonick, are the principal. Upon these and other smaller streams there are numerous sites for hydraulic works.

This town is accommodated with several turnpike roads; the Greenwoods turnpike, leading from New-Hartford, northwesterly, passes through this town; the Litchfield and Canaan turnpike, leading to Litchfield; and the Canaan and Salisbury turnpike, which unites with the last mentioned, near the old furnace in Salisbury.

The manufactures of the town are principally of iron, which constitute an important, and in general a profitable business. There are 8 Forges, 7 Anchor Shops, and 2 Furnaces. The ore used here is transported from Salisbury. The iron manufactures have developed an extensive field of industry, and are sources of considerable wealth. Besides these, there are 1 Cotton Factory, 1 Distillery, 4 Grain Mills, 1 Plaster Mill, 15 Saw Mills and 4 Carding Machines. There are a number of Limekilns in this town; and large quantities of lime are annually made, and sent to different places for a market.

In 1810, there were 2183 inhabitants in this town; and there are now about 300 Electors, 200 Militia, and 276 Dwelling houses.

The mercantile business is respectable, there being 9 Dry Goods and Grocery Stores in the town.

The civil or corporate divisions are 2 located Congregational Societies and 12 School Districts. Besides the located, there are 2 other religious Societies; one of Methodists and one of Friends, or Quakers. There are 12 primary Schools, one in each District; 3 Social Libraries, 3 Attornies, 2 Clergymen, and 2 practising Physicians.

This township was sold at New-London, at auction, in 1738; and the settlement commenced in June the same year. The first settlers were Daniel and Isaac Lawrence, and John Franklin; but they were soon joined by various others. The town was incorporated in 1739; and the first clergyman, the Rev. Elisha Webster, was settled in Oct. 1740.

COLEBROOK.

COLEBROOK, an elevated post township, is situated 31 miles northwest from Hartford, on the northern border of the county; bounded on the north by Massachusetts line, on the east by Hartland, in Hartford county, on the south by Winchester, and on the west by Norfolk. Its average length from east to west is 6 miles, and its average breadth 5 miles, containing about 30 square miles.

This township is embraced within the granitic district, which constitutes the height of land in the western part of the State. It is hilly and mountainous; and the soil is a hard, gravelly loam, and generally stony. It is in general rather cold and wet, but affords tolerable good grazing. There are some intervals which are well adapted to grass or mowing.

The dairy business is the principal agricultural interest of the town; and considerable quantities of butter and cheese are made annually by the inhabitants.

The natural growth of timber consists of oak, maple, beech, hemlock and other perennial trees; but the latter comprise a considerable proportion of the forests in this town.

The main branch of the Tunxis or Farmington river intersects the eastern section of the town, and affords most excellent mill seats and privileges for water works. Still river, a considerable branch of the Tunxis, washes its southeastern border; and another branch, called the Sandy river, runs through its interior. These two streams afford also numerous sites for mills and other hydraulic works.

The town is well accommodated with turnpike roads; the Albany turnpike leads through its eastern section; the Hudson turnpike thro' its southwestern; and the Hartland turnpike leads through the centre of the town from east to west; and the New-Haven turnpike from north to south; there is also the Still river turnpike.

The population of the town, in 1810, was 1243; and there are about 200 Dwelling houses, 200 Freemen or Electors, and 2 companies of militia.

The amount of taxable property, including polls, is $26,447; and the valuation or assessment of lands and buildings in 1815, which included 17,555 acres, amounted to $270,102, being an average of $15 47/100 per acre.

The most considerable manufacturing and mechanical employments are 1 establishment for the manufacture of Steel, 2 Scythe Factories, at which sleigh shoes and several other articles are manufactured, 1 Woolen Factory, 3 Tanneries, 1 Grain Mill, 1 Fulling Mill and Clothier's works, 1 Carding Machine, and 3 Manufactories of Wooden Ware, or Turning establishments. There are 4 Mercantile Stores.

The town contains 1 located Congregational Society & Church, and 1 Society of Baptists, 1 Social Library, and 8 School Districts and Schools.

The professional men are 2 Physicians, 2 Clergymen and 1 Att'y.

Colebrook was first settled in 1765, and was incorporated in 1779.

CORNWALL.

CORNWALL, a post township, is situated 38 miles west from Hartford, and 48 northwest from New-Haven; bounded on the north by Canaan, on the east by Goshen, on the south by Warren and Kent, and on the west by the Ousatonick river, separating it from Sharon.

Its average length from north to south is more than 9 miles, and its average breadth about 5 miles, comprising an area of about 46 square miles.

The township is hilly and mountainous; containing many elevated and continuous hills, and deep and extensive vales. Its geological character is primitive; the rocks consisting of granite, micaceous schistus, and some limestone in the vales. Several minerals have been discovered; in the west section of the town, there is a mountain, in which, at various places, there are veins of black lead ore. It has been used for marking, and some other purposes; but has not received that attention which is necessary to develope its quantity, richness or value. About two miles south of the principal settlement in the town, there is a bed of porcelain clay, of 5 or 6 feet in depth, 7 or 8 in width, and of several rods in extent. It is thought that the quality of the clay is as good as that of foreign countries; and, if properly manufactured, would afford excellent porcelain ware. There are also various indications of iron ore, at various places; but no mines have been opened or worked.

The soil is generally a gravelly loam; but in some sections of the vales it is a calcareous loam. It is warm, fertile and productive; being well adapted both to grain and grazing.

Among the natural growth of timber, oak, chesnut, maple and pine abound; there is also birch, ash, beech, &c., comprising every kind of wood, valuable for fuel, fencing or building.

The agricultural productions consist of wheat, of which considerable quantities are annually raised, rye, oats, hay, butter and cheese, of which considerable quantities are annually marketed abroad, beef, pork, wool, and some other articles.

The Ousatonick washes the western border of the town. Besides which, there are several small streams, affording many sites for water works.

Across the Ousatonick, there are several bridges; one on the Goshen and Sharon turnpike, called Hart's bridge; one on the road leading from this town to Ellsworth Society, in Sharon, called Lewis' bridge, at the village of that name; and one on the Sharon and Cornwall turnpike; these bridges are about 120 feet in length.

The town is accommodated with several turnpike roads; the Canaan and Litchfield turnpike crosses its northeast corner; the turnpike from Sharon to Poughkeepsie, after passing through Goshen, leads through the centre of the town east and west, and passes the north meeting-house; Cornwall and Washington turnpike leads through the town north and south, about one mile east of its centre; Warren turnpike runs north and south, on its west line; and Sharon and Cornwall turnpike east and west, near its south border.

About two miles from the north boundary of the town, and near its centre, east and west, there is a pond called Cornwall pond, being one mile in length, and half a mile in breadth, from which there is an outlet that affords numerous sites for mills and other waterworks. In the southeast corner of the town, there is also a pond of about one mile in length, and nearly half a mile in width. These ponds are stored with pickerel and trout; the latter are also taken plentifully in the small streams.

The manufactures and mechanical interests and trades in the town, are the following: 1 Woolen Factory, which employs about six hands, 2 Iron Forges, constantly in operation, 4 Distilleries, 2 of gin and 2 of cider brandy, 4 Tanneries, 3 Grain Mills, 2 Mills to clean clover-seed, 2 Oil Mills, 20 Saw Mills, 3 Fulling Mills and Clothiers' works, and 2 Carding Machines, for Customers. There are 2 Cabinet Makers, 4 House Joiners, 2 Carpenters, 2 Wheelwrights, 1 Carriage Maker, 6 Coopers, 7 Blacksmiths, 1 Mason and Bricklayer, 1 Hatter, 20 Shoe Makers and 5 Tailors. There are 4 Mercantile Stores and traders, and 4 Public Inns.

The population of the town, in 1810, was 1602; and there are about 250 Electors, 2 Companies of militia, one of about 80 members, and the other a Light Infantry Company of about 35, and about 200 Dwelling houses.

The amount of taxable property, including polls, estimated according to the laws for making up lists, in 1816, was $37,559; and the assessment of the lands and buildings of the town, in 1815, which comprised 23,484 acres, amounted to $490,696; being $20\frac{89}{100}$ dollars per acre. The assessment of the real estate of this town and Goshen, in 1799, amounted to $517,342; being only $17,646 more than the valuation of Cornwall alone, in 1815.

The town comprises 1 located Society and 11 School Districts. There are, however, 2 Congregational Churches, and a Society and Church of Methodists. There is a common or primary School maintained in each of the School Districts, a suitable portion of the year. Besides which there is a Foreign Missionary School, designed for the education and ecclesiastical instruction of foreigners, and is the only school of the kind in the United States.

It contains, at this time, 20 scholars from various parts of the world, some from the Sandwich Islands.

There are 3 Social Libraries, 1 Clergyman, 1 Attorney and 2 Physicians.

This township was divided into 53 shares or rights, and sold at public auction at Fairfield, in February 1737 or 1738, by a committee, consisting of John Barnes, Edmund Lewis and Ebenezer Silliman, appointed by the General Assembly for that purpose. The sale was effected, at $30 per right, with the reservation of one right for the support of the ministry, and another for the benefit of schools. In laying out the township, there was also a reservation of 384 acres for the benefit of Yale College.

The first settlement was made about the year 1738, probably in the spring of that year; and in 1740 there were 13 families in the town, previously to the arrival of John Dibble, with several others, from Stamford. Soon afterwards, Joshua Pierce removed from Pembroke, in Massachusetts, and settled in this town. The settlement soon became respectable and flourishing; and in 1741, a clergyman was ordained, being the first settled in the town.

BIOGRAPHY. Col. *Ethan Allen*, distinguished for his bravery, his adventures and his sufferings, during the revolutionary war, was a native of this town. Whilst he was a youth, his father removed to Vermont. In the year 1770, when the disturbances in that territory had assumed a serious aspect, Col. Allen first came into notice, from the bold and active part which he took in favour of the " Green Mountain Boys," as they were called, in opposition to the claims of the Government of the State of New-York. So obnoxious had he rendered himself, that an act of outlawry against him was passed by the Government of that colony, and 500 guineas were offered for his apprehension. But he had nothing to fear from these proceedings, as his party were too numerous and too faithful to the man who had been the great champion of their cause, to suffer him to be apprehended. During the period that this subject was agitated, in all the struggles which it occasioned, and in which Col. Allen took a part, he was uniformly successful.

On receiving the news of the battle of Lexington, the first hostile event of the revolutionary contest, Col. Allen determined to engage on the side of the colonies; and being hasty in his decisions, and desperately bold and determined in his enterprises, his ardour and attachment to the cause of his country were soon signalized by a daring and almost unexampled exploit. Soon after the affair at Lexington, a project had been consulted, to surprise and take the forts of Ticonderoga and Crown Point, by several gentlemen from Connecticut; and on being informed of this enterprise, Col. Allen engaged in it with his usual ardour and characteristic bravery, and being joined by Col. Arnold, this party of adventurers accomplished their object, without the loss of a man. In this affair, an incident occurred, which in a peculiar manner exemplified the character of Col. Allen. He rushed into the fort, at the imminent risk of his life, and demanded its immediate surrender. The astonished commander, equally filled with surprise and consternation, inquired "by what authority?" To this, Allen, without the least hesitation, replied, "in the name of the Great Jehovah and of the continental Congress."

In the autumn of 1775, he was sent into Canada, to observe the dispositions of the people in that province, and to endeavour to attach them to the American cause.

Whilst on this tour, Col. Brown proposed to him the project of an attack upon Montreal, which was eagerly embraced by Col. Allen. For the execution of this bold enterprise, he collected 110 men, nearly 80 of whom were Canadians; and with this little party, on the evening of the 24th of September, he crossed the river, expecting the co-operation of Col. Brown, in which, however, he was disappointed. In the morning he was attacked by a force of 500 men, a part of whom were Indians, and after an obstinate and desperate resistance, he was compelled to surrender. On falling into the hands of the British, he was put in irons, and treated with the greatest severity and cruelty. He was shortly after sent to England, as a prisoner, although not allowed the rights belonging to a prisoner of war, being after his arrival there confined in a castle near Falmouth. On the 8th Jan. 1776, he was embarked on board a frigate, destined for Halifax, and from thence proceeded to New-York. Here he was detained about a year and a half, and had an opportunity to witness the severe and inhuman manner in which the American prisoners were treated. He calculated that nearly 2000 of these unfortunate persons perished by hunger and cold, and from diseases which originated from the unwholesomeness of their provisions, and the impurity of their prison.

Col. Allen was exchanged in May 1778, and soon returned to Vermont; where, from his desperate exploits and extreme sufferings in the cause of his country, he was received with the most enthusiastic joy. He was soon after promoted to the rank of a Brigadier-General in the militia of that State. He acquired great influence in that section of the country, and was extensively active and useful during the remainder of the war.

Col. Allen possessed a mind naturally strong, vigorous and eccentric, but it had not been improved by an early education. He was brave in the most imminent danger, and possessed a bold, daring and adventurous spirit, which neither feared dangers nor regarded difficulties. He was also ingenuous, frank, generous and patriotic, which are the usual accompanying virtues of native bravery and courage. He wrote and published a narrative of his sufferings during his imprisonment in England and in New-York; comprising also various observations upon the events of the war, the conduct of the British, their treatment of their prisoners, &c. He died 13th Feb. 1789.

The Hon. *Heman Swift* was a resident of this town, and died here on the 14th Nov. 1814, aged 82 years. He was the son of Jabez Swift, and was born in Sandwich, Massachusetts, in 1733; soon after which, his father emigrated to this State, and settled in the town of Kent. During the French war, at an early age, Mr. Swift, the subject of this notice, entered the service, having the rank of a lieutenant in the provincial troops sent to the northern frontier. At an early period of the revolutionary war, he was appointed a colonel in the continental army, by the American Congress. He continued in the service until the termination of the war; and, throughout most of this arduous and distresing contest, he belonged to th main army, and executed the orers of its illustrious leader. H: was esteemed a good officer, ad was distinguished for his firmness, integrity, and strict regard to military discipline, and enjoyed the esteem and confidence of the Commander in chief. After the close of the war, having retired to his residence in Cornwall, he was soon appointed to various civil offices, under the Government of this State, and for twelve years in succession, was a member of the Council.

GOSHEN.

GOSHEN is an elevated post township, situated 32 miles west from Hartford, and 42 from New Haven; bounded on the north by Norfolk, on the east by Winchester and Torrington, on the south by Litchfield and Warren, and on the west by Cornwall. Its average length is about 9 miles from north to south, and its average breadth 4 and a half miles, comprising about 40 square miles.

This township is very elevated, and is undoubtedly the highest land in the State, but it is not generally mountainous; the surface being undulating affording an interesting diversity of hill and dale. Just north of the centre of the town, there is an elevated hill called Ivy mountain, which rises considerably above he general surface of the town, and is considered as the most elevated point of land in the State. It affords a most extensive and interesing prospect, in almost every direction; to the west is a view of the Catskill mountain for a considerable extent; its rugged features, and high and disorderly hills; and to the eas is a view of the elevated country east of Connecticut river.

The road called East-street is so situated upon a height of ground, as to divide the waters which descend into the Ousatonick and Waterbury rivers.

The geological character of the township is primitive; the rocs consisting of granite, gneiss and other original formations. The soil is a gravelly loam, deep, strong and fertile; and is admirably adapted to grazing; and hence, the dairy business is extensively and advantageously carried on, the products of which, consisting not only of butter and cheese, but of pork and lard, constitute the agricultural staples of the town. The growing of cattle and fattening of beeves, also receive considerable attention. This is one of the best towns for the dairy business in the State; and the farmers are generally wealthy and flourishing. In 1811, there was 380,236lb. of cheese marketed abroad from this town, which was much less than the whole quantity made; the consumption of the inhabitants, and sales at home being considerable. This quantity of cheese at 10 cents per pound, would have amounted to $38,023:60, a very considerable sum for the avails of a single staple. But neat cattle, and the various interests of the dairy business do not occupy the exclusive attention of the farmers of this town; sheep and the growing of wool, receive considerable attention, particularly since the merino breed has been introduced.

Of the natural growth of timber, the sugar maple prevails; and formerly, the industry of the inhabitants supplied large quantities of sugar, from the saccharine juice of this valuable tree.

There is no stream in Goshen, excepting one which rises in Norfolk, and runs across the northeast corner of the town, deserving the character of a river; but there are several small mill streams, having their sources in ponds and springs within the town, some of which afford good sites for water works.

There are five ponds in the town of different sizes, from one to three miles in circumference; the outlets of some of which afford excellent sites for hydraulic works. The stream which flows from one of these ponds in the western part of the town, is admirably calculated for water works, having an adequate supply of water at all times, and characterized by great uniformity; being neither affected by droughts, nor heavy rains occasioning freshets as in other streams. Upon this stream, there are now 2 Woolen Factories, a Carding Machine for customers, 2 Fulling Mills, a Grain Mill, Saw Mill, Trip Ham-

HARWINTON.

mer, a Machine for dressing flax and an Oil Mill, all situated within 50 or 60 rods of each other.

The turnpike road from Hartford to Sharon, and thence to Poughkeepsie, leads through the centre of this town; and one also from New-Haven to Albany, intersecting the former at right angles.

The more considerable manufactures and mechanical interests and employments are the following: 2 Woolen Factories, each employing from 15 to 20 persons; and it is estimated, that from 8 to 10,000lbs. of wool are manufactured annually at these establishments; the fabrics of which have justly acquired a considerable local celebrity, not only for durability, but for fineness and elegance of style. In addition to the Woolen manufactures, there are 2 Potteries, or manufactories of earthen ware, 2 Carding Machines, (besides those belonging to the two Woolen factories,) 3 Fulling Mills and Clothiers' works for customers, 2 Grain Mills, 5 Saw Mills and 5 Tanneries, mostly upon a small scale. There are in the town, 5 Mercantile Stores.

The population of the town, in 1810, was 1641; and there are about 350 Electors, 2 Companies of Militia, and about 240 Dwelling houses.

The amount of taxable property, including polls, in 1817, was $45,840. The assessment of lands and buildings, including 20,706 acres, amounted to $512,272; being 24\frac{74}{100}$ per acre.

The town contains 1 located Ecclesiastical Society and 8 School districts, which constitute its civil divisions; besides the located, there is a Society of Methodists, both of which are accommodated with houses for public worship. There is a primary School maintained in each of the School districts for a suitable portion of the year; besides which, there is usually a Grammar School in the centre of the town. There are 2 Clergymen, 2 Physicians and 1 Attorney.

The first settlement in Goshen commenced in 1738 or 1739, the township having been sold at New-Haven in 1737. The first settlers were principally from New-Haven, Wallingford & Farmington. From the elevated situation of the town, it has been remarkably healthy, having never been visited with epidemical or contagious diseases. The town was incorporated in October, 1749, being nine or ten years from the first settlement.

HARWINTON.

HARWINTON is a post township, situated in the southeastern section of the county, 23 miles from Hartford; bounded on the north by New-Hartford and Torrington, on the east by Burlington in Hartford county, on the south by Plymouth, and on the west by the Naugatuck river, which separates it from Litchfield. It is 6 miles in length, and 5 in breadth, comprising an area of 30 square miles.

The township is elevated and hilly; and its geological structure, both with respect to its rocks and soil, is of a granitic character; there are, however, some quarries of micaceous schistus, and other primitive rocks. The timber and forests consist principally of deciduous trees. The lands are best adapted to grazing, and the making of butter and cheese is a leading agricultural interest.

The town is watered, exclusive of the Naugatuck which washes its western border, by the Lead Mine river a branch of the Naugatuck, which runs through the interior of the township, and by numerous small streams.

The town is accommodated with the Hartford and Litchfield turnpike road, which leads through it; also by the Waterbury turnpike, leading to New-Haven. It contains one located Congregational Society, and one Society of Episcopalians. There is one small village of 15 or 20 Dwelling houses.

The manufactures and mechanical employments, exclusive of those of a domestic character, consist of 1 Tinware Factory, 3 Fulling Mills and Clothiers' Works, 3 Carding Machines, 4 Grain Mills and 2 Tanneries. There are 3 Mercantile Stores and 4 Taverns.

There are 11 School districts and common Schools, and 1 Academy in the town; 1 small Social Library, 2 Houses for Public Worship, 2 Clergymen and 1 Physician.

The population of the town, in 1810, was 1718; and there are 293 Dwelling houses, 240 Electors, and 1 Company of Militia.

The quantity of land included in the assessment, in 1816, was 17,069 acres, valued at $407,225; being an average of $23 $\frac{6}{10}$ per acre.

The general list of the town, including polls, is $36,648.

Harwinton was incorporated in 1737.

KENT.

KENT is a post township, situated in the southwestern section of the county, 45 miles from Hartford; bounded on the north by Sharon and Cornwall, on the east by Washington and Warren, on the south by New-Milford and Sherman, and on the west by the State of New-York; having an average length of nearly 8 miles, and an average breadth of more than 6 miles, containing 48 square miles.

The township is characteristically mountainous; and its geological structure consists principally of granite, although in some sections it is calcareous. Among its mineral treasures, iron ore is found in great abundance. Several mines have been opened and worked, from which it is estimated, that several thousand dollars worth of the ore is annually raised. There are seven forges that have been erected, and are usually in operation; all of which, it has been estimated, manufacture 100 tons of iron annually. These mines, & the manufactures and various interests which depend upon them, afford employment to industry, a stimulus to enterprise, and are sources of considerable wealth to the town.

The soil in this town varies, according to its geological structure. Upon the hills of granite, it is hard and gravelly, and in the limestone vales, it is a rich calcareous loam; the former affords tolerably good grazing, and the latter produces wheat, rye and grass. The timber is oak, chesnut, walnut, ash, &c.

This town is watered by the Ousatonick and its numerous branches, which afford many valuable sites for mills and other water works. It is accommodated by the Litchfield and New-Preston turnpike, which passes through its south section.

The population of the town, in 1810, was 1794; and there are now 200 qualified Electors, 2 Companies of Militia, & about 290 Dwelling houses.

In addition to the domestic manufactures of the town, and those of iron already noticed, there are 2 Grain Mills, 2 Fulling Mills and Clothier's works, 1 Carding Machine and 2 Tanneries. There are 3 Mercantile Stores.

The taxable property of the town, including polls, is $36,967; and the United States assessment, in 1816, was $414,278, being an average of more than $18 per acre for the quantity valued, which was but 22,764 acres. In 1799, this town, together with Warren, was assessed at $405,982.

Kent contains but one located Society; besides which, it has a Society of Episcopalians, and each of them has a house for public worship. It contains 10 School districts and Schools, 3 practising Physicians, 2 Attorneys and 1 Clergyman.

The town was incorporated in 1739.

NEW-HARTFORD.

NEW-HARTFORD is a post town, situated on the eastern border of the county, being 20 miles northwest from Hartford. It is bounded on the north by Barkhamsted, on the east by Canton, in Hartford county, on the south by Harwinton and Burlington, and on the west by Torrington. It is 6 miles in length from north to south, and nearly 6 miles in breadth from east to west, containing 34 square miles.

The Farmington or Tunxis river washes the eastern section of the town, and affords numerous sites and privileges for mills and other water works. The town is also watered by innumerable small streams, in almost every direction.

The township is hilly and mountainous, containing a range of mountain of considerable elevation, consisting of granite and other rocks of primitive formations. These ranges are covered with trees, and contain abundance of timber. The forests consist generally of deciduous trees, except in the northern part of the town, where the perennial or ever-green region of Connecticut commences. Here, but a few years since, was an extensive tract of forests, called "Green woods," but now they are reduced; roads having been opened through them; considerable portions cleared; and the wood upon what remains, is considerably diminished. These lands, formerly, were not considered of any value for cultivation, but are now more justly estimated. The soil in this ever-green district is a coarse, hard gravel, abounding with stone; and the land is not cleared or cultivated, without difficulty or labour; but when cleared, it will produce one crop of grain, and then makes indifferent pasturage.

In the other sections of the town, excepting the mountain, the soil is a gravelly loam, warm and fertile; it produces grain, but is best adapted to grass.

The Talcott mountain and Greenwoods turnpike passes through this town, in a northwestern direction. This is the principal road from Hartford, the eastern section of Connecticut, Rhode-Island and the southern part of Massachusetts to Albany, and the western district of New-York; and is one of the great avenues to the western country; and hence, this town has become a great thoroughfare for travelling. The Goshen and Torrington turnpike passes through the southern section of the town.

The population of New-Hartford, in 1810, was 1507; and there are now 200 Electors or Freemen, 2 Companies of Militia, and about 220 Dwelling houses.

The general list of the town, including polls, amounts to $31,434. The assessment of the United States, in 1815, was $343,940; being an average value of $17 per acre, for all the lands in the township. In 1799, this town, together with Barkhamsted, was valued only at $387,078.

In addition to the domestic manufactures of the town, there are 1 Tin Ware Factory, 4 Carding Machines, 4 Fulling Mills and Clothier's Works, 4 Distilleries, 3 Tanneries, 4 Grain Mills, 4 Saw Mills, 1 Ashery, and an extensive manufactory of machinery, including carding, shearing and spinning machines, &c. There are 3 Mercantile Stores in the town.

New-Hartford contains but one located Society, which has a house for public worship; it is divided into 8 School districts, in each of which there is a School maintained for several months in the year.

There are 2 small villages in the town, of about 20 houses each. There are 2 small Social Libraries 1 Clergyman, 2 Attornies and 1 Physician.

New-Hartford was incorporated in 1738.

NEW-MILFORD.

NEW-MILFORD is a large and flourishing post town, in the southwestern extremity of the county, 48 miles southwest from Hartford; bounded on the north by Kent, on the east by Washington, Roxbury and Southbury, on the south by Newtown and Brookfield, in Fairfield county, and on the west by New-Fairfield and Sherman. It has an average length of 13 miles, and an average breadth of 6 and a

NEW-MILFORD.

half miles, comprising an area of 84 square miles; being one of the largest townships in the State.

It is watered by the Ousatonick which intersects the town, and by two branches of the Aspetuck, a tributary stream of the Ousatonick. Upon these and other smaller streams, there are numerous sites and privileges for mills and other hydraulic works. There are two shad fisheries upon the Ousatonick; lamprey eels are also taken in great plenty. There are three bridges across this river, within this town. The section of the town which lies west of the Ousatonick, is watered by Rocky and Still rivers which intersect it, running in a northeasterly direction to the Ousatonick, into which they discharge their waters.

This township is hilly and broken, several mountainous ridges extending through it. These ridges consist of granite and micaceous schistus; the former is generally found upon their tops or summits, and the latter upon their declivities.

Quarries of the mica slate have been opened and worked; it makes excellent hearth-stones, &c. The vales in some sections of the town abound with limestone; and within these calcareous districts there are several valuable beds of marble, several quarries of which have been opened, and large quantities of the stone dislodged and raised, which is manufactured into slabs for use and market; for which purpose, there have been six saw-mills erected for sawing marble.

Among the minerals of the town are iron ore, in small quantities, porcelain clay, yellow ochre, and some silver ore ; a mine, containing small quantities of this ore, was formerly worked, but has long since been abandoned.

There are 4 Forges for the manufacture of iron; but the ore is principally brought from without the town.

This town contains 2 located Congregational Societies, 2 Societies of Episcopalians, 1 of Baptists and 1 of Quakers; all of which are accommodated with houses for public worship.

It contains also a pleasant and flourishing village, situated upon a flat or plain, bordering upon the Ousatonick. The village has 60 Dwelling houses, many of which are large, neat and handsome buildings, a Post office, several Mercantile Stores and Mechanics' Shops.

In this, as well as the other towns in the county, agriculture is the leading and principal business of the inhabitants. The lands, which are a sandy and gravelly loam, and some of them a calcareous loam, are in general, fertile and productive, affording wheat, rye, corn, oats and flax. The making of butter and cheese, beef and pork, and the growing of wool receive considerable attention.

The New-Preston turnpike road passes through this town.

In addition to the domestic manufactures, and those of marble and iron, already mentioned, there are 1 Woolen Factory, 1 Hat Factory, 4 Grain Mills, 4 Carding Machines, 6 Fulling Mills and 4 Tanneries. There are 7 Mercantile Stores.

The population of the town, in 1810, was 3537; and there are now about 500 qualified Electors, about 250 Militia, and 540 Dwelling houses

The amount of taxable property, including polls, is $74,857.

The valuation or assessment under the laws of the United States, in 1816, was $1,113,012; being an average value of $26\tfrac{74}{100}$ dollars per acre, for the whole quantity included in the valuation, which was 41,630 acres.

In 1799, the real estate of this town, together with Roxbury, was valued at $776,146.

There are, in this town, 16 School Districts and Schools, 4 practising Physicians, 3 Clergymen and 3 Attornies.

New-Milford was settled in 1713, and at that time belonged to the county of New-Haven. It was incorporated soon after, and was included within the county of Litchfield, when that was incorporated.

NORFOLK.

NORFOLK is an elevated post township, situated 35 miles northwest from Hartford; bounded on the north by the State of Massachusetts, on the east by Colebrook and Winchester, on the south by Goshen, and on the west by Canaan.

The township comprises an area of about 41 square miles; having an average length, from north to south, of about 9 miles, and a mean breadth of more than 4 and a half miles.

This township is elevated and mountainous, several considerable granitic ridges extending thro' it from northeast to southwest; and the general character of the surface consists of a succession of lofty hills.

The soil is a primitive gravelly loam, generally cold, stony, and unsuitable for arable purposes; but it has considerable depth and strength, and affords good grazing. In the north section of the township, the soil is warmer and more fertile.

The natural growth of timber here is principally oak and chesnut; but in the other and more considerable sections, the prevailing forests consist of sugar maple, beech and hemlock. Formerly, large quantities of sugar were made from the maple; more than 20,000lbs. having been manufactured in a single season. But for some years past the business has greatly declined; the forests having been cleared for improvement, by the progress of settlements, and destroyed extensively by the elements.

The dairy business comprises the principal agricultural interests of the town; considerable quantities of cheese, butter, pork, &c. being annually sent abroad for a market. In 1811, there were marketed 100 tons of cheese, at $160 per ton, making $16,000; six tons of butter, at $320, making $1920; 100 bbls. of pork, at $12 per barrel, producing $1200; and 100 head of beeves, averaging $20 per head, making $2000; the aggregate of which was $21,120. Considerable attention has been paid to sheep, there being, in 1811, 4000 in the town.

The town is watered by numerous small streams, the most considerable of which is Blackberry river, which rises within the township, and running through it northwesterly, passes into Canaan, and discharges its waters into the Ousatonick. This stream affords numerous excellent sites for hydraulic works falling near the centre of the town, over a ledge of rocks, of nearly 30 feet in height. There are several mills, manufacturing establishments, forges, &c. erected upon it. In the southern section of the town, the west branch of the Naugatuck has its source; in the eastern the Mad river, a branch of the Tunxis; and in the northeastern section the Sandy river commences, having its source in Benedict's pond. Besides this, there are several other ponds in the town, one of which forms the head of the west branch of the Naugatuck river, already noticed.

The Greenwoods turnpike, which was opened in 1800, leads through the centre of this town, and the Hartland turnpike, connects with this within this township.

The principal manufacture of the town is that of iron, of which there are 2 Forges, upon a considerable scale. They manufacture bar iron, anchors, mill irons, cart and waggon tire, sleigh shoes, &c. There are 2 Grain Mills, 1 Fulling Mill, and several Mercantile Stores.

In 1810, there were in Norfolk 1441 inhabitants; and there are now about 240 Dwelling houses.

about 200 Electors, 1 company of Militia, and part of several others.

The corporate divisions of the town are 1 located Ecclesiastical Society and 10 School Districts. There are 10 primary Schools, one in each District; 2 Social Libraries, 1 Physician, 1 Clergyman and 2 Attornies.

This township was sold in pursuance of a resolve of the General Assembly at Middletown, at public auction, in 1742. It was divided into 53 rights; one of which was reserved for the benefit of schools, one for that of the ministry, and one for the first clergyman. Such were the prejudices against this tract of land, that all the purchasers, except Timothy Hosford, of Windsor, who had received a deed of 400 acres, suffered their rights to become forfeited; thereby losing the first instalment of 40 shillings upon a right, which they had paid. Timothy Hosford, having retained his right, afterwards sold it to Titus Brown, who removed into the town about two years after the first sale. The Legislature, having failed in their first attempt to sell the town, after a lapse of 12 years, in 1754, a second time ordered its sale at public auction, at Middletown, excepting Brown's right. This attempt succeeded; and, soon after, (a settlement having been previously begun,) a number of families removed into the town, and the settlement made considerable progress. The first settlers were Titus and Cornelius Brown, from Windsor, and John Turner and Jedediah Richards, from Hartford. These located themselves upon Brown's right.

The town was incorporated in 1758, when there were 27 families; but from this period the settlement was very rapid, three years after, in 1761, there being 70 families. In this year the first clergyman was settled.

PLYMOUTH.

PLYMOUTH is a post town, situated in the southeast corner of the county, 24 miles from Hartford, and 30 from New-Haven; bounded on the north by Harwinton & Litchfield, on the east by Bristol, in Hartford county, on the south by Waterbury and Wolcott, in New-Haven county, and on the west by Watertown. Its average length is 5 and a half miles, and its average breadth nearly 5 miles, comprising 25 square miles.

The township is uneven and hilly. The soil is a gravelly loam; which, together with the rocks and stones, is of a granitic character.

The natural growth consists of oak, chesnut, maple, principally swamp maple, and some pine and hemlock.

The lands, when cultivated, produce rye, corn, oats and flax. They also afford tolerable grazing; and the making of butter and cheese, and beef and pork, are important agricultural interests. Of all these articles, there is annually a surplus raised, which is sent abroad for a market.

The town is watered by the Naugatuck, which washes its western section from north to south. This river here is a fine mill stream. There are also in the northern parts of this town, several small streams, which are branches of the Poquabuck.

The Waterbury turnpike leads through the town in a northerly and southerly direction; and the Hartford and Danbury turnpike in an easterly and westerly direction.

The manufactures and mechanical employments of the town, in addition to those of a domestic character, consist of 1 small Woolen Factory, 2 Wooden Clock Factories, upon a considerably extensive scale, 3 Grain Mills, 2 Fulling Mills and Clothiers' works, 2 Carding Machines and 4 Tanneries. There are 5 Mercantile Stores.

The population of the town, in 1810, was 1382; and there are 270 Dwelling houses, about 260 Freemen or Electors, and 2 Companies of militia.

The amount of taxable property, including polls, is $39,215; and the assessment, under the laws of the United States, in 1816, which included 18,070 acres, amounted to $577,386, being an average value of 31 dolls. 94 cts. per acre.

The town contains 1 located Congregational Society & Church, and 2 Episcopal Societies, each of which is accommodated with a house for public worship. It contains 12 School Districts and Schools, which are kept for several months annually.

There is a small village in the centre of the town, comprising 15 or 20 houses.

There are 1 Clergyman, 3 Physicians, and 1 Lawyer in the town.

Plymouth became an independent Society in 1739, belonging at that time to the town of Waterbury, and bore the name of Northbury. At this time Westbury belonged to this Society, but was afterwards incorporated as a distinct Society, retaining its name. Afterwards both of these Societies were incorporated as towns, the last mentioned by the name of Watertown, and the first or the Society of Northbury, in 1795, by the name of Plymouth.

There is a curious perpendicular, cylindrical excavation in a solid rock in this town, about three miles from the Meeting house, near the turnpike, about 21 feet above high water mark, in the Naugatuck river. This excavation is about 2 feet in depth, and 15 inches in diameter, and is supposed to have been made by the Indians.

ROXBURY.

ROXBURY is a small township, situated upon the southern border of the county, 46 miles from Hartford, and 32 from New-Haven; bounded on the north by Washington, on the east by Woodbury, on the south by Southbury, in New-Haven county, and on the west by New-Milford.

Its average length from north to south is 6 and a half miles, and its average breadth from east to west nearly 4 miles, containing about 26 square miles.

The township is diversified; being characterized with hill and dale. There are also some granitic ridges.

The soil is a gravelly loam, interspersed with some small tracts of sandy loam; it is considerably warm and fertile. The natural growth of timber consists of oak, walnut, chesnut and other deciduous trees.

The agricultural productions are such as are common to this district. The lands are well adapted to grazing; but afford considerable grain. The making of butter and cheese and beef and pork are the most considerable agricultural interests.

The geological structure of the town is generally granitic. Some other rocks are found; and there are some quarries of micaceous schistus. Mines of iron ore have been discovered, but they have received little attention.

The town is watered by the Shepaug, a considerable branch of the Ousatonick.

There are, in this town, 2 Grain Mills, 1 Carding Machine, 2 Fulling Mills and Clothiers' works, 1 Store and 1 Tavern.

The population of the town, in 1810, was 1217; and there are 200 Dwelling houses, 150 qualified Electors, and 2 Companies of Militia.

The amount of taxable property, including polls, is $25,833; and the assessment of the lands and buildings of the town in 1815, which included 13,257 acres, was $314,051; being an average of 23\frac{68}{100}$ per acre.

The township contains 1 located Congregational Society and Church, 1 Society of Episcopalians, and 1 of Baptists, which are accommodated with houses for public worship, 9 School Districts and Schools, and 1 Social Library.

The professional men are 1 Physician, 2 Clergymen and 2 Attornies.

Roxbury was originally a part of Woodbury, and was incorporated in 1801.

SALISBURY.

SALISBURY is a considerable and flourishing post township, situated in the northwest corner of the county and State, 47 miles from Hartford, and 60 from New-Haven; bounded on the north by Mount Washington and Sheffield, in Massachusetts, on the east by the Ousatonick river, which separates it from Canaan, on the south by Sharon, and on the west by the State of New-York. Its average length is 9 miles, and its average breadth about 6 and a half miles, comprising an area of about 58 square miles.

The township is broken, consisting of elevated hills and deep and extensive vales, generally of a calcareous character; this town being embraced within the limestone district of Connecticut, which is confined to its northwestern border, adjoining the State of New-York. The hills, and more elevated lands consist principally of granite, the calcareous rocks and soil being confined to the valleys and more level tracts.

The principal mineral in the town is that of iron ore, which is found in great abundance. In the western section of the town, three mines of iron ore have been opened and worked, from which large quantities of the ore are annually raised, which is used not only to supply the forges and furnaces which are in operation here, but a portion of it is conveyed to neighbouring towns. These mines are believed to be equal to any in the United States; the ore being very rich, and of an excellent quality. Near the centre of the town, there is also a mine of iron ore, which has been opened; and another in the northwest part of the township; from both of which comparatively small quantities of ore are annually raised. These mines are a source of considerable wealth, and afford a stimulus to enterprise and industry.

The soil of the township is either a calcareous loam, or a gravelly loam; varying, according to the geological character of the internal structure. The former is very rich and productive, and is admirably adapted to a grain culture, particularly wheat, of which it carries large crops. Rye, oats, Indian corn, barley, flax and peas are also cultivated with success. This is one of the best towns for grain in the State; and it is probable there is more wheat annually raised here than in any other. Grass also flourishes well in this town, and the lands afford excellent grazing; but the attention of the farmers has been principally directed to the cultivation of

SALISBURY.

wheat and other kinds of winter grain.

The Ousatonick river washes the eastern border of the town, and forms its boundary; and Salmon river, a small stream, runs thro' the town in a southeasterly direction, and discharges its waters into the Ousatonick. Upon Salmon river, there are a number of excellent sites for mills and other water works; and there are several bridges, across the Ousatonick, and a fall of the whole body of water of the river, of about 60 feet, which is a very considerable curiosity.

There are four ponds in the town, well stored with fish, particularly pike or pickerel; Northeast pond, Mountain pond in the west, Furnace pond in the south, and Long pond in the southwest section of the town.

Although the agricultural interests of this town are flourishing, and occupy a very great proportion of the attention and industry of the inhabitants; yet the advantages and facilities which it affords for various kinds of iron manufactures have not been neglected.

Of the manufactures of iron, there are 3 Forges, 2 Blast Furnaces, 1 Anchor and Screw Manufactory, 1 Scythe Manufactory, and 2 Shops with hammers, operated by water power, for the manufacture of Gun barrels, Sleigh shoes, Hoes, &c. In addition to these manufactures, there is 1 Button Factory, 4 Grain Mills, 4 Saw Mills and 2 Carding Machines. There are 5 Mercantile Stores.

The Salisbury and Canaan turnpike road leads through this town from east to west, but is a road of little public travel.

The population, at the census of 1810, was 2321; and there are 340 Dwelling houses, 264 Freemen or Electors, and 3 Companies of Militia.

The amount of taxable property, (estimated according to the laws for regulating lists,) including polls, is $51,626; and the valuation of the lands and buildings of the town, in 1815, which included 28,053 acres, amounted to $677,231; being an average value of $24\frac{14}{100}$ dollars per acre. In 1799, the valuation of Salisbury and Sharon together, amounted to $612,134; being about $65,000 less than the valuation of this town alone in 1815.

The town contains 1 located Congregational Society, and 1 of Methodists, both of which are accommodated with houses for public worship. There are also some Episcopalians.

There are 14 School Districts and Schools; 2 Social Libraries, one consisting of about 600 volumes, the other, which is for young persons, contains about 400 volumes, and was a present from the late Caleb Bingham Esq. of Boston; 5 Physicians, 4 Attornies and 1 Congregational Clergyman in the town.

Salisbury was first settled by three Dutch families from the State of New-York, in the year 1720, which was 12 years before the town was laid out. These families settled upon the border of the Ousatonick, in the vicinity of a considerable Indian settlement, consisting of peaceable and friendly natives. The township, having been granted to proprietors, was laid out into lots, in 1732, and the first settlement, under their authority, was in 1740. It was incorporated in 1741.

SHARON.

SHARON, a considerable and flourishing post township, is situated upon the western border of the county and State, 47 miles from Hartford; bounded N. by Salisbury, E. by the Ousatonick, which separates it from Cornwall, S. by Kent, and W. by the State of New-York. Its average length is about 9 miles, and its average breadth nearly 6 miles, comprising about 52 square miles.

Both the surface and soil of the township are strikingly diversified, and correspond with its geological character. Its eastern section abounds with elevated hills, and some granitic mountainous ranges, interspersed with which there are deep valleys.

This district affords good grazing; and some tracts are tolerably well adapted to grain. The soil is a gravelly loam, and considerably stony. The western section of the town, bordering upon the State of New-York, consists of an extensive calcareous vale, having a level or undulating surface, and a rich and fertile soil of calcareous loam.

This district is admirably adapted to grain, and produces excellent wheat, rye, corn and oats, & in great abundance. It is one of the richest and best tracts of land in the State for a grain culture. The soil in this section reposes upon a bed of limetone, and some rocks or quarries of marble have been discovered; and iron ore is supposed to exist in various places; but neither have been worked, or in any respect received much attention.

The natural growth of timber consists principally of oak, chesnut, walnut, ash and maple.

The Ousatonick river washes the eastern border of the town, and separates it from Cornwall. Across this stream there are several bridges. Its western section is watered by a small stream, called Oblong river.

Mudge's and Indian ponds are situated upon the western border of the town. The former is a considerable body of water, and the latter is partly in the State of New-York.

There are two turnpike roads which pass through this town; one leading to Hartford, and the other to New-Haven.

The town contains two parishes or located ecclesiastical Societies. Besides which, there is one Society of Episcopalians, and one of Methodists.

In the first local Society, there is a pleasant and considerable village, comprising 50 or 60 Dwelling houses, several of which are neat and handsome, 2 Churches, a Post office, and several Mercantile Stores.

The most considerable manufacturing establishment is a Duck manufactory, upon an extensive scale. There is something done at the Iron manufacture, there being 1 Forge; besides which there are 4 Grain Mills, 2 Carding Machines, 2 Distilleries for cider, and 5 Tanneries. There are 4 Mercantile Stores, and 3 Taverns.

The population of the town, in 1810, was 2706; and there are 380 Dwelling houses, 300 Freemen or Electors, and 3 Companies of Militia.

The amount of taxable property, including polls, is $55,503; and the valuation of lands and buildings, in 1815, comprising 29,388 acres, amounted to $695,302; being $23\frac{66}{100}$ dollars per acre. In 1799, the real estate of this town, together with Salisbury, was assessed, upon the same principle of valuation, at only $612,134; being $83,168 less than the valuation of Sharon alone in 1815. This is a very surprising rise of landed estate, in an inland and agricultural town, for the short period of 18 years.

There are, in the town, 15 School Districts & primary Schools, and an Academy for young gentlemen and ladies, 2 Social Libraries, 5 Physicians, 3 Attornies and 1 Clergyman.

Sharon was settled in the year 1738. In the spring of that year, 15 or 20 families removed there from Colchester and Lebanon, and commenced a settlement. The next year the settlement received considerable accession, by the emigration of several families from New-Haven, which rendered it quite respectable. The town was incorporated in Oct. 1739.

TORRINGTON.

TORRINGTON is a post town, centrally situated in the county, being 23 miles northwest from Hartford, & 7 miles northeast from Litchfield. It is bounded north by Winchester, east by New-Hartford, south by Litchfield and Harwinton, and west by Goshen. It is about 6 miles square, comprising 36 square miles, or about 23,040 acres.

The township is uneven, consisting of hill and dale; and the soil is a gravelly loam, mostly fertile and productive, and admirably adapted to grazing. The dairy business is carried on to considerable extent; which, together with the fatting of beeves and raising of neat cattle and sheep, are the principal agricultural interests of the town.

The forests, which are considerably extensive, consist principally of deciduous trees; although there are some evergreens interspersed.

The town is well watered by the east and west branches of Waterbury river.

There are two important turnpike roads passing thro' the town, and affording a facility to its intercourse and communication abroad; Goshen and Sharon turnpike, and Waterbury river turnpike.

The town contains 2 located Congregational Societies and Churches, and 1 Society of Baptists.

WOLCOTTVILLE, a village of 18 houses, has been built principally since 1802, and is an active, flourishing place. Its growth has been chiefly owing to the establishment of an extensive Woolen Factory, which now is owned principally by his Excellency, Oliver Wolcott. It is one of the largest establishments of the kind in the State; employing about 40 workmen, and manufacturing from 25 to 35 yards of broad cloth daily, of an average value of $6 per yard. The cloths made at this establishment have a substantial texture, and are manufactured in a style, scarcely inferior to the highest finished English cloths. This Factory was erected in 1813. There are also 1 Cotton Factory in this town, and 2 Grain Mills, 2 Fulling Mills and Clothier's Works, 1 Carding Machines, 5 Tanneries, 5 Mercantile Stores and 3 Taverns.

The population of the town, in 1810, was 1586; and there are now 250 Dwelling houses, 175 Freemen or Electors, 2 Infantry Companies of Militia, and a part of a Company of Cavalry.

The town contains 9 School districts and the same number of Schools, 2 Social Libraries, 3 practising Physicians and 3 Clergymen.

The amount of taxable property, including polls, is $40,886. The United States assessment, in 1815, was $446,965; being an average of 23 and a half dollars per acre, for all the lands in the town.

Torrington was incorporated as a town, in 1744.

BIOGRAPHY. The Hon. *Stanley Griswold*, a distinguished scholar, statesman and patriot, was a native of this town. His life was characterized with incident and vicisitudes. He was educated at Yale College, and having been regularly qualified therefor, was settled for several years as a Congregational Clergyman at New-Milford, in this county.

About the year 1804, he left his native State and established a patriotic and spirited weekly newspaper at Walpole, in New-Hampshire. In this situation he exhibited much talent and literary acquirements, and obtained considerable celebrity; there being at that time few ably edited newspapers in the United states. From this situation, in 1805, he was removed to the territory of Michigan, having received by Mr. Jefferson, then president of the United States, the appointment of Secretary of that territory. After this, he was appointed by Gov. Huntington of Ohio, a Senator in the Congress of the United States, to fill a vacancy; and subsequently, received the appointment of territorial judge, for the territory of Illinois. He died whilst in this situation, at Shawnetown, in 1815.

WARREN.

WARREN is an inconsiderable post township, having an elevated situation, 38 miles from Hartford, and 45 from New-Haven; bounded on the north by Cornwall, on the east by Litchfield, on the south by Washington, and on the west by Kent. Its average length from north to south is 5 miles, and its average breadth about 4 and a half miles, comprising about 23 square miles.

WASHINGTON.

The township is hilly and mountainous, and its rocks and soil are of a granitic character; of the former, however, there are some quarries of micaceous schistus, and the latter is a coarse gravelly loam. The natural growth consists of oak, walnut & maple; and the agricultural productions are grass, some grain, butter and cheese, and beef and pork.

The town is watered by the Shepaug, a considerable branch of the Ousatonick, which runs through the eastern section of the town, and by numerous small streams. Raumaug pond, a considerable body of water, is situated partly in this town, and partly in Washington.

There are 1 Forge, 1 Distillery, 1 Carding Machine, 1 Grain Mill, 1 Tannery, 2 Mercantile Stores and 2 Public Inns in the town.

The population of the town, in 1810, was 1096; and there are 120 Freemen or qualified Electors, 1 Company of Militia, and about 170 Dwelling houses.

The amount of taxable property, including polls, is $21,440; and the assessment in 1815, which included 13,884 acres of land, amounted to $222,961; being an average value of $16 $\frac{8}{100}$ per acre.

The town comprises 1 located Congregational Society & Church, 1 Society of Baptists, 8 School districts and Schools, 1 Grammar School and 1 Social Library. The professional men are 2 Physicians and 1 Clergyman.

Warren was incorporated as a town in 1786, previous to which it belonged to Kent.

WASHINGTON.

WASHINGTON is a post township, situated in the southwestern section of the county, 40 miles southwest from Hartford; bounded on the north by Warren, on the east by Litchfield and Bethlem, on the south by Woodbury and Roxbury, and on the west by New-Milford and Kent.

The average length of the township from north to south is about 7 miles, and its average breadth from east to west more than 5 miles; comprising an area of about 37 square miles.

A considerable proportion of this township is elevated and mountainous; several granitic ridges extending through its western and northwestern sections. Intervening between these ridges are calcareous vales of considerable extent. The other sections of the town present a surface consisting of a succession of hills and dales. Limestone abounds in many of the vales; and in these calcareous strata there are several quarries of marble, from which considerable quantities are raised, and two mills are constantly employed in sawing it. Iron ore has been discovered in various places; ochre, fullers' earth, and white clay, suitable for fine pottery, have also been found here.

The soil, corresponding with the geological character of the different sections of the township, is either a calcareous or primitive gravelly loam. The calcareous vales are fertile and productive in grain, and the ridges, hills and their declivities afford good grazing.

The dairy business affords the principal agricultural staples. Considerable quantities of grain, however, are raised, consisting of wheat, rye, corn and oats.

The town is watered by the Shepaug river, which intersects it, forming nearly two equal sections; by the Bantam, which runs through its north section, and by the Aspetuck, which has its source in Ramaug pond, in the northwestern border of the town. These streams afford numerous sites for hydraulic works.

This town is accommodated with the Litchfield and New-Milford turnpike, the New-Preston turnpike, and one leading to New-Haven.

The most considerable mechanical employments are the iron and marble business. There are 2 Marble Saw Mills, already noticed, 2 Forges, 1 Slitting Mill, 1 Nail Factory and 2 Trip Hammers. There are 4 Grain Mills, 2 Fulling Mills and Clothiers' works. 2 Carding Machines and 5 Saw Mills.

At the census of 1810, there were 1575 inhabitants; and there are about 240 Electors, 3 Companies of Militia, and about 230 Dwelling houses.

The amount of taxable property, including polls, in 1817, was $42,360; and the valuation of the lands and buildings of the town in 1815, which comprised 20,605 acres, amounted to $573,132; being an average of $28 per acre.

The corporate divisions are 2 located Congregational Societies and 11 School Districts. In addition to the located, there are 2 Episcopal Societies.

There are several Mercantile Stores, 2 Physicians, 1 Clergyman and 1 Attorney.

This town is of recent date, having been incorporated in 1779.

WATERTOWN.

WATERTOWN is a post township, situated in the southeastern section of the county, 26 miles from New-Haven, and 30 from Hartford; bounded on the north by Litchfield, on the east by West branch and Naugatuck river, which separates it from Plymouth and Waterbury, on the south by Waterbury and Middlebury, and on the west by Woodbury and Bethlem.

The township comprises an area of about 27 square miles; being of an average length of 6 and a half miles, and an average breadth of more than 4 miles.

It is generally uneven, or rather hilly; but some sections are level. Its geological character is granitic; being comprised within the district having this character, which includes the greater section of this county. There are, however, some limestone, and some tracts of calcareous soil; but a hard, dry, gravelly loam generally prevails.

WINCHESTER. 265

The natural growth consists of oak, maple, some beech, &c.

The lands are best adapted to grazing; but the different grains common to this county are cultivated.

The Naugatuck river washes the eastern border of the town. In addition to this, it is watered by numerous small streams.

The town is accommodated with two turnpike roads; one leading from Danbury to Hartford, and the other from Litchfield to New-Haven.

The population of the town, in 1810, was 1714; and there are 175 qualified Electors, 1 Company of Militia, and 250 Dwelling houses. The amount of taxable property, including polls, is $38,338. In 1816, there were 15,629 acres of land assessed in this town, which were estimated at $509,674; being an average value of $32 per acre.

The manufactures and mechanical employments, in addition to those of a domestic character, consist of 1 Distillery, 2 Grain Mills, 2 Carding Machines, 2 Fulling Mills and Clothiers' works and 2 Tanneries. There are 3 Mercantile Stores.

The town contains 1 located Congregational Society & Church, and 1 Society of Episcopalians, which is also accommodated with a house for public worship. It comprises 8 School Districts and Schools, and has 1 Social Library, 1 Physician, 1 Attorney and 2 Clergymen.

Watertown was incorporated in 1780.

WINCHESTER.

WINCHESTER is an elevated post township, situated 27 miles northwest from Hartford; bounded on the north by Colebrook, on the east by Barkhamsted, on the south by Torrington, and on the west by Goshen and Norfolk. Its average length is 6 and a half miles, from east to west, and its average breadth more than 5 miles, comprising about 35 square miles.

This township is situated within the evergreen district of the State, and is hilly and mountainous. Its geological character is primitive; the rocks and stones consisting of granite, mica slate, and other primitive formations, and the soil is a hard, coarse gravelly loam. The lands afford very good grazing; and the making of butter and cheese, and growing of cattle, together with some beef and pork, constitute the principal agricultural interests.

The natural growth of timber is maple, beech, oak and birch; but hemlock and other perennial trees constitute a considerable proportion of the forests.

The town is watered by two considerable mill streams, called Still and Mad rivers, which unite in its eastern section. These streams, particularly the latter, afford numerous excellent sites for hydraulic works.

Upon an elevated plain there is an interesting lake, or pond, which is one of the largest bodies of water in the State, being 3 and a half miles in length, and three fourths of a mile in width. The outlet of this lake presents a novel and romantic view. It consists of a small stream, compressed within a narrow channel, literally tossed from rock to rock, many having nearly a perpendicular fall, the whole descent being nearly a quarter of a mile, whence it unites with Mad river.

Upon this outlet, there are some of the best natural sites for hydraulic works in this State, or perhaps in the Union; several of which are occupied to advantage.

This town is justly celebrated for iron manufactures, which are a source of wealth and industry, and have promoted the growth of a considerable village. There are now 5 Smelting Forges, several of which carry on the business upon an extensive scale. The ore to supply these forges is brought principally from Salisbury, there being no mines in the town. In addition to the iron manufactures, there are 4 Carding Machines, 3 Grain Mills, 5 Tanneries, 3 Cider Distilleries, 1 Clock Factory, 1 Turnery, for the manufacture of Wooden Ware, 1 Scaleboard Factory, 3 Clothiers' works and Fulling Mills and 1 Oil Mill. There are 4 Mercantile Stores and 3 Taverns.

The population of the town, in 1810, was 1466; and there are about 230 Dwelling houses, 200 Freemen or Electors, 2 Companies of Infantry, and a part of a Company of Artillery, of Militia.

There are 2 located Ecclesiastical Societies or Parishes in the town, and 1 Society of Methodists. In the Society of Winstead, there is a small village, comprising several handsome Dwelling houses.

The Greenwoods turnpike, leading to Albany, passes through this section of the town. The Colebrook and New-Haven turnpike also leads through the western section of the town.

There are 9 School Districts and primary Schools, and 1 Academy or Grammar School, 2 Social Libraries, 3 Clergymen, 1 Attorney and 2 Physicians.

Winchester was incorporated in 1771.

WOODBURY.

WOODBURY is a flourishing post town, situated on the southern border of the county, 36 miles from Hartford, 25 from New-Haven, and 15 from Litchfield; bounded on the north by Washington and Bethlem, on the east by Watertown and Middlebury, in New-Haven county, on the south by Southbury, and on the west by Roxbury. Its average length, from north to south, is about 7 miles, and its average breadth from east to west, is nearly 6 miles, comprising about 41 square miles.

The face of the country is of an

BIOGRAPHY.

undulating character, being pleasantly diversified with hill and dale; upon the streams, however, there are intervals of considerable extent, which with some other tracts are level. The soil is generally a gravelly loam, warm and fertile; it is well adapted to grain, and carries good crops of rye, oats, Indian corn, &c. The lands are favourable for fruit, and there are many valuable apple orchards; so that the making of cider and cider spirits are important agricultural interests. Many of the farmers have small Distilleries upon their own estate, whereby they manufacture their cider into a spiritous liquor, called cider brandy.

The natural growth of timber is oak of the different kinds, maple, elm, ash, birch, walnut, chesnut and other deciduous trees.

The town is watered by three considerable branches of Pomperaug river, which unite their waters in its southern section. These streams afford some good mill seats, and for thier size, very extensive and valuable tracts of alluvial.

In this town, there are 2 located ecclesiastical Societies or Parishes, a Society of Episcopalians and some Methodists; 1 very pleasant village, containing 50 or 60 Dwelling houses, 3 Churches, 2 for Congregationalists and 1 for Episcopalians; a number of Stores, a Post office, & several professional offices.

The Danbury and Hartford turnpike road passes through the village, and the turnpike from Kent to New-Haven, through the town.

The manufactures and mechanical employments of the town, independent of those of a domestic character, consist of 2 Tinware Factories, 4 Clothier's works and Fulling Mills, 4 Carding Machines for wool, 3 Grain Mills, 3 Tanneries, and a number of cider Distilleries. There are 7 Mercantile Stores, 2 Taverns, 14 School districts and primary Schools, 1 Social Library, 3 Clergymen, 5 Attornies and 2 Physicians.

The population of the town, in 1810, was 1963; and there are about 300 Dwelling houses, 300 Freemen or Electors, and 2 Companies of Militia.

The amount of taxable property, including polls, is $42,246; and the valuation of the lands and buildings of the town, in 1815, for the levy of the direct tax of the United States, which comprised 19,528 acres, amounted to $604,175; being an average value of nearly $34 per acre. In 1799, the real estate of this town, together with Southbury, was apprised at $847,966.

Woodbury was incorporated in 1764.

BIOGRAPHY. Colonel *Henry Perry*, a youthful and gallant hero, who was killed on the confines of Mexico in 1817, whilst bravely contending for the cause of civil liberty in that interesting section of America, was from his earliest youth a resident in this town. Col. Perry was one of those heroic and chivalrous youth, whose courage springs from the noblest impulse of nature; an enthusiastic love of liberty, and a generous sympathy for all who are the unfortunate subjects of despotic power. He was engaged as a volunteer in the glorious defence of New-Orleans, and after the peace, joined the patriot army of Mexico; he had the command of a detachment of men under Mina, and was distinguished for his zeal, his courage and his enterprise during the short career of that unfortunate General, whose fate, and that of the gallant Perry's, were associated by that providence, which governs the destinies of man.

MIDDLESEX COUNTY.

MIDDLESEX, a pleasant maritime county, is centrally situated upon Connecticut river; bounded on the north by Hartford county, on the east by Hartford and New-London counties, on the south by Long-Island sound, and on the west by the county of New-Haven.

Its mean length from north to south is about 25 miles, and its mean breadth from east to west nearly 14 miles, comprising about 342 square miles.

The following TOPOGRAPHICAL AND STATISTICAL TABLE exhibits a view of the several towns in the county; their situation, with relation to Middletown; their population, according to the census of 1810; number of dwelling houses; religious societies; school districts, and post-offices.

Towns.	Post-offices.	Population.	Dwelling houses.	Religious societies.	School districts.	Distance from Middletown.
Middletown.	2	6332	800	11	26	
Haddam.	1	2205	387	3	13	8 m. S. E.
Chatham.	1	3258	453	6	15	1 m. E.
Durham.	1	1101	172	3	5	6 m. S. W.
East-Haddam.	1	2537	392	5	19	13 m. S. E.
Killingworth.	1	2244	320	6	15	20 m. S. E.
Saybrook.	2	3926	600	8	20	22 m. S. E.

This county has a very advantageous and pleasant situation, being intersected by Connecticut river, which gives it important commercial and other advantages. Its surface is greatly diversified, presenting almost every variety, from the lofty, rugged granitic ridges, to the delightful Connecticut river alluvial.

The extensive eastern granitic range of mountain passes through this county from a northeasterly to a southwesterly direction, rising upon the west side of Connecticut river, and extending into New-Haven county, towards the sound, where it subsides. Upon the east side of the river is a mountainous range, extending nearly parellel with the river, in a direction towards the sound, which, although not distinctly connected, appears to be a branch of the great eastern range. This, however, is mostly in New-London county. The first mentioned range forms the boundary between the granitic and argillaceous district upon Connecticut river; and the north section of this county, being the commencement of the argillaceous district, is a highly interesting country, having a beautifully undulating surface, and a rich and productive soil. The southern section being the tract south of the principal range, is of a granitic character, and generally hilly, rocky and broken, with the exception of the alluvial upon Connecticut river, and the flats upon the border of the sound.

The soil, corresponding with the geological structure of the county, in the northern section, is a rich argillaceous loam, interspersed with some excellent tracts of alluvial, and some small sections of sandy loam. In the eastern, middle, and more southern sections, the soil is a primitive gravelly loam, interspersed occasionally with small tracts of sand and alluvial.

The forests are deciduous, and considerably extensive; and the quality of the timber is excellent.

The agricultural interests of the county are respectable, and generally directed to the objects of the dairy business, and the raising of cattle and sheep. In the northern section of the county, considerable quantities of grain are raised; but in the other sections, little attention is paid to this branch of husbandry, and the grain raised is scarcely sufficient for the consumption of the inhabitants.

The waters of the county are abundant and valuable; and afford important advantages for the business of navigation, ship-building and fishing. Being intersected by Connecticut river, and its southern border washed by Long Island sound, this county unites greater advantages for navigation than any other in the State; there being but one town in the county but what is accommodated with navigable waters. Numerous small streams intersect and fertilize the different sections of the county, discharging their waters either into Connecticut river or Long Island sound. These streams abound with numerous sites for hydraulic works.

The commercial business of the county is important and flourishing, and is principally directed to a trade with the West-Indies, the southern States and New-York. Nearly 100 vessels of every description are owned in the county. Considerable attention is paid to the transportation of wood to the New-York market.

The shad fishery in Connecticut river is an extensive and important interest, and a source of great profit. Large quantities of shad are annually taken, which not only supply the immediate demand, but constitute a staple article for exportation.

This county possesses great advantages for ship-building; which, at different periods, has been extensively carried on.

There are several very valuable quarries in the county, which are a source of profit, and afford employment to considerable industry.

The manufactures of this county are respectable, and comparatively flourishing. The manufactures of woolen, of rifles, pistols, swords, ivory combs and button moulds are the most important. Several of these manufactures, particularly those of rifles, pistols and swords, have been carried to great perfection. There are, in this county, 3 Cotton Factories, 5 Woolen Factories, 17 Fulling Mills and Clothiers' works, 16 Carding Machines for customers, 43 Grain Mills, 1 Paper Mill, 1 Oil Mill, 1 Powder Mill, 1 Forge and 6 small Furnaces.

There are in the county of Middlesex, 18 School Societies, each of which is divided into a suitable number of School Districts, of which there are in all 113, and 42 Religious Societies, 99 Mercantile Stores, and 17 Social Libraries.

The population of the county, in 1810, was 20,723; and its aggregate list, of taxable property and polls, is $429,782.

The county was incorporated in 1785, previously to which, it belonged to the counties of Hartford, New-London and New-Haven; principally to the former.

MIDDLETOWN.

MIDDLETOWN, the semi-seat of justice, and the most considerable township of the county, is pleasantly situated upon the west side of Connecticut river, 31 miles from its mouth at Saybrook bar, according to the course of the river, 15 miles south of Hartford, 25 northeast of New-Haven, and 35 northwest of New-London, in north lat. 41° 35', west lon. 72° 54'.

The township is bounded on the north by Wethersfield and Berlin, in Hartford county, on the east by Connecticut river, which separates it from Chatham, on the south by Haddam and Durham, and on the west by Wallingford and Meriden, in New-Haven county.

Its average length from north to south is about 9 miles, and its average breadth from east to west nearly 7 miles, comprising about 58 square miles, or 37,120 acres.

This township comprises the southern section of the argillaceous district, upon the borders of Connecticut river; its geological character, surface and soil corresponding with the prevailing features of this district.

The surface is strikingly and pleasantly undulating and diversified, and the prevailing soil an argillaceous loam, rich and fertile, which reposes generally upon a bed of clay slate rock. But the western section of the township embraces the eastern branch of a greenstone range of mountain, being generally a succession, but in some places a continuity of elevated hills. In this district, the greenstone constitutes the upper stratum, and it is underlaid, or reposes upon argillaceous schistus.

The soil is favourable both for grain and grazing, and is well adapted to fruit, with respect to which the farmers have paid considerable attention, there being numerous apple orchards in the town; so that the making of cider is an important agricultural interest.

Of the grains cultivated, wheat, rye, Indian corn and oats are the principal; and of these the soil carries good crops. Grass, flax, some hemp, potatoes and other roots, culinary vegetables and summer and autumn fruits flourish well, under proper cultivation.

The waving and pleasantly diversified character of the country, the improved state of its cultivation, the richness and variety of its productions, and the majestic but pacific tide of the Connecticut, all of which are thrown under the eye of the beholder, placed upon many of the eminences, afford, in the summer season, most delightful and interesting landscapes.

About one mile below the city, upon the bank of the river, lead ore has been discovered, and a mine was opened and worked during the revolutionary war, but has since been abandoned. In this vicinity, there are also some indications of coal; several excavations have been attempted, which hitherto have proved unsatisfactory.

Besides the Connecticut, which washes the eastern border of the township, it is watered by two inconsiderable streams, called West and Little rivers. The former has its source in Guilford, a d runs thro' Durham and the southwesterly section of Middletown, maintaining a northeasterly course, until it unites with Little river, (which rises in Berlin, and runs in a southeasterly direction,) near the centre of the town, north and south, and about two miles west from Connecticut river, into which the waters of these united streams are discharged, between the city and the village called Middletown Upper Houses. These streams, particularly West river, afford numerous excellent sites for hydraulic works, many of which are advantageously and profitably occupied.

There are several shad and herring fisheries upon Connecticut river, and various small fish abound in most of the small streams.

In the western part of the town, near Meriden, there is a pond, called Black pond, which is also stored with fish.

There are seven turnpike roads communicating with Middletown; one leading to Hartford, one to Windham, one to Colchester, one to Saybrook, one to New-Haven, one to Meriden and one to Farmington.

The manufactures and mechanical establishments and employments of the town, inclusive of those in the city, consist of the following: 2 Woolen Factories, both upon a respectable scale, and the manufactures of which have acquired considerable reputation, and 2 Cotton Factories. Of iron manufactures, there are 1 Sword Factory, 1 Pistol Factory, and 1 Rifle Factory, all upon a considerable scale, and the articles manufactured at which, particularly Swords, have been esteemed equal in every respect, if not superior, to those imported. There are 6 Tin-ware Factories, 1 Silver plating Factory, 1 Button Factory, 3 Pewter Factories, 1 Comb Factory, 1 Paper Manufactory, 1 Powder Mill, 3 Rope walks, 1 Twine Factory, 1 Muff and Tippet Factory 3 Saddlers, 2 Cabinet Makers, and 2 Carriage Makers. There are 7 Grain Mills, 10 Saw Mills, 3 Carding Machines and 8 Tanneries.

There are, in the town, including the city, 11 Dry Goods Stores, 32 Grocery and Provision Stores, 2 Bookstores, 2 Druggist's Stores, 1 Hardware Store, 2 Crockery Stores, 1 Hat Store and 3 Lumber Yards.

The population of the town, in 1810, was 5382; and there are 700 Electors, 438 Militia, and about 800 Dwelling houses.

The civil divisions of the town are 4 located Ecclesiastical Societies or Parishes, 26 School Districts and an incorporated City. Besides the located, there are 3 Societies of Baptists, 1 of Episcopalians, 2 of Methodists and 1 of Independents, making 11 in the town, ten of which are accommodated with Churches, or houses for public worship; and, in each of the School Districts, a primary school is maintained.

There are 4 Social Libraries and 1 Circulating Library in the city; and, in the town, 6 Physicians, 10 Clergymen and 7 Attornies.

The amount of taxable property, including polls, is $113,896.

MIDDLETOWN CITY, incorporated in 1784, is delightfully situated upon the west bank of the river, near the centre of the township, upon its eastern border. It has a safe and commodious harbour, the river here having 10 feet of water at full tide, and is a port of entry. Its site is principally a gentle declivity; having a gradual ascent back from the river. It is built mostly upon eight streets, of which Main-street, being the great river road, is the principal. This street runs in a northerly and southerly direction, nearly parallel with the river; is well built, for nearly a mile in extent, and contains most of the public buildings and public offices; the two Banking houses, two Churches, the Naval office and Post office, a considerably extensive range of brick buildings, occupied principally for Stores, Washington Hotel, several elegant brick edifices, and a number of neat and handsome Dwelling houses, Stores, Mechanics' Shops, &c. Aside from the navigation interests, most of the mercantile business is done in this part of the city. Upon the margin of the river, is Water-street, running in a parallel direction, and affording a communication with the several wharves which have been built. The maritime business of the city is chiefly transacted in this street; but it contains few stores or other buildings either large or elegant. High-street has an elevated and prospective situation, more than 100 rods back from Main-street, upon the height of land, and runs in a parallel direction. This street is a delightful residence, affording a view of the other parts of the city, of the surrounding country, which, for beauty, richness and variety of rural scenery, is scarcely surpassed, and of the river for a considerable extent. There are a number of neat and handsome dwelling houses upon this street. These streets are intersected by several others, running from the river in a westerly direction. In the north section of the city is Green-street; the next south is Ferry-street, extending only from the river, or Water-street, to Main-street. This short street is tolerably well built, but its buildings are principally small and of wood. Washington-street intersects Main and High-streets south of Ferry-street. The Washington Hotel buildings are situated at the corner of this and Main-street. The western section of this street is elevated, and contains several pleasant residences. Court-street intersects Main-street near the centre of the city, and extends to High-street. The Court-House is situated upon this street.

The city contains about 350 Dwelling houses, and about 40 Mercantile Stores of every description; and, in 1810, it contained 2014 inhabitants, and has increased considerably since that period. It contains the Naval office, or Custom-house of the District, comprising the several ports upon the river, both in this county and the county of Hartford, a Post office, 5 Churches, one for Congregationalists, one for Episcopalians, one for Baptists, one for Independents and one for Methodists, a Court House, the Gaol of the county and an Alms-house.

There are, in the city, 2 Banks, one a branch of the United States Bank, established in 1817, the other incorporated by the State, in 1795, which has a capital of 400,000 dollars, a Marine Insurance Company, and a Newspaper establishment.

All the tonnage of the District is registered at the Naval office in this city, and, in 1815, amounted to 19,327 tons.

The city of Middletown possesses very considerable advantages for maritime commerce, but is less favourably situated for inland trade; the city of Hartford being but 15 miles above, upon the river, with several considerable towns farther up, deprives it, in a great measure, of the trade and commercial advantages of the country upon Connecticut river, north of that place. But it has a good harbour, and a depth of water admitting of large vessels, is of comparatively easy access from the ocean, and, in other respects, possesses advantages for maritime commerce, much greater than any other place upon the river.

In addition to the commercial advantages of the place, it unites many facilities for manufactures, was one of the first towns that disclosed a manufacturing spirit, and its establishments of woolen, cotton, swords, pistols and rifles, were among the first of the kind in the United States; and most or all of them have acquired a celebrity which has been attained by few others, and have contributed to the reputation and importance of the place.

For some time after the close of the revolutionary war, Middletown made little or no progress; and, for several years, actually declined in population; but for the last fifteen years it has been rising, has become a place of considerable importance, and has a fair

HADDAM.

prospect of a corresponding advancement in size, population and business, with the other commercial towns in the State.

Middletown was settled in 1651, the first settlers being principally from Hartford and Wethersfield, and some from England. The settlement soon after received considerable accession from Rowley, Chelmsford, and Woburn, in Massachusetts. The place was called Mattabesick by the natives, and received the name of Middletown from the General Court, in November 1653; at which time it was probably admitted to town privileges. In 1673, twenty years after, there were but 52 families or householders; and the township was divided into an equal number of shares. In a few instances, formerly, the General Assembly have held their sessions in Middletown; but no particular events have occurred here worthy of historic notice.

BIOGRAPHY. The Hon. *Titus Hosmer*, an eminent lawyer and statesman, was a native and resident of this town. He was one of the patriots of our glorious Revolution; having, at an early period, been a member of the Continental Congress. He died in 1781.

Hugh White Esq., the first settler of Whitestown, in the State of New-York, was a citizen of Middletown. He removed from this place with his family in 1784, and, penetrating beyond the Mohawk flats, which then formed a barrier to the western settlements, located himself at Sedaghquate, now Whitesboro' village, which, till then, had been the gloomy abode of wild beasts and savage men. For the first four years after the commencement of this settlement, its progress was rather slow and discouraging; yet, in 1788, it contained nearly 200 inhabitants; and the same year, the town of German Flats, comprising this settlement, was divided, and a new town established, which, in honour of this enterprising man, was called " *Whitestown.*" This township, with less than 200 inhabitants, comprised then almost all the western section of that State, which, in 1810, contained 280,319 inhabitants; being about 20,000 more than the whole population of Connecticut; so that Judge White, who survived this period two years, lived to see the dreary wilderness, into which he was the first man to penetrate, and which once bore his name, contain a greater population than his native State.

As was observed in his obituary notice, " Judge White may justly be considered as the *Patriarch*, who first led the children of New-England into the wilderness; and it may be truly said, that he lived to see and enjoy the promised land." He died in 1812, aged 80 years.

HADDAM.

HADDAM is a post township, situated upon the west side of Connecticut river, 8 miles from Middletown, and 23 from Hartford.

The tract of land between Middletown and Saybrook, embracing this township, was originally called the lands at Thirty mile Island, from the Island in Connecticut river of that name, (now Lord's Island,) north of the centre of the tract which was then thought to be 30 miles from its mouth, or the bar. These lands were owned and inhabited by the natives, of which there was a numerous, fierce and warlike tribe. In 1662, the Indian title to these lands was acquired by Matthew Allyn and Samuel Wyllys for thirty coats; not exceeding, probably, one hundred dollars in value. The same year, this purchase was disposed of to 28 persons, who immediately became actual settlers upon it. They were most, or all of them, from Hartford and its vicinity. The first settlement was made promiscuously in the town meadow; some families, however, located themselves on the plain below Mill creek, and were called the lower plantation. In October, 1668, six years only from the first settlement, the town was incorporated by the name of Haddam. At this time, this town belonged to the county of Hartford, and so continued until the formation of Middlesex county, in May 1785; previously to which, the judicial and other business had been transacted at Hartford, the seat of justice for the county. On the organization of the county of Middlesex, this town, on account of its central situation, became the semi-seat of justice for the county, & hath so remained ever since. In 1669, the original limits of this township were somewhat circumscribed by a resolution of the Assembly, ordering the division between this town and Saybrook and Lyme, of a tract of land embraced within the original purchase, which was considered as forming the boundaries of Haddam, but which was also claimed by these two towns.

At the present time, the mean length of this township is 7 miles, and its mean breadth more than 6 miles, comprising an area of 43 square miles.

This township is the commencement of the granitic district, extending to the mouth of Connecticut river. It is considerably rough and broken, being hilly and stony. There is but little alluvial upon Connecticut river, but the lands upon its borders are more smooth and better adapted to cultivation. Upon the branches of the Higganum, and upon Beaver brook, there are some small intervals, excepting which, the lands back from the river are generally rough, and cultivated only for grazing or timber. The prevailing soil is a gravelly loam, hard and dry. The forests are considerably extensive, and large quantities of wood are annually sent to market by the inhabitants, principally to New-York. The timber consists of hickory, oak and other hard wood. In 1807, there were 2000 cords carried from Higganum landing, the principal wood market, to New-York.

The agricultural productions consist principally of butter, cheese, beef and pork; some grain is raised, and a supply of potatoes and other esculent roots, vegetables &c.

There are several quarries of stone in this town, which, considering their vicinity to a navigable river, promise to be a source of wealth, permanent and inexhaustible.

The quarry below Haddam-street was opened about the year 1794. It is on a hill of considerable height, about 100 rods back from the river. The stones are usually a little below the surface, and are exhibited in nearly perpendicular strata. They are valuable for building, paving, &c. The bed is inexhaustible; and some years since, there were 80 or 90 hands employed in this quarry, and one opposite, on the east side of the river. These stones have been carried to various places in this State and Rhode-Island, to Boston, New-York, Albany and Baltimore for a market. They are sold by the foot of 4 inches thickness, from 17 to 20 cents; and of 2 inches thickness, for pavements, from 10 to 14 cents.

Besides the Connecticut which washes the eastern border of the township, it is watered by several small streams; the Higganum and its branches, Beaver brook and Pine brook. These streams afford various sites for mills and other hydraulic works. There are several ferries across Connecticut river in this town; Higganum ferry was granted to the town in 1763; and what are called Haddam ferry and Chapman's ferry are both private property. The shad fisheries in the Connecticut river in this town are very important, and a source both of industry and wealth; there are 16 or 17 different fisheries. In the season of 1814, it has been estimated that 130,000 shad were taken at the several fisheries in this town, although this was quite an unfavourable season; and it is supposed, that about 200,000 are annually taken. In 1802, there were 2300 taken at a single draught, of the seine used for the purpose.

From the maritime advantages of the town being situated upon a navigable river, it has from an early period done something at navigation and ship-building. For 60 or 70 years, a West India trade has been carried on, but upon a moderate scale. The coasting trade has been prosecuted more extensively. In 1814, there were owned in this town 1 Ship, 3 Brigs, 3 Sloops and 5 Schooners; amounting, in all, to 1597 tons. Ship-building has been regularly carried on for a length of time. Higganum landing has been its principal seat, although something has been done at other places.

The manufacturing and mechanical establishments and interests consist of 2 Clothiers' works, one of which fulls and finishes 4,500 yards of woolen cloth annually, 3 Carding Machines, 5 Grain Mills, 9 Saw Mills, 7 Tanneries, 1 Gin Distillery, 2 Cider Distilleries, 1 Machine for welding gun barrels and 1 Brick-yard. This brick-yard is half a mile from Higganum landing; the clay is taken from the bank of the river, and the brick are burnt upon a wharf; so that boats, and even vessels can approach so near, as to load the brick directly from the kiln.

The amount of taxable property, including polls, in 1816, was $40,571.

The population of the town, in 1810, was 2205; and there are about 250 Electors, 4 Companies of Militia, and about 390 Dwelling houses.

The town contains one located ecclesiastical Society, a Society of Baptists, and a Society of Methodists; 13 School districts and primary Schools.

There are 3 Churches; one for Congregationalists, one for Baptists and one for Methodists; one Social Library, one Clergyman, two Physicians and one Attorney.

CHATHAM.

CHATHAM is a flourishing post town, pleasantly situated upon the east side of Connecticut river, opposite Middletown, and 17 miles from Hartford; bounded on the north by Glastenbury, on the east by Marlborough and Colchester, on the south by East-Haddam and Haddam Neck, belonging to the town of Haddam, and on the west by Connecticut river.

The township has an average length of 9 miles, from north to south, and is more than 6 miles in breadth from east to west, comprising an area of about 56 square miles. The interior of the township is rough and broken, consisting of granitic hills, interspersed with inconsiderable vales. Upon Connecticut river, there is a considerable tract of alluvial, back of which, for nearly a mile, is an undulating argillaceous district, handsome and fertile, and corresponding with the geological character of the country upon Connecticut river. The termination of this tract forms the boundary between the argillaceous and granitic districts.

There are some valuable minerals in this town, the most important of which is cobalt ore. This valuable mineral has recently been discovered in several places in a mountain, called the Great Hill, about one mile from Middle Haddam Landing. It has been found in considerable quantities; and appearances authorize a belief of the mine's being extensive. The ore is found in a variety of forms and situations; sometimes embedded in masses of mica, having the figure of kidneys, sometimes surrounding garnets in clusters, sometimes it is discovered in hornblend, but most generally in micaceous veins, having a considerable dip. The ore of the different qualities that has been obtained, is generally combined with arsenic; but in some instances with arsenic and sulphur. This mineral is used extensively, and is very valuable in various manufactures; those of porcelain ware, linen, &c. The demand for these manufactures, in Great-Britain and Ireland, is supplied from Sweden and Germany. An oxyd of cobalt, called azure, is used in the china-ware manufactories in China, and is an important article of exportation to that country. They are at present supplied from Poland; but should this mine prove extensive, they might be supplied more directly, and upon more reasonable terms, from this country. This article, in addition to other important advantatages, would be, to a certain extent, a substitute for specie, in our trade with that country.

There is a very extensive and valuable quarry of freestone, situated upon the bank of Connecticut river, opposite Middletown, and below the bar in the river; so that vessels of 100 tons can load along side of the bank, near the quarry.

The strata of stone, forming the bed of this quarry, are a free sandstone, and can be worked and shaped with great facility. Very large quantities of stone are annually raised from this quarry, and sent to most of the principal cities in the Union for a market. For 14 years past, there have been employed in this quarry, yearly, from 40 to 60 labourers, and a number of teams. These quarries have been worked for about 150 years; but not extensively, until the last 30 years, since they have belonged to their present proprietors, Messrs. Shaler and Hall.

Although these stones are conveyed to most of the considerable cities in the Union, yet they are principally marketed at New-York, Boston and Savannah.

There are five different medicinal springs in this township; but their waters have not been subjected to chymical analysis, or their efficacy particularly ascertained.

Although most of this township is rough and stony, yet its agricultural interests are flourishing. The soil in the interior is in general a primitive gravelly loam, considerably warm and fertile, and well adapted to grazing. In the district upon Connecticut river, the soil is an argillaceous loam, rich and fertile, and suitable for a grain culture. In the interior, the forests are extensive, and the timber is of an excellent quality. The agricultural productions consist of rye, Indian corn, oats, flax, grass, cheese, butter, &c.

The most considerable stream of water within the town is Salmon river, which runs through its southeast section, and discharges itself into the Connecticut. Besides these, there are numerous small streams which water and fertilize the different sections of the town.

The Connecticut river, which washes the western border of the town, affords great advantages for commerce, fishing, &c. The principal harbour is at Middle-Haddam Landing, about 6 miles below Middletown. From this place, large quantities of timber, wood and lumber are shipped for New-York and Long Island. At this, and some other places in the town, ship-building has frequently been carried on to a considerable extent.

The shad fisheries in Connecticut river form an important business, and are a source of considerable wealth. There are 15 different fisheries.

The navigation business is respectable; there being 15 vessels owned in the town, employed principally in a trade to New-York and the southern States.

The town is accommodated with several turnpike roads; one leading to Windham, one to Colchester, and one other.

The manufactures and mechanical employments consist of 1

Woolen Factory, 1 Forge, 6 small Furnaces, for casting bells, cart and waggon boxes, &c., 6 Distilries, one of which, at Middle-Haddam Landing, is upon a considerable scale, 4 Tanneries, 8 Grain Mills, 12 Saw Mills, 3 Carding Machines and 4 Clothiers' works. The population of Chatham, at the census of 1810, was 3258; and there are about 525 Electors, 2 Companies of Infantry & 1 of Lt. Infantry of Militia, 453 Dwelling houses, 10 Mercantile Stores and 6 Churches.

The corporate divisions of the town consist of 3 located Congregational Societies and 15 School Districts. Besides the located, there are 2 Episcopal Societies and 1 of Baptists.

There are 15 primary Schools, one in each District, and an Academy or Grammar School in the first Society.

There are 5 Social Libraries, 3 Congregational, 1 Episcopal, and 1 Baptist Clergyman, 3 Physicians and 1 Attorney.

The amount of taxable property, including polls, as rated in the list, in 1817, was $53,616.

This town was incorporated in 1767, previously to which it belonged to Middletown.

DURHAM.

DURHAM is a post town, situated in the western section of the county 20 miles south of Hartford, and 18 northeast from New-Haven; bounded north on Middletown, east on Haddam, south on Guilford and Killingworth, and west on Wallingford.

This is a small township, averaging about 6 miles in length from east to west, and nearly 4 in breadth from north to south, comprising an area of about 23 square miles.

The prevailing character of the surface is undulating; exhibiting an agreeable and interesting diversity of moderate hills and gentle declivities and dales. The eastern and western borders are somewhat broken and mountainous.

This township is situated at the commencement of the argillaceous district extending to the north upon Connecticut river; being partly included within it, and partly within the granitic region which prevails upon the borders of Long Island sound. Within the clay slate strata, there is an exhaustless quarry of sandstone, which is a very valuable freestone.

The prevailing soil is an argillaceous loam, and a slaty or shistic gravel. It is generally fertile and productive. Upon the streams, particularly West or Middletown river, are considerable tracts of alluvial.

The lands are well adapted both to grazing and tillage, and also favourable for fruit.

The staple agricultural productions are rye, corn and flax.

Of the waters of the town, West river is the principal stream. It rises near the north line of Guilford, and runs northwardly through the town, embodying, in its course, most of the small streams, into Middletown, where it discharges itself into the Connecticut. It affords, within this town, very extensive meadows,

The Middletown and New-Haven turnpike leads through this town; the East-Guilford turnpike runs from that Society in Guilford, into the centre of this town; and there is a turnpike, commencing about half a mile south of the centre of this town, which leads to Haddam.

The principal manufacture is that of shoes; of which, for some years past, considerable quantities have been made, and sent to the southern States for a market. There are 4 Tanneries, 2 Grain Mills, 3 Saw Mills, 1 Carding Machine and 1 Cider Distillery.

The population of the town, in 1810, was 1130; and there are about 150 Electors, 2 Companies of Militia, and 172 Dwelling houses.

The aggregate list of the town, in 1816, including polls, was $26,609.

This town comprises but 1 located Ecclesiastical Society. Besides which, there is 1 Society of Episcopalians and 1 of Methodists. In the centre of the town, there is a small but pleasant village.

There are, in Durham, 3 Mercantile Stores, 6 common Schools, 1 small Academy, 2 Social Libraries, 1 Clergyman and 1 Physician.

The settlement in this town was commenced in the year 1699, and it was incorporated in 1708.

BIOGRAPHY. Gen. *James Wadsworth*, distinguished for his revolutionary services, was a native of this town. He was a General in the continental army, during the revolutionary war, and was esteemed a zealous patriot and a good officer. After the peace, he was for several years a member of the Congress organized under the Confederation. He died in 1817, aged 88.

EAST-HADDAM.

EAST-HADDAM is a considerable post township, situated upon the east side of Connecticut river, in the southeast section of the county, 13 miles southeast from Middletown, and about 27 from Hartford; bounded on the north by Chatham and Colchester, on the east by Colchester and Lyme, in New-London county, on the south by Lyme, and on the west, principally by Connecticut river, but partly by the Salmon river, separating it from Haddam Neck, belonging to the town of Haddam.

The average length of the township, from east to west, is nearly 8 miles, and its average breadth, from north to south, is about 6 and a half miles, comprising an area of about 50 square miles.

The face of the country presents the usual granitic features of this region, being rough, and of a mountainous character; but the soil, which is a primitive gravelly loam, is generally strong and fertile. There is some alluvial upon the borders of the streams, which, with some other small sections, is suitable for the cultivation of grain; but the principal part of the township is best adapted to grazing, and is too rough and stony for tillage. There is considerable timber in the town, which is of an excellent quality.

The agricultural interests and pursuits are principally directed to the dairy business, and the raising of cattle and sheep.

The waters of the town are abundant; it being washed upon its western border by the Connecticut, throughout most of its extent, and the residue by Salmon river. There are also several small streams which intersect and fertilize the different sections of the township, and afford numerous sites for hydraulic works.

Upon the Connecticut and Salmon rivers, there are several good harbours or landings, at which the commercial business is carried on, which consists principally in a trade with New-York and the southern States. Considerable quantities of wood are conveyed to the New-York market. The landing places afford great facilities to the business of ship building, which at some periods has received considerable attention.

The shad fisheries in the Connecticut constitute an important business, and are a source of considerable profit. They are six in number; and it has been estimated that the average quantity of shad, taken annually, is nearly 50,000.

The manufacturing and mechanical interests of the town are respectable. There are 1 Cotton Factory, 1 Woolen Factory, 3 Clothiers' works, 3 Carding Machines, 1 Oil Mill, 6 Grain Mills, 19 Saw Mills and 13 Tanneries.

There were 2537 inhabitants in this town, at the census of 1810; and there are about 300 Electors, 3 Companies of Militia, and about 390 Dwelling houses.

This town is accommodated with a turnpike road to Colchester, and the contemplated turnpike from New-Haven to Norwich will pass through it.

The civil divisions of East-Haddam are 3 located Congregational Societies and 19 School Districts. Besides the located, there is 1 Society of Episcopalians and 1 of Baptists.

There are 8 or 10 Mercantile Stores and 3 Social Libraries in the town.

The amount of taxable property and polls, in 1817, was $60,327.

This town was originally a part of Haddam; and for an account of its first settlement, we must refer the reader to that town. It was incorporated as a separate town in 1734.

BIOGRAPHY. Gen. *Joseph Spencer*, of this town, enjoyed a great share of public confidence in his day, and was honoured with many distinguished offices, both civil and military. During the French war, in 1758, he went into the northern army, having the rank of a major, and was soon promoted to a colonel, in which office he served the two succeeding years, and acquired considerable reputation. At the commencement of the revolutionary war, in 1775, he was appointed a Brigadier General, and, the subsequent year, a Major General in the Continental army. He resigned his commission in 1778, and the year after, was elected a member of the Continental Congress. He died in 1789, aged 75 years.

KILLINGWORTH.

KILLINGWORTH is a maritime post township, situated upon Long Island sound, 38 miles south-east from Hartford, 26 east from New-Haven, and 26 west from New-London; bounded on the north by Durham, on the northeast by Haddam, on the east by Saybrook, on the south by Long Island sound, and on the west by Hammonassett river, which separates it from Guilford.

The township is of an oblong figure, comprising an area of about 42 square miles, being about 13 miles in length, from north to south, and having a mean breadth of more than 3 miles.

The surface is various; the southern section of the township being level, the northern diversified with hill and dale, and it is rough and stony. Upon the border of the sound, there are large tracts of marine alluvial or salt marsh, comprising, as has been estimated, 1000 acres.

The soil is also various. The northern section is a gravelly loam; in other sections there are some tracts of sandy loam, and some argillaceous, and the marine alluvial already noticed.

Of the waters of the town, the Hammonassett river, which washes its western border, and the Menunketesuck, which runs through its eastern section, and discharges itself into Pochaug harbour, in Saybrook, are the most considerable streams. Besides these there are various small streams, which accommodate and fertilize the different parts of the town.

There is one harbour in the southern part of the town, tolerably safe and commodious; having seven and a half feet of water at common tides.

Some attention is paid to the business of fishing. Of the fish taken, are shad, black fish and shell fish. White fish are also taken very plentifully, for the purposes of manure.

There are eight small vessels belonging to the town, employed in the coasting trade. Wood and ship timber, of which the town affords large supplies, form a considerable item of exportation. They are sent principally to New-York. The wood is of an excellent quality, consisting mostly of walnut and rock oak.

Killingworth, as an agricultural township, does not unite superior advantages, or possess very ample resources for agricultural improvements and wealth. Some sections, however, are feasible, fertile and productive, and suitable for a grain culture; but many parts are rough and stony, and adapted only to grazing or the growth of timber.

The staple agricultural productions are Indian corn, some rye, oats, barley, the cultivation of which (although neglected in most other towns) forms a considerable interest, beef, butter and cheese.

The manufactures of the town, exclusive of those which form the products of domestic industry, are not very important or considerable. There are 1 Woolen Factory, 3 Fulling Mills and Cloth Dressing establishments, 2 Carding Machines, 8 Grain Mills and 6 Tanneries.

The civil divisions of the town consist of 2 located Congregational Societies and 15 School Districts. Besides the located, there are 2 Societies of Episcopalians and 1 of Baptists.

In the first located Society, there is a pleasant and interesting village, situated at the landing, upon the sound, and upon the great road leading from New-Haven to New-London. It comprises about 100 Dwelling houses, some of which are neat and handsome, a Post office, a Congregational Church, and several Mercantile Stores. It has a healthful, interesting and prospective situation; having, in the summer months, a salubrious sea air.

The population of the town, in 1810, was 2244; and there are about 400 Electors, 3 Companies of Militia, and about 320 Dwelling houses.

The aggregate list of the town, in 1816, was $52,751.

There are in Killingworth, 15 primary Schools, 1 Academy, 3 Houses for public worship, 1 Social Library, 9 Mercantile Stores, 8 Taverns or Public Inns, 3 Physicians, 2 Clergymen and 2 Attornies.

This township was called by the Indians Hammonassett, and was settled in 1663, by 12 families from Hartford, Windsor and Guilford.

The township was incorporated in 1703, by the name of Killingworth, although it was intended to have had the English name of *Kennelworth*, a mistake having been made in the record.

BIOGRAPHY. The Rev. *Jared Elliott*, D. D., was for many years a resident of this town. He was a man of genius and science; and invented or discovered the art of making sand-iron, being iron manufactured from black sand. This discovery was perfected in 1761; and he died in 1769, aged 78 years. He was a member of the Royal Society of London.

SAYBROOK.

SAYBROOK is an extensive maritime post township, situated at the mouth of Connecticut river, upon Long Island sound, 40 miles southeast of Hartford, 18 west of New-London, 34 east of New-Haven, and 70 southwest of Providence; bounded easterly upon Connecticut river, southerly upon Long Island sound, westerly by Killingworth, and northerly by the town of Haddam. The mean length of the township, from north to south, is about 11 miles, and its average breadth, from east to west, is more than 6 miles, comprising an area of about 70 square miles.

The general character of this township is rough, and considerably broken, being hilly and stony; but there are some intervals, and other sections that are level. Its geological features are primitive; the prevailing strata of rocks consisting of granite and micaceous schistus. Within these strata, there are, at different places, several valuable quarries of stone. The prevailing soil, which is a gravelly loam, is considerably fertile; it produces corn, some rye, oats, hay, &c. Indian corn and hay are among the staple productions, and are of the best quality. The lands

SAYBROOK.

are well adapted to grazing, and the dairy business is considerably attended to.

This township is very advantageously located, with respect to waters; being washed by Long Island sound upon its southern border, which is indented with numerous inlets, and by Connecticut river upon its eastern border, a distance of nearly 14 miles; besides which, there are several small streams that intersect the town. Of these, the most considerable are Chester river, which runs through the north Society; Pettipaug river, which discharges itself into the Connecticut; Oyster river, which discharges its waters into Long Island sound, and the Pochaug river, which waters the western section of the township. There are several harbours upon Connecticut river. The depth of water at the bar is about 12 feet at spring tides. There is a light-house at Lynde Point.

The navigation business of the town is considerable; there being 30 vessels of every description owned here, which are employed in the coasting trade. Ship building also receives considerable attention, particularly at the village of Pettipaug.

The shad fisheries in Connecticut river, within this town, are very valuable, a source of great wealth, and afford employment for considerable industry. The shad taken in this town are at least equal in quality to those taken at any other place upon the river, and are not surpassed by any in America. The quantities of shad taken in Connecticut river have considerably decreased, for some years past, and the price has proportionally advanced. Formerly, they were put up, or salted in barrels, without reference to the weight; but some years since, an act was passed by the Assembly, regulating the packing or salting of shad, which requires, that each barrel shall contain 200lbs. and be inspected, &c. These regulations have improved the quality of the shad, which are exported from Connecticut river, and given them a reputation surpassing that of any other, and a consequent higher price in market.

Salmon, which were formerly taken very plentifully in this river, have, for some years past, wholly disappeared. Some herring are taken in this town, which are salted, and fitted for the West India market. White fish are taken upon the shores of the sound, which are very valuable for the purposes of manure. They are sold for this object at $2 per thousand; at which price they are a cheap manure, their richness and efficacy being truly astonishing. The lightest soils, enriched with them, have produced 40 bushels of rye to the acre; and they have an equally advantageous effect upon the growth of corn, potatoes and other productions.

The interests of agriculture, navigation, fishing and commerce, engross most of the capital, industry and enterprise of the town; and its manufactures, exclusive of those of a domestic character, can claim only a very subordinate rank. There is 1 Ivory Comb Factory, upon a very extensive scale. Large quantities of ivory button moulds are also manufactured at this establishment. There are 3 Clothiers' works, 2 Carding Machines, 7 Grain Mills and 6 Saw Mills.

The mercantile business of the town is respectable, there being in the several Societies, 14 Dry Goods and Grocery Stores.

The civil divisions of the town consist of 4 Parishes or located Congregational Societies and 20 School Districts. Besides the located, there are 2 Societies of Methodists, 1 of Baptists and 1 of Episcopalians.

In the Society of Pettipaug, there is a considerable village, of the same name, situated at the landing, upon Connecticut river, eight miles from its mouth. This is a place of considerable commercial and navigation business. Ship building also is carried on here very extensively.

This village is memorable from the attack made upon it by the British, during the late war, and the entire destruction of the shipping in the harbour, which seems to have been the object of their *friendly* visit. This event occurred on the 8th of April, (being Good Friday, and a public Fast day,) 1814. A detachment from the British blockading squadron, then lying off New-London, consisting of several hundred soldiers and marines, made an excursion up the river, in six large barges, with muffled oars, and arrived at the landing in this village, about 3 o'clock in the morning. About 270 men were immediately landed, who rushed into, and took possession of the village. The commanding officer informed the inhabitants, that his orders were to burn the shipping, but not to molest the citizens, unless they were attacked.; in which case, he was ordered to destroy every house in the village. The suddenness and surprise of this irruption produced a scene of confusion, which obstructed the organization of any efficient means of resistance; and the party was left to proceed in their work of destruction. They burned all the vessels in the harbour, amounting to 23, and valued, subsequently, at $200,000. They also destroyed or stove several hogsheads of rum, and carried off several thousand dollars worth of cordage.

The population of the town, in 1810, was 3926; and there are about 450 Electors, 5 Companies of Militia, four of Infantry and 1 of Artillery, and about 600 Dwelling houses.

The aggregate list of the town, in 1816, was $75,857.

There are 2 Post offices in the town, one in the first Society, and the other in Chester; and, in addition to the county or public roads, it is accommodated with a convenient turnpike, leading thro' Haddam to Middletown; and another is now opening from this town to New-Haven.

There are, in this town, 20 primary Schools, 6 Clergymen, 5 Physicians and 1 Attorney.

This is one of the most ancient towns in the State. Lords Say and Seal and Brook, having purchased the tract of land upon the mouth of Connecticut river, previously to the year 1635, caused a fort to be erected at the Point, this and the succeeding year, in which a garrison of about 20 men was maintained. The garrison made

BIOGRAPHY.

some improvements; and it was contemplated immediately to prosecute the settlement. But the war with the Pequots, and the condition of the colony, retarded it. In the summer of the year 1639, Mr. George Fenwick, with his family, arrived in a ship from England, with a view to take possession of the country, and establish a settlement, in behalf of the purchasers or patentees thereof. A settlement was soon commenced, and in honour of their lordships, Say and Seal & Brook, was named Saybrook. Messrs. Fenwick and Thomas Peters, who was the first minister in the settlement, Capt. Gardiner, and Capt. John Mason, were among the first and principal settlers. The town was independent of the government of Connecticut, until after the purchase of Mr. Fenwick, in 1644. The first tax, levied by authority of the colony, was at the October session, the year after. Soon after this period, the settlement began to flourish; a number of families removing here from Hartford and Windsor. The original limits of the town extended upon the east side of the river, for several miles, and included a part of the town of Lyme.

BIOGRAPHY. Gen. *William Hart*, distinguished for his enterprise, as a merchant, his wealth, and the high estimation of his fellow-citizens, was a resident of this town. He was in the service, during the revolutionary war. In 1795, he, together with Oliver Phelps, and their associates, purchased of the Governor of this State the tract of land in the State of Ohio, called the "Western Reserve," amounting to about 3,300,000 acres; the consideration of which was $1,200,000.

Gen. Hart attained to a high rank in Society, and unusual public consideration; having, at one period of his life, for several years, been a candidate for Governor of this State. He died in 1817.

TOLLAND COUNTY.

TOLLAND, an inconsiderable and recently organized county, is situated in the northeastern section of the State; bounded on the north by the State of Massachusetts, on the east by Windham county, on the south by the county of New-London, and on the west by Hartford county.

The county of Tolland has an average length of more than 22 miles, and a mean breadth of about 15 miles; comprising an area of about 337 square miles.

The following TOPOGRAPHICAL AND STATISTICAL TABLE exhibits a view of the several towns in the county; their situation, with relation to Tolland, the seat of justice; their population, at the census of 1810; number of dwelling houses; religious societies; school districts, and post-offices.

Towns.	Post-offices.	Population.	Dwelling houses.	Religious societies.	School districts.	Distance from Tolland.
Tolland.	1	1610	300	3	13	
Bolton.	1	700	100	2	5	10 m. S. W.
Coventry.	1	1938	324	3	11	7 m. S.
Ellington.		1344	162	2	8	7 m. N. W.
Hebron.	2	2002	321	4	12	15 m. S.
Somers.		1260	200	1	9	10 m. N. W.
Stafford.	1	2230	320	5	19	8 m. N. E.
Union.		750	120	2	6	15 m. N. E.
Vernon.	1	827	135	1	6	8 m. S. W.
Willington.		1161	200	2	11	7 m. E.

Tolland county, as it respects its surface, soil and geological character, is divided into two distinct sections. The western section is a very handsome, level or undulating country, and as it is in location, so it appears to be in its character, an intermediate tract, between the argillaceous district upon Connecticut river, and the granitic region with which it connects upon the east. This tract is in general free from stone; and the soil, although generally shallow, and rather light, is warm, fertile and productive, being well adapted to the growth of grain, and affords great facility of cultivation. The eastern section embraces the extensive granitic range which extends through the State. This section is elevated and mountainous, and some parts of it cold and sterile. A considerable proportion of it has been suffered to remain to forests, which are more extensive here than in any other part of the State. The trees are of the deciduous species, and the timber is generally of an excellent quality. The improved lands, in this section of the county, afford tolerably good grazing ; but in general do not admit of a grain culture. Upon some of the streams, however, there are small intervals, suitable for arable purposes. In this section of the county, the agricultural productions consist of butter, cheese, cattle, sheep, beef, pork, and some others ; and in the western section, rye, corn and oats, constitute the staple productions.

The waters of the county consist of numerous small streams, and are principally embodied, in the eastern section, in the Willimantic and Hop rivers. These rivers and their numerous branches intersect and water a considerable proportion of the county. In the western and southern sections, the waters are principally embodied in the Scantic, Hockanum and Salmon rivers. The former of these streams has considerable tracts of alluvial, and the others afford many water privileges.

The manufacturing interests of the county are flourishing, and constantly extending ; developing new fields for industry and new sources of wealth. Domestic manufactures receive universal attention, and are an important source both of industry and economy ; the inhabitants being remarkable for their hardy and persevering habits of industry. Of the manufactures, those of cotton and iron are the most important. There are 9 Cotton Factories, 2 Forges and 3 Furnaces, most of which are upon a considerable scale. There are 11 Fulling Mills, 20 Carding Machines, 4 Woolen Factories, 36 Grain Mills, 2 Glass Factories, 3 Paper Mills and 2 Oil Mills. Recently, the manufacture of straw braid has been introduced, and receives great attention in some towns in the county. This business is the more important, as it contributes to the aggregate industry ; the labour being performed by those persons whose services are not usually profitably employed, and thereby avoids any interference with other departments of labour.

There are, in this county, 25 Religious Societies of every description, 14 School Societies, divided into a suitable number of School Districts, of which there are 100, and 10 Social Libraries.

There are about 40 Mercantile Stores.

The population of this county, in 1810, was 13,770 ; and the amount of taxable property and polls, in 1817, was $327,282.

This county originally belonged to the counties of Hartford and Windham, and was incorporated in 1786.

TOLLAND, the seat of justice for the county, is situated 18 miles east from Hartford, 52 northeast from New-Haven, and 42 northwest from New-London. It is bounded east on the Willimantic river, which separates it from Willington, west by Vernon and Ellington, south by Coventry, and north by Ellington. It contains about 36 square miles; being more than 6 miles in length, and 5 and a half miles in breadth.

The town is uneven and rough, being mountainous and stony. The soil is gravelly; but some of the valleys and borders of streams consist of loam which is warm and fertile.

The lands are best adapted to grazing, being too rough and stony for plowing, although some corn, oats, rye and flax are raised.

The forests, which are extensive, consist principally of oak and chesnut; comprising, however, various other deciduous trees.

The geological structure consists of granite, schistus and other rocks of a primitive formation. Large masses of granite appear upon the surface, some of which are detached and insulated, others of a connected stratum. Iron ore is found in many places in this range of mountains; but we have not ascertained that any has been discovered within this town.

There is a mineral spring in the town, the waters of which possess similar medicinal qualities to those of Stafford; but it has not acquired any celebrity abroad.

The town is watered by the Willimantic and the Skungamug rivers, and innumerable small streams. There are three bridges across the former, and four across the latter of these rivers.

Snipsick pond is a large body of water, being 2 miles in length, and 100 rods in width. There is also a pond called Skungamug in the town.

The civil divisions of the town are 1 located or Congregational Society and 13 School Districts.

In the centre of the town is a pleasant village, having an elevated and prospective situation. It is about half a mile in length, and contains a Court House and Gaol, for the county, 2 Churches, a Post office, and about 30 Dwelling houses, some of which are neat and handsome buildings.

There are several turnpike roads which pass through this town; Hartford and Tolland turnpike, leading from the former to the latter place, and from thence to Boston; Stafford turnpike, and Tolland county turnpike.

There were, in 1810, 1610 inhabitants in the town. There are now 250 qualified Electors, 3 companies of Militia and about 300 Dwelling houses.

There is 1 Furnace, for casting iron, 3 Grain Mills, 3 Saw Mills, 3 Distilleries, 3 Tanneries, 2 Fulling Mills, 1 Carding Machine and 4 Mercantile Stores.

There are 3 Churches; one for Congregationalists, one for Baptists and one for Methodists, 1 Social Library, 13 common or District Schools, 2 Clergymen, 3 Attornies and 4 Physicians.

The general list of taxable polls and estate of the town is $37,335.

Tolland was incorporated as a town in the year 1715.

BOLTON.

BOLTON is a small post township, 14 miles east from Hartford; bounded on the north by Vernon, on the east by Coventry, on the south by Hebron, and on the west by East-Hartford. The township contains an area of 16 square miles; being more than 5 miles in length and 3 in breadth.

This town is embraced within the granitic district of the eastern section of the State, has an elevated situation, and is hilly and stony. The soil is a coarse, hard, gravelly loam, rather cold and sterile. It however affords tolerable grazing; and the dairy business is the leading agricultural interest.

The natural growth of timber is oak, walnut, maple, chesnut, &c.; and the forests are considerably extensive. The farmers, in the fall and winter seasons, bring large quantities of wood to Hartford market.

A branch of Hop river runs through the northeastern section of the town, and a branch of Salmon river through the southwestern.

The Hartford and Norwich turnpike road leads through the centre of the town.

There are, in Bolton, 2 Grain Mills, 1 Fulling Mill and Clothier's works, 1 Tannery, 2 Mercantile Stores and 1 Tavern.

The population of the town, in 1810, was 700; and there are 100 Dwelling houses, 1 Company of Militia, and about 120 Electors

The town forms one located Congregational Society; and there is, besides, a small Society of Episcopalians. There are 5 School Districts and Schools, 1 small Social Library, 2 Physicians and 1 Clergyman.

Bolton was settled in 1716, and was incorporated in 1720.

COVENTRY.

COVENTRY is a post township, situated 18 miles east from Hartford; bounded on the north by Tolland, on the south by Hebron and Columbia, on the east by Mansfield, and on the west by Bolton and Vernon.

Its average length is 7 miles, and its average breadth about 6 and a half miles, comprising about 45 square miles.

The surface is uneven, or moderately hilly, and the soil a gravelly loam. The stones and rocks are granite and micaceous schistus.

The natural growth consists of oak, walnut, chesnut, butternut, sumach, &c.

The agricultural productions are grass, rye, corn, oats, butter, cheese, beef, pork, and some others; but the lands are best adapted to grazing, and the dairy business constitutes the principal agricultural interest.

The eastern border of the town is washed by the Willimantic, which forms its boundary. The Skungamug runs from north to south thro' the town, and, uniting its waters with another stream, forms Hop river; which, running eastwardly, washes the southern border of the town, and constitutes its boundary, or south line. It unites its waters with the Willimantic, which forms the southeastern corner of the township. There are a number of bridges across these streams; and they also afford numerous sites for mills and other water works, many of which are advantageously occupied.

There is a lake or pond in this town, called Wangumbog, a considerable body of water, being about 2 miles in length and 1 in width.

There are several turnpike and mail roads which lead through this town.

The manufactures and mechanical employments, exclusive of those of a domestic character, consist of 1 Cotton Factory, 2 Paper Mills, 1 Glass Factory, 1 Manufactory of Carding Machines, 3 small Distilleries, 5 Tanneries, 3 Grain Mills, 6 Saw Mills and 5 Carding Machines. There are 7 Mercantile Stores.

The population of the town, in 1810, was 1938; and there are 324 Dwelling houses, 366 Freemen or Electors, and 164 Militia.

The town is divided into three located Congregational Societies or Parishes, in each of which there is a small village and a Congregational Church.

It contains 11 School Districts and Schools, 2 Social Libraries, 2 Clergymen, 1 Attorney and 3 Physicians.

The general list of the town, including polls, is $52,833.

Coventry was settled in 1709; belonging then, and for a long time afterwards, to the county of Hartford, and incorporated in 1711.

BIOGRAPHY. Capt. *Nathan Hale*, a celebrated youthful hero, and martyr of the revolutionary war, was a native of this town. Capt. Hale received his education at Yale College, where he graduated in 1773. The ardent glow of patriotic feeling, and the deep interest which he took in the cause of his injured country, induced him, at an early period of the revolutionary war, to offer to it his services; and having obtained a commission, he entered the army in the capacity of a captain in the Light Infantry regiment commanded by Col. Knowlton, a very brave and distinguished officer, a succint account of whom may be found in this work, subjoined to the town of Ashford. After the unfortunate engagement upon Long Island, on the 27th of August, 1776, an immediate retreat to New-York was deemed the only expedient that could save the entire American army, consisting of about 9000 men, from falling into the hands of the enemy. This measure was planned and executed with great judgment, secrecy and success; all of the American forces having been safely conveyed to New-York, before the British had any knowledge of what was going on. Yet the suddenness of this movement, and the surprise which it must have occasioned with the British, gave Gen. Washington great solicitude to become acquainted with their situation subsequently to this unexpected event, and of their intended movements.

Gen. Washington communicated his views and wishes upon this subject to Col. Knowlton, whose regiment formed the van of the army, and requested him to devise some mode of obtaining the necessary information. Col. Knowlton, knowing the intelligence, the ardent patriotism, and the bold and adventurous spirit of Capt. Hale, submitted to him the views and wishes of the commander in chief. Capt. Hale, animated by a sense of duty, and pleased at an opportunity of signalizing his zeal in the cause of his country, he immediately offered himself as a volunteer for this difficult and imminently hazardous enterprise. Having disguised himself, he crossed to Long Island, explored and examined every part of the British army, and obtained the necessary information respecting their situation and subsequent operations. But, although successful in accomplishing the objects of his enterprise, he was not destined to return. He was apprehended, and carried before Sir William Howe, and circumstances affording such strong proof against him, and from the characteristic principles of integrity and honour, which governed his conduct, he frankly acknowledged who he was, and the objects of the service in which he was engaged. Sir William Howe immediately, without even the formality of a trial, ordered the provost marshal to have him executed the next morning. This cruel order was accordingly executed, under circumstances the most distressing, and by as unfeeling a savage as ever disgraced humanity.

Thus fell Nathan Hale, in the morning of life, and in the dawn of high promise, of reputation and honour to himself, and of usefulness to his country. The manner and circumstances of his death must ever be abhorrent to the feelings of humanity. He was treated in the most unfeeling and indecent manner; and every indulgence, every mark of sympathy and respect were denied him. He desired the attendance of a clergyman, which was refused. But what was more inhuman, the letters which he had written to his mother and friends, were destroyed on the morning of his execution. This savage outrage upon the feelings of humanity could only be equalled by the reason which was assigned for it; which was, "that the rebels should not know that they had a man in their army who could die with so much firmness." It is difficult to conceive of a situation more awful, or that in a more eminent degree was calculated to overcome the firmest mind. Among entire strangers, in the hands of his enemies, every face presenting the aspect of hostility, and without a single friend to sympathize with him or console him in this hour of trial, and subjected to contumely and reproach, having the opprobrious epithet of rebel bestowed upon him, he had nothing but the consciousness of his moral innocence, and the justness of the cause in which he was engaged, to sustain him; and these were sufficient. He met his fate with the most dignified composure and firmness. His last words were, "that he only lamented that he had but one life to lose for his country."

Capt. Hale possessed a fine genius, had received an excellent education, and disclosed high promise of future talents and usefulness. He was open, generous and brave, and enthusiastic in the cause of liberty and his country, in which he had engaged, and for which he was destined to die an early martyr. The fate of Hale, it will be observed, was in almost every respect strikingly similar to that of Major Andre. As it respects character, qualifications and personal interest, Hale would not suffer from a comparison with Andre. Yet, strange as it may seem, the fate of Andre, even in America, has been universally lamented, and his memory universally respected; whilst it is scarcely known that there was ever such a man as Nathan Hale. Andre has had a monument erected to his memory by his country, and the most distinguished honours and rewards conferred upon his family; but what has *our* country done for the memory of Hale? No stone, however humble, has been erected to it; no memorial has rescued it from oblivion; and no inscription has preserved his ashes from insult. Such is the influence of books, and the evil tendency of importing them, that while Nathan Hale, an American, an ardent revolutionary patriot, and who offered his life as a sacrifice to our liberties, is wholly unknown, the life, character and fate of Andre are familiar with almost every individual, however humble his situation, or limited his intelligence.

*Thus, while fond virtue wish'd in
  vain to save,*
*Hale, bright and generous, found
  a hapless grave.*
With genius' living flame his bosom glow'd,

*And science charm'd him to her
  sweet abode.*
*In worth's fair path his feet had
  ventur'd far,*
*The pride of peace, the rising grace
  of war.*
*In duty firm, in danger calm as
  ev'n,*
To friends unchanging, and sincere to heav'n.
*How short his course, the prize,
  how early won,*
*While weeping friendship mourns
  her fav'rite gone.*
                                DWIGHT.

The Hon. *Samuel Huntington*, late Governor of the State of Ohio, was a native of this town. He was the son of the Rev. Joseph Huntington, for several years a settled clergyman in this place, and distinguished for a posthumous work which he wrote, entitled "Calvinism improved," being a treatise upon the doctrine of universal salvation.

Samuel Huntington was educated at Yale College, where he graduated in 1785. In 1801, he removed to the State of Ohio, and settled near the village of Painesville, which at that time was a wilderness in the county of Geauga, upon the border of Lake Erie. During his residence in that State, he was appointed to a succession of important offices. He was a member of the convention which framed the constitution of that State, and a Senator in the first Legislature organized under it. He was afterwards appointed a Judge of the Superior Court, in which situation he continued until called to a more exalted station, being elected by the people Governor of the State. This office he held for some time, and discharged its important and responsible duties with equal credit to himself, and advantage to the interests of the State, which was rising rapidly into impórtance, and presented an extensive field requiring a judicious direction of authority for the developement of its resources, and the promotion of necessary improvements. He died at Painesville on the 7th of June, 1817, aged 49 years.

ELLINGTON.

ELLINGTON is situated 13 miles northeast from Hartford. It is bounded west by East-Windsor, north by Somers and Stafford, east by Tolland and Willington, and south by Vernon and Tolland.

The township is equivalent to about 34 square miles, but it is of an irregular figure, its greatest length being 9 miles, and its greatest breadth about 6 miles, and it comprises about 21,760 acres.

The township, in its western section, is generally level; a considerable portion of it being a plain, the soil of which is light, dry, and inclining to coarse sand or gravel, but is feasible, and considerably fertile. It is best adapted to grain, particularly rye, of which, when well cultivated, it carries good crops. It affords good pasturage for sheep, which receive considerable attention.

The eastern section of the town is broken, being hilly and stony; the soil of which is hard, coarse and gravelly.

There is a small but pleasant village in the centre of the town, having a Congregational Church, & a number of neat Dwelling houses.

In 1810, there were 1344 inhabitants in the town; and there are now about 175 Freemen, and 1 Company of Militia.

There are 1 Cotton Factory, 1 Distillery, 1 Grain Mill, 4 Saw Mills, 1 Tannery, 1 Carding Machine, and 3 Mercantile Stores.

There are in the town, 1 local or Congregational Society, 1 Society of Methodists, 8 District or primary Schools, 1 small Social Library, 1 Clergyman, 1 Physician and 1 Attorney, and 162 Dwelling houses.

The list of polls and taxable property of the town, is $34,529.

Ellington was originally a part of the township of East-Windsor, and was incorporated in 1786.

HEBRON.

HEBRON is a post township, situated 20 miles southeastwardly from Hartford; bounded on the north by Bolton and Coventry, on the east by Columbia and Lebanon, in Windham county, on the south by Colchester, in New-London county, and on the west by Glastenbury and Marlborough, in Hartford county. Its average length is 9 and a half miles, and its average breadth more than 4 miles, containing 42 square miles.

The township is uneven, being moderately hilly and diversified. The soil is a gravelly loam, and considerably fertile.

The geological character of the

town is principally granitic; but there are some micaceous schistus, and other rocks of a primitive formation.

The natural growth of timber is the same as is common to this region.

In a cultivated state, the lands produce corn, oats, some rye and flax, and afford tolerably good grazing.

Hop river washes the northeastern border of the town, and constitutes its boundary. This stream is a branch of the Willimantic. There are several small streams, which discharge their waters into Salmon river, that intersect the town.

North pond, a considerable body of water, is situated partly in this town and partly in Lebanon.

The turnpike road from Hartford to Norwich leads through the east section of this town; and one from Middletown to Providence through its centre.

The population of the town, in 1810, was 2002; and there are 330 Freemen or Electors, about 215 Militia, and 321 Dwelling houses.

The amount of taxable property, including polls, is $54,569.

There are in Hebron, 2 Woolen Factories, 2 Cotton Factories, both of which contain about 1000 spindles, 1 Paper Mill, 8 Cider Distilleries, 1 Tannery, 8 Grain Mills, 2 Carding Machines, 4 Fulling Mills and 7 Mercantile Stores.

The town contains 2 located Congregational Societies & Churches, 1 Episcopal Society and Church, and 1 Society of Methodists. It contains 12 School Districts & Schools, & 1 small village, situated in the centre of the town.

There are 4 Clergymen, 4 Physicians and 2 Lawyers.

Hebron was first settled in 1704; belonging then, and for a long time afterwards, to the county of Hartford. It was incorporated in 1707.

SOMERS.

SOMERS is situated in the northwest corner of the county, being 22 miles northeast from Hartford, 12 miles southeast from Springfield, in Massachusetts, and 56 miles west from Providence.

It is bounded north on Massachusetts line, south on Ellington, east on Stafford, and west on Enfield, in Hartford county.

The township is nearly 6 miles in length, with a mean breadth of about 5 miles, comprising an area of 28 square miles. The western section of the town is considerably smooth and level, being free from stone; and the surface is diversified with hills of a moderate elevation. The soil is a gravelly loam, interspersed with some tracts of argillaceous loam, rich and fertile, and well adapted to a grain culture. The eastern part of the town is hilly and mountainous, containing some heights of considerable elevation, affording an extensive and interesting prospect of Hartford, and the beautiful vale upon Connecticut river.

This mountainous tract is rough and stony, containing schistus, granite, and other rocks of a primitive formation. Some iron ore has been found, but not in great quantities. The soil in this part of the town is hard and gravelly; but it sustains some good orchards, and generally produces excellent pasturage.

The natural growth of the forests is chesnut, butternut, oak, elm, walnut, ash and other deciduous trees.

The town is well watered, being intersected with numerous small streams or brooks; and Scantic river runs through it. This, here, is a rapid stream, frequently overflowing its banks, and affords small tracts of alluvial.

Somers and Woodstock turnpike road, leading from Enfield bridge to Providence, passes thro' the centre of the town.

There were, in 1810, 1210 inhabitants; and there are now 135 qualified Electors, 145 Militia, comprising 2 companies, and 200 Dwelling houses.

The manufactures of the town are principally domestic. Most of the families manufacture a large portion of the coarser cloths for their own use, both woolen and linen, and also some of cotton. Other domestic manufactures receive attention, such as household furniture, casks, shoes, hats, straw bonnets, &c.

There is one small establishment of Woolen and Cotton manufacture. There are 3 Grain Mills, 4 Saw Mills, 1 Distillery, for grain, 6 for cider, 1 small Forge, 2 Tanneries, 1 Carding Machine and Clothier's works, 6 Mercantile Stores and 1 Druggist's Store.

The taxable polls and estate of the town, in 1817, was $31,434.

Somers forms but one located or Ecclesiastical Society, and contains one Congregational Church. There are a considerable number of Baptists, who, not being formed into a Society, are associated with the Baptist churches in the neighbouring towns.

The town contains 9 School Districts, in each of which a common School is maintained for several months in the year. There are 2 Social Libraries, 3 Attornies, 3 Physicians and 1 Clergyman.

Somers was incorporated as a town in 1734.

STAFFORD.

STAFFORD is an elevated post township, situated upon the northern border of the county and State, 26 miles northeasterly from Hartford; bounded on the north by Massachusetts line, on the east by Union and Willington, on the south by Willington and Ellington, and on the west by Ellington and Somers. Its mean length, from east to west, is 8 and a half miles, and its mean breadth, from north to south, more than 6 miles, comprising an area of about 53 square miles.

The general character of the township is that of an elevated, broken and mountainous country; but the western section is more conspicuously marked with these features.

Its geological structure is primitive; the rocks consisting of granite, micaceous schistus, and some

38

other original formations. The prevailing soil is a gravelly loam, hard and dry, but affording very good grazing.

There are several minerals in the town, of which iron ore is the most important, and abounds in various places. Several mines of it have been opened, which supply the furnaces that have been erected in the town. The ore used most, is called bog ore, and is of an excellent quality for casting.

In the northerly section of the township, there is a valuable quarry of white fire proof stone, admirably calculated for furnace hearths; for which purpose it has been an article of exportation. It is a source of wealth to the proprietor, as well as of convenience to the public.

The forests in this town, which are considerably extensive, consist of oak, walnut, maple, ash, chesnut and other deciduous trees.

The agricultural productions consist of beef, cider, cider brandy, butter, cheese, wool and some others. The lands are best adapted to grazing; and consequently the cultivation of grain receives but little attention.

The town is well watered by the Willimantic, its branches, and Roaring brook, which afford numerous interesting and valuable sites for hydraulic works, of which there are several upon the two branches of the Willimantic, in the vicinity of the mineral springs, that at some future period may promote the growth of a manufacturing village.

The mineral springs in this town have justly acquired considerable celebrity. There are two distinct springs, the medicinal qualities of which are considered as essentially different. One of them contains a solution of iron, sustained by carbonic acid gas, a portion of marine salt, some earthy substances, and what has been called natron, or a native alkali. This spring has been known and used for a length of time, and has been pronounced by chymists to be one of the most efficacious chalybeate springs in the United States. The other spring, the medicinal virtues of which were not known until about eight or nine years since, contains, according to the opinion of Professor Silliman, who examined it in 1810, a large portion of hydrogen gas of sulphur, and a small proportion of iron. These springs were known to the native Indians, who used to bathe in them and drink the waters. They first made them known to the English, soon after the settlement of the town. But they had not acquired much celebrity, until about the year 1765, when a case occurred, calculated to establish and extend their reputation. It was an effectual cure of a most obstinate cutaneous complaint, which had completely baffled all medicinal skill, and resisted all other applications. The publicity which was given to this case soon raised the reputation of these springs; and as a consequence of which, they immediately became a place of resort of persons afflicted with various diseases, and from almost every quarter. Since the reputation of the springs has been established, they have annually, in the summer season, been a place of much resort for the purposes of health or pleasure; and within the last five or six years, it has been estimated, that the number of visitors has annually been from six to nine hundred. The accommodations are ample and extensive; a very large and elegant building having been erected, which is occupied as a hotel and boarding house; besides which, there are several other boarding houses in the vicinity. Hitherto, the arrangements have been upon a scale of such liberality and amplitude, as to combine all the conveniences and most of the luxuries which are to be found at any watering place in the United States. It has been estimated, that for some years past, the receipts from visitors have amounted to five or six thousand dollars annually. The money, which is thus brought into the place from abroad, is a great advantage to the town, and one from which almost every class of citizens is in some measure directly or indirectly benefited; the farmer finds a market for small meats, vegetables, butter, poultry and other articles of his produce, and the mechanic for his industry.

This town is accommodated with several excellent turnpike roads. The great road from Hartford to Boston leads through it. Upon this road, the principal mail from Washington to Boston is conveyed; and the Boston and Hartford line of stages daily pass upon it. There is also a turnpike leading from Somers to Woodstock, and another leading from Norwich into Massachusetts, which pass thro' this town.

Stafford is considerably celebrated for its manufactures, particularly those of iron. The iron manufactures consist of refined iron, various kinds of castings, hollow ware, &c. There are 2 Forges and 2 Furnaces constantly in operation. The first furnace was built in 1779, is upon a large scale, and annually produces from 80 to 120 tons of hollow ware and other castings. Cannon, cannon shot or balls, and a variety of articles for manufacturing and other kinds of machinery, are cast at this furnace. The other furnace was erected in 1796, by a Company, of which Mr. Nathaniel Hyde is the principal. The products of this furnace have usually amounted to about 90 tons annually; and, with the exception of cannon, consist of all the varieties that are cast at the other furnace. In 1814, the price of hollow ware was 60 dollars per ton, and solid castings, 5 cents per pound.

Stafford castings are considered of an excellent quality, and esteemed softer and more ductile than any other in New-England. The ore is obtained from the mines within the town, is found in various places, and is called lowland or bog ore.

Besides the manufactures of iron, there are 2 Cotton Factories, 1 Manufactory of Clocks, 3 Clothiers' works, 2 Carding Machines, for customers, 3 Tanneries, 6 Grain Mills and 12 Saw Mills. In addition to these more important and laborious manufacturing employments, there are some which are attended to exclusively by females, of which the manufacture of straw braid is the most important. Large quantities of straw braid and bonnets are made and sent abroad for a market, which is equally important, regarded as a source of profit, or as a means of promoting female industry and habits of attention to business, and a consequent abstraction from light and frivolous occupations and amusements, or the more unwarrantable employment of local detraction. This manufacture is of recent date; and it has been estimated, that it already produces from 8 to $10,000 per ann.

The population of Stafford, in 1810, was 2355; and there are about 320 Dwelling houses, 300 Freemen or Electors, and 3 Companies of Militia.

The amount of taxable property, as rated in the lists, in 1816, was $39,293.

The civil divisions of the town are 2 located Ecclesiastical Societies or Parishes, and 19 School Districts. Besides the located, there is a Society of Baptists, a Society of Methodists and one of Universalists. These several Societies are all accommodated with houses for public worship. There is a primary or common School maintained in each of the School Districts for a suitable portion of the year.

There are, in the town, 6 Mercantile Stores, 9 Taverns, 2 Social Libraries, 3 Clergymen, 4 Physicians and 2 Attornies.

The settlement of this town commenced about the year 1718, having been surveyed that year. Of the first settlers, two were from Europe, Mr. Matthew Thompson and Mr. Robert White; the rest were from Hadley and Woburn, Dedham and Weymouth, in Massachusetts, Haverhill, in New-Hampshire, Windsor, Enfield and Preston, in this State. The first minister was settled in the town in 1723.

UNION.

UNION, an elevated interior township, is situated 33 miles northeasterly from Hartford, and 67 from New-Haven. It is bounded on the north by Massachusetts line, on the east by Woodstock, on the south by Ashford and Willington, and on the west by Stafford. Its extent, from east to west, is between 5 and 6 miles, and from north to south about the same; containing nearly 30 square miles, or about 19,000 acres.

The surface is broken, being hilly and rocky. Its geological structure consists of granite, micaceous schistus, and other primitive rocks, being a part of the granitic region composing the elevated tract in the eastern part of the State. Iron ore has been found in considerable quantities, but the mineralogy of the town has not been explored by the skilfulness of art, or with the judgment of scientific knowledge.

The soil is a mixture of loam and gravel. Its natural growth is oak, chesnut, walnut, beech, maple, ash, birch, wild cherry, pine and other perennial trees. The lands, when first cleared and cultivated, produce one heavy crop of rye, or wheat, and afterwards make good pasturing or mowing. They are also adapted to the growth of corn, oats, buck wheat, barley, flax, potatoes, &c. The apple tree flourishes well, and there are some orchards in the town.

Quinibaug river, (erroneously considered by most geographers to rise in Brimfield, in Massachusetts,) has its principal sources from two ponds, Mashapaug & Breakneck, both situated wholly within the town of Union. The Mashapaug branch of the Quinibaug river receives the waters of several small streams, having their sources within this town, and greatly exceeds, both in its size and the length of its course, the Brimfield branch. The Breakneck branch is also larger than that, having its source in Brimfield, and unites with the Mashapaug in Sturbridge.

Roaring river, a considerable branch of the Willimantic, and Bigelow and Still rivers, which unite in Ashford and form a considerable branch of the Shetucket, all have their sources in this town. These streams are plentifully stocked with trout, and afford many sites and privileges for mills and hydraulic works. The Mashapaug and Breakneck ponds alluded to are considerable bodies of water. They afford plenty of pike and perch; these excellent fish are also taken in a mill pond upon the Bigelow river.

The Mashapaug is a beautiful expanse of water, covering an area of 800 acres, and embosoms a small island, of about an acre, covered with wood, and having a character peculiarly romantic. Breakneck is of an oblong form, extending from north to south, about three fourths of a mile, having an outlet from its northern extremity, surrounded on all sides by its native forests. From the eastern side of this pond, the land rises with a gradual ascent, and is covered with valuable timber, forming a part of the extensive forests which the town contains. Its western borders are surrounded by a narrow skirt of meadow, thickly covered with spruce and cedar, behind which rises a bold, craggy ridge, bearing the name of the pond which it overlooks, covered with venerable oaks and pines; and was famous in former times, as being the haunt of wild beasts, and the noxious abode of the envenomed rattlesnake.

The town is accommodated with several good public roads; and Somers and Woodstock turnpike passes through it.

Union, in 1810, contained 752 inhabitants; and there are now about 100 qualified Electors, 1 Company of Militia and 120 Dwelling houses.

There are 2 Mercantile Stores, 9 Saw Mills, 1 Grain Mill and 1 Tannery.

There is 1 Congregational Society and Church, and 1 Society of Methodists, having a house for public worship, 6 District Schools and 1 Social Library. There is one Physician, who is the only professional character in the town, there being no Clergymen or Lawyers.

This town furnishes a striking example of the inequality and injustice of the principle of representation in this State, and of the prevalence of the "borough system" of England. Union, with a population of 752, and with a list of 17,000 dollars, has an equal representation with New-Haven, which has a population of more than 7000, and a list of $133,000; having more than nine times the inhabitants of Union, and paying nearly eight times the amount of taxes; and upon a more just principle of taxation, the difference in this respect would be more conspicuous.

Union was incorporated as a town in 1734.

VERNON.

VERNON, a small post township, is situated 12 miles north-east from Hartford. It is bounded on the north by Ellington, on the east by Tolland and Coventry, on the south by Bolton and East-Hartford, and on the west by East-Windsor and East-Hartford.

The town comprises an area of about 5 miles in length, and more than 3 and a half in breadth, containing 18 square miles.

The principal part of the town is uneven, being agreeably diversified with hill and dale. The eastern part is broken and mountainous, extending upon that mountainous range of country which constitutes the height of land between the Thames and Connecticut rivers, and directs the course of the streams. This mountain consists of granite, schistus and other original rocks. In the southeast part of this town, are quarries of a greyish slate stone, admitting of a smooth and even surface. These stones are well calculated to flag the side-walks in cities, and have been carried to Hartford for that purpose. The stone is a micaceous schistus, or mica slate, being composed of mica and quartz, and has a slaty structure. It is not found frequently upon the summit of the mountain, but upon its sides, forming gentle acclivities. When these rocks are found upon the summit of hills, they are generally round.

The soil is in general a gravelly loam, somewhat stony, yet considerably fertile.

Its natural and agricultural productions are similar to those of other towns in the county, and like them, agriculture is the principal employment of the inhabitants.

The most considerable streams in the town are Hockanum and Tankerooson, which are fine mill streams, and contain many good water privileges.

The Stafford and Tolland turnpike, which is a part of the great post road from Hartford to Boston, passes through the centre of this town.

The population of this town, in 1810, was 827; and there are now 135 Dwelling houses, one entire company of Militia and parts of several others.

There are 1 Woolen Factory, 2 Cotton Factories, one of which, it is believed, was the first establishment in the State, 3 Grain Mills, 6 Saw Mills, 2 Oil Mills, 1 Distillery, 1 Tannery, 4 Carding Machines and 1 Mercantile Store, in the town.

There are 6 District Schools, 1 Congregational Society and Church, 2 Social Libraries, 1 Clergyman and 2 Physicians. The amount of the general list of rateable polls and estate, is $27,444.

Vernon was first settled from East-Windsor, in 1716, being then a part of Bolton. It was incorporated as a town in Oct. 1808.

WILLINGTON.

WILLINGTON is situated 24 miles east from Hartford. It is bounded east on Ashford, west on Tolland, north on Stafford and Union, and south on Mansfield. It is nearly 8 miles in length, from north to south, and 4 and a half miles in breadth, from east to west, comprising about 35 square miles.

The surface is hilly and broken, and the soil a hard gravelly loam, abounding with stone.

This town lies within the granitic district of the eastern part of the State, which commences at Haddam, and extends through the State into Massachusetts.

The summit of the mountains and hills is generally covered with granite and micaceous schistus, and other rocks of a primitive formation also abound. Some of these stones contain large quantities of mica; and beds of iron ore have been discovered in this town.

The lands are best adapted to grazing, and afford many forests of good timber.

The Willimantic river, a lively mill stream, waters the western borders of the town, and divides it from Tolland. The Fenton is the next most considerable stream within the township. Across these two rivers there are a number of bridges.

The turnpike road, leading from Providence to Enfield bridge, passes through the centre of the town. The turnpike leading from Norwich to Monson, in Massachusetts, passes through the town.

It is a singular fact, that salmon, which have wholly deserted Connecticut river, are taken in the Willimantic, a small stream; but the course of this river, being rapid, its waters limpid, and its bed of stone and gravel, render it an inviting retreat for this excellent fish.

The population of the town, in 1810, was 1150; and there are now about 200 Freemen, 100 Militia and 200 Dwelling houses.

The manufactures of the town, in addition to those of a domestic character, are 1 Woolen Factory, 1 Glass Factory, 6 Grain Mills, 3 Tanneries, 5 Saw Mills and 3 Carding Machines.

The town contains 1 located Congregational Society, 1 Society of Baptists, and 11 District Schools. There are 3 Mercantile Stores, 2 Churches, 1 Social Library, 2 Clergymen and 2 Physicians.

The amount of the taxable polls and estate of the town is $26,276; and the valuation of real estate, $230,400.

The first settlement of the town was in 1720.

T. Young Pinx.t   I. Sanford Sculp.t

NEHEMIAH R. KNIGHT,
Governor of the State of Rhode-Island.

Hartford, Published by Wm. S. Marsh, for a Gazetteer of Rhode-Island 1819.

A

GENERAL GEOGRAPHICAL AND STATISTICAL VIEW

OF

THE STATE OF

RHODE-ISLAND.

The State of Rhode-Island is situated between 41 and 42° north lat. and between 3° 11′ and 4° east lon.; and is bounded on the north and east by the State of Massachusetts, on the south by the Atlantic ocean, and on the west by the State of Connecticut. The average length of the State, from north to south, is more than 42 miles, and its mean breadth is about 29 miles, comprising an area of 1225 square miles, inclusive of the waters of Narragansett bay, which comprise about 130 square miles.

The following TABLE exhibits a view of the counties in the State; the square miles in each; the number of towns; the seats of justice; the principal villages, &c.

Counties.	Square miles.	Number of towns.	Seats of justice.	Principal towns and villages.
Providence.	381	⁻0	Providence.	Providence, and Pawtucket vill.
Newport.	136	7	Newport.	Newport.
Bristol.	25	3	Bristol.	Bristol, and Warren village.
Kent.	186	4	E. Greenwich.	Greenwich, Apponaug and Pawtuxet villages.
Washington.	367	7	S. Kingston.	Wickford, Pawcatuck and Little RestHill villages.

Total 1095 square miles.

The natural features of this State are in some respects very peculiar. By casting a glance at the map, it will be perceived that the proportion which the waters bear to the land is much greater than in any other State in the Union; about one tenth part of the territorial limits of the State being water.

The continental part of the State possesses considerable uniformity, as it respects surface, soil and geological structure. There are no ranges of mountains in this section, or in any other part of the

State, nor any mountainous tracts; yet, with the exception of the immediate borders of Narragansett bay, and the Atlantic ocean, and some intervales upon the streams, it is somewhat of a rough country, being considerably hilly and rocky. This part of the State, exhibiting great uniformity, possesses a similar geological character; the rocks consisting of granite and other original formations. There are some level tracts upon the borders of Narragansett river, and some flats upon the shores of the Atlantic, in the southwest section of the State.

The most considerable eminences are Mount Hope, in Bristol, Hopkins' Hill, in West-Greenwich, and Woonsoket Hill, in Smithfield. There are also some hills of considerable elevation in Exeter. Rhode-Island, and most of the other islands in the Narragansett bay, disclose a geological structure, of the transition character, and present a surface generally undulating, and often highly picturesque and beautiful.

The mineral treasures of the State have not been explored by the lights of science, or the unerring hand of practical knowledge; but so far as they are known, they are not extensive or valuable. Iron ore is the most important mineral. It is found in Cranston, of an excellent quality, and in some other places in the county of Providence. Mineral coal is found at Portsmouth, upon Rhode-Island. Limestone abounds in the northeastern section of the State; and in these calcareous strata there are some excellent quarries of marble. Serpentine marble is also found at Newport; and there are in various places extensive quarries of freestone, valuable for building and other uses. Those in Johnston are the most important.

This State, considering the smallness of its dimensions, possesses ample resources for agricultural opulence. The soil, according to the operation of the established laws of nature, corresponding with the geological structure, exhibits considerable uniformity; being, in the continental section, generally, a primitive gravelly loam, which is deep, strong and fertile, but does not afford very great facilities of cultivation. It requires industry, and seems to bear the impress, illustrative of the justness of the declaration, that by the "sweat of the brow" man shall earn his bread. Upon Rhode-Island, the soil is of a shistic or slaty character, generally very fertile. In the county of Bristol, it is a rich garden mould; and in the northwestern section of the State there are some tracts possessing a soil which is hard, dry and sterile. There are some small tracts of sandy loam interspersed in various parts of the State, and some few pine plains. The proportion of alluvial is very inconsiderable; and there are no calcareous districts of any extent, and few argillaceous; although there are some small sections of the latter upon the borders of the rivers.

Natural and Agricultural Productions.—There are no extensive forests in the State; but what there are, are almost exclusively of the deciduous species of trees, of which, oak of the various kinds, chesnut and walnut are the most prevalent and important. There are, however, some small tracts of pine, and some of cedar. A great proportion of the forests are in the northwest section of the State, which affords a great supply of timber for ship building and other purposes. With the exception of some parts of the county of Newport, the forests are sufficient to supply the local demand both for timber and fuel. The islands in the Narragansett bay are mostly destitute of forest trees.

The agricultural productions of the State consist principally of the products of the grazing and dairy business. The counties of Washington and Newport will rank among the first grazing districts in the United States; the soil in these counties being generally a moist loam, which is deep, strong and fertile, affording abundant crops of grass and rich pasturage. These counties are distinguished for the extent and excellency of their dairies; they are also celebrated for their cattle and sheep. The farmers generally keep large stocks of valuable neat cattle, and have long paid great attention to the raising of sheep; and a peculiar and valuable breed of horses formerly were an object of considerable attention in the eastern section of Washington county. The various objects of the dairy business, and the raising of cattle and sheep, also form the leading agricultural interests in the northwestern section of the State.

Of the different kinds of grain cultivated, Indian corn, barley, oats and rye are principally attended to. Indian corn is cultivated in every part of the State, and barley extensively in the counties of Newport and Washington. The best townships for the cultivation of grain, are Middletown and Little-Compton, in Newport county; North and South-Kingston, in Washington county; Cranston, Smithfield and North-Providence, in Providence county; Warwick, in Kent county, and Barrington, in Bristol county. These and some other towns have a considerable proportion of arable land, which is well adapted to a grain culture, and is in a tolerable state of cultivation. In Bristol county, large quantities of onions are raised for exportation. In most sections of the State, the great convenience and value of fruit is duly appreciated, and is an object of proper attention. The most extensive and valuable apple orchards are in the towns of Smithfield, Johnston and Cranston, in Providence county; Middletown and Portsmouth, in Newport county; Warwick and Greenwich, in Kent county; and Hopkinton, in Washington county.

Waters.—The waters of Rhode-Island are abundant, and afford more extensive navigable advantages, than those of any other State in the Union. The Narragansett bay is one of the most beautiful sheets of water in the United States; is unrivalled for its navigable advantages, affording at all times a safe and ready communication with the ocean; and its shores, which are indented with innumerable bays and inlets, containing many excellent harbours. This bay also affords important advantages for the fishing business; it extends more than 30 miles into the interior of the State, and for this distance, affords superior advantages for ship navigation. The whole extent of the bay and river, from

Point Judith to Providence, is about 36 miles. The average breadth of the lower section of the bay is nearly ten miles; but the upper part is narrow. Exclusive of the islands, of which there are about fifteen in number, and some of considerable extent, the waters of the bay comprise an area of about 130 square miles. The principal harbours are Newport, which is one of the best in the world, Bristol, Providence, Wickford, Greenwich, Warren, Tiverton, Apponaug, Pawtuxet and Pawcatuck. These harbours afford facilities to the commercial interests of almost every part of the State.

The interior of the State is watered by numerous small rivers; the largest of which is the Seekonk, in the northeastern section. The principal branch of this river is the Pawtucket, a lively and valuable mill stream, affording numerous sites for hydraulic works, which are occupied to great extent. The Pawtuxet discharges its waters into the Narragansett, 5 miles below Providence. This stream is also distinguished for its numerous sites for mills and manufacturing establishments, and is unrivalled for the number of cotton factories erected upon it; there being forty upon this stream and its branches, and all within the distance of a few miles. This stream and its branches water a large proportion of the interior of the State. The Pawcatuck, which, near its mouth, is a considerable river, being navigable for vessels for five or six miles, together with its numerous branches, waters the southwestern section of the State. Its principal branches are the Wood and Charles rivers, which are convenient mill streams. The latter has its source in Warden's pond, a considerable body of water; besides which, there are numerous other fresh water ponds, which are generally well stored with fish.

The shores of the Narragansett bay, and the Atlantic border of the State, are indented with numerous inlets and salt water ponds, which are well stored with fish, and afford great facilities to the fishing business.

Climate.—Rhode-Island enjoys a salubrious climate, favourable to health and longevity. Being in the same parrallel of latitude, it corresponds with the climate of the State of Connecticut, in the vale of Connecticut river; although, perhaps, the islands and borders of the Narragansett bay may be somewhat milder. The winters in the maritime sections are evidently milder, and the seasons more uniform and temperate, than in the interior of New-England, in the same parrallel of latitude; and in these sections, the extreme heat of summer is allayed by the refreshing sea breezes. There is probably no section of the United States, that possesses a climate more favourable to health and human comfort, than the islands and borders of the Narragansett bay; and none, perhaps, affords a more agreeable residence, than some of the towns which line this beautiful sheet of water. Newport, from the salubrity of its climate, the beauty of its situation, and the various interesting objects and advantages which its maritime situation affords, is a place of extensive resort in the summer season, for the purposes of health and pleasure.

Roads and Bridges.—The roads of the State have been greatly improved within the last thirty years. In addition to the public roads, there are a number of good turnpikes, and several others in contemplation. Of these, the most important are a turnpike leading to Boston through Pawtucket village; one leading to Worcester county; one to Connecticut through Chepachet; one to Hartford, and one to Norwich. A turnpike is about to be constructed from Providence to Pawcatuck, and several other turnpikes are contemplated. There are good public roads from Providence to Bristol, Newport and Greenwich, and others in various parts of the State.

The most important and extensive bridge in the State is that which connects Portsmouth with Tiverton, at Howland's ferry. This bridge is constructed of stone, and is nearly 1000 feet in length. The next most important is Waybossett bridge, connecting the two divisions of the town of Providence. India and Central bridges across the Seekonk river, are considerable bridges. Besides these, there are numerous convenient bridges upon the different streams in every part of the State, affording to travelling and intercourse every facility and accommodation.

Fisheries.—The waters of the Narragansett, and its numerous bays, inlets and coves, afford a great variety of excellent and valuable fish, which in general are taken with great facility and success. The fishing business already employs considerable industry, and is capable of great extension. There are few sections in the United States which enjoy equal advantages for the fishing business; and by the direction of enterprise and industry to this channel, it might be rendered an important business, affording extensive employment, and become a source of great profit and wealth. The fishing business is carried on most extensively by the inhabitants of Block-Island, Wickford, Greenwich and Pawcatuck. At these places, considerable quantities are taken for exportation. Thirty-three boats, belonging to Block-Island, are engaged in the cod and mackerel fisheries. In addition to what are exported, large supplies are taken, not only at the aforesaid places, but by the inhabitants of all the towns and villages upon the shores of Narragansett bay and the borders of the Atlantic. These supplies comprise almost every variety of eatable fish, both of fin and shell, and contribute greatly to the means of subsistence, as well as to the luxuries of the table. The waters of the ocean form the great "common" of mankind, whose treasures are alike free to all.

Commerce and Navigation.—Although Rhode-Island is the smallest State in the Union, she claims a conspicuous rank, for mercantile industry and commercial enterprise. In no other State have the merchants engaged in foreign trade with more ardour, sagacity or intelligence; and no where have their efforts been crowned with greater success. Hence the immense accumulation of commercial capital in the maritime towns, which exceeds that of most other towns of their size. The foreign trade is not confined to any particular direction, but is carried on with almost every part of the world that offers a field for commercial enterprise. Considerable trade is carried on with the East Indies, South America, the Baltic and Mediterranean, and an extensive one with the island of Cuba. In addition to these, there is a brisk and profitable coasting trade maintained with the middle and southern States. The whole amount of tonnage belonging to the State, in 1819, was 39,044 tons, which is believed to be a greater amount, in proportion to the population, than is owned by any other State in the Union, with the exception of Massachusetts. There are now (1819,) about 670 mercantile stores of every description in the State ; a great number, for its size and population.

Manufactures.—In taking a view of the manufactures of this State, the cotton business claims the first attention. In the cotton manufacture, this, although the smallest State in the Union, ranks before any other. Considering the small beginning of this business and the difficulties which it has had to encounter, the progress which it has made and its present extension cannot but be regarded as a satisfactory evidence of its ultimate success, and must afford great gratification to the friends of American manufactures. Although it is nearly thirty years since the cotton spinning business was first commenced in this State, yet its progress, for a number of years, was extremely slow; and it did not receive much attention until about fifteen years ago. Since that period, although it has experienced various vicissitudes and several severe depressions, and at all times has had to contend with the most formidable foreign competition, supported by immense capitals, and aided by the general policy of the government, it has acquired a degree of maturity and importance, which authorize a belief that the business may be considered as permanently established. There are now more than 90 cotton mills or manufacturing establishments in the State. Many of these establishments are very extensive, and afford employment to a vast aggregate of industry ; some of them containing 6 or 7000 spindles. The fabrics manufactured at these establishments have become greatly improved within a few years, from experience and practical skill, and at present sustain not only a high reputation for their firmness of texture and durability, but also for the elegance of the style of manufacture. The amount of cotton goods manufactured at the various establishments in this State is immensely great, and constantly increasing. They are conveyed by land and water to most parts of the United States, and are constantly overcoming the prejudices of our citizens, and extending their reputation. Such is the condition of the cotton manufactures of this State, which yet are to be considered as in their infancy. As many, even at this time, are sceptical upon the subject of the permanent establishment of manufactures in this country, it may, perhaps, throw some light upon this subject, by comparing this view of the rise and progress of the cotton manufacture here with that of the same manufacture in Great-Britain. From the establishment of the first cotton mill propelled by water-power, by Sir Richard Arkwright, at Cromford, in Derbyshire, from the year 1771 to 1788, a period of 17 years, the number, in England, had increased only to 114. In Scotland, the first mill was erected in or about the year 1780; and in 1788 there were but 19. From these statements, it appears that the progress of the business was very slow in Great-Britain, for the first 17 years; and that, at this period, there were but few more water-power cotton mills in all England than there are now in Rhode-Island. When we consider the rapid extension which this business has received in Great-Britain, since 1788, forming at this time a great national interest, upon which a considerable proportion of the population of the country depends; may we not, without indulging the expectation of a progress equally rapid in this country, confidently rely upon the sure and steady advancement of this manufacturing interest, so important to our national prosperity and independence. If thirty years have produced such surprising results in Great-Britain, some of her largest towns having grown up with this business, may we not expect that the lapse of the same period will give to the manufactures of this country a vast extension; and that the manufacturing districts, particularly some sections of this State, will contain large and flourishing manufacturing towns, the seats of immense population, business and wealth. The woolen manufacturing business has received some attention in this State, although it holds but a very subordinate station, compared with the cotton business. There are at this time about 20 woolen foctories in the State, and 27 clothiers' works, for customers. Considerable attention is given to the various branches of the iron manufacture, in some sections of the State. There are three furnaces, one of which has been distinguished for the excellency of its castings, particularly cannon, two forges, three anchor shops and one gun factory. Considerable attention is also given to the manufacture of nails, scythes and some other articles in the iron business, in the northeastern section of Providence county. The distillation of spirit, both from domestic and foreign materials, is an important business in various parts of the State, particularly at Newport, where large quantities of rum are distilled for exportation. There are in all 12 rum distilleries, and several extensive gin distilleries. Ship building receives considerable attention in Providence, Newport, Bristol, Warren and Pawcatuck. The building of boats is carried on extensively in some sections of the State, particularly in Cumberland, where about 700 are annually made. As connected with the ship building and commercial interests, large quantities of cordage are manufactured in the commercial towns. The jewelry business receives great attention in Providence, where large quantities are manufactured for exportation. In Cumberland, there is an extensive marble manufactory, affording a great variety of articles for various uses, which are sent abroad for a market. The manufacture of lime is carried on extensively in Smithfield, and the products of the business are sent to various parts of the Union for a market.

In addition to the various manufacturing interests, there is a great amount of mechanical industry employed upon objects of general utility, and of domestic convenience and economy, particularly in the towns of Providence, Newport, Bristol, Warren and Pawtucket, and the villages in various parts of the State. There are in the State 140 grain mills and three paper mills.

Character of the Inhabitants.—From the necessary influence of moral causes, some of the most distinguishing traits of character in the inhabitants of this State can be traced to the circumstances attending the first settlement, and the peculiar opinions and prejudices of the first settlers. Among the characteristics most prominent, is that of the love of religious liberty, which pervades all classes. This just and liberal sentiment was implanted among the first settlers by the famous father and founder of the colony, the great apostle of religious liberty, Roger Williams. The Rev. Mr. Williams, and most of the first settlers of the colony, having been the victims of a spirit of religious persecution, which unfortunately prevailed in the colony of Massachusetts, adopted sentiments of great abhorrence of religious severity and intolerance, and a consequent respect for religious liberty and the rights of conscience. The spirit of religious liberty, which thus originated, and the existence of which was coeval with that of the colony, has been universally cherished, and at all times maintained an uninterrupted ascendency. The effects of this excellent and truly christian spirit have been most happy; it having secured to the State, from its first settlement to the present day, a degree of tranquillity and harmony among the various religious sects, which perhaps has not existed during the same period in any other community in Christendom. Was any wanted, this State would afford a satisfactory example of the salutary effects of legal and practical toleration in matters of religion and conscience. Another striking characteristic of the people of this State, which, however, they possess in common with their brethren of the other New-England States, is a spirit of enterprise and persevering habits of industry and economy. There is, perhaps, no community in the world, where the people exhibit more devotion to business, more intenseness of application, or more ardour and perseverance in pursuit of the various objects which occupy attention, than in Rhode-Island.

Enterprise is not checked from the want of objects. It opens new channels for business, and new fields for industry. The want of local advantages interposes no obstacles to its operations. These may be overcome by enterprise and industry; as in Holland, where the country itself has been almost rescued from the domains of the ocean, and where, although there is little or no grain raised, and no forests, there are innumereble distilleries and other manufactories, for which the country affords no facilities or advantages. The prosperity of a community does not so much depend upon the resources of the country, as it respects soil, waters, forests, &c. as upon the physical and moral resources of its inhabitants. Without the latter, the former are neglected and become useless; although it is evident. that when both are united, the results will be more important. This State possesses superior advantages as to navigable waters, and consequently for foreign trade; but its back country is very limited, affording but inconsiderable advantages for interior trade, which is generally considered as the support of foreign commerce. For manufactures, this State has some convenient waters or streams; but these give it no superior advantages, as like conveniences are to be found in most parts of our country. It is from the denseness and character of its population, that we are to account for its having become the seat of the cotton manufacture in America. It is that bold and active spirit of enterprise, and those indefatigable habits of industry, for which the people of this State are distinguished; which have originated, cherished, sustained, and which promise to bring to maturity this great and important national interest. It is with such a community, and such only, that manufactures can be maintained. Hence we conclude, that the influence of slavery, which produces the opposite of these characteristics and habits, will forever exclude manufactures from the southern States, and keep them dependent, even for the most common and necessary products of mechanical and manufacturing ingenuity and industry, upon the northern and middle States, or foreign countries. This will be one of the many evils of slavery.

Government.—The government of the State is, at the present time, founded on the provisions of the charter granted to the colony by Charles II, in 1663; being now the only State in the Union, which is without a written constitution of civil government.

The obligation of the charter, as a constitution of civil government, was necessarily abrogated by the declaration of independence, and the treaty of 1783, dissolving the political connexion of these colonies with Great-Britain. But by the common consent of the people, the form of the government, as established by the charter, has been preserved without any essential variation. The legislative power is vested in the General Assembly, consisting of two branches, the Senate and House of Representatives. The Senate consists of ten members, and the House of Representatives consists of two deputies or representatives from each town, with the exception of Providence, Portsmouth, Warwick and Newport; the three first of which are entitled to four representatives, and the last to six. The representatives are chosen semi-annually. The executive power is vested in a Governor; a Lieutenant Governor is also appointed, on whom this power devolves, in case of the office of Governor being vacated. The Governor and Lieutenant Governor have seats in the Senate.

There is a Treasurer, Secretary and Attorney General; who, together with the Governor and Lieutenant Governor, are chosen annually by the people or qualified electors of the State. There are annually two stated sessions of the legisature, in the months of May and October, and usually two adjourned sessions. The possession of a freehold is a necessary qualification to being admitted to the privilege of an elector.

The judicial power is vested in one supreme court, consisting of five Judges, whose jurisdiction extends throughout the State; the inferior or county courts, of which there is one in each county, comprising five Judges; and in single magistrates. Both the supreme and county courts hold two sessions annually in each county.

The municipal or local authority is vested in a town council, consisting of not less than five, nor more than seven freeholders, chosen annually by the freemen in their primary assemblies. This council possesses ample authority to manage the various concerns of the town, and to superintend all its local interests. The town council have also probate jurisdiction, and hear and determine all matters of a probate nature, which occur within their respective towns; an appeal being allowed in most instances to the higher courts. A town-clerk is annually chosen in each town, who is also clerk of the town council and of the probate court, and register of deeds for the town.

Institutions and Associations.—There are at the present time (1819) 33 incorporated banking institutions in this State, including the branch of the United States' Bank, at Providence. These banks are located as follows: seven at Providence, five at Newport, five at Bristol, three at Smithfield, two at Westerly, one at Warren, one at Pawtucket, one at Pawtuxet, one at Cranston, one at Gloucester, one at Burrellville, one at Scituate, one at Coventry, one at Greenwich, one at Wickford, and one at South-Kingston. Two of these institutions, one at Smithfield and one Bristol, have not yet commenced business.

The amount of banking capital here is doubtless much greater, in proportion to the population, than in any other State in the Union; although this excess is not as great as might be supposed, from the number of banks, as the banks of this State, possess, comparatively with those of most other States, but moderate capitals. The policy or expediency of extending the banking principle, so far as has been done in this State, and especially of doing this by the multiplication of institutions, as has been the case here, is at present, perhaps, to be regarded as problematical; as there may not as yet have been sufficient experience of this policy to authorize a satisfactory decision as to its utility. This State, we believe, affords the first example of a general distribution of banks, especially in agricultural places. It has been a common sentiment, that banking operations should be confined to commercial towns; but we see no good reasons for this opinion, which may, in some measure, owe its existence to the circumstance of the failure of some interior banks. But the operation of banks ought not to depend upon deposits, nor any other resource (as all others must be more or less precarious) than a substantial capital; and where this exists, it is difficult to conceive why banking operations cannot be as safely and as successfully carried on in an agricultural or manufacturing town as a commercial one, although the former may not admit of the same extent of business. The failure of interior banks has doubtless been owing to their having gone into operation without a specie capital. It is apparent that an agricultural district, of equal population and wealth with a commercial district, does not require the same extent of banking operations; yet, if monied institutions are considered as a convenience, and as contributing to the public prosperity, it is difficult to perceive the justness of that policy which would confine these advantages to particular sections, and to particular classes of citizens. The very appearance of a monopoly of privileges is objectional, and ought, as far as possible, to be avoided. This State is perhaps the only one which has attempted an experiment, as to the utility of the general distribution of banks; and so far as the trial has been made, it is believed that the result is satisfactory.

Besides the banking institutions, there are 10 Marine and Fire Insurance Companies, possessing, generally, ample capitals; six of which are in Providence, two in Newport, one in Bristol and one in Warren.

Militia.—The militia of the State are organized into one division, four brigades, and fourteen regiments; and, according to the last returns of the Adjutant-General, amount to 8350.

Population, &c.—The territorial limits of this State being very small, it became, at an early period, filled with inhabitants; and has, for the last fifty years, in common with the other New-England States, been a nursery for the western country, having afforded an immense number of emigrants. It has also furnished a large proportion of seamen; and the mercantile pursuits and habits, which extensively prevail, have occasioned considerable emigration to the commercial cities of the middle and southern States. From these causes, the increase of population, for the last fifty years, has been inconsiderable; although it is supposed that the rapid extension of the cotton spinning business, within the last ten years, has in some measure checked emigration, and promoted an increase of population. If this business continues to prosper, and receives that extension, which there is reason to expect, it must tend greatly to the increase of the population of the State. Rhode-Island contained, in the year 1730, 17,935 inhabitants; in 1774, 59,678; in 1782, 52,442; in 1790, 68,825; in 1800, 69,122; and in 1810, 76,931. The area of the State, exclusive of the waters, being estimated at 1095 square miles, gives a population of 70 to a square mile; so that this is unquestionably the most populous State, in proportion to its territorial limits, in the Union.

Literature, Primary Schools and Seminaries of Learning.—This State has not sustained a very high reputation for literature; and it has generally been considered, that what it possessed has been almost exclusively confined to the towns of Providence and Newport. How far this opinion may have been correct, at any former period, it is not necessary to inquire. It is, however, probable, that the subject of education, both in the higher and common branches, was formerly an object of less attention in this, than in most of the other New-England States. But, however education may have formerly been neglected, it is but just to observe, that for some years past it has received an increasing attention; and its importance seems to have been duly appreciated. Primary Schools have been established throughout the State, and perhaps are sufficiently numerous, and in general are under judicious and proper regulations. These schools are partly maintained by public contributions and partly by private subscription, from both of which sources sufficient pecuniary means are generally derived to afford them a good support. The whole number of primary schools in the State exceeds 250, which is a respectable number for its size, being more than eight to a town.

For instruction in the higher branches of education there are a number of seminaries established in different sections of the State. There are 12 or 13 academical Schools in the State; and it is gratifying to be able to add, that the number of academies is increasing; and as a consequence of this, that an attention to the higher branches of education is becoming more popular, and an object of more general attention. The number of young men who have received a college education has greatly increased within a few years, as appears from the increase of students, and the flourishing condition of Brown University. This institution, situated in a small State, and almost in the neighbourhood of two of the most distinguished Universities in the Union, in the two adjoining States, maintains a high reputation and a very respectable patronage, and is a very flourishing institution. For a description of it, the reader is referred to the article upon Providence.

Newspapers.—There are five newspapers printed in this State; three in Providence, of which two are semi-weekly papers, and two at Newport. These papers, it is understood, receive a respectable patronage; and there is an increasing taste among the people for newspaper reading; a circumstance, not altogether unimportant, as it respects the general improvement of society. The influence of newspaper publications, in "forming the public mind," not only upon political but upon moral, social, and, in some measure, upon scientifical subjects, by their contributing to create in the minds of youth a taste for reading, and a laudable desire for the acquisition of knowledge, is undoubtedly very great, and in general very salutary. The first newspaper printed in this State was the Rhode-Island Gazette, which was commenced in October 1732, at Newport; and the first paper published in Providence was in 1762.

Public and Social Libraries.—There are a number of extensive and valuable libraries in the State. The most ancient and important is that at Newport. This library, which was established as early as

1747, contains an extensive and valuable collection of ancient classical and theological books. There are several other valuable circulating libraries, and more than twenty social libraries, the most respectable and extensive of which is that of Providence; having a reading room connected with it. It is gratifying to learn, that the importance of the general distribution of books, as a means of disseminating knowledge, seems to be justly appreciated; and that there is a general disposition to encourage literary exertions; most useful publications having received a liberal patronage in this State. The diffusion of knowledge, from books and periodical publications, has the most happy influence upon society; as without these sources of improvement, it is impossible to overcome the stubbornness of ignorance, or to guard against rudeness of manners upon the one hand, or levity and frivolity upon the other.

Religion.—From the spirit of the people, the laws of this State have been remarkably liberal upon this subject; religion having from the first settlement been considered as a matter altogether abstract, and as no way connected with civil concerns. Under the influence of this just and fundamental opinion, the legislature has at all times disclaimed the right to interfere upon this subject; and consequently the laws have left religion where it always should be left, to stand upon its own foundation. In this respect, this State has made an important experiment, and affords an example of the justness of the principle which has been supported by some of the greatest and best men in the world, but unfortunately for a long time without any success, that Christianity will best answer the ends of its institution, and produce the most good in society, if left to itself. To the liberal character of the laws, and the prevailing spirit of the people, upon this subject, is in some measure to be attributed the great number of religious sects which for a long time have existed in this State. Of these sects, the Baptists have been and now are the most numerous, and the Friends or Quakers, the Congregationalists, the Episcopalians and the Methodists are numerous and respectable sects of Christians. Some of the Baptists profess the Arminian tenets, and others are of the Sabbatarian faith, and observe the seventh day, or the Jewish sabbath. Of the latter, the most numerous societies are in Hopkinton and Westerly. There are some few Unitarians; and it is supposed that this sect is increasing. There is one society of Moravians in Newport. All these different denominations have lived harmoniously together, each adhering to their own creed, and worshipping in their own way, but no one interfering in any way with the others. The clergy depend entirely upon individual contributions; yet it has been frequently and we believe very justly remarked, that they have generally received a very liberal support, and at all times maintained a suitable influence in society. The number of religious societies and churches has of late considerably increased. There are now more than 100 religious societies in the State, of every description, most of which are accommodated with houses for public worship.

History.—The design of this work admits only of a succinct notice of the most important historical events. An ample history of this State, to be written from authentic materials, is an object worthy the attention of any citizens of the State, possessing the necessary leisure and scientific acquirements for such an undertaking. Such is the perishable nature of human things, that facts, however important, are liable, even in a short period, to be partially lost; and the subjects with which they are connected, involved in great obscurity, unless they are collected and embodied, and recorded in a manner calculated to insure their preservation.

The country included within the limits of the State of Rhode-Island was originally principally occupied by the Narragansett tribe of Indians. This was one of the most numerous and powerful tribes that inhabited the coast of New-England. The Wamponogs inhabited the country of the eastern shore of the Narragansett. The precise period at which the Europeans became acquainted with the country upon the borders of the Narragansett, is not known; but it is believed, that it must have been soon after the first settlement at Plymouth. The first evidence that has been transmitted, of the Europeans having been acquainted with this country, is that of the murder of Captain Oldham at Block-Island, by the Indians, in 1635. The first permanent settlement appears to have been commenced in 1636, by the persecuted and celebrated Roger Williams. The Rev. Mr. Williams was forced to quit his family, in the greatest severity of the winter, and to flee from his persecutors into the wilderness, and seek an asylum among savages; by whom, it appears, he was received and treated with kindness and hospitality. In a short period, many others, who were obnoxious to the unfortunate spirit which prevailed in Massachusetts colony, followed the example of Mr. Williams; and a regular settlement was soon formed, which received constant accession, being an asylum for the persecuted and disaffected of every description. From these causes, the infant colony began to flourish at an early period, and soon became a nursery of the principles of religious liberty. Newport was settled in 1638, by Mr. Coddington and his associates. In 1643, Mr. Williams was sent to England, to obtain a charter for the civil government of the colony. In this object he succeeded, and the government was organized accordingly, and continued under the authority of this charter until the year 1663, when the famous charter of Charles 2d was granted, which has remained the basis of the government of the State until the present time. This charter contained only the outlines or form of the government, leaving the colony to adopt its own local regulations. As a matter of necessary consequence, the spirit of the people would show itself in their laws; and at an early period, the principles of religious liberty, and the rights of conscience were recognized and established, and have been ever since tenaciously maintained.

A considerable portion of the first settlers became Baptists, and this has ever since remained the most numerous denomination of christians in the State.

The colony continued to increase and flourish, and enjoyed comparatively a great portion of tranquillity, until the distressing Indian war, which was commenced in the year 1675, by the famous Indian sachem Philip, whose seat and residence was at Mount Hope. When the elements of war are once set in agitation, no human foresight nor prudence can guard against their extension. This war, which was by no means serious at first, being confined to a single tribe, was in its progress extended so as to embrace not only the Narragansetts, the most numerous and powerful tribe in New-England, but most of the other tribes in this region; it becoming a general war between all the European settlements, and with few exceptions, all the Indian tribes in New-England. From the threatening aspect of this war, uniting the hostility of almost all of the Indian tribes, the colonies were aroused to a sense of danger, and to great exertion. Accordingly, in December 1675, the famous Narragansett expedition was organized, consisting of a detachment of troops from the several New-England colonies. This expedition terminated, after a most desperate and obstinate engagement, in the capture of the Indian fortress, and nearly the entire destruction of their forces. This battle was fought on the 19th of December, and was the most sanguinary, as well as the most successful and important, that ever occured in the early wars with the natives. The troops of the colonies fought with the most desperate resolution and bravery, and sustained a severe loss; the Massachusetts forces having 31 killed and 79 wounded; and the Connecticut troops had 91 killed and wounded, among whom were seven distinguished officers.

Notwithstanding the severe loss of the Indians in this battle, it being estimated that 700 warriors were killed, and that about 300 died afterwards of their wounds, the war was not terminated until 1677; although Philip, who first engaged in it, and who instigated the other tribes to hostilities, was killed 12th of August, 1676. After the close of this war, this colony did not participate much in the subsequent wars with the Indians and French, owing principally to the circumstances of the colony's not being exposed, and the character of the inhabitants, a considerable proportion of them being Friends.

In the revolutionary war, this State took an active part; having at an early period disclosed a spirit of resistance to the unwarrantable acts of authority of the British government, and a determination to defend the rights of the colonies. She furnished, from the commencement to the close of the contest, her full quota of men; and her soldiers, for bravery and perseverance, ranked among the first in the Union. She had the honour also to afford a number of excellent officers, at the head of whom was Gen. Nathaniel Green, one of the most distinguished officers of the age. This State suffered severely during this war; her capital was for a long time in the possession of the enemy; and at the peace, its population was 3,769 less, than at the commencement of the war; the loss of property was also immense, and its business had almost entirely declined. Subsequently to the peace, every kind of business here, as well as in most of the other States, experienced great languor, and a general state of embarrassment and distress ensued. Commerce having been diverted from its former channels, and suffering from the general embarrassment, could not recover its activity. Anxious to alleviate this distress, the legislature had recourse to some miserable temporary expedients, which increased the evils they were intended to remedy, and public and private confidence became nearly destroyed; which, however, were restored by time, the great corrective of all sublunary evils.

Rhode-Island was the last of the original States which acceded to the constitution of the United States, which was not ratified until the 26th of May, 1790. The first bank was incorporated in 1791; since which, they have increased to 33. In 1804, the cotton spinning business first became an object of much attention in this State. In September, 1815, a tremendous gale occured, which did much damage to the towns upon the waters of the Narragansett bay. This State has had the honour of being the first in the Union, to repeal or modify its laws upon the subject of usury; thus affording an example of an enlightened policy, and a boldness of legislation; being the first to expunge from its statute book, laws founded in the prejudices of a barbarous age, and which are alike a violation of the principles of justice, and repugnant to sound policy.

A

TOPOGRAPHICAL AND STATISTICAL VIEW

OF THE SEVERAL COUNTIES, TOWNS AND VILLAGES

IN THE STATE OF

RHODE-ISLAND.

PROVIDENCE COUNTY.

PROVIDENCE, the most extensive and populous county in the State, is situated in its northern section; bounded on the north by the counties of Worcester and Norfolk, in Massachusetts, on the east by Bristol county, in Massachusetts, on the south by the county of Kent and the Narragansett river, and on the west by the State of Connecticut.

Its average length, from east to west, is nearly 22 miles, and its mean breadth, from north to south, is more than 17 miles; comprising an area of about 381 square miles.

The following TABLE exhibits a statistical and topographical view of the several towns in the county; their situation, with relation to Providence; population, according to the census of 1810; number of dwelling-houses; religious societies; schools; banks, and post-offices.

Towns.	P. O.	Pop.	D. H.	R. S.	S.	B.	Dist. from
Providence.	1	10,071	1300	8	5	7	Providence.
Burrellville.	0	1,834	300	2	10	1	20 m. N. W.
Cumberland.	1	2,110	309	4	9	0	8 m. N. E.
Cranston.	1	2,161	320	4	6	1	5 m. S. W.
Gloucester.	1	2,310	400	2	12	1	10 m. N. W.
Foster.	1	2,613	400	3	10	0	15 m. W.
Johnston.	0	1,516	233	2	7	0	5 m. W.
North-Providence.	1	1,758	316	3	8	1	4 m. N.
Scituate.	1	2,568	400	2	7	1	12 m. W.
Smithfield.	1	3,828	500	4	20	3	9 m. N.

The county of Providence is generally an uneven country; and some sections of it present very rugged features, being rocky and hilly; but no portion of it can be considered as mountainous.

Its geological character, especially in the western section, is primitive. The prevailing rocks are granitic. There are, however, some calcareous strata, or limestone, particularly in the northeastern section; and transition rocks are occasionally interspersed. The soil is generally a primitive, gravelly loam; but there are some sections of calcareous loam, some tracts of alluvial, in the southeast section, near the head waters of the Narragansett, and some small sections of plains, of a siliceous sand.

The mineralogy of the county is but imperfectly understood, having received but little attention. Iron ore of different qualities has been found in various places. The celebrated Hope furnace is supplied with ore of an excellent quality from this county. There are some indications of copper ore in some sections of the county. Limestone abounds in various places, and marble is found in these calcareous strata.

The forests of the county are considerably extensive, and the quality of the timber very excellent. The trees are principally deciduous; the most prevalent and valuable of which are oak, walnut and chesnut; but the forests comprise various others common to this region. Timber near the sea is observed to be firmer and less porous than that in the interior.

The principal agricultural interests arise from the grazing business; this being a leading system of husbandry. Considerable attention however is paid to the cultivation of grain, particularly Indian corn; barley and rye also are cultivated. The soil and climate are favourable for fruit; and there are many excellent orchards in some sections of the county. In the vicinity of Providence, considerable attention is paid to the cultivation of culinary vegetables, for the market at that place.

The agricultural interests of the county cannot be considered as very flourishing; although recently a spirit of improvement has disclosed itself, and has already produced valuable results in the important business of husbandry.

The extensive commercial and manufacturing interests of this county may have in some measure diverted the attention and industry of the inhabitants from agricultural pursuits.

The waters of the county are abundant, and afford many conveniences and advantages. Upon the southern border, are the waters of the Narragansett river and bay, which afford a safe and capacious harbour, and give great facilities to commerce and navigation.

In addition to the Providence or Narragansett river, are the Seekonk, which washes a part of the eastern border of the county, and its principal branch, the Pawtucket, which has also several branches. This is a valuable and interesting mill stream, almost unrivalled.

The next most considerable stream is the Pawtuxet, which forms a part of the southern boundary, and has its principal sources in this county. The Wanasquatucket and Mashasuck are valuable and interesting mill streams, affording numerous excellent sites for mills, manufacturing establishments and hydraulic works of every description, which are generally occupied. These streams discharge their waters into Providence Cove.

The commercial interests of this county are extensive, and are principally confined to the town of Providence; which, for commercial enterprise, activity and business, maintains a pre-eminent rank. Providence carries on a trade with almost every part of the civilized world. But the most important and extensive branches consist of a trade to the East-Indies, with the island of Cuba, and a coasting trade with the southern States, consisting principally of the exportation of the manufactures of the county, and the importation of cotton and some other southern staples.

But notwithstanding the commercial importance of Providence, the great interest for which this county is distinguished, and which seems destined to render it one of the most important and wealthy sections of the United States, is the cotton manufacture. When we consider that it is but about fifteen years since this business first received its principal impulse, the inauspicious circumstances under which it was commenced, the difficulties which it has had to encounter, from the want of practical knowledge, the prejudice which existed, the opposition from interest, arising from established commercial relations, the unequal competition which it has had to sustain with the British manufacturing interests; when we consider these and other circumstances, it must be a matter of surprise, that it has acquired the importance, and grown to the extent that it has. If the short and inauspicious period of a few years has produced such results, what may not be expected in half a century? Notwithstanding all the difficulties which have been experienced, there is no example in any other country, of a manufacturing interest, unaided by the power or resources of government, having grown to such importance in so short a period. This county and vicinity, having taken the lead of all other places in the Union, in the cotton manufacture, it is here that we must look for the Manchesters and Boltons of America; and Providence will thence become another Liverpool, the great depot of manufactures, which will be exported to every part of America, and to foreign countries. These views may be thought sanguine, but we trust that they are authorized by the example of England and other manufacturing nations, and the known enterprise and industry of our citizens. There are now 52 cotton factories in this county, of which a large proportion are upon an extensive scale, and are now in operation. Experience has greatly improved the skill necessary in the business; and cotton goods are now made, which, for style of manufacture, are scarcely inferior to British fabrics, whilst their texture is much more firm and substantial. This business at the present time employs a vast amount of capital, and an immense aggregate of industry.

Another important department of manufacturing industry is the jewelry business, which is carried on extensively in Providence. The iron manufacture is also of considerable importance, particularly the casting business, which is carried on extensively at the Hope furnace. Here, many of the cannon belonging to the navy of the United States were cast. There are also several nail factories, where considerable business is carried on. In some sections of the county, large quantities of lime are manufactured, which are sent abroad for a market. There is also an extensive marble factory in Cumberland, where large quantities of marble are manufactured for various uses, which are sent to Providence, Boston and other places for a market. The marble is obtained from the lime rock quarry in Smithfield. In Cumberland, the boat building business is carried on extensively. There are 19 shops engaged in the business; and about 700 boats are built annually.

The woolen manufacture receives some attention, there being 9 woolen factories in the county, and 13 cloth dressing establishments, for customers. There are in the county, 58 grain mills and 311 mercantile stores. There are 34 religious Societies of every description, 94 schools, which are provided with houses, 11 social libraries and 15 incorporated banks.

The population of the county, in 1790, amounted to 24,391; in 1800, to 25,854; and in 1810, to 30,769.

PROVIDENCE.

PROVIDENCE, an ancient, populous and wealthy commercial post township, and semi metropolis of the State, is situated in the southeastern section of the county, on the eastern border of the State, in north lat. 41° 51', and 71° 10' west lon., 30 miles north by west of Newport, 42 miles southwest of Boston, and about 70 miles east of Hartford, at the head of navigation, on the Narragansett or Providence river.

Providence is bounded on the north by North-Providence, on the east by the Seekonk river, which separates it from the State of Massachusetts, on the south by the Narragansett river and the town of Cranston, and on the west by Johnston.

Its average length, from east to west, may be about 4 miles, and its mean breadth more than 2 miles, comprising an area of about 9 square miles.

The town is divided into two nearly equal sections, by the Providence river and cove. The eastern section is generally elevated; and the geological structure and soil of a primitive character, the prevailing rocks being granite, and the soil a gravelly loam, considerably fertile, and very suitable for horticulture and the objects of husbandry, that invite attention in the vicinity of a market town. The

PROVIDENCE.

western section presents different geological features, being part marine alluvial, and part light sandy plains.

The waters of the town are abundant, and afford many conveniences, its eastern border being washed by the Seekonk, and most of its southern border by the Narragansett river, and the town intersected by the Providence cove and river, which form a capacious and excellent harbour, admitting of vessels of the greatest burthen. There is an extensive cove, which unites the waters of the Wanasquatucket and the Mashasuck, two convenient and interesting mill streams. Besides the great bridge, which unites the two sections, there are two convenient bridges across the Seekonk; one called the India bridge, and the other the Central bridge, in the eastern section of the town.

The fisheries of Providence are chiefly confined to the supplying the home consumption. The river and cove afford a tolerable supply both of fin and shell fish of the different kinds usually taken in the harbours and streams in New-England.

Providence is well accommodated with roads, affording great facilities to intercourse abroad. There is a turnpike road leading to Boston, called the Pawtucket turnpike; one leading to Worcester, called the Douglass turnpike; one to Connecticut, by the way of Gloucester; one to Hartford, thro' Scituate, and one to Norwich, thro' the same place. There are also good and convenient roads to Bristol, Greenwich and Taunton. A turnpike road is also in contemplation, to lead from this place to Pawcatuck, and thence to Stonington. Besides these, there are various other roads, all of which afford great facilities for travelling and intercourse, with an extensive interior country, rich in the resources of agricultural opulence and manufacturing industry.

The navigation and commercial interests of Providence are very important, and have been constantly increasing with the growth of the town, from its earliest settlement. The natural advantages of this place for commercial pursuits are considerable. But the extensive developement of its commercial interests, and its steady and growing prosperity, have proceeded principally from the enterprise and industry of the inhabitants. There are few towns in the United States where the merchants have been more distinguished for their intelligence, enterprise, industry and perseverance, than those of this town, or where commercial enterprise and exertions have been attended with more successful results. The idea of commerce has long been associated with that of wealth; and this may be true, in a local sense, although false, as applicable to a nation. The useful commerce of a nation is limited by the amount of its exports; and consequently its extent does not depend upon the capital and industry which it can command, but upon the aggregate enterprise and industry which are employed at home. But local advantages for business, abundant capital, and extraordinary commercial enterprise, may produce, for a single town, the most important and beneficial results. And hence Providence exhibits great commercial prosperity, and possesses an aggregate of wealth, which, perhaps, is not surpassed by any town of its size in the Union. Providence carries on a trade with most parts of the world; but, for some years past, the East-India trade has been the most important and extensive. There is supposed to be about 5000 tons of shipping employed in this trade. Next to this, the most important branches of foreign trade are a trade with the Baltic and north of Europe, and a trade with the island of Cuba. There is an active and extensive coasting trade carried on with the southern States, connected principally with the cotton business. There are 5 or 6000 tons of shipping supposed to be employed in this trade. The whole amount of shipping owned in Providence, in 1805, was 14,856 tons; and at the present time (1819) it amounts to 19,000 tons, and is constantly increasing. There are about 10 vessels constantly employed in the exportation of the products of the cotton manufactories in the vicinity of Providence. There are also a great number of packets, which ply constantly between Providence and Newport, Bristol, Warren, and the numerous villages on the shores of the Narragansett.

There are, in Providence, about 40 houses concerned in navigation, 20 wholesale and retail Dry Goods Stores, 10 houses engaged wholly in the sale of domestic Goods, 30 wholesale Grocery Stores, and 140 retail Grocery, Provision & Crockery Stores, 11 Druggists' Stores, 10 Jewelry and Watch makers' Stores, 6 Hard-ware Stores, 2 wholesale Crockery Stores, 4 Book Stores. 3 Paper Hanging Stores, 10 Shoe Stores, 6 Hat Stores and 3 Confectionary Shops or Stores.

The commercial interests of Providence are, to a certain extent, different from those of any other place in the United States; being connected with, and supported by the manufacturing interests in its immediate vicinity. The manufacture of cotton, in the neighbourhood of Providence, although it did not receive much attention, until about fifteen years since, now forms an important and growing interest, employing a vast capital, developing a new field for enterprise, and new sources of industry. Some idea can be formed of the progress of this business, from the fact, that in this short period, the cotton factories situated in this State, and in the adjoining States of Connecticut and Massachusetts, near the borders of this State, so that the business of all of them is principally transacted in Providence, have multiplied to the astonishing number of more than 100. From this view of the extension which has already been given to the cotton manufacture, it is evident, that if this business can be sustained, and continues to prosper, Providence must become a great depot of manufactures; and will, at no distant period, maintain the character in the United States that Liverpool does in England. And it is believed, that the success of this manufacture is no longer problematical; the practical knowledge which has been acquired, and the improvements which have been made, the results of experience, the high reputation which the fabrics have acquired, the favourable change which has taken place in the sentiments and habits of our citizens, and the trying vicissitudes and depressions which the business has encountered, seem to authorize the belief, that it has survived the crisis, and that it will become a permanent, extensive and important interest, affording both individual and national wealth and independence. The various interests and concerns, connected with the manufacture of cotton, already contribute greatly towards the business of this town. The importation of cotton, the exportation of the manufactures, vending of them at home, transportation, &c. have already become important and extensive branches of business. There are 5 Cotton Factories in this town, 2 Bleaching establishments and 3 Dye-houses. There are 2 Woolen Factories, 4 Rum Distilleries, 1 Gin Distillery, 1 Paper Mill, 1 Grain Mill, 1 Oil Mill, 2 Clothiers' works, 3 Rope walks and 2 Spermaceti works.

There is considerable ship-building carried on in Providence; but the most important manufacturing interest, next to that of cotton, is the jewelry business. There are 10 shops or manufactories engaged in this business, at most of which, large quantities of goods, of almost every description, in the jewelry line, are manufactured for exportation.

Providence is only a town corporation. The most compact part of it is divided into two nearly equal sections, by Providence river, which are connected by a bridge. It is built on about 50 streets, of which, the principal is Main-street, extending from Constitution hill to the lower part of the town. This street has a serpentine direction, and runs parallel with the river and cove, nearly through the town, in a northerly and southerly direction. An extension of this street, in the lower part of the town, is called Broadway. On Main-street, stand a number of the public buildings, and a considerable proportion of the stores and offices. This is the most ancient and populous street in the town, and in general is well built, and comprises a number of stately, elegant and durable brick edifices. Market-square extends from this street to the bridge, which connects the two divisions of the town.

Next to Main-street, the two most important streets are Waybossett and Westminster. The former has a serpentine direction, and is very populous. It branches from Westminster-street, near the bridge, and unites with it at Highstreet. This is a very active and busy street, possesses great wealth, a dense population, and is the seat of a considerable proportion of the commercial business of the town. Westminster-street extends in a direct line to High-street, is well built and populous, and comprises a number of stores. East Waterstreet, which has been principally built since the memorable gale, in September 1815, is the seat of extensive commercial business. Benefit-street is an elevated and prospective situation, to the east of Main-street. There are numerous other streets, many of which are well built and populous. Extensive improvements have been made upon the river, since the September gale, in 1815. Many additional wharves have been constructed, and existing ones enlarged and repaired. The general appearance of Providence is that of a growing, wealthy and flourishing commercial town, distinguished for its activity, diversity, and extent of business.

There are, in Providence, at this time, about 1300 Dwelling-houses, and more than 1000 other buildings. There are about 245 Mercantile establishments of every description, and 12 Public Inns.

Providence abounds with monied institutions. It possesses 7 Banks, viz. Providence Bank, having a capital of 422,000 dollars; Exchange Bank, with a capital of 400.000 dollars; Roger Williams Bank, with a capital of 150,000 dollars; Union Bank, with a capital of 250,000 dollars; Merchants' Bank, having a capital of 300,000 dollars; Eagle Bank, with a capital of 100,000 dollars, and a branch of the United States Bank.

There are 6 Insurance Companies; Washington Insurance Company, having a capital of 132,000 dollars; Peace Insurance Company, capital 70,000 dollars; Union Insurance Company, Eagle Insurance Company, capital 45,000 dollars; Columbian Fire Insurance Company, capital 100,000 dollars; and Mutual Fire Insurance Company. There are 15 Auctioneers and 1 Exchange-office.

There are, in Providence, 4 Printing-offices, 3 Newspaper establishments, 1 Public Library with a reading room connected with it, 5 Public Schools, which are well supported, and comprise usually about 1000 scholars. These schools are under judicious regulations, provided with good instructors, and, in general, well conducted, as primary schools. Besides these, there are a number of good private schools, for the instruction of both sexes, and some for the higher branches of learning. There is a charity school for people of colour, which is well attended.

Of the more important institutions of learning, there are 2 Academies, which are respectable and flourishing seminaries, and 1 University. An Academy also has recently been established by the Society of Friends. It is accommodated with a neat and commodious building, provided with good instructors, and is said to be very flourishing. Brown University, one of the most flourishing and respectable institutions in the United States, is located in this town. The College edifice is situated in Prospect-street, and has a very elevated and prospective site. It is a brick structure of 150 feet by 46, is four stories high, has 48 rooms for students, and eight large rooms for public uses. This institution was originally established at Warren, in 1764, and was removed to Providence in 1770. The present name of this institution was bestowed upon it, as a mark of respect to its principal benefactor. The President and majority of the Trustees are required to be of the Baptist denomination. The College authority consists of the President, Professors and Tutors. There are eight professorships; one of Mathematics and Natural Philosophy, one of Law, one of

Moral Philosophy and Metaphysics, one of Oratory and Belles-lettres, one of Anatomy and Surgery, one of Materia Medica and Botany, one of the theory and practice of Physic, and one of Chemistry. There are three Tutors. There is a valuable library belonging to the institution, of about 4000 volumes; in addition to which, a donation has recently been made by the late Rev. William Richards, of Lynn, in England, of 1200 volumes. The philosophical apparatus is extensive and complete. The number of students at the present time (1819) is about 126. There is a Grammar School connected with this institution, which comprises about 30 students.

There are, in Providence, 8 Religious Societies; 3 of Congregationalists, 2 of Baptists, 1 of Episcopalians, 1 of Friends, and 1 of Methodists. These several Societies are accommodated with houses for public worship, some of which are stately and elegant. The first Congregational church is a spacious stone edifice, constructed and finished in a style of great taste and elegance, and is a fine specimen of the arts. It stands on Benefit-street, and has an interesting and prospective situation. The first Baptist church, situated in Main-street, is a stately and superb edifice, very spacious; being about 80 feet square. The Episcopal church, situated also upon Main-street, is a large and elegant stone structure. Besides the churches, the public buildings consist of a Court house, Market house, Town house, a Theatre, a Gaol and Hospital.

The government of the town of Providence is vested in a Board, called the Town Council, consisting, usually, of five members, who are chosen annually by the people in their primary assemblies. One of the members officiates as president of the council. This town council possesses extensive and various powers; the police or internal concerns of the town being entirely entrusted to them. They have the care and direction of the town poor, or paupers, and the various concerns of the town. The annual expenditures of the town are about $25,000, inclusive of some appropriations for public improvements. The ordinary disbursements are principally for the maintenance of the town paupers, the support of the public schools, and maintaining and superintending the internal police of the town. The revenue is derived from direct taxes, licenses to retailers, and some other sources of indirect revenue.

History.—Providence was first settled in 1636, by that distinguished advocate of religious liberty, Roger Williams, and four associates. Mr. Williams was banished for heresy, by the government of the colony of Massachusetts, and was obliged to leave his family and connections in Salem, during the inclement season of winter, and seek an asylum in the wilderness, and among savages. He accordingly retired to Providence, then a frightful wilderness, and the abode of wild beasts and savages; who, however, were more humane than his persecutors, and received him with kindness and hospitality.

He purchased of the Indians a tract of land, and laid the foundation of the present town of Providence, which he appropriately named, regarding his preservation as the result of a providential interposition. The infant colony soon began to flourish, and exhibited great increase of numbers, which was in some measure the effect of the mistaken spirit of religious intolerance, which prevailed in the Massachusetts colony. Almost with the very commencement of the colony, very liberal and ample provisions were made for the security of religious liberty and the rights of conscience; so that the seeds of the principles of religious liberty, having been thus early implanted, have taken deep root, and produced, in each succeeding age, the salutary fruits of charity, peace, harmony, and a spirit of toleration, in matters of religion. The name of Roger Williams will be enrolled among the most early and distinguished founders of religious liberty. Mr. Williams became a Baptist, a short time after the commencement of the settlement of Providence, and was the principal founder of the first Baptist church. Providence suffered considerably in the Indian war of 1675, but has experienced few extraordinary vicissitudes or calamities, with the exception of the memorable gale, which occurred in Sep. 1815. This gale will long be remembered, as one of the most extraordinary and calamitous that was ever witnessed in New-England. It occurred on Saturday the 23d of September. A most furious storm commenced in the morning, the wind being in a southeasterly direction. Between 8 and 9 o'clock, the tide rose 12 feet higher than the usual spring tides; and, overflowing the usual barriers, the water rushed into the town, spreading devastation and ruin in every direction. The vessels were principally forced from their moorings, and driven with irresistible fury into the streets, or stranded at the upper end of the cove. The great bridge connecting the two sections of the town was swept away, and most of the wharves were destroyed. The water was precipitated with astonishing velocity and force, into the centre of the town, overturning stores, ware-houses, dwelling-houses and other buildings, sweeping their contents into the streets or the great cove. One church was entirely demolished. The whole town presented a scene of devastation and ruin; vessels, buildings, furniture and merchandize being thrown together in confusion and disorder; the expectations of youth, the reliance of age, and the industry of years, being, in some instances, swept away in a moment—a scene, solemn and impressive, affording the most conspicuous example of the weakness and impotence of man, and of his dependence upon "him who rides upon the wind, and directs the storm." The loss sustained by individuals was estimated at nearly a million and a half of dollars.

Biography. The Hon. *Stephen Hopkins*, a distinguished patriot and statesman, was a native of that part of Providence which now forms the town of Scituate. He was born in March 1707. In his youth, he disclosed high promise of talents, and soon became esteemed for his growing worth, his early virtues, and his regular and useful life. At an early period, he was appointed a Justice of the peace, was employed extensively in the business of surveying lands, and was appointed to various other offices, some of which were responsible and important; and he discharged the duties of all, with great ability and faithfulness, and with equal advantage to his own reputation and the public interest. In 1754, he was appointed a member of the board of commissioners, which assembled at Albany, to digest and concert a plan of union for the colonies. Shortly after this, he was chosen Chief Justice of the Superior Court of the colony of Rhode-Island; and in 1755, he was elevated to the office of chief magistrate of the colony, and continued in this dignified and important station about eight years, but not in succession. He was also for several years chancellor of the College. At the commencement of the difficulties between the colonies and Great Britain, Gov. Hopkins took an early, active and decided part in favour of the former. He wrote a pamphlet, in support of the rights and claims of the colonies, called "the Rights of the Colonies examined," which was published by order of the General Assembly. He was a member of the immortal Congress of '76, which declared these States, (then colonies) to be "free, sovereign and independent;" and his signature is attached to this sublime and important instrument, which has no example in the archives of nations.

Gov. Hopkins was not only distinguished as a statesman and patriot, but as a man of business; having been extensively engaged in trade and navigation, and also concerned in manufactures and agriculture. He was a decided advocate, and a zealous supporter, both of civil and religious liberty, a firm patriot, a friend to his country, and a patron of useful public institutions. He possessed a sound and discriminating mind, and a clear and comprehensive understanding; was alike distinguished for his public and private virtues, being an able and faithful public officer, and an eminently useful private citizen.

Gov. Hopkins finished his long, honourable and useful life, on the 20th July, 1785, in the 79th year of his age.

Dr. *Benjamin West*, a celebrated mathematician and astronomer, was for many years a resident of this town. He was born in Rehoboth, in Massachusetts, in the year 1730. Dr. West was entirely self taught. The scientific eminence to which he attained was the result of his vigorous native genius, and indefatigable application and perseverance. In early life, his advantages for obtaining an education were extremely limited; and he was also for a long period in very indigent circumstances. The obstacles, therefore, which circumstances threw in his way to the attainment of literary distinction, were of the most formidable nature; having to contend not only with the difficulties arising from the want of early opportunities and instruction, but subject to all the privations and embarrassments inseparable from poverty; and obliged to devote almost his whole time and attention, to procure a subsistence. But all these obstacles, as great as they were, were not sufficient to discourage him in his favourite pursuit, or to check the vigour of his mind; and under these embarrassments and difficulties, he made great progress in mathematics, which was his favourite science, and made extensive and solid acquisitions in general knowledge.

About the year 1753, he removed to Providence, where he opened a school; which, however, after some time, he relinquished, from an expectation of improving his pecuniary circumstances, and engaged in mercantile pursuits. While in this occupation, he opened the first book-store established at Providence. He continued in this business until the commencement of the revolutionary war, when his affairs having become embarrassed, he was obliged to retire from commercial business entirely, and seek some other employment for the support of his numerous family. While in commercial pursuits, he found some leisure, and pursued with great ardour his favourite study, the mathematical sciences. About the year 1763, he commenced the publication of an almanac, the astronomical calculations being designed for the meridian of Providence; and continued this publication annually, until about the year 1793. In or about the year 1766, he calculated an almanac for the meridian of Halifax; and he continued annually to furnish a copy of an almanac calculated for this meridian, until near the close of his life, in 1812, with the exception of a short period, during the revolutionary war. The transit of the planet Venus, which occurred on the 3d of June, 1769, and that of Mercury, which happened in November following, afforded him a favourable opportunity of establishing a more conspicuous reputation, as a mathematician and astronomer. As early as 1766, he made some very judicious observations upon a comet that appeared that year, which he communicated to Professor Winthrop of Cambridge.

He also furnished a communication for the Royal Society of London, on the subject of the aforesaid transit of the planets Venus and Mercury. About this period, the reputation which he had acquired led him to a correspondence with some of the most distinguished scientific characters in our country, upon various mathematical & astronomical subjects. In 1770, he received the honorary degree of Master of Arts from Cambridge College. During the revolutionary war, Dr. West was a zealous patriot; and Providence being a depot for military stores and supplies, for the American army, he was engaged in manufacturing clothing, for the public or continental troops, and continued in this occupation during most of the war. During this period, also, he persevered in his mathematical inquiries, with unabated ardour, and frequently favoured the public with the result of his investigations. In 1781, he was unanimously elected a member of the American Academy of Arts and Sciences, and received their diploma. Soon after this, he resumed his former occupation of instructing a school, and continued in this employment until 1786, when he was elected a Professor of Mathematics and Astronomy, in Rhode-Island College; but did not enter upon the discharge of the duties of his professorship, until 1788. During this interval, he officiated as Professor of Mathematics, in the Protestant Episcopal Academy at Philadelphia. Whilst here, he enjoyed the society, esteem and friendship of the first scientific characters in this metropolis; among whom were the immortal Franklin and Rittenhouse. In 1788, he entered upon the duties of his professorship; and at the commencement, in 1792, the degree of Doctor of Laws was conferred upon him, for his distinguished services to science and society. He continued in the situation of Professor of Mathematics and Astronomy, and discharged its important duties with great ability, and with equal credit to himself and advantage to the institution, until 1799, when he retired from a station to which he had imparted more honour than he had derived from it. In 1802, in consequence of his distinguished reputation and important services, he was appointed Post-master, at Providence. In this situation, he remained until his death, 13th August, 1813, in the 83d year of his age.

The life of Dr. West affords a conspicuous example, how much success, even in the higher objects of pursuit, depends upon ourselves; of the important results of persevering application, and that native genius, unassisted and without a guide to direct its course, is capable of overcoming all obstacles, and of attaining to the summit of human knowledge. Although Dr. West never attained to that distinguished pre-eminence in society, to which, from his genius, his learning and his patriotism, he was entitled, yet he acquired a distinction more novel and important, the reputation of being a mathematician, a philosopher, a patriot, a useful citizen and an honest man.

The gallant and much lamented Capt. *William Henry Allen,* a distinguished naval officer, who was mortally wounded on board the Argus sloop of war, in the action of the 14th August, 1813, in which the Argus was overpowered by a superior force, was a native of this town. He was the son of Gen. William Allen, a brave and distinguished revolutionary officer, and was born 21st October, 1784. In the morning of life, when the vigorous intellect of manhood had scarcely begun to expand from its germ, he disclosed the " bent of his mind," an uncommon ardour for distinction, and love of virtuous fame. At this early period, also, he discovered a surprisingly inquisitive mind, and a romantic inclination to visit foreign countries, and to become acquainted with the variety of character and manners, the result of different political and religious institutions, and various other moral causes, which belongs to the human family. It was from the influence of these dispositions and views, that he determined upon entering into the naval service of his country, which he accordingly did, in the month of May, 1800, in the capacity of a midshipman. In the month of August following, he embarked on board the frigate George Washington, commanded by Capt. Campbell, and sailed for Algiers. Under the instructions, and from the examples of this excellent officer, Capt. Allen made astonishing proficiency in naval tactics, and secured the confidence and esteem of his superior officers, and the approbation of his government. On the reduction of the navy, in 1801, Capt. Allen was retained in the service; and having previously arrived in America, he soon after embarked on board the frigate Philadelphia, for another cruise to the Mediterranean; and during this cruise, he visited Constantinople. He made several subsequent voyages to the Mediterranean, in the capacity of a midshipman, and had an excellent opportunity to gratify his curiosity and taste, by viewing the romantic and classical shores of the Mediterranean. In all these voyages, Mr. Allen conducted himself with propriety and fidelity, and manifested much devotion to the service and the interests of his country. In 1805, he was promoted to the rank of a Lieutenant in the navy, and was again destined to visit the Mediterranean, on board the frigate Constitution, then commanded by Capt. Rogers. During this voyage, he had an opportunity to visit the ruins of the ancient cities of Herculaneum and Pompeia, in Italy. Having again returned from the Mediterranean, Lieut. Allen was appointed third Lieutenant on board the Chesapeake, commanded by Capt. Barron; and whilst in this situation, he was destined to experience a mortification which he little expected. During that unfortunate and disgraceful affair between the Chesapeake and the English frigate the Leopard, Lieut. Allen, notwithstanding the situation in which he was placed, did not forget that he was an American officer; nor could he restrain the strong impulse of native bravery. He discharged the only gun that was fired by the American frigate on that occasion. At the commencement of the late war, Capt. Allen was employed as first Lieutenant on board the frigate United States, commanded by that distinguished officer, Com. Decatur, and was in the glorious action of the 25th Oct. 1812, which resulted in the capture of the Macedonian. In this splendid and almost unequalled engagement, Lieut. Allen was highly distinguished for his activity, skill and bravery, being the first opportunity he had had of displaying his superior knowledge in naval tactics, his ardent patriotism, and that undaunted courage, which formed the most conspicuous trait in his character. To him was confided the service of conducting the Macedonian into port; which, notwithstanding the difficulties and dangers that he had to encounter, he succeeded in doing; and, amidst the acclamations of thousands, safely anchored her in the harbour of New-York.

After a short repose, Lieut. Allen was promoted to the rank of Captain, and was assigned to the command of the Argus sloop of war, to conduct the American minister, the successor of Barlow, to France, and thence to cruise for the annoyance of the British commerce. This was a hazardous naval enterprise ; but Capt. Allen, considering that, whilst in the employ of his country, his services and his life, if circumstances required it, were to be devoted to her interests, engaged in it with great alacrity; and after a voyage of twenty-three days, anchored safely at Port L'Orient. From this place, he proceeded to cruise in the Irish channel ; where, after the most active and successful exertions in annoying the commerce of the enemy, and having captured or destroyed a great number of their vessels, almost within sight of their own shores, he fell in with the British ship Pelican, which he engaged, but was overpowered by a vastly superior force ; the Pelican being joined by another vessel during the action. In this action, which occurred on the 14th Aug. Capt. Allen was mortally wounded, and died on the 18th, at Mill Prison Hospital, in Plymouth, and was interred with military honours. This gallant and youthful hero was but 28 years of age at his death. His name will be enrolled in the catalogue of the naval heroes of his country ; and his fair fame, unextinguished by time, will beam like a star of the first magnitude, in the constellation of American patriots and heroes, which is destined to illume this western hemisphere.

BURRELLVILLE.

BURRELLVILLE, a town of recent date, is situated in the northwest corner of the State, about 20 miles northwest from Providence ; bounded north on Massachusetts, west on Connecticut, south on Gloucester, and east on Smithfield. It is about 12 miles in length, from east to west, and about 5 miles in breadth, from north to south, comprising about 60 square miles.

This township is rather rough, and the lands in general unfavourable for tillage ; but they are well adapted to grazing, and afford valuable timber, the forests being extensive. The soil is a primitive gravelly loam ; and the agricultural productions consist of butter, cheese, beef, pork, &c.

The most considerable stream in the town has its source in Allum pond, which is situated on the northern border of the town, and is partly in Massachusetts. This stream runs through the town in an easterly direction.

The population of this township, in 1810, was 1834 ; and it contains about 300 Dwelling houses, about 300 Electors, and 3 Companies of Militia.

The manufactures of the town are inconsiderable. There are 1 Woolen Factory, 2 Carding Machines and 2 Clothiers' works.

The mercantile business is respectable, there being five Stores and one incorporated Bank.

The amount of taxable property, according to the United States assessment, in 1815, was $335,540.

There are two Religious Societies, which are accommodated with houses for public worship, and ten regular schools. Burrellville belonged to Gloucester, until 1806, when it was incorporated as a separate town.

CUMBERLAND.

CUMBERLAND, a post township, is situated in the northeast corner of the State, about eight miles northeast from Providence; bounded east on Attleborough and Wrentham, in Massachusetts, north on Wrentham, Bellingham & Mendon, in Massachusetts, southwesterly on Pawtucket river, which separates it from Smithfield. It is of a very irregular figure, and was formerly called the Gore. It comprises an area of about 28 square miles.

There are some sections of the township that are level and favourable for tillage; but a considerable proportion of it is rough and broken, being hilly and rocky, and is reserved for forests and pasturage. It is estimated that there are about 5000 acres in the town, covered with forests. In the other sections, the soil is generally fertile, and affords the various productions common to this region. The cultivation of grain does not receive much attention. Hay, cider and fruit are the principal articles that are sent abroad for a market.

The waters of the town consist of the Pawtucket river, which washes its southwestern border, and numerous small streams, of which, Abbot's run, Mill and Peters' rivers are the most considerable. There are four bridges upon Pawtucket river; and these small streams afford numerous valuable sites for mills and manufacturing establishments.

The manufacturing spirit which prevails so extensively in this State, and which forms one of its principal characteristics, has produced important results in this town. There are 8 cotton manufacturing establishments, containing 5524 spindles. In one of these factories there are 30 water looms, and in another there are 12. The extensive and diversified application of mechanical power is truly astonishing. Every process, from the preparation of the raw material, to the last finishing which is given to the fabric, is, in a greater or less degree, facilitated and accelerated by it. The saving of labour, by the use of machinery, in these different processes, varies essentially; but in most of them it is immensely great. This reduces greatly the manual industry; yet, where business is carried on so extensively, a large aggregate of this is required.

Besides the manufactures of cotton, there are one Woolen Factory, two Clothiers' works and six Grain Mills.

The building of boats is an extensive business in this town. There are 19 shops engaged in it, which usually build about 700 boats annually. They are constructed principally of oak timber; some, however, are of pine, and some of cedar; they are of various sizes, and sell from 20 to 70 dollars each. The manufacture of nails was formerly an important business in this town.

At present, there is but one establishment, at which, from 15 to 30 tons of nails and brads are annually made, which are of an excellent quality, being a patent nail. There is also a marble mill in this town, where large quantities of marble are manufactured for various uses, and sent to Boston, Providence, Worcester and many other places, for a market. The marble is obtained at the limestone rock quarry, in Smithfield.

The population of this town, in 1810, was 2110; and there are 306 Dwelling-houses, 280 Electors, 3 companies of Militia, 1 Rifle company, and a part of a company of Cavalry.

The amount of taxable property, according to the United States assessment, in 1815, was $528,220.

The town is well supplied with schools, there being nine regular schools, which are accommodated with school houses. Besides which, there are several that are occasionally maintained in private houses. It is estimated that there are from 350 to 400 scholars usually receiving instruction in this town.

There are four Religious Societies; two of Baptists, one of Methodists and one of Friends, all of which are accommodated with houses for public worship.

The first settlement in this town was about the year 1710; and it was incorporated in 1746.

CRANSTON.

CRANSTON is a township situated about five miles southwesterly from Providence; bounded northerly on Providence and Johnston, easterly on Providence river, southerly on Pawtuxet river and the town of Warwick, and westerly on the town of Scituate. This township is about 7 miles in length, and about 4 and a half in breadth; containing about 19,448 acres.

The western section of the town is uneven, but the eastern section is generally level. The soil in the former is a moist loam; that of the western part of the latter, being the central part of the township, is rich and fertile, but the eastern part is light, and inclining to a siliceous sand. There is a mine of iron ore in this town, of an excellent quality for casting. Formerly, large quantities were raised, for the Hope furnace; and from this ore, many of the cannon in our navy were cast; particularly those used upon Lake Erie by the gallant Perry. The *metal* of Rhode-Island, was proved by the battle of Lake Erie to be of an excellent *quality.**

The agricultural productions consist of hay, Indian corn, rye, oats, barley, cider, potatoes, &c. From the vicinity of this town to Providence, particularly its eastern section, considerable attention is paid to the cultivation of culinary vegetables, for the Providence market.

The waters of the town consist of the Pawtuxet river, which

* *Commodore Perry is a native of Rhode-Island.*

forms a part of its southern boundary, and the Powchasset river, which runs through the town, and discharges itself into the former, about two and a half miles above the falls.

There are three bridges over the Powchassett, and one at the falls upon the Pawtuxet, which is maintained at the joint expense of this town and the town of Warwick.

The Providence and Norwich turnpike road runs upon the north boundary of the town, and a turnpike from Providence to Pawcatuck, which has been authorized, but is not yet opened, will lead through this town.

The manufacture of cotton is an extensive business in this town. There are seven Factories; one of which, the largest, contains 1224 spindles, and has 12 waterlooms; one 900 spindles; one 554; one 500; one 350; one 288, and one 192, making in all nearly 4000 spindles. These establishments afford employment to a great number of persons, and to an immense capital. They swell to a vast extent the aggregate industry, business and resources of the place. In addition to the cotton manufactures, there are three Woolen Factories in this town. There are one Gin Distillery, six Grain Mills and seven Mercantile Stores.

The population of the town, in 1810, was 2161; and there are about 320 Dwelling-houses, about 300 Electors, 3 Companies of Militia, and 1 chartered military company.

There are six school-houses and schools; one Social Library; four religious Societies, two of Baptists, one at the village of Pawtuxet and the other at the village of Knightsville, one of Friends or Quakers, and one of Methodists; all of which are accommodated with houses for public worship.

There is a Bank located at the village of Knightsville, having a capital of $75,000.

The amount of taxable property in the town is $577,798.

PAWTUXET, a pleasant and flourishing, commercial and manufacturing village, is situated upon the west side of Providence river or Narragansett bay, five miles below Providence, at the mouth of the Pawtuxet river, which forms a safe and commodious harbour. The village is built upon both sides of the Pawtuxet river, and is partly in this town and partly in Warwick. It contains about 110 dwelling houses, some of which are neat, and built in a handsome style, a Church, an Academy, called Pawtuxet Academy, comprising usually about 70 scholars, two flourishing Schools, a Post-office, an incorporated Bank, with a capital of $120,000, and about 1000 inhabitants.

Pawtuxet has considerable commercial and navigation business, and is a port of entry. But it is most distinguished for its manufactures, particularly those of cotton and woolen, both of which are carried on to a considerable extent. The woolen fabrics, manufactured here, have been considered as of a superior quality. There are two Woolen manufacturing establishments, one of which is called the Bellefonte Manufacturing Company. There are three Cotton Factories, one of which contains 1200 spindles; one 900 spindles, employed principally in spinning thread, and one of 350 spindles. There are one Gin Distillery, and three Grain Mills, two on the north and one on the south side of the river.

Upon the Pawtuxet river, there is a bridge, connecting the two divisions of the village. This is a lively and interesting river, affording numerous sites for hydraulic works, and which are probably occupied to a greater extent than those of any other stream in the United States; there being, upon the waters of the Pawtuxet, about 40 Cotton Factories, and various other manufacturing and mechanical establishments.

Cranston was formerly a part of the town of Providence, and was first settled by Roger Williams and his associates, whose posterity are now living here. Joseph Williams, a son of Roger Williams, lived and died in this town. The town was incorporated in 1754.

BIOGRAPHY. Among the citizens of this town, who were most distinguished for their talents, patriotism and public services, were *Joseph Harris* Esq. and *Nehemiah Knight* Esq. Although, during the revolutionary war, the inhabitants of this town were generally attached to the American cause, yet there were opposing interests and conflicting opinions that it was necessary to reconcile; and asperities of feeling, that were required to be conciliated. It was at this dark period of our history, when the clouds that appeared in our horizon were so charged with the electric fire of party spirit, as portended a war of political elements, that threatened to desolate society;—it was at this period that the patriotism and services of these compatriots and fellow-townsmen rendered them eminently conspicuous, and secured to their memories the respect and veneration of posterity. So great were their exertions, so extensive their influence, and so commanding their example, that the voice of opposition ceased, and and all became united in the cause of independence, and rallied round the standard of their country. The descendants of both these patriots are numerous and respectable. Among those of the latter, is the present chief executive magistrate.

GLOUCESTER.

GLOUCESTER is a post township, situated 16 miles from Providence; bounded on the north by Burrellville, on the east by Smithfield, on the south by Scituate and Foster, and on the west by the State of Connecticut.

The township has an average length of 12 miles, and a mean breadth of 5 miles, comprising an area of about 60 square miles.

The surface is generally uneven, and some sections rough and broken, being hilly and rocky. The forests are extensive and valuable, affording great supplies of timber for ship building and other uses. The grazing business constitutes the principal agricultural interest; but some grain is raised, and there are many excellent orchards.

Chepachet river, which runs through the centre of the town, is the most considerable stream. Upon this stream, near the centre of the town, is a considerable and interesting village, which is the seat of most of the business of the town. Here there are four Cotton Factories, comprising 2000 spindles; being all there are in the town. The mercantile business is mostly done here, and here also is located a bank, called the Franklin Bank. The famous Exchange Bank, which failed some years since, and occasioned nearly an entire loss to the holders of its notes, was established here. The present bank has a solid capital, and sustains a high credit.

The Providence and Hartford turnpike leads through this town, and passes by this village, which, from the stream upon which it is situated, is called Chepachet. The Rhode-Island and Connecticut turnpike leads through the southern border of this town.

Excepting the cotton business, the manufacturing and mechanical employments of the town are inconsiderable. There are two Clothiers' works and six Grain Mills. There are six mercantile Stores.

There are 2 religious Societies, 12 Schools and 1 Social Library.

The population of the town, in 1810, was 2310; and there are about 400 Dwelling-houses, 400 Electors, 3 companies of Militia, and 2 chartered companies, one of Infantry and one of Riflemen.

The amount of taxable property, according to the United States assessment, in 1815, was $568,660.

The settlements in this town commenced about the year 1700. The first settlers were the Inmans, Windsors, Smiths and Burlingames. One of the first settlers was a Frenchman, by the name of Tourtellot. The town was incorporated in 1730. It sends two representatives to the General Assembly.

FOSTER.

FOSTER, a considerable post township, is situated on the west section of the State, 15 miles from Providence; bounded on the south by the township of Coventry, in the county of Kent, on the west by the towns of Killingly and Sterling, in the State of Connecticut, on the north by Gloucester, and on the east by Scituate. The mean length of the township, from north to south, is more than 8 miles, and its mean breadth about 6 miles, comprising about 50 square miles.

This township is of a granitic geological character; and many sections of it present very rugged features, being hilly, rocky and broken. The soil is a primitive gravelly loam, generally deep and strong, affording good grazing; but the lands in general are too stony and rough for arable purposes. There are extensive forests in the town, particularly in its western section, which afford large supplies of valuable timber. The agricultural productions consist of the various articles of the dairy business, and a grazing system of husbandry.

The principal stream within the town, is the Ponongansett river, which has its source in a pond of the same name, in Gloucester. This stream is the principal branch of the Pawtuxet river; the latter of which empties into Providence river, about five miles below the town of Providence. Hemlock brook, a branch of the Ponongansett, rises in the interior of this township; and, after many windings, runs easterly into the border of the town of Scituate, where it unites with the Ponongansett. Moosup river, a branch of the Quinibaug, runs through the western part of this town, passing into Coventry, and thence into Connecticut. Upon these streams, there are numerous sites for mills and other water works.

The Providence and Norwich turnpike road runs about three miles through the southwesterly part of this town; and the Providence and Hartford turnpike leads through its north section. The mail stage passes daily (excepting Sundays) upon these roads; the principal eastern mail being conveyed upon these two roads alternately. Charters have been granted for two other turnpikes, one of which is contemplated to lead through the centre of this town, and to unite with the Providence and Hartford turnpike in Scituate, about eight miles from Providence. The other is to run further south, and unite with the Providence and Norwich turnpike, about 12 miles from Providence. Another turnpike has also been granted, which is to lead from the Friends' meeting house through the whole length of the town, intersecting the several turnpikes already noticed. This is to be called the Foster and Gloucester *Appian way*, from an idea that this may be the commencement of an artificial road, leading from Rhode-Island to Canada, which may bear some resemblance to the famous Roman road that bore this appellation, having been made by *Appius Claudius*. When these roads are completed, there will be few towns in the State better accommodated with roads.

Of the manufacturing and mechanical establishments in the town, there are 1 Cotton Factory, 1 Woolen Factory, 1 Clothier's Works, 1 Carding Machine, 11 Grain Mills, 13 Saw Mills, 3 Tanneries and 2 Trip hammer shops. There are 7 Mercantile Stores.

The population of the town, in 1800, was 2458; in 1810, it was 2601; and there are about 400 Dwelling houses, about 450 Freemen or Electors, and 4 Companies of Militia, besides 2 chartered Companies; one called the "Foster safe Guards," and the other, being partly composed of inhabitants of Scituate, the "Scituate and Foster Independent Rifle Company."

There are 10 Schools usually maintained, which are provided with houses, and one Social Library, comprising a valuable collection of books. There are three religious Societies, two of Baptists and one of Friends, all of which are provided with houses for public religious worship.

The amount of taxable property, according to the United States assessment in 1815, was $342,070.

In the year 1662, William Vaughan, Zachariah Rhodes and Robert Westcot, purchased of the Indians a tract of country called Westquanaug, bordering easterly on Providence. This was called the

West-Quanaug purchase, and comprised nearly the southern half of the town of Foster. A number of individuals of Newport were afterwards associated with the first purchasers, among whom were Gov. John Cranston, Caleb Carr, Thomas Clark, William Foster, Clement Weaver, Aaron Davis, John Jones and Latham Clark, most or all of whom have now descendants in the town. In 1707, this purchase was divided by lot among 29 proprietors, but the first settlement was not commenced until 1717. The first settler was Ezekiel Hopkins, whose descendants are now very numerous in the town; there are also here a number of the descendants of the two Governors, John Cranston and Samuel Cranston.

Foster was incorporated with Scituate in 1730, forming the western section of that township, which was divided in 1781, when the western setion was incorporated as a separate town, by the name of *Foster*, which it received from the Hon. *Theodore Foster*, who for many years was a senator in the senate of the United States, and who is now an inhabitant of the town.

JOHNSTON.

JOHNSTON is a township situated 5 miles from Providence; bounded northerly on Smithfield, northeasterly on Wanasquatucket river, which separates it from North-Providence, east on Providence, south on Cranston, and west on Scituate. It contains about 17 square miles; being more than 4 miles from east to west, and about 4 from north to south.

This township is of a primitive, granitic structure, and its surface is interspersed with hill and dale. There are several valuable quarries of freestone in the town, suitable for building and other uses. They not only afford a supply for the demand in the town. and in the immediate vicinity, but are sent abroad to a distance; having, in some instances, been exported to Savannah. Stone also, suitable for furnace hearths, having great capacity to sustain fire, have been found. Limestone is also found at what is called Border Rock, from which large quantities of lime are made.

Although the surface is uneven, the soil is generally good. It is best adapted to grazing, but affords good crops of Indian corn; barley, oats and buckwheat are also cultivated to advantage. Potatoes are also raised in abundance, and are an article of exportation. The town is favourable for fruit, and contains many valuable orchards. Large quantities of cider are made, which is an article of exportation.

The most considerable streams in the town are the Wanasquatucket, which washes its northeastern border, the Powchassett, which runs through the town from northwest to southeast, and a branch of this stream, called Cedar brook, which empties into the Powchassett near the south boundary of the town, adjoining Cranston. These streams afford numerous advantages for the milling and manufacturing business. There are four Cotton Factories in the town; one called the Union Factory, having 1500 spindles, and one the Merino Factory, having 612 spindles. The woolen business is also carried on at this establishment; for which purpose, there are 280 spindles. Here also are 12 water looms, which usually weave 40 yards each in a day. There are five Grain Mills and six mercantile Stores in the town.

In 1810, there were 1516 inhabitants in this town; and there are 238 Dwelling houses, about 230 Freemen or Electors, and 2 companies of Militia.

The amount of taxable property, according to the assessment of the United States, in 1815, was $427,950.

There are seven regular schools which are provided with houses; and several other schools are occasionally maintained.

There are three religious societies; two of Baptists and one of Friends.

Johnston originally belonged to the town of Providence, and was incorporated as a distinct township in 1759.

NORTH-PROVIDENCE.

NORTH-PROVIDENCE is a post town, situated four miles north from Providence; bounded on the north by Smithfield, on the east by the Seekonk river, which separates it from Massachusetss, on the south by Providence, and on the west by the Wanasquatucket river, which separates it from Johnston.

The average length of the township is about 6 miles, and its mean breadth more than 2 and a half miles, comprising an area of about 16 square miles.

The surface of this township is uneven, consisting of moderate elevations and gentle declivities. The rocks are primitive and transition; some limestone is found.

The prevailing soil is a gravelly loam, which is interspersed with tracts of sandy loam, and some of calcareous. The forests consist of oak, walnut and some pine; and the agricultural productions, of grass, hay, corn, some rye, potatoes, vegetables and fruits, for Providence market.

The waters of the town consist of the Seekonk river, which washes its eastern border; the Wanasquatucket, which forms its western boundary; and the Mashasuck, which intersects the interior of the township. These streams afford numerous sites for hydraulic works, some of which are almost unrivalled. There are some valuable shad and herring fisheries in the Seekonk.

The town is accommodated with the Pawtucket & Providence turnpike, leading to Boston, and the Douglass turnpike.

In 1810, there were 1758 inhabitants in this town; and there are about 316 Dwelling-houses, 200 Electors, & 2 companies of Militia.

The amount of taxable property, according to the assessment of the United States, in 1815, was $556,970.

SCITUATE.

This town is distinguished for its manufactures, particularly those of cotton, which form an important interest. There are 10 Cotton Mills or Factories, some of which are among the largest and most ancient in the State. The extent of this business, having concentrated a large capital, and an immense aggregate of industry, has, within the last thirty years, given rise to a large and flourishing village. The village of Pawtucket is situated in the northeast section of the town, four miles northeast of Providence, on the border of the Seekonk river; its site being principally the declivity of a hill, and it is highly romantic and picturesque. The river here affords numerous natural sites for manufacturing establishments, mills and hydraulic works of almost every description, which are scarcely rivalled, and which are occupied to a great extent. The rapid march of manufacturing and mechanical industry, which the short annals of this place disclose, has few examples in our country, and has produced one of the most considerable and flourishing manufacturing villages in the United States. The river here forms the boundary line between the two States, and the village is built upon both sides of it; being partly in Rhode-Island and partly in Massachusetts. That part of the village which is in this State is principally built on four streets; and comprises 83 Dwelling-houses, 12 mercantile Stores, 2 Churches, a Post-office, an incorporated Bank, an Academy, and two or three flourishing Schools. Of the 10 Cotton Mills in the town, three are at this place, and upon an extensive scale. There are six shops engaged in the manufacture of machinery, having the advantages of water-power, and various other mechanical establishments, affording extensive employment, and supporting a dense population. Upon the Massachusetts side of the river, there is a village of nearly equal size and consequence, for its manufacturing and other interests.

Besides the cotton business, there are in the town 2 Furnaces for casting, 1 Slitting Mill, 2 Anchor Shops, 1 Cut-nail Factory, 2 Screw Manufactories, 3 Grain Mills, 1 Clothier's works and 1 Carding Machine.

There are in the town, 14 mercantile Stores. There are 3 Religious Societies and Churches, two for Baptists and one for Episcopalians, two Academies & 8 Schools, including those in Pawtucket village. North-Providence sends two representatives to the General Assembly.

This town was originally a part of Providence, and was incorporated in 1767.

SCITUATE.

SCITUATE is a considerable post township, situated twelve miles west from Providence; bounded on the north by Gloucester, on the east by Johnston, on the south by Coventry, and on the west by Foster. Its average length, from north to south, is about

3 miles, and its average breadth more than 6 miles, comprising an area of about 50 square miles.

The surface is diversified with hills and dales, and some sections are rough and broken. In the west part of the town there is a valuable quarry of freestone, suitable for building, from which large quantities are raised, and transported to Providence and other places at a distance.

The prevailing soil is a primitive, gravelly loam, and is best adapted to grazing; and, in general, the land is too rough and rocky for tillage; some grain however is raised.

The agricultural productions consist of Indian corn, oats, barley, potatoes, flax, beef, pork, butter, cheese, and some others.

The township is watered by two small streams, one of which rises in its north eastern section, near Maswanshecut pond; the other has its source in Punnongansett pond, in Gloucester, runs through Foster, and entering this town upon its western border, unites with the first mentioned stream; whose united waters form the north branch of Pawtuxet river.

The town is accommodated with two turnpike roads; one leading from Providence to Hartford, and the other from the same place to Norwich.

In 1810, there were in this town 2568 inhabitants; and there are about 400 Dwelling houses, about 420 Freemen or Electors, and five companies of Infantry and one company of Cavalry, of Militia.

The amount of taxable property, as assessed by the United States, in 1815, was $650,980.

Scituate claims a respectable rank among the manufacturing towns in the State. There are four Cotton Factories and one Woolen Factory here. There are also two Clothiers' works and nine Grain Mills. There are five mercantile Stores and one incorporated Bank.

There are two religious Societies, one of Baptists and one of Friends, seven primary Schools, and an Academy is about to be established, the building for which is now erecting, and two Social Libraries.

This town belonged, at an early period, to Providence; and was incorporated as a separate town in the year 1731.

SMITHFIELD.

SMITHFIELD is a large and flourishing post township, situated nine miles northwest of Providence; bounded northeasterly by Blackstone or Pawtucket river, which divides it principally from Cumberland, northerly by the State of Massachusetts, westerly by Burrellvile and Gloucester, south and southeasterly by Johnston and N. Providence.

The average length of the township is about 10 miles, with a mean breadth of 6 miles, comprising an area of 60 square miles.

This township has generally an undulating surface, presenting an agreeable diversity of moderate eminences and gentle declivities; but in some sections it is considerably rough and broken. Its geological structure comprises numerous calcareous strata. In these strata, four quarries have been opened, and large quantities of limestone raised, which has been manufactured into lime. It has been estimated that from 40 to 50,000 casks have been made annually, the principal part of which is exported to the southern States for a market. One of these quarries affords limestone of a peculiar character; the lime made of which is of the very best quality, and commands an extra price. This stone also makes a good cement. The manufacture of lime is an important and extensive business, and affords employment to a great number of persons. There is also a quarry of white stone at what is called Woonsoquett hill, that sustains heat remarkably well, which renders it very valuable for furnace hearths; for which purpose it has been transported by land from 50 to 60 miles. About two miles distant from this, there is a quarry, containing excellent whetstones, for edge tools. Large quantities are annually wrought into a suitable shape for that use, are transported into various parts of the Union, and are in high estimation.

The soil is a gravelly and sandy loam, with some sections of a calcareous loam. It is generally rich and fertile, although in some places it has been reduced by an exhausting system of cultivation. The lands are generally warm, and favourable for most kinds of vegetation. There are, however, some low and marshy tracts, which are generally appropriated to mowing, and afford good crops of grass. The forests are not extensive, but are sufficient to supply the inhabitants with fuel and timber, and for the consumption occasioned by the lime manufactories, which afford a considerable market for this article.

The agricultural productions consist of the various articles common to the climate; Indian corn, rye, some wheat, barley, oats, potatoes, some flax, beef, pork, butter, cheese, apples, cider and hay.

But few of these productions form articles of exportation. Considerable quantities, however, of potatoes, cider, apples and hay are sent to the southern markets. The agricultural interests of the town are not very flourishing, considering the natural resources of the soil; the industry of the inhabitants being in some measure diverted from agriculture, by the extensive cotton manufactures, and the attention that is paid to the lime business, which constitutes an important interest.

The waters of the town consist of the Pawtucket, which washes its northeastern border, and a branch of this river, nearly of equal size, which intersects the town, discharging its waters into the former, in the northern section of the town. After the union of these streams, the Pawtucket is from one to two hundred feet in width. At some seasons of the year, it usually overflows its banks, and has been known to rise from 15 to 20 feet above its usual height. There are five bridges upon the Pawtucket,

SMITHFIELD. 347

and several upon the branch stream. Besides these, there are numerous small streams, some of which afford valuable sites for mills and manufacturing establishments, which are mostly occupied. In the south part of the town, within about four miles of Providence, there is a considerable body of water, called Scotch Pond. It is nearly a mile in length, about half a mile in width, and of great depth. What is memorable in this pond, is the steep descent of its shores, particularly that adjoining the old post road from Providence to Worcester. Cases have occurred, of persons being drowned in attempting to water their horses at this pond.

There are three turnpike roads that pass through this town, all leading from Providence; one is called Loisquissett, which meets the post road from Worcester, about 9 miles from Providence; one is called the Douglass turnpike, leading directly from Providence to Douglass; and the other is called the Powder-mill turnpike, leading to Connecticut.

The cotton manufactories of this town are important and extensive. There are nine Factories, all of which contain about 11,000 spindles. About one half of these belong to one factory, owned by Almy, Brown and Slater. This establishment is situated upon the aforesaid branch of the Pawtucket river, about one mile and a half from its junction, being an excellent site for hydraulic works. At this place, there is a large and flourishing village, called Slatersville, comprising from six to eight hundred inhabitants. This village is of recent date, having grown up with the manufacturing business, which may be considered as the parent of it. It is impossible to contemplate such a village as this, without the most pleasing sensations and reflections. What a seat of wealth, a focus of activity, and a nursery of industry! What a display of mechanical ingenuity, and what a developement of the importance and influence of the useful arts! What a combination and variety of operations, what diversity of employment, and what a number of distinct and curious processes are comprised in the manufacture of those fabrics requisite to supply the wants which the refinements of society occasion! Who can look upon such manufacturing villages as this, without regarding them as the germs of the future Manchesters of America?

In addition to the cotton factories, which have been noticed, there is one other extensive establishment, called the Mammoth Factory, containing from 6 to 8000 spindles, which is supposed to be within the bounds of this town; but this admits of doubt; as the line between this State and Massachusetts, at this place, has not been definitely settled. This establishment is owned by Butler, Wheaton & Co. of Providence.

In addition to the cotton manufactures, there are one Paper Mill, two Distilleries, two Scythe Manufactories, where large quantities of scythes are annually made for exportation, one Gun Factory, eleven Grain Mills, the greater part of which are on streams affording a sufficient supply of water, and one Fulling Mill and Clothiers' works.

The mercantile business of the town is respectable, there being 11 Stores. There are two Banks in this town, and a charter has been obtained for one more.

The population of Smithfield, in 1810, was 3828; and there are about 500 Electors, more than 500 Dwelling houses, 5 companies of Militia, and 2 chartered companies.

The town is well supplied with schools, there being 20 regular schools, which are provided with suitable houses, and are maintained nearly through the year. Besides which, there are several schools kept in the winter season in private houses. There are also two Academies; and another has recently been incorporated. There are 4 religious Societies; one of Friends or Quakers, which is the largest, one of Baptists, one of Methodists and one of Christians; and there are four churches, two of which belong to the society of Friends. There are four Social Libraries.

There is a remarkable fall of water upon the Pawtucket river, called Woonsoquett falls, which is considered as quite a curiosity. The fall is about 20 feet, is not perpendicular, but over a precipice of rocks for some distance. The fall of the water upon these rocks through a succession of ages, has occasioned numerous excavations, all of which are smooth and circular, and some of them very large, being sufficient to contain several hogsheads.

The taxable property of the town, by the United States assessment of 1815, was $830,960.

Smithfield belonged originally to the town of Providence, and was settled about the same time, but was not incorporated as a town, until 1730.

BIOGRAPHY. The Rev. *Elisha Thornton*, of this town, was an eminent minister of the gospel, belonging to the Society of Friends, and was alike distinguished for his exemplary and useful life, and for his scientific acquirements. He was self-taught, having had but little advantages as to education, in early life. But such was the native vigour of his mind, and his insatiable thirst for knowledge, that he became an eminent mathematician and practical astronomer, and for several years was Preceptor of a school, which sustained a high reputation.

Daniel Mowry Esq. of this town, late a member of Congress, possessed superior talents, and was an ornament to his profession. But he was not more distinguished for his talents than for his benevolent and friendly disposition, and for his eminently useful life.

NEWPORT COUNTY.

NEWPORT is a maritime commercial county, situated in the southeastern section of the State, and is composed principally of detached and insulated sections, being separated by the waters of Narragansett bay. The whole territorial limits of the county, exclusive of the waters intervening between its different divisions, comprise about 136 square miles.

The following TOPOGRAPHICAL AND STATISTICAL TABLE exhibits a view of the number of towns in the county; their situation, with relation to Newport; their population, according to the census of 1810; number of dwelling houses; religious societies, schools; banks, and post-offices.

Towns.	P.O.	Pop.	D.H.	R.S.	Sch.	Ban.	Dist. from Newport.
Newport.	1	7097	1100	10	29	5	
Jamestown.	0	564	70	1	2	0	3 m. W.
Little-Compton.	0	1553	230	2	7	0	8 m. N. E.
Middletown.	0	976	160	1	5	0	3 m. N. E.
New-Shoreham.	0	722	128	1	0	0	24 m S.S.W.
Portsmouth.	1	1795	250	2	7	0	8 m. N. E.
Tiverton.	1	2837	400	7	11	0	13 m. N. E.

The most important and extensive section or division of this county is Rhode-Island, from which the State takes its name. This delightful and interesting island is situated in the Narragansett bay, near its southern extremity and connexion with the sea. The island is about 15 miles in length, from northeast to southwest, and has a mean breadth of about 2 and a half miles, comprising about 37 square miles. The surface of the island presents a most interesting diversity, consisting of moderate eminences and gentle declivities, which afford the most charming and beautiful landscapes.

The geological structure of the island is of the character denominated transition; and the prevailing strata of rocks are schistus or slate; but there are some calcareous strata, and the surface exhibits various other rocks and stones. In these calcareous strata, some specimens of very rich and elegant serpentine marble have been discovered; and that valuable mineral, fossil coal, is supposed to exist in great abundance. Two mines or pits have been opened, and considerable quantities of coal obtained. The quality of it is thought to be improving. It has been exported to New-York and elsewhere.

The soil is very rich and productive, being an admixture of schistic gravelly loam, with a vegetable mould. It is well adapted both to a grain and a grass culture, affording excellent crops of Indian corn, barley and grass. The cultivation of barley, which has been recently introduced, is found to be a great improvement upon the former mode of husbandry, and is beginning to receive general attention, being a very profitable crop, and at the same time attended with little exhaustion to the soil.

The next most important division of the county is the continental section, comprising the towns of Tiverton & Little-Compton. This is the most extensive section, and is separated from Rhode-Island by the Seconnet river or passage. A part of this section discloses similar geological features to Newport; but the northern section is a primitive granitic district, being rough and broken, unsuitable for cultivation, and principally appropriated to forests, which are extensive and valuable. Cannanicut, Prudence and Block islands constitute the remainder of the county, which, with the exception of the latter, have a similar geological character to Rhode-Island.

From the local situation of this county, being surrounded by navigable waters, which intersect it in various directions, forming numerous insulated divisions, it unites superior advantages for navigation, commerce and the fishing business. And hence, these have been leading interests with the people of this county, from its earliest settlement. Although neither commerce nor the fishing business has been pursued to that extent, or acquired that importance, which, from local advantages, might have been expected; yet, considering the vicissitudes which this county has experienced, both of these interests are very respectable. The maritime commercial interests consist principally of a trade to the island of Cuba, and a coasting trade, mostly directed to the southern States. There is, however, some trade to the Baltic and the north of Europe. The amount of shipping at this time is about 10,950 tons.

The fishing business, with the exception of that of Block-Island, which is very important, is chiefly directed to supply the home consumption. That of the latter is carried on to a great extent, and with great success. Large quantities of fish are taken, which form an important article of exportation. The fishing business in this county is capable of great extension, and might be made a capacious field for enterprise and industry, and a source of ample profit.

The agricultural interests of this county are respectable. The leading pursuits of husbandry heretofore have been directed to the dairy business, and the raising of sheep; but for some time past these interests have been rather upon the decline, and the cultivation of grain has received more attention, particularly barley, the cultivation of which has been recently introduced, and it is found to be a very profitable and advantageous crop. Barley, it is believed, is cultivated more extensively here, than in any other section of the Union. Indian corn also is raised in considerable quantities and to good advantage. Fruit likewise receives considerable attention. The manufacturing interests of the county, although they will not sustain a comparison with those of some other sections of the State, are however very considerable for the advantages which it possesses; there being no rivers of any extent, and consequently few sites for hydraulic works. The most important branch of manufacturing business is the manufacture of rum, which is carried on considerably extensively at Newport. There are seven distilleries engaged in the business at that place. The manufacture of cordage is carried on to a considerable extent at Newport, and ship-building also receives some attention, particularly of that description of vessels intended for packets. Boat building is likewise attended to.

There are in the county three Cotton Factories, two Woolen Factories, one Duck Factory, four Clothiers' works and 28 Grain Mills, a large proportion of which are Wind Mills. There are about 160 Mercantile Stores of every description, 24 Religious Societies, about 61 Schools, 5 Social Libraries and 5 incorporated Banks.

The population of the county, in 1790, was 14,300; in 1800, 14,845; and in 1810, 16,294.

NEWPORT.

NEWPORT, an ancient commercial post town, and semi-metropolis of the State, is situated in the southwest section of Rhode-Island; 30 miles south by east of Providence, and 75 miles southwest from Boston. The township lies in an irregular, and somewhat of a semicircular form, and may be about 6 miles in length upon an average estimation, and more than a mile in breadth, comprising about 8 square miles.

The surface of the town is pleasantly diversified, presenting a succession of beautiful and prospective eminences, and gentle and interesting declivities. Its gelogocal structure, and the prevailing strata of rocks are of the transition character, and consist principally of schistus or slate, interspersed with which there is some granite; limestone also abounds in some sections, and in the calcareous rocks serpentine marble has been found, of a very rich and elegant quality.

The soil is a schistic gravelly loam, generally deep and rich, and productive both in grass and grain. It is also very favourable for fruit, and the various objects of horticulture. The original forests were of the deciduous species, but there are none now of much extent. The agricultural interests are considerably flourishing. Among the objects of husbandry, the culture of barley, which has been recently introduced, sustains a conspicuous place. This is a profitable crop, and deserves to be encouraged and extended. Indian corn and hay are cultivated with success; and vegetables and fruit for the Newport market.

The waters of the town, for

beauty and convenience, are unrivaled. The Narragansett bay affords, at this place, one of the most excellent harbours in the United States. It is in a semicircular form, and of safe and easy access; sufficiently capacious to contain whole fleets, and has sufficient depth of water for vessels of the largest burthen.

The harbour is defended by Fort Wolcott, erected upon Goat Island. Another fort has been erected, called Fort Adams; and there was a fort erected during the late war, called Fort Green. These forts are kept in good repair, & are well provided with ordnance, barracks and magazines; and they are garrisoned with a detachment of United States troops. In addition to these, some works were commenced for the defence of the harbour, some years since, on Rose Island, but have never been completed.

The fisheries of Newport are very valuable, and a source of subsistence, convenience and wealth. There is probably no fish market in the world that is better supplied; that affords a greater variety, or fish of better quality. Nearly sixty different kinds of eatable fish, comprising almost every species of fin and shell, have been exhibited in Newport market. This great supply of fish is a convenience to all; but is of the greatest advantage to the poor, affording them a sure and cheap means of subsistence. The fishing business, also, opens an extensive field for industry; but is capable of great extension, and might be rendered an important business, and a source of great profit. Few places are more advantageously situated, or unite more advantages for the fishing business, and a spirit of enterprise and perseverance, directed in this channel, would raise it to an important interest; affording immense wealth to individuals, employment to thousands, and contributing essentially to the general prosperity. The business, at present, is chiefly directed to furnishing a supply for the market in this town, and the villages on the shores of the Narragansett.

The commercial interests of the town, although they have declined at some periods, are now very respectable. Previously to the revolutionary war, there were but few towns in the colonies, whose commerce was more extensive or flourishing than Newport. More than 100 sail of vessels were owned here, at an early period; but the revolutionary war destroyed the sources of the trade of this town, and for some time subsequently its commerce continued to decline. Within the last fifteen years, it has experienced various vicissitudes, but it is now considerably revived. At this time (1819) there are 10,951 tons of shipping owned here. The trade of Newport has no particular direction; it maintains some trade with the East Indies, some with the north of Europe, and considerable with the Island of Cuba; but the most important is a coasting trade with the middle and southern States. The last branch of trade is supposed to be increasing. In addition to the other navigation interests, there are a number of regular packets that ply between this port and New-York, Providence and the numerous villages

NEWPORT.

and ports upon the shores of the Narragansett.

The manufacturing interests of Newport are not very important or extensive; nor can this be a matter of surprise, considering the maritime situation and habits of the place, and the want of advantageous sites for manufacturing establishments, which can scarcely be expected upon an island affording only small streams. The most important manufacturing interest is that of domestic spirits, which are made principally from foreign materials. There are 7 rum distilleries in Newport, at which large quantities of rum are distilled, most of which is sent abroad for a market. There is also one gin distillery; and the manufacture of cordage receives considerable attention, there being five rope walks. Ship building is carried on to some extent; and boat building likewise receives considerable attention. There are 1 Duck Factory, 4 Tanneries and 5 Grain Mills.

There are in Newport about 1100 Dwelling houses, 140 Mercantile Stores of every description, and numerous Mechanics' shops; the town being well supplied with mechanical industry. Some branches of mechanical business are carried on to considerable extent, affording more than a supply for home consumption.

There are in Newport 10 Religious Societies, and about 30 Schools for the primary branches of education; in some of which also. the higher branches are taught. These schools are generally well conducted, and contain a great number of scholars. There is one Academy and two Social Libraries, one of which contains 3000 volumes. There is also one public Library, a very ancient establishment, which was founded and incorporated as early as the year 1747. It contains about 700 volumes, most of which are large and valuable folios. Among this collection, is a bible that was printed as early as 1487; one of the most ancient volumes in the United States. A neat and commodious edifice was erected for the Library, as early as the year 1748.

The compact part of the town of Newport is built upon a beautiful site, being a gentle declivity facing the harbour, in a southwesterly direction. The principal street is Thames-street, which extends more than a mile in length, from a northwest to a southeasterly direction; it is well built, and contains a dense population. The houses on this street have an ancient appearance, but most of them are in good repair. This street is the seat of a large proportion of the commercial business. Next to the Thames, the most important is Broad-street, commencing at the public square, and extending in a northeasterly direction. This is the main road to Boston and Providence, and is a seat of considerable business. Spring-street runs south of the public square, parallel with Thames-street. Washington-street extends from the long-wharf across the point. This street has a most beautiful and prospective situation. The public or Washington square is a very handsome area in front of the State-House. In addition to these, there are numerous other streets most of which are well built, and seats of considerable business. There are in Newport ten Churches, and a Jewish synagogue, which is kept in good repair, but is not now used as a house for religious worship. Four of the Churches are for Baptists, 2 for Congregationalists, 1 for Episcopalians, 1 for Friends, 1 for Methodists and 1 for Moravians. The other public buildings are a State house, which is an ancient, but very respectable brick edifice fronting the public square; the Library building already noticed, a Market house constructed of brick, a Theatre and an Almshouse. The town is accommodated with about 30 wharves.

There are in Newport 4 Bookstores, 2 Newspaper establishments and 5 incorporated Banks; the Rhode-Island Bank established in 1795, with a capital of $100,000; Newport Bank established in 1803, capital $120,000; Rhode-Island union Bank in 1804, capital $200,000; New-England commercial Bank, and Merchants Bank. There are two Insurance Companies.

In 1752, a Marine Society was established here, for the relief of distressed widows and orphans, whose husbands and fathers had been mariners, and other individuals in distressed circumstances.

Previously to the American revolution, Newport was the fourth commercial town in the colonies, and at one period contained more than 9000 inhabitants. It had the appearance, and sustained the character of a rich and flourishing commercial city, nearly one hundred years since. Its principal streets have been paved for more than 80 years. It is believed, that there is no town within the present territorial limits of the United States, that has experienced so many, and so great vicissitudes as Newport. It is now supposed to be increasing in population and business, and is evidently gradually rising from its former decline. It has been suggested, that this town was an eligible situation for manufactures; but we think not. The local situation of the place, and the maritime habits of the inhabitants, which are the result of local influence, and are of long standing, seem to interpose a barrier to a manufacturing spirit; and to the diversion of industry from established occupations, to a channel so essentially different; and this opinion does not rest merely upon argument, but upon experience and the known results of like causes. If we look to Europe, (and who does not look there for examples?) we shall perceive, that upon the sea board, there are few if any manufacturing towns; her Birminghams and Sheffields are in the interior. And as like causes produce like effects every where, it can scarcely be doubted that this will be the case in America. Newport, situated as it is, almost forming a part of the domains of the ocean, seems destined to reap its principal harvest from this element. Its local situation gives it superior advantages for maritime pursuits, either the fishing business or foreign commerce and navigation. The fishing business, here, particularly invites attention, and is capable of great extension. There are many examples in the United States, of bold but judicious enterprise, and persevering industry in this branch of business, being crowned with the most successful results; and it is by no means improbable, that this town, by well directed enterprise in the fishing business, and other maritime and commercial pursuits, may again experience its former prosperity, and attain to that population, wealth and commercial consequence and business, to which, by its superior natural advantages, it seems to be destined.

Newport was first settled by William Coddington and his associates, in 1638. The growth of the town was so rapid for the first hundred years, that in 1738 it contained seven worshipping assemblies; and there were about 100 sail of vessels owned here.

Newport suffered severely during the revolutionary contest, and for a long time was occupied by the enemy. It suffered severely also in common with the other towns upon the shores of the Narragansett, in the memorable September gale of 1815. Extensive damage was done to the wharves, stores, and shipping in the harbour; and what added greatly to the affliction, several lives were lost.

In this town, there is now standing an ancient stone mill, the erection of which is beyond the date of its earliest records; but it is supposed to have been erected by the first settlers, about 180 years ago. It is an interesting monument of antiquity.

Newport is celebrated for the pleasantness and beauty of its situation, and is equally distinguished for the salubrity of its climate, being considered as one of the healthiest towns in the United States. From these circumstances, and from the inviting objects which it affords, from its local and maritime situation, it is, during the summer months, a place of great resort from the southern and middle States, for the purposes of health and pleasure. From the facts here noticed, Newport may be considered as the Montpelier of America. N. lat. 41° 29′, W. lon. 71° 17′.

JAMESTOWN.

JAMESTOWN is an insulated township, situated on Connanicut Island, in Narragansett bay, about 3 miles west of Newport, and 30 south of Providence. Jamestown includes the whole of Connanicut Island, and is about 8 miles in length, from north to south, and has a mean breadth, from east to west, of nearly one mile, comprising about 8 square miles.

The geological structure and rocks of the island are similar to those of Rhode-Island. The soil is a rich loam, and peculiarly adapted to grazing. It is likewise productive in grain, especially barley and Indian corn. The agricultural interests, which occupy almost exclusively the attention of the inhabitants, consist principally in the various objects connected with the grazing business, and the cultivation of barley and Indian corn. Considerable attention has been bestowed heretofore upon the raising of sheep, on this island; but this at present is an object less attended to. The concerns and interests of husbandry in general exhibit a flourishing aspect, the inhabitants being industrious, economical and persevering agriculturalists.

The town is accommodated with two ferries, one to Newport and the other to South-Kingston; and the principal road extends across the island, communicating with these ferries. At the southern extremity of the Island, at a place called Beaver tail, stands a light-house.

The population of the island, at the last census, in 1810, was 504; and there are about 60 or 70 Dwelling-houses, 1 Religious Society and Church, 2 or 3 Schools and School-houses, 50 or 60 Electors, 1 Grain Mill, and 1 company of Militia.

This town sends two representatives to the General Assembly.

This island was purchased of the Indians, as early as 1657, and Jamestown was incorporated in 1678.

LITTLE-COMPTON.

LITTLE-COMPTON is a wealthy maritime and agricultural township, situated in the southeastern extremity of the county and State, 30 miles southeast of Providence; bounded on the north by Tiverton, on the east by the State of Massachusetts, on the south by the Atlantic ocean, and on the west by the east passage of the Narragansett bay. The average length of the township, from north to south, is about 7 miles, and its mean breadth, from east to west, is 4 miles, comprising an area of about 28 square miles.

The form of the southern section of the township is that of a peninsula, inclining to a point. The surface is pleasantly diversified. The soil is a deep loam, rich in agricultural resources, and the means of wealth derived from this branch of industry.

The agricultural productions are abundant, and consist of the various articles common to this region. This town is one of the most flourishing agricultural districts in the State. Barley constitutes a staple production, large quantities of it being raised. Horticulture also receives considerable attention, various culinary vegetables being raised for marketing.

The manufactures of the town are wholly of a domestic character, which are extensive and important, the inhabitants being distinguished for their habits of industry and economy, and their social and moral virtues.

The population of the town, in 1810, was 1553; and there are about 230 Dwelling-houses, 225 Freemen or Electors, two companies of Militia and a part of another company.

There are 2 Religious Societies, one of Congregationalists and one of Friends, 7 Schools and 1 Social Library. There are 4 Mercantile Stores and 6 Grain Mills. This town sends two representatives to the General Assembly.

Little-Compton was settled in 1674, by Capt. Church and his associates. The Indian name was Seconnet.

MIDDLETOWN.

MIDDLETOWN, the central township of Rhode-Island, is situated two miles N. E. from Newport, and about 28 miles southeast from Providence. It is bounded northwest by the Narragansett bay, northeast by Portsmouth, southeast by the east passage of Narragansett bay, and southwest by Newport.

The length of the town, from northwest to southeast, is about five miles, and it has a mean breadth of nearly two and a half miles, comprising an area of about 12 square miles.

The surface is undulating and diversified, affording numerous pleasant and interesting landscapes. The soil is a rich loam, very productive, and under a high state of cultivation; and the lands maintain a very high estimation.

The forests are inconsiderable, and principally consist of oak and walnut.

The agricultural interests of the town are very flourishing. The leading objects of husbandry are the dairy business, hay, the culture of Indian corn and barley, and the raising of supplies for Newport market. The article of barley, the cultivation of which has been but recently introduced, has become a leading agricultural production, and probably receives more attention here than in any other part of New-England. The orchards of this town are very valuable, and are not only a source of convenience, but form a considerable important agricultural interest. The people of this town are principally agriculturists; and are distinguished for their habits of industry and economy, and the uniformity, plainness and simplicity of their manner of living.

There are few subjects of statistical or local detail in this town; being situated in the vicinity of a large commercial town, most of the mercantile, mechanical and professional business is transacted at Newport.

Middletown is accommodated with two good roads, both leading from Newport to the upper end of the island.

There is one Religious Society in this town, and five Schools.

The population, in 1810, was 976; and there are about 160 Dwelling-houses, 2 companies of Militia, and 115 Electors. Middletown sends two representatives to the General Assembly.

The town was incorporated in 1743.

NEW-SHOREHAM.

NEW-SHOREHAM, a township in the county of Newport, consists of the island of Block-Island. This island lies in the open sea, 15 miles S. S. W. of Point-Judith, and about 12 miles southerly of the nearest part of the continent. It extends north and south about eight miles, and is from two to four in breadth. A chain of large ponds extends from the north end to nearly the centre. These, with several separate and smaller ones, compose about one seventh part of the island. The land, in general, is high, and in some parts very uneven, being diversified with abrupt hills and narrow dales.

The soil is various—sandy, loamy and gravelly. Its agricultural productions are corn, barley and potatoes. It is no longer "famous for its cattle, and sheep, and butter and cheese," as formerly; the land being more generally converted from pasturage to tillage. It is entirely destitute of forests. Considerable quantities of peat are produced, which is the only fuel. The stones are granite in detached nodules, none of very large size. There being no nucleus or rocky foundation, the land is constantly washing away by the surges of the ocean. In process of time, the island must totally disappear, and its present site constitue a shoal, where the tenants of the waters will feed, and fishermen resort. There is no ship harbour; the boats are obliged to be hauled on shore in bad weather. In the season of fishing, 33 boats, from 14 to 30 feet keel, and about 190 men, are employed in taking cod and mackerel. It contains 128 Dwelling-houses; and at the last census there were 722 inhabitants, 140 of which are freemen or voters. It pays the hundred and nineteenth part of the State taxes, and sends two representatives to the General Assembly. There is one company of Militia, organized by law, but it is never called upon to do military duty. There is one Meeting-house and one Religious Society of the Baptist order. There are two Windmills and four retail Stores. Its aboriginal name was *Manisses*. It was settled in 1661, and incorporated in October, 1672.

PORTSMOUTH.

PORTSMOUTH is a post township, situated upon the northern section of Rhode-Island; bounded on the north by Mount Hope bay, on the east by the Seconnet or east passage, on the south and southwest by Middletown, and on the west by the Narragansett bay.

The length of the township, from northeast to southwest, is about 8 miles, and it has a mean breadth of more than 2 miles, comprising about 17 square miles.

The surface is generally elevated and prospective, affording pleasant and interesting landscapes. The geological structure is similar to that of the rest of the island; the prevailing rocks being schistus or slate. The internal structure comprises extensive strata of mineral coal, which are supposed to be four miles in extent. Two pits have been opened, and considerable quantities have been raised. The quality of the coal is supposed to be improving, as the mine is extended; and it is believed, that it will eventually be a source of great profit, and of extensive public utility.

The soil is various in different sections of the island. There are some tracts of shistic gravel, and some of argillaceous loam. In general, it is very productive, and well adapted to grass and a grain culture.

The lands are mostly in a state of cultivation, the forests being very limited, and sustaining a high price. The leading objects of husbandry are the dairy business, and the raising of grain; of which, barley and Indian corn are the principal. The raising of sheep, which formerly received much attention, has for some years past been more neglected. The soil and climate are favourable for fruit, and the orchards are extensive and valuable.

From the maritime situation of this town, being surrounded by water upon almost every side, its fisheries are extensive and valuable, affording employment to considerable industry.

The navigation business is inconsiderable. There are, however, a few coasting vessels owned in the town.

Its mechanical and manufacturing interests, likewise, are not very important. There are 2 Woolen Factories, 1 Cotton Factory, 8 Grain Mills and 2 Clothiers' works.

There are, in the town, 4 Mercantile Stores, 2 Religious Societies and Churches, 7 Schools and 1 Social Library.

The population of the town, in 1810, was 1795; and there are about 250 Dwelling houses, 220 Electors, and 2 companies of Militia. This town sends four representatives to the General Assembly.

Prudence, and several other small islands, are attached to this town. Prudence Island is situated in Narragansett bay, opposite the northern section of Portsmouth. This island is about 6 miles in length, and has a mean breadth of about three-fourths of a mile, comprising about four square miles. The soil is excellent, affording abundant crops both of grass and grain. The land is principally owned in Providence. There are, upon this island, about 17 families.

Portsmouth was one of the original towns contained in the charter of the State of Rhode-Island, granted by Charles II. in 1663.

TIVERTON.

TIVERTON is a post town, the most extensive in the county, situated in the southeastern section of the State, 24 miles southeast of Providence, and about 13 northeast of Newport; bounded on the north and east by the State of Massachusetts, on the south by Little-Compton, and on the west by the eastern passage of the Narragansett bay and Mount Hope bay.

The township is more than eight miles in length, from north to south, and about 5 miles in breadth, from east to west, comprising 42 square miles.

The surface is generally diversified with hill and dale; but there are some sections that are rough and rocky. The prevailing geological structure is granitic. The soil is somewhat various, corresponding with the geological character, but is principally a gravelly loam, and is considerably fertile both for grass and grain.

The forests, in some sections of the town, are extensive and valuable, the prevailing timber being oak, hickory and some other deciduous trees, and is of an excellent quality, especially for ship timber.

The agricultural productions of the town are such as are common to this region, consisting of barley, Indian corn, hay, and the products of the grazing and dairy business.

The waters of the town are abundant and valuable, affording great conveniences, having an extensive coast, bordering on the east passage of the Narragansett and Mount Hope bay, affording safe and navigable waters for vessels of the largest size. It is supposed, that the waters of this town afford superior advantages for the naval depot which is contemplated to be established by the government of the United States, in Narragansett bay. Besides the navigable waters, there are several considerable and valuable ponds, which are well stored with fish.

There is an extensive and convenient stone bridge, which unites this town with Rhode Island. This bridge is a solid and durable structure, nearly 1000 feet in length, and provided with a draw, which prevents its being an obstruction to navigation. This bridge sustained considerable damage from the memorable September gale, but has since been repaired.

The fisheries of the town are extensive and valuable, affording employment to considerable industry, which in general is productive of handsome profit.

The commercial interests of this town are considerably important; there being usually 20 vessels either owned or employed here, and a considerable proportion of the population is engaged in seafaring pursuits. Ship building is occasionally carried on.

The manufacturing business also receives some attention. There are 2 Cotton Factories, 2 Clothiers' works and 6 Grain Mills.

There are, in the town, 8 Mercantile Stores of every description, 7 or 8 Religious Societies, which are generally accommodated with houses for religious worship, and 11 Schools.

The population of the town, in 1810, was 2837; and there are about 400 Dwelling houses, 4 companies of Militia and about 340 Freemen or Electors.

There are two small villages in the town, one of which is at the bridge or Howland's ferry. This town sends two representatives to the General Assembly.

Tiverton originally belonged to Massachusetts, and was not annexed to Rhode-Island until 1746.

BRISTOL

COUNTY.

BRISTOL, an inconsiderable commercial county, is delightfully situated on the peninsula, between Mount Hope bay and the upper waters of the Narragansett bay; bounded northwesterly and northeasterly by Massachusetts, southeasterly by Mount Hope bay, and southwesterly by Narragansett bay.

This county possesses but small territorial limits, but is populous and wealthy. Its mean length, from northeast to southwest, is more than 8 miles, and its mean breadth, inclusive of rivers and inlets, may be about 3 miles, comprising an area of nearly 25 square miles.

The following TOPOGRAPHICAL AND STATISTICAL TABLE exhibits a view of the towns in the county; their situation, with relation to Bristol, the seat of justice; population, according to the last census; dwelling-houses; religious societies; incorporated banks, and post-offices.

Towns.	Post-offices.	Population.	Dwelling-houses.	Religious societies.	Banks.	Dist. from Bristol.
Bristol.	1	2693	450	4	5	
Barrington.	1	604	100	1	0	7 m. N.
Warren.	1	1775	230	2	1	4 m. N.

This county comprises a very interesting tract of country, and has a local situation, which is almost unrivalled; its southeastern border being washed by Mount Hope bay, and its southwestern by the Narragansett bay, two beautiful bodies of water.

The surface is in general moderately uneven, exhibiting a pleasant and interesting diversity; but in the southeastern section there is a beautiful eminence of considerable altitude, called Mount Hope, celebrated in the early history of New-England, being the seat of the distinguished and heroic Indian chief, Philip. In the northern section of the county there is a level tract of considerable extent.

The geological structure is generally primitive, and the prevailing strata of rocks are granite. But the northern section of the county, being of a smooth and level surface, discloses indications of a different geological structure. The soil is generally a deep, rich, gravelly loam, interspersed, in the northern section, by tracts of sandy loam, and some of siliceous sand.

BRISTOL COUNTY.

The natural growth of forest trees was of the deciduous species; but there are no considerable forests at this time.

The leading agricultural interests consist of the grazing business, and the culture of barley, Indian corn and rye. Horticulture receives great attention, particularly in Bristol, where onions constitute a staple commodity, and form an important article for exportation.

The waters of this county are unrivalled for their beauty and navigable advantages. Every town is accommodated with navigable waters and convenient harbours. Its interior waters do not afford many sites for hydraulic works.

The fishing business is not pursued very extensively, being confined principally to supplying the home consumption.

The commercial and navigation business of this county constitute its most important interest. There are probably few sections of our country, which have been more distinguished for commercial enterprise, or where its results have been more important. A great proportion of the population is engaged in sea-faring pursuits; and the people are distinguished for their bold and adventurous commercial spirit, and for their hardy and persevering habits in this department of industry. It is believed, that there is no section of the United States, of equal population, which possesses as much shipping that is engaged in foreign trade as this county; and there is probably no other where this business is pursued with so much ardour and success. The amount of shipping owned here in 1819, was 9,093 tons. The trade of this county is not confined to any particular direction, but is extended to various parts of the world. An extensive and important trade is carried on with the island of Cuba, and a coasting trade of considerable extent with the southern States and elsewhere.

The manufacturing interests of the county are very inconsiderable; there being few streams affording facilities for mechanical or manufacturing operations. There is, however, considerable mechanical industry of different descriptions; and ship building has at some periods received great attention. There being little done in any department of manufacturing, there are, in this county, few local interests requiring description, and few objects of statistical detail. There are, in the county, 3 Grain Mills, 3 Distilleries, about 67 mercantile establishments of every description, and five incorporated Banks; and a charter has been granted for another.

There are 7 Religious Societies, two Academies, four or five public Schools, and about twelve private Schools.

The population of the county, in 1790, was 3211; in 1800, 3801; and in 1810, 5072.

This county originally belonged to the colony of Massachusetts, and was attached to the State of Rhode-Island in 1746.

BRISTOL is an ancient, wealthy commercial post township, port of entry, and seat of justice of the county, situated on the eastern shore of the Narragansett, adjoining the waters of Mount Hope bay, in north lat. 41° 40'; bounded on the north by Warren, on the east, partly by Massachusetts, and in part by Mount Hope bay, and on the south and west by the Narragansett bay. The average length of the township, from north to south, is more than five miles, and its mean breadth more than two miles, comprising an area of about twelve square miles.

This township is a very interesting tract of country, having a charming situation, and washed, upon its southern and western borders, by the most beautiful sheets of water in the world. Its surface, with the exception of Mount Hope, a considerable eminence in the southeast section of the town, is uneven, exhibiting a pleasant diversity. Some sections however are somewhat rocky.

Mount Hope is a beautiful eminence, affording an interesting view of the bay to which it gives name, and of the waters and islands of the Narragansett, and all their variegated scenery. It is also renowned in the annals of the early wars with the natives, as the seat of the celebrated Indian sachem Philip.

The geological structure of the township is primitive, the rocks being principally granitic. The soil is a deep, gravelly loam, very fertile and productive.

The agricultural interests are flourishing, the lands being in a high state of cultivation. Among the objects of husbandry, the cultivation of onions receives great attention, large quantities being annually raised for exportation; and it is believed, that the quantity of this article raised here, exceeds that of any other town in the United States, with the exception of Wethersfield, in Connecticut.

The waters of Bristol are unrivalled, for their beauty, or the navigable advantages which they afford. Bristol bay or harbour lies in form of a basin—is capacious and safe—of easy access—and affords sufficient depth of water for vessels of the largest size.

The fisheries of this town afford a plentiful supply for the inhabitants, and some articles for exportation.

Commerce is the leading business of this town, and its commercial interests hold the first rank. There is probably no town in the Union, of the same population, possessing a more extensive, active or profitable commerce. The merchants of Bristol are distinguished for the boldness of their commercial enterprise, the extent of their capital, and their persevering industry. When it is considered, that this place has no local advantages for interior trade, that it has little or no back country, and has no other important sources of wealth but foreign commerce, it affords the most striking example of the important results of commercial enterprise and industry; and that the want of superior local advantages interposes no insuperable barrier to the successful operation of these causes. The trade of this town is carried on with various parts of the world; but the most important branch of it, perhaps, is that to the island of Cuba, where many of the merchants have sugar and coffee plantations. The amount of the article of molasses, imported in 1818, was 1,013,820 gallons. In addition to the trade with the island of Cuba, there is a profitable and considerably extensive trade carried on with the Baltic, the Mediterranean, and various other places. There is also an extensive coasting trade maintained with the southern and middle States. The amount of shipping owned in Bristol district, in 1819, was 9093 tons.

The manufacturing and mechanical industry of the town is inconsiderable, with the exception of what is employed in ship building, which at some periods has been carried on to considerable extent, and other objects connected with the navigation business. The most important manufacture is the distillation of spirits, there being two extensive rum distilleries.

The population of Bristol, in 1810, was 2693. It has greatly improved since; and there are about 450 Dwelling houses, 300 Electors or Freemen, and 4 Companies of Militia.

There are, in the town, 35 mercantile Stores of every description, 21 Ware-houses, many of which are very extensive, 3 Grain Mills and 2 Rope-walks. There are four Religious Societies.

The compact part of the town of Bristol is built upon a beautiful declivity, fronting the bay or harbour, and facing to the west. It contains more than 300 dwelling-houses, and 13 streets, three of which are the principal, running north and south. These are intersected at right angles by the others, which run east and west. Many of the streets are well built.

The houses are in general neat and handsome buildings; and there are some superb and splendid edifices, finished in superior style and elegance. In a central part of the town is a spacious public square.

There are four Churches; one for Congregationalists, one for Episcopalians, one for Baptists and one for Methodists, a Court-house, where the legislature occasionally holds its sessions, an Academy and Market-house. There are one public School, one charity School, and six private Schools. There are four incorporated Banks, and a charter has been granted for the fifth, and a Marine Insurance Company with a respectable capital. About one mile east of the town, on a prospective and beautiful eminence, is the country seat of James De Wolf Esq. which, for elegance of style, neatness, the general splendour of its appearance, and the beauty and expensiveness of the various improvements, will rank among the first in our country. Bristol sends two representatives to the General Assembly.

Bristol, for a long time after its settlement, formed a part of the colony of Massachusetts, and was under its jurisdiction, until the settlement of the boundary line in 1746, when it was annexed to Rhode-Island. Bristol suffered severely during the revolutionary war, part of the town being burnt by the British. It also suffered considerably by the memorable September gale, in 1815.

BARRINGTON, a small agricultural post township, is situated in the northern section of the county, 7 miles from Providence; bounded on the northwest and northeast by the State of Massachusetts, on the southeast by Warren, and on the southwest by the Narragansett river. The average length of the township may be about 3 miles, with a mean breadth of nearly the same, comprising an area of about 8 square miles. The surface is generally level, and the soil a light, but fertile sandy loam, well adapted to a grain culture; rye, Indian corn and barley being cultivated with success. Sea weed is used extensively as a manure, and has been of great utility in enriching the land. The agricultural interests are considerably flourishing, and the various objects of husbandry constitute the principal occupation of the inhabitants.

The town is well watered by an inlet of the Warren, & by Palmer's river, and its southwestern borders are washed by the waters of the Narragansett. There is a convenient toll bridge, connecting this town with Warren. The waters of the Narragansett afford a plentiful supply of fin and shell fish for home consumption.

The manufacturing and mechanical industry of the town is inconsiderable; some attention, however, is paid to the manufacture of salt; there being one establishment that manufactures 1200 bushels annually.

The population of Barrington, in 1810, was 604; and there are nearly 100 dwelling houses, one religious Society and Church, two public Schools, one company of Militia, 70 or 80 Electors, and two Mercantile Stores.

In the eastern part of this town, there is a cove of considerable extent; which, from the remains of timber, is supposed to have been a pine and cedar forest, and to have been burnt by the Indians at an ancient period, long before the first settlement of this country. The adjoining waters having broken over their usual barriers, this tract became immersed, and now is covered with water of considerable depth. Cedar and pine timber are obtained from the bottom of the cove, for fencing and fuel.

This town sends two representatives to the General Assembly.

Barrington originally belonged to the State of Massachusetts, and was attached to the State of Rhode-Island in 1746, and was incorporated as a town in 1771.

WARREN.

WARREN, a small but pleasant & populous post township, is located upon the southeast side of Warren river, 11 miles southeast of Providence, & 19 miles from Newport; bounded west and north by Palmer's river, east by the State of Massachusetts, and south by Bristol. Its extent is about two miles north and south, and more than two east and west, comprising an area of more than four square miles.

This is a pleasant and interesting township, having a beautiful situation. The surface is undulating, affording very delightful landscapes. The soil is a rich mould, very fertile and productive. The various objects of husbandry, common to this district, are attended to; Indian corn, rye, barley, oats and potatoes, are cultivated with success. Horticulture also receives great attention; among the objects of which, the cultivation of onions is the most important. All kinds of culinary vegetables are raised in abundance. Fruit is also an object of general attention, and the town affords a great variety.

This town, for one of its size, maintains considerable commerce, and is a place of activity and business, and of considerable wealth. The trade is various; and, as it respects its direction and character, corresponds with that of other places upon the waters of the Narragansett. There are 30 vessels owned here, comprising about 3000 tons of shipping.

The manufacturing and mechanical business of the town is inconsiderable, with the exception of ship building, which has occasionally been carried on to considerable extent. There are two Distilleries, one of rum and one of gin, and three Grain Mills, two of which are wind mills, and one a tide mill.

The village, or compact part of the town, is built upon an interesting site, upon the southeast side of Warren river, having a moderate elevation and facing the harbour, which is safe and commodious, and has sufficient depth of water for vessels of 300 tons. There are 12 wharves, upon all of which there are store houses. There are two principal streets, intersected by several cross streets. There are in the village 180 Dwelling houses, and 40 other buildings, about 30 Mercantile Stores of every description, 2 Churches, an Academy, one public and several private Schools, one Social Library, one incorporated Bank and one Marine insurance office. There are two Religious Societies, one of Baptists and one of Methodists.

The population of the town, in 1810, was 1775; and there are about 230 Dwelling houses, 175 Electors, 2 Companies of Militia and one chartered Company.

Warren sends two representatives to the General assembly.

This town, for a long time after its settlement, was a part of Swanzey, in Massachusetts, and under the jurisdiction of that State. It was incorporated as a separate town, by its present name, in 1746.

KENT COUNTY.

KENT is an agricultural and manufacturing county, centrally situated on the western shore of the Narragansett, and is bounded on the north by the county of Providence, on the east by the Narragansett bay, on the south by Washington county, and on the west by the State of Connecticut. Its average length is nearly 20 miles, and its mean breadth more than 9 miles, comprising an area of 186 square miles.

The following TOPOGRAPHICAL AND STATISTICAL TABLE exhibits a view of the several towns in the county; their situation, with relation to East-Greenwich, the seat of justice; their population, according to the census of 1810; number of dwelling-houses; religious societies; schools; banks, and post-offices.

Towns.	P. O.	Pop.	D. Hou.	Reli.	So.	Sch.	Ban.	Dist. from
East-Greenwich.	1	1530	210	4		6	1	E. Green.
Coventry.	1	2923	350	5		3	1	10m.N.W.
Warwick.	1	3757	520	5		10	2	4 m.N.
West-Greenwich.	0	1619	220	*		*	0	8 m.W.

The geological structure of this county is primitive, the prevailing strata of rocks being granitic; which, however, are interspersed with various other rocks. The surface is generally uneven, and some parts of the county are rough and broken, especially the western section. The eastern section, however, is diversified with many tracks which present a level surface. The soil, corresponding with the geological structure, is either a primitive gravelly loam, or a sandy loam, and is generally strong and productive, particularly in the eastern section. There are some small tracts of alluvial.

The forests consist of deciduous trees, and are sufficiently extensive to afford a supply for the local demand, both for fuel and timber.

The agricultural interests are of a character corresponding with those of this district generally, consisting of the various objects of the grazing business, and the cultivation of Indian corn, rye, &c. In the eastern section of the county the orchards are extensive, and a source of convenience and profit.

Although there is no want of industry, the agricultural interests of the county are not very flourishing. There is an apparent want

* See Appendix.

of enterprise in this department of industry, and of a spirit of agricultural improvements.

This county, in common with the rest of the State, enjoys the advantages of the waters of the Narragansett bay, which, within the limits of this county, afford several good harbours, the principal of which are the Pawtuxet, (which, however, is not entirely in this county,) the Apponaug and the Greenwich harbours. The other waters of the county are principally embodied in the Pawtuxet river and its branches, which water a large portion of the northwestern section of the county. This is a beautiful mill stream, unrivalled for its advantageous sites for manufacturing establishments and other hydraulic works.

The fisheries of the county afford employment to considerable industry; and the fish taken not only supply the home consumption, but constitute a considerable article of exportation.

The commercial and navigation interests of the county are not very extensive, and are mostly confined to the coasting business. There are about 20 vessels owned in the county.

Next to agriculture, manufactures constitute the most important and extensive interest in the county. The cotton manufactures of this county claim the first rank. This business being carried on more extensively here than in any other county in the Union of the same population and extent. There are in the county 28 cotton mills, many of which are upon an extensive scale; which, considering the short period since this business commenced, and the difficulties that it has had to encounter, from foreign competition and the prejudices of our own citizens, cannot but be regarded as a gratifying result, and a satisfactory evidence that this great and important interest will become permanently established in this country.

In addition to the cotton factories, there are in this county, exclusive of West-Greenwich, 2 Woolen Factories, 2 Clothiers' works, 1 Anchor Forge, 1 Paper Mill, 1 Gin Distillery and 17 Grain Mills. There are 59 Mercantile Stores of every description, 4 incorporated Banks, 14 Religious Societies and 24 Schools.

In 1790, the population of the county was 8848; in 1800, 8487; and in 1810, 9830.

EAST-GREENWICH.

EAST-GREENWICH is a post township and seat of justice of the county, situated upon the western shore of the Narragansett bay, 13 miles south of Providence; bounded northerly on Warwick, easterly on the Narragansett bay, southerly on North-Kingston, and westerly on West-Greenwich. The township contains an average length of 6 miles, and an average breadth of 4 miles, comprising an area of about 24 square miles.

The surface is uneven, and in some sections rather rough and stony, being of a primitive geological character. No minerals have been discovered. The soil, which is a primitive gravelly loam, is considerably fertile, affording good grazing, Indian corn, barley and potatoes. Rye is also raised, but is a less certain crop. There are numerous orchards in the town; and it has been distinguished for the excellent quality of its cider.

The natural growth of timber is deciduous; and although there are no considerable forests in the town, yet there is a supply of oak and chesnut timber for fuel, fencing, building and other uses.

The town is well watered, being washed upon its eastern border by the waters of the Narragansett, and its interior intersected by the Maskachug and Hunt's rivers, two inconsiderable streams. Upon each of these streams is a bridge of the same name.

There is one excellent harbour, being safe at all times, has 15 feet of water at high tides, and will admit of ships of 500 tons burthen.

The fisheries are confined principally to the taking of cod and munhaden. There are about 1200 quintals of cod taken annually, and about 1000 barrels of munhaden. The whale fishing was formerly prosecuted here; but for some time past it has been abandoned.

The commercial business is not very considerable, and is confined to a coasting trade. There are 10 vessels owned here.

Of manufacturing and mechanical establishments, there are one Cotton Factory, containing 340 spindles, and five Grain Mills.

In the northeastern section of the town is an ancient and pleasant village, which contains a Courthouse, a Bank, an Academy, and a number of Dwelling-houses and Stores, and is the seat of considerable commercial and other business. The legislature occasionally holds its sessions at this place.

In 1774, there were 1663 inhabitants in the town; and in 1810, 1539; and it contains about 210 Dwelling-houses, 220 Electors, and 2 companies of Militia, besides one chartered company, called the "Kentish Guards." This company was established in the year 1774, and proved a nursery of officers in the war of the Revolution; having furnished, during that memorable contest, one Major-General, one Brigadier-General, three Colonels, one Major, and no less than thirty subordinate officers. The Major-General was Nathaniel Green, one of the most distinguished officers in the revolutionary war. The Brigadier-General was James M. Varnum; the Colonels, Christopher Green, Archibald Crary, and Adam Comstock; and the Major, John S. Dexter.

The taxable property of the town, is $263,158.

There are 6 Ware-houses and 20 Retail Stores in the town.

There are 4 Religious Societies; two of Baptists, one of Congregationalists and one of Friends, and three Churches. There are five Schools, besides the Academy, and one Social Library.

This town was incorporated in 1677, and had been settled but a few years at that period.

COVENTRY.

COVENTRY is an interior manufacturing post township, situated in the northwestern section of the county, 10 miles southwest from Providence; bounded northerly on the towns of Cranston, Scituate and Foster, easterly on Warwick, southerly on West-Greenwich, and westerly on the State of Connecticut.

The length of the township, from east to west, is about 12 miles, and its mean breadth about 6 miles, comprising an area of 72 square miles; being one of the largest towns in the State.

The principal section of this township presents primitive rugged features, being hilly and rocky. Some sections, however, are level, and possess a sandy soil. In the granitic sections the soil is a primitive gravelly loam, strong and fertile, being well adapted to grazing, and affording good crops of Indian corn, rye, potatoes, &c.

The dairy business is the leading agricultural pursuit; and the the town is celebrated for the excellent quality of the cheese made here. About three-fourths of the land is under a state of improvement, and the residue has been reserved for forests. The natural growth of timber is of the deciduous species.

This town is not accommodated with any navigable waters, but is intersected by several small streams, the most considerable of which is the south branch of the Pawtuxet river. Besides this is Flat river, and several other small streams. The Pawtuxet and some of the other streams afford numerous excellent sites for hydraulic works.

This town is justly distinguished for its manufactures, particularly those of cotton. The number and extent of its factories rank it among the first of the cotton manufacturing towns in the State. It contains 12 cotton mills or manufacturing establishments, all of which comprise about 10,000 spindles. The largest of these establishments are the Washington, the Coventry and the Arkwright Manufacturing Companies. Besides the cotton factories, there are one paper-mill, two clothiers' works, and ten grain mills.

There is considerable mercantile business in the retail line, there being 16 Stores in the town.

There is a flourishing manufacturing village situated on the south branch of Pawtuxet river. It contains 3 cotton mills, one of which comprises 1300 spindles. A large machine shop, for the manufacture of cotton and other machinery, and a weaving shop is established here, with water-power looms, on Gilmore's plan.

It contains from 40 to 50 dwelling-houses, a School-house, 4 merchants' stores, and a number of other buildings. The bank of Kent is located here, being 13 miles from Providence.

The population of the township, in 1810, was 2929; and there are 400 Freemen or Electors, about 350 Dwelling-houses, and 5 companies of Militia.

There are five Religious Societies; four of Baptists and one of Methodists, all of which are accommodated with houses for public worship, 8 Schools and School-houses, and 1 Social Library.

WARWICK. 371

This town was distinguished for its patriotism and services during the revolutionary war. In General Sullivan's expedition upon Rhode-Island, when nearly all of the militia of the State were called upon, the companies in this town rallied with great alacrity, there being in the whole town but five delinquencies, which were occasioned by religious scruples, the individuals being Friends or Quakers. The first settlement of Coventry is not known. It was incorporated in 1742.

WARWICK.

WARWICK is a flourishing manufacturing post township, situated five miles southwesterly of Providence; bounded north on Cranston, east on Narragansett bay, south on East-Greenwich, and west on Coventry.

The western section of the township is elevated and hilly; some of the eminences affording a view of the principal part of the State; but the eastern section is generally level. It has an average length, from east to west, of more than 8 miles, & an average breadth of nearly 7 miles, making about 54 square miles.

The prevailing soil, which is a primitive gravelly loam, is strong and productive, affording grain of the different kinds, vegetables, &c. and being also well adapted to grazing. The town is well supplied with timber, consisting of oak, walnut, chesnut, &c.

The Pawtuxet river is the largest stream in this town. The southwest branch of this stream has its source, consisting also of several branches, in Exeter, West-Greenwich and Coventry. The northwest branch rises in Scituate, and forms a junction with the southwest branch in this town, near the northwest corner, forming the Pawtuxet, which discharges its waters into Narragansett bay, at the village of Pawtuxet, which is in the northeast corner of the town. Upon this river are five bridges. But what renders it more conspicuous is, its excellent sites for hydraulic works, and the great number of cotton factories which have been erected.

There are several good harbours, the principal of which is Apponaug, about one mile from the village. It is spacious and safe, affording a depth of water sufficient for vessels of any size. Vessels of from 20 to 50 tons come up to the village. The fisheries in Narragansett bay are considerably important. From 1000 to 2000 barrels of munhaden are put up annually for exportation.

Among the manufacturing towns in the State, this claims a preeminent rank. There are 15 Cotton Factories, containing between 17 and 18000 spindles. The establishments are principally on the Pawtuxet river.

In the southern section of the town is the pleasant village of Apponaug, 10 miles S. S. W. from Providence. It is the principal village in the town of Warwick, containing upwards of 50 houses, mostly new, and very compact. Its public buildings are a Baptist Meeting house and Academy. A Bank, called the Warwick Bank, was established in this town in 1818, and located in this village. The Post-office, called the Fulling Mill post-office, is also located here.

Within a mile from the village of Apponaug may be seen a huge rock, so completely balanced upon another, and its equilibrium so exact, that a boy 14 years of age may set it in such motion that the contact or collision caused thereby, produces a sound somewhat like that of a drum, but more sonorous, which in a still evening may be heard a distance of six or eight miles. Hence, from time immemorial, it has gone by the name of the Drum rock. From the ponderous weight of that part which is thus nicely balanced, it is generally believed, that no other than the hand of nature ever could have done it. Yet some are inclined to believe, that it was thus placed by the herculean labour of some tribe of the natives. There remains no doubt, but that this was a place of their resort or encampment; and that the *Drum Rock* served them either to give an alarm in case of *danger*, or to call the tribe together from their daily avocations. This rock is considered as a great curiosity, excites much attention, and consequently is at the present day a place of much resort, particularly in the pleasant season of the year.

In addition to the cotton manufacture, there are 2 Woolen Factories, 1 Anchor Forge, 1 Gin Distillery, and 12 Grain Mills.

The commercial and navigation business is respectable. There are 10 vessels owned here, engaged principally in a coasting trade. There are 20 Dry Goods and Grocery stores, and 3 Druggists' stores.

In 1810, there were 3757 inhabitants in this town; and there are 520 Dwelling houses, 450 qualified Electors, and 5 companies of Militia, besides 2 independent companies.

There are two incorporated Banks in this town; one at the village of Pawtuxet, and one at Warwick.

There are 5 Religious Societies, 2 of Arminians, 1 of Baptists, 1 of Friends and 1 of Methodists; 10 Schools and 2 Social Libraries.

BIOGRAPHY. Col. *Christopher Green*, a very distinguished revolutionary officer, of his rank, was a native of this town. He was born in the year 1737. With only the advantages of a common education, he became an excellent scholar, particularly in mathematical sciences. From the natural vigour of his mind, the solid and useful acquisitions which he had made, and from his correct deportment, he acquired, at an early period, the confidence of his fellow-citizens, and was elected a representative of his native town in the General Assembly of the colony, for several years in succession. At the commencement of the revolutionary war, in 1775, he was chosen a Lieutenant in a military company, called the "Kentish Guards." In May, 1775, he was appointed a Major in a military detachment which was raised for the defence of the State, and shortly after accepted a Captain's commission in a regiment raised by the State of Rhode-Island for the continental service, and joined the Canadian expedition under Gen. Montgomery. In the ill-fated attack upon Quebec, in which the brave Montgomery lost his life, Capt. Green was taken prisoner, and remained with the British as a prisoner of war, for some time. On being exchanged, he joined the army, and in 1777, was appointed to the command of a regiment, and was selected by Gen. Washington to take charge of Fort Mercer, commonly called Red Bank. In the attack upon this fort by a superior force, Col. Green made a gallant defence, which established his reputation as a brave, judicious and faithful officer.

After having performed various services in Rhode-Island, in 1781, Col. Green was assigned to the command of the advanced guard of the army, which was stationed upon the border of Croton river, in the State of New-York. While in this situation, he was surprised in the night by a party of American royalists, and assassinated in the most brutal manner. This melancholy event occurred on the 13th May, 1781, and in the 45th year of his age. Thus died the gallant and heroic Green, a martyr to the cause of his country.

Col. Green possessed an active and energetic mind, and a great share of native bravery. He was a worthy citizen, an ardent patriot, and an excellent soldier.

Major-General *Nathaniel Green*, one of the most distinguished officers of the Revolution, was a native of this town. It will not be expected to find here a biography giving an ample view of the life and character of Gen. Green, whose history is identified with that of his country, during the most important period of her annals. A work of this description, we understand, is shortly to appear, from the pen of Judge Johnson of South-Carolina. This notice, from our prescribed limits, must be confined to a few prominent facts.

Gen. Green was born in the year 1741. His parents belonged to the denomination of Friends; and having little prescience of the exalted destiny of their son, bestowed little care upon his education; his early advantages having been very inconsiderable. He obtained, however, the rudiments of a common education, and some knowledge of the Latin language, at an early period; and having a vigorous mind, and a strong inclination for the acquisition of knowledge, he obtained, subsequently, by close application, having the aid of a small library, a respectable education for business, and a competent share of general knowledge. At an early period, he removed to the town of Coventry. where he soon became distinguished for his talents, and the general propriety of his conduct; and his being elected by the people to represent them in the legislature of the State, is an evidence of the high estimation in which he was held. He was first elected to this office in or about the year 1770, and was re-elected for five years in succession. This being the period immediately preceding the commencement of the revolutionary contest, was one of peculiar difficulty and importance. In the year 1775, when the difficulties between Great-Britain and her colonies had assumed a hostile aspect, and when the clouds which thickened in our political horizon portended a war of resistance to arbitrary authority, and when the strong arm of power seemed to be outstretched, to check the progress which the spirit of liberty was making in this country, General Green was among the patriots of that day, who perceived that, if this spirit was suffered to be put down by force, and the just rights of the colonies trampled under foot, the liberties of his country would be lost forever. So conspicuous were his ardour and patriotism for the cause of liberty and the just rights of his country, that he was appointed, at the commencement of hostilities, a Brigadier-General, and assigned to the command of the three regiments furnished by the State of Rhode-Island for the general defence. He led the troops under his command to Cambridge, and was present during the evacuation of Boston by the British troops.

Gen. Green's ardent patriotism, and the high promise of military talents which he early disclosed, did not pass unnoticed, but secured to him the confidence of the commander in chief, and the guardians of the public welfare. On the 26th of August, 1776, he was appointed by Congress Major-General in the Continental army; and the winter following, he distinguished himself in the well conducted and fortunate actions at Trenton and Princeton. At the battle of Germantown, he commanded the left wing of the army, and was signalized for his activity, bravery and skill. In March, 1778, he was appointed Quarter-master General, which situation he accepted, on condition that his rank in the army should not be effected by it.

About the middle of the same year, an attempt was made by the Americans, relying upon the co-operation of the French fleet, to relieve Newport. Gen. Green held a command under General Sullivan, who was entrusted with conducting this enterprise, which, although it failed, afforded an opportunity to Gen. Green to display his military talents; and he acquired great credit, for the coolness and skill with which he conducted the retreat of the American army.

After a series of disasters in the southern department, the command was bestowed upon Gen. Green. He arrived at head-quarters on the 2nd December, 1780, and found only the skeleton of an army, and that in a destitute condition. But with this remnant of an army, destitute of every thing, dispirited, and without any confidence in themselves, the natural consequence of a succession of disasters, he had to oppose a powerful army, elated with victory. After some delay, required for the recruiting of the army and obtaining necessary supplies, he sent a detachment of troops, under the command of Gen. Morgan, which obtained a victory over the enemy at the Cowpens, that effectually checked the progress of the British in that section of the country. Having received considerable reinforcements, the succeeding spring he found himself in a condition to meet the enemy, which he did at Guilford, in North-Carolina, and fought the well known battle at that place. This was one of the most obstinate, and perhaps one of the best fought actions that occurred during the war. Gen. Green displayed great courage, determined perseverance and superior military skill. Although this action was not decisive, in its immediate consequences, it not only checked the progress of the enemy, but led to an evacuation of that part of the country by the British troops. Gen. Green's next object was to drive the British from South-Carolina; and after repeated movements and various success, having nearly succeeded in compelling the enemy to retire from the interior of the State, he was obliged to retreat before a vastly superior force; the British having received reinforcements from Europe. In September, 1781, Gen. Green obtained a decisive victory over the British at Eutaw springs, which terminated the war, in the interior of the Carolinas. In this action, Gen. Green displayed his characteristic bravery, and distinguished military talents, which were duly appreciated by Congress, that body having, as a testimony of the high sense which they entertained of his good conduct and superior generalship in this engagement, presented him with a British standard and a gold medal.

Gen. Green continued in the field until the objects for which his country had taken up arms were accomplished, and the rights and independence of the colonies, recognized, in the treaty of peace of 1783, when he retired to his native State, where he continued until 1785; when he emigrated to Georgia, where he had a considerable estate, not far distant from Savannah. Here he passed his time as a private citizen, occupied with domestic and other private concerns. As he was walking, one remarkably hot day, without an umbrella, the intense rays of the sun overpowered him, and occasioned an inflammation of the brain, of which he died, June 19th, 1786, in the 47th year of his age.

Gen. Green possessed a humane and benevolent disposition; yet he was resolutely severe, when the maintenance of discipline rendered severity necessary. Among the constellation of heroes and patriots, with whom he was associated in the glorious cause of defending the liberties and independence of his country, there was none that displayed more determined firmness, and few more prudence and foresight.

As a soldier, Gen. Green will rank among the first of his age. The prominent characteristics of his mind fitted him in a peculiar manner for a military character. To the most determined resolution and the most indefatigable perseverance, he united an active and comprehensive mind, full of expedients, and never disconcerted by difficulties; and to the most daring courage he united superior military skill and extensive practical knowledge. Among the many distinguished individuals engaged in the same cause, few acted their part with more credit and honour to themselves or usefulness to their country, than Gen. Green. As his life was devoted to the cause of liberty and his country, his name will rank among the first of the heroes and patriots of the Revolution, and be revered by his country to the latest posterity.

WEST-GREENWICH.

WEST-GREENWICH is an agricultural township, situated in the southwest section of the county, about 18 miles southwest from Providence; bounded on the north by Coventry, on the east by East-Greenwich, on the south by Exeter, in Washington county, and on the west by the State of Connecticut. The length of the township, from east to west, is about 12 miles, and its mean breadth about 3 miles, comprising an area of about 36 square miles.

This township possesses a primitive geological character; its surface presents a diversity of hill and dale. There is one considerable eminence called Hopkins' hill, which affords an interesting prospect of the surrounding country. The natural and agricultural productions of the town correspond with those of this region generally.

The waters of the south branch of the Pawtuxet river, have their source in this town; and the western section is watered by Wood river and its branches.

The contemplated turnpike road from Providence to Pawcatuck, will lead through this town.

The population of East-Greenwich, in 1748, was 766; in 1774, 1764; in 1782, 1698; in 1790, 1756; in 1800, 1759; and in 1810, 1619; there are about 220 Dwelling houses, & 3 companies of Militia.

West-Greenwich sends two representatives to the General Assembly.

This town originally belonged to East-Greenwich, and was incorporated as a separate town by its present name, in 1741.

WASHINGTON COUNTY.

WASHINGTON is a maritime county, situated in the southwestern section of the State; bounded on the north by Kent county, on the east by Narragansett bay, on the south by the Atlantic ocean, and on the west by the State of Connecticut. The average length of the county, from east to west, is about 20 miles, and it has a mean breadth of more than 18 miles, comprising about 367 square miles.

The following TOPOGRAPHICAL AND STATISTICAL TABLE exhibits a view of the several towns in the county; their situation, with relation to South-Kingston, the seat of justice; their population, according to the census of 1810; number of dwelling-houses; religious societies; banks, and post-offices.

Towns.	Post-offices.	Population.	Dwelling houses.	Religious societies.	Banks.	Dist. from S. Kingston.
South-Kingston.	1	3560	400	4	1	
Exeter.	0	2254	311	1	0	10 m. N. W.
Charlestown.	1	1174	220	1	1	10 m. S. W.
Hopkinton.	1	1774	230	4	0	13 m. W.
North-Kingston.	1	2957	391	5	1	8 m. N. E.
Richmond.	1	1330	230	*	*	7 m. W.
Westerly.	1	1911	250	2	2	20 m. S. W.

The geological character of this county is primitive; the rocks consist of granite and other original formations. The surface is generally diversified with moderate hills and narrow dales; there are, however, some considerable eminences in the northwest section of the county, and some flats of considerable extent in the south section, bordering upon the Atlantic. The prevailing soil is a primitive gravelly loam, strong and fertile; there are some considerable tracts of sandy loam, and some of alluvial. The forests of the county are of the deciduous species, and in most sections afford a supply both for fuel and timber, for the local demand. The various objects of the grazing business form the leading agricultural interests of the county. A considerable section of this county was formerly called the Narragansett country, and was celebrated for an excellent breed of pacing horses; the other section was called the Shannock country, and was equally distinguished for a valuable breed of neat cattle. This

* See *Appendix*.

county still maintains a high reputation as a grazing district, and affords many extensive and valuable dairies. But the agricultural interests are not confined exclusively to the objects of the grazing business; in some sections of the county, considerable attention is paid to the cultivation of grain, particularly Indian corn and barley; some rye also is raised. Although there may be some want of enterprise and a spirit of agricultural improvements, yet the inhabitants are distinguished for their habits of industry and frugality, and in general enjoy their necessary results, health and competence.

The waters of the county are extensive & important, possessing a maritime border upon the Atlantic ocean & the Narragansett bay, of more than 50 miles extent. There are, however, but 2 or 3 harbours; the principal of which is Wickford, in the northeastern section of the county; the next most important is the Pawcatuck. The principal interior waters of the county are embodied in the Pawcatuck river, which forms part of the western boundary of the State. The principal branches of the Pawcatuck are the Wood and Charles rivers; which, with their tributary streams, water a large proportion of the western section of the county, and afford numerous sites for mills and other hydraulic works.

There are, in the county, several salt and fresh water ponds, which are well supplied with fish.

The fisheries of the county are extensive and valuable, affording employment to considerable industry, which is usually well rewarded. The fish taken, not only supply the home consumption, but constitute an article of exportation. The fishing business is carried on principally at the villages of Wickford and Pawcatuck.

The commercial and navigation interests of the county are not very extensive or important, and are confined principally to the aforesaid villages.

At these and other places in the county, there are from 20 to 25 vessels owned. Although the commercial business carried on within the county is not very considerable, yet its maritime situation has had its natural influence upon the habits of the people; a considerable portion of whom are employed in seafaring business.

The manufacturing interests of the county are inconsiderable, and consist principally of the woolen and cotton manufactures, and the business of ship building. Besides these, there is considerable mechanical industry in the various departments of mechanical business.

There are in the county, exclusive of those in the town of Richmond, which have not been received, 17 Religious Societies, 52 Schools, 5 incorporated Banks, 67 Mercantile Stores, 5 Cotton Factories, 7 Woolen do. 34 Grain Mills, 8 Clothiers' Works and 2 Forges.

The population, in 1774, was 13,867; in 1782, 13,133; in 1790, 18,075; in 1800, 16,135; and in 1810, 14,962. From this view of the population of the county, at these several different periods, it appears that it has suffered greatly by emigration.

SOUTH-KINGSTON.

SOUTH-KINGSTON, a post town and seat of justice of the county, is situated 30 miles south-west from Providence; bounded on the north by Exeter and North-Kingston, on the east by the Narragansett bay and the Atlantic ocean, on the south by the Atlantic, and on the west by Charlestown and Richmond. This is the largest township in the State, being about 11 miles in length, from north to south, and nearly $8\frac{1}{2}$ in breadth, from east to west, comprising an area of about 92 square miles.

This is a flourishing agricultural township; it is of a primitive geological character, having generally an uneven surface. The rocks consist of granite and other primitive formations. The prevailing soil is a gravelly loam, generally strong and fertile. It is adapted both to grazing and a grain culture, affording many excellent dairy farms, and producing good crops of Indian corn, barley, oats and rye. The dairy business constitutes the leading agricultural interest, and is carried on advantageously, and to considerable extent.

The town is extensively accommodated with navigable waters; its eastern and southern borders being washed by the Atlantic ocean and the Narragansett bay. Its interior is watered by numerous small streams, but there are none deserving the character of rivers. In the northeast part of the town, upon the Narragansett bay, there is a good harbour. There is one large salt pond, called Point-Judith pond, and about twenty fresh water ponds, some of which are of considerable size, one containing three or four thousand acres.

The fisheries are of some importance. Upon the shores of the Narragansett, and in the salt pond, considerable quantities of alewives, bass, perch and smelt are taken. Between one and 2000 barrels of alewives are annually put up for exportation; and large quantities of bass are marketed at Providence, Newport, and frequently at New-York.

Exclusive of the fishing business, the maritime interests of the town are inconsiderable, although a considerable proportion of the inhabitants are engaged in seafaring pursuits abroad.

The mercantile business is confined principally to the retail trade, engaged in which there are eight stores.

The manufacturing and mechanical employments of the town are inconsiderable. There are eight Grain Mills and two Clothiers' works.

Near the centre of the township is a small but pleasant village, called "Little rest hill." It has a prospective and interesting site, and contains about 25 Dwelling-houses, a Court-house, in which the courts for the county are held, and which is occasionally occupied by the legislature, an incorporated Bank, and an Episcopal Church. There is another small village, called Tower Hill.

The population of the town, in 1810, was 3560; and there are about 400 Dwelling-houses, about the same number of Electors, and 5 companies of Militia.

The taxable property exceeds $700,000.

There are, in the town, 4 Religious Societies, two of Friends, one of Episcopalians and one of Baptists. There are 4 Schools.

This town was first settled about the year 1670, then being a part of the town of Kingston, which, in about the year 1723, was divided into two towns, the southeast section was called South-Kingston, and the other North-Kingston.

EXETER.

EXETER is an agricultural township, situated 24 miles southwest of Providence; bounded on the north by West-Greenwich, on the east by North-Kingston, on the south by South-Kingston, Richmond and Hopkinton, and on the west by the State of Connecticut.

This township comprises extensive territorial limits, having an average length of more than 12 miles, and a mean breadth of more than 5 miles, comprising an area of about 66 square miles.

The surface, soil and geological features of this township correspond with this district generally. The rocks are primitive, the soil a gravelly loam, and the face of the country uneven, exhibiting a diversity of hill and dale.

The natural and agricultural productions also are such as are common to this region. The various objects of the dairy business, and the cultivation of Indian corn, rye and oats constitute the principal agricultural interests.

The contemplated road from Providence to Pawcatuck will lead through this town.

This town is not accommodated with any navigable waters. Its western section is watered by Wood river and its branches, which intersect it in various directions. This stream affords some good sites for hydraulic works.

The cotton spinning business constitutes the principal manufacturing interest. There are 2 Cotton Factories, containing about 360 spindles each. There are one Woolen Factory, one Clothier's works and ten Grain Mills.

The population of the town, in 1810, was 2254; and there are 296 Electors, 311 Dwelling-houses and 3 companies of Militia.

The amount of taxable property is $200,078.

There are one Religious Society and Church, 20 primary Schools and 3 Mercantile Stores.

Exeter was incorporated the 5th of December, 1743.

CHARLESTOWN.

CHARLESTOWN is a post township, situated 40 miles southwest from Providence; bounded on the north by Charles river, which separates it from Richmond, on the east by South-Kingston, on the south by the Atlantic ocean, and on the west by Westerly.

The township is between six and seven miles square, and nearly in a square form, comprising an area of about 43 square miles, including its waters, of which there are five considerable ponds, two salt, and three fresh water, all of which, it is estimated, contain about 7 square miles. These ponds are called Charlestown, Conaquetogue, Posquissett, Watchaug and Cochumpaug. The two first are salt water, and the three latter fresh water ponds.

Between the two first mentioned ponds there are communications with the sea, which are occasionally closed by sand. The entrance into Conaquetogue pond is sometimes of sufficient depth to admit of vessels of from 15 to 20 tons; but that into Charlestown pond only admits of small open boats. In these ponds, and in the sea, considerable quantities of fish are taken; the most important are codfish, haddock, black fish, mackerel, blue fish, white fish, scupaug, (an Indian name,) bass, perch and alewives.

Charles river, which has its source in Warden's pond, in South-Kingston, washes the northern border of the township. This stream, after affording several sites for hydraulic works, unites with Wood river from the north, forming Pawcatuck river, which discharges its waters into Fisher's Island sound.

The township, as it respects its surface and soil, is considerably diversified. Bordering upon the sea, for about two miles in extent, there is a level tract, possessing a fertile soil, and affording a facility of cultivation. Back of this is a tract of about the same extent, which is elevated and rough, being hilly and rocky; so much so as to render it in a great measure unfit for cultivation. It however affords valuable forests, which comprise oak of the various species, chesnut, walnut, maple, ash, birch, and white and yellow pine. In the north section, the soil is generally light, but carries tolerable crops of rye and Indian corn.

The agricultural productions consist of rye, corn, oats, barley, potatoes, beef, pork, butter & cheese.

There are no manufacturing establishments in this town, although there is considerable manufacturing industry. Large quantities of cotton cloth are usually wove here in families, for the manufacturing establishments in other towns. For several years past, about 3000 pair of coarse wool stockings have been manufactured here for the New-York market.

The mercantile business is inconsiderable. There are six retail Stores, which employ but small capitals, and do but little business.

The population of the town, in 1810, was 1174; and there are about 220 Dwelling-houses, 170 Electors, and two companies of Militia.

There is one Religious Society of Baptists, which have two places for religious worship. There are ten primary schools usually maintained in the winter season; and in the summer there are several female schools for instruction in reading, writing and needlework. It must, however, be acknowledged, that there is less attention paid to the subject of education than its importance demands.

Having noticed what belongs to civilized man, we cannot pass over the aboriginal inhabitants. Here are the remains of the famous Naragansett tribe of Indians, once sovereigns of immense domains, once powerful in peace and terrible in war, not only to neighbouring tribes, but to the primitive European settlements. Where is this numerous and powerful nation, which once "possessed the earth?" They have passed away like a dream, and the places that knew them know them no more. Their fishing ponds have become ports of entry, and their hunting grounds fruitful fields. The remains of this tribe at this place amount to about 100, nearly all of whom are intermixed with the whites and negroes. They are an abject race, strongly attached to spiritous liquors, subsisting miserably upon the rents of their lands, which are all leased out, and occasional personal labour. They possess, however, some of the traits of their ancient character; they are hospitable, and notwithstanding their wretched situation, they are seldom guilty of theft, although in other respects they seem to have little sense of moral principle. They still own about 3000 acres of land, extending through the centre of the town, north and south. It is in a bad state of cultivation, and in general greatly impoverished by a system of bad husbandry, and the mismanagement of tenants. It is naturally good land, and adapted to a grain culture, and affords at the present time tolerable crops of corn and rye.

They are governed by laws enacted by the General Assembly; which, however, are distinct from the general laws of the State. Their lands are secured to them, not being subject to be alienated; and they are not allowed the privilege of selling their wood and timber. This latter regulation, however, is violated with impunity. No process can issue against them for debt; and any officer issuing such process is subjected to a fine. Negroes, intermarrying with the tribe, are allowed the same privileges and exemptions. In some instances, their marriages are sanctioned by conformity to the laws; but in general they pursue the primitive custom of "taking a wife" without ceremony. Several years ago, the most intelligent, active and industrious emigrated to Oneida, where they had lands given them by that tribe. Those disposed to emigrate may lease their lands for ten years; after which, it descends to the heir at law, which is the next of kin. The Indians choose annually, from among themselves, a council, consisting of five members, which, with the approbation of an agent, appointed by the General Assembly, have heretofore had the management of affairs relating to the poor, leasing tribe lands, and the lands of absent individuals. But, from an accumulation of expense in the agent's department, that office has lately been discontinued; and the council now have the sole management of the affairs of the tribe. There are no distinctions of "chiefs" among them at the present time; but 50 or 60 years since, some of them were invested with regal dignity, with considerable ceremony.

Charlestown, including Richmond, was separated from Westerly, and incorporated in 1738. The date of the first settlement is not known; but perhaps was as early as the incorporation of Westerly, in 1669.

HOPKINTON.

HOPKINTON is an interior post township, situated 30 miles southwest of Providence; bounded northerly by the town of Exeter, easterly by Wood river, which separates it from Richmond, southerly by the town of Westerly and Pawcatuck river, and westerly by North-Stonington, in the State of Connecticut.

Its average length, from north to south, is more than 8 miles, and its mean breadth is about 4 miles, comprising an area of about 34 square miles.

The north section of the town is rough and broken, and presents primitive geological features. The soil here is a gravelly loam, well adapted to grazing. The south section of the town is smooth and level, and the soil well adapted to a grain culture. Grass also grows well, and most other crops. In the north part, there is considerable wood and timber, of the deciduous species. There are many valuable apple orchards, and considerable quantities of cider are made.

The principal waters of the town are embodied in Wood river, a small stream which washes its eastern border, and empties into the Pawcatuck at the southeast corner of the town. This is a valuable mill stream. A part of the southern border of the town is washed by the Pawcatuck, in which shad, alewives and many other kinds of small fish are taken; these are the only fisheries the town affords. There are several ponds in the township.

This town, possessing no navigable waters, maintains but little commerce. There are seven mercantile stores engaged in the retail business.

The contemplated turnpike road from Providence to New-London will lead through the centre of this town.

The are some manufactories in the town. Two Forges have been erected upon Wood river. Besides which, there are 3 Woolen Factories, 2 Clothiers' works, 5 Grain Mills and 10 Saw Mills.

The population of the town, in 1810, was 1774; and there are 220 Freemen or Electors, 230 Dwelling-houses, and 3 companies of Militia, and one chartered company.

The amount of taxable property is $250,000.

There are 4 Religious Societies, three of Baptists, and one of Friends, all of which are accommodated with houses for religious worship, 6 regular Schools, besides several others which are occasionally maintained.

Near the centre of the town, there is a small village, which is the seat of most of the commercial and mechanical business.

The first settlement of this town was about the year 1660; and it was incorporated in 1757.

NORTH-KINGSTON.

NORTH-KINGSTON, a wealthy and flourishing maritime post township, is situated 20 miles southwesterly from Providence; bounded northerly by East-Greenwich and Warwick, easterly by Narragansett bay, southerly by South-Kingston, and westerly by Exeter. Its average length is about 8 miles, from east to west, and its mean breadth about 7 miles, comprising about 56 square miles.

The face of the country is generally uneven, being diversified with hills and dales. The northern section, however, is level.

The geology of the township is primitive; and there are several quarries of excellent freestone, for building and other purposes.

The soil in the northern section is a sandy loam, well adapted to a grain culture, particularly Indian corn; and the southern section is a gravelly loam, affording good grazing.

The agricultural productions consist of Indian corn, rye, wheat, buck-wheat, barley, beans, peas, potatoes and some others common to this region.

There are some forests in the town, which afford a supply of wood and timber for ordinary uses, and for ship building, &c.

This town enjoys the advantages of the waters of the Narragansett bay, which wash its eastern border; and its interior is watered by numerous small streams, the most considerable of which are the Pettequamscust, or Narrowriver, which has its source in this town, and runs southerly thro' South-Kingston, and discharges itself into the ocean; the Annoquetucket, which is a valuable mill stream, and the seat of a number of mills and factories; and Hunt's river, which runs upon the northern boundary of the town. In the first of these streams, large quantities of bass, perch, smelts and alewives are taken.

There is a safe and convenient harbour at Wickford, having a sufficient depth of water, and situated 8 or 9 miles north of the Beaver Tail light-house, and so near the ocean as seldom to be obstructed by ice in the winter season. Besides this, there are in the town two other harbours, Cole's harbour and Allen's harbour.

The fishing business forms a considerable interest in this town. It is carried on upon Nantucket shoals, the Grand Banks, the Streights of Belle-Isle, off Block-Island, Sandy-Hook, &c. There are generally from 6 to 10 vessels employed in this business.

There is considerable commercial and navigation business, the latter of which consists principally of a coasting trade. There are from 15 to 20 vessels owned in the town; and there are 35 stores of every description.

The manufacturing interests are considerably important. There are 2 Cotton Factories, containing, both of them, 1164 spindles, one Gin Distillery, situated in the vicinity of Wickford village, 2 Woolen Factories, 3 Clothiers' works and 6 Grain Mills.

WICKFORD, in this town, is a large and flourishing village, situated on the west side of the Narragansett bay, about 22 miles southwest from Providence, and 15 northwest from Newport, having a pleasant and interesting site, upon a peninsula or point of land. There are in the village about 90 Dwelling-houses, 30 Mercantile Stores, and a considerable number of workshops and other buildings. There are here three houses for public worship; one for Separate Baptists, which is a new, large and elegant building, one for Episcopalians, a handsome edifice, and one for Friends; an Academy, called the Washington Academy, the building for which is a substantial and elegant edifice, 60 feet by 30, delightfully situated upon an eminence, out of the village, encircled with rows and groves of trees, exhibiting a romantic, rural and picturesque appearance. There is a valuable library attached to this Academy; and it is usually attended by from 50 to 60 students. There is a Bank located at this village; and the Gin Distillery already noticed is established here. The town-house, where the electors' mteeing are held, is at this place.

This is the seat of most of the commercial and navigation business. A trade is carried on with the West-Indies and south-America, and a coasting trade with the southern and eastern States. The fishing business also, which has been noticed, is carried on from this village. There is likewise a number of packets that ply regularly between this village and Newport, Providence, Bristol and the other commercial places upon Narragansett bay. The harbour is spacious, safe and accessible at all seasons of the year.

The population of this town, in 1810, was 2957; and there are about 450 Electors, 391 Dwelling-houses, four companies of Militia and one Independent company.

There are five Religious Societies, one of Baptists, one of Separate Baptists, one of Episcopalians, one of Friends and one of Methodists, all of which have houses for public worship, and the Society of Baptists have two.

There are 12 Schools, exclusive of the Academy, at the village of Wickford.

On the post road, between the village of Wickford and East-Greenwich, there is a cleft of a rock, in which there are several holes, in the shape of the human foot; one of which is called the "Devil's foot," and is twenty inches in length; the others are of a less size. There are various other impressions, some exhibiting the figure of a dog, all of which have the appearance of having been made when the rock was formed, and before it acquired a perfectly indurated character.

This town was incorporated in the year 1674.

RICHMOND.

RICHMOND is an interior post township, centrally situated in the county, 30 miles from Providence; bounded on the north by Exeter, on the east by South-Kingston, on the south by Charles river, which separates it from Charlestown, and on the west by Wood river, which divides it from Hopkinton. Its average length, from north to south, is nearly 7 miles, and its mean breadth, from east to west, is more than 6 miles, comprising about 40 square miles.

The physical features of this township accord with those of this district generally; having a primitive geological structure, and the surface being generally uneven, but interspersed with some level tracts, and the soil is a gravelly loam.

The forests consist of trees of the deciduous species; and the agricultural productions are butter, cheese, Indian corn, and some others. The various objects of the grazing and dairy business form the leading agricultural interests.

The town is well watered by the two principal branches of the Pawcatuck, Wood and Charles rivers; one forming the western and the other the southern boundary of the town. The latter of these streams has several branches, which water the interior of the township. These two rivers and their branches afford numerous sites for hydraulic works.

There are in the town three Cotton Factories, one Woolen do. one Clothier's works for customers, six Grain Mills and seven Mercantile Stores.

The population of Richmond, in 1774, was 1257; in 1800, 1368; and in 1810, 1330; and there are about 230 Dwelling-houses, 2 companies of Militia, 160 Electors, three Religious Societies, one of Baptists, one of New-Lights, and one of Friends, 3 regular Schools and School houses, besides several others which are occasionally maintained.

The amount of taxable property is $370,380.

Richmond sends two representatives to the General Assembly. It was incorporated in 1747.

WESTERLY.

WESTERLY is a maritime post township, situated in the southwest corner of the State, 36 miles southwest from Providence, and 35 west by south from Newport; bounded on the north by the Pawcatuck river and the town of Hopkinton, on the east by Charlestown, on the south by the Atlantic ocean, and on the west by the Pawcatuck river, which separates it from the State of Connecticut. Its extent is more than six miles east and west, and nearly the same north and south, comprising about 36 square miles.

This township, though not mountainous, is considerably rough and broken, the surface presenting primitive and somewhat rugged features. The soil, which is generally a gravelly loam, affords, as it respects the quality of it, most of the varieties from a fertile mould to a soil lean and sterile. In some sections of the town, barley is cultivated to advantage. Some Indian corn is also raised; but the staple agricultural product consists of cheese. The lands being in general best adapted to grazing, the dairy business is carried on extensively and to great advantage.

The town is well accommodated with navigable and other waters. Its southern border is washed by the Atlantic ocean, and its western by the Pawcatuck river. This stream has its source in Warden's pond, in South-Kingston; and although small at first, and having but a short course, yet being swelled by numerous tributary streams, and having the advantages of tidewater, it becomes a navigable river. It forms a part of the boundary line between Richmond and Charlestown, and between this town and Hopkinton. There are seven bridges upon this river, within this town, the largest of which is in the village of Pawcatuck. This bridge, connects this town with Stonington, in Connecticut. The east part of it was built and is maintained by this State, and the west part by the town of Stonington. This river is navigable for vessels of 80 tons, as far as Champlin's wharf, four miles from the ocean, and for sloops of 30 tons, at high water, two miles above, to the village of Pawcatuck. This river affords a great variety of scale and shell fish, and in great abundance.

The village of Pawcatuck is situated upon the west side of this river, about six miles from its mouth. There is a small settlement also upon the opposite side, in the town of Stonington. There are in the village about 50 Dwelling-houses, 8 Mercantile Stores, an extensive Woolen Factory, the building of which is a substantial stone structure, 64 feet by 36, and four stories in height, two considerable Tanneries, and several work-shops for mechanical purposes. Here also are two incorporated Banks; the Washington Bank, established in 1800, with a capital of $75,000, and the Phœnix Bank, in 1818, having a capital of $60,000. There are two Academies established here, which are under good regulations, and afford great facilities to the youth of this place and vicinity, of obtaining an education, with convenience and economy. There is one Social Library established here.

This is an active and flourishing village, containing about 400 inhabitants. In connection with agriculture and the mechanic arts, it carries on a brisk coasting trade; and at the present time the Labrador fishery, which was formerly prosecuted with success, is reviving and promises again to become an important and profitable business. Ship building is likewise carried on here, at some periods, to considerable extent; ships of 300 tons have been built, and conducted to the ocean during flood tides. About three miles northeasterly of Pawcatuck bridge, upon the river of the same name, at a place called Potter's hill, in this town, there are one Cotton Factory, containing about 1000 spindles, a Grain Mill, Saw Mill and Clothiers' works.

The population of this town, in 1810, was 1911; and there are 2 Religious Societies, 250 Dwelling houses and 4 Companies of Militia.

This town sends two representatives to the General Assembly.

Westerly was incorporated in 1669, being the first town incorporated in the State after the obtaining of the charter of Charles II, in 1663, and then embraced the whole extent of country which is now comprised in this town, Charlestown, Richmond and Hopkinton. These several towns have been set off and incorporated at different periods, which of course has greatly reduced the original territorial limits of this town.

APPENDIX.

State of Connecticut.—Since the work was written, some alterations have been made as to its civil or corporate divisions; and the seat of justice in one county has been changed. At the May session of 1819, a new town was incorporated, by the name of *Salem;* being composed of the south section of Colchester, the northeast section of Lyme, and the northerly section of Montville. The centre of the township of Salem is about 29 miles southeast from Hartford. Its dimensions are about six and a half miles by five and a half. It contains about 150 dwelling houses, from 1000 to 1200 inhabitants, and between 150 and 200 Electors. The town is accommodated with a post-office, and the turnpike road from Hartford to New-London passes through it. By a general provision in the new Constitution of the State, the town is entitled to but one representative in the popular branch of the General Assembly.

During the same session of the Legislature, the seat of justice for the county of Windham was removed from the town of Windham to Brooklyn, a more central town, situated upon the Quinibaug river, 45 miles from Hartford.

Weston, FAIRFIELD COUNTY.—There are 22 school districts and the same number of primary schools in this town.

Some additional information respecting the Mohegan Indians in Montville.—The tract of land which they inhabit contains about 2400 acres, bordering upon the river Thames, on its west side, and forming the northeast corner of the town of Montville. It is bounded north upon Trading Cove and Trading Cove brook, and is intersected by the turnpike road between the cities of Norwich and New-London. The soil is generally of a good quality for arable purposes, pasturage and mowing, but is in a bad state of cultivation, owing to its having been long tenanted by persons having no interest in the inheritance. In the year 1791, these lands were apportioned among the tribe, with the exception of about 500 acres which were reserved in a farm, the rents of which are applied to the contingent charges arising from age, sickness and infirmity, incident to this irregular and improvident people. Their number, in 1808, was 71, and in 1818, 52. About two-thirds consist of females. The character of the Mohegans is peaceable, patient, generous, hospitable, and thoughtless of tomorrow. They are without enterprise, being neither hunters nor fishermen—are not inclined to dishonesty, but much given to intemperance. As the descendants of the subjects of Uncas, they are attached to the government and the white people of Connecticut, and have a strong adherence to all ancient customs of their own. The concerns of this tribe are managed by a board of overseers, appointed by the General Assembly.

State of Rhode-Island.—Some further particulars relating to the town of West-Greenwich have been received since the work went to press. There are in this town 250 electors, one religious society, and a part of several others, one regular school, kept throughout the year, and several usually maintained in the winter seasons in different sections of the town. There are five small cotton factories, all of which contain about 2000 spindles, connected with which are a bleach house and several dye houses. There are 10 grain mills, 1 clothier's works and 9 mercantile stores.

ERRATA.

In a work of this description, comprising a vast collection of facts, it will not be a matter of surprise, that a considerable number of errors should have escaped detection. Such of them as have been discovered, and are deemed material, are corrected here; but being unwilling to swell the errata, the errors merely verbal are left for the reader to correct himself.

Page 33, in the County Table, after East-Windsor, read '2 Post-offices.'
Page 36, line, 29th, after and, read 'which.'
Page 62, line 23d, for 8 or 10, read '6 or 8.'
Page 92, line 12th from bottom, after one, read 'of which.'
Same page, second column, after the word with, for *William Davy and Mr. Murray*, read '*Messrs. Davie and Murray.*'
Page 94, line 14th, for *all*, read 'most of.'
Page 104, line 2nd from bottom, 2nd column, for *building*, read 'buildings.'
Page 128, line 17th from bottom, for *dome*, read 'dove.'
Page 162, bottom line, 2nd column, for 4000, read '2400.'
Page 180, for the boundaries of the town of Huntington, in the text, substitute the following; bounded northwest by Newtown, northeast and southeast by the Ousatonick river, which separates it from Oxford, Derby and Milford, south and southwest by Stratford, Trumbull and Weston.
Page 249, bottom line, for 350, read '250.'
Page 271, 2nd column, 11th line from bottom, for 42, read '41.'
Page 305, 2nd line, after east lon. read '*from Philadelphia.*'
Page 324, for the dimensions of the town of Providence, instead of 4 miles in length, and 9 square miles, substitute '3 miles in length, and 7 square miles.
Page 355, bottom line, for for *social*, read '*circulating.*'
Page 368, line 9th, before 28, insert the words '*more than.*'

N. B.—The number of the *line* is understood as being from the top of the page, unless mentioned as being from the bottom; and where the *column* is not mentioned, it is the first column in the page.

This index lists all people and places mentioned in the text.

ABBOT'S, Run 336
ADAMS, 161 Andrew 235 Judge 149 Pres 161
ALBANY, 61 70 71 77 81 238 243 249 252 266 277 331
ALDEN, Roger 118
ALLEN, Capt 334 335 Col 245-247 Ethan 245 Lt 334 Mr 334 Wm 333 Wm Henry 333
ALLEN'S, Harbor 384
ALLYN, Matthew 276 Mr 239 Pelatiah 238
ALMY, 347
AMES', Lake 164 Pond 164
AMHERST, Gen 84
ANDRE, Maj 294
ANDREWS, Nehemiah 81
ANDROSS, Edmund 32 175
ANNOQUETUCKET, River 384 Stream 384
APPONAUG, 305 308 371 372 Harbor 308 368 371 Village 305
ARKWRIGHT, 370 Richard 310 311
ARNOLD, Benedict 144 Col 246
ASH, Creek 172 River 169
ASHFORD, 41 63 202 207 211 216 218 225 292 300 301 303

ASPETUCK, River 253 264
ATHENS, 123
ATTLEBOROUGH, 336
ATWATER, Joshua 109
AUSTIN, William 239
BABCOCK, Elisha 188 Mr 188
BACKUS, Azel 240 Dr 240 Sylvanus 220
BACON, Pierpont 152
BACON'S, Bridge 209
BALD, Mountain 5
BALDWIN, Abraham 122 188 Miss 188
BALTIMORE, 277
BANKS, Joseph 156
BANTAM, 233 River 232 264
BARKHAMSTEAD, 60
BARKHAMSTED, 8 76 80 229 237 251 265
BARLOW, 119 188-190 335 Joel 187 Mr 187 188
BARNES, John 245
BARRINGTON, 307 361 365
BARRON, Capt 334
BATES', Pond 210
BAXTER, Simon 81
BEAVER, Brook 276 277 Pond 99 Stream 160
BEAVER TAIL, 356 384

BECKWORTH, Maj 155
BELLAMY, Dr 240
BELLEFONTE, 338
BELLE ISLE, 384
BELLINGHAM, 336
BENEDICT, Joel 218
BENEDICT'S, Pond 255
BENNETT'S, Bridge 183
BENNINGTON, 145
BERKSHIRE, County 229
BERLIN, 5 9 15 16 33 41 55 60 71 84 85 89 100 125 271 272
BETHLEM, 8 229 231 239 263 264 266
BIGELOW, River 207 301 Stream 207
BINGHAM, Caleb 259
BISHOP, Abraham 102 187 Berkley 104 James 102 Samuel 112
BISSELL, 66
BLACK, Pond 272
BLACKBERRY, River 241 255
BLACKHALL'S, Pond 160
BLACK ROCK, 7 169 Harbor 7 169 172
BLACKSTONE, River 345
BLACKWELL'S, Brook 208
BLANFORD, 77
BLOCK ISLAND, 309 318 350 357 384
BOLTON, 61 62 69 74 288 291 295 302 303
BORDER, Rock 342
BOSTON, 13 41 63 72 100 102 104 203 207 216 219 223 225 227 277 279 290 299 302 309 324 325 337 343 351 353 374
BOZRAH, 139 146 150-152 162 214

BRANFORD, 93 95 100 109 114 119 120 130 133 174 Harbor 95 River 95
BRATTLEBORO, 41
BREAKNECK, Pond 301 River 301
BRIDE, Pond 160
BRIDGE, Stream 160
BRIDGEPORT, 7 13 15 169 179 181 183 195-199 Borough 1 Harbor 7 169 195 196 199
BRIMFIELD, 228 301 River 301
BRISTOL, 33 57 58 60 71 84 137 256 305 306 308 309 311 312 314 315 325 326 361 363 365 385 Bay 363 County 305-307 361 Harbor 308 363
BROCKWAY, 160
BROCKWAY'S, Ferry 160
BROOK, Lord 286 287
BROOKFIELD, 5 168 177 178 182 183 252
BROOKLYN, 8 202 208 211 212 217 218 220-222 388
BROWN, 347 Col 246 Cornelius 255 Titus 255 University 316 328
BULL, Epaphras W 53
BULL'S, Pond 182
BUNKER, Hill 221
BURLINGAME, 340
BURLINGTON, 15 33 58-60 71 249 251
BURNHAM, Rev Mr 57 58
BURR, 228
BURRELLVILE, 345
BURRELLVILLE, 314 321 335 339
BUSHES, Landing 179

BUTLER, 347
BUTLER'S, Bridge 209
BYRAM, River 169 180
CAMBRIDGE, 51 221 332 374
CAMPBELL, Capt 334
CANAAN, 9 15 112 113 229 232 240 243 244 254 255 258 259
CANANDAIGUA, 88
CANNANICUT, Island 350
CANTERBURY, 9 149 153 158 202 205 208 209 211 217
CANTON, 9 33 59 60 76 83 237 251
CAPE COD, 142
CARR, Caleb 342
CASE, Amos 239
CAT, Hole Pass 126
CATSKILL, Mts 231 248
CAUDATOWA, 192
CEDAR, Brook 342 Pond 160
CENTRAL, Bridge 309 325
CHAMPLIN'S, Wharf 387
CHAPMAN, 277
CHARLES, River 308 378 380 381 385 386
CHARLES I, King Of England 109
CHARLES II, King Of England 180 313 318 359 387 King Of Great Britian 17
CHARLESTON, 154
CHARLESTOWN, 377 379 380 385-387 Pond 381
CHATHAM, 5 8 74 82 151 269 271 278 281
CHELMSFORD, 218 275
CHELSEA, 140 147 148 Landing 140 147 148
CHEPACHET, 309 340 River 340
CHERSEY'S, Pond 61

CHESHIRE, 5 9 57 84 85 93 99 109 115 124 125 133 135-137
CHESTER, 286 River 285
CHITTENDEN, Thomas 123
CHURCH, Capt 356
CLAPP, Thomas 106
CLARK, Latham 342 Thomas 342
CLEAVELAND, 53
CLERC, Mr 49
CLOYNE, 104
COCHUMPAUG, Pond 381
CODDINGTON, Mr 318 William 355
COLCHESTER, 82 139 147 150 151 159 162 214 261 272 278 279 281 282 295 388
COLE'S, Harbor 384
COLEBROOK, 8 80 229 232 237 238 242 254 265 266
COLUMBIA, 202 204 210 214 291 295 County 11 District Of 220
COLUMBIAN, Gardens 107
COMSTOCK, 160 Adam 369
COMSTOCK'S, Ferry 160
CONAQUETOGUE, Pond 381
CONCORD, 175
CONNANICUT, Island 355
CONNECTICUT, 305 308 309 319 321 325 326 335 339-341 347 367 370 376 377 380 386 388 Colony 32 River 2-6 8-11 14 32-36 38-42 48 50 51 56 61 62 65 67 68 72 74 75 77 81 83 85 River 89-91 94 97 140 147 159 160 203 204 226 231 248 269-272 274-282 284 285 River 286 288 296 302 303 308
CONSTITUTION, Hill 327
COOK, Capt 155

COPPER, Hill 79
CORNWALL, 5 15 229 240 243
    247 247 250 260 262 Pond 244
COSCOB, Landings 179
COVENTRY, 16 210 216 288 290
    291 295 302 314 340 341 344
    367 370 371 373 376
COWPENS, 374
CRANBERRY, Pond 232
CRANSTON, 306 307 314 321
    324 337 342 370 371 John 342
    Samuel 342
CRARY, Archibald 369
CREKER'S, Brook 200
CROTON, River 373
CROWN, Point 246
CRYSTAL, Pond 207
CUMBERLAND, 311 321 324 336
    345
CUTLER, Timothy 106
CUVIER, 39
DABOLL, Nathan 157
DAGGETT, Naphtali 106
DANBURY, 1 9 15 41 53 59 71
    168 170 176 178 179 182 183
    186 191 198 200 201 256 265
    267
DAVENPORT, John 109 Mr 135
DAVEY, William 92
DAVIE, Mr 390
DAVIS, Aaron 342
DAVY, 39 William 390
DAY, Jeremiah 106
DECATUR, Com 334
DEDHAM, 63 300
DEERFIELD, 40
DERBY, 6 93 95 99 100 116 128
    129 131 132 136 180 196 390
    Landing 95 Turnpike Bridge 99
DETROIT, 53

DEVIL'S, Foot 385
DEWOLF, James 364
DEXTER, John S 369
DIAMOND, Pond 75
DIBBLE, John 245
DIESKAU, Baron 206
DISTRICT, Of Columbia 190 220
DORCHESTER, 90
DOUGLASS, 223 325 343 347
DRAGON, Bridge 99 120
DRUM, Rock 372
DUMMER, Jeremiah 104
DURHAM, 15 52 120 121 130 133
    269 271 272 280 283
DUTCHESS, County 11
DUTCH POINT, 32 51
DWIGHT, 294 Dr 105 113 Pres
    113 174 Timothy 106 112
DYER, Col 206 Eliphalet 206
    Thomas 206
EAST, River 121 Rock 94 96 103
    124
EASTABROOKE, Samuel 210
EAST GREENWICH, 305 367 368
    371 376 383 385
EAST GUILFORD, 121 281
EAST HADDAM, 8 151 159 239
    269 278 281
EAST HARTFORD, 5 9 16 33 38
    61 74 291 302
EAST HAVEN, 93 95 109 114 119
    130
EAST WINDSOR, 9 14 33 38 58
    61 64 65 67 90 295 302 303
    390
EATON, Gen 227 228 Gov 109
    135 Mr 109 Samuel 109
    Theophilus 109 William 227
EDWARDS, Jonathan 67 Timothy
    67

EGG, Harbour 142
EIGHT, Mile River 159 160 Mile Stream 160
ELLINGTON, 9 288 290 295-297 302
ELLIOTT, Jared 284
ELLS, Ozias 239
ELLSWORTH, 244 Oliver 92
ELY, 160
ELY'S, Ferry 160
ENFIELD, 9 10 14 15 34 67 85 226 239 296 297 300 303 Bridge 10 297
ERIE, Lake 294
EUTAW, 375 Springs 375
EXETER, 224 306 371 376 377 379 380 384 385
FAIRCHILD, Robert 30
FAIRFIELD, 1 9 13 113 168 170 178 182 184-186 194 197 199 200 235 245 County 1 15 116 131 132 168 229 252 388 Village 173
FAIRWEATHER'S, Island 172 195
FALLS, Stream 160
FARMINGTON, 2 8 9 34-36 38 41 56-61 71 83-85 89 90 99 100 115 124 249 272 River 6 36 59-61 71 77 81 83 91 238 242 251
FENTON, River 303 Stream 216 303
FENWICK, George 287 Mr 287
FISH, Pond 216
FISHER'S, Island 154 165 381 Island Sound 154 165 381
FITCH, James 104 149 Thomas 104
FIVE, Mile River 181 185 213 223
FLAT, River 370

FORT, Adams 352 Crown Point 246 Green Griswold 144 155 352 Mercer 373 Montgomery 221 Stoddard 236 Ticonderoga 246 Trumbull 144 Wolcott 352
FOSTER, 321 339 340 344 345 370 Theodore 342 William 342
FOUR, Mile River 159 Miles Stream 160
FRANKLIN, 139 146 150 152 158 205 214 333 John 242
FRENCH, River 203 204 223
FRESHWATER, Stream 36
FUGILL, Thomas 109
FURNACE, Pond 259
GALE, 154
GALE'S, Ferry 154
GALLAUDET, Mr 49 Thos H 49
GARDINER, Capt 287
GARDINER'S, Lake 150 162
GEAUGA, County 294
GENESEE, 88
GEORGETOWN, 190
GEORGIA, 123 188 224
GERMAN, Flats 275
GERMANTOWN, 374
GIBBS, George 104
GIDDINGS, Joshua 81 Thomas 81
GILBERT, Matthew 109
GILMORE, 370
GLASTENBURY, 34 61 74 82 89 278 295
GLOUCESTER, 314 321 325 335 336 339-341 344 345
GOAT, Island 352
GOFFE, 109
GOODRICH, Chauncey 52
GOODYEAR, Stephen 109
GORE, 336
GORHAM, Mr 88

GOSHEN, 8 229 231 234 243 244 245 247 252 254 261 265
GOULD, James 233
GRANBY, 5 9 34 36 60 76 80 83 85 86 90 124 237
GRAND, Banks 384
GRANVILLE, 88
GRAVES, Sterling 81
GREAT, Hill 278 Pond 232
GREAT BRITAIN, 32 51 54 207 310 311 331
GREEN, Capt 373 Christopher 369 372 Col 373 Gen 373-375 Nathaniel 319 369 373
GREENE, Gen 123
GREENFIELD, 113 170 173 175 176 186 Hill 171 174 175 Hill Village 171 173 174
GREENSFARMS, 175
GREENSTONE, Mountain 83 96 Range 94
GREENWICH, 7 168 169 179 193 305 307-309 314 325 Harbor 7 169 308 368
GREENWOOD, 81
GREENWOODS, 238 241 251 252 255 266 Mountain 4
GREGSON, Thomas 109
GRISWOLD, 139 153 158 163 164 209 217 224 Fort 144 155 Gov 161 Matthew 149 161 Roger 161 Stanley 262
GROSVENOR, Thomas P 220
GROTON, 8 139 141 144 154 162-165
GUILFORD, 7 8 15 93-95 100 114 120 174 188 272 280 281 283 284 375 Borough 1 Harbor 7 Harbour 95

HADDAM, 1 5 8 94 269 271 275 280-284 826 303 Neck 278 281
HADLEY, 50 109 300
HAERLEM, Heights 208
HALE, 294 Capt 292 293 Nathan 292 294
HALIFAX, 332
HALL, Mr 279
HALSEY, Col 84
HAMDEN, 5 15 16 85 93 95 96 109 115 124 130 136 239
HAMILTON, College 240
HAMMONASETT, River 95
HAMMONASSETT, 284 River 120 121 283
HAMPDEN, 33
HAMPTON, 202 204 207 208 211 216 218
HANOVER, 41 215
HARDY, Commodore 145 Thomas 166
HARRIS, Joseph 339
HART, Gen 287 Jonathan 58 Maj 58 William 88 287
HART'S, Bridge 244
HARTFORD, 1 4 5 10 13-17 21 32 33 36 38 55-61 63-67 71 72 74-77 80-82 84 85 89 90 95 100 108 114-116 119-121 124-128 130-134 136 137 141 142 146 147 148 150-154 158-160 162-164 167 175 176 178-184 186 188 191 192 193 195 199 204 205 207-214 216-219 222 223 225 231-234 237 239 240 242 243 247 249 249-252 254-258 260-267 271 272 274-276 278 280 281 283 284 287 290 291 292 295-297 299 300 302 303

HARTFORD (continued)
309 324 325 340 341 345 388
Bridge 10 48 City 1 45 County
1 9 14 15 33 61 93 115 125 137
139 151 229 242 249 251 256
269 271 288 County 289 295
296 Ferry 62 Museum 49 50
HARTLAND, 34 76 80 237 238
243 255
HARVARD, College 145
HARWINTON, 60 229 231 232
249 251 256 261
HAVERHILL, 300
HAYNES, Mr 51
HEBRON, 74 82 151 210 214 288
291 295
HEMLOCK, Brook 341
HIGGANUM, Landing 276 River
276 277 Stream 277
HIGHLANDS, 221
HILLHOUSE, James 101
HOCKANUM, River 6 61-63 289
302 Stream 36 302
HOG, Pond 160
HOLLENBACH, River 241 Stream
241
HOLMES, Dr 131
HOOKER, Mr 51 90
HOP, River 7 127 203 210 211 289
291 296
HOPKINS, 119 Dr 53 54 Ezekiel
342 Gov 331 Lemuel 53 136
Stephen 330
HOPKINS', Hill 306 376
HOPKINTON, 163 307 317 377
380 383 385-387
HOSFORD, Timothy 255
HOSMER, Titus 275
HOWE, William 293
HOWLAND, 309

HOWLAND'S, Ferry 309 360
HUDSON, 41 243 River 97 221
HULL, Gen 53 William 118
HUMBOLDT, 39
HUME, 10
HUMPHREY, Daniel 118 David
117 118 Gen 119
HUMPHREYSVILLE, 17 100 117
118
HUNT'S, River 369 384
HUNTINGTON, 116 168 180 183
194 199 390 Gen 145 Gov 262
Jedediah 145 Joseph 294
Samuel 149 161 294
HYDE, Nathaniel 299
ILLINOIS, 262
INDIA, Bridge 309 325
INDIAN, Attawanhood 149 Islands
114 Momauguin 109 Montowese 109 Owaneco 149 Philip
319 361 363 Pond 260 Sassacus
144 Totanimo 64 Uncas 149
206 388
INDIANS, Mohegan 149 163 206
388 Narragansett 318 319 381
Pequot 144 149 174 175 287
Podunk 64 67 Rippowam 194
Tunxis 72 Wamponog 318
INGERSOLL, Jared 110
INMAN, 340
IVES, John 239
JAMESTOWN, 349 355
JAY, Mr 92
JEDYARD, John 155
JEFFERSON, 161 Mr 118 190 236
262 Pres 161 190 Thomas 111
JEWETT'S, City 153
JOHNSON, Judge 373 Wm 206
JOHNSTON, 306 307 321 324 337
342 343-345

JONES, Israel 239 John 342
JORDAN, River 167
JUDD, Maj 73 74 William 73
KARPPI, Wendy 13
KENDALL, John 81
KENNELWORTH, 284
KENSINGTON, 57 58
KENT, 5 15 192 229 243 247 250 252 260 262 263 267 370 County 305 307 321 340 367 377
KILLINGLY, 5 8 202 208 209 212 217 218 222-224 340 Pond 213
KILLINGWORTH, 7 100 120 174 269 280 283 284 Harbor 7
KING, Jonathan 239
KINGSTON, 380
KIRBY, Col 235 236 Ephraim 235
KNIGHT, Nehemiah 339
KNIGHTSVILLE, 338
KNOWLTON, Col 292 293 Thomas 208
KOSCIUSKO, 118
LAKEERIE, 53 145 337
LAMBERT'S, Cove 165
LANCASTER, 81
LANMAN, James 30
LAWRENCE, Daniel 242 Isaac 242
LEAD MINE, River 250
LEARNED, David 224
LEAVENWORTH'S, Bridge 181
LEBANON, 8 63 147 150-152 202 204 210 211 214 234 261 295 296
LEDYARD, 156 Col 155 John 155 157
LEE, Ann 69 70
LEFFINGWELL, Thomas 149
LENOX, 41

LEWIS, Edmund 245 Village 244
LEWIS', Bridge 244
LEXINGTON, 221 246
LIEUTENANT'S, River 160 Stream 160
LISBON, 139 146 152 153 158 164 205 209
LITCHFIELD, 1 3 15 35 50 60 71 100 137 149 231 239 241 244 247 249-251 256 261 262 263-266 County 1 33 58 60 80 81 93 127 132 137 168 178 182 192 229 254 Village 1 233
LITTLE, Compton 307 349 350 356 359 Mount Tom 231 Pond 232 Rest Hill 305 379 Rest Hill Village 305 River 203 209 212 219 272
LOISQUISSETT, 347
LONG, Bridge 99 Pond 259
LONG ISLAND, 97 144 196 221 279 292 293 Sound 1 3 4 7-9 14 93-95 98 108 114 117 119-121 128 139-143 159 160 165 167-170 174 179 181 184 185 191 193-196 203 269 270 280 283-285
LONGMEADOW, 67
LORD'S, Island 276
LOUISBURG, 198
LOUISBURGH, 67
LOUIS XVI, 188
LUDLOW, Mr 175
LYMAN, Gen 87 88 Phineas 87
LYME, 3 4 81 139 140 142 151 159 160 162 167 276 281 287 388
LYNDE, Point 285
MAD, River 137 255 265 266
MAINE, 13 70 97

MAMACOCK, Stream 160
MANISSES, 358
MANSFIELD, 9 15 16 130 202 204 207 211 216 291 303
MANSFIELD'S, Bridge 130
MARLBOROUGH, 5 34 74 76 82 151 278 295 Pond 82
MASHAPAUG, Pond 301 River 301
MASHASUCK, River 323 325 343 Stream 323 325
MASKACHUG, River 369
MASON, Capt 174 175 John 149 206 287
MASSACHUSETTS, 1 13 33 40 51 70-72 76 80 81 85-88 90 124 149 159 166 174 205 210 218 223 225-227 232 240 242 252 254 288 296 297 299 300 303 305 310 312 318 319 324 326 329 330 335 343-345 347 356 359-365 Colony 51 Commonwealth Of 1
MASWANSHECUT, Pond 345
MATTABESECK, 109
MATTABESICK, 275
MEIGS, Josiah 187
MENDON, 336
MENUNCATUCK, River 95
MENUNKATUCK, River 121
MENUNKETESUCK, River 283
MERIDEN, 15 56 57 84 85 93 115 125 133 135 271 272
MIANNUS, River 169 193
MICHIGAN, 262
MIDDLE, Haddam Landing 278-280
MIDDLEBURY, 93 131 127 132 135 264 266

MIDDLESEX, 94 County 1 9 14 33 82 93 94 133 139 151 269 276
MIDDLETOWN, 1 2 4 5 13 15 16 17 40 41 56-58 60 82 84 85 89 94 100 109 113 114 120 125 130 133-135 137 151 205 211 255 269 271 275 276 278-281 286 296 307 349 357 358 City 1 273 Mountain 4 River 280 Upper Houses 272
MILFORD, 5 7 9 10 93 95 96 110 116 118 128 129 136 137 174 390 Harbor 7 95 129
MILL, Creek 276 River 32 36 38 40 41 46 51 56 95 98 99 115 124 125 169 172 193 194 200 336 River Harbor 169 172 River Village 173 174 Stream 211 336
MINA, 268 Gen 268
MINER, Nathaniel 166
MISSISSIPPI, 236 River 88
MISSOURI, 57
MIX, John 106 Mr 106 107
MIX'S, Museum 106
MOHAWK, Flats 275
MOHEGAN, Indians 149 163 206 388
MOMAUGUIN, 109
MONSON, 303
MONTGOMERY, Fort 221 Gen 373
MONTOWESE, 109
MONTREAL, 220 246
MONTVILLE, 139 146 150 151 154 159 162 164 167 388
MOOSUP, River 203 217 222 341 Stream 203

MORGAN, Gen 374
MOUNT, Carmel 124 Hope 306
   319 358 363 Hope Bay 358-361
   363 Hope River 207 Hope
   Stream 207 216 Lamentation
   125 Pleasant 97 101 Prospect
   231 Tom 3 231 Tom Pond 232
   Washington 258
MOUNTAIN, Pond 259
MOUNT VERNON, 119
MOWRY, Daniel 348
MUDDY, Brook 223 225 226
MUDGE'S, Pond 260
MURRAY, Mr 92 390
MYSTIC, 7 141 154 Harbor 7 141
   River 141 154 165
NACHAUG, River 7 205 211 216
   Stream 205
NAMEAUG, 144
NANTUCKET, Shoals 384
NARRAGANSET, 225
NARRAGANSETT, 144 308 318
   377 Bay 305-309 320 338 349
   352 355-361 363 367 368 371
   377-379 383-385 Indians 318
   319 381 River 306 308 309 318
   321 322 324-326 352 353 355
   363 365-367 369
NARROW, River 384
NATCHEZ, 88
NAUGATUCK, River 6 94 116
   117 127 132 135 137 230-232
   249 250 255 256 264 265
NECK, Bridge 99
NEWAMSTERDAM, 32
NEWBRITAIN, 57 58
NEW CANAAN, 15 168 181 184
   193 200
NEW FAIRFIELD, 168 177 178
   182 191 192 252

NEWGATE, Prison 30 78 79 238
NEW HAMPSHIRE, 11 70 100
   215
NEW HARTFORD, 16 59-61 229
   232 237 238 241 249 251 261
NEW HAVEN, 1 2 4 7 13 15-18 21
   32 34 41 46 55-58 60 67 71 73
   74 81 84 85 89 90 93 95 114-
   117 119 120 122 124-137 141
   142 147 151 154 159 164 167
   168 170 174-176 179 180 183
   184 187 188 193-196 199 200
   208 231 232 239 243 247 249
   250 254 256-258 260-262 264-
   267 271 272 280-284 286 290
   300 302 Bay 98 99 119 130
   City 1 101 Colony 17 18
   County 1 4 15 33 85 93 133
   183 229 256 257 266 269 271
   Harbor 7 95 Village 135
NEW LONDON, 1 7 13 41 63 75
   82 95 108 139 141 146 147
   149-151 154 155 160 162 163
   165 167 202 204 205 242 271
   283 284 286 290 383 388 City
   1 County 1 14 33 82 139 205
   224 269-271 281 288 295
   Harbor 7 141 172
NEWMAN, Francis 109 Robt 109
NEW MILFORD, 5 9 15 100 110
   132 178 179 182 192 196 199
   229 232 250 252 257 262 263
   264
NEW NETHERLANDS, 180
NEW ORLEANS, 57 236 268
NEWPORT, 131 305 306 308 309
   311-318 324 326 342 349 351
   355-357 359 365 374 379 384-
   386 County 305 307 349
   Harbor 308

NEW PRESTON, 251 253 264
NEW ROXBURY, 226
NEW SHOREHAM, 349 357
NEWTON, 72
NEWTOWN, 9 51 90 110 131 132 168 177-181 183 186 196 199 252 390
NEW YORK, 1 3 11 13 14 32 41 57 60 70 88 95 100 108 116 117 121 129 132 142 148 154 165 166 168-174 177-182 184 185 191-196 200 203 220 229 231 240 245 246 250 252 258-260 270 276 277 279 282 283 292 349 352 373 379 381
NIANTIC, 7 141 159 Bay 141 159 160 Harbor 7 141 River 140 167 Stream 160
NIPSUCK, 75
NISKEUNA, 70
NORATON, River 169 193
NORFOLK, 8 15 77 81 229 238 240-242 247 248 254 265 County 321
NORTH, Pond 296
NORTHAMPTON, 41
NORTHBURY, 257
NORTH CAROLINA, 375
NORTHEAST, Pond 259
NORTHFIELD, 56
NORTH HAVEN, 3 93 99 109 119 124 130 133
NORTH KINGSTON, 307 368 377 379 380 383
NORTH PROVIDENCE, 307 321 324 342 343 345
NORTH STONINGTON, 8 139 153 154 163-165 224 383
NORTON, Mr 239

NORWALK, 7 168 170 178 181 184 186 192 193 199-201 Harbor 7 169 River 181 185 186 191 201
NORWICH, 1 7 15 16 41 63 100 104 108 139 141 142 145 146 150-153 158 162 164 167 203 204 209-211 216 219 222 226 236 282 291 296 299 303 309 325 338 341 345 388 City 1 147 Harbor 141 Little River 150 Pond 160
NOSOTEN, River 181
NOVA SCOTIA, 57
OBLONG, River 260
OHIO, 11 31 53 88 110 145 294
OLD, Mill Creek 196 Mill Village 196 198
OLDHAM, Capt 318
ONEIDA, 382 County 240
ONION, River 123
ONTARIO, County 88
ORLEANS, 236
ORONOQUE, 198 Village 198
OUSATONICK, 3 97 255 Mountain 3 River 3 5 6 9 10 14 93-95 116 117 127-129 131-133 168 169 174 177 178 180 181 River 182 183 192 194 196 230 232 240 241 243 244 248 251 253 257-260 263 390
OXFORD, 8 93 116 127 131-133 135 136 180 390
OYSTER, River 285
PAINESVILLE, 294 295
PALMER, Amos 167 Nathan 221
PALMER'S, River 365
PARSON, Gen 112
PATTAGAWONSET, Pond 160

PATTERSON, Edward 56 Mr 57
PAUCAMACK, Pond 224
PAUCATUCK, Bay 165 River 141 163 165 166
PAUG, Pond 134
PAUGASSETT, 118
PAWCATUCK, 305 308 309 311 325 338 376 378 380 387 Bridge 387 Harbor 308 378 River 378 381 383 386 Village 305
PAWTUCKET, 305 312 314 325 343 344 346 River 308 322 336 345 347 348 Village 305 309
PAWTUXET, 305 308 314 338 371 372 Harbor 308 River 308 323 337-339 341 345 368 370 371 376 Village 305
PEMBROKE, 245
PENNSYLVANIA, 11
PEQUANOCK, River 195 199 Stream 199
PEQUONACK, River 169
PEQUOT, Indians 144 149 174 175 287 River 146 Swamp 173
PERRY, 268 Col 267 Commodore 337 Henry 267
PETERS, Thomas 287
PETERS', River 336
PETIPAUG, River 285
PETTEQUAMSCUST, River 384 Stream 384
PETTIPAUG, 286
PHELPS, Charles 166 Maj Gen 84 Noah 84 Oliver 88 287
PHILADELPHIA, 7
PHILIP, 319 361 363
PIERCE, Joshua 245
PIERSON, Abraham 106
PINE, Brook 277 Rock 96

PIPER'S, River 89
PITKIN, William 64
PLAINFIELD, 9 202 208-210 212 217 222 224
PLYMOUTH, 15 51 58 135 137 149 229 231 249 256 264 318 335 Colony 51
POCHAUG, Harbor 283 River 140 225 285 Stream 153 224
PODUNK, Indians 64 67 Stream 36 65
POINT, 196 Judith 308 357 379 Judith Pond 379
POMFRET, 8 202 207-209 211 212 218 223 225
POMPERAUG, River 94 133 230 239 267
PONONGANSETT, River 340 341
POOL, At Nipsuck 75
POQUABACK, Stream 36 59 60
POQUABUCK, River 256
POQUATANOCK, River 140
POQUATONUCK, River 154
POQUONOCK, 92 River 154
PORTSMOUTH, 306 307 309 313 349 358
POSQUISSETT, Pond 381
POTOMAC, River 57
POTTER, James 192
POTTER'S, Hill 387
POUGHKEEPSIE, 244 249
POWCHASSET, River 338
POWCHASSETT, River 342 Stream 342
POWTATUCK, 184 River 183
PRESTON, 139 146 147 153 154 158 162-164 300
PRINCETON, 374
PROVIDENCE, 13 41 147 153 158 165 203-205 207 208 212 213

PROVIDENCE (continued)
217-219 222 223 225 226 284
296 297 303 305 308 309 311-
317 321-324 335-345 347 348
351-353 355 356 357 359 365
367 368 370 371 376 379 380
383-386 390 County 305-307
311 321 Cove 323-325 Harbor
308 River 322 324 325 327 337
338 341
PRUDENCE, Island 350 359
PUNNONGANSETT, Pond 345
PUTNAM, Gen 118 119 220-222
Israel 219 220
PUTNEY, 198 Village 198
PYNCHEON, John 87
PYQUAG, 90
QUANADUOK, Bridge 165
QUANDUCK, Stream 222
QUASEPAUG, Lake 127 Pond 127
QUEBEC, 57
QUINAPAUG, Pond 121
QUINIBAUG, Pond 213 River 3 6
7 9 140 153 158 164 203 204
208-210 212 213 217 218 219
223 224 226 River 301 341 388
QUINIPIACK, 109 River 3 84 95
96 98 99 100 115 119 120 126
130 133 134
RAMAUG, Pond 264
RAUMAUG, Pond 263
READING, 168 175 177 180 183
186 191 199 200
RED, Bank 373
REEVE, Judge 233 236 Tapping 233
REHOBOTH, 166 331
RHODE ISLAND, 1 3 10 14 63 73
139 158 163 165 198 202 212
213 217 222-224 252 277 389

RHODES, Zachariah 341
RICHARDS, Jedediah 255 William 329
RICHMOND, 377 379 380 382 383 385 387
RIDGEFIELD, 168 177 178 182 186 191 200
RIMMON, Falls 116
RIMMON'S, Falls 137
RIPPOWAM, Indians 194
RITTENHOUSE, 333
ROARING, Brook 75 298 River 301
ROCKY, Hill 4 89 River 182 253
RODGERS', Pond 160
ROGERS, Capt 334
ROSE, Island 352
ROWLEY, 275
ROXBURY, 5 72 132 220 229 252 257 263 266
SACHEM'S HEAD, 7 95 121 Harbor 7 95 121
SAINTCLAIR, Gen 58
SALEM, 70 200 220 232 329 388
SALISBURY, 5 9 15 123 229 240 241 258 260 261 266
SALMON, Brook 36 75 76 77 River 6 151 259 281 282 289 296
SALTONSTALL, Lake 114 120 Pond 120
SAMP, Mortar Rock 171 Rock 171
SANDWICH, 247
SANDY, Hook 384 River 243 255
SASCO, River 172
˙SASSACUS, 144
SAUGATUCK, 7 Harbor 7 169 172 River 169 170 172 184-186 191 200 Village 173 174
SAVANNAH, 154 279 342

SAY, Lord 286 287
SAYBROOK, 6 16 38 104 149 160
    161 269 271 272 276 283 284
SCANTIC, River 6 34 65 67 68
    289 297 Stream 36
SCITUATE, 314 321 325 330 337
    339-342 344 370 371
SCOTCH, Pond 347
SEAL, Lord 286 287
SECONNET, 356 Passage 350 358
    River 350
SEDAGHQUATE, 275
SEEKONK, River 308 309 322
    324 325 343 344
SHALER, Mr 279
SHANNOCK, 377
SHARON, 9 229 243 244 249 250
    258-261
SHAWNETOWN, 262
SHEFFIELD, 41 258
SHEPARD, Joseph 239
SHEPAUG, River 6 94 133 230
    232 257 263 264
SHERMAN, 5 168 182 192 250
    252 Roger 110 111
SHETUCKET, River 3 6 7 140 146
    147 152 158 203 205 212 301
SILLIMAN, Ebenezer 245 Prof 40
    298
SIMSBURY, 9 15 34 35 60 61 71
    76 77 82 90 124 239
SKUNGAMUG, River 290 291
SLATER, 347
SLATERSVILLE, 347
SMALLEY, Dr 58
SMITH, 340
SMITH'S, Pond 160
SMITHFIELD, 306 307 311 314
    321 324 335-337 339 342 343
    345

SNIPSICK, Pond 290
SOMERS, 5 9 67 226 288 295-297
    299 301
SOUND, 143
SOUTHBURY, 6 8 9 93 127 131
    132 183 252 257 266 267
SOUTHERTON, 166
SOUTHINGTON, 9 15 34 56-58
    71 84 115 124 125 137
SOUTH KINGSTON, 305 307 314
    356 377 379-381 384-386
SOUTHWICK, 85 86 Pond 86 232
SPALDING, Asa 149 187
SPENCER, Joseph 282
SPRINGFIELD, 41 70 85 296
STAFFORD, 5 8 15 41 63 207 216
    288 290 295-297 300 302 303
    Spring 290
STAMFORD, 7 168-170 175 179
    181 184 193 235 245 Harbor 7
    169 Mill River 181
STANFORD, River 169
STARKE, Gen 145
STEEL, John 51 90
STEPNEY, 89
STERLING, 202 212 217 222 224
    340
STEUBEN, County 88
STEWARD, Mr 49
STEWART, Mr 47
STILES, Dr 105 131 Ezra 106 131
    Isaac 131 Pres 113
STILL, River 169 177 178 207 238
    242 253 265 301 Stream 207
STONEY, River 36
STONINGTON, 7 8 13 139 141
    154 163 164 325 387 Borough
    1 165 Harbor 7 141 165
STONY, River 86
STRATFIELD, 175

STRATFORD, 9 10 128 129 168-170 174 180 194 199 235 390 Sound 169
STRONG, Nathan 53
STURBRIDGE, 301
STUYVESANT, Peter 180
SUFFIELD, 5 9 10 34 36 67 68 76 85 90 226 239
SUFFOLK, 227
SULLIVAN, Gen 371 374 John L 50
SWANZEY, 366
SWIFT, Heman 247 Jabez 247 Mr 247
SWIGHT, Doct 105
TALCOTT, 71 Mt 71 72 252
TALMADGE, Col 118
TANKEROOSON, River 302 Stream 302
TAUNTON, 325
THAMES, River 4 6 7 140-143 146-148 154 159 162 164 167 302 388
THIMBLE, Islands 114
THIRTY, Mile Island 276
THOMPSON, 7 63 202 204 212 218 223 225 226 Matthew 300
THOMPSON'S, Bridge 99
THORNTON, Elisha 348
TISDALL, Mr 55 Thomas 54
TIVERTON, 308 309 349 350 356 359 Harbor 308
TOLLAND, 1 8 63 288 290 291 295 302 303 County 1 33 67 82 139 151 202 207 288
TOMLINSON, 99 Bridge 120 Isaac 99
TOMLINSON'S, Bridge 99
TORRINGTON, 8 229 231 238 247 249 251 252 261 265

TOURTELLOT, 340
TOWER, Hill 379
TRACEY, Uriah 187
TRACY, Mr 236 Uriah 236
TRADING, Cove 388 Cove Brook 388
TRENTON, 374
TRUMBULL, 119 168 180 194 199 390 Gov 214 215 Jonathan 214
TRYON, Gov 110 221
TUNXIS, Indians 72 River 6 9 34-36 59 60 71 72 77 83 91 92 230 238 242 251 255
TURNER, John 255 Nathaniel 109
TURNPIKE, Bridge 120
TYRON, 176
UNION, 8 207 225 288 297 300 303
VARNUM, James M 369
VAUGHAN, William 341
VERMONT, 11 100 123 227 245 247
VERNON, 288 290 291 295 302
VERONA, 200
VIRGINIA, 118
VOLUNTOWN, 153 163 202 217 222 224
WABASH, River 58
WADSWORTH, Col 52 Daniel 72 James 281 Jeremiah 51 52
WADSWORTH'S, Pond 72
WALDO, Dr 222
WALLINGFORD, 3 9 15 57 93 100 109 114-116 124 125 127 130 133 249 271 280
WALPOLE, 63 262
WAMPONOG, Indians 318
WANASQUATUCKET, River 323 325 342 343 Stream 323 325

WANGUMBOG, Lake 292 Pond 292
WAPAWAUG, River 129 137
WARDEN'S, Pond 308 381 386
WARDLEY, James 69 Jane 69
WAREHOUSE POINT, 6 66
WARHAM, Mr 90
WARREN, 229 231 243 244 247 250 251 262 263 305 308 311 312 314 315 326 328 361 363 365 Harbor 308 River 365 366 Village 305
WARWICK, 307 313 337 338 367 368 370 371 383
WASHINGTON, 3 5 15 100 123 145 161 227 229 231 232 239 244 250 252 257 262 263 266 299 370 Bridge 10 129 County 305 307 367 376 377 Gen 118 119 215 221 292 373 George 334 Pres 145 161 189 Square 353
WATCHAUG, Pond 381
WATERBURY, 15 53 85 93 115 126 127 131 135-137 250 256 257 261 264 River 135 248 261
WATERFORD, 139 141 154 159 162 167
WATERTOWN, 127 135 175 229 231 239 256 257 264 266
WATTS, Dr 188
WAYBOSSETT, Bridge 309
WEAVER, Clement 342
WEBSTER, Elisha 242
WERNER, 39
WEST, Benjamin 331 Bridge 99 Dr 331-333 Meadow 97 River 94 95 97-99 137 272 280 Rock 94 96 103 115 124
WESTCHESTER, 152 County 179

WESTCOT, Robert 341
WESTERLY, 165 314 317 377 380 382 383 386
WESTERN, Mountain 3
WEST GREENWICH, 306 367 368 370 371 376 380 389
WEST HAVEN, 98
WESTON, 168 170 175 180 183 186 199 200 388 390
WEST POINT, 112 221
WEST QUANAUG, 341 342
WETHERSFIELD, 9 17 32 34 38-40 50 56 58 74 271 275 363
WEYMOUTH, 300
WHALEBONE, Stream 160
WHALEY, 109
WHEATON, 347
WHEELOCK, Eleazer 215 John 215 Pres 215 Rev Mr 215
WHITE, Hugh 275 Judge 275 Plains 187 Robert 300
WHITEFIELD, Henry 122
WHITESBORO, 275
WHITESTOWN, 275
WHITING, Col 206 Nathan 206
WHITNEY, Eli 125
WICKFORD, 305 308 309 314 378 384 385 Harbor 308 378 384
WILDER, Joseph 239
WILLIAMS, Col 206 Eliphalet 65 Elisha 90 106 Joseph 339 Mr 318 330 Rev Mr 312 318 Roger 312 318 329 330 339
WILLIMANTIC, River 7 203 205 211 216 289-292 296 298 301 303 Stream 205 211 303
WILLINGTON, 7 207 216 288 290 295 297 300 303
WILTON, 168 181 184 191 199 200

WINCHESTER, 8 15 229 232 237 238 242 247 254 261 265
WINDHAM, 1 9 16 41 82 147 152 158 204 209-212 214 216 272 279 388 County 1 16 33 139 151 152 158 163 202 217 288 289 295 388
WINDSOR, 9 14 17 32 34 36 38 40 66 76 81-83 85 88 90 175 227 234 238 255 284 287 300 340
WINSTEAD, 266
WINTHROP, Prof 332
WINTONBURY, 92 River 40
WOBURN, 275 300
WOLCOTT, 58 84 93 115 135 137 256 Alexander 187 Eratus 67 Gov 234 235 Oliver 30 104 187 234 262 Roger 67 234 Wm 67
WOLCOTTSVILLE, 17
WOLCOTTVILLE, 261
WOOD, River 308 376 378 380 381 383 385 386
WOODBRIDGE, 8 93 95 99 109 115 116 124 128 131 135 136
WOODBURY, 9 100 127 132 133 229 239 240 257 258 263 264 266
WOODS, River 40
WOODSTOCK, 8 147 158 202 207 209 210 218 223 225 297 299-301
WOONSOKET, Hill 306
WOONSOQUETT, Falls 348 Hill 346
WOOSTER, David 198 Gen 198
WOPOWAUG, River 94
WORCESTER, 63 202 219 325 337 347 County 227 309 321
WORTHINGTON, 57 58
WRENTHAM, 336
WYLLYS, Samuel 276
YALE, College 27 31 32 49 103 Elihu 104
YANTIC, River 140 146 147 150 152
YORK, 118
ZOAR, Bridge 181

www.ingramcontent.com/pod-product-compliance
Lightning Source LLC
Chambersburg PA
CBHW071015240426
43661CB00073B/2298